SHAPERS
─── OF THE ───
GREAT DEBATE
─── ON THE ───
CIVIL WAR

SHAPERS

—— OF THE ——

GREAT DEBATE

—— ON THE ——

CIVIL WAR

A BIOGRAPHICAL DICTIONARY

Dan Monroe and Bruce Tap

Shapers of the Great American Debates, Number 6
Peter B. Levy, Series Editor

GREENWOOD PRESS
Westport, Connecticut • London

For Brenda and Julie

Library of Congress Cataloging-in-Publication Data

Monroe, Dan, 1961–
  Shapers of the great debate on the Civil War : a biographical dictionary /
Dan Monroe and Bruce Tap.
      p. cm.—(Shapers of the great American debates, ISSN 1099-2693 ; no. 6)
    Includes bibliographical references and index.
    ISBN 0-313-31745-3 (alk. paper)
      1. United States—History—Civil War, 1861–1865—Biography—
  Dictionaries. 2. Politicians—United States—Biography—Dictionaries. 3.
  United States—History—Civil War, 1861–1865—Causes. 4. Slavery—Political
  aspects—United States—History—19th century. 5. United States—Politics
  and government—1861–1865. 6. United States—Politics and government—
  1849–1877. I. Tap, Bruce. II. Title. III. Series.
  E467.M77   2005
  973.7'092'2—dc22   2005006191

British Library Cataloguing in Publication Data is available.

Library of Congress Catalog Card Number: 2005006191
ISBN: 0-313-31745-3
ISSN: 1099-2693

First published in 2005

Greenwood Press, 88 Post Road West, Westport, CT 06881
An imprint of Greenwood Publishing Group, Inc.
www.greenwood.com

Printed in the United States of America

The paper used in this book complies with the
Permanent Paper Standard issued by the National
Information Standards Organization (Z39.48–1984).

10 9 8 7 6 5 4 3 2 1

CONTENTS

SERIES FOREWORD

American history has been shaped by numerous debates over issues far ranging in content and time. Debates over the right, or lack thereof, to take the land of the Native Americans, and the proper place and role of women, sparked by Roger Williams and Anne Hutchinson, respectively, marked the earliest years of the Massachusetts Bay Colony. Debates over slavery, the nature and size of the federal government, the emergence of big business, and the rights of labor and immigrants were central to the Republic in the nineteenth century and, in some cases, remain alive today. World War I, World War II, and the Vietnam War sparked debates that tore at the body politic. Even the Revolution involved a debate over whether America should be America or remain part of Great Britain. And the Civil War, considered by many the central event in American history, was the outgrowth of a long debate that found no peaceful resolution.

This series, *Shapers of the Great American Debates*, will examine many of these debates—from those between Native Americans and European settlers to those between "natives" and "newcomers." Each volume will focus on a particular issue, concentrating on those men and women who *shaped* the debates. The authors will pay special attention to fleshing out the life histories of the shapers, considering the relationship between biography or personal history and policy or philosophy. Each volume will begin with an introductory overview and include approximately twenty biographies of ten to fifteen pages, an appendix that briefly describes other key figures, a bibliographical essay, and a subject index. Unlike works that emphasize end results, the books in this series will devote equal attention to both sides, to the "winners" and the "losers." This will lead to a more complete understanding of the richness and complexity of America's past than is afforded by works that examine only the victors.

Taken together, the books in this series remind us of the many ways that class, race, ethnicity, gender, and region have divided rather than united the inhabitants of the United States of America. Each study reminds us of the frequency and variety of debates in America, a reflection of the diversity of the nation and its democratic credo. One even wonders if a similar series could be developed for many other nations or if the diversity of America and its tradition of free expression have given rise to more debates than elsewhere.

Although many Americans have sought to crush the expression of opposing views by invoking the imperative of patriotism, more often than not Americans have respected the rights of others to voice their opinions. Every four years, Americans have voted for a president and peacefully respected the results, demonstrating their faith in the process that institutionalizes political debate. More recently, candidates for the presidency have faced off in televised debates that often mark the climax of their campaigns. Americans not only look forward to these debates, but they would probably punish anyone who sought to avoid them. Put another way, debates are central to America's political culture, especially those that deal with key issues and involve the most prominent members of society.

Each volume in the series is written by an expert. While I offered my share of editorial suggestions, overall I relied on the author's expertise when it came to determining the most sensible way to organize and present each work. As a result, some of the volumes follow a chronological structure; others clump their material thematically; still others are separated into two sections, one pro and one con. All of the works are written with the needs of college and advanced high school students in mind. They should prove valuable both as sources for research papers and as supplemental texts in both general and specialized courses. The general public should also find the works an attractive means of learning more about many of the most important figures and equally as many seminal issues in American history.

Peter B. Levy
Associate Professor
Department of History
York College

ACKNOWLEDGMENTS

Several individuals played a role in the writing of this book. Albert Castel read several chapters and offered a number of insightful comments. His careful reading of the manuscript resulted in the elimination of several errors. Merton Dillon offered a number of helpful suggestions on the chapter on Harriet Beecher Stowe. We appreciate the attention both Robert W. Johannsen and Mark Plummer gave to the manuscript.

INTRODUCTION: WHAT WERE THE GREAT DEBATES?

The American Civil War was the single most tumultuous event in American history. The four years of war between the firing on Fort Sumter and the surrender of Robert E. Lee and the Army of Northern Virginia at Appomattox produced over 620,000 deaths and thousands more wounded, almost as many as all other American wars combined. Almost every family in the United States had an immediate and personal connection to battlefield fatalities. For years after the conflict, Civil War veterans, for instance, could be singled out because of physical deformities or a missing limb. The emancipation of some 4 million slaves had profound consequences on Southern society, promising freedom and opportunities for blacks while traumatizing white Southerners faced with the fundamental reordering of social structures. In addition to death and the psychological trauma that affected thousands of families throughout the North and South, the physical destruction suffered by the Southern states in particular was drastic, so much so that it would take the region several decades to recover from the physical impact of the war. During the last year of the war, in particular, the Union armies of Sherman and Sheridan worked with devastating efficiency in the destruction of Southern resources. Union hosts systematically destroyed bridges, railroads, farm equipment, and factories.[1]

For over 100 years, historians have debated the causes of the American Civil War. Some historians have seen the war exclusively in terms of the debate over slavery. Others have focused on the cultural differences between the regions; an industrializing North was no longer compatible with a rural, agricultural South. Historian Charles Beard, for instance, saw the war as the second American Revolution, whereby an industrial North triumphed over an agricultural South. Others have seen the war as the result of a debate over states' rights versus the strong central authority of the national government. Finally, a whole generation of revisionist historians saw the war as an unnecessary consequence of fanaticism—Southern fire-eaters and zealous Northern abolitionists. The war, according to this viewpoint, was the result of inept politicians incapable of negotiating compromise on pivotal issues. In the words of James Garfield Randall, a "blundering generation" created the war. In reality, the war was the outcome of many great debates, issues that had been controversial for decades in the young republic. While historians will continue to debate the origins and causes of the war, few can doubt the statement of historian William Gienapp, who writes, "As such, the Civil War constituted the greatest single failure of American democracy."[2]

The war did answer a constitutional question that was inherent from the young republic's beginning, namely, within a federal system of government, where power was shared between various levels of authorities (local, state, and national), what level of government held ultimate authority? Beginning already with anti-Federalist opponents of the Constitution, those suspicious of expanding federal power answered the question by positing the supremacy of state governments. Argued in the Virginia and Kentucky resolutions of 1798 and later perfected by such Southern political figures as John C. Calhoun, the so-called compact theory of government asserted that the United States was, in fact, a league of sovereign states. The whole was not greater than the parts; each individual state had the right and authority to negate legislation that it found obnoxious to its interest. As Thomas Jefferson stated in a draft of the Kentucky resolutions, "and that whensoever the general government assumes undelegated powers, its acts are unauthoritative, void, and of no force." Ultimately, a state could opt out of the federal union through the act of secession. By 1828 South Carolina's John C. Calhoun had developed a full-blown theory of nullification that he outlined in the "South Carolina Exposition and Protest."[3] Proponents of nullification believed that each state had the authority to interpret the constitutionality of acts of Congress. If a state believed an act or law was unconstitutional, it could "nullify" the law and it would, in theory, become inoperative for the state.

Conversely, proponents of a more nationalist interpretation stressed the ultimate supremacy of federal authority over that of individual states. When the Federal Union was created, a new entity, indivisible, and clearly superior to any of its parts, was created. The founders of the country had never intended for states to have the option of secession, this viewpoint maintained, because that would have included a national right to self-destruction or suicide. The primacy of the Union was expertly articulated by the legendary orator, Daniel Webster, when, while in the Senate, he replied to a speech by South Carolina Senator Robert Y. Hayne that stressed a states' rights interpretation of the Constitution. For Webster, the Union existed prior to the Constitution and states were, therefore, subservient to it. Webster, according to Merrill D. Peterson, "raised the idea of Union above contract or expediency and enshrined it in the American heart. Liberty was identified with the Union, the Union with Liberty; together they defined American nationhood." The tragedy of the American Civil War was that the debate over this issue was ultimately resolved only after much bloodshed and loss of life.[4]

The question of the supremacy of state or national authority periodically erupted at critical junctures in American history, and in a very real sense, ideological consistency was not always apparent. Probably the most important feature of the states' rights position was the republican argument that focused on the potentially tyrannical power of a strong central government. This was obviously on the minds of the revolutionary generation as they revolted from what was considered a tyrannical central government, and the same attitude was apparent in the almost paranoid revulsion of centralized authority in the arguments of the anti-Federalist opponents of the Constitution. States' rights proponents, primarily Jeffersonian republicans, used the compact theory to discredit the Federalist Alien and Sedition Acts. In 1832 South Carolina states' rights republicans used Calhoun's theory of nullification when they attempted to negate the tariff of 1832 and threatened secession. Tough rhetoric by President Andrew Jackson and compromise measures enacted by Congress temporarily averted a crisis. After the Mexican War, when the admission of California threatened to upset the sectional balance between the free and slave states, Southern states' rights advocates organized the Nashville convention to discuss possible courses of action—including the threat of secession. Defused by the Compromise of 1850, talk of secession was temporarily squelched; however, it would reassert itself routinely during the tumultuous 1850s. With the formation of the Republican Party, an avowedly Northern sectional party, and the election of a Republican candidate to the presidency in 1860, Southern states' rights advocates believed they had to strike before the opportunity for action was gone.[5]

It would be a distortion to assert that only Southerners, and Democrats at that, used the argument of states' rights to advance their political interest in the years before the war. In fact, in 1814, during the War of 1812, disgruntled Federalists talked of seceding from the Union and creating a New England Confederation. While the December 1814 meeting of Federalists at Hartford, Connecticut, squelched extremist talk of secession, the right of states to nullify offensive legislation was affirmed. Again during the 1850s, when a strengthened national Fugitive Slave Law, the principal result of the Compromise of 1850, forced Northern citizens to assist federal marshals in the apprehension and return of escaped slaves, nine Northern state legislatures passed personal liberty laws to protect fugitive slaves from federal power. If examined closely, the question of states' rights was often tied to the issue of slavery. Extreme states' rights advocates were at the forefront of the demand for a *federal* slave code for national territo-

ries, while members of the Republican Party, the so-called party of consolidation, might position the authority and rights of Northern state legislatures against the national government when an opportunity to deal a
blow against slavery was possible.[6]

The issue of slavery was intimately connected with divisions in American society. Behind the abstract constitutional debates about states' rights
and national authority lurked this peculiar institution, a term Southerners
used to describe the uniqueness of slavery. Uneasily recognized in the Constitution, the institution of slavery was part of the fabric of the American
republic. While many of the Founding Fathers were clearly uncomfortable
with the institution, they felt it better to compromise than jeopardize the
strength and vitality of the young republic. Black abolitionist leader Frederick Douglass, for instance, would state that the Constitution's failure to
use the word *slave* demonstrated the founders' ambivalence toward slavery. Unrealistically expecting the institution to fade away, the popularity of
cotton production in the early nineteenth century quickly rejuvenated slavery and helped foment its transformation from a necessary evil to a positive good. Bolstered by a host of pseudo-scientific arguments that "proved"
black inferiority, Southerners constructed elaborate positive affirmations
for their labor system. Indeed, some theorists went even further. During the
late 1850s, for instance, Virginian George Fitzhugh argued that slavery
ought to be the natural condition of all labor.

Exacerbating conflict in American society during the antebellum period
was the abolitionist movement. If slavery had remained, as some of the
founders imagined, a fledgling institution in decline, the abolitionist movement would have never become as high profile and controversial as it did.
With the rise of cotton and the rebirth of slavery, however, there were some
individuals in the antebellum United States who were awakened to the inherent inequity and brutality of the slave system. The birth of the abolitionist movement sparked a spirited debate on the institution of slavery that
would rage for some thirty years.

As significant as the abolitionist movement was, it remained an essentially
fringe movement in the 1830s and the early 1840s. Many considered abolitionists dangerous fanatics, whose ideas threatened the very fabric of American society. In some Northern cities, abolitionists were the targets of riotous
crowds who periodically attacked antislavery zealots along with Northern
free blacks. Contributing to the ineffectiveness of abolitionism was internal
division. Antislavery advocates aligned with Massachusetts abolitionist
William Lloyd Garrison, developed a strategy of moral suasion, rejected the
Constitution as illegitimate because it sanctioned slavery, and, thereby, repudiated the political system as a legitimate means of bringing about the desired goal of the abolition of slavery. Political abolitionists, represented by
the likes of Gerrit Smith, Salmon Chase, and Joshua Leavitt, disagreed with
Garrison and formed the Liberty Party to advance antislavery ideas and prin-

ciples at the ballot box. While Garrison's followers were immediatist, who rejected all compromise as illegitimate, political abolitionists, while recognizing the evil of slavery, also recognized the necessity of compromise and making alliances with political elements that did not wholeheartedly endorse the abolitionist crusade. At the ballot box, the Liberty Party was insignificant, however, garnering a smattering of votes in the 1840 and 1844 presidential elections, while failing to take a single electoral vote.[7]

It would be a mistake to see the antislavery movement as motivated by the desire to bring about equality and civil rights for African Americans. Among antislavery advocates were those who supported social, political, and economic rights for African Americans; however, at the same time, antislavery sentiment in the North was often tinged with racism and antiblack attitudes. Racism pervaded many Northern communities, and discriminatory laws and social practices hampered the small Northern free black community. Even antislavery advocates accepted notions of Anglo-Saxon superiority as championed by politicians such as Missouri's Thomas Hart Benton. "Civilization, or extinction, has been the fate of all people who have found themselves in the track of the advancing Whites," Benton wrote in 1846, "and civilization, always the preference of the Whites has been pressed as an object, while extinction followed as a consequence of its resistence. The Black and Red races have often felt their ameliorating influence." Even such radical abolitionists as Unitarian minister Theodore Parker believed that African Americans were passive and unassertive. Black abolitionist Frederick Douglass would often complain that the Republican Party's antislavery sentiments were tinged with antiblack prejudice that sought to keep African Americans out of the Northern society altogether.[8]

Had it not been for the annexation of Texas in 1845 and the subsequent Mexican War in 1846, abolitionism might have remained mired in obscurity in American history for many years. The Mexican War, however, brought the United States vast new territories. How those territories were organized and whether slavery would be allowed into the territories now became an important political issue. Beginning with the introduction of the Wilmot Proviso in August 1846, an amendment to a House appropriations bill that forbade the introduction of slavery into any territories conquered from Mexico as a result of the war, the issue of the disposition of slavery in the territories of the United States remained divisive, confrontational, and, ultimately, an unsolvable problem for the political system of the young republic. Almost all of the major political confrontations of the 1850s—the Kansas-Nebraska Act of 1854, which repealed the Missouri Compromise of 1820 and made possible the spread of slavery in the Louisiana territory, the Dred Scott decision of 1857, which declared that African Americans were not citizens of the United States, the battle over the ratification of the Lecompton Constitution of 1857–1858, whereby a proslavery Constitution was foisted upon the residents of Kansas—centered on this divisive issue. Obviously, there were other issues. As ethnocultural historians rightly observe, important wedge social issues—such as temperance, sabbatarianism, and anti-Catholicism—often riveted local communities and were at the forefront of local elections. Nevertheless, without downplaying any of these other issues, the centrality of the slavery issue cannot be underestimated.[9]

At the end of the Mexican War, three distinct positions emerged with respect to the status of slavery in the territories. Some Northern Democrats joined with Conscience Whigs and members of the newly organized Free Soil Party to endorse the well-established principle of congressional oversight of the territories—including crafting laws and conditions for slavery. Founded upon congressional power granted in Article 4, Section 3 of the Constitution, this position had the virtue of precedent on its side. As early as 1787, when Congress passed the Northwest Ordinances, it prohibited the introduction of slavery into these territories north of the Ohio River. Again, in the Missouri Crisis of 1820, Congress once again set rules and conditions upon the introduction of slavery in federal territories. While some may not have agreed with the exclusion of slavery from the territories, few, if any, denied that Congress had the right to regulate the peculiar institution.[10]

Southern Whigs, Democrats, and their allies in the North endorsed a second position. Expertly articulated by such apostles of Southern rights as John C. Calhoun, Robert Barnwell Rhett, and William Lowndes Yancey, this position focused on the assertion that federal territories were the common property of the states. The general government was merely a caretaker for the states. Since slavery was legal in Southern states, it would be a denial of equal rights to prevent Southerners from taking slave property into federal territories. As a result, Calhoun and others argued that Congress had no power to interfere with the institution of slavery in federal territories. The only opportunity to exclude slavery was when the territory was ready for statehood and a constitution was formed; then, and only then, could slavery be legally excluded. In the late 1850s, this position became more extreme with prominent Southern senators demanding a federal slave code for the territories.

Northwestern Democrats such as Lewis Cass of Michigan and Stephen A. Douglas of Illinois developed a middle course between these two extremes. Derisively called *squatter sovereignty* by opponents, this position asserted the fundamental rights of territorial settlers to create and adjust their own institutions through the ballot box and their own territorial legislatures. Rooted in American traditions of self-government and republicanism, this position potentially satisfied Southerners by forbidding Congress to legislate on slavery while, at the same time, endorsing democratic principles of self-rule. The fundamental flaw in the position was when self-rule began. Exactly how many residents of a territory were needed before important decisions on local laws and customs could be formulated? If slavery was allowed by one legislature, could it be made illegal by another? Would there be any stability in such an environment? Although the Compromise of 1850 temporarily resolved the outstanding issues of slavery in the territories, some historians regarded the compromise as merely a temporary interlude in an ongoing conflict.[11]

For many Americans, it seemed as if two separate and distinctive cultures were emerging in the United States. Although prior to the Mexican War, one historian observed that nationalism was strong in the South, by the 1850s it seemed to some as if two Americas were developing. While it would certainly be an exaggeration to characterize the North as urban and industrialized, it had undergone many more changes in this regard than the South. Historian Charles Sellers has elaborately demonstrated the social and economic changes that occurred in various communities throughout the North as a result of the penetration of the market economy. Many Northern political leaders captured the spirit of Northern society by endorsing the so-called free labor argument. The market economy had created a dynamic society where one could rise in society through hard work, thrift, and sobriety. By contrast, the South and slavery, according to this argument, bred a system that was static and caste oriented. In a speech that captured the sentiments of many, prominent New York Republican Senator William Henry Seward made the case for Northern distinctiveness and superiority, and argued that the two systems were mutually antagonistic. "It is an irrepressible conflict between opposing and enduring forces," maintained Seward, "and it means that the United States must and will, sooner or later, become entirely a slave-holding nation, or entirely a free labor nation."[12]

While the South was certainly capitalistic, it did not experience the penetrating power of the market economy as did the North. It remained more traditional, more rural, more folk, and, of course, more wedded to the peculiar institution. If such Northern leaders as Seward and Abraham Lincoln saw the South as benighted and backward, Southern leaders and intellectuals regarded the evolving Northern commercial-industrial society as, in the words of Thomas Hobbes, brutish, nasty, and mean. Regarding the drudgery of Northern workers as little better than wage slavery, writers such as George Fitzhugh and William Grayson argued that plantation slavery was far less brutal than Northern free labor. "Free laborers have not a thousandth part of the rights and liberties of negro slaves," maintained George Fitzhugh. "Indeed, they have not a single liberty, unless it be the right or liberty to die." For Southern political leaders, writers, and clergymen, the more decentralized, plantation-based, rural culture of the South was superior to the brutal laissez-faire society that had developed in the Northern states.[13]

Were the differences between North and South real? Obviously, a host of statistical data supports the contention that the North was much more industrialized than the South, had more urban development, and, particularly due to immigration, a much more heterogeneous complexion than the more homogeneous South. The two regions also developed different political orientations or points of view. "They came down to two fundamental and competing points of view over the nature of government," writes William C. Davis, "between those who favored stronger central authority ideally to promote the strength, security, and prosperity of all, and those who preferred limited government to favor greater local control in the individual states, so that the people who best knew their own local interests could better serve them."[14]

It was during the 1850s that the position between the two regions began to harden. While some historians have focused on ethnocultural conflicts as the major engine of political fighting during the 1850s, these conflicts, while significant, scarcely account for the hardening of regions and the mutual distrust that developed between the North and the South. When the Whig Party disintegrated in the aftermath of the Kansas-Nebraska Act, the eventual formation of the Republican Party was taken by Southern political leaders as evidence of a conspiracy, a black Republican conspiracy to keep slavery out of the territories and eventually to use the power of the federal government to abolish slavery throughout the South. The success of Republican candidate John C. Frémont in 1856, the raid of John Brown on Harpers Ferry in 1859, and the eventual election of Lincoln to the presidency in 1860—without even being on the ballot of any state in the Deep South—was evidence of the black Republican conspiracy. "The history of the Abolition or Black Republican Party," noted the New Orleans *Daily Crescent*, ". . . is a history of repeated injuries and usurpations, all having in direct object the establishment of absolute tyranny over the slave-holding states." For Southern radicals, known as fire-eaters, the only legitimate way to protect the institution of slavery was disunion and Southern independence.[15]

Conversely, antislavery politicians in the Free Soil Party and then the Republican Party developed the powerful image of the Slave Power conspiracy, using it to interpret some of the pivotal events of the 1850s, including the Kansas-Nebraska Act, the Dred Scott decision, the battle over the Lecompton Constitution, and finally the demand for federal protection for slavery in the territories of the United States. Indeed, from the Mexican War on, antislavery advocates interpreted political events through the dire lens of a proslavery conspiracy. According to this viewpoint, powerful Southern slaveholders, holding disproportionate power in the South and in the national government, willfully manipulated political policy to benefit the peculiar institution. In 1852, Indiana antislavery advocate George W. Julian denounced the Slave Power in numerous speeches delivered to antislavery audiences throughout the Midwest. "The powers of the government are in their keeping, and they determine all things according to the counsels of their own will," Julian told one audience. "They say to the politicians of the North 'Go,' and he goeth; to the Northern priest, 'Do this,' and he doeth it." And in the 1858 senatorial race in Illinois, Republican candidate Abraham Lincoln availed himself of this colorful image to advance his cause:

> But when we see a lot of framed timbers, different portions of which
> we know have been gotten out at different times and places and by
> different workmen—Stephen [Douglas], Franklin [Pierce], Roger
> [Taney], and James [Buchanan], for instance—and when we see these
> timbers joined together, and see they exactly make the frame of a
> house or a mill . . . in such a case, we find it impossible not to believe
> that Stephen and Franklin and Roger and James all understood one
> another from the beginning, all worked upon a common plan or draft
> drawn up before the first blow was struck.[16]

Ultimately, the outcome of the controversial events and debates of the 1850s would be determined by war. While the question as to the war's inevitability remains debatable, force decided all the outstanding issues between the two regions. The events leading up to war and the failure to negotiate a compromise to avert war are discussed in almost every chapter of the present volume. Once war began between the North and the South, each region faced internal dissent and challenges to its war goals. In the North, the Lincoln administration initially rallied most citizens by a popular appeal to restore the Union while leaving the peculiar institution alone. When ideology and necessity eventually prompted the preliminary Emancipation Proclamation after the battle of Antietam and ultimately the Emancipation Proclamation on January 1, 1863, Democratic critics emerged, popularly known as Copperheads, to challenge the new direction of the war. Enraged that the war was now waged for the abolition of slavery and upset at Lincoln's seeming disregard for civil liberties, Democratic Copperheads, beginning in earnest in the fall of 1862, began publicly challenging the policies of the president. Such political leaders and journalists as Clement Vallandigham, Charles Lanphier, Daniel W. Voorhees, and Samuel Medary charged that the Lincoln administration had perverted a war to restore the Union and replaced it with an illegitimate, revolutionary struggle to abolish slavery. Suspicious of the increasing power of the federal government, Copperhead critics also charged that the war was establishing a tyrannical central government that threatened the republican fabric of the young nation. While ultimately not convincing to the majority of Northerners, antiwar sentiment threatened to unravel the Union war effort at critical junctures during the war. After the disasters of Fredericksburg and Chancellorsville, Union military victories at Gettysburg and

Vicksburg stemmed the tide of rising Copperheadism and probably prevented the election of peace Democrats Vallandigham and George W. Woodward as governors of Ohio and Pennsylvania respectively. In the late summer of 1864, as mounting Union casualties dampened Northern morale and threatened the reelection of Abraham Lincoln, the fall of Mobile Bay and Atlanta once again turned back the rising tide of antiwar sentiment.[17]

If the goals of the war were controversial and divisive in the North, so, too, was the manner of waging war. Beginning with conciliation, Northern political and military leaders assumed that the secession was an emotional response that would eventually lose steam and subside. Once fighting broke out in the aftermath of Sumter, the worst course of action would be to unnecessarily antagonize Southern civilians by taking their property, liberating their slaves, and threatening their persons. Such policy was typified by Northern military leaders such as General George McClellan, who, as late as July 1862, urged a policy designed to shield Southern civilians from the harsher aspects of war. As Northerners settled in for a long war, however, political and military leaders emerged with different points of view. This military leadership reflected the change in the views of the dominant Republican political leadership. While early on, many Republicans settled for conciliation in their attempt to restore the Union, Southern resistance and victories caused a reversal of such opinions. Military leaders such as Generals Ulysses Grant, Philip Sheridan, and William Tecumseh Sherman developed a new style of warfare, aimed at making Southern civilians suffer and, hopefully, convincing them of the utter folly of resistance. Sherman, perhaps more than any other Union general, developed the rhetoric that symbolized this harsher version of warfare. "You cannot qualify war in harsher terms than I will," Sherman remarked to one correspondent. "War is cruelty and you cannot refine it." By the time the war had entered its third full year, Sherman and Grant had embarked on a style of warfare designed to convince Southern civilians not to support the Confederate government of Jefferson Davis. Government property was confiscated and, if not usable, destroyed; such supporting infrastructure as railroads was incapacitated, while Southern civilians willingly and unwillingly contributed to the maintenance of Union armies through liberal foraging policies. By the last year of the war, Sherman's armies' march through Georgia and the Carolinas inflicted unmeasurable hardship on civilians. The attitude of many Northerners evolved accordingly.[18]

In the South, war waged for the supremacy of states' rights and home rule seemed compromised by the centralizing tendencies of the Jefferson Davis administration. Faced with an administration that was forced on occasion to suspend the right of habeas corpus and that, more than once, initiated a federal conscription, Southern purists, like Democratic Copperheads, accused Davis and the Confederacy of abandoning and compromising the very principles it was fighting to maintain. Led by Confederate

Vice President Alexander Stephens, Joe Brown, Zebulon Vance, and William W. Holden, these critics of the Davis administration questioned the validity of the war and Davis's leadership on the grounds that it sacrificed the very reasons for Southern independence. In a speech delivered in March 1864, Stephens reminded Georgia legislators, "But as a parting remembrance . . . I warn you against the most insidious enemy which approaches with her syren song, 'Independence first and liberty afterward.' It is a fatal delusion. Liberty is the animating spirit, the soul of our government, and like the soul of man, when once lost is lost forever." Ironically, in early 1865, the Davis administration, backed by the Confederate Congress, approved a measure to emancipate male slaves who volunteered for military service. Like Northern Copperheads, critics of Jefferson Davis argued that the means of waging war were destroying the purpose of the war.[19]

Once the guns fell silent and the armies of Robert E. Lee and Joseph Johnston had surrendered, the pivotal issue of the Reconstruction of Southern states came to the forefront. Had states really opted out of the Union? Would they simply be readmitted? Could the Northern government place conditions and requirements on readmittance? If so, what were these conditions, and who ultimately controlled the reconstruction process: Congress or the president? While the end of the Civil War decisively answered the question as to the practical consequences of secession, it introduced a series of complicated constitutional questions that have not totally been answered even today. Democrats and Conservative Republicans shared minimalist goals for Reconstruction that imposed few conditions on seceded states and provided few rights for African Americans. They argued that secession was a theoretical and constitutional impossibility. Since states were never really out of the Union, Reconstruction would be simple, straightforward, and uncomplicated. On the other hand, radical Republicans, motivated by higher moral ideas, had loftier goals, demanding more conditions on seceded states and many more rights for recently emancipated slaves. Such radicals as Thaddeus Stevens, for instance, argued that states had de facto left the Union and could be treated as conquered provinces, with Reconstruction requirements imposed as the spoils of victory. So divisive were the questions of Reconstruction that it brought the nation to another constitutional crisis, the first impeachment of a president. While Andrew Johnson escaped conviction, the significance of impeachment in the Reconstruction period was the tipping of political power into the hands of Congress and away from the executive branch.[20]

As a number of historians point out, the American Civil War brought about a greater centralization of political authority than heretofore in the history of the young republic. As is often the case with war, the power of the national government was greatly expanded. Historians also emphasize that change in the country's character. Focusing on Lincoln's Gettysburg Address, for instance, many emphasize the subtle way in which a league of equal states became a sovereign nation. "The ideological groundwork for an activist government that would protect the weak and promote equality," comments George Fletcher, "was forged in the sufferings of both strong and weak in the killing fields of Gettysburg and Antietam." While these ideals were obviously not fully realized, the notion of the federal government as playing a role in the guarantee of equal rights was obviously created during the Civil War.[21]

The historical figures singled out in this volume had something to say on all of the themes mentioned in this introduction. While the selection of some might be considered arbitrary and unfair, they were selected for this volume because they participated in the public discussion on almost all of the controversial issues of the day. They had strong opinions on whether states could secede from the Union and on whether state power was ultimately subordinate to federal power. On the issue of slavery, some were abolitionists, some were primarily antiextensionists, while others believed that slavery was a beneficent institution that had the sanction of Almighty God. When the war erupted, these figures had well-articulated positions as to how the war ought to be waged and for what purpose. After the Confederate surrender at Appomattox, these individuals had definite ideas on how the peace should transpire, how the Southern states might be integrated back into the Union, and what rights African American might enjoy in a postemancipation society. Indeed, it is no exaggeration to state that many of the figures covered in this volume played a significant role in articulating what type of republic the United States ought to be after the Civil War had ended.

The figures singled out in this volume contributed to the great debates in very public ways. Through speeches, books, articles, letters, public debates, and actions, these individuals were interwoven in the public discourse of these issues during the Civil War era. They were not passive observers, but energetically engaged in the issues of the day. Some were legislators, helping determine the legislative agenda of the nation. Some were military figures whose actions and ideas were instrumental during the war. Some military figures, such as George McClellan, were prominent political figures in addition to their military roles. Others were journalists and publicists whose ideas helped shape public opinion. New York *Tribune* editor Horace Greeley, for instance, participated in the public discussion of practically every major social, political, economic, and military idea that was publicly debated during the Civil War era. Others in this volume were agitators and activists, whose actions played an important role in the direction of events. Harriet Beecher Stowe, for instance, may have made the largest single contribution to bringing about sectional discord with the publication of *Uncle Tom's Cabin*. Stowe's novel was arguably the most highly visible literary attack on the peculiar institution, reaching a multitude of Americans through both the stage and written form. Activist John Brown published nothing; however, his actions in Kansas Territory in the mid-1850s and his daring raid on Harper's Ferry in 1859 polarized the nation more powerfully than the words or speeches of any journalist or politician.

In every sense of the word, the figures chosen for this volume were shapers of the great debate during the Civil War era. Tragically, the participants in the great debates could not peaceably resolve their differences. They argued forcefully for the positions that they endorsed; however, they were unsuccessful in negotiating compromises that might have averted war. Their unfortunate failure precipitated the most catastrophic event in American history.

NOTES

1. James McPherson, *Battle Cry of Freedom: The Civil War Era* (New York: Oxford University Press, 1988), 818–19; and idem., *Ordeal by Fire: The Civil War and Reconstruction* (New York: Alfred A. Knopf, 1982), 486–89. Sherman estimated that his army destroyed 100 million on his march to the sea. See Albert Castel, *Articles of War: Winners, Losers, and Some Who Were Both in the Civil War* (Mechanicsburg, PA: Stackpole Books, 2001), 227.

2. James A. Rawley, *Race and Politics: Bleeding Kansas and the Coming of the Civil War* (Lincoln: University of Nebraska Press, 1969); and Charles and Mary Beard, *The Rise of American Civilization*, 2 vols. (New York: Macmillan, 1927), 2:54–55. For examples of revisionism, see Avery Craven, *The Coming of the Civil War*, 2nd rev. ed. (Chicago: University of Chicago Press, 1957); idem., *The Repressible Conflict* (Baton Rouge: Louisiana State University Press, 1939); James G. Randall, *Lincoln the Liberal Statesman* (New York: Dodd, Mead & Company, 1947), 36–64; Brian Holden Reid, *The Origins of the American Civil War* (London and New York: Longman, 1996), 3–17; and William E. Gienapp, "The Crisis of American Democracy: The Political System and the Coming of the Civil War," in *Why the Civil War Came*, ed. Gabor Borritt (New York: Oxford University Press, 1996), 81.

3. "The Kentucky Resolutions of 1798," in *The Causes of the Civil War*, ed. Kenneth M. Stampp (Englewood Cliffs, NJ: Prentice Hall, 1959), 34–35 (quote, 35); and "South Carolina Exposition and Protest," in *A More Perfect Union: Documents in American History*, ed. Paul F. Boller Jr. and Ronald Story, 2nd ed. (Boston: Houghton Mifflin Company, 1988), 1:125–27. For a discussion on the Kentucky and Virginia resolutions, see, for instance, Noble E. Cunningham Jr., *In Pursuit of Reason: The Life of Thomas Jefferson* (New York: Ballantine Books, 1987), 216–20.

4. Merrill D. Peterson, *The Great Triumvirate: Webster, Clay, and Calhoun* (New York: Oxford University Press, 1987), 170–80 (quote, 178).

5. For discussions of republicanism, see Bernard Bailyn, *The Ideological Origins of the American Revolution* (1967; reprint, Cambridge, MA: Harvard University Press, 1992); Drew R. McCoy, *The Elusive Republic: Political Economy in Jeffersonian America* (Chapel Hill: University of North Carolina Press, 1980); and Dan Monroe, *The Republican Vision of John Tyler* (College Station: Texas A&M University Press, 2003). On the nullification crisis, see William W. Frehling, *Prelude*

to Civil War: The Nullification Controversy in South Carolina, 1816–1836 (New York: Harper & Row, 1965); Merrill D. Peterson, The Olive Branch and Sword—The Compromise of 1833 (Baton Rouge: Louisiana State University Press, 1982); and Richard Ellis, The Union at Risk: Jacksonian Democracy, States' Rights, and the Nullification Crisis (New York: Oxford University Press, 1986).

   6. McPherson, Ordeal by Fire, 79–80.

   7. For a recent study on slavery, see Ira Berlin, Many Thousands Gone: The First Two Centuries of Slavery in North America (Cambridge, MA: Belknap Press, 1998). On abolitionism and political abolitionism, see the following: Victor B. Howard, Conscience and Slavery: The Evangelistic Calvinist Domestic Missions, 1837–1861 (Kent, OH: Kent State University Press, 1990); Herbert Aptheker, Abolitionism (Boston: Twayne Publishers, 1989); and Daniel J. McInerney, "A Faith for Freedom: The Political Gospel of Abolition," Journal of the Early Republic 2 (Fall 1991): 371–93. On the Liberty and Free Soil Parties, see Richard Sewell, Ballots for Freedom: Anti-Slavery Politics in the United States 1837–1860 (New York: W. W. Norton & Company, 1976). See also Eric Foner, The Story of American Freedom (New York: W. W. Norton & Company, 1998), 84–88.

   8. Thomas Hart Benton, "The Destiny of the Race," in A More Perfect Union, 1:139–42 (quote, 140–41). On Theodore Parker, see Paul E. Teed, "Racial Nationalism and Its Challengers: Theodore Parker, John Rock, and the Antislavery Movement," Civil War History 41 (June 1995): 142–60. On the views of Douglass, see William S. McFeely, Frederick Douglass (New York: W. W. Norton & Company, 1991), 189–90. See also Eugene W. Berwanger, The Frontier against Slavery: Western Anti-Negro Prejudice and the Slavery Extension Controversy (Urbana: University of Illinois Press, 1967).

   9. On territorial expansion, see Michael A. Morrison, Slavery and the American West: The Eclipse of Manifest Destiny and the Coming of the Civil War (Chapel Hill: University of North Carolina Press, 1997), 13–14, 82–84. Ethnocultural interpretations of conflict of the 1850s abound. See Joel H. Silbey, The Partisan Imperative: The Dynamics of American Politics before the Civil War (New York: Oxford University Press, 1985); Michael Holt, The Political Crisis of the 1850s (New York: John Wiley & Sons, 1978); and William E. Gienapp, The Origins of the Republican Party, 1852–1856 (New York: Oxford University Press, 1987).

   10. The three positions on the fate of slavery in the territories are expertly discussed in Allan Nevins, Ordeal of the Union: Volume One, The Fruits of Manifest Destiny, 1847–1852 (New York: Charles Scribner's Sons, 1947), 26–32.

   11. Indeed, one historian calls the Compromise of 1850 the armistice of 1850. See William W. Frehling, The Road to Disunion: Secessionists at Bay, 1776–1854 (New York: Oxford University Press, 1990), 487–510. Also see Morrison, Slavery and the American West, 130–36.

   12. David Potter, The Impending Crisis, 1848–1861 (New York: Harper & Row, 1976), 12–13; and the William H. Seward quote is from Democracy on Trial: A Documentary History of American Life, ed. Robert W. Johannsen, 2nd ed. (Urbana: University of Illinois Press, 1988), 135–44 (quote, 138). The best expression of the free labor argument remains Eric Foner, Free Labor, Free Soil, Free Men: The Ideology of the Republican Party before the Civil War (New York: Oxford University Press, 1970). On economic changes in antebellum society, see Charles E.

Sellers, *The Market Revolution: Jacksonian America, 1815–1846* (New York: Oxford University Press, 1991).

13. George Fitzhugh, *Cannibals All! Or Slaves without Masters* (Cambridge, MA: Belknap Press, 1988), 19. Also see Emory Thomas, *The Confederate Nation, 1861–1865* (New York: Harper & Row, 1979), 9–10.

14. William C. Davis, *Look Away! A History of the Confederate States of America* (New York: Free Press, 2002), 9.

15. Gienapp, "The Crisis of American Democracy," 91; Eric Walther, *The Fire Eaters* (Baton Rouge: Louisiana University Press, 1992), 6–7; and New Orleans *Daily Crescent*, November 13, 1860, quoted in Stampp, *Causes of Civil War*, 29.

16. Morrison, *Slavery and the American West*, 160–61; William Gienapp, "The Republican Party and the Slave Power," in *Race and Slavery in America: Essays in Honor of Kenneth Stampp*, ed. Robert H. Abzug and Stephen E. Maizlish (Lexington: University of Kentucky Press, 1986), 51–78; David Brion Davis, *The Slave Power Conspiracy and the Paranoid Style* (Baton Rouge: Louisiana State University Press, 1969); George W. Julian, "The Strength and Weakness of the Slave Power—The Duty of Anti-Slavery Men," in *Speeches on Political Questions* (Westport, CT: Negro University Press, 1970), 70; and Robert W. Johannsen, ed., *The Lincoln-Douglas Debates of 1858* (New York: Oxford University Press, 1965), 18.

17. On antiwar sentiment in the North, see Frank L. Klement, *The Copperheads in the Middlewest* (Gloucester, MA: Peter Smith, 1972); idem., *Lincoln's Critics: The Copperheads of the North* (Shippensburg, PA: White Mane Books, 1999); and Joanna D. Cowden, *"Heaven Will Frown upon Such a Cause as This": Six Democrats Who Opposed the War* (New York: University Press of America, 2001). On the election of 1864, see Albert Castel, *Winning and Losing in the Civil War: Essays and Stories* (Columbia: University of South Carolina Press, 1996), 15–32; and David E. Long, *The Jewel of Liberty: Abraham Lincoln's Re-election and the End of Slavery* (New York: Da Capo Press, 1994). Northern politics during the American Civil War are also expertly discussed in Mark E. Neely Jr., *The Union Divided: Party Conflicts in the Civil War North* (Cambridge, MA: Harvard University Press, 2002). On the nature of Democratic suspicions of centralized power and tyranny, see also Jean H. Baker, *Affairs of Party: The Political Culture of the Northern Democrats in the Mid-Nineteenth Century* (Ithaca, NY: Cornell University Press, 1983), 147–59.

18. Sherman quote is from Michael Fellman, *Citizen Sherman: A Life of William Tecumseh Sherman* (New York: Random House, 1995), 182. Conciliation and union policy toward Southern civilians are documented in *The Hard Hand of War: Union Policy toward Southern Civilians, 1861–1865* (Cambridge: Cambridge University Press, 1995); and Charles Royster, *The Destructive War: William Tecumseh Sherman, Stonewall Jackson, and the Americans* (New York: Alfred A. Knopf, 1991). Various war issues and challenges are discussed in Garbor S. Borritt, ed., *Lincoln the War President: The Gettysburg Lectures* (New York: Oxford University Press, 1992). McClellan's attitude toward the style of warfare is best exemplified in his Harrison's Landing letter. See McClellan to Abraham Lincoln, July 7, 1862, in *The Civil War Papers of George B. McClellan: Selected Correspondence 1860–1865*, ed. Stephen W. Sears (New York: Da Capo Press, 1992), 344–45.

19. Stephens quote is from *The Union in Crisis, 1850–1877*, ed. Robert W. Jo-

hannsen and Wendy Hamand Venet (Acton, MA: Copley Publishing Group, 2003), 278. The issue of Confederate emancipation is covered in Robert F. Durden, *The Gray and the Black: The Confederate Debate on Emancipation* (Baton Rouge: Louisiana State University Press, 1972). The conflicts and struggles of the Confederacy are also discussed in William C. Davis, *The Cause Lost: Myths and Realities of the Confederacy* (Lawrence: University Press of Kansas, 1996).

20. Studies on the Reconstruction are too numerous to list; however, the issues surrounding wartime reconstruction are expertly discussed in William C. Harris, *With Charity for All: Lincoln and the Restoration of the Union* (Lexington: University of Kentucky Press, 1997). One of the most comprehensive volumes on reconstruction remains Eric Foner, *Reconstruction: America's Unfinished Revolution, 1865–1877* (New York: Harper & Row, 1988).

21. George P. Fletcher, *Our Secret Constitution: How Lincoln Redefined American Democracy* (New York: Oxford University Press, 2001), 4–6 (quote, 8). See also Gary Wills, *Lincoln at Gettysburg: The Words That Remade America* (New York: Simon & Schuster, 1992).

JOHN BROWN
(1800–1859)

A Bloody Career

LIFE

John Brown was born to Owen and Ruth Brown on May 9, 1800, in Torrington, Connecticut. Owen Brown was the product of a difficult youth. His father died after brief service in the Continental Army when Owen was five, leaving his large family utterly impoverished. After a childhood marked by hunger and privation, Owen began working as an itinerant cobbler at age twelve. He moved to Simsbury, Connecticut, where he attended a Congregational Church and purportedly learned that slavery was a mortal sin. Hard work and thriftiness enabled him to present enough of a figure to marry Ruth Mills, the daughter of a Congregational minister, in 1793. They moved to Norfolk, Connecticut, where Owen worked as a tanner and cobbler. The death of two children at very young ages prompted them to move to Torrington in 1799. John Brown's birth followed in the next year.

John Brown grew to manhood in a strict Congregationalist and Calvinist household. He learned to obey the commandments, keep the Sabbath, and pray with regularity. Owen was a strict disciplinarian who felt no reluctance to whip his children when caught in a misdeed. Slavery, young Brown learned, was a terrible sin and those victimized by it were to be pitied. Further, his father believed that the American republic was the divinely blessed vehicle for the Second Coming of Jesus Christ, a unique nation that slavery blighted. Owen was also possessed of the restlessness characteristic of the age. In June 1805, he moved his family to Ohio. The Browns settled in Hudson, near Cleveland. Owen reestablished his tanning business, and he farmed and raised livestock.

Tragedy revisited the family in December 1808 when Brown's mother died soon after the birth and death of an infant daughter. His mother's death traumatized Brown, who plunged into an abyss of despair. He became an ill-tempered youth given to rough behavior, a poor and disruptive student at the rude frontier school he attended. His father remarried to a young bride for whom Brown held little affection. Business began to keep Owen from home, and he confessed that his absences harmed his son. Brown abandoned his studies and joined his father in the tanning business. During the War of 1812, he drove cattle to the Michigan frontier for sale to American troops. While on one of these trips, Brown saw a master viciously beat his slave, an event that made a distinct impression and gave life to his father's admonitions on the evils of slavery.

Brown briefly flirted with agnosticism, then fervently embraced the Calvinism of his father and, after a profession of faith, joined the Congregational Church in Hudson. He determined on a career in the ministry and briefly attended schools in Massachusetts and Connecticut before lack of funds and health problems drove him back to Ohio in 1817. An imperious and self-assured young man despite that setback, Brown could not abide working for his father, so he opened his own tannery and lived in a cabin with his adopted brother Levi Blakeslee. Bursting with energy, Brown soon had other men working for him in his business. He also learned surveying, a practical trade on the frontier. He hired a woman to keep his cabin clean and was smitten with her daughter, Dianthe Lusk. They married on June 21, 1820, and their union produced seven children, though two died. Brown aspired to genteel business success: he taught Sunday School at his church, joined the Masons, and compelled his tannery employees to attend morning prayer services he conducted himself. He was equally strict with his own children, expecting them to obey him and the dictates of religion.

Restless and anxious to make his own mark, Brown traveled to Randolph County, Pennsylvania, in 1825, where he found good timber for a tanning business. In May of the following year, he moved his family to Pennsylvania and started his tannery. Brown quickly became a leading citizen, employing ten to fifteen men in his business. He also surveyed the area and became the postmaster for the community, which was called New Richmond. In 1832, he helped organize a Congregational Church in New Richmond and in the absence of a minister, Brown delivered stern sermons. He relied on the Old Testament, much of which he seems to have committed to memory, and on the fiery sermons of Jonathan Edwards. Brown's God was the wrathful deity of the Old Testament who punished transgressors, rather than the forgiving savior of the New Testament.

Brown's business fortunes peaked during his first few years in Pennsylvania and then went into a precipitous decline from which he never emerged. A man of great energy who could work tirelessly, Brown was given to manic enthusiasm yet he lacked the good judgment that, coupled to his hard work ethic, would have led to prosperity. Brown's decline began when he contracted the ague, or malaria, in 1831. For the remainder of his life, Brown endured periodic bouts of the ague. His illness lasted into 1832 and kept him from properly managing his business affairs. His wife Dianthe, exhausted from childbearing, died in August 1832 soon after delivering an infant who also died. Brown bore his afflictions stoically with Christian resignation, and he soon found his second wife, Mary Day, in the same manner as he had discovered his first: Mary was the sister of a woman who Brown hired to keep house after Dianthe's death. They married on June 14, 1833. Mary was a stout woman fit to endure life with a restless dreamer and poor provider. She had been raised to act as a traditional wife, and so she would until Brown's death in 1859, bearing thirteen children during their marriage, six of whom reached adulthood. With a new wife, six children, and his business in tatters, Brown moved back to Ohio in May 1835.

A series of business failures followed. Brown immediately became involved in the speculative fever in land values that swept the country. He borrowed and spent recklessly on land, hoping to sell as values rose and take a profit while repaying his notes. His partner urged him to sell in 1836, but Brown, who always felt he knew better in all matters than anyone else and would accept no advice, held on. The Panic of 1837 followed, land values plummeted, and Brown was ruined. He then attempted a cattle partnership in 1838–1839, but it too failed. Besieged by creditors, Brown declared bankruptcy in September 1842. The next year, he began tending sheep for Simon Perkins and eventually entered into a partnership. Brown became convinced that textile manufacturers were not paying a fair price to wool producers. His solution was to establish himself as a representative factor for wool growers; he would evaluate and grade the wool, then sell it for an appropriate price.

In 1846, the firm of Perkins and Brown opened in Springfield, Massachusetts, and Brown put his theory into effect. His effort proved disastrous. He was as industrious as ever, but obstinate in his pricing. He did not understand the vagaries of the market, where prices fluctuated with supply and demand, and textile manufacturers simply refused to purchase wool at the rates Brown had set. By 1848, Perkins and Brown was failing. In an effort to save the enterprise, Brown came up with a bizarre scheme to ship the wool to England, where he believed better prices waited. He traveled there himself in August 1849, but ended up selling the wool at a loss. The firm closed in 1850, $40,000 in debt, and Brown endured protracted litigation as his creditors sought redress for losses.

While failing at his various business ventures, Brown had become a committed antislavery activist. The 1830s marked the emergence of the abolition movement and leaders such as William Lloyd Garrison. Brown read Garrison's abolition newspaper, the *Liberator*, and witnessed abolition debate and controversy in Ohio. Disputes between advocates of immediate emancipation and those of more moderate sentiments who favored colonization occurred in colleges such as Western Reserve and the Lane Seminary. Brown's father Owen was a trustee at Western Reserve. He resigned from the board after it reprimanded professors who advocated immediate emancipation. Owen Brown became a supporter of the more progressive Oberlin College.

The antislavery fervor affected Brown, who already had a marked distaste for slavery. In January 1837, Brown attended an abolition meeting in Cleveland, serving on a correspondence committee that petitioned the Ohio legislature to repeal state black laws (laws that codified legal discrimination against black Americans). At a memorial meeting in Hudson held later that year to honor the memory of abolitionist newspaperman Elijah Lovejoy, who had been murdered by a mob in Illinois, Brown impulsively leapt to his feet and vowed to make freeing slaves his life's mission. A contemporary said of Brown, "He was eccentric, but not crazy. He had a consuming idea in life, and that was to free the black man. He had no other aim." Brown also advocated equality of treatment for black people. In 1838, while living in Franklin Mills, Ohio, Brown insisted that black citizens sit in the pews at the local Congregational Church; they had been forced to cluster at the doorway. The hypocrisy of church members in Franklin Mills turned Brown away from established religion, though he continued to be a fervent Christian.[1]

While living in Springfield, Massachusetts, Brown attended abolition meetings, but never joined an organization. While Garrison and others advocated nonviolence, Brown was prepared to countenance armed, violent resistance. Indeed, he criticized Northern free blacks for being too submissive, too tolerant and accepting of white prejudice. In November 1847, Brown met the famed escaped slave and antislavery orator Frederick Douglass, to whom he outlined a plan to create an armed force of men and establish it in the Alleghany Mountains to assist escaped slaves. Brown argued that the value of slaves would decline as more and more escaped, assisted by his armed men. Douglass wondered if it would be better to persuade slaveholders to abandon slavery without recourse to violence, though he later accepted the necessity of violence to end slavery, a change in attitude some have attributed to Brown's influence. In the end, slavery would be abolished. Perhaps influenced by the militant Henry H. Garnet, whom he had also met, Brown advocated black resistance as a way to boost blacks' self-respect. He did not, unlike other abolitionists, believe that slave owners could be persuaded to voluntarily abandon slavery. As his wool business collapsed, Brown met Gerrit Smith in the spring of 1848. A wealthy philanthropist and antislavery advocate, Smith had set aside 100,000 acres in the Adirondack Mountains in New York for free black settlers. Brown suggested that he move to the town of North Elba in the region and act as a mentor to the black settlers. He could teach them to farm, become self-sufficient, and create a model black community whose existence would be a rebuke to the Southern argument that dependence and slavery were the natural condition for blacks. Smith agreed, and Brown relocated his family to North Elba in May 1849.

After returning to North Elba from his disastrous business trip to England in September 1850, Brown endured protracted litigation. Outraged at the reinvigorated Fugitive Slave Act that was part of the Compromise of 1850, Brown formed a militant group that he called, with Old Testament fervor, the United States League of the Gileadites. The group's goal was to resist enforcement of the act on Smith's land. A number of free blacks became members of Brown's group. In 1854, Brown was in Ohio, where he ended the last vestiges of his business relationship with Perkins, and then he returned to North Elba and his family at the hardscrabble farm he had established. That same year, the Kansas-Nebraska Act passed Congress and was signed into law by President Franklin Pierce. Angry at the repudiation of the Missouri Compromise in the act and anxious to keep Kansas free, emigrant aid companies formed in the North to spur settlement of the territory by those of Free Soil sentiments. A race of sorts began as North and South vied to populate the territory with antislavery and slavery partisans.

Brown's sons Aaron, Salmon, Frederick, Jason, and John Jr. decided to make a fresh start in Kansas. In the spring of 1855, they migrated to Kansas Territory, where they built a settlement called Brown's Station near Osawatomie on North Middle Creek. Brown had at first rebuffed his sons' entreaties to join them. Later, he changed his mind and decided to go to Kansas temporarily, as he intended that Mary and his minor children remain at the North Elba farm. In May, John Jr. wrote his father an inflammatory letter describing the precarious condition of his family and other Free Soil settlers as proslavery toughs from Missouri crossed the border and threatened them. He urged his father to bring weapons so that they could defend themselves. Brown reacted vigorously. He went to Gerrit Smith and to an abolition convention meeting in Syracuse, New York, and solicited donations. He took the funds raised, purchased arms and ammunition, and in October 1855, Brown was in Kansas with a wagonload of weapons and goods.

Brown's appearance energized his family, who had been listlessly residing in tents and lean-tos. He took charge, constructing cabins, harvesting the crops his sons had planted in the spring, and generally getting the homestead in shape. As winter approached, the murder of a Free Soil settler sparked tension in Lawrence, a city that was a bastion of Free State sentiment. When the territorial governor called out the notoriously proslavery militia, Free State men rushed to the defense of Lawrence. Brown armed his sons and fifteen other men and rode to the city. He was commissioned a captain of the First Brigade of Kansas Volunteers. Negotiations ensued that calmed tempers before outright violence broke out, and Brown's militia unit was disbanded. He and his family spent a hard winter eating cornmeal cakes.

The next year brought renewed violence. A Free State legislature convened in Topeka in March 1856, defying the existing proslavery legislature. Brown's son John Jr. had been elected a delegate to the convention and also to the command of the local Free State militia unit, called the Pottawatomie Rifles. Tensions ran high in the spring. Proslavery settlers in the vicinity of Pottawatomie Creek threatened their Free State neighbors. After a proslavery sheriff was shot, some 400 armed Southerners marched to Kansas in early May. Soon after, Lawrence was sacked, an event that made news across the United States. Brown and his sons, hearing that Lawrence was again in danger, had rushed to its defense with Brown attaching himself to his son's Pottawatomie Rifles. While en route to Lawrence on May 22, the men learned they were too late: the city had already suffered attack. Uncertain whether to proceed, John Jr. called a halt for the evening. Brown, always in favor of precipitate action, was incensed and spent an evening fuming about the campfire. The following day brought word of the brutal beating of antislavery Massachusetts senator Charles Sumner on the floor of the U.S. Senate, news that convinced Brown that proslavery settlers had to be taught a lesson.

Brown asked for volunteers to undertake a secret mission. His son refused to release any of his men to his father, and the two argued. In the end, Brown departed on a wagon loaded with broadswords he had acquired from a defunct filibustering group in Ohio. Several of his sons and a few other men joined him. He planned to murder proslavery settlers on Pottawatomie Creek. Though these settlers had evidently threatened their Free State neighbors, Stephen Oates has correctly noted that if Brown and his sons had really been fearful of their neighbors they would not have ridden off to Lawrence, leaving female family members unprotected at Brown's Station. There was little of self-defense in the murders that followed. On the evening of May 24, 1856, Brown and his followers went killing, hacking up five proslavery men with broadswords after hauling them out of cabins in the dark of night. Pleas for mercy from family members of the men were ignored; Brown himself shot one man in the head as a coup de grâce. Having committed the bloody deed, Brown and his men rode back to rejoin the encamped Pottawatomie Rifles. The men of the company were outraged at the murders, fearing retaliation, and settlers at Osawatomie subsequently denounced the killings at a conciliation meeting. Witnesses to the murders identified Brown and his men as the culprits, arrest warrants were issued, and Brown and his sons became fugitives.

A summer of violence followed in which Brown and his family participated. Raiders from Missouri burned Brown's Station in early June, scattering or stealing what livestock the Browns possessed. Brown and other

Free State men skirmished with a small force of Missourians near Prairie City, at the so-called Battle of Black Jack. In August, Brown raided proslavery settlements on Sugar Creek. In response, Missourians raided into Kansas, targeting Osawatomie and Brown himself. On August 30, 1856, Brown's son Frederick was shot dead as the Missourians attacked, dispersing Brown's force. Brown again went into hiding, though he emerged in Lawrence in early September 1856, where city residents welcomed him with cheers. Brown was portrayed in some Northern newspapers as a kind of warrior-saint, and he probably saw himself as just that, the living and scourging instrument of a just God angry at the abomination of slavery.

Convinced he was an avenging angel destined to free the slaves, Brown began mulling over his plan to establish a guerrilla bastion in the mountains of western Virginia to assist and encourage escaped slaves. In October 1856, he left for the east with the ostensible goal of raising money for the Free State cause in Kansas, but also with his Southern offensive in mind. Brown met with and secured a letter of introduction from Salmon P. Chase, the governor of Ohio. In January 1857, Brown was in Boston where Franklin B. Sanborn, a leader of the Massachusetts State Kansas Committee, befriended him. Quite taken with Brown's obvious zeal and force of personality, Sanborn helped him make useful contacts among those with antislavery convictions and the wealth to support them. Brown met William Lloyd Garrison, Theodore Parker, Amos A. Lawrence, Samuel Gridley Howe, George Luther Stearns, and Wentworth Higginson. With Gerrit Smith, Parker, Howe, Sanborn, Stearns, and Higginson became the so-called Committee of Six who supported Brown's endeavors. These men pledged to help Brown, and he was given money and 200 rifles. He also met Charles Sumner and, at Brown's request, Sumner displayed the blood-smeared coat he had worn when Preston Brooks assailed him in the Senate. Brown reverently fingered the gruesome artifact of a Slave Power attack on a democratic representative.

Brown subsequently went on a speaking tour of New England and New York, raising funds for his Kansas defense effort. At Concord, Massachusetts, Brown met Ralph Waldo Emerson and Henry David Thoreau, and he told the former that he revered the Bible and the Declaration of Independence and thought violent death preferable to violating the tenets of either. Brown was prepared for and even welcomed bloodshed. He ordered pikes from a Connecticut contractor, and he met a soldier of fortune named Hugh Forbes, whom Brown envisioned as a drillmaster for his forces. Forbes agreed to help and went off to Tabor, Iowa, where Brown hoped to gather and train his forces. Brown believed that freed slaves, untutored in the cumbersome process of loading and firing muskets, could fight effectively with medieval pikes. That Brown would seriously consider the obsolete pike as a weapon for insurrection illustrates the paucity of clear thinking that typified the entire undertaking.

In the ensuing two years before Brown's quixotic raid on Harpers Ferry, Virginia, he struggled to put his violent messianic vision into effect. He went back to Kansas and recruited men before returning east for more fundraising. In January 1858, Brown met with Frederick Douglass and outlined his plan for an incursion in the South. Douglass thought the plan dubious and his houseguest tiresome on the subject, but he allowed Brown to stay in his home for a number of weeks, and while there, Brown drew up a constitution for the provisional government he expected to establish in a mountain redoubt. In May, Brown was in Chatham, Ontario, Canada, where a meeting of free blacks ratified Brown's proposed constitution and elected "cabinet ministers" to the provisional government. With his increasingly grandiose visions seemingly moving forward, Brown prepared for action, but the plan was delayed after a disaffected Hugh Forbes appeared in Washington, D.C., and revealed Brown's intentions to Senator Henry Wilson. Brown's supporters feared that the revelations would compromise them, and Brown acceded to their request that he not act for a year. They urged him to return to Kansas and give the lie to Forbes's claim of a pending raid in the South. Brown dutifully went back to Kansas and staged a raid in Missouri, freeing slaves and damaging property. He left Kansas in January 1859 with the freed slaves, intending to march them to freedom in Canada, a goal he accomplished without being molested by legal authorities. He stopped briefly in Cleveland, where he witnessed protests against the Slave Power and heard militant talk from the free black community. Stephen Oates has argued that these events probably gave Brown the impression that his Virginia raid would have widespread support in the North. Brown also concluded that Southern blacks would be just as militant as those in the North. Both assumptions were wrong.

After final visits with his supporters in Boston and with his family in North Elba, Brown put his plan into effect. In July 1859, he was in Harpers Ferry. He rented a farmhouse in Maryland seven miles from town. His men slowly began joining him in the weeks to come, some twenty in all including Brown and his sons. Brown's plan was to seize the government armory at Harpers Ferry, drawing escaped slaves and antislavery whites to him, as he believed these groups would flock to his support and defense. He would arm the new converts and march through the South, freeing slaves, seizing government armories when he needed weapons and ammunition, and disappearing into the mountains when necessary. The plan had terrible flaws. Harpers Ferry was a poor choice as the jumping-off point for Brown's design. Ringed with hills at the juncture of the Shenandoah and Potomac Rivers, the town was isolated and indefensible to a military force in possession of the surrounding hills. The mountainous terrain of the region was not suited to extensive plantations with the correspondingly large slave workforces whom Brown hoped to attract to his command. Further, Virginia had not forgotten the Nat Turner revolt of more than a quarter century previous and was prepared to suppress a slave insurrection. In short, the mere selection of Harpers Ferry placed Brown at a severe disadvantage before his effort even began.

The attack was doomed to failure and the fatal result for Brown and his men predictable. Brown's sons worried that they would be trapped in Harpers Ferry, but their father's faulty judgment ruled the day. He had convinced himself that he was an avenging Moses, God's chosen come to punish the slaveholders and free the slaves, a reenactment of the events described in the Book of Exodus in the Bible. On October 16, 1859, Brown and his men swarmed into Harpers Ferry, seizing the armory and related facilities. Hostages were taken, including Lewis W. Washington, a relative of George Washington, and Brown purportedly confiscated and buckled to his waist a sword that Frederick the Great had given to George Washington and that had been in Lewis Washington's possession.

A train came chugging into town and Brown, with consistent foolishness, permitted it to leave. The act contradicted the effect of Brown's instructions to cut the telegraph wires. The train's crew gave the alarm, and in remarkably quick fashion an angry swarm of Virginia militia poured into town and bottled up Brown and his men. With retreat cut off, and his men under heavy fire, Brown seemed baffled. Instead of a welcoming host of escaped slaves and antislavery whites, Brown had drawn angry militiamen who, fired up with whiskey, wanted blood and were disinclined to give quarter. Brown tried to parley, and he had hostages, but his emissaries carrying a white flag were fired upon and seriously wounded. The bloody farce ended soon after federal troops under the command of Colonel Robert E. Lee arrived. Lee ordered U.S. Marines to bayonet-charge the building in which Brown had barricaded himself and some of the men. Brown was clubbed unconscious in the assault. Most of his men were killed, wounded, and captured.

In the wake of the successful assault, Virginia governor Henry Wise, Virginia senator James M. Mason, and others interrogated Brown. Though he had fought for hours and had been knocked senseless in a bloody assault, Brown's composure and demeanor impressed even his hostile captors. He appeared calm and in command of himself, and he answered questions firmly and with a certain aplomb. Brown recognized that his moment of fame had arrived; his fate assured, for the fiasco could only end in death, Brown acted and accepted the role of martyr. He told his captors that he was an instrument of Providence working on behalf of the oppressed slaves. Brown denied that he sought a slave uprising, a patent falsehood, and he also claimed that he had received no support, trying to protect the Committee of Six and others. Unfortunately for Brown, in yet another lapse in judgment, he had left a cache of documents at his Maryland farm complete with letters from his closest supporters and detailed plans. Virginia authorities secured the documentation of Brown's folly.

Governor Wise insisted that Brown and his surviving men be tried in Virginia, and the process was speedy because there was concern that Brown would be lynched before a regular judicial proceeding could begin. Brown was spirited to Charleston, Virginia, where Judge Richard Parker presided over a Virginia circuit court that was in session. Brown was scheduled for trial a mere week after his capture and examined by a magistrate on October 25, 1859. The following day, a jury charged Brown with murder, conspiracy to foment a slave revolt, and treason against the state of Virginia. The trial that followed was a mere formality; it would have been impossible for an impartial jury to be empanelled in Virginia, now hysterical at the prospect of impending abolitionist raids and slave revolts. The sole surprise at trial was an attempt by Brown's counsel to have him declared insane. Brown rebuked his counsel for making the claim, and new defense attorneys took over, though Judge Parker refused to delay the trial. On November 2, 1859, Brown was found guilty and sentenced to death by hanging on December 2, 1859. Brown made a stirring oration prior to sentencing, declaring that his actions were based on Christian principles. He used the last month of his life to write eloquent letters from confinement, and he rebuffed plans to spring him from jail that would have been unlikely to succeed in any event. Brown recognized the value of his martyrdom and hoped his death provoked a civil war that would end slavery. The afternoon before his execution, his wife Mary arrived in Charleston and spent a few hours with him. The following day, Brown was hanged, and his body turned over to his widow. She returned the corpse to North Elba after removing Brown from the Southern coffin in which he had been placed. Brown was interred on his farm on December 8, 1859, next to a massive boulder.

PRINCIPAL IDEAS

John Brown was given to manic enthusiasms throughout his life, but his zeal was not matched with a corresponding degree of wisdom. He displayed tremendous energy in his business ventures but ultimately failed because of bad judgment and timing. Deeply religious, adhering to a Calvinist faith, Brown eschewed the established church because of racism that congregations had displayed toward blacks. Though a Calvinist, he fervently embraced abolition, a reform effort that reflected a belief in the perfectibility of man that was fundamentally at odds with his faith. Nominally apolitical, Brown's insistent advocacy of racial equality, shown by his willingness to live and work with his black neighbors in New York, was in fact a form of political radicalism, a reproof to contemporary politics and societal norms, both of which were profoundly racist. Imbued with his reading of the Old Testament, Brown accepted that bloodshed was necessary for slavery to end, and he came to see himself as an instrument of God to bring about that purpose. When his ill-conceived plan failed, Brown willingly assumed the role of martyr—there was little else left for him to do—and he hoped his rash acts would foment sectional tensions and ultimately civil war. Brown's raid provoked hysteria in the South and damaged Unionist sentiment. Though initially condemned in the Northern press as a criminal, Brown's courageous behavior after capture and eloquent perorations at his trial won him favorable press coverage, an increasingly positive Northern reaction that further enraged a jittery South. The raid on Harpers Ferry helped doom the Union, and in 1861, Brown's bloody vision came to pass.

CONCLUSION

Brown's postelection interview with Governor Wise and Senator Mason revealed his state of mind. Always attracted to the Old Testament and its theme of redemption through violence and destruction, Brown convinced himself that he too had become an instrument of a wrathful God. The overthrow of slavery was his task, and he set about it with the same manic energy he had brought to every other of his life's endeavors. Though some have suggested that Brown acted to redeem a failed life, he had in fact long been committed to emancipation and black equality and civil rights. His raid was the culmination of his life's work rather than a precipitate act to rehabilitate it. He was unsuccessful, though only in an immediate sense, for the actions he took at Harpers Ferry fulfilled the apocalyptic warnings fire-eaters had been uttering throughout the previous decade. Attitudes in both the North and the South hardened. While never inevitable, Brown's raid made more likely the tragic clash of arms.

NOTE

1. Stephen Oates, *To Purge This Land with Blood: A Biography of John Brown* (New York: Harper & Row, 1970), 53.

FURTHER READING

W.E.B. Du Bois, *John Brown* (1909; reprint, New York: Kraus-Thompson, 1973); Stephen B. Oates, *To Purge This Land with Blood: A Biography of John Brown* (New York: Harper and Row, 1970); Merrill D. Peterson, *John Brown: The Legend Revisited* (Charlottesville: University of Virginia Press, 2002); and John Stauffer, *The Black Hearts of Black Men: Radical Abolitionists and the Transformation of Race* (Cambridge, MA: Harvard University Press, 2002).

JAMES BUCHANAN
(1791–1868)

Too Late to the Prize

LIFE

James Buchanan's father and namesake had emigrated from Ireland in 1785 and quickly proved himself a hardworking and capable businessman. He went to work at a trading post located in a mountain passage in Pennsylvania that was called Stony Batter, working for the owner John Tom. Industrious and thrifty, the elder James bought out his boss to acquire the trading post in 1787. The following year he married a young woman he had met in York County, Elizabeth Speer. Their first child, a girl named May, was born in 1789 but soon died. The future president, James Buchanan, arrived on April 23, 1791, his appearance a welcome comfort for a mother still grieving the loss of her firstborn. Buchanan biographer Philip Klein has argued that Elizabeth Buchanan treated her son with special attention to compensate for the death of her daughter. Five baby girls succeeded the birth of James, so he continued to occupy a cherished place in his parents' affections as the only surviving son and heir until the birth of his brother in 1805.

Buchanan was the older brother surrounded by adoring younger sisters for most of his boyhood and youth, an experience that left him with a pronounced sense of self-assurance that could be mistaken for arrogance. The family moved to Mercersburg, Pennsylvania, and James attended school in town, learning Greek and Latin as was customary. It became apparent that James had intellectual gifts, another spur to his ego, and his father determined to send him to higher education with the eventual goal of a career in law. In September 1807, Buchanan entered Dickinson College in Carlisle, Pennsylvania, beginning his studies at the rank of junior. Initially a devoted student, Buchanan soon discovered that his fellow students appreciated and rewarded not studiousness among friends, but troublemaking, drinking, and smoking. To conform, Buchanan adopted the habits of the rowdies, though he retained his faculties enough that he still earned high academic standing at the close of his first year. However, his behavior had drawn the unwelcome attention of the authorities, and soon after he returned to Mercersburg at the end of the academic year, he was expelled from the college. The intervention of a member of the board of trustees got him reinstated, and he was permitted to return, finish his senior year, and graduate in September 1809.

Three months after leaving Dickinson, Buchanan had moved to the Pennsylvania capital of Lancaster and embarked on a legal apprenticeship with a prominent attorney, James Hopkins. He was admitted to the bar three years later and made a brief trip to Kentucky that convinced him that he was overmatched against seasoned western lawyers like Henry Clay. He returned to Pennsylvania and started practicing law in Lancaster in February 1813. Buchanan's father had been a staunch Federalist, and the son adopted those principles and the party that represented them. Buchanan viewed entry into politics as a good method for attracting paying clients. He was selected as a candidate for the state legislature in August 1814 by the local Federalist organization that dominated Lancaster. He briefly served in the militia that same month when local units rode to the defense of Baltimore against the British in the War of 1812. As a state legislator, Buchanan served on the judiciary committee and assiduously tended the legislative needs of his district. He angered local Federalists, frightened at the prospect of a British invasion, when he spoke against a conscription bill, but redeemed himself with a slashing 1815 Fourth of July speech in which he assailed the Republicans and called Thomas Jefferson a "philosophic visionary."[1]

Buchanan's political career proved a boon to his legal practice. Democrats in the state legislature had taken to impeaching Federalist judges to get them off the bench. When he was impeached, Judge Walter Franklin chose Buchanan as his defense attorney. Buchanan argued that it was a violation of the separation of powers for Democrats to impeach a judge because they disagreed with his rulings. He successfully defended Franklin from three consecutive impeachment attempts, winning acquittal on each occasion and making his legal reputation. After his dramatic victories for Franklin, Buchanan began his ascent to wealth as clients sought his services. He was always careful about his money, investing it with prudence and care, and he delighted in the minor bookkeeping his personal finances required. He became something of a social lion, recognized as an up-and-coming young man, and he attended fashionable events and met the wealthy and the powerful. He became engaged to Ann Coleman, the cousin of a woman who his law partner Molton C. Rogers was seeing. Ann's father had earned a fortune in the iron business, and was a hard man who suspected the motives of Buchanan's interest in his daughter. James and

Ann became engaged in the summer of 1819, but soon had a falling out when Ann questioned his fealty to her after a long period of work kept him from seeing her with any regularity. After the breakup, which left Buchanan dismayed and puzzled, in December 1819 Ann traveled to Philadelphia to divert herself from the emotional tempest. She took ill and died suddenly while in the city, passing from life with breathtaking speed and no warning.

The death of Ann Coleman is considered a seminal event in James Buchanan's life. In the immediate aftermath, many in Lancaster blamed him for causing her death, perhaps due to intense sorrow at the end of her engagement; some wondered if she had committed suicide. Ann's death and Buchanan's involvement were much discussed, and the controversy threatened to ruin his career. The Coleman family exacerbated the problem when they denied Buchanan's request to participate in Ann's funeral, an unfeeling decision that also tarred Buchanan in Lancaster for culpability in her death. The loss of Ann and the ugly rumors that followed it dogged Buchanan for life and caused him to turn inward. His mother had been a devout believer, and Buchanan now accepted the religious fatalism that she espoused, that whatever tragedy occurs was God's will, and the believer could do little else than accept and live. Though he had other romances and enjoyed the company of women throughout his life, he never married and remained a bachelor. As he aged, he increasingly came to view a prospective wife as a nursemaid and cook more than a lover, an attitude that no doubt hampered his ability to convince a woman to marry him once she understood this. "I feel that it is not good for a man to be alone and should be astonished to find myself married to the same old maid who can nurse me when I am sick, provide good dinners for me when I am well, and not expect from me any very ardent or romantic affection," he wrote in 1843. It is hardly surprising that no woman ever took him up given his cold, emotionally distant mind-set.[2]

Buchanan returned to Lancaster and immersed himself in his work, riding out his grief for Ann and the unflattering rumors, allowing his industriousness to define him rather than idle gossip. He ran successfully for Congress in 1820, entering the House in the midst of the presidency of James Monroe and the no-party Era of Good Feelings. In his first term, Buchanan quickly earned the respect of other congressmen with his strong speaking voice, easily heard in the House chamber, and his lawyer's penchant for mastering facts and wielding them in debate. When William Lowndes, a respected figure, took ill, he asked Buchanan to deliver his speech in defense of War Secretary John C. Calhoun, an indication that Buchanan's talents had been recognized. His voting reflected attitudes that would soon be associated with the emerging Jacksonian Democratic Party. He opposed a bankruptcy bill and approved President Monroe's veto of internal improvements legislation. He also diligently labored for his district and in consequence was reelected to the seat, breaking a local tradition that called for congressmen to step down after a single term.

The disputed presidential election of 1824 roiled Pennsylvania politics and Buchanan's political career. He found himself drawn to Andrew Jackson, and he disliked John Quincy Adams, though Jackson and Buchanan developed a somewhat testy relationship after an incident related to the disputed election. Buchanan approached Jackson for a pledge that he had no plans to appoint his rival John Quincy Adams as secretary of state, information that Buchanan planned to give to Henry Clay in an effort to draw Clay to the Jackson camp, a gambit that failed when Clay threw his support to Adams, who subsequently won the election in an extraordinary vote in the House of Representatives. Jackson, embittered at the outcome, later suggested he had been approached by a congressman from the Clay forces with an offer, the kind of offer his partisans were characterizing as a corrupt bargain. Buchanan was forced to issue an awkward public letter denying the corrupt bargain imputation while maintaining his continuing support for Jackson. The difficulty between the two men was smoothed over but not forgotten, and both never completely trusted the other again.

Buchanan meanwhile sought control of the pro-Jackson forces in Pennsylvania, advocating a political union between Germans in the east and Scotch-Irish in the west, a political faction dubbed the Amalgamators. In 1828, Buchanan ran for reelection for Congress as a Democrat, abandoning his outmoded Federalist label, and winning again after a bitter campaign. His hopes that Jackson would reward him and the Amalgamators with patronage appointments were dashed, as Jackson appointed members of another Pennsylvania Democratic faction, the so-called Family Party that had been allied with John C. Calhoun, to significant posts in his administration. Buchanan often found himself buffeted by the factional conflicts of the Pennsylvania Democratic Party, his appeals for unity failing. When Jackson later broke with Calhoun, the Family Party's influence in the administration waned, and Buchanan found himself touted as a possible vice presidential running mate with Jackson. His hopes were dashed when, at the end of May 1831, Jackson offered to appoint him American minister to Russia, a post generally considered a political graveyard where presidents consigned rivals or nuisance politicians. Buchanan believed Jackson wanted him out of Pennsylvania so his allies could build a political organization geared to the election of his chosen successor, Martin Van Buren. Despite his disappointment and misgivings, Buchanan accepted the post.

Buchanan left for Europe in the spring of 1832, spending a fortnight in England enjoying the social life before continuing on to St. Petersburg, where he arrived on June 2, 1832. For the next six months, Buchanan labored to induce the suspicious Russian czar and his ministers to conclude a commercial treaty with the United States. He finally succeeded by suggesting that the czar sign the treaty on his birthday, December 18, 1832, a prospect that delighted the emperor and got the treaty clear of delays. His mission accomplished, Buchanan left Russia in August 1833, with Jackson's approval, and toured Europe, meeting and taking the measure of giants such as Talleyrand and Lord Palmerston. Philip Klein has argued that Buchanan had taken the St. Petersburg appointment, a potential political graveyard, and turned it to his advantage with his successful treaty negotiations. He had also been fortunately out of the country during the nasty Bank War and nullification controversies. His acquaintance with royalty convinced him that he had the mettle and intellect for the presidency. He arrived in Philadelphia at the end of November 1833 and was elected to the Senate the following year in December 1834 after Jackson cleared a path for him by appointing Pennsylvania senator William Wilkins to the Russia Mission. He was reelected to the Senate in 1836 and 1842.

As a senator, Buchanan could not compete in legislation achievements or public accolades with senatorial giants like Henry Clay and Daniel Webster. However, he did become chairman of the Senate Foreign Relations Committee, where he supported American expansion. Though there was considerable sentiment in Pennsylvania in favor of the national bank, Buchanan opposed it and endorsed President Van Buren's subtreasury scheme, arguing that the national bank was too powerful and a threat to liberty. Philip Klein has argued that Van Buren modeled his subtreasury plan on suggestions that he elicited from Buchanan. Buchanan had a constricted Jacksonian view of the government and his role as a senator, believing, for example, in the doctrine of instruction that held that a senator had to vote in accordance with the wishes of the state legislature or resign. In consequence, when the Whigs won the Pennsylvania state legislature in 1840 and instructed him to support Whig legislation in the Senate, Buchanan voted as ordered, sometimes after giving a speech condemning his own vote, an absurd situation. He thus aped the ideological rigidity that characterized many Southern politicians, choosing an unwavering allegiance to an abstract principle that when acted upon led to a practical absurdity. Buchanan shared his quarters with Democratic Alabama senator William R. King, an arrangement that prompted speculation about his possible homosexuality then and now, though there is no way to prove or disprove the charge. The two senators were so close they were called "the Siamese Twins," and Buchanan unsuccessfully promoted King as a replacement for Richard M. Johnson as Democratic candidate for vice president in 1840. Though he abhorred slavery, Buchanan considered the institution entirely legal under the Constitution, and he condemned the abolition movement.

Van Buren offered Buchanan the post of attorney general in 1839, but Buchanan refused the offer in part because he wanted to remain in the Senate. He also had presidential ambitions of his own, though he preferred to publicly pretend to be uninterested in the White House while privately writing dozens of letters touting his candidacy to political contacts across the country, whose addresses he kept in journals for the purpose. He also hoped to unite the Pennsylvania Democratic Party behind him as a necessary precursor to any bid for the 1844 nomination. However, the party was so riven by competing factions that Buchanan despaired and formally withdrew as a candidate on December 14, 1843. When the Democratic National Convention chose dark-horse candidate James K. Polk in May 1844, Buchanan worked to make Polk's free trade record palatable in Pennsylvania by assuring Pennsylvanians that Polk was sound on the tariff. Polk won the state by a narrow margin.

Buchanan's reward for that loyal service came when Polk named him secretary of state in February 1845. The choice made a great deal of sense for Polk because Buchanan had been a successful diplomat and had met his European counterparts, and the appointment appeased the Pennsylvania Democratic faction Buchanan represented. Buchanan was delighted with the appointment, the most prestigious in the cabinet, and he purchased a spacious house on F Street in anticipation of entertaining the foreign diplomatic corps and members of Congress and the government. Polk and Buchanan subsequently had an often difficult relationship. Buchanan, always conscious of his superior intellectual gifts, believed he knew more about foreign affairs than Polk and tended to be condescending with the president. Polk, a proud man, sensed the slight, determined to have his way as president, and obstinately rejected what Buchanan considered his well-founded criticisms of Polk's proposals. Polk asked all his cabinet appointees to swear off any pursuit of the 1848 nomination, but Buchanan refused to give a blanket promise. He still had the presidency as a future goal and was not above placing himself in the public eye on certain issues to advantage even if in doing so he embarrassed the president.

His tenure as secretary of state was an eventful one, and the workload consequently so onerous that Buchanan complained that he labored like a "galley slave." His tempestuous relationship with Polk was in evidence on virtually every foreign affairs issue. Polk ordered Buchanan to take charge of negotiations with Britain over the disputed Oregon Territory. When the British ambassador summarily rejected Buchanan's offer to settle the boundary at forty-nine degrees, Polk ordered Buchanan to withdraw the offer and prepare a detailed defense of the American claim to the entire territory. Buchanan did as ordered, but he privately urged the president to continue to pursue the original compromise because he believed that if war became necessary, the American cause would have a higher moral standing if based on an insistence on a compromise proposal rather than an aggressive land claim. The dispute was eventually settled on the basis of Buchanan's original proposal in June 1846. Buchanan believed that Polk's intransigent posture before the final settlement was a ploy to give him credit for the treaty and compromise rather than the secretary of state.[3]

Buchanan also differed with Polk on policy regarding the war with Mexico that began in April 1846. Once the war started, Polk did not wish to bind or restrict himself in any manner that might prevent him from winning the maximum indemnity from Mexico in the form of territory. Yet Buchanan advocated a public statement of administration policy that declared the war as purely defensive, a suggestion the president and Cabinet rejected. He considered it unwise to invade deep into Mexico, thinking it best only to occupy the territory intended to be annexed, but as the war progressed and American forces won victory after victory, Buchanan altered his opinion and endorsed greater territorial conquest, a change in attitude that Polk found annoying. When Buchanan's chief clerk in the State Department, Nicholas Trist, negotiated a peace treaty of more modest territorial gains than Polk and others thought the success of American arms warranted, Buchanan condemned the agreement and advised against sending it to the Senate. Buchanan recognized the utility of a public face in favor of aggressive expansion for a candidate for the Democratic presidential nomination. Central America and Cuba interested Buchanan too, and he pursued, unsuccessfully, the purchase of Cuba from Spain. He secured transit rights across the Panamanian Isthmus, considered an important concession for an emerging American commercial empire in the Pacific.

Buchanan's term as secretary of state, with its incessant labor amid war, aged him. He was soon known as "Old Buck," abandoning the nickname of his political and personal youth, "Jimmy." Nonetheless, he continued to pursue the presidency in both 1848 and 1852. Starting in December 1847, he held weekly dinners at his home in Washington, D.C., for important and influential Democrats and members of the government in an attempt to charm them into backing his candidacy. To deal with the crisis engendered by the status of slavery in the territory acquired from Mexico, Buchanan proposed that the Missouri Compromise line be extended to the Pacific Ocean. His foe for the Democratic nomination in 1848, Lewis Cass, argued that slavery ought to be left to the decision of the settlers in the territories, the doctrine of popular sovereignty. In May 1848, the Democratic National Convention selected Cass and popular sovereignty. Though disappointed at his failure, Buchanan later thought it fortunate that he did not have to face the Whig juggernaught of Mexican War hero Zachary Taylor, who was elected president in 1848.

Buchanan returned to Pennsylvania in 1849, gave up his home in Lancaster, and purchased a country estate outside of town that he called Wheatland. He invited fellow politicians and friends to visit him, and he enjoyed the role of semiretired statesman and convivial host, ever ready with a bottle of Madeira. His charming and attractive niece, Harriet Lane, joined him and acted as a hostess, a task she would later perform at the White House. He kept up a vigorous correspondence in an effort to keep his name in the forefront for the Democratic presidential nomination in 1852. He felt decidedly uncomfortable with the Compromise of 1850, considering it overly optimistic to suggest, as supporters did, that it was a final settlement of the slavery agitation. Buchanan thought that popular sovereignty was a mistake, and that Congress did have the power to legislate for the territories. Throwing the slavery issue to the people of the territories only would, in Buchanan's opinion, lead to conflict. Eventually, Buchanan felt compelled to publicly support the Compromise to maintain his political viability, but he privately continued to have reservations about the measures.

Democrats turned to Franklin Pierce as their presidential nominee in 1852, as Buchanan was again passed over. When Free Soil partisans tried to split the Democratic vote in the subsequent campaign in Pennsylvania, Buchanan worked for Pierce. He accused Whig nominee, Winfield Scott, of harboring intentions to repeal the Fugitive Slave Law and thereby unravel the Compromise of 1850, which had restored at least a veneer of sectional amity. He tried to suggest that a vote for Pierce was a vote to uphold the Compromise. After his election victory, Pierce ignored Buchanan's patronage requests, offering him instead the post of minister to Great Britain. Buchanan initially refused to accept, as to do so would place him in an awkward position with friends who had been rejected for federal positions. He also worried that Secretary of State William Marcy intended to conduct the most glamorous negotiations in Washington, leaving Buchanan with little chance for distinction. He finally accepted, only to learn that Pierce was primarily motivated by a desire to remove Buchanan from Pennsylvania politics. Buchanan also made the mistake of naming the flamboyant and erratic New Yorker Daniel Sickles as legation secretary, an appointment that brought Buchanan much grief.

Buchanan's tenure at the Court of St. James was a stormy one. It began on an inauspicious note when Secretary of State William Marcy ordered U.S. diplomats to refrain from court dress, a policy that outraged British society and public opinion, which equated ostentatious plumery and golden braid with respect for the queen and Parliament. Without appropriate attire, Buchanan could not attend the opening of Parliament, and he risked being mistaken for a servant. Yet Queen Victoria did not mind if Buchanan appeared in a black coat with a modest sword strapped to his waist to distinguish him from the help, his solution to the problem. The queen also delighted in the company of Harriet Lane, who charmed London and court society. So the incident passed, but was an ill portent. Pierce had internalized the Democratic penchant for expansionism and wanted the British to abandon any possessions in Central America and give the United States a free hand in the region. He also intended to acquire Cuba, preferably by purchase, but by intrigue or violence if necessary. Buchanan strongly favored acquiring Cuba but had reservations about Pierce's means to attain the desired end. Pierce intended to send a three-man diplomatic mission to Spain with a cash offer for Cuba and a threat of filibusters if the Spanish balked. Buchanan thought it better to avoid the bluster, particularly public threats, and work within confidential negotiations.

Agitation over the Kansas-Nebraska Act compelled Pierce to give up his Cuba commission, but Marcy ordered Buchanan and his ministerial colleagues in France and Spain, John Y. Mason and Pierre Soulé, to meet in Paris to concert policy leading to acquiring Cuba. Buchanan objected to the meeting as unnecessary and bound to generate negative publicity and wild rumors about pending American aggression. The meeting would only make impossible the kind of confidential negotiations Buchanan advocated. Why not simply correspond via the diplomatic pouch? Marcy insisted, though he did agree to Buchanan's suggestion that the meeting place be moved to Ostend, Belgium. The resulting manifesto, which Buchanan wrote based on policy notes provided by Soulé, provoked sensational and damaging criticism when later published in the New York *Herald*. Daniel Sickles also harmed the prospects for success when he traveled through Europe making fantastic claims about pending American action. He had earlier angered British public opinion and ruined any usefulness he had as a diplomat when he refused to stand for a toast to the queen during a London dinner. His penmanship was so bad that clerks had to be detailed to recopy his letters, a uniquely poor gift for an antebellum diplomat. Sickles was a disaster, and Buchanan sought and obtained his resignation from the legation. Buchanan wanted to work offstage with Spanish bondholders, who might be delighted at the prospect of a large cash payment to the Spanish treasury that could then pay interest on bonds. But the negative publicity made businessmen reluctant to involve themselves.

Buchanan returned to the United States in the spring of 1856, replaced as minister by George M. Dallas. He had told friends at the beginning of his term as minister that he would not be a candidate for president in 1856. As it became increasingly clear that Pierce was discredited, Buchanan had a change of heart, and by January 1855 he had reversed himself and was a candidate. Once again, a diplomatic mission had proven a blessing to Buchanan's career. In his absence, Pierce had endorsed Stephen A. Douglas's Kansas-Nebraska Act, which organized the territories of Kansas and Nebraska at the price of repealing the Missouri Compromise to earn Southern congressional votes. Explicitly ending the compromise generated considerable outrage in the free states, and civil war erupted in Kansas between proslavery Southern settlers and Free Soil Northern settlers. Buchanan avoided any association with the political imbroglio and resulting violence. He now appeared in New York Harbor the very model of the disinterested, elderly statesman prepared to forego a well-earned retirement to perform a final patriotic service to the nation by guiding it away from the sectional conflict toward which it was drifting. Buchanan received the Democratic nomination in June 1856, accepting a popular sovereignty plank in the platform even though he once had little use for the doctrine.

He did no campaigning, retiring to his Wheatland estate, though he did write numerous letters encouraging his minions to greater efforts. Buchanan and the Democrats portrayed the election in stark terms, as a choice between union and disunion. The South, it was believed, would never accept the election of the Republican candidate, John C. Frémont, so a vote for Buchanan was a vote for a continued Union and a rebuke to a dangerously radical, abolition-based political party. Many former Whig conservatives were persuaded to support Buchanan out of concern for the constancy of the nation.

Elected in November 1856, Buchanan pledged to end sectional tensions. "The great object of my administration will be to arrest, if possible, the agitation of the slavery question at the North, and to destroy sectional politics," he intoned. With that goal in mind, Buchanan involved himself in the Dred Scott case then pending in the U.S. Supreme Court, urging the justices, through his friend Justice John Catron, to settle forever the question of slavery's status in the territories. He also wrote Pennsylvanian and Supreme Court Justice Robert Grier, asking him to back a broader opinion. Grier agreed and became the only Northern justice to join the majority decision, announced on March 6, 1857, that denied Scott's citizenship, ruled the Missouri Compromise unconstitutional, and declared slavery constitutionally protected in the territories. Buchanan had thrown in a line in his inaugural address anticipating the court's ruling, saying that the status of territorial slavery was a matter for the courts. When the opinion came down, Republicans and others charged that Buchanan was a willing tool of the Slave Power conspiracy that sought to remove all restrictions on slavery and nationalize it. Any hopes that the Supreme Court could tamp down sectional tensions with a decision favoring the South were dashed, though Buchanan probably did not recognize the reality for a time.[4]

Buchanan's cabinet appointments reflected his intention to dominate his administration. He was a seasoned politician who had always been extremely confident of his abilities, to the point of arrogance, and he had finally reached his long-sought goal. He did not intend to cede an inch of his presidential prerogatives. He settled on the aged Michigan senator and former presidential contender Lewis Cass as secretary of state, after Cass agreed to a largely ceremonial role with Buchanan and various clerks running the State Department. Buchanan felt himself an expert on foreign affairs, and he intended, once he had tamped down sectional troubles, to move aggressively in Central and South America. So he retained the foreign policy portfolio. His other appointees were largely minor politicos who shared his Southern appeasement–minded views on the slavery issue. Four Buchanan cabinet members, Howell Cobb, John B. Floyd, Jacob Thompson, and John C. Breckinridge, later served the Confederacy.

Buchanan's presidency was tumultuous and plagued with problems from the beginning. The president-elect visited Washington in January 1857 to consult with party leaders and picked up a debilitating case of dysentery from the faulty pipes of the National Hotel. His malady tormented him for months, so much that he had a physician on hand at his inauguration to tend him if he collapsed. His personal secretary and nephew, Esridge Lane, also contracted the National Hotel disease and died in April 1857. Buchanan recovered and spent the first months applying himself to the problem of distributing patronage posts. If he was to have any chance of forming a national party organization loyal to him, it was crucial to place his loyalists in positions of influence and power. Buchanan has been faulted for bungling this important task. First, accustomed to the necessity of reading the diplomatic correspondence at the State Department, he immersed himself in the minutiae of federal patronage, examining applications for even minor posts, tasks that should have been delegated for the sake of his health and sanity. In short, he punished himself by fretting over who to put in as assistant postmaster of obscure frontier towns. Second, he failed to reward loyalists, particularly Pennsylvanians, and thereby created an impression of ingratitude. John W. Forney, for example, had labored as a Buchanan newspaper editor and political aide for many years and thought he deserved a suitable reward. Buchanan did not help him, and Forney defected to the camp of Stephen A. Douglas. For his part, Douglas complained that Illinois and other western states did not receive their fair share of appointments, and he was embarrassed when Buchanan appointed his father-in-law to a minor treasury post. It seems that Buchanan created as many enemies as friends, and powerful ones at that, with his appointments.

In August 1857, the New York Stock Exchange collapsed, banks had already begun to fail, and a tide of economic retrenchment swept the country, an event dubbed the Panic of 1857. The ensuing depression created considerable hardship, particularly in the North as prices for farm products plummeted and unemployment increased in urban centers. Buchanan clung to his archaic Jacksonian views, a preference for hard money or specie over paper notes and a pronounced reluctance for any intervention on the part of the federal government to get the economy moving again. Buchanan held Jackson's skeptical opinion of the constitutionality of federal internal improvement spending or public works projects in modern parlance. Consequently, he did nothing to alleviate the economic downturn or the resulting suffering, preferring to ride out the depression for the sake of the crabbed Democratic orthodoxy on the Constitution.

Since the passage of the Kansas-Nebraska Act, Kansas had become a battlefield between Free Soil Northerners and proslavery Southerners, with each side prepared to employ violence to graft their views upon the Kansas Constitution and government. The conflict had consumed three territorial governors. Buchanan had earlier predicted that the Cass-Douglas policy of popular sovereignty would lead to conflict; now, as president, he had to find a solution to the resulting mess. He turned to a seasoned politician for territorial governor. Robert J. Walker had been a senator and treasury secretary during the Polk administration, and he reluctantly accepted a post that he considered beneath him for patriotic motives. Walker had Buchanan's pledge that a statewide plebiscite had to be held on any proposed Kansas constitution. He traveled to Kansas in late spring 1857 and had the bad judgment to declare in his first address that slavery could not exist in Kansas Territory for climatological reasons. Southerners accused Buchanan of appointing a territorial governor of Free Soil sentiments, and the president was forced to repudiate Walker's remarks.

When the proslavery government scheduled elections for delegates to a constitutional convention, Free Soil settlers determined to boycott the voting registration process and election. It was unfortunately common for citizens of neighboring Missouri, a slave state, to cross the porous border and vote in Kansas elections, giving the proslavery minority a boost, hence the unwillingness of Free Soil elements to participate. Nevertheless, the election of delegates proceeded without the participation of the Free Soil majority. The resulting constitutional convention, held in the fall of 1857 in Lecompton, Kansas, produced two constitutions, a proslavery constitution and a supposedly antislavery constitution, though its strictures were so watered down and the amending process so difficult that slavery would continue in Kansas regardless of which constitution was adopted. Walker concluded that rather than vote on the product of the tainted convention, the entire process had to be restarted. Buchanan refused to countenance such a course. He always felt that the South was the aggrieved party in the sectional troubles, a victim of a radical, agitating abolition movement. He was also obsessed with legal form; the federal government recognized the Lecompton government, which had produced a constitution. By contrast, he compared the unauthorized Topeka government to the Hartford Convention of antiwar Federalists that met during the War of 1812.

Buchanan's insistence on Lecompton led to a split in the Democratic Party, the last national political organization, a rift that would plague the 1860 Democratic National Convention. The president's own territorial governor, Robert Walker, advised abandoning the Lecompton Constitution, and when Buchanan refused, Walker resigned in December 1857. That same month, Stephen A. Douglas had a stormy interview with Buchanan at the White House. Douglas considered the constitution and the flawed process that gave birth to it a violation of popular sovereignty and the rights of the Free Soil majority in Kansas. Douglas faced a reelection battle in 1858, with the Lecompton Constitution tremendously unpopular in Illinois; he could ill afford to endorse it. Buchanan's failure to consult Douglas, the chairman of the Senate's Territorial Committee, also irritated the Illinois senator. Buchanan told Douglas that he intended to make the admission of Kansas under the Lecompton Constitution an official Democratic Party measure, and warned the Illinois senator of dire consequences if he opposed the measure. He would break Douglas as Andrew Jackson had broken his opponents. Douglas responded with a put-down that echoes to this day: "Mr. President, I wish you to remember that Gen. Jackson is dead, sir." Douglas became an administration opponent, fixing Buchanan in the minds of many Northern citizens as an ally of Southern extremists.[5]

In February 1858, Buchanan presented the Lecompton Constitution to Congress after it had been approved in a December plebiscite that the Free Soil majority boycotted. Free Soil forces held their own plebiscite in January, and the constitution was overwhelmingly rejected. No matter, Buchanan felt: the Lecompton territorial government had followed the legally sanctioned process, and the Free Soilers who refused to participate had only themselves to blame. With administration backing, the Lecompton Constitution passed the Senate. The House was a different matter, where Northern Democrats joined Republicans to block the measure. Buchanan vigorously employed all the tools at the disposal of the executive branch to facilitate legislative logrolling, promising government contracts or jobs or threatening to take them away. Despite strenuous efforts, the best that Buchanan could manage was compromise legislation that sent the Lecompton Constitution back to Kansas for yet another plebiscite, with the offer of a large federal land grant as an inducement for Kansans to approve. The Free Soil majority participated in the August election, ignored the land grant bribe, and rejected the Lecompton Constitution. Buchanan later claimed credit for pacifying Kansas, yet he had alienated the Douglas faction of the Democratic Party with his unwavering support of Lecompton, and Southern Democrats, who had demanded the admission of Kansas as a slave state, were also displeased with the president.

In addition to an economic depression and Kansas, Buchanan also aggressively moved to reestablish federal authority in Utah Territory. Mormons had fled to the region in the late 1840s, trying to escape anti-Mormon violence in Illinois and Missouri. Brigham Young had led the exodus, and he had been named territorial governor by President Millard Fillmore. Young also controlled the church, and the territory became a de facto theocracy. Federal officials who exercised their duties in a manner that defied Young and the church had been harassed and threatened, including federal judges. The Mormon practice of polygamy, taking multiple wives, repulsed national sensibilities, and unflattering tales of polygamous unions were a staple in newspapers. Buchanan received reports of the defiance of federal authority and Young's autocratic rule. He appointed a new territorial governor and slate of officials, and sent them to Utah with a federal army of 2,500 troops. Young and the Mormons soon accepted U.S. authority, and Alfred Cumming replaced Young as territorial governor, though Young and the church retained great influence.

Buchanan had been an exponent of expansionism, had kept the State Department under his control, and intended to be an activist president in regard to the acquisition of territory. Foreign affairs made up a considerable portion of his annual messages to Congress. Jean Baker has argued that the common historical perception of Buchanan as a timid, irresolute president is belied by his aggressive foreign policy. He repeatedly pressed Congress for an appropriation with which to purchase Cuba, meeting failure each time. He wanted to reassert the Monroe Doctrine in Central America, perhaps as a precursor to American expansion in the region. Britain gave up its claims to certain islands to Honduras and Nicaragua in response to Buchanan's bluster. When forces in Paraguay fired on an American vessel, the president sent the nineteenth-century equivalent of a naval task force of nineteen warships to compel better behavior. He requested congressional funding for a punitive expedition against the province of northern Mexico. The president did not neglect the Pacific region, sending another military force under Winfield Scott to secure American rights in the Northwest, and his diplomats concluded pacts with China and Japan. Congress foiled his most aggressive schemes by denying funding, a practice made simpler after strong Republican gains in the 1858 elections gave them control of the House. With majority control, Republicans launched a committee investigation, under John Covode, of Buchanan's lobbying efforts on Kansas. Covode found numerous instances of government money and patronage employed to influence the vote. In the president's defense, Philip Klein has argued that Buchanan wanted to end the slavery debate before it wrecked the Union and was willing to countenance any means to effect that end. The president deeply resented the committee report, which Republicans gleefully distributed, and relations between the administration and Congress were poisoned. Two cabinet members, Jacob Thompson and John B. Floyd, were also implicated in corrupt practices. Any possibility of adventurous foreign schemes largely vanished.

Buchanan refused to run for reelection in 1860, honoring his pledge to serve a single term. He could not countenance Stephen A. Douglas, with whom he had feuded since their quarrel over Lecompton in December 1857. Administration hostility toward Douglas helped bring about the disastrous breakup of the Democratic National Convention at Charleston in April 1860 and the eventual nomination of two separate candidates. Buchanan supported the Southern Democratic candidate, his vice president John C. Breckinridge, and endorsed federal protection for slavery in the territories, the demand that had sundered the party convention. In the 1856 election, Buchanan and the Democrats had portrayed the choice as between union and disunion because the "black" Republican Party was so radical and so bent on harming the South that secession would follow a Republican victory. His rhetoric now helped insure that unfortunate outcome in the event of the success of the Republican nominee, Abraham Lincoln.

Lincoln's triumph began the sad denouement of Buchanan's presidency and with it the end of the Union and the descent of the country into sanguinary civil war. Buchanan's behavior in the final months of his administration has earned him considerable criticism, and it is largely to this period that he owes his reputation for vacillation and fecklessness. In November, South Carolina called a secession convention to meet the following month, and it was clear that the state intended to part from the United States. It was also clear that South Carolina's secession-minded officials regarded U.S. forts and installations within the state's borders as an affront and planned to occupy them under the new "national" authority. Buchanan held a series of cabinet meetings in November to endlessly discuss the crisis, seeking also an opinion from his attorney general, Jeremiah Black, on presidential powers to deal with a seceded state. He had the example of Andrew Jackson as a model: when South Carolina had similarly threatened to defy the authority of the federal government during the Nullification Crisis, Jackson had insisted in no uncertain terms that federal authority would be enforced, at the point of a bayonet if need be. He isolated South Carolina and effectively prevented other Southern states from joining with it to create a confederacy. Unlike Jackson, his opposite in temperament, Buchanan equivocated. In his annual message to Congress in December 1860, he declared that secession was unjustified because Lincoln as president-elect posed no threat to slavery. He blamed the abolition movement for sectional conflict and condemned it yet again. He also said that the federal government lacked the authority to force a sovereign state to remain in the Union, though he somewhat contradictorily pledged to defend federal property in the event of attack. He subsequently met with South Carolina representatives and apparently gave them a pledge not to reinforce the federal forts in Charleston, South Carolina. Buchanan retreated into an extreme constitutional literalism to justify near-total inaction while a secession movement gathered strength and proceeded to act and set up an alternative government and nation.

Buchanan eventually was forced to act, albeit in a modest manner. At the beginning of 1861, goaded by members of his Cabinet, he agreed to send supplies to Fort Sumter, located in Charleston Harbor, after the commander of the American garrison moved his men to the more defensible fort in the harbor from vulnerable shore installations. A merchant vessel, rather than a warship, was dispatched. When it arrived in Charleston Harbor on January 8, 1861, shore batteries fired upon it and the captain turned the ship about and fled. With that, Buchanan's efforts to assert federal power in the South ended. He had tried to foster support for a constitutional convention that would address Southern grievances and hoped to enlist the assistance of President-Elect Lincoln in bringing about the scheme. Lincoln was cool to the idea because he refused to countenance any expansion of slavery. Frustrated at Lincoln's rebuff, and beset with a hostile Congress, Buchanan remained inert for the remaining weeks of his administration, allowing the Confederate government precious time to organize itself unmolested, and doing little to resist the seizure of federal arsenals and military installations throughout the South. When he turned over the executive office to Lincoln in March, he left the new and untried president a divided country, a disaster that he did nothing to prevent or even inhibit.

After the beginning of civil war in April 1861, Buchanan's reputation was savaged, and he continued to be flayed in the newspapers and public opinion throughout the conflict. He was tarred for his long history of pro-Southern attitudes, and he received threats to his life and property. He was a traitor at best or a dupe at worst, according to the current wisdom. Buchanan loyally supported the Union after the war began, denouncing officers who resigned commissions to join the Confederacy, yet his actions did not stem the abuse. Congress revoked his franking privileges, and his portrait was removed from the Capitol Rotunda. He was officially disgraced and a pariah. Anxious to answer his critics, Buchanan combed through his correspondence and official papers for material that he crafted into a book-length response. Recognizing that releasing a defense of his actions during the war might be personally disastrous, he withheld publication until the end of hostilities. His unconvincing apologia and explanation, *Mr. Buchanan's Administration on the Eve of the Rebellion*, appeared in 1866. Buchanan blamed everyone but himself for the disastrous war: Congress for refusing to compromise, and his Cabinet and military officials for bungling the Fort Sumter crisis. He criticized subordinates for failing to take actions that were more properly his responsibility as president. He subsequently worked with writer James F. Shunk on an autobiography, but Shunk never produced a manuscript. James Buchanan lived quietly at his Wheatland estate until his death on June 1, 1868.

PRINCIPAL IDEAS

Despite his intellectual gifts and vanity, and his years of service as a diplomat and politician, Buchanan remained provincial in his philosophic outlook, adhering to the ancient Jeffersonian-Jacksonian creed he had adopted early in his career. He had a suspicion of industrialization and a romantic affection for the agrarian life, as evinced in the purchase of his Wheatland estate to which he repaired on his retirement. Buchanan remained true to his principles throughout his life, outlining them again in an 1867 letter a year before his death. He affirmed that a literal reading of the Constitution was absolutely necessary to guard against the threat of a consolidated federal power that would trample the rights of the states and people. In Buchanan's traditional view, the Founding Fathers' great fear was a federal government that grew into a dictatorship with steady accretions of power to match the growth in the country's population and wealth, and with state governments reduced to little more than ciphers. The Constitution was created to protect against tyranny by specifically enumerating the powers of the federal government, reserving all unmentioned powers to the states. In Buchanan's conception, it was a document written not to enhance rights, but to restrain federal power. He particularly touted the Tenth Amendment, which specifically reserved the rights of states.[6]

His traditional Jeffersonian philosophy formed the basis for his actions as a legislator and an executive, tempered always by a degree of moderation and pragmatism. He opposed a bankrupt bill to allow relief for debtors because he thought property rights were the foundation of a civil society; human nature was fundamentally base, and therefore absolving defaulters would only encourage greater fraud. On the tariff, an important concern in Pennsylvania with its iron industry, Buchanan evinced moderation, favoring tariff rates on items in a manner that would encourage the creation and growth of a national market impervious to the vicissitudes of foreign wars and economic turmoil. Rates should not be unjust to one particular region or industry, but rather at levels that maximized national harmony. He honored the archaic doctrine of instruction, that a senator had to obey the dictates of the state legislature that had elevated him to the Senate, to the point of voting for measures he had denounced. He thought the Bank of the United States had some merit, as well as a limited run of paper money to insure liquidity in a growing economy. Yet, he recognized that Andrew Jackson had made condemning the bank a test of party loyalty, so he publicly criticized it as a threat to liberty. He probably helped craft Martin Van Buren's subtreasury scheme, the Democratic alternative to a national bank. He supported the right to petition Congress during the gag rule controversy—an 1830s congressional rule that prohibited the reading of abolition petitions—but he blamed the abolition movement for the controversy and urged that petitioning Congress not be abused by what he saw as a radical and crass political movement. He thought slavery undesirable in the abstract, but felt that the South had a constitutional right to the institution. Buchanan always manifested a pronounced pro-Southern tilt: he shared a room at a Washington boardinghouse with a Southern senator and found attractive the romanticized agrarianism of plantation society. Throughout his political career, he viewed the South as the aggrieved party in the sectional crisis and blamed the abolition movement for fomenting the trouble. He emerged in the 1840s as a leading exponent of efforts to acquire additional territory, particularly in Central and South America. His concern with the imperialism of foreign nations such as Great Britain was one reason for his advocacy of expansion; another may have been his desire to placate the South with additional territory out of which could be carved slave states. He also recognized the utility of such aggressive nationalism for a presidential run.

CONCLUSION

James Buchanan achieved his long ambition when he won election to the presidency in 1856. He arrived at the White House completely divorced from both the rising progressive, Free Soil sentiment of the North and the increasingly fanatical proslavery sentiment of the South. His years overseas immediately preceding his executive tenure and his ancient Jeffersonian-Jacksonian beliefs were ill suited to the crises he soon faced. He also always harbored considerable sympathy for the Southern sense of grievance in American political life. When the time emerged for strong presidential leadership, Buchanan equivocated and allowed the Confederacy invaluable time to create unmolested a functioning government. He became the subject of considerable abuse after he left office in consequence of his perceived mishandling of the sectional dispute.

NOTES

1. Philip Shriver Klein, *President James Buchanan: A Biography* (University Park: Pennsylvania State University Press, 1962), 22.
2. Klein, *President James Buchanan*, 156.
3. Klein, *President James Buchanan*, 193.
4. Klein, *President James Buchanan*, 261–62.
5. Robert W. Johannsen, *Stephen A. Douglas* (New York: Oxford University Press, 1973), 586.
6. James Buchanan, *The Works of James Buchanan*, ed. John Bassett Moore (Philadelphia: J.B. Lippincott, 1908–1911), 11:439–42.

FURTHER READING

Jean A. Baker, *James Buchanan* (New York: Henry Holt, 2004); Michael J. Birkner, ed., *James Buchanan and the Political Crisis of the 1850s* (Selinsgrove, PA: Susquehanna University Press, 1996); James Buchanan, *The Works of James Buchanan*, ed. John Bassett Moore, 12 vols. (Philadelphia: J.B. Lippincott, 1908–1911); J. Buchanan Henry, ed., *The Messages of President Buchanan* (New York: n.p., 1888); Philip S. Klein, *President James Buchanan: A Biography* (University Park: Pennsylvania State University Press, 1962); and Elbert B. Smith, *The Presidency of James Buchanan* (Lawrence: University Press of Kansas, 1975).

SALMON CHASE
(1808–1873)

Striving for Freedom

LIFE

Salmon Chase was born on January 13, 1808, in Cornish, New Hampshire, the son of a prosperous farmer, Ithamar Chase, and his wife Janette Ralston Chase. Salmon was Ithamar and Janette's eighth child. He enjoyed his first eight years of childhood within the bucolic confines of a thriving New England farm, under the supervision of a kind father and mother who emphasized education and religion. Disaster befell the family when Ithamar made the ill-advised decision to sell his farm and take up the glass-making trade. He moved his large family to the town of Keene, New Hampshire, in late 1815. The War of 1812 had driven up the price of glass, but the peace treaty signed soon after Ithamar jumped into the business led to steep price declines as cheaper British glass imports appeared on the market. His speculative venture in tatters, Chase's father succumbed to despair and depression. A stroke felled him in August 1817.

With her husband dead and eight children to raise, Janette Chase faced a terrible trial, yet she managed to continue Salmon's education. She dispatched Chase to teacher Josiah Dunham, who ran a school in Windsor, Vermont; there Chase learned Latin and devoured Federalist newspapers, his first taste of the political world that would so consume his life. Returning to Keene, Chase studied with Zedekiah Barstow before his hard-pressed mother determined to send him off to live with his uncle, Philander Chase, an Episcopal bishop who had a school in Worthington, Ohio. The young lad departed for the frontier region in April 1820 at twelve years of age.

Chase passed formative years with his uncle, and his biographers have concluded that Philander had a profound influence on his nephew and charge, for good or for ill. Stern, demanding, and a believer in the virtues of corporal punishment and verbal bullying, the bishop pushed Salmon to excel in his studies. Young Chase had both chores and scholastic labor to perform each day, and if he failed to measure up in the execution of either, he was severely punished. Under his uncle's rigorous supervision, Chase's religious faith blossomed, as did a prodigious drive for achievement and advancement. Twin and seemingly contradictory impulses in Chase's character emerged: religious zeal and driving ambition. In 1822, Chase followed his uncle to Cincinnati after Philander accepted the position of president of Cincinnati College. When his uncle resigned the next year, Chase returned to Keene. He became a teacher and, when he imitated the harsh methods of his uncle, he was sacked for being too rough on his pupils.

Chase attended Royalton Academy, and then entered Dartmouth College in 1824. Gifted with a strong intellect, Chase considered his colleagues less talented than himself. Revivalism and religious enthusiasm swept the campus, which probably reinforced Chase's existing religiosity. He graduated in 1826, rejecting a career in the ministry as too likely to leave him in provincial parishes. He decided to try again as a teacher, and he traveled to New Jersey, Virginia, and Maryland in search of a promising venue for a school. Finding nothing, Chase landed in Washington, D.C., in the charge of another uncle, Dudley Chase, who represented Vermont in the Senate. Chase placed notices for his school in the *National Intelligencer*, but could attract no pupils; he ended as a teacher in a school already established under Alexander Plumley.

Two of Chase's students were sons of Attorney General William Wirt. Chase became friendly with the Wirt family and soon found himself enveloped in the warm embrace of a patrician Virginian's household, escorting Wirt's daughters to Washington social functions and attending parties and receptions at the Wirt home. An immensely accomplished lawyer who also played at politics and wrote biography, Wirt possessed everything Chase desired: erudition, professional and political success, and a warm, loving family. Wirt's example inspired Chase to consider a legal career, and he asked his newfound patron if he could study law under him. As a sitting attorney general, Wirt had no time for students, but he was fond of Chase and agreed to take him. Chase pursued a course of self-study in the law, working at it with what was his typical zeal, studying before and after his classes and on Saturdays.

Chase was examined for his bar license on December 14, 1829, before members of the District of Columbia Circuit Court, including Judge William Cranch. Andrew Jackson had been inaugurated as president earlier that year, and Chase found the new administration's leveling tendencies abhorrent. His friends had been prominent members of the previous administration, but now his friend and patron Wirt was out of office. Like many young lawyers of the time, Chase decided to pursue his fortune in the West, specifically Cincinnati, Ohio, where he had briefly resided with his uncle. He departed the national capital and arrived in Cincinnati on March 13, 1830.

Chase had chosen to make his professional start in a riverine city that traded heavily with the slave-dominated South and was consequently loath to disturb the sensibilities of Southern business partners. Chase diligently worked to establish himself as a lawyer. He earned admission to the Ohio bar in June 1830 and embarked on a series of legal partnerships, the most fortunate of which was with Daniel T. Coswell, the solicitor of the local branch of the Bank of the United States. Coswell helped Chase with contacts in the banking community, and the latter was soon doing considerable banking and commercial business. He worked with an almost fanatical doggedness and tenacity, often laboring seven days a week. Though he had received an excellent education by the standards of his time, he embarked on continued study of literature, the Bible, and foreign languages, the kind of perpetual self-improvement common among young men on what was then the nation's frontier. He helped found a lyceum and delivered lectures himself. He published articles in the *North American Review*, and with almost Herculean energy, he produced an updated version of the *Ohio Statutes*. His prodigious vitality, imposing intellect, and obvious talent soon made Chase a sought-after lawyer in the booming commercial center.

Chase attempted to recreate the comfortable family life that his mentor Wirt enjoyed. Tragedy marred his efforts. He married Catherine Jane Garniss in 1834, but she died of peritonitis in the wake of the birth of their first child while Chase was on a business trip. He drowned in sorrow for having been absent when his new wife succumbed, for pursuing his business goals when he should have been at her side. Upon returning home, he sat up with the corpse for a considerable period of time as if to beg the lifeless form for forgiveness. The child, a girl named Catherine, survived until 1840, dying after contracting scarlet fever from her maternal grandfather. Chase had two more wives and five more children. Both of his subsequent wives, Eliza Ann Smith and Sarah Bella Dunlop, died, Eliza in 1845 and Sarah in 1852. Only two of Chase's children survived to adulthood, the beautiful and talented Catherine, called Kate, whom Eliza bore in 1841, and Janette Ralston, called Nettie, whom Sarah bore in 1847. Kate Chase grew into an attractive young woman who became her father's political confidant and advisor.

The first decade of Chase's legal career in Cincinnati coincided with the rise of the abolition movement, heralded by the establishment of William Lloyd Garrison's abolition newspaper in Boston, the *Liberator*. John Quincy Adams, displaced from the presidency by someone he regarded as a frontier ruffian, Andrew Jackson, won election to the U.S. House of Representatives and began his long campaign to present abolition petitions, which were barred in that legislative body after Southern congressmen insisted on a rule that automatically tabled such petitions. For his part, what

Chase had seen of slavery in Washington, D.C., he did not like. He thought slavery ought to be abolished in the capital of a free republic, and he considered it an impediment to economic progress, an archaic labor system in an age brimming with progress. He also considered slavery immoral. However, Chase's contact with the commercial and banking world made him leery of the abolition movement with its demands for immediate emancipation. That smacked of anarchy, and the practical-minded Chase believed, if the slaves were ever freed, pervasive white racism necessitated the colonization of the freedmen.

The white majority demonstrated its antipathy to abolitionists and black Americans in Cincinnati in the summer of 1836. An anti-abolition mob sacked the printing office, which produced editions of James G. Birney's abolition weekly, the *Philanthropist,* and a recently abandoned black shantytown was razed to the ground. The crowd sought out Birney himself to tar and feather him, but fortunately he was not in town. Chase helped the local antislavery society recover damages from the mob's leaders. The next year, Chase appeared as counsel for Birney in another case that biographer John Niven characterized as an important moment for Chase's life. Birney had a servant, named Matilda, who was an escaped slave. Her status was discovered; she was seized by a slave catcher, a profession quite active in areas of Ohio that bordered slave states; and Birney wanted Chase to defend him against charges of harboring an escaped slave. Chase argued that Ohio was free territory and had been since the Northwest Ordinance; the Constitution did not sanction slavery, and indeed, the founders had not intended that the federal government support the institution. He also suggested that, since slavery violated natural rights, it could only exist where legally enforced. Slavery was purely a local institution. Once Matilda moved to free territory, she had ceased to be a slave because Ohio had no laws to enforce that unnatural condition upon her. Though the judge ruled for the slave catcher, condemning Matilda to a miserable fate in the Deep South and leveling a fine on Birney, the Ohio Supreme Court later reversed the verdict.

After defending a prominent leader of the abolition movement, Chase was identified as an abolitionist, a label that hurt his standing with conservative Whigs. He nevertheless continued to act as counsel for other runaways, cementing his reputation as somewhat radical on slavery. John Niven has suggested that Chase chose to make a grandiloquent argument on slavery when a narrower defense might have had a better chance of actually freeing Matilda. Chase had demonstrated a recurring character trait: he had pursued a moral goal with regrettable means. The woman, Matilda, had been sacrificed, a mere vehicle that allowed Chase a stage from which to make his argument for free territory and free labor. Chase recognized that opposition to the spread of slavery was the issue of the future, and it appealed as well to his moral zeal. He had been a nominal Whig, serving briefly on the Cincinnati city council, but he went into the Liberty Party because of his profound and religiously based abhorrence of slavery. He adopted some of the principles that Democrats espoused, such as states' rights and a preference for hard money or specie rather than paper currency. Chase wanted the Liberty Party to drop its extreme abolitionism and link itself to the Democratic Party, to become a vehicle for reform and antislavery within a more mainstream and powerful national party. Through the 1840s, Chase described his cardinal principles as ending slavery in the District of Columbia and the territories, leaving slavery alone where it existed, and prohibiting the expansion of slavery. He continued to argue that the Constitution did not sanction slavery and neither had the founders, and he also suggested that a conspiracy of Southern slave owners was working to take control of the federal government and make it serve their interests.

Chase had an opportunity to put his theories into practice in 1848 when a faction of the New York Democratic Party, angry with the Polk administration on patronage and other matters, nominated former president Martin Van Buren as a Free Soil candidate for the presidency. Chase had previously called a Free Soil convention to meet in Columbus, Ohio, on June 20, 1848, and he maneuvered the resulting meeting into endorsing the old warhorse Van Buren. He then chaired the national Free Soil convention at Buffalo, New York, in August. Chase had hit upon a formula to give antislavery wide appeal, at least in the North: emphasize the benefits to whites of restricting slavery rather than the benefits to blacks, an explicit acknowledgment of the pervasiveness of white racism.

Chase undertook his first statewide speaking tour of Ohio in support of the Free Soil ticket. Despite his strenuous labors, the major parties, Democrat and Whig, retained the loyalty and votes of the majority of voters, and Van Buren fared poorly. However, the Free Soil movement managed to elect eleven members to a closely divided Ohio legislature, giving them the power to determine which party, Whig or Democrat, would organize the state legislature. Chase began angling for the U.S. Senate seat and in pursuit of that goal, he cut a deal with Democratic leaders. In return for voting to organize the House under Democratic control, the Free Soilers would get a few minor offices, the repeal of Ohio's black laws, and the election of Chase to the Senate. For their part, Democrats received patronage and lucrative state contracts. Chase won election, but many Whigs forever considered him a man willing to sacrifice principle for personal ambition, a practitioner of the "corrupt bargain."

Chase's term in the U.S. Senate was in many respects disappointing. He had reached a political pinnacle through a third party, the Free Soil movement, and he hoped to fashion a new political party composed of antislavery men united around traditional Jeffersonian Democratic principles. However, Chase's deal with the Democrats alienated Whigs, and Democrats were not about to abandon their party for an uncertain political amalgamation under Chase's leadership. Chase accordingly found his design frustrated during most of his Senate years. Although he voted with the Democrats on procedural votes, he was nonetheless excluded from the Democratic caucus. He was denied any significant committee seat, receiving what to him was a humiliating offer to serve on a minor committee that dealt with Revolutionary claims. As a junior senator, Chase participated little in the great debate on Henry Clay's compromise proposals, but he opposed the compromise as too deferential to the South. He dismissed the contention of Stephen A. Douglas and others that slavery could not spread to the West because climate and other factors were inhospitable. On the contrary, Chase contended that with irrigation, slavery could flourish in the region, so Douglas's confident prediction that it could not survive in the West, and therefore that restricting it was unnecessarily inflaming the national debate, was flat wrong.

Chase's most dramatic and fame-inducing moment in the Senate came when he was a prominent leader of opposition to Stephen A. Douglas's Kansas-Nebraska Act. Introduced in January 1854, Douglas's bill organized the Nebraska Territory but also included an explicit repeal of the Missouri Compromise and its prohibition against slavery. Chase and other foes of slavery's expansion composed a public letter in opposition to Douglas's bill, a letter that Chase substantially reworked from a draft written by Joshua Giddings. Titled "Appeal of the Independent Democrats in Congress to the People of the United States," it savagely condemned Douglas for abandoning the sacred Missouri Compromise for the sake of appeasing Southern politicians. Chase manfully faced Douglas's wrath in the Senate, deliberately cultivating a calm demeanor in the face of abusive criticism delivered by the enraged, red-faced Illinois senator. Though the bill passed and received President Franklin Pierce's signature, Chase had gained national stature in his opposition.

Chase now had an issue behind which he had a real chance to realize his long-held dream of creating a new political coalition behind antislavery, Free Soil ideology. His new anti-Nebraska coalition triumphed in the 1854 Ohio state election, and the following year Chase was elected to the first of two terms as governor of Ohio. He became a leader in the formation of the new Republican Party in 1856, though he did not win the party's first presidential nomination, which went to John C. Frémont. As governor, Chase resisted the enforcement of the federal Fugitive Slave Act and supported the free Kansas movement. He even met with Kansas ruffian and radical abolitionist John Brown. Chase's high national profile made him a leading contender for the Republican presidential nomination in 1860, but his effort floundered because of the perception that he was too radical to win the general election. The Ohio legislature elected him to the Senate again, and later he was named a member of the Peace Commission that met in Washington, D.C., early in 1861 in a futile attempt to forge a compromise to stave off civil war.

Chase's relationship with the new president, Abraham Lincoln, was defined by several parameters. First, Chase had an exalted opinion of himself and a grievance. He had, in his mind, created the Republican Party with his Free Soil ideology and his advocacy of political fusion. He had been the first Republican governor and a leading presidential contender. He keenly felt the loss of the nomination to Lincoln, who had, after all, been defeated in his Senate contest with Stephen A. Douglas two years previous while Chase had been twice elected governor of Ohio. When Lincoln summoned Chase to Springfield, Illinois, after his election victory, Chase took the measure of the man who had wrested the prize from him. Chase was not impressed. With his awkward height and homely appearance, Lincoln represented the archetype of the ungainly frontier lawyers Chase had bested throughout his career. Still, Lincoln's deferential manner and soothing directness initially disarmed Chase.

Ever mindful of status, Chase hoped for the most prestigious cabinet post, secretary of state, but found to his dismay that Lincoln intended him for treasury or war. He grew more peevish when Lincoln informed him that he could not offer him either post pending word from others. His dignity a bit ruffled, Chase took his leave and awaited events. In March 1861, Lincoln sent Chase's nomination for secretary of the treasury to the Senate without consulting Chase further, so Chase learned that he was a member of Lincoln's cabinet in the newspaper. He subsequently met with Lincoln and remonstrated with the president for his backhanded manner of acting, but Lincoln persuaded him to take the post.

With the advent of the war, Chase shouldered the terrific burden of running the Treasury Department at a time of unprecedented government spending. The years immediately preceding the war had been marked by deficits and declining government revenues brought on by a depression and lower tariff rates. Chase had represented bankers in Cincinnati but he was not a financier, and he also held archaic hard-money Jacksonian beliefs incompatible with the necessity to create innovative financial solutions to pay for the war. Chase initially determined to borrow to finance the immediate demands on the U.S. Treasury after the opening of hostilities in April 1861. He browbeat New York financiers into supporting a bond issue, but required payment in specie, which kept currency tied up in government coffers instead of circulating in the economy as would have been possible if the funds had been deposited in a bank. As a result, specie became increasingly scarce and with the spate of bad news for the Union at the end of 1861, the Ball's Bluff disaster, and McClellan's stagnant army, banks started suspending specie payments. It appeared that an inability to pay for vital war supplies might paralyze the Union government.

The crisis forced Chase to abandon or at least modify his Jacksonian preference for hard money, and he endorsed legislation, the Legal Tender Act, that provided for the printing and use of paper currency, the so-called greenbacks. He had also authorized the brilliant financial promoter and Philadelphia banker, Jay Cooke, to handle the government's bond sales. Cooke's patriotic appeal to sell federal bonds, wrapping them in the flag, coupled with lower bond denominations, proved to be a spectacular success. Chase also proposed a number of financial reforms that were eventually enacted into law. The Union government also established the first income tax and raised tariff rates, measures that gave the financial community confidence that the federal government was soundly managed and could be trusted to meet its debt obligations. By contrast, the Confederate government simply printed currency and drifted into the abyss of intractable galloping inflation, a major factor in its demise.

In the first year of the Lincoln administration, Chase quickly became an influential cabinet official. With his immense self-confidence and commanding presence, he established himself as a rival for the president's attention with the veteran politician turned secretary of state, William H. Seward. Chase proved helpful on both military matters and with the border states. Simon Cameron, the war secretary, struggled to cope with the blizzard of administrative details that came with mobilizing and deploying masses of troops, and he leaned on Chase for considerable assistance. Cameron's weakness gave Chase influence in military appointments, and he successfully pushed Ohioans for important posts, such as Irvin McDowell, George B. McClellan, and William Rosecrans. Chase's knowledge of Kentucky, because he spent much of his career in Cincinnati close to the border, led Lincoln to seek his advice on the border states, at least initially.

Unfortunately for Chase, his Ohioans fared poorly in military command. Irvin McDowell was a fine staff officer, but a mediocre field commander. He earned blame for the Union defeat at Bull Run in July 1861 and for gaffes as a corps and army commander the following year. After McClellan scored early success in western Virginia, Chase assiduously pushed him forward as the logical successor for the superannuated army chief, Winfield Scott. Chase grew frustrated with General McClellan's deliberativeness as a commander, his discourteous treatment of the president and Cabinet, and his conservative Democratic views on the war's goals and race issues. Chase also, like Lincoln, opposed McClellan's grand ocean-borne flanking maneuver to the peninsula east of Richmond, Virginia, as that route left Washington uncovered in the face of a Confederate army. Rosecrans too was faulted for lack of aggressiveness. Chase suffered some loss of face as a military advisor to the president in consequence of the foibles of the Ohioans he backed for high military commands. After the vigorous attorney Edwin M. Stanton, another Ohio native, replaced the incompetent Cameron at the War Department, Lincoln largely ceased to consult Chase on military affairs. Chase learned after the fact about the appointment of John Pope as commander of the Army of Virginia, and later of Ambrose Burnside replacing McClellan as head of the Army of the Potomac.

As the nation's chief financial officer, Chase knew only too well the devastating financial effects of every Union military setback. Anxious for success, convinced that only aggressiveness in command could bring victory, Chase blamed Lincoln for the Union Army's lackluster performance, forgetting that he had been an early booster of mediocrities such as McDowell and McClellan. Chase also thought Lincoln moved too slowly against slavery and was too conservative in his race and Reconstruction policies. Convinced he could provide better leadership, and always in pursuit of the presidency, Chase encouraged the view that the president was a bumbler and the Cabinet divided because of the excessive influence of conservatives, specifically William H. Seward. His treasury duties required Chase to work closely with important congressional leaders, and he gave his opinions without hesitancy. He also tried on two occasions to organize a petition drive within the Cabinet to force Lincoln to remove McClellan, really an attempt to reduce the president to a mere creature of his Cabinet ministers. Both efforts failed because other Cabinet members, such as Navy Secretary Gideon Welles, refused to countenance them.

The potency of Chase's complaints to members of Congress became apparent when, after the disaster at Fredericksburg in December 1862, a committee of Republican senators called on Lincoln and demanded that he restructure his Cabinet beginning with the firing of Secretary of State Seward. The senators told the president that Seward disrupted the Cabinet unity necessary for the successful prosecution of the war, an argument straight from Chase. However, the iron-willed president refused to be driven. Lincoln arranged a meeting of the Cabinet and the senatorial scolds, and, in front of all, bluntly asked Chase if the Cabinet lacked unity. Chase meekly confessed that the Cabinet had agreed for the most part. Chase's congressional supporters felt the treasury secretary had duped them. His reputation for honest dealing suffered considerably; his naked ambition for the presidency had been exposed. Chase sent in his resignation to Lincoln, as had Seward, but the president declined to accept either. Lincoln had neatly avoided a trap while retaining the services of two able men, both of whom represented divergent wings of the Republican coalition.

For the remainder of his tenure as treasury secretary, Chase continued to differ with Lincoln. He tried to move the administration in a more radical direction on Reconstruction policy, repeatedly urging Lincoln to drop restrictions in his emancipation policy and embrace a broad black franchise, and he attempted to control Reconstruction in Louisiana through his treasury agents. He quarreled with Lincoln over the patronage appointments in his department, particularly those associated with the port of New York City. In the fall of 1863, Chase gave a series of speeches in Ohio and

Indiana, outlining his opinions on Reconstruction. He had, in effect, opened a campaign for the Republican presidential nomination in 1864. Soon after, Chase's congressional supporters, including Kansas senator Samuel Pomeroy, sent out a pamphlet highly critical of Lincoln and touting Chase for president. When the Pomeroy circular came to Lincoln's attention, Chase was forced to apologize to the president and again offered his resignation. Lincoln kept him on, but when the two differed over another patronage appointment in June 1864, leading Chase to again resign, expecting to be retained, Lincoln abruptly accepted his contentious secretary's withdrawal. Chase had not anticipated his removal—resignation threats were simply a bullying tactic he employed—and he suddenly found himself plunged into an unwelcome retirement.

In the end, Lincoln chose to be magnanimous to Chase, a duplicitous cabinet member and intriguer who sought to undermine the administration and president he served in order to advance his own presidential ambitions. Yet he had performed ably as treasury secretary, as Lincoln frankly acknowledged, and remained a leading figure in the Republican Party. Chase tried to re-earn the president's gratitude if not trust by endorsing and campaigning for Lincoln in the fall of 1864 with the goal of convincing the president to nominate him to the Supreme Court, a post that in the antebellum period did not preclude a presidential run. Supreme Court Justice John McLean, whom Chase knew personally, had pursued a presidential nomination while a member of the court. After Chief Justice Roger Taney died, Lincoln gratified Chase's desire and appointed him as Taney's replacement on December 6, 1864. Four months later, Chase administered the oath of office to Andrew Johnson in the wake of Lincoln's assassination at the hands of John Wilkes Booth. Within weeks of Johnson's unexpected ascension to the presidency, Chase embarked on a tour of the defeated South, traveling along the east coast, stopping to visit Charleston and other places of interest in the late war before heading on to Mobile and New Orleans. He witnessed the almost complete breakdown of law and order in the region, and the state of near anarchy in many places convinced him of the necessity of a lenient policy with regard to a settlement of the conflict. He peppered President Johnson with letters, advancing again and again his belief that universal black suffrage should be the centerpiece of Reconstruction policy, coupled with a broad, generous amnesty. Johnson had every intention of leniency, as time would prove, but he ignored Chase's advice on black suffrage.

As chief justice during the contentious Reconstruction period, the politically astute Chase sought to steer the court down a moderate path between the feuding Congress and president. During his tenure, the court ruled in *Ex Parte Milligan* (1866) that civilian courts had jurisdiction over military commissions when civilian courts were still functioning, freeing a number of Democrats imprisoned during the war for seditious activities. The court ruled in *Texas v. White* (1870) that secession was impossible because the Union was inviolable, and it also declared certain test oaths unconstitutional. Yet Chase also worried that the Congress had gone too far in its attempt to curb the power of the executive branch; specifically, he thought the Tenure of Office Act was unconstitutional. The Tenure of Office Act required Senate approval of Cabinet removals. Chase believed the president had the constitutional right to dismiss Cabinet officials without any reference to the Senate. When the Republican House impeached Johnson, the Constitution required Chase as chief justice to preside over the president's 1868 trial in the Senate. He agreed to his role, but he insisted that the trial be conducted as a judicial proceeding and that he rule on evidence and witnesses, conditions to which the congressional leadership grudgingly acceded. Chase felt isolated throughout the trial in the clubby Senate, Johnson was finally acquitted in a close vote, and important precedents were set for the conduct of future impeachment trials. For example, Chase insisted the Senate act in some manners as a court.

The presidential hunger never left Chase, and he unsuccessfully angled for the Democratic nomination in 1868. The Democratic leadership could not accept him as a candidate, as his support for black suffrage was a crippling barrier for most Democrats. In 1870, Chase had a heart attack, later followed by another heart attack and a stroke, and his health went into irreparable decline. His figure became wizened, his once-robust frame having disappeared, though he gamely continued his work at court after his stroke with slurred speech and diminished abilities. He suffered another and final stroke and died on May 7, 1873.

PRINCIPAL IDEAS

Chase's deep religious faith animated his aversion to slavery, and his legal training engendered a respect for law and order that made him wish to oppose it in a fashion that did not controvert the law and the Constitution. He also recognized that the abolition movement, dominated as it was by ministers and pious laypeople, was of limited utility when confronting what to him seemed an organized proslavery conspiracy bent on controlling the federal government. Chase drew on arguments previously advanced by abolitionists such as James G. Birney, but he molded and shaped those opinions to create something distinctly his own. Citing numerous antislavery statements, Chase argued that the Founding Fathers never approved of slavery and hoped that it would disappear from the United States sooner rather than later. He noted the antislavery pronouncements of Thomas Jefferson and others, and similar sentiments embodied in the Declaration of Independence and the Northwest Ordinance. The Constitution too had not sanctioned slavery despite the fugitive slave clause, and therefore the federal government had no business promoting it. Slavery was unconstitutional in areas or territories under the control of the federal government, such as the District of Columbia. Local regulations governed slavery, and without them a slave reverted back to his or her natural state, freedom.

That slavery existed in the national capital was the product of the malign influence of the Slave Power, the small group of Southern slaveholders who were actively seeking to subvert the original intent of the founders and turn the Constitution and the federal government into institutions under their dominance. Eric Foner has argued that Chase more than anyone else planted the image of the Slave Power conspiracy in the Northern consciousness, as well as his conception that the founders had been antislavery in opinion and had placed the institution on the path to extinction. "Freedom is national; slavery only is local and sectional," Chase had intoned in the Senate, and his conclusion became a slogan for the fledgling Republican Party.

CONCLUSION

In Salmon P. Chase, deep religious feeling matched an equally great ambition. His relentless pursuit of the presidency harmed his reputation when he acted in a duplicitous manner as a member of the Lincoln administration. Still, his ability to craft an antislavery ideology that seemed conservative when compared with the radical pronouncements of abolitionists helped encourage broad participation in the movement to restrict and ultimately end slavery.

FURTHER READING

Frederick J. Blue, *Salmon P. Chase: A Life in Politics* (Kent, OH: Kent State University Press, 1987); Salmon Chase, *Inside Lincoln's Cabinet: The Civil War Diary of Salmon P. Chase*, ed. David Donald (New York: Longmans, Green, 1954); Eric Foner, *Free Soil, Free Labor, Free Men: The Ideology of the Republican Party before the Civil War* (New York: Oxford University Press, 1970); and John Niven, *Salmon P. Chase: A Biography* (New York: Oxford University Press, 1995).

JEFFERSON DAVIS
(1808–1889)

Stubborn Resolve for States' Rights

LIFE

Jefferson Davis was the son of Samuel Emory Davis and Jane Cook Davis. Samuel was a Revolutionary War veteran who fought in the bitter campaigns in Georgia and South Carolina. Davis always revered his father's service in the Glorious Cause, referring to it in political speeches. After the Revolution, Samuel received a land bounty in Wilkes County, Georgia, where he scratched out a farm. Like many of his generation, Samuel was a restless wanderer, forever in search of more fertile fields over the next hill. He cleared land, established a homestead, and then moved and repeated the process elsewhere. Though he had accumulated 4,000 acres in Georgia, Samuel moved his family to Kentucky in 1793, eventually settling in Christian County, where he farmed and ran a tavern. His tenth and last child was born there on June 3, 1808, named Jefferson after Samuel's political idol Thomas Jefferson. He then moved the family to Louisiana and finally to Wilkinson County, Mississippi. Samuel had gradually accumulated a modest workforce of around a dozen slaves. With his slaves, he cleared a farm he called Poplar Grove and raised cotton. Jefferson Davis spent his boyhood at the small Mississippi farm, the adored last child of middle-aged parents, surrounded by slaves and the plant and harvest cycle of cotton growing.

Samuel and Jane were intent on a good education for Jefferson. He received lessons in a log cabin school in Wilkinson County, but his father wanted more professional instruction for his son. In July 1816, Jefferson enrolled at St. Thomas College in Washington County, Kentucky. He spent two years at St. Thomas, learning a classics- and language-based curriculum. His parents missed him terribly and insisted that he return to Mississippi in 1818. Young Jefferson briefly attended a school in Washington,

Mississippi, before an academy opened in Wilkinson County. He attended the Shaw Academy until 1823. At that point, his father and older brother, Joseph, a prominent lawyer in Natchez, decided to send Jefferson to the renowned Transylvania University in Lexington, Kentucky. Jefferson was a successful student at Transylvania. He was popular, and his academic record was good in the classics-based curriculum. However, the death of his father in 1824 ended his sojourn at Transylvania. His elder brother Joseph assumed the role of surrogate father to Jefferson, and he arranged for the young man's enrollment at the military academy at West Point. Although reluctant to leave Transylvania, Davis bowed to his brother's wishes.

Davis's four years at West Point were not distinguished. He was not adept at mathematics, an important subject at the engineering school. He willingly violated the rigid rules of behavior, earning scores of demerits, and he even came perilously close to expulsion for a visit to the notorious Benny Haven's tavern near campus. With his poor behavior and low marks, Davis finished twenty-third in a class of thirty-three in June 1828. Unlike Robert E. Lee, whose outstanding mathematical skills and sterling behavior were rewarded with assignment to the engineers, Davis went to the infantry. While at the academy, Davis befriended Southerners for the most part, men like Leonidas Polk and Albert Sidney Johnston. He later touted the academy for inspiring cadets to think of themselves as Americans rather than citizens of a particular state or region. Yet, as a cadet, he had mostly Southern friends and criticized "Yankee" cadets for what he deemed excessive parsimony.

After graduation and spending leave with his family, Davis reported for duty at Jefferson Barracks in St. Louis, Missouri, in January 1829. Davis spent the next six years in the army, acting in the diverse roles typically given to junior officers: quartermaster and commissary, recruiter, adjutant, supervisor of various work crews and projects, and pursuer of deserters. He was assigned in 1829 to Fort Crawford in Michigan, where he supervised the construction and improvement of forts. While in the army, Davis had a slave as his personal servant, James Pemberton, whom his father had bequeathed to Davis in his will. As an officer, Davis was of slight build, though physically robust. He had a reputation for good manners but also for a temper and sharp retorts if angered. He was immensely self-assured and tended to believe himself correct in all matters.

Davis could be prickly, and that landed him into trouble on two occasions while in the army. He was named adjutant to Colonel Henry Dodge in 1834, but was soon reassigned after he quarreled with the colonel, though the latter had promoted him to first lieutenant and adjutant. After his regiment was ordered to Oklahoma Territory to intimidate the Indians, Davis was court-martialed for insubordination. Acquitted early in 1835, his narrow escape helped him determine to leave the army. He had also met and fallen in love with Sarah Knox Taylor, the daughter of Zachary Taylor, his commanding officer in Michigan Territory and the future president. Colonel Taylor did not approve of his daughter marrying a penniless infantry lieutenant, so Davis and Knox, as Sarah was called, conducted their romance in secret. Nevertheless, they were determined to be married.

Joseph Davis, Jefferson's elder brother, had established himself as a successful planter and attorney in Mississippi. He offered to set Jefferson up as a planter as well. Anxious to marry Knox Taylor and perhaps hoping that his change of professions would earn her parents' approval of their union, Jefferson accepted his brother's offer. He took charge of 900 acres on the Mississippi River, fertile soil in an area called Davis Bend. The plantation was named Brierfield. With that, Jefferson married Knox on June 17, 1835, in Louisville, Kentucky. They journeyed by steamboat south to Davis Bend, the site of their new home, and then later that summer south to Louisiana to visit Jefferson's sister. Tragedy soon visited the young newlyweds. Both Jefferson and his bride contracted malaria in the fetid Louisiana summer. Jefferson survived, but Knox Taylor died on September 15, 1835, at the age of twenty-one.

The tragedy and disease forever marked Davis. Losing his wife so soon after their marriage left Davis crushed with overwhelming grief, and he was subject to periodic malarial bouts for the remainder of his life. The plans for the future they had happily made together, the children they would raise, the good times to come—all the dreams were entombed in Sarah Knox Taylor's grave. Davis biographer William C. Davis has noted that Knox had been reluctant to travel south during the deadly summer yellow fever season. Davis had persuaded her it was safe, though he knew it was not; he was simply anxious to get married and have his wife with him. Her subsequent death must have preyed on his conscience, so much so that William C. Davis has suggested that to deal with the guilt, Jefferson Davis became even more stubborn in his belief in his own infallibility in all matters. After Knox's death, Davis had land to clear for cotton cultivation at Davis Bend, but he felt unable to proceed. He spent the winter of 1835 in temperate Cuba, trying to reestablish his emotional and physical health.

In early 1836, Davis recovered his emotional equilibrium, returned to Mississippi, and set about clearing the land at Brierfield for cotton. With the financial help of his brother, he purchased sixteen slaves at Natchez. He then appointed his manservant James Pemberton as overseer, and the slaves under Pemberton's supervision prepared the acreage for cotton. Davis resided at his brother's plantation, Hurricane, which was nearby. Strangely, Joseph Davis retained title to the property Jefferson called his own. The land was quickly profitable, the rich Delta soil producing a good cotton crop in 1837. While living at his brother's Hurricane mansion, Davis met the woman who became his second wife. Varina Howell was the daughter of William B. Howell, a not particularly successful Natchez businessman and a friend of Joseph. Varina was invited to visit Hurricane, where she met Jefferson. She initially found him a bit off-putting with his strong self-assurance and tendency to believe his every opinion the only one thinkable. Spending two months in his company at the plantation estate brought her around. They were married on February 26, 1845, in Natchez. Varina was a few months shy of her nineteenth birthday when she married Jefferson, who was nearly thirty-seven. William Cooper has argued that in the antebellum South, the husband-wife relationship was analogous to that of a parent and child. The difference in age between the newlyweds may have accentuated that cultural phenomenon in the Davis' marriage; Davis became both father and husband to Varina. He signed a note to her just before the wedding ceremony, "Uncle Jeff." After their wedding, Davis arranged for a steamboat trip down the Mississippi to New Orleans and, in a bizarre twist, the couple stopped at the grave of Jefferson's first wife to decorate it with flowers. If Varina visited Knox's grave with her new husband, it must have struck her as a peculiar event for her honeymoon.

The Davis marriage and the family pocketbook prospered, as the Brierfield plantation, worked by slaves, was tremendously profitable. According to William Cooper, the slaves at Brierfield were well treated. With the advent of his political career, Davis was absent much of the time in Washington, and overseers and his brother Joseph kept his plantation in working order. The slaves were given decent if spartan food. They were allowed religious services on the Sabbath, and slave families were recognized. Davis constructed a slave hospital for the sick, and Varina nursed those who were ill when she was in residence. Cooper concluded that Davis was a humane master, if such could be possible, but that the Davis family subsequently exaggerated their commitment to the slaves' welfare. The plantation was immensely profitable. Varina estimated that their annual income was in the $35,000–40,000 range.

Davis's first years as a planter had also marked the beginning of his political career. He read voraciously and discussed current events with Joseph. Both men were Democrats, staunch states' rights men who revered the Virginia and Kentucky resolutions and admired Andrew Jackson. Jefferson was selected as a delegate to the Mississippi Democratic state conventions of 1840 and 1842. The following year, he was abruptly drafted to run for the state legislature late in the campaign. He debated the famed Whig orator Seargent S. Prentiss and though he lost the race, he earned respect and recognition. In 1844, Davis was chosen as a presidential elector at large. He favored Calhoun, arguing with the sectional animus that marked his career that it was time for a Southern president. Davis also claimed that Southern coastal defenses had been neglected while those of the Northeast had been lavished with federal funds. He traveled throughout Mississippi in support of James K. Polk, who had won the Democratic nomination over Calhoun and others, from June to November 1844.

The following year, Mississippi Democrats nominated Davis for an at-large congressional seat, and he campaigned as a traditional states' rights Democrat who favored strict construction of the Constitution. He denounced the national bank, the tariff, and the Whig economic agenda. However, he also pledged to get a fair share of federal largesse for Mississippi, noting that he intended to work for the establishment of a federal navy yard on the Mississippi Gulf Coast. Davis was elected to Congress in November 1845. Later that month, John C. Calhoun stopped in Vicksburg, and Davis gave a gushing welcoming address that left little doubt that he considered himself a Calhoun disciple. For his part, Calhoun spent more time with Varina then Jefferson, enjoying the charms of the pretty young wife.

Davis journeyed to the Capital in late November and was sworn in as a member of the Twenty-ninth Congress on December 8, 1845. He arrived at a time of tension with Mexico and Britain. The former was angered at the annexation of Texas in March 1845, while tension existed with Great Britain over competing claims to the Oregon Territory. Davis delivered a speech on Oregon in the House of Representatives in February 1846. He portrayed the settlement of Oregon by American immigrants who intended to farm as a more noble fate for the region than to remain the fur-bearing province of the British Hudson's Bay Company. Settlement benefited mankind; fur trading, the few stockholders of the company. He endorsed President Polk's efforts to negotiate a settlement with the British. Davis also signaled his strong adherence to strict construction orthodoxy in a speech opposing the Rivers and Harbors Bill, a federal appropriation to improve navigation on rivers and in harbors. Davis objected because there was no specific language in the Constitution authorizing expenditures for rivers and harbors. His attitude was not unusual in the Democratic Party. Indeed, President Polk vetoed the Rivers and Harbors Bill for constitutional objections.

Davis did not simply oppose and obstruct as a congressman. He became and remained a strong proponent of the Smithsonian Institution. He praised West Point for the superb training provided to the men who, despite fearful odds, bested the Mexican army when war between the two countries began in May 1846. He devoted much time to constituent service, advocating Mississippians for federal appointments. Often he labored into the night on his correspondence, and he dutifully presented private petitions on the House floor. While Jefferson labored for Mississippi, Varina relished the Capital's social whirl. She enjoyed clever men and women and facile conversation, both of which were present in the drawing rooms of the national city. She could be blunt and rude in expressing her opinions, and consequently earned the enmity of some.

The coming of the Mexican War interrupted Davis's congressional career. He immediately offered himself for service should Mississippi be called on to furnish regiments for the conflict. Polk authorized one regiment for the state, which became the First Mississippi, and the men elected Davis as colonel. A horrified Varina opposed her husband's return to the army, but Davis insisted. He could not have been unaware of the political advantages of successful wartime service in a culture that revered martial prowess.

Davis's regiment was shipped to Mexico and to the army under the command of his former father-in-law, Zachary Taylor. Davis and Taylor had been reconciled before the war, and Taylor came to regard Davis in a kind manner. Davis and his command, known as the Mississippi Rifles, distinguished themselves in hard fighting in two battles, Monterrey and Buena Vista. At Monterrey, Davis and the Rifles fought house-to-house in the city. When fighting ended, Taylor named Davis to a commission that arranged for a controversial armistice with the Mexican commander, General Pedro de Ampudía, that President Polk later repudiated. At Buena Vista in February 1847, Davis and the First Mississippi played a vital role in repulsing Mexican attacks. Davis suffered a nasty musket wound to his foot; he was hobbled for two years in consequence. Painfully wounded though he was, the war proved immensely valuable to Davis's political standing. When he returned to Mississippi in June 1847, he was a war hero with an assured political future in the state. He was appointed to the U.S. Senate in August 1847 to replace the deceased Jesse Speight. The Mississippi legislature subsequently elected him to the Senate in January 1848.

Davis arrived in the Senate just as the acquisition of territory from Mexico exacerbated sectional tensions. He served on the Military Affairs, Library, and Pensions Committees, and the Smithsonian Institution's Board of Regents. As a disciple of John C. Calhoun, Davis pitched into the political struggle over whether to allow slavery into the new territories and the West. The passage of the Wilmot Proviso in the House, which would have prohibited slavery in the territories, made clear that the South's equality in the Senate was vital to the preservation of slavery. Davis argued for admitting slavery into the Oregon Territory. He thought the only suitable compromise was to extend the Missouri Compromise line to the Pacific Ocean. Presumably, then, slave states below the line would be admitted to the Union in concert with free states carved from territory above the line, and the Senate balance would be maintained.

Given his attitude, Davis opposed President Zachary Taylor's plan to immediately admit California as a free state. Despite political differences, Davis and Taylor continued to have a warm personal relationship, and when Taylor became fatally ill in July 1850, Davis and his wife Varina kept vigil at his bedside. Davis also opposed Henry Clay's grand design for a compromise in 1850 because he did not think it was an equitable arrangement. The admission of California and potentially other free states would end the Southern bulwark in the Senate, while the supposed concession to the South, a reinvigorated Fugitive Slave Law, was unenforceable in the North. He condemned the abolition movement, which he saw as the source of all the sectional controversy, and he urged the South to unite for the protection of its constitutional rights.

Davis debated and battled the other Mississippi senator, Henry S. Foote, who favored Clay's compromise. Both men criss-crossed Mississippi on speaking tours, Davis denouncing the compromise as inequitable and maintaining the South had to unite to uphold its rights in the face of an aggressive abolition movement in the North. He called Foote a submissionist. For his part, Foote supported the compromise and Union and called Davis a disunionist. Davis always maintained that while secession was legal, he did not support it. Secession was a last resort. Still, his many speaking tours of Mississippi in which he denounced Northern aggression and compromise efforts undoubtedly helped create a prosecession climate that eventually prevailed in the state's public opinion.

Mississippi governor John A. Quitman was a Democrat and avowed secessionist who called for a state convention that would decide whether the state would leave the Union. The election for delegates to the convention was scheduled for September 1851. Davis, Foote, and Quitman campaigned in the summer; when the Union and compromise cause championed by Foote won a majority of delegates, Quitman resigned as the Democratic gubernatorial candidate. The state Democratic Party drafted Davis as a replacement candidate. Foote, running as the candidate of a Union ticket, defeated Davis in November.

After Franklin Pierce was elected president of the United States in 1852, he wished to construct a Cabinet composed of Democrats who had favored and those who had opposed the Compromise of 1850. Davis immediately came under consideration for the post of secretary of war. With his West Point education, distinguished record in the Mexican War, and chairmanship of the Senate Committee on Military Affairs, Davis was an obvious choice. Pierce summoned Davis to Washington, where he accepted the War Department charge in March 1853. Pierce came to rely on Davis. William Cooper has suggested that the death of a young son between election and inauguration traumatized Pierce and led him to lean on Davis. Whatever the motive, the two developed a close friendship, a relationship that gave Davis considerable influence in the administration.

As administrator of the War Department, Davis embraced every detail; indeed, he oversaw virtually every matter that came within the department's province. He worked long hours until his health began to suffer, then moderated his work habits. He had a penchant for involving himself in trivialities that were more properly dealt with by clerks or subordinate officers. For example, when West Point cadets wrote for permission to grow facial hair, Davis personally answered. Given his willingness to countenance such inconsequential matters, it is hardly surprising that his schedule was constantly full. His failure to delegate seems more a weakness than strength.

Davis placed his imprimatur on a number of areas. He was fascinated with new technology and innovations in military tactics and strategy, meeting with inventors who offered the latest in military weaponry. Davis approved the rifle for production by U.S. armories in 1855, replacing the antiquated smoothbore musket. He subsequently commissioned the writing of a new tactical field manual to take account of the deadly efficiency of the rifle. He also sent observers to the Crimean War, who returned and produced a report that catalogued the battle tactics and methods in use in Europe. He broadened the curriculum and lengthened the term required for a degree at West Point. He introduced camels to the service as ideal for crossing the deserts of the West. The camels were purchased in the Middle East and successfully employed on an experimental journey between Texas and California. Unfortunately, Congress allowed funding for the camels to lapse.

Davis supported building military installations and forts to aid settlement in the West. He convinced Congress to increase the size of the regular army; four regiments were created in 1855. The pay scale was improved in an effort to increase retention levels of military personnel. He supported federal involvement in the construction of a transcontinental railroad, something of a departure from strict construction, though Davis did not notice any inconsistency. He commissioned surveys of the frontier West to determine the best route for the railroad. The Pierce administration purchased land from Mexico that extended the U.S. border further south to facilitate a southern direct route to the Pacific. Nevertheless, the terrain surveys that Davis commissioned revealed a number of possible transcontinental routes, but Davis publicly endorsed the southern route, which followed much of the thirty-second parallel. Davis's sectional bias was ever present in his public career.

Throughout his tenure at the War Department, Davis remained a close advisor to Pierce. In 1854, he helped win the president's backing of the Kansas-Nebraska Act, with an explicit repeal of the Missouri Compromise. Davis naturally approved of opening the territory to slavery, which had been prohibited there for more than thirty years. He lobbied congressmen for the bill, which became an administration measure once Davis won Pierce's imprimatur. He thereby helped usher in the final sectional political crisis that ended in civil war.

Davis longed to return to the Senate and made clear his ambition to friends and supporters in Mississippi, and in January 1856, the Mississippi legislature elected him. He resigned as war secretary in March 1857 and was sworn in as senator. He was again chosen as chairman of the Military Affairs Committee. He continued his lifelong advocacy of Southern rights, battling for the proslavery cause in Kansas and against Stephen A. Douglas and popular sovereignty. The new Republican Party, dedicated to resisting the expansion of slavery, horrified Davis. In speeches to Mississippi audiences, Davis would salute the Union, but then declare that the election of a Republican president in 1860 would warrant secession. He warned Mississippians to prepare for that eventuality by building railroads and munitions factories. War, he insisted, was preferable to submission to tyranny. The John Brown raid on Harpers Ferry in 1859 vindicated Davis's apocalyptic warnings in the minds of many Southerners and seemed to offer proof of the necessity to prepare for conflict. Davis supported Democratic presidential candidate John C. Breckenridge in 1860. He could hardly have been surprised with the ensuing secession of Southern states, Mississippi included, after the election of Abraham Lincoln. The establishment of a Confederate government followed.

When the Provisional Confederate Congress elected Davis president, he received the news at Brierfield with grim resolve. He probably would have preferred a commission as general-in-chief of the Confederate Army; his wife maintained that army command would have suited him better. Nevertheless, he felt honor bound to accept the charge and left for Montgomery, giving speeches when called upon along the way in which he gave vent to bloody-mindedness, promising to give his last drop of blood for independence. He was sworn in February 18, 1861. In his inaugural address, Davis was both belligerent and conciliatory. He maintained that Northern aggression had led to secession and that independence was irrevocable. In a thinly veiled effort to husband foreign support, he noted that any interference with the cotton trade would harm the economies and people of the world. While insisting that the South wanted only peace and free trade, Davis repeatedly asserted the new country's willingness to embrace war if necessary. While claiming that he preferred militia, Davis said circumstances demanded a standing professional army and navy, and he called for the creation of both. It was a beginning full of martial overtones.

As president, Davis manifested the same traits as the administrator of the Confederate government as he had as war secretary under Pierce. Obsessively detail oriented, Davis passed judgment on matters large and small. His most recent biographer found Davis's annotation on reams of official correspondence that had flooded into the government with the president personally approving such minutiae as a lieutenant's transfer from one army unit to another. Davis considered the War Department his special province by virtue of his training, experience, and the ongoing war, and he often usurped duties that should have been handled by the war secretary. His inability to delegate and his desire to pass judgment on trivial matters kept his schedule full, and he worked arduous hours throughout the war. Beyond Davis's penchant for burying himself in paperwork, other problems hampered the administration of the Confederate central government. The president tended to indecisiveness. While draining his energies on trivialities, he allowed important decisions to drift. Unlike Lincoln, who made most of the important decisions with little Cabinet consultation, Davis held long cabinet meetings to discuss a subject, often concluding the meeting without resolving the problem under consideration.

Davis and the new Confederacy soon faced the war for which he had defiantly avowed his willingness to shed blood. The federal fort in Charleston Harbor, Fort Sumter, was an intolerable affront to South Carolina and the Confederacy. Davis tried negotiating the fort's abandonment, sending three commissioners to Washington, D.C., to treat with the Lincoln administration. The commissioners received no encouragement from Lincoln, but received private assurances from Secretary of State William H. Seward that the fort would be abandoned. When Lincoln moved to resupply the fort, Davis felt he had been duped. The fort's mere existence in Charleston Harbor insulted Southern honor. Now, Lincoln had, in Davis's mind, tweaked his nose. After lengthy Cabinet meetings in early April, the president ordered an attack on the fort. For the sake of honor and because his new nation seemed bent on a clash of arms, Davis embraced the onus of commencing hostilities.

The first year of war revealed the weaknesses and inherent contradictions that doomed the South. Davis struggled with them all. In some ways, his style of leadership, which alternated between imperiousness and indecisiveness, exacerbated problems. Yet it may also be true that Davis's intense willpower kept the fledgling government from disintegrating. The problems were manifold. Davis was head of a government founded on the fundamental principle of state sovereignty. It now faced the necessity of centralized control to meet the military challenge of a vastly more powerful foe. Davis implemented laws that drafted men into the Confederate Army, suspended the writ of habeas corpus, established martial law, and confiscated property. These bold measures inflamed states' rights opposition to Davis and his administration. Opponents included prominent governors, like Joseph Brown of Georgia; members of the Confederate Congress such as Texas senator Louis T. Wigfall; and even the vice president, Alexander Stephens. Davis willingly embraced any measure that aided the fight for independence even if it violated principles he had spent his political life upholding.

Though Davis accepted the increased central control that the war necessitated, he provided no strategic direction for the war effort. Leading a nation that stressed the importance of state sovereignty, it may have been impossible for Davis to impose some overall strategic vision on the independence campaign. He did urge his generals to take the offensive, correctly recognizing that retaining the initiative would make it difficult for the Union enemy to take offensive action. He also wanted to carry the war into Northern territory, as he felt that the ensuing chaos and damage would strengthen peace sentiment in the North as well as provide a measure of retribution for the depredation Union armies had wreaked on Southern soil. Seizing territory also could influence pro-Southern feeling in the border states and might convince foreign powers such as Britain and France to side with the Confederacy. Robert E. Lee shared these sentiments. While Davis preferred to defer to local commanders on tactical actions, there were clear instances when he should have directly ordered a Confederate general to pursue a desired course. For example, the president ordered General Joseph Johnston to assist General John C. Pemberton's Confederate Army, hemmed in at Vicksburg, Mississippi, by General Ulysses S. Grant's Union army. Johnston pleaded lack of men and inability to do much, though he did eventually attack Grant to little purpose. Davis should have ordered Johnston and Pemberton to unite their armies and attack Grant, clearing up any ambiguity about whether Pemberton was obligated to cling to Vicksburg and dismissing Johnston's typical worries.

The president's indecisiveness could be costly. In 1863, General Braxton Bragg had lost the confidence of his fellow officers in the Army of Tennessee. Davis had been deluged with complaints about Bragg, and he determined to assess the situation himself. In October 1863, the president visited the army, where he personally interviewed Bragg and other officers. Though convinced of the depth of anti-Bragg sentiment in the army, Davis allowed Bragg to retain command. In an ensuing Union attack on Bragg's position at Missionary Ridge, which lay on the Tennessee-Georgia border, the army performed poorly because many officers had no confidence in Bragg's plans and dispositions. Despite a formidable natural defensive line, the Army of Tennessee was decisively defeated. Change had been necessary, but the president failed to do what was required.

Davis liked to be kept informed of his generals' plans. Early in the war, Joseph Johnston was alienated from Davis when he was not made the senior Confederate officer by date of rank. He concluded that the Confederate president had insulted him and wished him ill. As the commander of Confederate forces facing McClellan's Army of the Potomac, Johnston's animus led him to withhold information regarding his plans from Davis. The Confederate president was naturally anxious for some idea of what his general intended to do to keep McClellan's horde away from the Confederate capital city of Richmond, Virginia. Davis was taken by surprise when Johnston finally launched an attack against McClellan on May 31, 1862. When Johnston was wounded in action, Davis named Robert E. Lee, who had been the nominal commander of Confederate armies, as his replacement.

Unlike Johnston, Lee kept Davis informed of his plans, his situation, and the status of the army. He met regularly with Davis when the tactical situation allowed to discuss offensive and other operations. Like Davis, he recognized the value of offensive operations. When Lee took the Army of Northern Virginia north into Maryland in 1862 and into Pennsylvania in 1863, he had the support of Jefferson Davis. Lee demonstrated his tactical brilliance in command of the army, and Davis came to regard him as indispensable. After the unsuccessful Pennsylvania campaign with Lee rebuffed at Gettysburg, Lee offered his resignation. Davis would not consider it. The president appreciated Lee's audacity and his devotion to the Confederate cause. He sought to assist him and his army in every possible way.

Davis believed that the Confederate independence struggle demanded total commitment, and he took George Washington as a model. Personal considerations or ambitions had to be swept aside. Those who, in Davis's opinion, valued personal matters above the national interest, he treated with scorn. After Joseph Johnston threw a fit over precedence of rank and expressed his anger in an intemperate letter to Davis, the president never had much regard for him. (He continued to employ Johnston in various commands for lack of a better alternative.) He quarreled with Confederate General P.G.T. Beauregard too over what Davis considered petty matters. Politicians too felt Davis's wrath. The president's tendency to demand absolute fealty to the cause alienated some who fell short of his high standard. He lacked the political and personal skills to accept flawed individuals who, though possessed of imperfections that Davis found vexing, might still have rendered good service to the cause.

Davis and the Confederate government were forced to abandon Richmond in early April 1865, as Grant flanked Lee and forced the remnants of the Army of Northern Virginia out of their entrenchments near Petersburg. Davis scurried off with the files of the government and some of its treasure. Incredibly, even after Lee surrendered what had been the most successful Confederate army, Davis continued to speak of victory and the continuation of the Confederate nation. His statements at the time bordered on the irrational, though he did foreswear as uncivilized a continuing guerrilla war. Davis was eventually captured, along with Varina, with whom he had met on the trail. As Union cavalry overran his campsite, Davis fled his tent clad in a cloak and ladies' shawl that his wife had thrown around his shoulders. He was captured in that undignified garb.

The federal government imprisoned Davis for two years in Fortress Monroe, a military prison located in Virginia on the Chesapeake Bay. Lincoln had been assassinated on April 14, and many believed Davis was involved. There is, however, no convincing evidence of a link between John Wilkes Booth and his co-conspirators and Jefferson Davis. The former president of the Southern Confederacy was indicted, but the trial was eventually dropped. It would have been difficult to empanel an impartial jury in Virginia, where the case had to be heard.

Davis spent time in Canada and Europe while the legal process ground to a conclusion. He then accepted a position as president of the Carolina Life Insurance Company with offices in Memphis. Like Robert E. Lee, Davis had been offered the presidency of Southern colleges and universities, but unlike Lee, who accepted the presidency of Washington College,

Davis declined such offers. He chose the insurance post because it was more financially rewarding. Unfortunately, Davis resigned from the company after quarreling with the board of directors, and other business investments and arrangements were equally unsuccessful. With little money and no prospects, Davis decided to write his war memoirs. He ensconced himself at the estate of an admiring widow, Sarah Dorsey, who believed him a great hero and allowed him free room and board. A horrified Varina refused to visit the estate, called Beauvoir, but eventually dropped her objections to the unusual arrangement. Davis received a substantial advance for his memoir from New York publisher D. W. Appleton, and his two volumes, *The Rise and Fall of the Confederate Government*, sold well. In another bid to recoup his fortunes, Davis sued his late brother's granddaughter for control of his former plantation, Brierfield. He was successful, but the plantation was never profitable. Sarah Dorsey died of breast cancer in 1879, leaving Beauvoir to Davis, much to the chagrin of her surviving relatives.

As Davis aged, he became the exemplar of the Lost Cause, a rallying point for those who remained devoted to the Confederacy and the ideals for which it had stood. Davis remained publicly silent on the issues of the day, but privately his opinions were unchanged. He still considered secession honorable and constitutional. He continued to believe blacks genetically inferior, and black suffrage and citizenship a mistake. He detested the state Reconstruction governments and rejoiced at their downfall and the consequent reestablishment of white supremacy and the Democratic Party. He died on December 6, 1889.

PRINCIPAL IDEAS

Davis was a staunch defender of the institution of slavery on constitutional and what he called humanitarian grounds. He contended that the Constitution explicitly sanctioned slavery; it acknowledged slaves in representation, in taxation, and in mandating the return of fugitive slaves. It was recognized in treaties and in the clause mandating the end of the slave trade after twenty years. Like John C. Calhoun, he thought slavery should be vigorously defended as a positive, civilizing experience for slaves. Blacks were inherently inferior, Davis argued, and slavery gave them sustenance while civilizing them. He condemned Southerners who conceded that slavery was a curse for giving encouragement to what he considered the dangerously radical abolition movement. Davis argued that self-interest prompted planters to keep their slaves healthy and contented. Self-interest dictated decent food, housing, and civilizing influences for the slave workforce. He denied charges that Bibles were kept from slaves, or that slaves were prohibited from learning to read. To the contrary, Davis claimed, the slaves were given instruction in Christianity and otherwise educated.

The American republic, according to Davis, was a creation of sovereign states who had ceded specific powers to the federal government carefully enumerated in the Constitution. Any power not explicitly delegated in the Constitution was retained by the states, and Davis strongly objected to any assumption of rights or powers based on a creative reading of a constitutional clause. He viewed the sectional crisis through a prism based on a strict constructionist view of the Constitution, strong advocacy of states' rights, and a positive opinion of the slave system. Given those views, the crisis seemed to him a product of repeated Northern trenching on Southern constitutional rights and the rule of law. He considered Northern objections to slavery in the territories and resistance to the enforcement of the Fugitive Slave Law evidence of a willingness to trample on the South. The territories had been acquired with the blood and treasure of all the states, and were therefore the common property of every state and could not be organized without reference to Southern constitutional prerogatives. He never felt comfortable with Stephen A. Douglas's advocacy of popular sovereignty, which allowed the residents of a territory to decide the slavery issue for themselves. By the end of the 1850s, Davis advocated explicit federal legal protection for slavery in the territories. He also regarded Northern criticism of slavery as an affront to Southern honor; it was an offensive suggestion that he and others who owned slaves were in essence bad men engaged in an immoral practice. The abolition movement was to blame for the sectional tensions that beset the nation, being unwilling to accept that the Constitution permitted slavery in the Southern states and, further, that slavery actually benefited blacks.

Though Davis was a strong defender of Southern rights, his years at West Point and service in the army led him to revere the Union. He admired and revered George Washington and the legacy of the American Revolution. In 1858, he traveled to New England for rest and respite from summer's heat, and while in the region, spoke feelingly for a resolution of sectional animosities and continued Union. Unfortunately, Davis believed his conception of the Constitution and states' rights to be unassailably correct, which left little room for compromise.

CONCLUSION

Jefferson Davis brought both strengths and weaknesses to his leadership of the Confederacy in the Civil War. He had a penchant for circular cabinet discussions that resolved nothing, had a pronounced tendency to wallow in details best left to subordinates, and at times tended to put off decisions. He also worked incessantly and was devoted to his duties, and his stubbornness and inflexible resolve probably prolonged the life of the Confederate government. He continued to affirm the correctness of his views on state sovereignty and race after the war, becoming a symbol of the Lost Cause.

FURTHER READING

William J. Cooper Jr., *Jefferson Davis, American* (New York: Random House, 2000); idem., *Jefferson Davis: The Essential Writings* (New York: Modern Library, 2003); Jefferson Davis, *The Papers of Jefferson Davis*, ed. Haskell M. Monroe et al., 11 vols. (Baton Rouge: Louisiana State University Press, 1971–); Varina Davis, *Jefferson Davis, Ex-President of the Confederate States of America: A Memoir by His Wife*, 2 vols. (New York: Belford Co., 1890); William C. Davis, *Jefferson Davis: The Man and His Hour* (New York: HarperCollins, 1991); and Herman Hattaway and Richard E. Beringer, *Jefferson Davis, Confederate President* (Lawrence: University Press of Kansas, 2002).

STEPHEN A. DOUGLAS
(1813–1861)

"Let the Voice of the People Rule"

LIFE

Stephen Douglas was born on April 23, 1813, in the small town of Brandon, located in western Vermont, just east of the Green Mountains. The Douglas family came from Puritan roots. The first Douglas, William, immigrated to the American colonies in 1640 from England. Douglas's father, Stephen Arnold, was a prominent Brandon physician. Douglas never knew his father, who died of a stroke when young Stephen was just two months old. "I only speak of my father," Douglas wrote in 1838, "as I have always heard others speak of him, for he died when I was only two months old, and of course I cannot recollect him." Douglas's mother was Sarah Fisk, the daughter of Nathaniel Fisk, a longtime Brandon resident. After the death of Douglas's father, Sarah, along with Stephen and older sister, Sarah, were forced to leave Brandon and settled on a nearby family farm, where they resided with Sarah's brother Edward Fisk.[1]

The young Douglas worked the farm with his uncle, whom he did not particularly appreciate. "I had no great aversion to working on the farm," Douglas later recollected, "nor was I much dissatisfied with my good old uncle, but thought him a rather hard master, and unwilling to give me those opportunities for improvement and education that I thought I was entitled to." The drive and ambition that so characterized Douglas's public career were clearly discernible before he entered adulthood.[2]

At fifteen, dissatisfied with Uncle Edward, Douglas left home for Middlebury, Vermont, where he became apprenticed to Nahum Parker, a local cabinetmaker. While Douglas felt challenged and contented with the work, he did not get along with Parker and subsequently returned to Brandon, where he became apprenticed to another cabinetmaker. Illness, however, interrupted Douglas's work. Once recovered, he was advised to abandon his chosen profession and, consequently, enrolled in the Brandon Academy where he began studies in Latin and mathematics.

1830 was an eventful year for the seventeen-year-old Douglas. His mother and sister married a father and son, Gehazi and Julius Granger of New York. Along with his new family, young Stephen moved to Canandaigua, New York, in the Finger Lakes region. Douglas enrolled in the Canandaigua Academy, where he remained a student until 1832. Established in 1795, the academy was an excellent school for the study of classics, mathematics, logic, and rhetoric. With a remarkable memory and excellent debating skills, Douglas was an above-average student who received an above-average education that was to serve him well in his later political career.

After graduation, the ambitious young Douglas, not yet twenty, was determined to make his mark in the world. Despite the protests of his mother, Douglas, a little over five foot tall and weighing scarcely 100 pounds, left home with $300 in his pocket. Determined to study law and realizing that state requirements were far more lax in western states, Douglas set his course westward.

Arriving in Cleveland in late June 1833, Douglas commenced law studies with attorney Sherlock Andrews. However, a four-month bout with "bilious fever," or inflammatory rheumatism, interrupted Douglas's studies and drained most of his financial resources. Deciding to move west, Douglas eventually landed in Jacksonville, Illinois, where he arrived with little money and few prospects. Out of necessity, Douglas opened up a school in the small town of Winchester, several miles southwest of Jacksonville. He attracted some forty students in December 1833. Despite his humble beginnings in Illinois, Douglas looked optimistically to the future and quickly demonstrated a feeling of pride for his new home. "I have become a *Western* man [and] have imbibed western feelings principles and interests," Douglas reported to brother-in-law, Julius Granger, shortly after arriving in Illinois.[3]

Once a resident of Illinois, it did not take the energetic Douglas long to make a name for himself. Respected Jacksonville attorney Murray McConnell told Douglas that a law license was not needed to practice before the justice of the peace. After briefly teaching school in the nearby town of Winchester, Douglas decided to pursue a career in the law. Despite McConnell's advice, he decided to get a law license because they were easy enough to obtain. In March 1834, Douglas was granted a law license after he successfully passed an oral examination by Illinois Supreme Court Justice Samuel D. Lockwood. Unable to find a law partner, Douglas established his own practice in Jacksonville. As it turned out, Stephan Douglas was not interested in law but politics. Douglas's involvement in local party activities would set him on a course that would lead to one of the most popular and controversial careers in antebellum American politics.

From his Vermont days, Douglas was drawn to the party of Andrew Jackson. The West offered him numerous opportunities for political involvement. While Illinois was heavily Democratic in the 1830s, Jacksonville was made up of many New Englanders who were not enthralled with Andrew Jackson. Although the Whig Party had not yet emerged, a faction of the Democratic Party popularly known as the "milk and cider" faction leaned toward positions hostile to Jackson, such as support for the second Bank of the United States. The young Douglas quickly established a reputation for himself as a spirited debater, a defender of Old Hickory and the core principles of the Democratic Party. Douglas earned the nickname "Little Giant" when he successfully defended Jackson's record against a number of anti-Jackson speakers at a Jacksonville political gathering.

Douglas's skills as a public speaker as well as his personal charm led to a quick succession of public offices. In 1834, Douglas was elected states attorney for the First Judicial District, comprising eight counties in west-central Illinois. In 1836, he was elected to the state legislature as a representative from Morgan County. In 1837, Douglas resigned the seat when newly elected President Van Buren appointed him register of the Springfield Illinois Land Office. In 1838, Douglas set his sights on Congress and the Third Congressional seat. In a tightly contested election, Douglas was narrowly defeated by John T. Stuart, a prominent Springfield attorney and law partner of Abraham Lincoln. Douglas contemplated challenging the election results and even wrote Washington *Globe* editor, Francis Preston Blair, contending that many Whig justices had failed to accept votes cast for him. Whig threats to challenge the votes of many immigrant voters, however, may have persuaded Douglas to abandon his case.[4]

As a rising young leader of the Illinois Democratic Party, Douglas played an important role in the campaign of 1840. Governor Thomas Carlin rewarded his hard work with an appointment to the post of secretary of state. Scarcely interested in the mundane duties of this office, Douglas did not remain in this position for long. Fearful that a Whig-dominated Illinois Supreme Court might rule that numerous aliens were voting illegally, the Democratic legislature passed a judiciary reform bill with a view toward protecting immigrant voting, an important element of Democratic electoral strength. Several Democrats were appointed by the legislature to the newly created seats on the court, including Douglas, who, at age twenty-seven, was the court's youngest member. As a Supreme Court justice, Douglas was responsible for the Fifth Illinois Judicial Circuit. During his tenure on the court, Douglas resided in the Mississippi River town of Quincy, one of the major cities on the circuit.

Known for the rest of his career as Judge Douglas, the Little Giant was an unlikely appointee to the state's highest bench. Although he had a law license and practiced for several years, even by his own admission, Douglas's knowledge of the law was limited. His court was known for its casual and informal manner. Nevertheless, as with most of the offices he occupied, Douglas discharged his duties energetically. Members of both parties were impressed at the way Douglas dispatched his cases, and, during his brief tenure on the court, he wrote twenty-two majority opinions.

In 1843, Douglas took a major step forward in his political career when Fifth District Democrats nominated him as their candidate for the U.S. Congress. When he learned of his nomination, Douglas resigned from the bench. His Whig opponent, Quincy attorney Orville Hickman Browning, was no match for the Little Giant. A formidable stump speaker who was comfortable on the campaign trail and mingling with the people, Douglas was a better campaigner than the more reserved Browning. The campaign centered on traditional issues that divided Whigs and Democrats, with Douglas arguing against high protective tariffs and the reestablishment of a national bank. When ballots were cast in the fall, the Little Giant was elected by a majority of 461.

As a first-term congressman, Douglas moved quickly to advance the interests of his constituents as well as gain the confidence of his fellow legislators. His maiden speech in the House was spirited advocacy of a refund bill for then-General Andrew Jackson. The bill's purpose was to reimburse Jackson for a $1,000 fine imposed on him for illegally declaring martial law in New Orleans in 1815. Another major goal was the advancement of internal improvements that many of his Illinois constituents desired, particularly improvements for the Illinois River. This goal, however, eluded Douglas in his early congressional career.

Douglas's entrance into the Washington political scene came during an explosive and exciting time in the young Republic's history. The annexation of Texas was prominently featured in the presidential election of 1844, and Democrats nominated former Tennessee Governor James K. Polk who favored the annexation of Texas and territorial expansion. Whigs nominated Henry Clay who was much more ambivalent on the issue of the annexation of Texas—which was eventually annexed in March 1845 by a joint resolution of Congress. During the campaign, Douglas quickly became one of the foremost Democratic spokesmen for territorial expansion. Douglas's vision for the country was to make it "an ocean bound republic." His aggressiveness in foreign policy made him bitterly Anglophobic. In Douglas's eyes, it was Great Britain that threatened American expansion across the continent. This same aggressiveness brought him into conflict with President James K. Polk. While Polk also endorsed territorial expansion, practical considerations forced the president to moderate his demand—much to the disappointment of Douglas. When Polk compromised with the British over the Oregon Territory, agreeing to compromise at the forty-ninth parallel instead of insisting on acquiring all of the Oregon Territory, Douglas was disappointed. Similarly, when war broke out with Mexico in 1846, Douglas fervently believed that all of Mexico should become part of the United States. When Polk signed the Treaty of Guadalupe-

Hidalgo in 1848, gaining for the United States the territories of California, New Mexico, and Utah, Douglas felt the country had been cheated out of the just spoils of war.

Although disappointed in Polk's action with respect to territorial expansion, Douglas did not break with the president. When Pennsylvania Congressman David Wilmot introduced a proviso to an appropriations bill that would exclude slavery from all territories gained from Mexico, Douglas did not join other western Democrats in a revolt against the Polk administration. He believed, and would continue to believe, that introducing slavery into national politics was a dangerous distraction.

Before the military action in Mexico had concluded, Douglas became a senator, chosen by the Illinois legislature in December 1846. At age thirty-three, he was one of the youngest senators in Washington, D.C. The change in legislative body did not change Douglas's political principles. In the Senate, as in the House, Douglas remained an ardent defender of the administration's war policy against Mexico and a bitter critic of antiwar Whigs.

As the territory acquired from Mexico at the war's conclusion introduced slavery in national politics, Douglas remained convinced that the issue of slavery was an ideological distraction that would prevent the country from developing, organizing its territories, and expanding. For him, the geographical conditions of most of the West precluded the survival of the peculiar institution; therefore, the emotional debate over slavery was unnecessary. In the Senate, Douglas now turned his attention to negotiating a successful compromise to an issue that threatened to divide the Union. As chairman of the Committee on Territories, Douglas had the task of providing organization to the residents of the territories; however, since antislavery advocates were determined to prevent slavery from occupying the lands won from Mexico, they were unwilling to allow territorial organization to take place unless the Wilmot Proviso was adopted. Douglas tried to mediate the dispute by proposing that the Missouri Compromise line be extended to the Pacific coast; however, his attempt proved unsuccessful as Northern Free Soilers blocked this maneuver.[5]

With the discovery of gold in California in 1849, the necessity of finding a solution to the organization of new territories became urgent. As people streamed into California, its residents demanded organization. Yet with the complicated slavery issue so intertwined in the debate over the organization of new territories, the nation seemed dangerously close to disintegration. In an effort to bridge this gap, a number of congressional leaders tried to come up with a solution that would solve the outstanding issues between the North and South. Veteran Kentucky Senator Henry Clay took all of these measures and combined them into one bill, popularly known as the omnibus bill. The bill consisted of five parts:

1. The immediate admission of California as a state with or without slavery, as its people saw fit.

2. The abolition of the slave trade in Washington, D.C.

3. The organization of New Mexico and Utah without reference to slavery.

4. Settlement of the Texas border question in favor of the New Mexico territory. Previously, Texas claimed ownership of large portions of New Mexico. The compromise settled this dispute by denying this ownership in exchange for financial compensation to the state of Texas.

5. A new, stronger, federal Fugitive Slave Law.

Debate raged throughout the spring and summer of 1850. In the end, however, the omnibus bill failed because it united extremists in both sections against compromise.

After a disappointed Clay left Washington, Douglas took over management of the omnibus bill and employed an entirely different strategy. Realizing that combining the measures had unified the opposition, Douglas decided to break apart the omnibus bill into separate bills. In such fashion, he was able to fashion majorities for the passage of each element of the compromise, a feat that was accomplished by the early fall of 1850. With the compromise intact, Douglas hoped that the slavery issue would recede from public view, and by early 1851, he was convinced that he was right. "Public opinion is becoming sound and enlightened upon this question [slavery]," Douglas wrote one correspondent, "and the abolitionists are already reduced to a state of despair."[6]

For many years, Stephen Douglas lived the life of a Washington bachelor. His lifestyle was typically masculine in a political environment that glorified masculine values such as aggressiveness and assertiveness. All that changed on April 7, 1847, when Douglas married Martha Martin. The two met through the efforts of North Carolina Congressman David Reid, a colleague of Douglas in the House. Martha was Reid's niece and the daughter of prominent planter Robert Martin. Marriage smoothed over some of Douglas's rough edges. Martha gave birth to two sons, Robert and Stephen. Through his marriage to Martin, Douglas became the manager of a Mississippi plantation on the Pearl River. Robert Martin wanted to give the plantation to Douglas; for political reasons, Douglas made sure the property was put in his wife's name, although he managed the plantation for 20 percent of its annual profits. For years afterward, Douglas was subject to false allegations of slave ownership.[7]

The early 1850s saw Douglas continue to gain prominence in national affairs. In 1852, he was a leading candidate for the Democratic nomination for president. He was a favorite of the so-called Young America movement. Fervently nationalistic and expansionistic, the Young America movement demanded bold and vigorous leadership in contrast to the "old fogy" leaders of the party. One particular ally of Douglas, Kentucky newspaper editor George Nicholas Sanders cost Douglas the nomination. While Sanders denounced the candidates in his newspaper, party leaders assumed that Douglas authorized the attacks, and this united them against a Douglas nomination and for the dark-horse nomination of New Hampshire's Franklin Pierce.[8]

Douglas's political disappointment was soon followed by personal disappointment. In early January 1853, Martha died after giving birth to the couple's third child, a daughter. A few weeks later, the infant daughter also passed away. This tragedy put Douglas into a deep depression. Abandoning his political duties, he rejuvenated by taking a long trip to Europe. When he returned to his Senate duties in December 1853, he embarked on the last phase of his career, a phase that was marked by bitter controversy, political realignment, and violent partisanship.

For many years, Douglas's efforts to organize western territories had been hampered by squabbles over the slavery issue. In his opinion, important American expansion and development were being thwarted. The construction of a Pacific railroad, the peopling of the West, and the growth of American state and commerce were being held hostage by this issue. Twice before, Douglas has tried to organize the Nebraska Territory in Congress only to be defeated. When Iowa residents, through their representative, August Dodge, clamored again for territorial organization for Nebraska, this time Douglas made a bold move to advance the cause of westward expansion.

Douglas knew that Southern senators would undoubtedly vote against the organization of the Nebraska Territory because it was part of the Louisiana Territory to which the Missouri Compromise strictures applied. In particular, Missouri Senator David Atchison, president pro tempore of the Senate, was intent on blocking organization until his slaveholding constituents had the right to settle the Nebraska Territory with their slaves. Douglas hoped to organize the Nebraska Territory according to the principles of the Compromise of 1850—what Douglas called popular sovereignty. However, Southerners could not be persuaded to support the bill until the Missouri Compromise was explicitly repealed. In the initial bill, Douglas was deliberately ambiguous, leaving Northerners and Southerners to draw their own conclusions about the legality of slavery during the territorial phase. Southerners suspected that unless the Missouri Compromise was explicitly repealed, the assumption might be that slavery could not come into the Nebraska Territory until the advent of statehood. At the insistence of Kentucky Whig Senator Archibald Dixon, Douglas was forced to formally repeal the Compromise of 1820 in the final version of the bill. Under the Missouri Compromise of 1820, all portions of the Louisiana territory north of the latitude 36°30' were closed to the expansion of slavery. The final version of Douglas's bill overturned this prohibition. This repeal was the price of Southern support. According to Douglas, this would raise a "hell of a storm." With the support of the Pierce administration, the Kansas-Nebraska bill was now made a test of Democratic fidelity.[9]

While antislavery senators, led by Salmon Chase, Charles Sumner, and others, protested vehemently against the bill, and public protests abounded in Northern cities (Douglas said he could see himself by the light of his own effigy), the bill easily passed the Senate. A few months later, skillfully managed by Douglas's lieutenant, William A. Richardson, the bill narrowly passed in the House and was signed into law by President Pierce. The Kansas-Nebraska bill shook up an already tottering two-party political system, encouraging the formation of new political coalitions. It also, however, encouraged competition for control of the Nebraska Territory. In particular, the plains of Kansas (the final bill had carved two territories out of the area: Kansas and Nebraska) saw Missourians and Northern antislavery emigrants struggling for control. The confrontation was intense and in some cases violent.[10]

With violence and contention taking place in Kansas, Democrats turned to the 1856 presidential race looking for a stronger leader to replace Pierce. Knowing that his eagerness for the nomination in 1852 was his undoing, Douglas had publicly maintained a position of apathy toward the nomination. As early as 1853, he had written close associate Charles Lanphier, editor of the Illinois *State Register,* "Let us leave the Presidency out of view for at least two years." Few people took Douglas at his word. By early 1856, Douglas was downplaying his earlier disavowals of the nomination. Douglas's principal competition was the U.S. minister to England, James Buchanan, who was aided by two powerful allies, Senator John Slidell of Louisiana and Senator Jesse Bright of Indiana—Douglas's principal rival for control of patronage in the Northwest. As in 1852, Douglas once again withdrew after several ballots at the Cincinnati convention. Rather than divide his beloved party, Douglas pledged his delegates to Buchanan, hoping that in return, Buchanan would give him a large amount of influence in his administration. In addition, since the party platform endorsed popular sovereignty as defined by the Kansas-Nebraska Act, Douglas also felt that his principles were vindicated.[11]

Affairs in the Kansas Territory would dominate the Buchanan administration. For over a year prior to the election of 1856, Kansas had been the scene of violence and controversy. After the passage of the Kansas-Nebraska bill, Missourians poured across the border, hoping to establish slavery in the new territory. Many Northerners settled the area as well, encouraged by antislavery groups such as the New England Emigrant Society. Initially Missourians predominated and could have fairly won the first election for a territorial legislature. However, as time passed, Free State settlers had a numerical majority. Proslavery forces, however, were determined to win, and nothing was left to chance. In the first elections for the territorial legislature, proslavery forces won an overwhelming victory; however, it was later shown that almost 5,000 fraudulent ballots were cast on behalf of proslavery candidates. Predictably, the territorial legislature adopted a constitution that incorporated the slave code provisions modeled after the State of Missouri. Free Soil settlers, led by Charles H. Robinson and James H. Lane, refused to accept what they considered the results of a fraudulent election and established a rival "Free Soil" government at Topeka. As the year 1856 passed, the violence and emotional rhetoric increased. A succession of Pierce-appointed governors seemed incapable of dealing with the situation.[12]

James Buchanan's presidency was marked by turbulence and increasing controversy over affairs in Kansas. Just after his inauguration, the U.S. Supreme Court ruled on the controversial Dred Scott decision, determining that Dred Scott, as a black man, was not a citizen and not entitled to sue for his freedom in federal court. More importantly, however, Chief Justice Roger B. Taney also commented on the constitutionality of the Missouri Compromise, declaring that a congressional prohibition on slavery in any federally owned territory was unconstitutional because it deprived citizens of property without due process of law. Not only did the decision render the Republican position on slavery problematic, but it also made Douglas's popular sovereignty questionable. If Congress could not legally exclude slavery from a territory, could a territorial legislature exclude it, as Douglas maintained?

Buchanan's course on Kansas was equally disturbing. As early as his inaugural address, the president made clear that his interpretation of popular sovereignty was decidedly Southern: there could be no exclusion of slavery from a territory until the state was ready to come into the Union. In other words, the territorial legislature was not empowered to exclude slavery from a territory, as Douglas maintained. The exclusion of slavery could only occur once the territory was ready for statehood and adopted an antislavery constitution. Nevertheless, to help quell the controversy, Buchanan appointed Mississippi Democrat Robert Walker as governor of Kansas and charged him with the responsibility of overseeing Kansas's organization for statehood. Walker took the job with one stipulation: that the people of Kansas be given an opportunity to ratify the constitution in a fair election.

Early on in the Kansas controversy, Douglas blamed the troubles on "Republican" agitators. During the period of the drafting and ratification of the constitution, however, he became convinced that fair play was not being observed and that popular sovereignty was not being allowed to operate. In February 1857, the territorial legislature authorized a constitutional convention to draft a constitution for Kansas. It was obvious to slavery supporters that a fair election would result in the admission of a free state. Since the majority of Free State settlers were ignored in the election of delegates, proslavery forces controlled the convention, which met in the small town of Lecompton. When the elections for territorial legislature in the fall of 1857 revealed a strong Republican majority, the convention devised a trick whereby the constitution would be voted on, but slavery could not be excluded from the state. Voters were given a choice to vote for the constitution "with" or "without" slavery. Not only were the residents prevented from a vote on the entire constitution, even if they decided for the constitution "without" slavery, but also slaves brought into Kansas during the territorial stage were protected under law. The Lecompton Constitution was accepted with slavery in December 1857 in an election marred by irregularities and boycotted by large numbers of Free State settlers. When the Topeka government held its own election to ratify the document in early 1858, it was overwhelmingly defeated. This simply confirmed what Douglas had concluded some weeks earlier: the Lecompton Constitution made mockery of popular sovereignty.[13]

Before the opening of Congress in December 1857, Douglas met with Buchanan and strongly urged him to reject ratification of the Lecompton Constitution. Buchanan not only refused, but also threatened Douglas with punishment if he dared challenge the administration on the issue. Never one to bend to threats, Douglas now allied with Republican senators and led the fight against Lecompton in the Senate. Although unsuccessful in the Senate, anti-Lecompton forces prevailed in the House and the measure went down in defeat. Douglas's actions had important implications for his political future. His actions during Lecompton made him the persona non grata of the Buchanan administration. Douglas was prepared for his fate, telling one inquisitor, "I have taken a through ticket, and checked all my baggage." The president used his powers of patronage to chastise the Little Giant, and powerful administration allies began to exert their influence to engineer Douglas's defeat in his bid for reelection in 1858.[14]

Although eastern Republicans led by Horace Greeley recommended that Illinois Republicans unite behind the Little Giant, Illinois Republicans were too suspicious of their longtime political nemesis and nominated Springfield attorney Abraham Lincoln to oppose Douglas's reelection bid in 1858. To punish Douglas, President Buchanan's supporters organized the so-called National Democrats (or Dannites), who eventually nominated their own candidate, Sidney Breese, to oppose Douglas. In addition, Buchanan's representatives continued to pressure Democratic officeholders in Illinois, demanding a declaration of political sympathies. Administration supporters replaced those professing loyalty to Douglas. In a curious combination of ideological opposites, National Democrats and Republicans informally worked together in the common cause of defeating the Little Giant.[15]

Once the campaign got into full swing in the summer of 1858, Lincoln began to follow Douglas from town to town. Eventually Lincoln challenged Douglas to a series of debates. Douglas, much more popular than Lincoln, had much to lose from such a format, while Lincoln had much to gain. Yet to refuse the challenge would expose Douglas to charges of cowardice, so he eventually proposed a series of seven debates to be held in each Illinois congressional district.

Douglas used a number of strategies in the debate to discredit Lincoln. First and foremost, he painted Lincoln as a dangerous abolitionist whose "black Republican" doctrines would inaugurate racial amalgamation and bring about civil war. Focusing on Lincoln's remarks on the Declaration of Independence, Douglas accused Lincoln of supporting the social, political, and racial equality of the races. In the Negrophobic 1850s, such a strategy, while crude in contemporary terms, was effective. Lincoln was often hard-pressed to explain what impact his opposition to slavery would have on African American political and social status. Douglas also claimed that Lincoln was a consolidationist who could not abide any differences in local customs, laws, and traditions. Taking aim at Lincoln's "House Divided" speech, Douglas claimed that the founders had created a nation half free and half slave, that such a nation could survive in perpetuity, and that it was up to residents of each state and each territory to decide on the appropriateness of slavery. To these charges, Lincoln's replies were more effective. He countered that the founders had never intended that slavery exist forever and had taken steps early on to prevent its spread. Taking aim at Douglas's cherished popular sovereignty, Lincoln argued that the national government and the democracy were so corrupted that it was no longer possible for the residents of a territory to keep slavery out, particularly in light of the Dred Scott decision. To this, Douglas responded with the famous Freeport Doctrine, arguing that local residents of a territory could prevent the introduction of slavery by refusing to adopt positive measures to protect the peculiar institution. In the end, the way Illinois had been apportioned as a result of the 1850 U.S. Census gave Douglas an edge. While Lincoln and the Republican ticket outpolled Douglas statewide, the south and central portions of Illinois, where Douglas was popular, had the majority of seats in the Illinois legislature. In early January 1859, Douglas was reelected to a third Senate term by a vote of 54–46.

Returning to the Senate in 1859, Douglas was now subjected to severe punishment by a vindictive Buchanan administration. Not only was he stripped of his chair of the Committee of Territories, but angry Southern Demcrats also subjected him to a number of attacks in the Senate. Upset by Douglas's Freeport Doctrine, Southern senators began to make extravagant demands on behalf of slavery, including the request for a federal slave code for all territories of the United States. For Douglas, the best chance for vindication was the 1860 Democratic presidential nomination. If he could gain the nomination, he might be able to unite the party, steer it away from Southern extremists, and defeat the Republicans in the 1860 election.

Southerners began campaign already in the winter of 1859–1860, offering resolutions in the Senate demanding a federal slave code for the territories. Indeed, by the time of the Democratic convention in Charleston in April 1860, this demand would be the condition of Southern participation in the Democratic Party. Douglas, on the other hand, made it clear that he would not accept the nomination on a platform that he could not support. He felt the key to political success was positioning himself between Northern and Southern extremists. "We must make war boldly against the *Northern abolitionists* and the Southern *Disunionists*," he told Charles Lanphier, "and give no quarter to either." While Douglas supporters came to the convention confident of victory and with strong support in North, the attitude of Southerners would have a great deal to do with the convention's outcome; particularly significant was the pledge of several state conventions to walk out if a federal slave code for the territories was not adopted. At the convention, Southerners controlled the platform committee and adopted a majority report that adopted a federal slave code plank. When the majority of the delegates voted instead for the minority platform, which reaffirmed Douglas's position of popular sovereignty, the delegates of seven Southern states, led by famous fire-eater William Lowndes Yancey, bolted the convention. Since the convention rules required the nominee to obtain two-thirds of all delegate votes, the withdrawal of Southern delegates stalemated the convention.[16]

Democrats agreed to meet at Baltimore a few weeks later; however, no agreement could be reached with the delegations of dissident Southern states. This time, however, Douglas's supporters agreed that a majority, not two-thirds, would be enough to nominate; hence, the Little Giant finally achieved his political dream of a presidential nomination. A divided party, however, tarnished his dream. Delegates from the South met at Richmond shortly thereafter and nominated John C. Breckinridge as their presidential candidate.

The two Democratic candidates joined Republican Abraham Lincoln and John Bell of the border state Constitutional Union Party in the 1860 general election. Douglas focused his attention on presenting himself as a moderate alternative between Southern extremists and a Northern abolitionist. In a departure with tradition, Douglas took to the campaign trail personally—something many considered as vulgar and unpresidential. For Douglas, the decision to campaign was linked to his belief that the Union was in peril. After the first returns were announced in October and Lincoln's election appeared imminent, Douglas continued on the campaign trail, making a swing through the South. Speaking in a number of major Southern cities, Douglas's message was that Lincoln's election did not justify secession. As he told a group of New Orleans citizens, "Nothing has yet occurred to release any citizen from the oath of fidelity to the Constitution of the United States, which is the *supreme law* of every State and of every citizen."[17]

While Lincoln's election depressed Douglas, he now became a principal proponent of compromise in the ensuing secession crisis and a leading proponent of Kentuckian John J. Crittenden's compromise measures. Crittenden's proposals included a constitutional amendment prohibiting the abolition of slavery in the states where it presently existed as well as extending the Missouri Compromise line to the Pacific Ocean. When Crittenden's measures failed to pass in the winter of 1860–1861, Douglas placed the blamed squarely on Republicans. On Christmas Day, 1860, Douglas told Charles Lanphier, "The fact can no longer be disguised that many of the Republican Leaders desire war & Disunion under the pretext of saving the Union." When Lincoln was inaugurated in March 1861, Douglas nonetheless supported the new president. Prior to the inauguration, he announced that he would support Lincoln on the constitutional discharge of his office, despite opposing his administration on most partisan issues.[18]

When it looked as if the Lincoln administration might abandon Fort Sumter in an effort to conciliate the border states, Douglas was an enthusiastic supporter of compromise and any effort to avoid civil war. Once the firing on Sumter took place, however, Douglas met Lincoln at the White House to pledge his unqualified support for restoration of the Union. He supported Lincoln's call for troops, only disagreeing with the number that Lincoln asked for—Douglas believed 200,000 was more realistic than Lincoln's call for 75,000. To shore up wavering Democrats in his own state, Douglas traveled to Illinois, where he addressed the Illinois state legislature to rally support for the Union, claiming that in the present crisis there were only patriots and traitors.

Shortly after his address in Springfield, Douglas's health began to fail. Undoubtedly this was the result of overexertion on the campaign trail and an unhealthy lifestyle, and Douglas was bedridden in Chicago with acute rheumatism. For three weeks, the Little Giant battled the illness, rallying from time to time and then declining. Finally, on June 3, with second wife Adele Cutts Douglas (whom Douglas had married in 1857), sons Robert and Steven, and a Roman Catholic priest present, Douglas passed away. Ironically, Douglas passed away prior to the first battle of a fratricidal conflict that he had tirelessly striven to avoid.

PRINCIPAL IDEAS

Although Douglas was not a "philosopher" and left no great legacy of published works, his political career was shaped by a number of important concepts. Douglas began his political career as an orthodox Jacksonian Democrat. As a member of the Democracy, Douglas believed that his party represented the common people, while the Whig Party stood for wealth and property. "It is not, fellow citizens, to be disguised," Douglas told an Illinois audience, "that in this country . . . there are two opposing parties. The one, the advocates of the rights of the People; the other, the advocates of the privileges of Property." For Douglas, to be a Democrat entailed the belief in a number of specific doctrines. As opposed to the centralizing tendencies of the Whig Party, what Douglas referred to as consolidation, the democracy stood for a national government that was limited in scope and shared power with state and local government. It implied a strict construction of the Constitution, meaning the federal government was only to do what it was specifically authorized to do by the Constitution. Hence, exorbitant taxation for internal improvements or the creation of the National Bank, were, for Douglas, not only illegitimate but also unconstitutional.[19]

Despite Douglas's emphasis on the limits of national power and the rights of states, his devotion to the Union was, nevertheless, central to his political philosophy. He never accepted the compact notion of government as advocated by Southern rights advocates such as John C. Calhoun, whereby states could nullify federal legislation and ultimately secede from the Union voluntarily. Nothing demonstrates Douglas's commitment to the Union more than his public position during the secession crisis. During the presidential election of 1860, Douglas frankly told one Southern audience in Norfolk, Virginia, that secession was not justified by Lincoln's election, in the absence of an unconstitutional act on his part. Douglas also added that in case a state did secede, the federal government was justified in using military force to coerce the state back into the Union. After the Confederate guns fired on Fort Sumter, Douglas was even more explicit. In one of his last letters, written to Illinois Democrat Virgil Hickox, Douglas wrote,

> I know of no mode by which a loyal citizen may so well demonstrate his devotion to his country by sustaining the Flag, The Constitution and the Union, under all circumstances and under evry [sic] Administration regardless of party politics against all assailants at home and abroad. The course of Clay and Webster towards the Administration of General Jackson in the days of Nullification presents a noble and worthy example for all true patriots.[20]

Coupled with Douglas's devotion to the Union was his belief in Manifest Destiny. In today's self-conscious, cynical age, the notion of Manifest Destiny is greeted with a good deal of derision and skepticism. For Douglas, however, the notion that the United States was a unique, republican nation and an example to decrepit European monarchies was something he took very seriously. Throughout his career in both the House and the Senate, he endorsed territorial expansion and denounced foreign powers, particularly Great Britain, that he felt would limit American expansion. Early in his House career, Douglas claimed that the United States should be an "ocean-bound republic." To James Polk, just prior to the Mexican War, he wrote, "The Northern Provinces of Mexico including California ought to belong to this Republic, and the day is not far distant when such a result will be accomplished."[21]

In the 1850s, some of Douglas's most controversial measures, such as the Kansas-Nebraska Act, were justified by the necessity of territorial expansion. To a group of St. Joseph, Missouri, residents, Douglas justified the attempt to organize the Nebraska Territory in terms of the desirability of national expansion:

> To the States of Missouri and Iowa, the organization of the Territory of Nebraska is an important and desirable local measure; to the interest of the Republic it is a national necessity. How are we to develop, cherish and protect our immense interests and possessions on the Pacific, with a vast wilderness fifteen hundred miles in breadth, filled with hostile savages, and cutting off all direct communication. The Indian barrier must be removed. The tide of emigration and civilization must be permitted to roll onward until it rushes through the passes of the mountains, and spreads over the plains, and mingles with the waters of the Pacific.[22]

The doctrine most commonly associated with Stephen Douglas is popular sovereignty. There is nothing complicated or mysterious about Douglas's belief on this score. Simply put, it was his genuine belief that the residents of territories, like the residents of states, had the power to determine their own laws, customs, and institutions. "The great fundamental principle of our Government," Douglas declared at the Galesburg, Illinois, debate in 1858, "is that the people of each State and each Territory shall be left free to decide for themselves what shall be the nature and character of their institutions. When this Government was made, it was based on that principle."[23]

For Douglas, popular sovereignty not only had the virtue of consistency with the principles of the Founding Fathers but also had the potential to solve the sectional squabbles over slavery that were preventing the organization of territories and western expansion that he deemed fundamental to the American mission. For over 100 years, historians have debated the motives of Douglas in backing the controversial Kansas-Nebraska Act. Some have emphasized Douglas's possible presidential aspirations and the need to satiate the South. Others have focused on Douglas's desire for the construction of a transcontinental railroad along a central route and, furthermore, have accused the Little Giant of having pecuniary motives in the bill. It is important to remember, however, that the Kansas-Nebraska bill must be seen within the context of Douglas's vision of an expanding, developing republic. The slavery controversy was hampering westward expansion, and Douglas believed he had found a formula to thwart extremists

in both parties whose political agendas threatened the health of the republic.[24]

Stephen Douglas's views on slavery are as complicated as they are mis-
understood. Historians such as Allan Nevins have contributed to misconceptions about Douglas's beliefs. Nevins accused Douglas of having a
purely materialistic conception of slavery: if it paid, it was good, but if it
did not pay, it was not good. In the 1858 senatorial debates, Lincoln made
similar charges when he claimed that Douglas did not care whether slavery was voted up or down. The reality was much more complex than the
dismissive attitude of Lincoln and such historians as Nevins.[25]

As a man of his times, Douglas's views on slavery and race were shaped
by racial attitudes that he shared by the majority of his contemporaries.
Douglas viewed African Americans through the spectrum of inferiority, and
he believed that the American republic was not intended to include blacks
as citizens. This point was repeated in every one of the debates with Lincoln. At Charleston, Illinois, Douglas stated,

> I say that this Government was established on a white basis. It was
> made by white men for the benefit of white men and their posterity
> forever, and never should be administered by any except white men.
> I declare that a negro ought not to be a citizen, whether his parents
> were imported into this country as slaves or not, or whether or not
> he was born here. It does not depend upon the place a negro's par-
> ents were born, or whether they were slaves or not, but upon the fact
> that he is a negro, belonging to a race incapable of self-government,
> and for that reason ought not be on an equality with white men.[26]

Still, this callous, indifferent attitude about the peculiar institution can
be tempered with another point of view. In a conversation with friend Murray McConnel's grandson, Douglas allegedly condemned slavery as immoral; yet, at the same time, he was not willing to violate the Constitution
in order to get rid of slavery. According to McConnel, Douglas had no real
desire to repeal the Missouri Compromise in his Kansas-Nebraska bill;
however, he felt loyalty to his party, and the party leaders demanded repeal as their support for sponsoring the Kansas-Nebraska bill. "But what
can I do?" Douglas allegedly stated. "All my life I have been a party man."
Since Douglas believed that the slavery issue was compromising the important goals of territorial expansion, his public positions on slavery were
calculated to give a symbolic gesture to the South while in reality preserving the territories of the West for freedom. Douglas was aware that the
bulk of potential western settlers were Northerners with no particular attachment to slavery. At the same time, he shared the popular belief that
slavery could not survive in the West for reasons of climate and geography.
"The cry of the extension of slavery has been raised for mere party pur-

poses by the abolition confederates and disappointed office seekers. All candid men who understand the subject admit that the laws of climate, and production, and of physical geography . . . have excluded slavery from that country [the western territories]."[27]

In Douglas's opinion, Northern antislavery advocates simply had to bide their time and make symbolic gestures to the South (which in the long run would be practically meaningless), and all would come out right. The great goal of national expansion would transpire, the growth of slavery would be stymied, but the South would not be unnecessarily ridiculed and attacked during the process. While African Americans would still occupy a subordinate position in American society, Douglas did not envision that the institution would expand and flourish in the West. His apparent apathy toward the moral dimension of slavery was as much for political affect as it was born out of genuineness. Above all, Douglas saw the debate over slavery as potentially dividing the Union, and he regarded the perpetuity of the Union as more important than the debate over slavery.

CONCLUSION

Stephen Douglas was undoubtedly the most dominant political figure of the 1850s. Motivated by devotion to the Union and territorial expansion, Douglas pursued a political course calculated to advance the interests of the nation while avoiding the divisive issue of slavery. Unfortunately for Douglas, he miscalculated the fervor that motivated antislavery forces in the North. Instead of quelling sectional tensions, Douglas's principal political actions in the 1850s had the effect of inflaming these same sectional tensions. His actions during the election of 1860, the secession crisis, and the aftermath of Fort Sumter demonstrated to all the priority of the Union in his thoughts and actions. While his views on race appear callous if not downright racist according to contemporary standards, it must be remembered that Douglas typified an age and a time when Negrophobia and racial hatred were widespread and the publicly stated positions of numerous politicians, scientists, and journalists. An optimist and advocate of American exceptionalism, Douglas's faith in the American republic was not diminished even on his deathbed, when the American nation was on the verge of dissolution.

NOTES

1. "Autobiographical Sketch," September 1, 1838, in Robert W. Johannsen, ed., *The Letters of Stephen A. Douglas* (Urbana: University of Illinois Press, 1961), 56–68. The original spelling of the Douglas family name was Douglass. Stephen changed the spelling to a single "s."

2. "Autobiographical Sketch," September 1, 1838, in *Letters of Stephen A. Douglas*, 57.

3. Douglas to Julius N. Granger, December 15, 1833, in *Letters of Stephen A. Douglas*, 3.

4. Douglas to Francis Preston Blair, November 2, 1838, in *Letters of Stephen A. Douglas*, 69.

5. Douglas had been appointed chair of the House Committee on Territories in 1845 and then chair of the Senate Committee on Territories when he entered the Senate in 1847. See Robert W. Johannsen, *Stephen A. Douglas* (New York: Oxford University Press, 1973), 219.

6. Douglas to Thomas Settle, January 16, 1851, in *Letters of Stephen A. Douglas*, 207. See also Douglas to Charles Lanphier and George Walker, August 3, 1850, in *Letters of Stephen A. Douglas*, 191–93.

7. For details on Douglas's connection to the Mississippi plantation, see Douglas to Charles H. Lanphier, August 3, 1850, in *Letters of Stephen A. Douglas*, 189–91.

8. For instance, see Douglas's apology for Sanders's editorial in the *Democratic Review* to Massachusetts Democrat Caleb Cushing. See Douglas to Caleb Cushing, February 4, 1852, in *Letters of Stephen A. Douglas*, 237. See also Douglas to George Nicholas Sanders, February 10, 1852, and April 15, 1852, in *Letters of Stephen A. Douglas*, 239, 246–47.

9. The literature on the Kansas-Nebraska Act is voluminous. Besides the biographies of Douglas already cited at the end of this chapter, see also Frank H. Hodder, "The Railroad Background of the Kansas-Nebraska Act," *Mississippi Valley Historical Review* 12 (June 1925): 3–22; James C. Malin, *The Nebraska Question, 1852–1854* (Ann Arbor, MI: Edwards Brothers, 1953); Allan Nevins, *The Ordeal of the Union: A House Dividing* (New York: Charles Scribner's Sons, 1947), 80–91; Roy F. Nichols, "The Kansas-Nebraska Act: A Century of Historiography," *Mississippi Valley Historical Review* 43 (September 1956): 259–80; P. Ormand Ray, "The Genesis of the Kansas-Nebraska Act," *American Historical Association Annual Report* (1914): 259–80; James Ford Rhodes, *The History of the United States from the Compromise of 1850*, ed. and abrdg. Allan Nevins (1907; reprint, Chicago: University of Chicago Press, 1966); and Robert R. Russel, "The Issues in the Congressional Struggle over the Kansas-Nebraska Bill," *Journal of Southern History* 29 (May 1963): 187–210.

10. On the transformation of the party system, see the following works: Brian Holden Reid, *The Origins of the American Civil War* (New York: Addison Wesley Longman, 1996), 131–77; Joel Silbey, *The Partisan Imperative: The Dynamics of the American Politics before the Civil War* (New York: Oxford University Press, 1985); William Gienapp, *The Origins of the Republican Party, 1852–1856* (New York: Oxford University Press, 1987); Michael Morrison, *Slavery and the American West: The Eclipse of Manifest Destiny and the Coming of the Civil War* (Chapel Hill: University of North Carolina Press, 1997); and David Potter, *The Impending Crisis, 1848–1861* (New York: Harper & Row, 1976). Chase, Sumner, and several other antislavery congressmen penned the "Appeal of the Independent Democrats," which appeared in major newspapers. Highly critical of Douglas, it accused the Illinois senator of sacrificing the principles of the Missouri Compromise for the sake of Southern support for the 1856 Democratic presidential nomination.

11. Douglas to [Charles H. Lanphier], November 11, 1853, in *Letters of Stephen A. Douglas*, 267.

12. For information on Kansas and the Lecompton Constitution, see James McPherson, *Ordeal by Fire: The Civil War and Reconstruction* (New York: Alfred A. Knopf, 1982), 92–93.

13. McPherson, *Ordeal by Fire*, 102–5.

14. Douglas quotation from Horace Greeley, *Recollections of a Busy Life* (New York: J. B. Ford and Company, 1868), 356. At least one historian maintains that Buchanan's use of the patronage system against Douglas is overrated. See David E. Meerse, "Buchanan, the Patronage, and the Lecompton Constitution: A Case Study," *Civil War History* 41 (December 1995): 291–312.

15. On the role of Greeley and eastern Republicans, see David Herbert Donald, *Lincoln* (New York: Simon & Schuster, 1995), 204–5; and Jeter Allen Isely, *Horace Greeley and the Republican Party, 1853–1861: A Study of the New York Tribune* (New York: Octagon Books, 1965), 244–45.

16. Douglas to Charles H. Lanphier, July 5, 1860, in *Letters of Stephen A. Douglas*, 498.

17. "To Ninety-six New Orleans Citizens," [November 13, 1860], in *Letters of Stephen A. Douglas*, 499–503 (quote, 500).

18. Douglas to Charles H. Lanphier, December 25, 1860, in *Letters of Stephen A. Douglas*, 504. On the Crittenden proposals, see McPherson, *Ordeal by Fire*, 135–36.

19. "To the Democratic Republicans of Illinois," [November 1837], in *Letters of Stephen A. Douglas*, 42. Like many Democrats from western states, Douglas did support internal improvements in specific circumstances, particularly as they enhanced the business climate and opportunities of the State of Illinois.

20. Douglas to Virgil Hickox, May 10, 1861, in *Letters of Stephen A. Douglas*, 511–13 (quote, 512–13).

21. Douglas to James Polk, August 25, 1845, in *Letters of Stephen A. Douglas*, August 25, 1848, 119–20.

22. Douglas to J. H. Crane, D. M. Johnson, and L. J. Eastin, December 17, 1853, in *Letters of Stephen A. Douglas*, 268–72 (quote, 270).

23. Robert W. Johannsen, ed., *The Lincoln-Douglas Debates of 1858* (New York: Oxford University Press, 1965), 218. On popular sovereignty, also see Harry V. Jaffa, *A New Birth of Freedom: Abraham Lincoln and the Coming of the Civil War* (Lanham, MD: Rowman & Littlefield, 2000), 473–88; and Robert W. Johannsen, *The Frontier, The Union, and Stephen A. Douglas* (Urbana: University of Illinois Press, 1989), 120–45.

24. See previously cited materials in note 9.

25. Nevins, *Ordeal of the Union: A House Dividing*, 107–9; and Johannsen, *Lincoln-Douglas Debates*, 225.

26. *Lincoln-Douglas Debates*, 196. For the viewpoint of many Midwesterners toward African Americans, see, for instance, V. Jacque Voegeli, *Free but Not Equal: The Midwest and the Negro during the Civil War* (Chicago: University of Chicago Press, 1967); and Frank L. Klement, *Lincoln's Critics: The Copperheads of the North* (Shippensburg, PA: White Mane Press, 1999), 109–17.

27. Major George Murray McConnel, "Recollections of Stephen A. Douglas," *Journal of the Illinois State Historical Society* 4 (1900): 49; and Douglas to the editor of the Concord, New Hampshire *State Capitol Reporter*, February 16, 1854, in *Letters of Stephen A. Douglas*, 289. For a provocative analysis of Douglas's

views, see James L. Huston, "Democracy by Scripture versus Democracy by Process: A Reflection on Stephen A. Douglas and Popular Sovereignty," *Civil War History* 43 (1997): 189–200.

FURTHER READING

Gerald M. Capers, *Stephen A. Douglas: Defender of the Union* (Boston: Little, Brown, 1959); William J. Gardiner, *Life of Stephen Douglas* (Boston: Roxburgh Press, 1905); Robert W. Johannsen, *Stephen A. Douglas* (New York: Oxford University Press, 1973); Allan Johnson, *Stephen A. Douglas: A Study in American Politics* (1908; reprint, New York: Da Capo Press, 1970); George Fort Milton, *The Eve of Conflict: Stephen A. Douglas and the Needless War* (New York: Octagon Books, 1934); and Damon Wells, *Stephen Douglas: The Last Years, 1857–1861* (Austin: University of Texas Press, 1971).

FREDERICK DOUGLASS
(1817–1895)

From Slavery to Freedom

LIFE

Unlike many Americans, Frederick Douglass was never quite sure of his age. The prominent African American leader estimated that he was born in February 1817, but was never completely sure of the exact year or day of his birth. "It has been a source of great annoyance to me, never to have a birthday," Douglass purportedly stated. Born on the eastern shore of Maryland, at Tuckahoe, Talbot County, Frederick's mother was Harriet Bailey; however, his father was not known. Because of his light complexion, Douglass assumed that his father was white. "My father was a white man," states Douglass. "He was admitted to be such by all I ever heard speak of my parentage." Indeed, many of his slave contemporaries believed that his master, Aaron Anthony, was his father. Douglass had few memories of his mother, who lived on a different plantation and rarely had time to visit the young Douglass. Instead, his grandparents, Betsy and Isaac Bailey, raised the young slave. Isaac Bailey was a free black, while Betsy Bailey, a field hand, played a major role in the life of young Douglass.[1]

Douglass belonged to Captain Aaron Anthony and was often referred to as "Cap'n Ant'ney Frd." Anthony was a small slaveholder who owned perhaps 20–30 slaves and lived in a nearby mansion known as Wye House, the primary estate of Anthony's boss, Colonel Edward Lloyd. Anthony's principal occupation was running the estate of Lloyd, a prominent local planter who owned perhaps 1,000 slaves. Douglass described Aaron Anthony as an "overseer of overseers." Douglass's early years were carefree enough living under the supervision of his grandparents; however, in 1824, at the age of six, Douglass was taken to the Wye House by his grandmother. Here he was reunited with his brother Perry and sisters Elizabeth and Sarah—siblings who he barely knew and who would never play a prominent role in his life.

While living at Wye House, Douglass lived a life mixed with boyhood frolicking but also racked with hunger and occasional abuse. The slave charged with raising Douglass, Aunt Katy, routinely punished the rambunctious youngster by withholding food from him. Fortunately for Douglass, Captain Anthony's daughter, Lucretia (married to Captain Thomas Auld), took a special liking to the bright young slave and often supplied him with food and other treats that made up for the stinginess of regular rations and the spiteful actions of Aunt Katy.

Although Captain Anthony and his overseers rarely physically abused Douglass, he was nevertheless exposed to the brutality of the slave system early on. Not only did he witness savage whippings administered by Captain Anthony and Colonel Edward Lloyd, but he also was familiar with the brutal exploits of some of Captain Anthony's overseers. Perhaps the most callous event recalled by the young Douglass was the cold-blooded murder of a slave named Demby by overseer Austin Gore. The slave had dove into a nearby pond to avoid capture by Gore. The blunt overseer shot the defenseless slave when he refused to come out from the water. "His mangled body sank out of sight," Douglass recalled, "and blood and brains marked the water where he had stood." For Douglass, the lesson from this event as well as others was that the life of a slave was of little value in the world of white planters. "It was a common saying, even among little white boys," Douglass noted, "that it was worth a half-cent to kill a 'nigger,' and half-cent to bury one."[2]

Douglass's life took a turn for the better when Master Thomas Auld decided to send the young boy to Fells Point, a shipping district of Baltimore, where he lived with Auld's brother Hugh and wife Sophia. Frederick's job was to take care of the Auld's young son, Tommy; however, he was treated as one of the family and cared for in a much better fashion than he had experienced at Wye House. Sophia Auld, in particular, treated Douglass as if he were a son. "I was utterly astonished at her goodness," Douglass noted. "I scarcely knew how to behave towards her. She was entirely unlike any other white woman I had ever seen . . . my early instruction was all out of place. The crouching servility, usually so acceptable a quality in a slave, did not answer when manifested toward her." For the first time in his life, Douglass had suitable clothing, food, and shelter. When Captain Anthony died in November 1826, Douglass's life in Baltimore was jeopardized. Sent back to Wye House because Anthony had failed to provide a will, the young slave was assigned to Thomas Auld, who sent Douglass back to Fells Point to live again with Hugh and Sophia.[3]

Unfortunately, Douglass's positive experience in Baltimore did not last. When Sophia began teaching the young slave to read, Hugh Auld intervened, telling his wife that it was inappropriate and illegal, and would prevent Frederick from knowing his station in life. "If you teach that nigger [Douglass] how to read," Hugh warned, "there will be no keeping him. It would forever unfit him to be a slave." From that day forward, Douglass noticed a change in the behavior of Sophia. She became less kind, more arrogant and demanding. For Douglass, this was proof positive that the institution of slavery poisoned the attitudes and action of whites. At the same time, however, Douglass was determined to become educated and, in effect, prove his master right. "From that moment," Douglass recalled, "I understood the pathway from slavery to freedom. It was just what I wanted, and I got it at a time when I least expected it."[4]

From that day forward, Douglass applied himself to reading, copying from Tommy Auld's spelling book as well as picking up what he could from playmates in the street. He was successful. Eventually the young scholar purchased a copy of the popular *Columbian Orator*, which familiarized him with some of the greatest orators of the time; he also began to pick up information from the newspaper. From newspapers and conversations, he became familiar with the word *abolition*, although he struggled at first to comprehend its meaning. Eventually he learned about the abolitionist movement and its opposition to chattel slavery. As a young child, Douglass had questioned the morality of the slave system; now, as a young teenager in Baltimore, he understood that he was not alone in his moral opposition to the slave system. Reinforcing his opposition to slavery was religion. Douglass converted to Christianity while a young teenager, becoming involved in a local African Methodist Episcopal church. One African American minister, Uncle Lawson, had a significant impact on the young slave, telling him that God would undoubtedly deliver him from slavery. "The *Lord* can make you free, my dear," Father Lawson advised Douglass, "all things are possible with Him; only have *faith* in God."[5]

Douglass's time in Baltimore quickly came to an end. Perhaps Hugh Auld became concerned with the company that Douglass kept. Baltimore had a substantial free black population, and Auld may have been concerned about the impact this free black community might have on an intelligent, aggressive character like Frederick. For whatever reason, in 1833, Douglass was sent back to the eastern shore and the St. Michael's plantation of Thomas Auld. Unfortunately for Douglass, his benefactor, Lucretia Auld, had died and Thomas had taken a new wife, Rowena Hamilton. The new wife was not at all sympathetic to Douglass or the plight of slaves in general. When Douglass began teaching a Sunday school class for a group of young slaves, Thomas Auld and local slaveholders broke up the class. Worried that Douglass was demonstrating an independent spirit inconsistent with the status of a slave, Thomas leased Douglass to a local slave breaker, Edward Covey. It was Covey's job to crush the spirit of resistance growing in the young slave's bosom.

For the first time in his life, Douglass was now a field hand, expected to labor at the behest of the brutal Edward Covey. While working for Covey, Douglass was routinely beaten; however, an event happened in the summer of 1834 that Douglass regarded as the turning point in his life. While assisting with threshing operations in the hot August sun, Douglass collapsed from sunstroke and was unable to work. Covey, who routinely spied on slaves to make sure they were working, discovered Douglass in a weakened condition, but savagely beat the teenaged slave, assuming that Douglass was slacking to avoid work altogether. In a weakened and almost delirious condition, Douglass ran off, making his way through the woods to Master Auld's St. Michael's plantation. While Douglass expected little sympathy from Auld on moral grounds, he did believe his master would intervene strictly from the standpoint of economic self-interest—Covey was mistreating his slave property. Instead, Auld told Douglass that he deserved the beatings and that he was to return to Covey the very next morning.

Begrudgingly, Douglass returned to Covey's plantation. The following Monday while Douglass performed early morning chores in the stable, Covey surprised the slave, catching him from behind and trying to tie Douglass with a rope. Douglass shocked the slave breaker by striking back, grabbing Covey by the neck. "My resistance," Douglass recalled, "was so entirely unexpected, that Covey seemed taken aback. He trembled like a leaf." After grappling with Douglass for almost two hours and failing to elicit the assistance of other slaves under his supervision, Covey gave up. Douglass finished his time at Covey's working hard, but never was he beaten again. "This battle with Mr. Covey was the turning-point in my career as a slave. . . . I was *nothing* before; *I was a man* now."[6]

When Douglass finished his year at Covey's, he was contracted to work for William Freeland, a considerably gentler slaveholder. While work conditions improved markedly, Douglass would not accept his position as a slave. "I will give Mr. Freeland the credit of being the best master I ever had, *till I became my own master.*" Douglass quickly became the leader of a gang of slaves, setting up school and teaching the others to read. Eventually, the group of slaves, led by Douglass, hatched a plot to escape from slavery; however, somehow word of the plot was leaked to area slaveholders, who sent authorities to Freeland's plantation, arrested the suspects, and transported the slaves to nearby Easton, where they were held in jail. As the ringleader, Douglass feared that his master would be forced to sell him to the Deep South. Indeed, when Thomas Auld let Douglass languish in jail much longer than his fellow conspirators, Douglass was certain of this unpleasant fate. Instead, Auld eventually retrieved Douglass and was determined to send him again to Baltimore. As an incentive, Thomas promised to emancipate Frederick at age twenty-five—provided that the unruly slave became more compliant to his master's wishes.[7]

In Baltimore, Douglass once again lived in the home of Hugh Auld and began work as an apprentice caulker in the shipping yards. Tension between white workers and slave and free black laborers, however, led to trouble for Douglass. After Douglass received a brutal beating at the hands of fellow white caulkers, Hugh Auld moved Douglass to the shipyard where he worked. Auld had tried to use the legal system to receive compensation for Frederick's beating. Ironically, the grounds for which Auld sought compensation were the very reason he could not use the legal system. Frederick was considered property, not a human being capable of giving testimony against white witnesses.

During these Baltimore days, Frederick did have increased contact with the shadowy world of free blacks. Indeed, it was during this time that he met his wife-to-be Anna, who was working as a free black domestic servant. Moving in the circle of free blacks made Douglass more anxious to be free. At first, he longed to have the privilege often accorded many urban slaves, namely, Douglass wanted to hire his time. Under this arrangement, slaves would make their own living and working arrangements, returning a set amount of money to their master each week. Douglass asked Thomas Auld to be hired out when the latter visited Baltimore on one occasion, but he refused Douglass's request. A few months later, however, Douglass had worked out an agreement with Hugh Auld whereby he could make his own living arrangements in exchange for payment of a fixed amount each week to Auld. During this period Douglass also began putting money away and planning his flight north to freedom.[8]

Finally, on September 3, 1838, Douglass executed his escape along with his wife Anna. Having purchased freedom papers from a free black sailor, Douglass embarked on a night train to Wilmington, Delaware, and from there ferried across the Susquehanna River to Philadelphia. From Philadelphia, he moved on to New York, where he stayed with free black David Ruggles. From there, with the help of Quaker friends, Douglass finally arrived in the shipping town of New Bedford, Massachusetts. During the journey, Douglass and Anna were married. While Douglass had originally taken the surname Johnson, he eventually decided on Douglass, based on the Sir Walter Scott poem "Lady of the Lake."

New Bedford was a bustling town of 12,354, with a free black population of 1,051. Douglass initially earned his living by doing odd jobs such as woodcutting and caulking at the shipyard; however, a lesson learned early on in New Bedford was that racial discrimination was not the monopoly of Southern slaveholders. Indeed, Douglass's job at the shipyard as a caulker did not last due to discrimination on the part of white workers, so he eventually took a job in the whale refinery of George Howland. Douglass would stay in New Bedford for almost three years. Here, two of his children were born: Rosetta (June 24, 1839) and Lewis Henry (October 9, 1840). Bigger things were in store for this recently escaped slave, and when Douglass was invited to attend a Massachusetts Anti-Slavery Society meeting in Nantucket on August 16, 1841, his life was about to take its most significant turn since his escape from slavery.

According to Douglass, Quaker abolitionist William C. Coffin overheard Douglass speaking to friends at a local New Bedford church and, on that basis, invited Douglass to the Nantucket meeting. Also attending were such antislavery luminaries as William Lloyd Garrison and Wendell Phillips. Invited to speak, Douglass initially struggled. "I trembled in every limb," he later recalled. Yet Douglass got his message across, and at the conclusion of the meeting, John A. Collins, an agent of the Massachusetts Anti-Slavery Society, offered him a position in the Massachusetts group. Moving to Lynn, Massachusetts, Douglass began a new career as a paid abolitionist orator.[9]

For the next several years, Douglass spent considerable time on the road, traveling through the East and Midwest as an antislavery speaker. Because he was black, Douglass obviously attracted considerable attention in a Northern society that was thoroughly Negrophobic. Even more controversial were some of Douglass's traveling companions such as Abby Kelly, a female abolitionist. Douglass and his cohorts were subjected to all sorts of rumors regarding sexual impropriety. Perhaps the greatest discovery Douglass made was that while he was no longer a slave, he was not free from constant and pervasive racism in Northern society. Indeed, Douglass quickly encountered discrimination when he refused to use the Jim Crow car on the Boston-to-Portland railroad. When the railroad superintendent refused to allow the train to stop in Douglass's hometown of Lynn, public pressure was brought to bear on the railroad since many of Lynn's citizens were inconvenienced. Eventually Douglass and the City of Lynn would win out; however, the practice of discrimination was something Douglass experienced time and again at almost all points of his life.

Douglass's message to listeners throughout the Midwest and East not only denounced Southern slavery but also racial discrimination generally. In many locales, his message was not favorably received, and upon occasion, bitter Northern audiences attempted to physically disrupt Douglass's meetings. In September 1843, for instance, Douglass and his fellow travelers were assaulted in Pendleton, Indiana, when a group of rowdy whites attacked Douglass during an antislavery rally. Not only was Douglass knocked out, but also his right hand was broken in the melee.

According to Douglass biographer William McFeely, William Lloyd Garrison recognized that Douglass was an antislavery superstar. For that reason, he arranged for Douglass to tour and lecture in Ireland, Scotland, and England in 1845. Indeed, Douglass was gaining popularity, having just set down the story of his life and escape from slavery in the *Narrative of the Life of Frederick Douglass: An American Slave*, which had sold 4,500 copies by the fall of 1845. However, Douglass mentioned an alternative reason for the trip abroad in *The Life and Times of Frederick Douglass*. This was Douglass's fear that his popularity might lead to his kidnapping and return to slavery. "I became myself painfully alive to the liability which surrounded me," Douglass admitted, "and which might at any moment scatter all my proud hopes, and return me to a doom worse than death."[10]

After numerous successful speaking engagements in such places as Cork, Edinburgh, and Glasgow, Douglass eventually returned to the United States in early 1847. His trip increased his popularity immensely and gave him numerous international contacts, including such well-known British politicians as John Bright. As a result of wide exposure, Douglass's friends were able to gain support and raise $1,250 in order to purchase his manumission from Thomas Auld. On December 12, 1846, a deed of manumission was filed in Baltimore County courthouse. When Douglass returned to his Lynn, Massachusetts, home, he did so as a free man.

Douglass returned from England a changed man in many respects. For many years, Douglass had chafed under the paternalism exhibited toward him by his antislavery colleagues. While in England, Douglass had toyed with the idea of striking out on his own and had raised £500 to help with the task. After much thought, Douglass relocated to Rochester, New York; purchased a home; and established his own paper, the *North Star,* along with partners Martin Delany and William Nell. Publishing his first issue on December 3, 1847, the *North Star* never boosted enough subscribers to make it profitable. As a result, the paper was always dependent upon charitable donations to survive. Among the most prominent sponsors of Douglass and the *North Star* was Gerrit Smith, a wealthy abolitionist who resided in Peterboro, New York. Douglass's decision to strike out on his own did alienate him from his former patron, William Lloyd Garrison, and his supporters.

Smith's sponsorship of Douglass had a major impact on the new editor's perception of antislavery politics. William Lloyd Garrison fervently believed that since the Constitution sanctioned slavery, abolitionists should not participate in the political system. "I was then," recalled Douglass, "a faithful disciple of Wm. Lloyd Garrison, and fully committed to his doctrine touching the pro-slavery character of the Constitution of the United States, also the *non-voting Principle* of which he was a known and distinguished advocate." Smith, on the other hand, was already prominently involved in the activities of the Liberty Party and would also play a prominent role in the formation of the Free Soil Party in 1848. He argued, along with other political abolitionists, that nothing in the Constitution was meant to sanction the institution of slavery. Where it existed, it was through local means only. Nothing in the Constitution warranted the use of federal power to support or bolster the peculiar institution. By the early 1850s, Douglass had come around to the political abolitionism of Smith, Salmon Chase, Charles Sumner, and other prominent antislavery advocates.[11]

During the 1850s, Douglass continued to travel the antislavery lecture circuit. He now was a political advocate of antislavery politics and would eventually identify with the Republican Party. In his paper, he publicly challenged the moral suasionist position of William Lloyd Garrison and, in many respects, became the mouthpiece of Gerrit Smith's positions. His language turned violent upon occasion. In an August 11, 1852, speech in Pittsburgh, Douglass told his audience, "The only way to make the Fugitive

Slave Law a dead letter is to make a half dozen or more dead kidnappers."
Douglass backed up his opposition to the Fugitive Slave Law with actions,
making his Rochester home a stopping point for fugitive slaves on their
way to Canada.[12]

Douglass also attracted attention on a more personal level. At several
junctures in his life, he became involved with single white women. After
Julia Griffiths, a young English reformer who Douglass had met in England, arrived in Rochester to help Douglass edit the *North Star*, the gossip began to fly. When the two traveled together, flaunting social
convention, Douglass's friends became upset that he was damaging the antislavery cause by such seemingly scandalous behavior. Eventually Griffith
would marry and return to England; however, Douglass would cultivate
other friendships that would lead to the same criticism. His friendship with
Ottilia Assing, a wealthy German benefactress, created similar rumors and
gossip.

Perhaps the most controversial event of the 1850s was Douglass's involvement with radical abolitionist John Brown. Douglass originally met
the peculiar abolitionist in 1847 when visiting Springfield, Massachusetts.
Although not particularly impressed by Brown's home or personal groom-
ing, Douglass did appreciate the abolitionist's sincerity, simplicity, and hatred of slavery. Brown told Douglass of his plan to liberate slaves and form
a haven for runaways in the Appalachian Mountains. How seriously Douglass took Brown's plan is debatable; however, Brown did visit Douglass
from time to time in Rochester. Brown did not really share with Douglass
how the details of his plans were changing. Nor was Douglass one of the
secret six associated with Brown's October 1859 raid in Harpers Ferry.
Nevertheless, Douglass was implicated in the plot when he met Brown in
Chambersburg, Pennsylvania, just a few days before Brown's attack. When
apprised of Brown's plan, Douglass urged against it, sensing that the plan
was doomed to fail. When Brown was arrested, a letter from Douglass was
found on Brown's person. Douglass quickly retreated to Rochester, but,
fearing arrest, moved on to Canada and then to England. He returned to
the states only when he received the news of the death of his daughter
Anna. Douglass admired Brown. "Had some men made such a display of
rigid virtue, I should have rejected it as affected, false, and hypocritical, but
in John Brown, I felt it to be real as iron or granite."[13]

When the South seceded from the Union and conflict erupted at Fort
Sumter, Douglass was a forceful advocate of transforming the purpose of
the conflict from restoration of the Union to the abolition of slavery. In ret-
rospect, Douglass was relieved that the South rejected all Northern overtures for compromise and conciliation during the winter of 1860–1861, for
it would eventually lead to the abolition of slavery. "Happily for the cause
of human freedom, and for the final unity of the American nation," Douglass commented, "the South was mad, and would listen to no concessions."

Douglass's opinion of Republican President Abraham Lincoln was complex and ambiguous. For Douglass, slavery ought to be forthrightly attacked not only because it was wrong, but also as a matter of pragmatic policy. *"The simple way, then, to put an end to the savage and desolating war now waged by the slaveholder,"* Douglass asserted, *"is to strike down slavery itself,* the primary cause of that war." Lincoln undoubtedly came to this conclusion early on in the conflict; however, a principal concern was to unite diverse elements of war support throughout the war. As a result, the president felt that he must wait for the appropriate moment to act. When that moment finally came after the Battle of Antietam, Lincoln acted, issuing the preliminary emancipation proclamation and then the final Emancipation Proclamation on January 1, 1863. Despite his criticism of Lincoln's caution, Douglass complimented the president when he believed he had done the right thing. Despite the limited nature of the proclamation, Douglass looked beyond it. "Its meaning to me was the entire abolition of slavery, wherever the evil could be reached by Federal arms, and I saw that its moral power would extend much further."[14]

Douglass played a major role in advancing the cause of arming African American troops, arguing that blacks ought to be given the opportunity to contribute to their freedom. Undoubtedly pressured by their father's role in recruitment, Douglass's two eldest sons, Lewis and Charles, enlisted in the 54th Massachusetts. Although Douglass was pleased with the administration's decision to use black troops, he was not content with the unequal pay or the lack of protection afforded potential African American prisoners of war. Threatened with execution or reenslavement by the rebel government of Jefferson Davis, African American troops were particularly vulnerable when they fell into enemy hands. Indeed, so upset was Douglass with the Lincoln administration's inaction with respect to black prisoners of war that he threatened to stop his recruitment efforts. He complained bitterly to George Stearns that the administration had betrayed its commitment to African American soldiers by failing to retaliate on behalf of black soldiers. When Lincoln finally did take action, Douglass, as in the case of emancipation, was able to credit the president for righting a wrong.[15]

As previously stated, Lincoln's relationship to Douglass was complex. Douglass, for instance, visited the White House on a couple of occasions and was warmly greeted by the president. At their first meeting, Douglass noted, "I at once felt myself in the presence of an honest man—one whom I could love, honor, and trust without reserve or doubt." At the same time, Douglass often strongly disagreed with the president. After the war, he noted his faith in Lincoln "was often over taxed to the uttermost." Remembering that Lincoln was willing to return fugitive slaves, Douglass recalled that the president was not particularly concerned about the black race. "To protect, defend, and perpetuate slavery in the states where it existed Abraham Lincoln was not less ready than any other President to draw the sword of the nation." Briefly in 1864, Douglass was ready to join other radical Republicans in jettisoning Lincoln for another candidate; however, when the Democrats nominated McClellan, Douglass quickly fell in line behind Lincoln. While disagreeing with the president on many issues, Douglass believed that despite his shortcomings, Lincoln hated slavery, and Douglass credited him with endorsing a policy that led to the abolition of the peculiar institution in the United States. "Though the Union was more to him than our [black] freedom or our fortune, under his wise and beneficent rule we saw ourselves gradually lifted from the depths of slavery to the heights of liberty and manhood."[16]

With the surrender of Confederate forces imminent, Douglass's thoughts turned to Reconstruction. Wanting nothing elaborate, Douglass did not demand excessive compensation for newly emancipated slaves. As he had made his own way, he would require the same of former slaves. At the same time, realizing the spirit of racism that characterized both North and South, Douglass hoped that political leaders would aggressively protect the rights of blacks. Most important was suffrage. "Without this," Douglass argued, "liberty is a mockery." Writing shortly after the war, Douglass remarked, "The true way and the easiest way is to make our government entirely consistent with itself, and give to every loyal citizen the elective franchise,—a right and power which will be ever present, and will form a wall of fire for his protection." Other than citizenship and the right to vote, Douglass felt blacks wanted nothing more than the freedom to make their own way society, whether freedom led to success or failure.[17]

Like many radicals, Douglass was quickly disillusioned with President Andrew Johnson. While the former Tennessee senator had remained loyal to the Union and even promised to be a Moses to newly freed slaves, he quickly let optimistic radicals down. His commitment to newly freed blacks was limited to the Thirteenth Amendment without regard to protecting their civil rights or extending the elective franchise. When Douglass led a delegation of blacks to lobby the president for the elective franchise and in opposition to black codes adopted by many Southern states, Johnson was noncommittal. "I know that d———d Douglass," Johnson remarked. "He's just like any nigger, and he would sooner cut a white man's throat than not."[18]

For obvious reasons, Douglass supported the agenda of the radical Republicans in Congress and the election of Ulysses Grant as president in 1868. While hoping for a lucrative patronage position under Grant that would never materialize, Douglass did witness the election of several African Americans to the Senate and House of Representatives. After locating his family to Washington, D.C., and involving himself in a new publication, the New Era, Douglass finally got a minor political office, appointed as a secretary to a presidential commission charged with investigating the feasibility of annexing the island of Santo Domingo. Members of the committee, including Douglass, favored annexation. A treaty of annexation had previously been defeated in the Senate, largely through the efforts of Charles Sumner. Usually an ally of the Massachusetts radical, Douglass found himself at odds with his longtime political friend.

Similarly, Douglass found himself at odds with Sumner and other radical Republicans who bolted the party in the Liberal Republican revolt. Tired of scandals in the Grant administration and the continuation of Reconstruction in the South, Liberals united with the Democrats and nominated Horace Greeley on a program pledged to honest government and reconciliation with the South. For Douglass, loyalty to Grant and the Republican Party was still the best way to advance the cause of African Americans. As a result, he never endorsed the Liberal revolt and continued to urge fellow African Americans to support Republican candidates. Indeed, Douglass's speech in New Orleans at an 1872 convention of black voters was an important step in holding black voters in the Republican Party. Douglass argued, "There was no path out of the Republican party that did not lead directly into the Democratic party."[19]

During the 1870s, Douglass finally received some measure of recognition for his unswerving loyalty to the Republican Party. After presiding over the disastrous Freedman Bank and watching the New Era slide into financial insolvency, Douglass was rewarded for his vigorous assistance to the campaign of Rutherford B. Hayes in 1876. While the disputed election signaled the end of Reconstruction in the South and the gradual erosion of the status of African American citizenship, Douglass was appointed marshal of Washington, D.C. Largely a ceremonial role, Douglass had to suffer indignities at this position, as he was not allowed to stand next the president at official functions and gatherings. When James Garfield was elected in 1880, Douglass's appointment as marshal was not renewed. Instead, he was offered and accepted the less prestigious appointment as register of deeds. While the position paid less, Douglass did have some patronage powers and was able to appoint members of his family to positions within his office.

A number of other important milestones transpired for Douglass during the 1870s. Despite financial setbacks, his political appointments along with continued revenue from lecture fees allowed Douglass to move into a more prestigious home in Uniontown, named Cedar Hill. Toward the end of the decade, in 1877, Douglass visited his childhood neighborhood, traveling to Talbot County, Maryland. In fact, Douglass was invited to visit his old master, Thomas Auld, who, nearly eighty years old, was on his deathbed. It was an emotional meeting. Douglass even apologized to Auld for incorrectly accusing his former master of mistreating his grandmother in old age. While not giving an inch on the immorality of slavery, Douglass did deliver a less critical judgment on his former master. "He was to me no longer a slaveholder either in fact or in spirit," Douglass recalled, "and I regarded him as I did myself, a victim of the circumstances of birth, education, law, and custom."[20]

On August 4, 1882, Anna Douglass died at the age of sixty-nine. Although Douglass wrote little about his loyal wife and seemed to put his career over his marriage, his sadness seemed genuine. In fact, so genuine was his grief that he spent a good deal of 1883 at the Maine resort of friends, Frank and Martha Greene. However, by early 1884, Douglass had taken a new wife and caused a sensation in the process, marrying a younger clerk who worked in his office as register of deeds, Helen Pitts. Many disapproved of the marriage because Pitts was white. This included Helen Pitts's father, Gideon, as well as members of Douglass's family, particularly his daughter Rosetta. Douglass had little time for politics and public affairs in the mid-1880s as he spend a considerable time traveling with his new wife, taking an extended honeymoon trip to New York, Michigan, and New England, and then an extended trip abroad, visiting Europe, Africa, and the Middle East.

Some historians criticize Douglass for insensitivity to the plight of African Americans in the South in the aftermath of the election of Hayes in 1876. While it is true that Douglass seemed to have little in common with working-class and poor black tenant farmers in the South, it is somewhat unfair to charge that he was blind to the slowly eroding position of African Americans in the United States. When the U.S. Supreme Court struck down the Civil Rights Act of 1875 in the infamous Civil Rights Decision of 1883, Douglass published a forceful critique of the court, characterizing the decision as a new Dred Scott decision and urging the country to overturn the decision as it had Dred Scott. In other respects, however, Douglass did seem oblivious to the obvious erosion of African American power in the South. When thousands of black Southerners decided to combat discrimination in the South by relocating to Kansas in the West, Douglass opposed the movement as misguided. Proponents of the exodus, claimed Douglass, argued "that no emancipated and persecuted people ever had or ever could rise in the presence of the people by whom they had been enslaved, and that the true remedy for the ills which the freedman were suffering, was to initiate the Israelitish departure from our modern Egypt to a land abounding, if not in 'milk and honey,' certainly in pork and hominy." As Douglass had escaped slavery and climbed the latter of success, so, too, he reasoned, should his Southern brethren.[21]

Still loyal to the Republican Party, Douglass was rewarded by newly elected president Benjamin Harrison with an appointment as minister to Haiti. Douglass and his wife moved to Port-au-Prince in October 1889. The Haitian government was in the throes of revolutionary struggle between factions headed by General François Legitime and Florvil Hyppolite. By the time Douglass arrived, Hyppolite's faction prevailed. Perhaps Douglass's most trying time in Haiti was his participation in negotiations for the use of a naval base on the island. "Assisting" Douglass in the negotiations was Rear Admiral Bancroft Gheradi, a tactless, brazen imperialist who tried to force the Hyppolite government to capitulate to American demands through intimidation and saber rattling. In the end, despite Douglass's best efforts, Gheradi's stupidity caused negotiations to fail. Amid criticism that he overlooked the faults of Hyppolite because he was black, Douglass resigned his position on July 30, 1891.

During his last years, Douglass updated and republished his *Life and Times of Frederick Douglass* in 1892, worked for the Haitian government at the 1892 Chicago World's Fair, and participated in one last crusade, joining with a young Ida B. Wells in criticizing the rise of lynching in the Southern states. In July 1892, Douglass penned an article in the *North American Review* entitled "Lynch Law in the South," and he arranged a public lecture for Wells in Washington, D.C., in February 1893. At the Colored Peoples' Day celebration during the Chicago World's Fair, Douglass delivered a forceful, impromptu speech after being heckled after he began his prepared speech, "The Race Problem in America."

Douglass's last days were spent in the context of his conscious awareness of the deteriorating condition of Southern blacks. While Douglass still clung to the ideals of the Republican Party and resisted the notion of racial solidarity in politics, blacks suffered wholesale disenfranchisement in the South while being increasingly subject to mob, vigilante justice. Douglass's last speech, "The Lessons of the Hour," highlighted what he considered the disgraceful position of many blacks in Southern society. For Douglass, the end would come on February 20, 1895. He had just returned from attending a women's rights convention in Washington, D.C. He collapsed and died later that day at his home at Cedar Hill. Buried at Mount Hope Cemetery, Douglass's funeral was attended by numerous dignitaries including Ohio Senator John Sherman and U.S. Supreme Court Justice Harlan Marshall. The most popular and prolific African American of the nineteenth century had passed away.

PRINCIPAL IDEAS

Nature of Chattel Slavery

Immorality of Slavery

From his earliest days on the plantation, Douglass sensed the injustice, the immorality, and the utter unfairness of the slave system. Even as a young boy, growing up somewhat sheltered from the harsher realities of slavery, Douglass sensed that all was not right in the world. "I was a slave," Douglass asserted, "born a slave—and though the fact was incomprehensible to me, it conveyed to my mind a sense of utter dependence on the will of *somebody* I had never seen; and, from some cause or other, I had been made to fear this somebody above all else on earth." Even as a child, Douglass could never rationalize the rightness of the slave system. "I could not reconcile the relation of slavery with my crude notions of goodness."[22]

How could a system be judged humane and moral that did not consider slaves as human beings? Not only were slaves denied the rights of free person such as voting, serving on juries, and the right to own property, as Douglass discovered in Baltimore, but he could not even get satisfaction when beaten to a bloody pulp by white workers because his testimony would not be accepted in a court of law. Indeed, as a child growing up on the plantation of Colonel Lloyd, Douglass witnessed savage beatings and outright murders—murders that went unpunished because they were not considered murders, since they involved the taking of the life of a chattel slave. Taking issue with contemporary proslavery apologists, Douglass denounced the slave system as fundamentally immoral. Because it was based on immoral principles, Douglass also endorsed a different standard of morality in dealing with slavery and slaveholders. For Douglass, any law or regulation passed on behalf of slavery could be rightfully and purposefully ignored.

Brutality of the Slave System

Douglass's condemnation of the slave system as barbaric and brutal was based on his own suffering and his observation of cruelty inflicted on fellow slaves. "I am not from any of those States where slaves are said to be in their most degraded condition; but from Maryland, where Slavery is said to exist in its mildest form," Douglass told one New York City audience, "yet I can stand here and relate atrocities which would make your blood boil at the statement of them." Although Douglass himself was rarely whipped as a young slave, he rarely got enough to eat and Aunt Katy, as punishment for misbehavior, denied him food. Douglass did personally observe calculated acts of cruelty that were routinely directed at slaves. There was the case of Uncle Barney, who kept the horses for Colonel Lloyd. When Colonel Lloyd was displeased with the upkeep of the horse, he would force Uncle Barney to remove his shirt, kneel, and be whipped until his flesh bled. There were also savage beatings administered on slaves by overseers. In some cases, beating resulted in murder. Even the most savage beating, however, was justified on the grounds that an unpunished slave would quickly become an unmanageable slave. When Colonel Lloyd questioned one overseer, Austin Gore, who had killed a recalcitrant slave, Gore defended his actions, arguing "that if one slave refused to be corrected, and escaped with his life, the other slaves would soon copy the example; the result of which would be, the freedom of the slaves, and the enslavement of the whites."[23]

"It is the boast of slaveholders that their slaves enjoy more physical comforts of live than the peasantry of any country in the world," Douglass noted. "My experience contradicts this." This was the argument that proslavery apologists like William Grayson, George Fitzhugh, and others would make. It also would be the argument of twentieth-century historians such as Ulrich Bonnell Phillips. Indeed, even sophisticated historians such as Robert Fogel, Stanley Engerman, and Eugene Genovese have attempted to balance the brutality of slavery by presenting examples of its more positive features. Douglass would have none of it. For Douglass, the food was poor and inadequate. Living conditions and clothing were squalid and insufficient. Why did slaves rarely complain about their treatment? For Douglass, it was a self-defense mechanism. If a slave were to complain about his or her treatment and the master found out, that slave would risk punishment, perhaps even being sold to the Deep South. Indeed, even the Christmas respite was a calculated swindle on the part of slaveholders. By encouraging drunken frivolity, slaveholders tricked their slaves into forgetting about their real problems. "Judging from my own observation of experience," Douglass noted, "I believe those holidays were among the most effective means in the hands of the slaveholders of keeping down the spirit of insurrection among the slaves." He added, "These holidays served the purpose of keeping the minds of the slaves occupied with the prospective pleasures within the limits of slavery."[24]

Slavery and the Family

For Douglass, the most disturbing aspect of chattel slavery was the negative impact that it had on family life. Drawing on his experience, Douglass could make a compelling case. He did not know who his father was, though it was thought to be a white man, possibly even his master. His mother, Harriet Bailey, was a shadowy figure, rarely present in his life. While his grandparents were a particularly strong force in his life, Douglass was separated from them at an early age. Of his brothers and sisters, Douglass knew who they were but never developed particularly close relations with them. While a number of historians have pointed out that the slave family was stronger and more resilient than many supposed, Douglass based his argument entirely on personal experience.[25]

While a number of historians point out that slaveholders often encourage the development of marriage and nuclear families among their slaves, Douglass argued that this was rarely the case in eastern Maryland. "Marriage—as imposing obligations on the parties to it—has no existence here [on the plantation], except in such hearts as are purer and higher than the standard of morality around them." For Douglass, perhaps the best demonstration of his point was the way in which white slaveholders discouraged young, attractive slave women from courtship and marriage. In one instance, Douglass tells of the plight of an attractive slave woman, Esther, who was prevented from courting her beau by Colonel Lloyd. What was

Colonel Lloyd's motive? According to Douglass, it was his own lustful passions whereby he would corrupt the young slave girl as well as lighten the black race. Douglass notes,

> It is one of the damning characteristics of the slave system, that it robs its victims of every earthly incentive to a holy life. The fear of God, and the hope of heaven, are found sufficient to sustain many slave-women, amidst the snares and dangers of their strange lot; but, this side of God and heaven, a slave-woman is at the mercy of her owner. Slavery provides no means for the honorable continuation of the race.[26]

Finally, Douglass noted the perpetual threat of the disruption of the family unit. As in Harriet Beecher Stowe's *Uncle Tom's Cabin*, every slave had the fear of being sold down the river. Being sold to the Deep South might be a way to deal with a disobedient slave. After Douglass's first escape attempt was foiled, he fretted lest Thomas Auld yield to communal pressures that suggested that recalcitrant, revolutionary slaves be shipped to the Deep South. "The ever dreaded slave life in Georgia, Louisiana, and Alabama,—from which escape was next to impossible—now in my loneliness stared me in the face."[27]

Even the moderate, well-behaved slave could never live in security. As Douglass witnessed early in life, when his master died all of his possessions—slaves included—were divided between surviving heirs. The division of the estate could be a particularly traumatic time. Families could be split at a whim, and there was nothing the slave could do about it. Douglass described it as follows:

> After the valuation, then came the division. I have no language to express the high excitement and deep anxiety which were felt among us poor slaves during this time. Our fate for life was now to be decided. We have no more voice in that decision than the brutes among whom we were ranked. A single word from the white men was enough—against all our wishes, prayers, and entreaties—to sunder forever the dearest friends, dearest kindred, and strongest ties known to human beings.[28]

Slavery and Religion

Particularly irksome to Douglass was the use that Southern apologists for slavery made of the Christian religion. For him, defenders of slavery perverted the teachings of the Bible. As a young teenager, Douglass converted to Christianity and was determined to convert all mankind. "I loved all mankind—slaveholders not excepted; though I abhorred slavery more than ever. My concern was, now, to have the world converted." Douglass believed that Christianity and the teachings of the Bible clearly outlined the evil of slavery. Douglass was surprised and hopeful when Master Thomas Auld converted to Christianity. "If he has got religion," thought I, "he will emancipate his slaves; and if he should not do so much as this, he will, at any rate, behave toward us more kindly, and feed us more generously than he has heretofore done." But Douglass was quickly disappointed. He was unsparingly critical of the way that Southern slaveholders used the Christian religion to justify the peculiar institution.[29]

For Douglass, religion in the South was a complete and utter sham. Outwardly, Thomas Auld, and many slaveholders like him in Douglass's views, distinguished themselves by their public acts of piety and devotion. Yet Douglass forcefully complained that it was nothing but rank hypocrisy:

> His house [Master Auld's] was, literally, a house of prayer. In the morning, and in the evening, loud prayers and hymns were heard there, in which both himself and his wife joined; yet, *no more meal* was brought from the mill, *no more attention* was paid to the moral welfare of the kitchen; and nothing was done to make us feel that the heart of Master Thomas was one while better than it was before.

So too did Douglass note that despite his master's conversion, he would not allow Douglass to teach Sunday school or be taught. When Douglass attempted to start a Sunday school, his master, as previously noted, led the charge to shut it down. According to Douglass, his master's actions after his conversion were worse than ever. While whipping Douglass's cousin, Henny, a physically handicapped slave, Auld would quote passages of scripture: "That servant which knew his lord's will, and prepared not himself, neither did according to his will, shall be beaten with many stripes."[30]

What irked Douglass the most was the way in which slaveholders perverted and twisted the teaching of the gospel in order to justify a barbaric and immoral labor system. Hence, slaveholders would encourage slaves to get drunk or immorally cohabitate in order to increase the number of the master's slaves, while, at the same time, maintaining that it was wrong and revolutionary to teach a slave to read the Bible. "I assert most unhesitatingly that the religion of the south is a mere covering for the most horrid crimes," Douglass noted, "a justifier of the most appalling barbarity,—a sanctifier of the most hateful frauds,—and a dark shelter, under which the darkest, foulest, grossest, and most infernal deeds of slaveholders find their strongest protection."[31]

Douglass and Antislavery Politics

For Douglass, escaping slavery and living in the North taught him some powerful lessons with respect to racial prejudice. Southern slaveholders did not have a monopoly on racism, as Douglass quickly found out shortly after arriving in Bedford. Throughout the North, African Americans were regarded as second-class citizens, subject to a barrage of legal restrictions ranging from prohibitions on certain types of trades, denial of the elective franchise, and segregation in places of public accommodation. As several scholars of the antebellum United States have noted, antislavery sentiment was often motivated by the desire to be free of African Americans altogether. Some point out that it was no accident that the colonization of free blacks was a solution favored by a seemingly large segment of antislavery advocates.[32]

The basis for Douglass's antislavery message was the immorality of slavery, which was predicated on the oneness of the human race and the equality between blacks and whites. In speeches and lectures delivered throughout the North, Douglass contested the work of so-called scientists and ethnologists whose crude and unpolished observations tried to prove that blacks were not completely human. For Douglas, only the woefully ignorant or stubborn could deny the humanity of blacks. "Tried by all the usual, and all the *un*usual tests, whether mental, moral, physical or psychological [*sic*]," Douglass contended, "the Negro is a Man." To counter Southern apologists of slavery and their claims of black inferiority, Douglass claimed a connection between blacks and the oldest and most developed of ancient civilizations, Egypt: "And a direct relationship may be claimed by the Negro race to That Grandest of all the Nations of Antiquity, the Builders of the Pyramids."[33]

If whites and blacks sprang from a common humanity, one race should not be inherently subordinate to another. Douglass believed that talent, hard work, even advantages from family and birth, would mean that there would always be rich, poor, and middling classes; however, for rich and poor to be defined strictly in terms of color was the result of the unjust institution of chattel slavery. Having established the immorality of slavery and the equality of the races, what was the best means of eliminating slavery?

Since Douglass's involvement in the antislavery movement began in William Lloyd Garrison's Massachusetts Anti-Slavery Society, his early views on abolitionism stressed the immediate abolition of slavery through nonviolent and nonpolitical means. As Garrison viewed the Constitution as illegitimate because it supposedly sanctioned slavery, he spurned political activity as equally illegitimate. Throughout his travels and lectures in the East and Midwest, Douglass parroted the views of his mentor Garrison and other such antislavery giants as Wendell Phillips.[34]

As Douglass began to distance himself from Garrison, Phillips, and the New England branch of the antislavery movement, his thinking on antislavery politics began to change. Most influential in this transformation was New York abolitionist Gerrit Smith. The upstate New Yorker was a wealthy landowner who patronized Douglass's antislavery paper, *North Star*. He also forcefully argued, along with other political abolitionists associated with first the Liberty Party and then the Free Soil Party, that the Constitution was not a proslavery document. Nowhere in the Constitution was slavery accorded a national status. To the extent that slavery existed, it was purely a local institution that the Founding Fathers clearly intended to die out over time.

Douglass was initially curious about, but not totally convinced by, this line of reasoning. In early 1851, Douglass asked Smith whether his interpretation of the Constitution hinged on some technical flaw or language in the document that Smith exploited to give the Constitution an unintended antislavery character that was wholly different from the intent of the founders. Indeed, at a Syracuse, New York, meeting to oppose the Fugitive Slave Law, Douglass stated that Smith "did not believe the Constitution was anti-Slavery—he wished he could." However, by May 1851, Douglass told Smith that he had abandoned the Garrisonian position that the Constitution was proslavery. When Smith ran for Congress and was elected in 1852, Douglass was a warm supporter and his paper, *North Star*, fervently supported the radical abolitionist. During the remainder of the 1850s, Douglass became an avid proponent of using politics to combat the peculiar institution.[35]

In many of his speeches, Douglass combined the antislavery precepts of Smith along with the transcendental absolutism of Thoreau, referencing a "higher law" that preempted state and national laws that supported slavery. "He who has God and conscience on his side," Douglass told a Pittsburgh audience, "has a majority against the universe." In a scathing critique of Roger B. Taney and the Dred Scott decision, Douglass displayed the character of many of his antislavery arguments. The decision, according to Douglass, directly contradicted the antislavery spirit of the Founding Fathers. "It is an open rebellion against God's government," he charged. Arguing that the Constitution and the Declaration of Independence were both antislavery documents, Douglass predicted a day when the Dred Scott case would be overturned and the institution of slavery overthrown in the United States. Douglass wondered why the Constitution did not ever use the word *slave,* arguing that "law is in its nature opposed to wrong, and must everywhere be presumed to be in favor of the right." For Douglass, there was nothing proslavery about the Constitution. The preservation of slavery was the result of the way the Constitution was administered, not any inherent defects in the instrument.[36]

Douglass's Ideas on Race in Post–Civil War Society

In many respects, Frederick Douglass embodied the free labor ideology advanced by leading Republican antislavery advocates. For many members of the Republican Party, slavery was certainly a moral wrong; however, it was also an economic and social evil because it stymied innovation and advancement. Slavery, they argued, created a static, caste-based society where laborers were stuck on the bottom rung of the social ladder with little prospect of advancement. The crime of slavery was that it deprived the laborer of the fruits of his work, depriving him of the opportunity of rising. In a speech in honor of John Brown, Douglass summarized the case against Southern slaveholders:

> He [the slaveholder] has become harder and harder, with every appeal made to his sense of justice, with every appeal made to his humanity, until at length he has come even to confront the world with the pretension that to rob a man of his liberty, to pocket his wages, or to pocket the fruits of his labor without giving him compensation for his wages . . . is not only right according to the laws of the land, but that it is right and just in the sight of the living God.[37]

In the aftermath of slavery, what were the expectations of Douglass in a postslavery society? During and before the war, Douglass resisted and opposed every emancipation plan that contained a colonization component. Not only was colonization an explicit statement of racial inferiority, but it was also patently unjust in Douglass's eyes, ignoring the fact that blacks had been in the country for a longer period of time than many whites. Douglass envisioned a multiracial society that would eventually be color-blind, based on the notion of a common humanity that united various racial and ethnic groups. His goal was not segregation but full integration and eventual assimilation. "He [the African American] will be absorbed, assimilated, and will appear finally, as the Phoenicians now appear on the shores of the Shannon, in the features of a blended race."[38]

Douglass's vision for American society continued to be shaped by notions of upward mobility. As previously indicated, there was a role for the federal government in this process; however, it was not to provide newly emancipated slaves with preferential treatment. While Douglass did accept the role of such agencies as the Freedmen's Bureau that would function in a transitional period between slavery and freedom, in the long run, Douglass expected African Americans to stand on their own feet, as he had, and succeed or fail, depending upon their own efforts and talents. Douglass succinctly summarized his vision in a speech before the Massachusetts Anti-Slavery Society during the war:

> Everybody has asked the question; and they learned to ask it early of the abolitionist, "what shall we do with the Negro?" I have had but one answer from the beginning. Do nothing with us! Your doing with us has already played the mischief with us. Do nothing with us! . . . And if the Negro cannot stand on his own legs, let him fall also. All I ask is, give him a chance to stand on his own legs! Let him alone! . . .

If you will only untie his hands, and given him a chance, I think he will live.[39]

To the extent that government would assist newly emancipated slaves integrate into free society, its role was largely as a guarantor of equal opportunity and access. Although Douglass was disappointed when the Johnson administration took back Southern lands that had been redistributed to newly emancipated slaves, this type of economic assistance was not his central emphasis. As a result, Douglass was an outspoken advocate of the Fourteenth and Fifteenth Amendments, as these guarantees of citizenship and the elective franchise were, in his opinion, pivotal to giving African Americans some semblance of equal opportunity in free society. In particular, Douglass stressed the connection between African American success and the franchise. "The true way and the easiest way is to make our government entirely consistent with itself," Douglass argued, "and give to every loyal citizen the elective franchise,—a right and power which will be ever present, and will form a wall of fire for his protection."[40]

Once these basis rights were established, it was also crucial that Congress and federal authorities ensure that African American rights be protected and preserved. "The black man is not a free American citizen in the sense that a white man is a free American citizen," Douglass remarked, for "he cannot protect himself against encroachments upon the rights and privileges already allowed him in a court of justice without an impartial jury." Douglass was a vigorous advocate of the Ku Klux Klan acts passed by Congress during the Grant administration, which allowed the federal government to intervene and prosecute individuals or groups that interfered with the civil rights of others, especially newly enfranchised African Americans, as well as the last piece of civil rights legislation of the Civil War era: the Civil Rights Act of 1875. Passed largely to honor the memory of the recently deceased Charles Sumner, the law guaranteed all persons, regardless of race, access to all places of public accommodation as well as made it a crime to deny blacks participation on juries.[41]

When the Supreme Court struck down the Civil Rights Act of 1875 in its 1883 Civil Rights decision, Douglass was a vigorous and vociferous critic. In essence, the court maintained that the law was unconstitutional because the federal government was not authorized to regulate the behavior of its citizens with respect to racial relationships. "In humiliating the colored people of this country, this decision has humbled the Nation," Douglass asserted. "It gives to a South Carolina or a Mississippi Railroad Conductor, more power than it gives the National Government." For Douglass, the court's logic suggested that rights guaranteed by the Fourteenth Amendment could be eradicated by individual actions, just so long as states did not participate in the process.[42]

During the 1880s and 1890s, as it became increasingly apparent that the position of African Americans in the South was rapidly eroding, Douglass continued to cling to his vision of the federal government as the guarantor of equal opportunities for blacks. While many states were busily stripping away the elective franchise and other rights, Douglass spoke out against popular prejudices against blacks as well as the increasing popularity of lynch mobs. What was the solution? Douglass hoped that a general spirit of progress and enlightenment in the nineteenth century would slowly erode popular prejudices against his people; however, on the eve of his death, he had few real solutions. Spurning the separatism of emerging black leaders such as Booker T. Washington, Douglass continued to put forth the model of integration and a color-blind society, based on individual initiative with the federal government guaranteeing equality of opportunity and a level playing field. When he died in 1895, Douglass's goals were largely unrealized.[43]

CONCLUSION

Frederick Douglass was arguably the most notable African American of the nineteenth century. A man of incredible talents, his story of escape from slavery to a position of prominence in American culture is among the most important success stories in all of American history. A powerful critic of the institution of slavery, Douglass was an important voice for change in the nineteenth-century United States, not just among African Americans but also within the larger American culture generally. While some historians have criticized Douglass for his failure to identify with the plight of African Americans in the South in the aftermath of Reconstruction and for his continued devotion to the Republican Party even after that party had largely abandoned its historic commitment to the cause of African Americans, in reality, Douglass had few choices. Determined that African Americans never be denied seats at the table of American democracy, Douglass never abandoned his forceful demand that the nation live up to the ideals put forth by the Declaration of Independence and the Founding Fathers. That such rhetoric had few listeners at the end of the century is more a reflection of the failures of a nation and not the individual.

NOTES

1. Frederic May Holland, *Frederick Douglass: The Colored Orator* (1891; reprint, Westport, CT: Negro University Press, 1970), 7 (first quote). Materials for this essay are derived from the following sources: Frederick Douglass, *Narrative of the Life of Frederick Douglass, An American Slave*, ed. with intro. by Houston A. Baker Jr. (New York: Penguin Books, 1982); idem., *My Bondage and My Freedom*, new intro. by Philip S. Foner (New York: Dover Publications, 1969); and idem., *The Life and Times of Frederick Douglass* (New York: Citadel Press, 1983). Second Douglass quote is from *Narrative of Frederick Douglass*, 48.

2. *Narrative of Frederick Douglass*, 67, 69.

3. *Narrative of Frederick Douglass*, 77.

4. *Narrative of Frederick Douglass*, 78.

5. *Life and Times of Frederick Douglass*, 84.

6. *Life and Times of Frederick Douglass*, 137, 140.

7. *Life and Times of Frederick Douglass*, 121.

8. The world of free African Americans in the South is well documented in Ira Berlin, *Slaves without Masters: The Negro in the Antebellum South* (New York: Oxford University Press, 1974).

9. *Life and Times of Frederick Douglass*, 216–17 (quote, 216).

10. *Life and Times of Frederick Douglass*, 236.

11. *Life and Times of Frederick Douglass*, 265–67 (quote, 265–66); F. Douglass to Gerrit Smith, January 21, 1851, in *Frederick Douglass: Selected Speeches and Writings*, ed. Philip S. Foner, abridged and adapted by Yuval Taylor (Chicago: Lawrence Hill Books, 1999), 171.

12. "Fugitive Slave Law," Pittsburgh, August 11, 1852, in *Selected Speeches and Writings*, 207.

13. *Life and Times of Frederick Douglass*, 281–82.

14. *Life and Times of Frederick Douglass*, 337, 360; and "How to End the War," *Douglass's Monthly*, May 1861, in *Selected Speeches and Writings*, 448.

15. See for instance, F. Douglass to G.L. Stearns, August 1, 1863, in *Selected Speeches and Writings*, 538–39.

16. *Life and Times of Frederick Douglass*, 351–52; "Oration in Memory of Abraham Lincoln, April 14, 1876," *Selected Speeches and Writings*, 616–24 (quotes, 618, 619, 620); and Douglass to Theodore Tilton, October 15, 1864, *Selected Speeches and Writings*, 571–72.

17. "What the Black Man Wants," pamphlet in the Frederick Douglass Papers, Library of Congress, Manuscript Division, 36–39 (quote, 36); and "Reconstruction," in Foner, *Selected Speeches and Writings*, 593 (quote). The latter item was originally printed in the December 1866 of the *Atlantic Monthly*.

18. Quoted from James McPherson, *Ordeal By Fire: The Civil War and Reconstruction* (New York: Alfred A. Knopf, 1982), 498.

19. *Life and Times of Frederick Douglass*, 424.

20. *Life and Times of Frederick Douglass*, 447.

21. *Life and Times of Frederick Douglass*, 436.

22. *My Bondage, My Freedom*, 45, 90.

23. "My Slave Experience in Maryland," in John W. Blassingame, ed., *The Frederick Douglass Papers, Series One: Speeches, Debates, and Interview, Volume 1: 1841–1846* (New Haven, CT: Yale University Press, 1979), 1:29; and *Narrative of Frederick Douglass*, 67.

24. *My Bondage, My Freedom*, 100; and *Life and Times of Frederick Douglass*, 144. On the work of twentieth-century historians of slavery, see, for instance, Ulrich Bonnell Phillips, *American Negro Slavery* (New York: D. Appelton and Company, 1918); Eugene Genovese, *Roll, Jordan, Roll: The World the Slaves Made* (New York: Vintage Books, 1976); Robert William Fogel and Stanley L. Engerman, *Time on the Cross: The Economics of American Negro Slavery* (New York: University Press of America, 1984); and John Blassingame, *The Slave Community: Plantation Life in the Antebellum South*, rev. and exp. ed. (New York: Oxford University Press, 1979).

25. For instance, see Herbert G. Gutman, *The Black Family in Slavery and in Freedom, 1750–1925* (New York: Vintage Books, 1977).

26. *My Bondage, My Freedom,* 85–87 (quote, 86).

27. *Life and Times of Frederick Douglass,* 173.

28. *Narrative of Frederick Douglass,* 90.

29. *My Bondage, My Freedom,* 167, 194.

30. *My Bondage, My Freedom,* 197, 201.

31. *Life and Times of Frederick Douglass,* 149–50; and *Narrative of the Life of Frederick Douglass,* 117.

32. Recently this characterization of the colonization movement has been challenged. See Douglas R. Egerton, "Averting a Crisis: The Proslavery Critique of the American Colonization Society," *Civil War History* 43 (1997): 142–56. On Northern attitudes toward free blacks, see, for instance, Leon Litwack, *North of Slavery: The Negro in the Free States, 1790–1860* (Chicago: University of Chicago Press, 1960); Leonard P. Curry, *The Free Black in Urban American, 1800–1860: The Shadow of a Dream* (Chicago: University of Chicago Press, 1981); and Waldo E. Martin Jr., *The Mind of Frederick Douglass* (Chapel Hill: University of North Carolina Press, 1984), 109–35.

33. Frederick Douglass, "The Claims of the Negro," pamphlet in Frederick Douglass Papers, Library of Congress, 5, 25. See also "The Slanderous Charge of Negro Inferiority, December 11, 1845," in Blassingame, ed., *The Frederick Douglass Papers,* 1:97–102. The Egyptian argument is also detailed in Peter P. Hinks, *To Awaken My Afflicted Brethren: David Walker and the Problem of Antebellum Slave Resistance* (University Park: Pennsylvania State University Press, 1997), 175–87.

34. The various views of contending antislavery factions is discussed throughout Richard H. Sewell, *Ballots for Freedom: Anti-Slavery Politics in the United States, 1837–1860* (New York: Oxford University Press, 1976).

35. "Resistance to Blood-Houndism, January 7–8, 1851," in Blassingame, ed., *The Frederick Douglass Papers,* 2:278; Douglass to Gerrit Smith, January 21, 1855, May 21, 1855, and November 6, 1852, all in Foner, *Selected Speeches and Writings,* 171–72, 174–75, 210–11.

36. "Fugitive Slave Law," Pittsburgh, August 11, 1852, in Foner, *Selected Speeches and Writings,* 209; and "The Dred Scott Decision," in the Frederick Douglass Papers, Library of Congress, 28–45 (quote, 39).

37. Speech on John Brown, Tremont Temple, Boston, December 3, 1860, in Foner, *Selected Speeches and Writings,* 418. The best single work on the Free Labor ideology is Eric Foner, *Free Soil, Free Labor, Free Men: The Ideology of the Republican Party before the Civil War* (New York: Oxford University Press, 1970).

38. "The Future of the Colored Race," in Foner, *Selected Speeches and Writings,* 591.

39. "What the Black Man Wants," 39.

40. "Reconstruction," in Foner, *Selected Speeches and Writings,* 593 (reprint from the December 1866 issue of *Atlantic Monthly*).

41. Frederick Douglass, "Give Us the Freedom Intended for Us," in Foner, *Selected Writings and Speeches,* 612–14 (quote, 613). This piece was originally published in the *New National Era* (December 5, 1872).

42. "Civil Rights Cases, 1883," 4–13 (quote, 8), Frederick Douglass Papers, Library of Congress.

43. Douglass to Francis J. Grimke, January 19, 1886, in Foner, *Selected Writings and Speeches*, 695; and "Lynch Law in the South," in Foner, *Selected Writings and Speeches*, 746–50 (originally published in the July 1892 edition of the *North American Review*).

FURTHER READING

David B. Cheesebrough, *Frederick Douglass: Oratory from Slavery* (Westport, CT: Greenwood Press, 1998); Philip S. Foner, *Frederick Douglass* (New York: Citadel Press, 1969); Frederick May Holland, *Frederick Douglass: The Colored Orator* (1891; reprint, Westport, CT: Negro University Press, 1970); Nathan Huggins, *Frederick Douglass: Slave and Citizen: The Life of Frederick Douglass* (Boston: Little, Brown & Co., 1980); William McFeely, *Frederick Douglass* (New York: W. W. Norton & Company, 1991); Dickson J. Preston, *Young Frederick Douglass: The Maryland Years* (Baltimore: Johns Hopkins University Press, 1980); and Eric J. Sundquist, ed., *Frederick Douglass: New Literary and Historical Essays* (Cambridge: Cambridge University Press, 1990).

GEORGE FITZHUGH
(1806–1881)

The Fear of Freedom

LIFE

Virginia's George Fitzhugh was the South's best-known proslavery theorist of the antebellum period. Born on November 4, 1806, in Prince William County, Fitzhugh was the son of Dr. George Fitzhugh and Lucy Stuart Fitzhugh. The family had been in the American colonies since the 1670s, when William Fitzhugh migrated to Virginia from England and settled in Stafford County on the Potomac River. The elder George Fitzhugh owned a modest plantation in King George County; however, when he died in 1825, the plantation was sold for cash. As a result, the younger George Fitzhugh grew up in extremely modest circumstances. Educated in one-room schoolhouses known as field schools, Fitzhugh eventually read law with local attorneys and became sufficiently familiar with Virginia law to obtain his license. In 1829, Fitzhugh wedded Mary Metcalf Brockenbrough. Through his marriage, Fitzhugh inherited a ramshackle plantation at Port Royal, Caroline County, Virginia.

The particular circumstances of Port Royal society played a significant role in shaping Fitzhugh's later thinking and writing. The home of agrarian thinkers such as John Taylor, Port Royal was a tobacco town that had seen better days. Its population was equally divided between whites and blacks; however, the proportion of free blacks was steadily increasing, undoubtedly the result of the steady decline of land fertility and the unprofitability of slavery. The fear of a rising population of free blacks was a relatively common fear in many states of the upper South and was accompanied by a variety of stereotypes of free African Americans, focusing particularly on indolence, promiscuity, and criminality.[1]

The Fitzhughs had nine children at Port Royal, although two died in accidents and did not live to adulthood. Although Fitzhugh practiced law in

Port Royal, he was not overly enthusiastic about his profession and, consequently, his family struggled financially. Preferring the contemplative life of study, abstract discussion, and writing, Fitzhugh used his idle time to develop his ideas on slavery, the South, and its social, political, and economic structures. In the 1850s, he would emerge as an important spokesperson for the slave system, publishing articles in major Southern papers such as *De Bows' Review* and the Richmond *Examiner* as well as his two principal monographs, *Sociology for the South* (1854) and *Cannibals All!* (1857). While Fitzhugh's works were widely read and disseminated, influential Northern writers and political figures such as Abraham Lincoln would wildly exaggerate the extent of Fitzhugh's influence among the Southern populace.[2]

Fitzhugh wrote in a South that was increasingly under the influence of such proslavery theorists as William Grayson, Thomas R. Dew, Josiah Nott, and others. Influenced by crude theories of ethnocentric classifications and unsophisticated biological theories, these thinkers constructed elaborate theories of black inferiority under the guise of scientific theory. While Fitzhugh's mature thought would emphasize the class origins of slavery instead of racial inferiority, his thought definitely assumed, like many proslavery apologists, that slavery was a positive blessing. "You, and Hughes, and I," Fitzhugh remarked to fellow writer George Frederick Holmes in 1855, "in the last year, it seems to me, have revolutionized public opinion at the South on the subject of slavery. Then, not one person vindicated slavery in the abstract—now all endorse my book and thereby endorse slavery in the abstract."[3]

George Fitzhugh belonged to the Democratic Party. Although he was politically active, Fitzhugh was never interested in political office and never ran for any elective position. Fitzhugh, however, maintained political connections through his work for Southern newspapers. Beginning in the early 1850s, Fitzhugh became a regular contributor to such Southern papers as the Richmond *Examiner*, *De Bow's Review*, and the *Southern Literary Messenger*. His articles reached a fairly prominent audience of Southern writers and included George Frederick Holmes, James DeBow, and Edmund Ruffin, among others.

Fitzhugh's most significant works were written during the 1850s and included a pamphlets entitled "Slavery Justified by a Southern" (1849), and "What Shall Be Done with the Free Negroes," which appeared in the May 2, 1851, edition of the Richmond *Examiner*. His two principal books, *Sociology for the South* and *Cannibals All!* sold modest amounts of copies and were widely reviewed throughout Northern and Southern newspapers. Representing a defense of the slave system and an attack on the inequities of free society, Fitzhugh's monographs were disputed and resented by many Northerners.

While Fitzhugh rarely wandered from his Port Royal home, he made one trip to the North, coming to Hartford, Connecticut, in March 1855 as an invited speaker for the town's lyceum. In a lecture entitled "The Failure of Free Society," Fitzhugh repeated many of the arguments that he had aired in *Sociology for the South*. When veteran abolitionist Wendell Phillips gave a scathing reply to Fitzhugh's lecture on the subsequent evening, Fitzhugh was in the audience. During his only trip to the North, Fitzhugh visited New York City and radical abolitionist Gerrit Smith at Peterboro, New York. Ironically, Smith had married one of Fitzhugh's sisters. While disagreeing vehemently with Smith's position of slavery and society, Fitzhugh respected his New York relative as a man of principle and integrity. The trip north helped convince Fitzhugh of the correctness of his positions. For Fitzhugh, Northern society was becoming scandalously secularized, and the extreme poverty in some sections of large cities reinforced his position that the plight of African American slaves was better than that of laboring whites.

In July 1857, Fitzhugh received a political appointment, taking a position as law clerk in the office of Attorney General Jeremiah S. Black. As a loyal Virginia Democrat, the appointment was a presumed payback for Fitzhugh's loyal service to the party. Moving to Washington, Fitzhugh worked primarily on the issue of California land claims. The fact that Fitzhugh needed the position, which paid him $1,600 per year, was an indication of just how financially strapped the writer was. After one year, Fitzhugh's position was eliminated as a result of budgetary restraints. To make ends meet, he was forced to remain active in writing. In 1859, Fitzhugh became literary editor for *De Bow's Review* and, in 1860, he delivered a series of lectures in Fredericksburg, Virginia, on anti-abolitionism and Horace Greeley's connection to French radical philosopher Charles Fourier. Greeley was a leading advocate of the ideas of Fourier in the United States; Fitzhugh's lectures were intended to discredit Fourier, who advocated organizing society into unconventional small communities known as phalansteries. By linking Greeley to such radical social ideas, Fitzhugh also intended to discredit the controversial *New York Tribune* editor, who was also a well-known antislavery advocate and member of the Republican Party.

Despite his criticism of the North, Fitzhugh was not an avid supporter of secession until after the election of Abraham Lincoln in 1860. Viewing war as invigorating for society, Fitzhugh also viewed it largely as a clash of cultures, pitting a traditional cavalier culture of the South against a Puritan, Enlightenment society of the North. Resettling his family in Richmond in early 1862, Fitzhugh spent the majority of the war years as clerk in the Confederate Department of Treasury.

After the war, unlike many Southerners, Fitzhugh seemed to accept the finality of Southern defeat. Taking a position in the Freedmen's Bureau, Fitzhugh actively worked as an advocate for blacks. His sympathy, however, was born of racism and paternalism, viewing African Americans as children who would become naturally indolent and impoverished if left alone. As radical Republicans began to seize control of Reconstruction, Fitzhugh became more pessimistic, arguing that the South ought to be free to deal with blacks on its own and fearing that Republican sponsorship of black rights would lead to violence and terror in the South.

Moving back to Port Royal at the end of 1866, Fitzhugh continued to write, working for *De Bow's Review* until the death of James De Bow in 1867. He then wrote for *Lippincott's Magazine* in 1869–1870. In 1872, Fitzhugh published his last article in *Southern Magazine*. Shortly thereafter, Fitzhugh's health began to decline, largely as the result of excessive insomnia. After his wife passed away in October 1877, Fitzhugh moved to Frankfort, Kentucky, and lived briefly with son R. H. Fitzhugh. In 1880, he moved to Huntsville, Texas, where he lived at the home of his daughter, Mariella Foster. His health continued to deteriorate in Texas, and eventually the Southern writer went blind. Fitzhugh passed away on July 29, 1881, just a few months before his seventy-fifth birthday.

PRINCIPAL WORKS, IDEAS, AND SIGNIFICANCE

Sociology for the South

Published in 1854 by the Richmond book company Adolphus Morris, *Sociology for the South* did not contain a lot of fresh material; rather, it was a compilation of miscellaneous newspaper articles that Fitzhugh had composed over the years. The organization is somewhat scattered with excessive repetition of Fitzhugh's principal point, namely, the superiority of slave society over free society. The work shows the influence of English philosopher Thomas Carlyle, whom Fitzhugh read extensively in the early 1850s. A leading critic of the French Revolution, Carlyle criticized liberal economic theory as unduly harsh on the English laboring classes.

According to Fitzhugh, the so-called free societies of the Northern United States and western Europe gave rise to a destructive individualism that pitted the strong against the weak. Built on the laissez-faire philosophy of the Scottish economic theorist Adam Smith, these modern commercial societies, according to Fitzhugh, deployed a philosophy of free trade and limited government. For Fitzhugh, these societies were fundamentally different from the traditions of medieval times when society was ruled by the feudal kings and Roman Catholic Church. Medieval society, for Fitzhugh, was more benevolent and was characterized by a more conciliatory class structure. In traditional society, the rich and strong had obligations toward the poor and weak. Indeed, as Fitzhugh read history, slavery was ingrained into the best societies of the past. It was the way that the stronger cared for and protected weaker members of society. In modern society, according to Fitzhugh, the strong destroy the weak and the rich despoil the poor. "And thus," wrote Fitzhugh, "whether between nations or individuals, the war of free trade is constantly widening the relative abilities of the weak and the strong."[4]

Free trade and laissez-faire capitalism, for Fitzhugh, had encouraged an aggressive, destructive individualism, whereby the interest of self becomes paramount. Wrote Fitzhugh, "*Laissez-faire*, free competition begets a war of wits, which the economists encourage, quite as destructive to the weak, simple and guileless, as the war of the sword." Free societies encouraged the rich to dispossess the poor. "This war of the rich with the poor, and the poor with one another," wrote Fitzhugh, "is the morality which political economy inculcates."[5]

Fitzhugh believed that traditional societies, represented by medieval feudalism and, most importantly, the agrarian South, were superior to modern societies that had evolved from the Reformation and the European Enlightenment. In traditional societies, each social class had obligations to the other social classes, and every social class was mutually subordinate to the church and state. Instead of exploiting the weak, members of the upper classes had an organic bond to weaker members of society. For Fitzhugh, slavery typified the kinship between the classes, for "benevolent" slaveholders cared for the needs of each slave "not according to his labor, but according to his wants."[6]

By contrast, "free" society was characterized by crime, disorder, starvation, and uncertainty. In free societies, the individual was glorified, social obligations between the classes were nullified, and each individual was at war with his or her neighbor. According to Fitzhugh, the direct result of freedom was increased pauperism, social turmoil, and higher prison populations. Since workers could be displaced whenever an economic downturn occurred, the poor were forced to resort to petty crime to survive, which ultimately increased the prison population. Whereas slaves had the security of home, clothing, and food, no such safety net existed for unemployed Northern workers. Class warfare characterized the North as opposed to class conciliation in the South. According to Fitzhugh, "We deny that there is a society in free countries."[7] By "society," Fitzhugh meant a social structure in which the rich had obligations to the less fortunate. Free countries lacked "society," according to Fitzhugh, and the various social classes warred against each other, with the rich often exploiting the poor.

Why was Northern society deluged with all sorts of utopian commutarian ideas and experiments in the mid-nineteenth century? According to Fitzhugh, it was the recognition by many intellectuals that laissez-faire society had destroyed all sense of community and replaced it with a harsh Hobbesian competition, where life was brutish, nasty, and mean. How much better was slavery, Fitzhugh wondered, the oldest and best form of socialism? For Fitzhugh, the majority of African Americans were much better suited to slavery. Why? Lacking intelligence, they would perish in a free society where they had to depend entirely on their own wits. However, Fitzhugh also maintained that the average Northern laborer fared little better in the competitive wars of the political economy, and ended up as slaves in a real and practical sense. "Three-fourths of free society," maintained Fitzhugh "is slaves, no better treated, when their wants and capacities are estimated, than Negro slaves."[8]

Fitzhugh saw the free, acquisitive society of the North as the antithesis of all traditional values; moreover, he saw laissez-faire as a threat to those institutions that historically restrained human selfishness, namely, the state and the church. The state exists to maintain order and supply necessary governance as a way to restrain the baser instincts of men. "The world," states Fitzhugh, "wants good government and plenty of it—not liberty." Disagreeing with the basic premise of limited government, Fitzhugh saw a strong state as supporting class cooperation and preventing a war of the rich against the poor. Reinforcing the state was the Christian religion, which also emphasized the obligations of the rich and powerful to the weak and poor. Fitzhugh saw the institution of slavery as sanctioned by Christianity because it forced powerful masters to care for the members of the lower classes. "As a slave," Fitzhugh noted, "he will be beloved and protected, whilst free, he will be hated, despised, and persecuted."[9]

For Fitzhugh, the evidence overwhelmingly suggested that free society was an unmitigated disaster. Exploitative, usurious, and unfeeling, free society not only increased the ranks of paupers and prisons, but also destroyed the institutions that historically had provided support, comfort, and protection for the weak. Competition was the greatest evil of the laissez-faire world; unrestrained competition would eventually kill off free African Americans and irreparably degrade the white working classes. While Northern abolitionists posed as the benevolent benefactors of African American slaves, in reality, they were their greatest enemies. Ironically, it was the Southern slaveholder who was the greatest ally of slaves. "The Southerner is the negro's friend, his only friend. Let no intermeddling abolitionist, no refined philosophy, dissolve that friendship."[10]

Cannibals All!

Fitzhugh followed *Sociology for the South* with his equally controversial *Cannibals All! Or Slaves without Masters*, published in 1857. Employing many of the same arguments as the earlier work, *Cannibals* was less original, containing numerous passages quoted verbatim from scholarly works, newspapers, or intellectual journals. Haphazardly organized, the work emphasized many of the same points over and over again.

As in *Sociology for the South*, Fitzhugh's principal aim was a justification of slave society, arguing that the slaves of the South were much better treated than Northern laboring classes. Arguing the essential amoral nature of Northern laissez-faire capitalism, Fitzhugh maintained that Northern society was revolutionary and destroyed traditional institutions of social control such as the church and family. By so doing, it also obliterated any sense of noblesse oblige between members of the upper and lower classes, encouraging instead a brutal relationship of exploitation. For Fitzhugh, Northern industrial laborers were slaves without masters, lacking direction and basic material comforts that slaves took for granted.

Tracing the rise of laissez-faire capitalism with the demise of feudal serfdom, Fitzhugh believed that the European laboring classes were much better cared for as serfs than as proletarians. "All writers agree," Fitzhugh comments, "there were no beggars or paupers in England until the liberation of serfs." For Fitzhugh, the motto of free society was unbridled selfishness, regardless of the impact on others. He wrote, "Duty to self is the first of duties: free society makes it the only duty." Slave society, however, was characterized by an entirely different and Christian principle. "Christian morality is the natural morality in slave society, and slave society is the only natural society."[11]

Throughout the work, Fitzhugh emphasized repeatedly the superiority of slave diet, living, and working conditions as opposed to that of Northern proletarians. For him, slavery was a natural extension of family and created a bond of mutual obligation between master and slave. Bound in this relationship, the exploitation of the master over the weaker and less intelligent slave could be checked and limited. Viewing society as hierarchical and connected, Fitzhugh deplored the Enlightenment attempt to view humans as equal and isolated. Attacking fellow Virginian Thomas Jefferson for his egalitarianism, Fitzhugh wrote, "He was the genius of innovation, the architect of ruin, the inaugurator of anarchy. His mission was to pull down, not to build up." Beginning with the Reformation and continuing through the Enlightenment, modern society, for Fitzhugh, overemphasized individualism and competition. The result was the harsh, brutal society that had emerged in much of Europe and was developing in the Northern United States.[12]

While Fitzhugh believed the enslavement of African Americans was justified on the basis of inferiority, in most of his writings, he also argues for the class origins of slavery. In other words, the institution of slavery was not inherently racial. Northern Republicans, such as Abraham Lincoln, seized on this point in an effort to popularize and justify the antislavery principles of the Republican Party. Although he believed that blacks might be treated differently than whites in slavery, the natural and preferred condition of all labor was slavery. Historian John Ashworth notes, "Those southerners who had defended black slavery while admitting its inapplicability to whites, he [Fitzhugh] maintained, were guilty of the most spurious reasoning." For Fitzhugh, slavery was simply the social mechanism whereby the strong and rich were obligated to care for the weak and poor. Slavery was not essentially a racial institution, but based on class distinctions.[13]

CONCLUSION

Many Northern journalists and political figures gave far more weight to Fitzhugh's standing in the South than he legitimately deserved. Despite dubious research methods and limited knowledge of Northern society, many of Fitzhugh's comments and criticism obviously touched a nerve among educated Northerners. While exaggerated, some of Fitzhugh's comments were on the mark, revealing a seamier side to Northern industrial growth that few wanted to acknowledge. Of course, undercutting Fitzhugh's penetrating criticisms of Northern society was his obvious blindness to the shortcomings of the slave system. Ignoring rampant cruelty and inhumane living and working conditions, Fitzhugh painted an idealized version of slavery that existed nowhere except in the mind of George Fitzhugh and in the pages of his manuscripts. As a biased apologist for slavery, however, Fitzhugh's reasonable criticisms of Northern society were often overlooked and ignored. As numerous historians point out, Fitzhugh's comments on the Northern proletariats were as penetrating and devastating as the comments of Karl Marx, even if they came from an entirely different set of suppositions.

NOTES

1. On the perception of free blacks in the South, see Ira Berlin, *Slaves without Masters: The Free Negro in the Antebellum South* (New York: Oxford University Press, 1974).

2. For Lincoln on Fitzhugh, see David Donald, *Lincoln* (New York: Simon & Schuster, 1995), 187, 191–92; Harry V. Jaffa, *A New Birth of Freedom: Abraham Lincoln and the Coming of the Civil War* (New York: Rowman & Littlefield Publishers, 2000), 166; Allen C. Guelzo, *Abraham Lincoln: Redeemer President* (Grand Rapids, MI: William B. Eerdmans Publishing Company, 1999), 136–38; and Stephen Oates, *With Malice toward None: The Life of Abraham Lincoln* (New York: Harper & Row, 1977), 137, 140, 152, 179.

3. Fitzhugh quote from Fitzhugh to George Frederick Holmes, March 27, 1855, Holmes Letter Book, Duke University Library, quoted from Eugene Genovese, *The World the Slaveholders Made: Two Essays in Interpretation* (New York: Pantheon Books, 1969), 130. The Hughes referred to in the quoted material is George W. Hughes. There are any number of relevant sources that discuss Fitzhugh and other proslavery thinkers: William Sumner Jenkins, *Pro-Slavery Thought in the Old South* (Chapel Hill: University of North Carolina Press, 1935); Clement Eaton, *The Freedom-of-Thought Struggle in the Old South* (New York: Harper Torchbooks, 1964); John McCardell, *The Idea of a Southern Nation: Southern Nationalists and Southern Nationalism, 1830–1860* (New York: W. W. Norton & Company, 1979), 49–50, 70–91, 150–51; John Hope Franklin, *The Militant South, 1800–1861* (Urbana: University of Illinois Press, 2002); and Eugene Genovese, *The Southern Front: History and Politics in the Cultural War* (Columbia: University of Missouri Press, 1995), 79–91.

4. *Sociology for the South, or the Failure of Free Society* (New York: Burt Franklin, n.d.), 13. The following works were also consulted in connection with Fitzhugh: Drew Faust Gilpin, *A Sacred Circle: The Dilemma of the Intellectual in the Old South, 1840–1860* (Baltimore: Johns Hopkins University Press, 1977), 127–31; Genovese, *The World the Slaveholders Made*, 118–19, 128–31, 151–64; and John Ashworth, *Slavery, Capitalism, and Politics in the Antebellum Republic, Volume 1: Commerce and Compromise, 1820–1850*, 229–46. On Thomas Carlyle, see L.C.B. Seaman, *Victorian England: Aspects of English and Imperial History, 1837–1901* (London: Methuen, 1973), 300, 303; and Wish, *Propagandist of the Old South*, 64, 172, 224, 241, 265–67.

5. *Sociology for the South*, 21, 22–23.

6. *Sociology for the South*, 29.

7. *Sociology for the South*, 32.

8. *Sociology for the South*, 86.

9. *Sociology for the South*, 107.

10. *Sociology for the South*, 95.

11. *Cannibals All!* 108, 218.

12. *Cannibals All!* 135. See also Ashworth, *Slavery, Capitalism, and Politics*, 231–32.

13. Ashworth, *Commerce and Compromise*, 236. Lincoln's "A House Divided," speech in 1858 seemed influenced by Fitzhugh's contention that the natural condition of all labor was slavery. See Robert W. Johannsen, ed., *The Lincoln-Douglas Debates of 1858* (New York: Oxford University Press, 1965), 14.

FURTHER READING

Robert Saunders Jr., "George Fitzhugh," in *Encyclopedia of the American Civil War*, ed. David S. and Jeanne T. Heidler (Denver: ABC-Clio, 2000), 2:702–3; Harvey Wish, *George Fitzhugh: Conservative of the Old South* (Charlottesville: University of Virginia Press, 1938); idem., *George Fitzhugh: Propagandist of the Old South* (Baton Rouge: Louisiana State University Press, 1943); and C. Vann Woodward, "George Fitzhugh, *Sui Generis*," in *Cannibals All! Or Slaves without Masters*, ed. C. Vann Woodward (Cambridge, MA: Belknap Press, 1960).

HORACE GREELEY
(1811–1872)

The Eccentric Genius

LIFE

Horace Greeley was born on February 3, 1811, on a farm close to Amherst, New Hampshire, one of five children. His father, Zaccheus Greeley, was plagued by financial setbacks that may have been a product of excessive drinking, while his mother, Mary Woodburn Greeley, was a jovial farm woman who enjoyed dancing and singing. Mary Greeley became progressively withdrawn as she grew older and the family's prospects dimmed. Horace was called "Hod" as a boy, and he demonstrated considerable intellectual precocity and little athletic prowess. Perhaps in consequence of his clumsiness and intelligence, he read a great deal and supplemented the rude education he received with constant self-study. His father had to give up his farm in 1820, and the family moved several times in search of better prospects before settling near Westhaven, Vermont. With his affinity for books and reading, Horace decided to learn the printing business, and in 1826 he walked a dozen miles to East Poultney, Vermont, and inquired for employment at the offices of the *Northern Spectator*. The editor, Amos Bliss, admired the boy's evident seriousness and agreed to take him on as a printer's apprentice for a period of five years.

At the age of fifteen, Greeley began to learn the newspaper business from the basement of the profession, setting type for each run of the paper. Bliss also asked him to summarize articles borrowed from other papers, a typical practice so as to economize space, and the experience taught him the value of precise language. He worked for the *Spectator* until it went out of business in 1830, then returned to his family at the Pennsylvania farm to which they had moved. He worked for a local enterprise, the *Erie Gazette*, for several months before determining to try employment in New York City, where he relocated in August 1831. He found work with a printer and toiled relentlessly at his profession at various newspapers including the *Evening Post, Spirit of the Times, Morning Post,* and the *Commercial Advertiser.* In 1833, Greeley started his own printing office with Francis V. Story as a partner; after Story's untimely death, Jonas Winchester replaced him. Greeley sought self-expression and founded a weekly as a vehicle for his commentary on current events and literature, the *New Yorker.* Never profitable with the weekly alone, Greeley relied on the printing business to keep his enterprise solvent.

In the pages of the *New Yorker,* Greeley dispensed his wisdom in editorials, expressing an enthusiasm for reform and education that was tempered by a flinty New England conservatism. He embraced many of the reform enthusiasms of the 1830s and 1840s, including temperance, vegetarianism, and communitarianism. He endorsed an end to imprisonment for debt, a fate that his father narrowly avoided, and he condemned both slavery and the abolition movement. His traditionalism manifested itself in his hidebound attitude toward women, who he believed should remain at home and without even legal ownership of property brought into the marriage. While personally living out his reform zeal at a boardinghouse organized on the ideas of Sylvester Graham—a vegetarian diet of bran bread and vegetables—he met his future wife, Mary Youngs Cheney, whom he called "Molly." A teacher, she taught briefly in Warrenton, North Carolina, before they married on July 5, 1836. Mary found marriage to Greeley difficult, as he was consumed with the newspaper business and politics, working constantly and becoming a scarce presence in their house.

With his emphasis on reform while preserving certain traditional norms and societal order, Greeley naturally gravitated to the Whig Party, and he became friendly with Thurlow Weed, the great political puppet master of New York politics. Greeley's partnership with Jonas Winchester had ended, and with the Panic of 1837, he teetered on the brink of bankruptcy. Just in time, Weed approached Greeley in late 1837 with an offer to publish a campaign sheet that would assist the 1838 New York gubernatorial campaign of William H. Seward, and Greeley agreed, putting out the *Jeffersonian* beginning in February 1838. He spent considerable time in Albany working on the paper and covering the state legislature, laboring constantly to earn enough to support his family. He purportedly began wearing a white coat to ward off the chill as he endured countless river voyages between Albany and New York City. His white duster and white chin whiskers became personal trademarks. He again put out a campaign weekly in 1840 to aid William H. Harrison's presidential run, called the *Log Cabin,* which did so well that Greeley continued to publish it after Harrison's victory over incumbent Martin Van Buren. His success prompted demands for Greeley to publish a Whig daily newspaper in New York City, an idea that he had previously suggested to Weed and Seward only to be rebuffed. Pushing forward nonetheless, Greeley began publishing the *New York Tribune*, the first issue of which appeared on April 10, 1841.

The *Tribune*, in a matter of years, became one of the most influential newspapers in the United States. Greeley struggled at first to make the paper a success. His cause was tremendously aided when Thomas McElrath joined him as a partner and in essence business manager in July 1841. McElrath had a reputation for sober business acumen, and his presence at the *Tribune* reassured the conservative Whig business community that the newspaper was not another radical sheet. Greeley had immense skills as a newspaperman, and his paper reflected his active mind, crusading spirit, and lively interest in the world. Although he always considered the moral reformation of the lower classes an important goal, he also recognized the value to a newspaper's profitability of printing the grisly details of a murder or sex crime. He also was a good judge of writing talent, hiring some of the best writers of the era, including Charles A. Dana, Bayard Taylor, Solon Robinson, and Margaret Fuller. He used the pages of the *Tribune* to advance his progressive reforms, and his natural optimism about the country's prospects seemed to capture what was referred to as the "spirit of the times." He was also enough of a conservative to reassure the more traditional elements of the Whig Party and thereby retain their support and patronage, though this would wax and wane.

His main preoccupation continued to be politics. When Henry Clay broke with John Tyler over the president's repeated vetoes of Clay's national bank bill, Greeley supported Tyler for a time, eventually abandoning the erstwhile Whig president in September 1842. Greeley then supported Clay for president in 1844, as Clay's program of economic nationalism appealed to Greeley, who preferred to stress the tariff and internal improvements to avoid the divisive slavery issue that he feared would split the Whig Party. When Texas annexation became the focal point of the 1844 campaign, Greeley was dismayed, as he feared that acquiring additional territory could disrupt sectional amity and prolong the institution of slavery for another century. His fears were well placed, as events proved. He actively supported Clay in the campaign, speaking at rallies and writing and distributing campaign literature, to no avail as Democrat James K. Polk was victorious. In addition to his constant presence in national politics, Greeley labored to reform New York City, attacking corrupt city officials and supporting measures such as more humane policies at the city jail and better schools.

He opposed the Mexican War and supported the proviso of David Wilmot that would have prohibited slavery in any territory acquired during the war. Greeley began advocating homestead legislation, which granted free land to settlers, seeing such a policy as a solution to overpopulated cities that spawned criminal and immoral behavior. He initially supported fierce war opponent Thomas Corwin for president in 1848, then backed alternative candidates to the eventual Whig nominee, Zachary Taylor. Greeley gave Taylor little support, withholding his endorsement until September 1848. Tired of being a spectator, he had repeatedly pressed his Whig patrons, Thurlow Weed and William H. Seward, for an office. Weed had him elected to fill the unexpired congressional term of David S. Jackson, who was unseated when the House refused to certify his election, and Greeley served in the final session of the Thirtieth Congress. In his brief tenure in the House of Representatives, Greeley managed to alienate his congressional colleagues with a slashing attack on the practice of padding mileage reimbursements, calling his fellow congressmen "mileage elongators." He satirized the twisting, back-and-forth routes to the Capitol that were claimed to increase reimbursement payments. He also introduced homestead legislation, as well as bills to reform the navy by ending flogging and the grog ration, cut back the size of the army, and rename the country "Columbia." His legislative record bespeaks his reformist impulses, wide interests, and eccentric genius. His actions also annoyed Weed and Seward, who increasingly viewed Greeley as wild and uncontrollable, an unreliable character given to flights of unreality that could end in political disaster for them and for the Whig Party.

Greeley and the *Tribune* continued to prosper. The newspaper issued stock in 1849 and continued to increase in subscribers and influence. By the end of the 1850s, the *Tribune* would have a circulation of 300,000. With prosperity came the end of Greeley's once ever-present financial woes. He traveled to Europe in 1851 and wrote an account of his sojourn called *Glances at Europe*. He and Molly had lived in New York City for years, but Greeley had a reverential opinion of farming and the agrarian scene, and this outlook prompted him to purchase a farm near Chappaqua, New York, in 1853. His wife became increasingly emotionally volatile, perhaps unhinged by her frequent miscarriages, Greeley's workaholic schedule, and consequent neglect. The Greeleys suffered tragedy as parents, as only two of their nine children survived. Having become a popular figure for his reformist zeal and entertaining editorials, Greeley took to the lecture circuit, where he could earn fat fees and supplement his income; hence, he was often away from home. Perhaps in response to her husband's manic activity, Molly traveled to Europe.

Greeley actively participated in the political battles that presaged civil war. No fan of Zachary Taylor, he opposed the president's plan to end the divisive battle over the territories by quickly admitting California, preferring Henry Clay's more elaborate compromise plan. Since William H. Seward supported Taylor, Greeley's stand put him at odds with his longtime allies. With Taylor's death and the passage of a strong Fugitive Slave Act as part of the final compromise, Greeley lost his zeal for the political deal with slave states. Glyndon Van Deusen has argued that after the Compromise of 1850, Greeley concluded that secession threats from the South were mere bluster to force the North into accepting undesirable legislation such as a reinvigorated Fugitive Slave Law, and he subsequently adopted a highly skeptical attitude to future legislative compromises. He also consistently overestimated the strength of Southern Unionism.

Greeley supported Winfield Scott in 1852, though he found much about the Whig Party that angered him, deploring Whig resistance to homestead legislation and continued support for the Compromise of 1850. He had become a leading foe of the enforcement of the Fugitive Slave Law, and he had concluded that slavery should be abolished. After Scott's defeat and amid the gradual disintegration of the Whig Party, Greeley drifted into independent status, promoting various reforms rather than the agenda of a political party. He annoyed Thurlow Weed when he supported candidates who backed prohibition without reference to party. For his part, Greeley was angry at Weed and Seward for what he regarded as their tacit support of his newspaper rival, the *New York Times*, which had begun publishing in 1851. Greeley viewed the introduction of the Kansas-Nebraska Act in Congress in January 1854 as a chance for a new political beginning. He strongly opposed the legislation as a transparent effort to add slave territory and eventually slave states to the Union and thereby bolster flagging Southern political strength in the national government. Greeley hoped that opponents of slavery's expansion could coalesce into a new political party organized on the principles of temperance and antislavery. He backed efforts to flood Kansas Territory with Free Soil settlers and supported anti-Nebraska fusion political organizations and tickets, which were coalitions of former Whigs, Democrats, Know-Nothings (also known as the American Party), and Free Soilers united in resistance to the extension of slavery.

Thurlow Weed and his political cohorts resisted abandoning the New York Whig Party in 1854 and rebuffed Greeley's ambition to win the nomination for governor. Feeling unappreciated and preferring a new political organization, Greeley strongly criticized the refusal of Weed and other New York Whigs to face the reality that the times and the issues required a fresh start. He increasingly viewed himself as independent from Seward and Weed, and in time he would criticize Weed for corruption and Seward for excessive conservatism. Greeley's desire for a new party became fact when the New York Republican Party was created in September 1855, with Greeley acting as chairman of the platform committee at the new party's convention. He wanted a broad coalition for the party, while old Whigs like Weed were reluctant to countenance moves that might dilute their influence.

The Republican Party became Greeley's great cause as he supported its first presidential nominee, John C. Frémont, in 1856. Greeley had concluded that a Slave Power conspiracy centered in the South sought to wrest control of the national government from the progressive Northern masses, and the Republican Party was the vehicle to resist the central goal of the slaveocracy, the expansion of slavery into new territory out of which additional slave states could be created to equalize the political balance in American government. Greeley covered the civil war in Kansas as a battle between the forces of light, the Free Soil settlers, and the forces of darkness, those who favored the Lecompton Constitution. He backed Seward's Senate proposal to admit Kansas under the Topeka Constitution (free-state constitution) and called President James Buchanan a tool of the slaveocracy. When Albert Rust, an Arkansas Democratic congressman, attacked Greeley with his cane out of anger from some criticism that had appeared in the *Tribune*, Greeley, who was not seriously injured, said he had been assaulted by a border ruffian, a term used to characterize proslavery guerrillas in the Kansas debacle.

In the two years leading up to the election of 1860, Greeley, anticipating Republican victory, moderated his rhetorical barrages at the South and stressed that the region had little to fear from a Republican president. Reflective of his lack of understanding of the South, he hoped that the Republicans could make inroads there. When Democratic senator Stephen A. Douglas broke with James Buchanan over the Lecompton Constitution, Greeley supported Douglas for reelection in 1858 and advised Illinois Republicans to do likewise. Always an advocate of an ever-expanding Republican Party, Greeley hoped Douglas and his supporters would abandon the Democrats. Illinois Republicans ignored Greeley's advice, nominated Abraham Lincoln for the Senate seat, and waged a spirited but unsuccessful campaign against Douglas. After Lincoln's defeat, Greeley criticized the state party for ignoring his counsel, and he subsequently supported Missouri attorney general Edward Bates for the Republican presidential nomination in 1860. Such slights were not forgotten by Lincoln and his friends.

In 1850, Greeley traveled to California and wrote numerous, engaging columns about the trip and the country. His letters appeared as a book titled *Overland Journey*. In February 1860, Greeley was one of the hosts for Abraham Lincoln's famed speech at the Cooper Union in New York, and though he admired Lincoln's rhetoric, he continued to tout Bates in the *Tribune*. Greeley attended the Republican National Convention in Chicago, where his efforts helped derail William H. Seward's candidacy, which greatly angered his former compatriots Weed and Seward. Lincoln received the nomination rather than Bates and went on to win the general election. When Lincoln elevated Seward to the cabinet as secretary of state, Greeley made another unsuccessful bid for elective office, failing to win the vacant Senate seat. With threats of secession in the offing, Greeley published an editorial on November 9, 1860, suggesting that the wise course would be to allow Southern states to leave the Union, for in time Southern Unionism would reassert itself and each seceded state would rejoin the United States. Greeley consistently overestimated the depth of Southern Unionism, and his editorial was roundly denounced. He felt that Lincoln was too in-experienced and unsophisticated for the task at hand and would be dom-inated by more savvy politicians like William H. Seward. Always skeptical of the efficacy of political deals with the slaveocracy, he did not support last-minute compromise efforts by John J. Crittenden and others.

After the outbreak of the war in April 1861, Greeley backed the war ef-fort, though his actions throughout the war could charitably be described as mercurial at best. Never a champion of Abraham Lincoln, he alternated from lashing the president for incompetence to praising him. After Gree-ley hurt himself on his farm in May, and his deputy Charles A. Dana took charge in his absence, the *Tribune* strongly advocated aggressive offensive action to quickly end the war. The resulting pressure was one reason for the ill-conceived Union attack in July, which resulted in a repulse and Con-federate victory at Bull Run. Greeley and the *Tribune* were harshly criti-cized for advocating forward movement, and advertising revenue and subscriptions sharply declined. Returning to the helm at the newspaper, Greeley sent Lincoln a bizarre letter in which he suggested an armistice, the first of many defeatist pronouncements he would utter during the conflict that typically came after a Union defeat or other difficulty. Lincoln ignored Greeley's suggestion, and publicly Greeley continued to support the war. He pledged to refrain from criticizing the army, a pledge soon forgotten.

Greeley had stressed the importance of restoring the Union as the para-mount goal of the war, but he soon decided that slavery had been the cause of all the nation's current problems and had to be eliminated. He viewed emancipation as an important war measure that would quickly end the re-bellion if implemented, and he criticized Lincoln for timidity when he re-versed the premature emancipation efforts of certain Union generals. Greeley argued his case in his famous editorial, "Prayer of Twenty Mil-lions," which appeared in August 1862, in which he argued that 20 mil-lion Northern citizens wanted Lincoln to end slavery. The president was already moving in the direction Greeley desired, but he responded by af-firming his commitment to saving the Union. The eventual Emancipation Proclamation pleased Greeley, though he wished for a speedier end to slav-ery.

The hideous casualties and immense expense of the war shocked and un-nerved Greeley, and prompted him to urge peace negotiations or an armistice. After Republican setbacks in the 1862 elections and stunning Union defeats at Fredericksburg and Chancellorsville, Greeley touted for-eign mediation of the conflict by France or another willing power. He sug-gested that emancipation might be given up as an inducement to the South to return to the Union and end the war. He recovered his senses for a time after the Union victories at Gettysburg and Vicksburg, but the savage ca-sualties of the Wilderness campaign in 1864 prompted the reappearance of Greeley's pessimism. He actively supported efforts to dump Lincoln as the

Republican nominee in 1864, continuing into September. Greeley's hostility to Lincoln had been in part driven by his writing of a history of the rebellion, a chore he had labored at for eight months and that apparently reminded him of why he disliked the president. The fall of Atlanta helped end the movement to dump Lincoln and brought Greeley back into the Lincoln camp, and he subsequently supported the president's Reconstruction policy, which fit with Greeley's own desire for a lenient attitude toward the South.

A few days before Lincoln's tragic assassination, Greeley published an editorial recommending a general amnesty for the South, and he later suggested that the region might be pacified by a policy that offered amnesty in exchange for Southern acceptance of black suffrage. He embraced amnesty for Jefferson Davis and got the former Confederate president a good lawyer, and traveled to Richmond to provide security for Davis's bail. Sentiments such as these made him a natural ally of the new president, Andrew Johnson, and Greeley supported Johnson's tendency to placate Southern white racist opinion rather than advance black civil rights. The veto of the Freedmen's Bureau was a turning point for Greeley, who worried that Johnson intended to completely abandon the former slaves. He became a persistent critic of the president, supporting his radical foes, the Tenure of Office Act, and impeachment. He backed Ulysses S. Grant's candidacy for the presidency, though without any great enthusiasm. Grant wanted Greeley's support or at least Greeley defanged, and once he became president, he offered the newspaperman appointment as minister to Great Britain and met with him on at least two occasions to solicit Greeley's input on patronage and other matters. Greeley refused to join the administration.

Grant's overtures had the desired effect for a time, as the *Tribune* loyally supported the former general turned political leader. In the end, however, Greeley became a Grant foe for several reasons. He disliked the general on a personal level. He also could not conceive of any value to the continued military occupation of the South; Greeley had a long history of preferring reductions in military spending and force size. He also worried about excessive government debt, which a large standing army could generate. He thought the state Reconstruction governments had been fiscally irresponsible to the point of being discredited, and he thought Southern white rule was a reality that had to be accepted. He also sensed the waning of his influence in New York political circles and was angered at perceived slights in patronage appointments.

The result was Greeley's quixotic campaign for the presidency in 1872 as the candidate of both the Democratic and anti-Grant Liberal Republican parties. Greeley campaigned on national reconciliation, touting the greatness of the United States, a nationalist appeal that he hoped would unite the country behind him and a crusade to heal the wounds of civil war and reconstruction. He had spent his career savagely attacking Democrats, many of whom now regarded his appearance as their new champion as an unconvincing transformation. Greeley was viciously lampooned in the cartoons of the brilliant Thomas Nast, who portrayed the editor as a betrayer of Abraham Lincoln, shaking hands with John Wilkes Booth. Greeley conducted a spirited campaign, delivering more than 200 stump speeches, but he could not best the man who had accepted Robert E. Lee's surrender at Appomattox. Tragically, his wife died a few days before the election, adding to the gloom that came on Election Day, a landslide victory for Ulysses S. Grant. Despondent and overwhelmed with the defeat, Mary's death, and the future prospects of the *Tribune*, Greeley gave into despair and had to be admitted to a sanitarium at Pleasantville, New York. He died on November 29, 1872.

PRINCIPAL IDEAS

Coming into his professional maturity in an era that featured a number of reform movements, Horace Greeley embraced many of the solutions on offer for American ills. Fundamentally, Greeley believed in the perfectibility of man, and though a Christian, he believed that eliminating harmful environmental and other influences could improve humankind. He touted the temperance movement, vegetarianism, reform of city government, and tolerance toward immigrants. Intensely nationalistic, Greeley showered praise on American writers and tried to promote American literature as an equal of the best European writing. He embraced the Whig economic agenda of tariff, internal improvements, and a national bank; he particularly associated the tariff with national progress. Free trade, to Greeley, was a recipe for chaos and foreign dominance of key industries. In time, Greeley believed, the necessity for protection would fade as the citizenry completed the transformation to an industrial power.

He had at first condemned the abolition movement as too radical. But in the 1850s, Greeley came to view slavery as a grave threat to the nation and thought it had to be abolished, though typically in a gradual fashion. Though concerned with the plight of blacks, he viewed slavery as a reactionary institution that was an obstacle to national greatness and societal improvement, that is, he worried more about the larger implications of the institution of slavery rather than black rights.

He viewed the population as a possible threat to the continuance of the republic, a potential angry mob that might fall into the clutches of a demagogue and become a tool for dictatorship. His preventative was education and moral instruction. He supported the common school system, and he backed temperance and other moral reforms. Ultimately, Greeley gave up the Whig distribution policy for homestead legislation that granted free land, in part because he wanted to move the poor out of cities and into the pastoral beauty of the American West. On the frontier, the downtrodden could start new and virtuous lives raising crops and children, a vision that harkened to Greeley's early support of the communitarian movement as advanced by Charles Fourier and Albert Brisbane. The town of Greeley, Colorado, was founded with help from Greeley and along similar principles. Interestingly, Greeley's zeal to reform never extended to women's rights, as he contended that women were not interested in voting. He tended to be more sympathetic to management than labor, arguing that the two antagonists had to work cooperatively while denouncing strikes, labor's most potent tool for forcing concessions. He was in many respects a typical Whig, suspicious of the mob and concerned with maintaining social order and stability, and his reform proposals were always moderate in intent.

CONCLUSION

Horace Greeley's intellectual energy and enthusiasm made the *New York Tribune* one of the most influential newspapers in the decade preceding the Civil War. His gifts were matched with flaws that precluded success in elective office, much to his chagrin. Yet Greeley helped form the consensus against slavery's extension, a necessary precursor to the ultimate demise of the institution that oppressed millions of African Americans. Unfortunately, he did not insist on the enforcement of black civil rights in the Reconstruction South.

FURTHER READING

William Harlan Hale, *Horace Greeley: Voice of the People* (New York: Harper, 1950); Erik S. Lunde, *Horace Greeley* (Boston: Twayne, 1981); Suzanne Schulze, *Horace Greeley: A Bio-Bibliography* (Westport, CT: Greenwood Press, 1992); and Glyndon G. Van Deusen, *Horace Greeley: Nineteenth-century Crusader* (Philadelphia: University of Pennsylvania Press, 1953).

ANDREW JOHNSON
(1808–1875)

The Challenge of Impeachment

LIFE

Seventeenth president of the United States Andrew Johnson was born in Raleigh, North Carolina, on December 29, 1808. The capitol of North Carolina was at that time a primitive town of about 1,000 inhabitants, of which approximately 300 were African American. Johnson was the second son of Jacob Johnson and Mary McDonough Johnson. Johnson had an older brother, William, and a sister, Elizabeth, but the latter died in early childhood. Johnson's parents were hardworking but poor and illiterate. Jacob Johnson worked as a porter at the local bank, while Mary, popularly known as "Polly," worked as a seamstress. Tragedy struck the Johnson family shortly after Andrew's third birthday when Jacob Johnson unexpectedly passed away. The elder Johnson apparently died of complications after he rescued passengers in a capsized boat from a nearby pond. Now even more impoverished, Mary quickly remarried, turning to Turner Daughtry, a man of questionable habits who did little to improve the family's financial condition. As a result, Mary was forced to sign apprenticeship agreements with a local tailor, James Selby, for both William and Andrew. Forced to work at the age of ten, Johnson would not spend a single day of his life in school.[1]

Johnson was forced to flee Raleigh in 1824 when his brother, he, and a group of boys ran afoul of the law. For some reason, the boys had a dispute with a local widow and, as a result, threw pieces of wood at her house. When the widow threatened to prosecute the offenders, Johnson and his brother fled to Carthage, North Carolina, and then to Lauren in northwestern South Carolina. In both places, Johnson worked at his acquired trade, tailoring. James Selby posted a notice of the runaways that clearly identified Andrew as the leader. Describing him as "very fleshy, freckled face, light hair, and fair complexion," Selby offered a $10 reward for the capture of the runaway apprentices, but also added "or I will give the above Reward for Andrew Johnson alone."[2]

Tired of living as a fugitive, Johnson returned to Raleigh several months later in an effort to make peace with Selby, who had moved twenty miles outside of the city. The latter, however, was uncompromising, refusing to allow Johnson to serve additional time for money owed. Fearing capture and imprisonment, the young tailor headed west, traveling over the Appalachian Mountains into neighboring eastern Tennessee. After stops in Knoxville, Tennessee; Mooresville, Alabama; and Columbia and Rutledge, Tennessee, Johnson eventually found a permanent home in the eastern Tennessee town of Greeneville. The small town of 3,000 seemed ideally suited for Johnson. With the picturesque Smoky Mountains in the background, the town was culturally sophisticated for its size, boasting several churches, a library, and two colleges. More significantly, the town had only one tailor—and he was elderly.

Johnson quickly established himself in Greeneville, aligning himself with a wealthy benefactor, Joseph Brown. When the latter purchased a suit from the new tailor and recognized its superior quality, Johnson's tailoring business began to thrive, allowing him to reinvest profits in real estate. Amorous pursuits also occupied the young tailor as Johnson met Elizabeth McCardle, the daughter of a local shoemaker. The two quickly fell in love and were married. The Johnsons had five children: Martha (1828), Charles (1830), Mary (1832), Robert (1834), and Andrew or "Frank" (1852). While Elizabeth was a supportive and caring wife during the Johnsons' fifty-year marriage, she was seldom in the spotlight, preferring the private sphere to the rough-and-tumble world of politics.

While Johnson's tailoring business thrived, the young tailor also had ambitions for a political career. Although he had never spent a single day in school, Johnson nevertheless learned to read. While his writing was always poor, Johnson developed into an effective and dynamic public speaker. Using his speaking skills, Johnson's political career took off quickly as he served as an alderman as early as 1829 and was then elected mayor of Greeneville in 1834. In 1835, Johnson ran for state legislature and to the surprise of many was elected by a substantial majority. Opposition to internal improvements, a popular issue in mountainous east Tennessee, diminished Johnson's popularity in the district, and he did not run for reelection in 1837, choosing instead to concentrate on supporting his growing family. At the same time, the taste of politics was in Johnson's mouth and he would shortly move back into the public sphere, never returning to tailoring.

Johnson's early partisan affiliation was ambiguous. While a staunch supporter of Andrew Jackson, he nevertheless supported Tennessee native and Whig candidate Hugh Lawson White for president in 1836. When Johnson chose to run for the state legislature again in 1839, he ran as a states' rights Democrat, and, from that day forward, never wavered in his political affiliation. Winning election in 1840 to the state senate, Johnson's most notable action was participation in the controversial legislative session of 1841–1842. Leading a group of Democrats known as "the immortal thirteen," Johnson and his cohorts blocked the election of both U.S. senatorial candidates by refusing to attend legislative sessions, thus preventing a quorum. Johnson's action earned him respect and standing among Democrats, while enraging Whig opponents.

As a committed, if not fervent, Democrat, Johnson demonstrated an ideological consistency that was traceable from his earliest political campaigns for state office and remained with him until the presidency. First and foremost, Johnson stood for the advancement of common people over privilege and aristocracy. Even before his identification as a Democrat, Johnson favored the abolition of the Electoral College and the direct election of the president by popular vote. "The president should at all times be made by the people," Johnson complained to George W. Jones, "and I would prefer an amendment to the Constitution of the United States to that affect, so as the people could vote directly for president & vice president." Additionally, Johnson opposed public spending for internal improvements while demonstrating an almost fanatical devotion to economy in government spending. Like all of his Democratic contemporaries, Johnson believed in white supremacy. As a Southerner, he ardently defended the peculiar institution from the onslaughts of Northern abolitionists.[3]

Eventually Johnson tired of Nashville and state politics and set his sights on Washington, D.C., and national office. Determined to stay in politics and out of tailoring, Johnson ran for the House of Representative in 1843 and, to the surprise of many of his enemies, defeated fellow Democrat John Aiken. Johnson would serve five successive terms in the House before being gerrymandered out of his seat in 1852. Opponents of Johnson in the Tennessee legislature, led by Gustavus A. Henry, enlarged Johnson's congressional district, turning it into a safe Whig district. During these years, he pursued issues consistent with his Democratic principles such as economy in government, opposition to Whig financial ideas, as well as support for the Mexican War and territorial expansion. During his House years, Johnson also became an advocate of homestead legislation, a measure that made him somewhat unpopular in the South because of its later Free Soil connotations. Life in Washington was not all that satisfying for Johnson. In particular, the Tennessee representative was lonely for his wife Elizabeth, who remained in Greeneville and did not visit Johnson during his entire time as a member of the House.

Johnson's rise to political power created numerous enemies in east Tennessee. William G. "Parson" Brownlow was the Tennessee tailor's most formidable opponent. The editor of the Jonesboro *Whig,* and later the editor of the Knoxville newspaper, the *Whig*, Brownlow was a Virginia native who had migrated to Tennessee. A fervent evangelical Methodist, Brownlow hated abolitionists and Democrats. Opposing Johnson in the election of 1840, Brownlow despised his political tactics, particularly the way Johnson appealed to common folk. During the 1840s, the parson frequently attacked Johnson, accusing his father of thievery and calling Johnson an illegitimate son. "*You*, a living mass of *undulating* filth, a political *Skunk*— a creature who is indebted for his very existence, to the moral putrification on which he feeds," Brownlow wrote in one letter to Johnson. "such a sin-poluted soul as this talk about other men being unworthy of his 'steel!'" Yet Johnson seemed to best Brownlow time and time again, not only proving that he was not illegitimate, but also defeating Brownlow when up for reelection in 1845. Not only would Johnson increase his majority by several hundred votes, but the failure of Brownlow to meet Johnson in debate also provided additional vindication.[4]

While popular in eastern Tennessee, Johnson lacked standing with party leaders in Washington, D.C. Although a James Knox Polk supporter, Johnson alienated the Tennessee governor by initially backing Lewis Cass for president in 1844. Likewise, he clashed with Southern leaders in Congress, most prominently Jefferson Davis, when the latter extolled the virtues of a professional military and made a derogatory reference to tradesmen, including tailors in his negative comments. While Johnson did enthusiastically support the Mexican War and dutifully opposed the Wilmot Proviso, he continued to earn the distrust of many prominent Democrats who believed that Johnson was an unprincipled demagogue. Eventually Johnson's Tennessee opponents thwarted their nemesis when they successfully redrew the First Congressional District, making it a Whig district and preventing Johnson's reelection in 1852.[5]

Johnson, however, quickly turned the tables on his political opponents, Democrat and Whig, when he successfully snatched the Democratic gubernatorial nomination in 1852. In a grueling campaign in the summer of 1853, Johnson defeated Whig candidate Gustavus A. Henry, whom Johnson accused of conspiring to enlarge his First Congressional District, thereby causing Johnson's defeat in 1851. This allowed Johnson to level the charge of the "henry-mander" against his opponent in the gubernatorial race. Johnson would win reelection in 1855, defeating Whig opponent Meredith Gentry, whom Johnson attacked as an aristocrat with connections to the Know-Northing Party (the popular term for the American Party, which organized on the basis on anti-immigrant and anti-Catholic principles). Since the governor of Tennessee lacked a number of fundamental executive powers, such as a veto, Johnson's power as governor was extremely circumscribed. Nevertheless, Johnson worked hard at his official duties, remaining in Nashville and absent from Greeneville for months at a time. As governor, Johnson spoke on issues he had supported in Congress, including limited spending, opposition to internal improvement, the defense of slavery, and support of federal homestead legislation. Choosing not to seek reelection in 1857, Johnson instead sought and was subsequently elected U.S. senator on October 8.

Returning to Washington in December 1857, Johnson was once again alone. Although Eliza would visit him in 1860, she failed to move to Washington and Johnson occupied rooms by himself at the St. Charles Hotel at 53rd and Pennsylvania. Once again, Johnson championed such issues as economy in government and homestead legislation. Since the right to expand slavery into the territories was dearly important to many Southern legislators, Johnson's devotion to homestead legislation was not popular with many Southern senators, who saw such legislation as serving the interests of the Northern Republican Party. As a result, Johnson faced hostile opposition from many of his Southern cohorts. On occasion he quarreled violently with Jefferson Davis, James S. Green of Missouri, Louis T. Wigfall of Texas, and fellow Tennessee senator John Bell. Eventually the House and Senate passed a modified version of a homestead bill, which was promptly vetoed by President Buchanan on June 22, 1860, who argued that the bill's provision for free distribution of federal lands was unconstitutional.

As 1860 was a presidential year, Johnson entertained ambitions for high office. The favorite son of his native Tennessee, Johnson advocated popular sovereignty and opposed the demand for a federal slave code for territories of the United States. Hoping for the vice presidential slot on a Stephen A. Douglas ticket, Johnson was disappointed with the Democrats' inability to unite on a platform and candidate. While he would eventually support the candidacy of John C. Breckinridge, throughout the campaign of 1860, Johnson urged Democrats to merge their two tickets to prevent the election of a Republican president. When Lincoln's election sent off secession fervor in the South, Johnson chose a course of action that would eventually lead him to the presidency of the United States.

Andrew Johnson was shocked and outraged by the course of the fire-eaters during the secession crisis. Although an orthodox Southerner on the question of the morality of slavery, Johnson sincerely believed that slavery was much more secure within the framework of the Union. While he strenuously opposed the Republican Party and Abraham Lincoln, Johnson nevertheless did not believe that Lincoln's election warranted disunion. Like Andrew Jackson, Johnson was a proslavery Democrat who rejected the doctrine of secession. "If the doctrine of secession is to be carried out upon the mere whim of a state," Johnson told the Senate in a popular December 18, 1860, speech, "this Government is at an end." In Johnson's opinion, talk of secession was little more than disloyalty. "It is treason, and nothing but treason," Johnson argued, "and if one State, upon its own volition, can go out of this Confederacy without regard to the effect it is to have upon the remaining parties to the compact, what is your Government worth?"[6]

Johnson devoted the majority of his time in Washington during the winter of 1860–1861 to compromise. He strongly endorsed the Crittenden compromise measures, hoping they would provide adequate security for slave property, thereby convincing worried Southerners that the incoming administration could not move against the peculiar institution. "If Tennessee can be held firm for the present," Johnson told one correspondent, "She can hereafter be made to perform a Conspicuous part in Savi[n]g the Country from Civil and Servild [sic] war." When compromise measures failed, Johnson blamed Southern fire-eaters who he claimed were never serious about compromise. Still, he was determined to keep Tennessee within the Union despite the opposition of prominent Tennessee Democrats—including Governor Isham Harris.[7]

When firing erupted at Fort Sumter, Johnson quickly returned to his native Tennessee in an effort to stem the tide in favor of secession. On his way back, he faced down hostile crowds at Lynchburg, Virginia. With the exception of his native eastern Tennessee, Johnson met hostile crowds throughout the state and was routinely denounced. While Johnson's opposition to secession did make friends out of such former east Tennessee enemies as William G. Brownlow and Whig Congressman Horace Maynard, as a whole, Unionist sentiment in the state was in the minority. After a special convention had voted for withdrawal from the Union, the Tennessee electorate ratified the vote on June 8. Although eastern Tennessee remained Unionist, Johnson felt that it was unsafe for him to remain in Tennessee as Confederate troops were promptly stationed in the area. Johnson quickly made his way back to Washington, D.C., where he and Horace Maynard became the principal spokespersons for Union intervention in east Tennessee.[8]

As the only senator for a seceded state to remain in Congress, Johnson became a celebrity in the North. During the secession crisis, many of his speeches were carried in national newspapers, and he was a much sought-after political speaker. As a senator without a constituency, Johnson still took his senatorial responsibilities seriously. Since he regarded secession as illegal, Johnson viewed himself as the duly constituted representative of the people of Tennessee. As a critic of abolitionists and supporter of slavery, Johnson was also determined to ensure that the war was fought for the correct purposes. To that end, Johnson collaborated with Kentuckian John J. Crittenden in the formulation of the Crittenden-Johnson resolution. Introduced and overwhelmingly supported by Congress in the summer of 1861, the resolution framed the war's purpose as restoration of the Union and having nothing to do with the abolition of slavery.

During his tenure as a war senator, Johnson became a member of the controversial Joint Committee on the Conduct of the War. Formed in the aftermath of Union defeats at Bull Run, Wilson's Creek, and Ball's Bluff, the Republican members of the committee were critics of the Lincoln administration and suspicious of the commander of the Army of the Potomac, General George Brinton McClellan. Johnson shared these suspicions. Even though McClellan was a prominent Democrat, Johnson participated in committee investigations of the Army of the Potomac in the winter of 1861–1862 with an enthusiasm that impressed his fellow Republican committee members. In early February 1862, for instance, Johnson interviewed McClellan with Committee Chair Benjamin F. Wade of Ohio. The fiery Ohio senator launched a rhetorical salvo against McClellan's lack of earnestness, and McClellan received little sympathy from fellow Democrat Johnson. When Johnson succeeded Lincoln as president, his participation on the Committee on the Conduct of the War gave him acceptance among radical Republicans.[9]

Johnson's work as a wartime senator, however, was short-lived. After Union military successes in the West, Abraham Lincoln tapped him to be military governor of Tennessee on March 4, 1862. Union occupation of Tennessee was precipitated by the fall of Fort Donelson in February 1862. Since Nashville was located on the Cumberland River, continued Confederate control of the capitol was problematic. As Confederate troops under Albert Sidney Johnson withdrew from Tennessee, Governor Harris abandoned the city. When Johnson arrived in Nashville, he found the city dominated by secessionists. Johnson moved quickly to make the capitol a Unionist stronghold, closing secessionist papers, jailing citizens who refused to take a loyalty oath to the Union, and appointing only loyal Unionists to government positions, including east Tennessee Unionists Horace Maynard and William G. Brownlow.

Consistent with his position on slavery heretofore, Johnson promised loyal Tennessee slaveholders the protection of federal law for their slave property. Once President Lincoln issued the preliminary emancipation proclamation, Johnson asked the president to exempt Tennessee. Since Johnson's request was consistent with the provisions of the proclamation, it did not liberate any Tennessee slaves. While Johnson would eventually change his position on the issue of slavery, at this stage of the conflict, he continued to endorse a policy of the restoration of the Union as the war's principal purpose.

During his tenure as governor, Johnson frequently quarreled with Union military commanders in the West. Showing a persistent distrust of West Point educated soldiers, Johnson particularly disliked Don Carlos Buell, the commander of the department of Ohio and one of the leading generals in the West. When Braxton Bragg's Army of Tennessee invaded Tennessee and Kentucky in September 1862, Buell angered Johnson when he advised the abandonment of Nashville. Johnson refused and eventually was given enough troops to secure the capital. Even more frustrating to the military governor was Buell's indifference to the fate of east Tennessee. Despite repeated attempts to get Buell to send troops to his native region, nothing happened. In fact, not until the summer of 1863, long after William Rosecrans had replaced Buell, would Union forces under Ambrose Burnside liberate the Unionist population in the eastern part of the state.

As military governor, Johnson was also intimately connected to the issue of wartime Reconstruction. On the issue of Reconstruction, Johnson saw eye to eye with Lincoln. Johnson believed that seceded states had never really left the Union; consequently, their restoration to the Union, in Johnson's eyes, should be a relatively easy and uncomplicated process. After Lincoln unveiled the contours of his Ten Percent Plan, the president urged Governor Johnson to bring Tennessee back into the Union. The Ten Percent Plan stipulated that whenever 10 percent of a seceded state's 1860 registered voters took oaths of allegiance to the United States, this group of citizens could form a state government that would be granted recognition by the president. The oath of allegiance stipulated recognition of all laws of the United States and acceptance of all presidential proclamations regarding slavery. Because pro-Confederate sentiment remained dominant in the state, Johnson proceeded slowly. In fact, when Johnson accepted the vice presidential nomination in 1864, he had not finished the job of Reconstruction, nor had Tennessee abolished slavery or formed a new constitution. These were tasks for the future.[10]

How Johnson came to be the vice presidential nominee of the Republican (now called the Union) Party is still subject to historical speculation. While Hannibal Hamlin was a popular enough vice president, Lincoln was interested in strengthening his position among Democrats; therefore, overtures were made to a number of prominent war Democrats including Daniel Dickinson of New York, Daniel Sickles, and Benjamin F. Butler, the colorful politician turned general. After delegates unanimously renominated Lincoln, a similar motion to renominate Hamlin was defeated. Johnson emerged as the leading candidate to replace Hamlin, and eventually the convention made his selection unanimous.[11]

Johnson's participation in the campaign was an unprecedented departure from tradition. Prior to the election of 1864, only one other candidate campaigned on his own behalf—Stephen Douglas during the election of 1860. Equally remarkable was Johnson's embrace of emancipation during the election. Previously a bitter Negrophobe who fought for the restoration of the Union and not the abolition of slavery, Johnson, in a remarkable speech delivered in Nashville on October 24, 1864, now told African Americans that he would be their Moses and help lead them out of slavery. Then early in 1865, Johnson witnessed the end of military government in Tennessee as a special convention abolished slavery as well as nominated and elected William G. Brownlow as governor.

Johnson's service as vice president got off to a rocky start. On Inauguration Day, March 4, 1865, Johnson was still recovering from a bout with typhoid fever. The previous night, he had drunk several rounds of whiskey with journalist John W. Forney. In the morning, Johnson did not feel well. To steady himself, Johnson took a couple of glasses of whiskey prior to inauguration ceremonies at the Capitol. The whiskey had a noticeable effect on the new vice president. When it was his turn to speak, he delivered a long incoherent tirade, punctuated with such uncouth phrases as "I'm a going to tell you." An embarrassed President Lincoln pulled a parade marshal aside and instructed, "Do not let Johnson speak outside." Johnson was ridiculed in the press for his behavior, and some powerful Washington figures immediately called for his resignation; however, the controversy eventually subsided.[12]

Johnson's tenure as vice president was short-lived, for late in the evening on April 14, he was awakened by a knock at the door at his room in the Kirkwood House on Pennsylvania Avenue. It was former Wisconsin Governor George Farwell, a friend of Johnson's. The president had been shot, Farwell told a stunned Johnson. Neither man realized the danger the vice president had avoided. John Wilkes Booth had targeted Johnson along with other members of the cabinet. The man assigned to kill Johnson, George Atzerodt, had gotten drunk instead of trying to kill the vice president. Unaware of the Booth plot, the two men hurried over to the house across from Ford's Theater where Lincoln was temporarily housed. When Lincoln passed away early the next morning, the Tennessee tailor was sworn in as the nation's seventeenth president.

While a Southern Democrat, Andrew Johnson assumed the presidency with the enthusiastic support of many Republicans. Indeed, radical Republicans, who had quarreled frequently with Lincoln over the issues of emancipation and reconstruction, were among the new president's most enthusiastic supporters. Given Johnson's racial prejudice and well-known Jacksonian views, Johnson's good relationship with the radical wing of the Republican Party might seem puzzling. During the secession crisis, however, Johnson had earned admiration from many Republican quarters for his denunciation of secession and his refusal to abandon his senate seat once the war began. As a member of the Joint Committee on the Conduct of the War, Johnson had rubbed elbows with such prominent Republican radicals as Benjamin F. Wade, Zachariah Chandler, Indiana's George Washington Julian, and Pennsylvania's John Covode. Committee members were impressed with Johnson's determination to vigorously prosecute the war and his impatience with conservative generals of the McClellan stripe. As military governor of Tennessee, Johnson had shown the same dogged determination to punish traitors and establish a loyal government in the state. As vice president and immediately after assuming the presidency, Johnson continued to make strong statements, denouncing secession as treason and promising to punish those guilty of treason. As Ben Wade remarked in an oft-quoted phrase, "Johnson, we have faith in you. By the Gods, there will be no trouble now in running the government."[13]

By the end of the year, however, radical Republicans were united in their distrust of Johnson. What had Johnson done to alienate these same radicals who welcomed him with open arms in April? Radical Republicans soon discovered that beneath Johnson's surface of tough talk about punishing traitors was a political philosophy wholly at odds with the that of Republican Party. With the collapse of the Confederacy practically coinciding with Johnson's ascension to the presidency, the question of Reconstruction philosophy was fundamental. In this respect, Johnson stressed his agreement with the views of his predecessor. "Johnson remade his predecessor in his own image," notes Brooks Simpson, "and used Lincoln's name as he used the Constitution—as a justification of his actions and nothing more." The most significant point of agreement between Lincoln and Johnson was their belief that secession was a legal fiction. States, in fact, had never been out the Union; rebellious individuals had temporarily gained control of state governments. Since states had never been out of the Union, the process of readmittance ought to be simple and uncomplicated—as was Lincoln's Ten Percent Plan. Johnson's notion of Reconstruction was fundamentally different than that of a Charles Sumner or a Thaddeus Stevens, who, while differing on particulars, stressed the notion that states had gone out of the Union and, therefore, Reconstruction ought to be an arduous process whereby the federal government could lay down a number of conditions for readmittance to the Union. For Johnson, a state would be required to ratify the Thirteenth Amendment, repudiate Confederate debt, and repeal its ordinance of secession; however, stipulating black suffrage and requiring the appropriation of plantation lands for newly emancipated blacks was not only politically unwise, but also, in Johnson's view, constitutionally incorrect.[14]

While Republican radicals believed that Johnson's vindictive rhetoric revealed a commitment to a punishing peace that would incorporate a radical social-political agenda, Johnson was quietly hatching his own strategy to unite the country and ensure his election to the presidency in 1868. In order to do this, Johnson hoped to precipitate fundamental political realignment, uniting conservative Republicans as well as Northern and Southern Democrats in a grand conservative majority, dwarfing the political potency of Republican radicals. Johnson's first major statement on Reconstruction came with his North Carolina proclamation. Originally drafted by Secretary of War Edwin Stanton, Johnson revised Stanton's work and issued his proclamation on May 29. While the document technically only applied to the reconstructed government of North Carolina, the proclamation was an obvious model of presidential Reconstruction. A general amnesty was announced and all property was restored to rightful owners, slaves excepted. Although amnesty was declared, the proclamation stipulated fourteen classes of persons not covered under amnesty provisions including Confederate military officers, Confederate political officeholders, and persons who owned at least $20,000 in property. Rights could be restored through a presidential pardon. Once the legal voters in 1861 formed a Republican constitution, North Carolina could be restored to the Union. Since African Americans were not legal voters in 1861, Johnson's plans excluded them.

Predictably, radical Republicans were angered. Chief among them was Thaddeus Stevens. The outspoken Pennsylvania Republican had earlier warned Johnson about excluding Congress from the Reconstruction process. "Better call an extra session [of Congress]," he warned Johnson on May 19, 1865, "than to allow many to think that the executive was approaching usurpation." Charles Sumner also expressed outrage at the proclamation, telling English liberal John Bright, "There is immense disappointment in Johnson's Proclamation for the reorganization of North Carolina, excluding colored persons. This is madness." Still, it was relatively early in the game. Most Democrats were encouraged, while moderate and conservative Republicans were willing to take a wait-and-see approach.[15]

By the end of 1865, many Republicans were increasingly nervous. Following the North Carolina model, Johnson adopted similar policies toward the former Confederate states of Mississippi, South Carolina, Florida, Georgia, Alabama, and Texas. In each case, states were to ratify the Thirteenth Amendment, repudiate Confederate debt, and nullify respective ordinances of secession. While an opponent of black suffrage, Johnson had even made a diplomatic appeal to the provisional governor of Mississippi, William L. Sharkey, on behalf of black suffrage for literate African Americans. By endorsing limited black suffrage, Johnson hoped to convince the radicals that the Southern states were on the right track. By the time Congress assembled in December, the "fruits" of Johnson's policies were apparent. South Carolina refused to repudiate Confederate debt, while Mississippi refused to ratify the Thirteenth Amendment. Both states neglected to repeal secession ordinances. Elections for representatives and senators showed continued Southern defiance. Individuals excluded from holding office under the president's proclamation were sent to Washington, perhaps the most prominent being former Vice President of the Confederacy Alexander H. Stephens. Gearing up for a potential battle, Republicans in Congress formed the Joint Committee on Reconstruction; however, instead of appointing a known opponent of Johnson such as Thaddeus Stevens as chair, Republicans chose the moderate Maine Republican William Pitt Fessenden. While disappointed with Johnson, most Republicans were still willing to reach out for compromise.[16]

Understandably, many Northerners took an unfavorable view of these developments. They seemed to indicate that the former states of the Confederacy had not accepted defeat and instead remained defiant and rebellious. Additionally, the treatment of newly emancipated African Americans concerned Northerners. In the aftermath of emancipation, many Southern states passed so-called black codes to regulate former slaves. Although a few features of the black codes were positive, providing for such things as property ownership and legal marriages, other aspects were primarily intended to control blacks and were little more than disguised slavery. The most egregious features of the codes punished vagrancy, prohibited interracial marriages, and allowed for segregation in public places. While Northerners were not particularly progressive on racial issues, as evidenced by the persistent discrimination toward African Americans living in the Northern states, many did believe that the Southern states should behave with a modicum of fairness toward former slaves. Southern stubbornness on the issue of race slowly moved Northern public opinion toward the positions endorsed by Republican radicals.[17]

In early 1866, Republican moderates tried to reach out to Johnson, looking for compromise and common ground. The president, however, was not predisposed to negotiate. A dogged fighter who had defied party leaders and powerful enemies his entire political career, Johnson lacked the capacity to compromise; he would rather hold out for what he believed was right. When it came to the issue of African American civil rights and suffrage, Johnson stuck to his Jacksonian states' rights principles, arguing that states should determine what rights blacks should have and that it was unconstitutional for the federal government to force states to adopt provisions such as black suffrage.

In February and March 1866, Illinois Senator Lyman Trumbull, chair of the Senate Judiciary Committee, lobbied Johnson to sign legislation on two separate occasions. The first measure was a bill to indefinitely extend the life of the Freedmen's Bureau, a federal agency created in 1865 to assist former slaves make the transition from slavery to freedom. Trumbull's bill would have given the bureau 3 million acres of land to redistribute to Southern blacks as well as establish military courts to ensure that the civil rights of former slaves were protected. Johnson opposed the bill on the grounds that it was special legislation for blacks and unnecessarily enhanced military power; however, when Trumbull lobbied him to sign the bill, his response was ambiguous, leading Trumbull to believe that the president would support the bill. Consequently, Johnson's veto of the bill on February 19, 1866 not only angered some of the Cabinet officers but also genuinely shocked Trumbull and many Republicans in Congress. In this instance, Republicans were not able to muster the votes to override the veto; however, the president's course of action was quickly pushing moderate Republicans into the radical camp.[18]

In an extemporaneous speech delivered to a crowd of supporters outside of the White House on February 22, 1866, Johnson vehemently denounced

Thaddeus Stevens, Charles Sumner, and the Joint Committee on Reconstruction. A few weeks later, Trumbull was promoting the Civil Rights Act of 1866, which was designed to counteract the black codes. The measure made African Americans citizens entitled to all civil rights including the right to own property, the right to make contracts, and equal access to the judicial system. Once again, on March 27, 1866, Johnson vetoed the measure stating that it was an unwarranted attack on states' rights. This time, however, both houses of Congress overrode the presidential veto, and the Civil Rights Act became law. For many in Congress, it seemed that Johnson was unwilling to compromise. "Johnson would not cooperate," historian Hans Trefousse observes, "no matter what measures Congress might devise."[19]

In order to ensure that the Civil Rights Act of 1866 could not be repealed by another Congress or diluted by a nonsupportive president, Republicans in Congress were determined to frame the major features of the bill as a constitutional amendment. The Fourteenth Amendment was the outcome. The handiwork of the powerful Joint Committee on Reconstruction, the amendment ensured that all persons born in the country or naturalized were citizens—including African Americans. As citizens, they were guaranteed equal protection under the law, and their civil rights could not be circumvented without due process of law. The amendment also deprived persons who had violated an oath to uphold the Constitution from holding any state or federal office. The legitimacy of Confederate debt was explicitly repudiated. Although black suffrage was not mandated, any state that circumscribed the rights of an adult male to vote would have its representation in Congress reduced accordingly. Hence, any seceded state that did not enfranchise adult black males would have its representation in Congress and the Electoral College reduced accordingly. The Republican Congress had announced its "terms" to the seceded states of the South. As historian Albert Castel remarks, "In effect, the amendment constituted the peace terms of the North, of Congress, and the Republican party." Unfortunately, President Johnson still stubbornly clung to a Jacksonian notion of states' rights and would not support the amendment. His course of action would become increasingly offensive to Republicans in Congress, eventually resulting in impeachment and prompting a tumultuous constitutional crisis.[20]

As previously noted, Johnson hoped to bring about a substantial political realignment, uniting conservative Republicans along with Democrats in a new party of conservatives. His plans took a major step forward on August 14, 1866, when his political advisors organized the National Union Convention in Philadelphia, popularly known as the arm-in-arm convention. Consisting of two delegates from each congressional district and U.S. territory, along with four at-large delegates, Johnson's intent was to unite conservatives across the country into a new political organization of the center. In reality, the convention was primarily Democratic and the majority of Republicans boycotted the convention, with radical Republicans concluding that the whole scheme was proof of Johnson's disloyal and traitorous intentions. The association of notorious Copperheads with the convention, such as Ohio's Clement Vallandigham and New York's Fernando Wood, seemed to prove the less than patriotic sentiments of the convention.[21]

Shortly after the arm-in-arm convention, Johnson undertook an extensive speaking campaign in an effort to defeat the radical Republicans in the fall elections. Popularly known as the "Swing round the Circle," Johnson began in upstate New York, headed west toward Chicago, then southwest to St. Louis, and then back to Washington, D.C. Throughout his political career, Johnson had thrived on making extemporaneous speeches, defying hostile audiences, and triumphing over his enemies. Despite repeated warnings from Cabinet officers and political advisors about the danger of impromptu outbursts, Johnson could not contain himself. While responding to a hostile crowd in Cleveland, Johnson denounced the Republican radicals, even suggesting that Thaddeus Stevens and Charles Sumner ought to be hanged. Scenes such as these were repeated throughout the trip, and Johnson was widely ridiculed in the press for such outbursts. In the end, the speaking trip cost Johnson politically as Republicans overwhelming swept the fall elections. Armed with an overwhelming majority in Congress, Republicans were now more than equipped to best the hostile executive.[22]

A defeated Johnson was still determined to contest Republican radicals. He hoped to hamper the radicals long enough for public opinion to reassert itself—public opinion, he believed, that would stop short of requiring the South to grant suffrage to African Americans. In his annual message delivered in early December 1866, Johnson seemed conciliatory; however, privately he conceded nothing, convinced that public opinion would eventually sustain him, not the Republican radicals.

When Southern states began rejecting the Fourteenth Amendment, Republicans, led by Thaddeus Stevens, took action. A series of military Reconstruction acts were passed in early 1867. The first was designed to establish a process for reorganizing Southern state governments. It abolished current Southern governments and divided the South into five military districts, governed by generals appointed by the president. While disenfranchising all officials who had violated an oath to uphold the Constitution, the law spelled out a process whereby states could come back into the union. District generals were to call for a convention to form new constitutions, with black males allowed to participate in the process. When Johnson predictably vetoed the measure on March 2, 1867, Republicans overrode the veto a few hours later. Eventually, three additional Military Reconstruction Acts were passed. Each was passed over a presidential veto.[23]

Along with the Military Reconstruction Acts, radical Republicans also sponsored a couple of other provisions designed to reign in executive power. The Tenure of Office Act stipulated that no official appointed with Senate approval could be removed and replaced unless the Senate concurred. This measure was widely viewed as protection for War Secretary Stanton, who had distanced himself from the president's policies; however, the measure was ambiguously worded and it was not completely clear if it applied to the current secretary of war, since Lincoln had appointed him to office. Additionally, the Army Appropriation Act specified that all of the president's orders to the army had to pass through the general-in-chief, then Ulysses S. Grant. With the South divided into military districts, it was still the president who would appoint military commanders for each district. This bill made sure that Grant, who was becoming more sympathetic to the radicals, might deter the president from issuing commands that might conflict with the wishes of Congress. The president vetoed each of these measures; however, Congress subsequently overrode each veto.

Throughout 1867, there was a small but determined minority in the Republican Party dedicated to the impeachment of the president. Radicals like Thaddeus Stevens believed the president deserved impeachment on the grounds that he was deliberately thwarting the will of the people. Stevens's argument was that impeachment was political, not judicial. Others, such as Ohio's James Ashley, were motivated by theories that bordered on the absurd. Ashley developed the novel and bizarre theory that every vice president who succeeded to the presidency must be implicated in the death of the president. Most Republicans members of Congress, however, seemed more comfortable with the judicial view of impeachment, namely, that the president ought not be impeached unless he was guilty of a high crime or misdemeanor. In early 1868, Johnson would finally present Republican radicals with a pretext for impeachment.

For well over a year, Andrew Johnson and Edwin Stanton had been at odds. The conflict between the two became a source of irritation for Johnson. When Attorney General Henry Stanbery, for instance, delivered opinions on the scope of the military Reconstruction acts, Stanton stubbornly disagreed, denying the president any real authority in Reconstruction and persistently opposing his authority to make military appointments. While the Tenure of Office Act was passed with Stanton in mind, Johnson was finally determined to get rid of his disloyal subordinate. When the president discovered that Stanton had collaborated with congressional Republicans in crafting the Third Military Reconstruction Act, he was determined to remove him from office. With Congress out of session, Johnson suspended Stanton from his position and appointed Grant as interim secretary of war on August 12, 1867. Johnson then moved against Philip Sheridan, removing the controversial general, a favorite of radical Republicans, from command of the Texas-Louisiana military district and replacing him with the more moderate George Thomas. The removal of Sheridan was followed by the removal of Carolina District Commander Daniel R. Sickles, another general Johnson felt was too committed to implementing radical policies in the Southern states.[24]

Fall electoral setbacks for the radicals emboldened Johnson. Of particular note was the unpopularity of a number of state measures for black suffrage. Despite the removal of Stanton and popular generals from office, by the end of 1867, the impeachment movement seemed to have run out of gas. In the House, the judiciary committee had finally adopted articles of impeachment by a vote of 5–4; however, the committee failed to convince the House of Representatives to endorse an impeachment effort. Consequently, the resolutions were rejected by a vote of 57–104. At this time, most Republican congressmen believed that the president, while endorsing repugnant policies, had committed no crime or misdemeanor. Although there were still ardent advocates of impeachment, the Republican majority in Congress was not yet interested in impeaching a president.

Events in early 1868 would quickly change the opinions of Republican legislators, and it was the attitude of Johnson, emboldened by his interpretation of public opinion, that would prompt these changes. In early January, interim Secretary of War Grant informed Johnson that if the Senate did not concur in the suspension of Stanton—a requirement of the Tenure of Office Act—that he would no longer serve as interim Secretary of War. Grant was worried about the legal consequences of violating the Tenure of Office Act. While Johnson did not object to Grant's future course of action, he believed that he had secured a promise from Grant to hold the war office just long enough for the president to name a new secretary of war and prevent Stanton from reoccupying the war office. According to Johnson, his principal motivation was to challenge the constitutionality of the Tenure of Office Act and get the controversy into the courts, where he believed the law would be overturned.

On January 13, the Senate passed a resolution rejecting the suspension of Stanton. On January 14, Grant returned to the War Department and turned his keys over to Acting Assistant Adjutant General E. D. Townsend. When Stanton showed up an hour later and took possession of the war office, Johnson felt that Grant had betrayed him, despite the fact that Grant had no idea that Stanton was waiting in the wings to take back the department. When Johnson subsequently removed Stanton from office on February 21, 1868, and tried to replace him with General Lorenzo Thomas, the impeachment movement was reenergized. This time it would not subside.

Following a resolution introduced by Pennsylvania radical, John Covode, on February 24, the House passed an impeachment resolution by a vote of 126–47 and a committee was chosen to draft impeachment charges. The committee was made up of Thaddeus Stevens, John J. Bingham of

Ohio, James F. Wilson of Iowa, and George Boutwell of Massachusetts. Eventually, this committee drafted eleven separate articles of impeachment. The first eight articles were essentially variations on the theme of Johnson's alleged violations of the Tenure of Office Act. The ninth article detailed Johnson's alleged attempt to subvert the Army Appropriation Act. A tenth article accused the president of attempting to discredit Congress with unflattering speeches. An eleventh article, often referred to as the omnibus provision, reiterated all of the other articles. Crafted by Thaddeus Stevens, historians generally believe it was the strongest element of a weak case.

In a dramatic scene on March 4, impeachment managers marched to the Senate where they delivered the articles of impeachment before their congressional colleagues. Each senator was then sworn in as a juror under the direction of Chief Justice Salmon Chase. Andrew Johnson was summoned to appear before the Senate for his trial on March 13. For his part, the president quickly assembled a talented and diverse legal team consisting of Attorney General Henry Stanbery, Benjamin C. Curtis, William Evarts, Thomas A. R. Nelson, Jeremiah Black, and, after the latter resigned, William Groesbeck. Because of Johnson's propensity to get carried away in public speeches and interviews, his legal advisors insisted that he give no public interviews during the impeachment trial.

The central issue of the impeachment trial was the Tenure of Office Act. It, after all, precipitated the crisis, and it was central in the articles of impeachment. Johnson's argument was that the law was unconstitutional. Although Johnson did try to remove Stanton from office, his intent was to test the constitutionality of law in the courts. As a result, Johnson's lawyers argued that the president had committed no crime. Moreover, even if the law was constitutional, Johnson and his attorneys argued that the law did not apply to Stanton because Lincoln, not Johnson, appointed him. Since Johnson had not actually removed Stanton from office, how could he be charged with violating the law? Finally, Johnson's attorneys argued that this impeachment attempt was political and not judicial. Johnson had committed no impeachable offense. Nor was Johnson's criticism of Congress an impeachable offense; on the contrary, it was simply an expression of the president's right to make political pronouncements. Hence, there was no plausible reason to remove the president from office.[25]

In a trial that lasted a full forty-five days, Johnson also made a number of moves behind the scenes to placate moderate Republicans who did not really want to vote for conviction. First, there was the nomination of Major General John Schofield as secretary of war, something that appealed to the moderate Republicans. Second, Johnson reached out to critical senators whose votes were pivotal in procuring an acquittal. One such senator was Edmund G. Ross of Kansas. Ross promised a vote to acquit if Johnson were to submit to Congress new state constitutions for South Carolina and Arkansas.[26]

After John J. Bingham presented the concluding argument before the Senate on May 7, the Senate voted on May 16. Since there was great doubt about the eventual outcome, proponents of impeachment conducted a frantic campaign in the last days to gather votes, exerting a great amount of pressure on so-called moderate senators such as William Pitt Fessenden of Maine, James Grimes of Iowa, Lyman Trumbull of Illinois, and Ross. Votes were to be taken on each article of impeachment, and the first article voted on was the eleventh article. The Senate voted 35–19; Johnson escaped conviction and removal by a single vote. And so it was on every subsequent vote until, after the vote on the fifth article, a motion was made to dismiss the case. Johnson had survived the impeachment crisis and would finish out his term of office.

While some scholars focus on the importance of the Ross vote, historians such as Hans L. Trefousse argue that any number of moderate Republicans were ready to change their vote in order to acquit the president. As before, many moderate Republicans felt that Johnson's actions and policies, while politically repugnant, did not rise to the level of impeachable offenses. Undoubtedly another principal reason for opposition to a vote of conviction was their fear of a Ben Wade presidency. As president pro tempore of the Senate, Wade was next in the line of presidential succession. Throughout the years, Wade had made numerous enemies, and his radical positions on such issues as labor and women's rights genuinely concerned some moderates. Finally, many Republicans felt that the removal of Johnson from office would have a negative effect on financial markets as well as the nation's morale.

Once acquitted, Andrew Johnson still had several months left in office. Some radicals continued to stir the impeachment pot; however, most Republicans in Congress were content to let the seventeenth president finish out his term without incident. Johnson, however, still had ambitions of outright election to the presidency in 1868 and actively sought the Democratic presidential nomination. A presidential amnesty proclamation in the summer of 1868 was intended to gain favor with the Democratic Party in the South; however, it was in the North where Johnson needed support. In order to curry favor with Democratic leaders, Johnson was expected to jettison William H. Seward and Treasury Secretary Hugh McCulloch, both offensive to many Democrats. When Johnson refused to dismiss two loyal subordinates, his chances for the nomination were gone and it was instead given to former New York governor Horatio Seymour.

Johnson spent his remaining time in office trying to curb what he considered Republican excesses; however, his vetoes continued to be overridden and the Republican Congress used the Tenure of Office Act to inhibit his powers of patronage. The election of Grant to the presidency later that year was difficult to swallow. Bitter rivals, the popular general had now bested his former boss. Adding insult to injury, Grant refused to pick up the outgoing president in his carriage for the inauguration day ceremony, breaking with tradition.

After residing briefly at the home of John Coyle, the owner of the *National Intelligencer*, Johnson returned to his Greeneville, Tennessee, home. Tragedy soon struck as his eldest son, Robert, committed suicide after a long battle with alcoholism. Despite this tragedy, the former president was still consumed by ambition and was determined to return to Washington, D.C., as an U.S. senator. With numerous opponents in the state legislature, Johnson was initially thwarted in his attempt to gain a seat. He was undeterred. After he survived a cholera attack in 1873, the following year the term of his bitter opponent, Parson Brownlow expired. This time Johnson prevailed and was elected to the Senate on January 5, 1875, on the fifty-fourth ballot. It was sweet revenge.

Johnson returned to Washington a few months later in March, and on March 22 took the floor to denounce President Grant for his Reconstruction policies in the South. Johnson's triumph, however, would prove short-lived. On the way home from Washington that summer, Johnson traveled to the home of his eldest daughter in Carter's Station, Tennessee, when he suffered a paralytic stroke. Just a scant two days later, the seventeenth president passed away. Wrapped in a U.S. flag with a copy of the Constitution in his coffin, the last Jacksonian was buried in Greeneville, Tennessee.

PRINCIPAL IDEAS

The Jacksonian Persuasion

Historian Kenneth Stampp has described Andrew Johnson as the "last Jacksonian Democrat." Indeed, from his earliest involvement in political affairs, Johnson espoused Jacksonian principles and beliefs that he carried with him throughout his political career. At the core of his belief system was a commitment to the sanctity of the common person and a refusal to endorse any belief or measure that hinted at privilege or an unfair advantage based on wealth or some other unnatural distinction. "I am a mechanic, *a plebian mechanic*," Johnson told one correspondent during his tenure as governor of Tennessee. He was "not ashamed nor afraid to own it, in or out of office; but on the contrary feel proud that it is so, and never recur to the period when I was an indentured apprentice, a journeyman, and then the proprietor of my own shop."[27]

Johnson consistently endorsed positions throughout his political career that sought to spread democratic principles and advanced the Jacksonian agenda as opposed to the principles of the Whig Party. For instance, early in the 1830s, he advocated the abolition of the Electoral College and the direct election of senators. He opposed the protective tariff on the grounds that it unfairly robbed the working classes of money for the benefit of an elite business class. A persistent theme throughout Johnson's political career was the notion of limited government. In no area did Johnson more consistently apply this principle than when public expenditures were involved. A vigilant steward of the people's money, Johnson time and again spoke for economy in expenditure and frugality in government. Johnson, for instance, objected to public expenditures for the pavement of Washington, D.C., streets. Part of his objection was based on constitutional grounds, but he also was concerned lest the central government have too much power to deprive the people of money. Johnson insisted that public expenditures be rigorously justified to the people. When the government paid for the funeral expenses of John Quincy Adams, Johnson introduced an amendment requiring an explanation of all expenses. "The great mass of the people," he told the House, ". . . ought to be informed how their money was appropriated."[28]

For Johnson, the quintessential example of his commitment to Jacksonian principles was his long-term sponsorship of homestead legislation. While many politicians in the South opposed homestead legislation, Johnson consistently endorsed the principle and saw it as a logical extension of his Jacksonian commitment to common folk. As a member of the House of Representatives, Johnson first introduced homestead legislation into Congress in 1846. Although he was ultimately unsuccessful in getting a bill signed by the president, Johnson worked on this provision as a legislator from 1846 to 1851 and then as a U.S. senator from 1857 until the coming of Civil War. Although his bill went through various renditions with numerous amendments, the essential features would provide 160 acres to qualified heads of family who were naturalized citizens and would make a commitment to live on the property for at least five years.

As previously mentioned, Johnson was repeatedly attacked by Southern congressmen for this measure, which was seen as potentially dangerous to slavery because it would people the western territories with small farmers of Free Soil proclivities. Johnson saw the measure as a way to elevate ordinary Americans. "You have granted an immense amount of land to railroads on this principle, and now why do not do something for the people?" Johnson reasoned with fellow senators. For Johnson, the measure was far from a giveaway program. Instead, by encouraging the cultivation of the vacant land, the measure would stimulate commerce and enterprise, swelling public coffers rather than draining them. "He is enabled to buy more land than he was before," Johnson asserted, referring to the homesteader, "and thus he contributes more to the support of his Government." To the argument that Free Soil legislation was an inherently Republican provision, Johnson saw no inconsistency in small Southern slaveholders immigrating into the territories and transplanting the peculiar institution alongside them.[29]

Slavery and Race

Johnson's thinking on slavery and race was typically Southern, and he took great pains during his political career prior to the war to remain orthodox on the slavery issue. Growing up in North Carolina and Tennessee, he was conscious of his own modest social standing. At the same time, he no doubt took comfort in the fact that he was not at the bottom rung of the social scale. Though he owned slaves, Johnson never had an enormous financial stake in the peculiar institution. He always maintained a belief that African Americans were innately inferior to whites. Even after his conversion to an antislavery position during the war, his belief in innate black inferiority would dominate his postwar views on race relations and help poison his relationship with congressional Republicans. As a Southern representative to Congress, Johnson was always eager to establish his orthodoxy on the slavery issue.

In defending the peculiar institution, Johnson employed arguments that were popular among many Southern apologists for slavery. One such argument held that slaves in the United States were far better off than in their native continent of Africa. During a stump speech at Raleigh, Tennessee, Johnson asserted that "the negro here in the state of slavery [is] in a far better condition than the native African at home." Johnson also maintained, like other Southern apologists, that the real warfare existed in the North between capital and labor. "Capital at the North is the oppressor of the laboring man," Johnson told the Senate. "There is where the oppression is; there is where the irrepressible conflict exists. It is between the dollars and cents of the North and the free labor of the North, not between slave labor and free labor." Chiding Republicans such as Illinois' Lyman Trumbull for hypocrisy in the way Trumbull's own state of Illinois discriminated against free blacks, Johnson argued that the Founding Fathers had in no way intended the Declaration of Independence to include slaves.[30]

Unlike Southern fire-eaters, however, Johnson did not embrace the position that the federal government was obligated to protect slavery in federal territories. Despite supporting Breckinridge for president in 1860, Johnson's position on the important issue of slavery in the territories was similar to that of Northern Democratic leader Stephen A. Douglas. "My position is that Congress has no power to interfere with the subject of slavery," Johnson told one audience, "that it is an institution local in its character and peculiar to the States where it exists and no other power has the right to control it." Johnson resented Republicans because they would not only exclude slavery from the territories but would also eventually attempt to exclude it from states altogether. "They now Seemingly [sic] confine their intentions to excluding Slavery from the Territories merely; but once successful, they Cannot, and will not stop at the Territories, but will be pressed into the States." At the same time, Johnson believed that the position of Southern fire-eaters was too extreme and controversial. Instead, it would do well to simply allow the people to decide whether they would or would not have slavery. "It is for the people and not the Congress of the United States to decide," Johnson told his Senate colleagues. For Johnson, as for Douglas, the nation could exist half free and half slave. To break up the Union for either the defense of slavery or its abolition made little sense.[31]

Reconstruction

"General, there is no such thing as reconstruction," Johnson told John A. Logan in an interview in May 1865. "These states have not gone out of the Union, therefore, reconstruction is unnecessary." This simple statement provides the pivotal clue to understanding the debate over Reconstruction between Andrew Johnson and his Republican antagonists. What confused many Republican radicals were the numerous statements Johnson made at the end of the war that suggested a desire to impose a punishing peace on the rebellious states. "But, I say treason is a crime—the highest crime known to the law," Johnson told a delegation of Pennsylvanians led by Simon Cameron. The pivotal mistake here was to interpret Johnson's heartfelt desire to punish some of the principal leaders of the rebellion as a desire to affect a radical social and political revolution in the South—something that offended the conservative, Jacksonian instincts of the president. Throughout the struggle over Reconstruction, Johnson believed that he represented the views of Lincoln. "The Executive (my predecessor as well as myself) and the heads of all the Departments have uniformly acted upon the principle that the Union is not only undissolved, but indissoluble."[32]

Many Republicans mistook Johnson's transformation on the emancipation issue during the war as an indication that he might be willing to entertain basic social and political rights for newly freed slaves, perhaps even suffrage. In reality, Johnson's views of African Americans had changed little even after his commitment to emancipation. He continued to view blacks as inferior, childlike, and incapable of self-government. Nor did he envision a major federal commitment to former slaves. As he told one delegation of black ministers, "I want to impress this upon you[r] minds, that freedom simply means liberty to work and enjoy the product of your own hands." When Johnson received numerous reports from the South that freedom was often interpreted as freedom from work, this reinforced deeply held opinions concerning black indolence and slothfulness. In his view, any attempt to empower African Americans with the vote universally was foolish and doomed to failure. "But if anything can be proved by known facts, if all reasoning upon evidence is not abandoned," Johnson told Congress, "it must be acknowledged that in the progress of nations Negroes have shown less capacity for government than any race of people. No independent government of any form has ever been successful in their hand."[33]

While Johnson's decision not to compromise with congressional Republicans was shortsighted and ultimately led to the impeachment controversy, his decision to use the office of the presidency to thwart congressional Reconstruction was sound from a constitutional standpoint, even if foolish from a practice and ethical perspective. For Johnson, the Military Reconstruction Acts were blatantly unconstitutional. "I would be unfaithful to my duty if I did not recommend the repeal of the acts of Congress which place the Southern states under the domination of military masters." According to Johnson, many acts of Congress were intended to limit executive prerogative and power; they had to be resisted for the good of the office and the country. The Tenure of Office Act was one example; another was the Command of Army Act. When Johnson removed generals from command of the military districts of the South, he did so at great risk to himself. Accused of deliberately obstructing congressional reconstruction, the president replied to his critics by asserting that he was merely exercising executive prerogatives. The failure of the Senate to convict him during the impeachment trial demonstrated the strength of Johnson's argument from a constitutional standpoint.[34]

CONCLUSION

Andrew Johnson's rise to the presidency was one of the greatest success stories in American history, but also one of the greatest tragedies. While Johnson's succession to the presidency was greeted with enthusiasm and optimism, he left office with the mark of impeachment upon him. Indeed, historians generally regard his presidency as an out-and-out failure. When he returned to Greeneville, Tennessee, in 1869, he was something of a political pariah. Republicans understandably hated him; however, even Democrats were not eager to embrace him and, accordingly, passed him over for Horatio Seymour as their standard bearer in 1868.

Historians are more supportive of Johnson's forceful defense of constitutional prerogatives during his presidency. The seventeenth president surely was within his constitutional rights to assert and use the powers of his office. Similarly, the majority of historians also believe that the impeachment case against Johnson was weak. It was purely political, for the president had not taken a bribe nor committed a high crime or misdemeanor. Unfortunately, that is not the entire story, for it overlooks what Johnson did to provoke the Republican Congress in the first place. His refusal to compromise on any positive measure for the advancement of African Americans beyond the Thirteenth Amendment did major damage to the nation and his presidency. His vetoes of both the Civil Rights Act of 1866 and the extension of the Freedmen's Bureau, which were not the extreme measures of Radical Republicans hell-bent of social revolution but simply sensible, just, and equitable measures that probably met with the wishes of most Northerners, were ill-timed. The fact that Johnson may have been on strong constitutional ground during the impeachment crisis does not excuse his earlier behavior. In a very real sense, Johnson brought impeachment upon himself. Failure to compromise with political opponents ruined what could have been a magnificent presidency.

NOTES

1. Mary Johnson committed Johnson to Selby in 1818; however, the actual indenture was not filed until February 18, 1822. See "Indenture to James J. Selby," February 18, 1822, in *The Papers of Andrew Johnson, Volume 1, 1822–1851*, ed. Leroy P. Graf and Ralph W. Haskins (Knoxville: University of Tennessee Press, 1967), 1:3.

2. "Notice of Runaway Apprentices," June 24, 1824, in *Papers of Andrew Johnson*, 1:3–4 (quote, 3).

3. Johnson to George W. Jones, December 25, 1836, in *Papers of Andrew Johnson*, 1:18.

4. William G. Brownlow to Johnson, [December 13, 1843], *Papers of Andrew Johnson*, 1:122–30 (quote, 123). For more information on Brownlow, see E. Merton Coulter, *William G. Brownlow: Fighting Parson of the Southern Highlands* (Knoxville: University of Tennessee Press, 1937).

5. See, for instance, Johnson to Robert B. Reynolds, September 9, 1843, in ibid., 121.

6. "Speech on Secession," December 18–19, in *Papers of Andrew Johnson*, 3:3–51 (quoted materials, 9, 22).

7. Johnson to Sam Milligan, January 13 [1861], in *Papers of Andrew Johnson*, 3:164. On the Crittenden Compromise, see Brian Holden Reid, *The Origins of the American Civil War* (London: Longman, 1996), 280–81, 288–92.

8. Conflict in east Tennessee during the Civil War is discussed extensively in Noel C. Fisher, *War at Every Door: Partisan Politics and Guerrilla Violence in East Tennessee 1860–1869* (Chapel Hill: University of North Carolina Press, 1997). Also see Noel C. Fisher, "Definitions of Victory: East Tennessee Unionists in the Civil War and Reconstruction," in *Guerrillas, Unionists, and Violene on the Confederate Home Front*, ed. Daniel E. Sutherland (Fayetteville: University of Arkansas Press, 1999), 89–112.

9. For Johnson participation in committee work, see Bruce Tap, *Over Lincoln's Shoulder: The Committee on the Conduct of the War* (Lawrence: University Press of Kansas, 1998). See also T. Harry Williams, "Andrew Johnson as a Member of the Joint Committee on the Conduct of the War," *East Tennessee Historical Publications* 12 (1940): 70–83.

10. Some of the issues that affected both Johnson and Lincoln with respect to wartime reconstruction are discussed in William C. Harris, *With Charity for All: Lincoln and the Restoration of the Union* (Lexington: University of Kentucky Press, 1997), 40–46, 50–53.

11. Probably the single best source on this controversy is Don E. Fehrenbacher, "The Making of a Myth: Lincoln and the Vice-Presidential Nomination in 1864," *Civil War History* 41 (December 1995): 273–90.

12. Lincoln comment quoted from David Herbert Donald, *Lincoln* (New York: Simon & Schuster, 1995), 565. Charles Sumner was one Republican who hoped that Johnson would resign. For his response to Johnson's inaugural speech, see David Donald, *Charles Sumner and the Rights of Man* (New York: Alfred A. Knopf, 1970), 218–19.

13. Wade quoted in Tap, *Over Lincoln's Shoulder,* 243.

14. Brooks Simpson, *The Reconstruction Presidents* (Lawrence: University Press of Kansas, 1998), 72.

15. Thaddeus Stevens to Johnson, May 16, 1865, *Papers of Andrew Johnson,* 8:80–81 (quote, 80); and Charles Sumner to John Bright, June 5, 1865, *The Selected Letters of Charles Sumner,* ed. Beverly Wilson Palmer (Boston: Northeastern University Press, 1990), 2:303–5 (quote, 303).

16. On the Joint Committee on Reconstruction, see Eric Foner, *Reconstruction: America's Unfinished Revolution, 1863–1877* (New York: Harper & Row, 1988), 239.

17. On black codes, see for instance, James McPherson, *Ordeal by Fire: The Civil War and Reconstruction* (New York: Alfred A. Knopf, 1982), 511–12; and Eric Foner, *Reconstruction,* 199–201, 208–9.

18. For a concise summary of the Freedmen's Bureau extension, see Albert Castel and Scott L. Gibson, *The Yeas and the Nays: Key Congressional Decisions 1774–1945* (Kalamazoo, MI: New Issues Press, 1975), 83–84.

19. Castel and Gibson, *The Yeas and the Nays,* 84–85; McPherson, *Ordeal by Fire,* 515–16; and Hans L. Trefousse, *Impeachment of a President: Andrew Johnson, the Blacks, and Reconstruction* (Knoxville: University of Tennessee Press, 1975), 42. The veto of the civil rights act was the first presidential veto ever to be overridden.

20. Albert Castel, *The Presidency of Andrew Johnson* (Lawrence: Regents Press of Kansas, 1979), 74. On the Fourteenth Amendment, also see McPherson, *Ordeal by Fire,* 516–18.

21. Those who praised the convention were markedly conservative, such as Secretary of the Interior, Orville Hickman Browning, who had earlier praised Johnson for his vetoes of the Freedmen's Bureau extension as well as the Civil Rights Act of 1866. See *The Diary of Orville Hickman Browning,* ed. James G. Randall and Theodore C. Pease (Springfield: Illinois State Historical Library, 1925), 2:62–63, 68–69, 89–90.

22. Foner, *Reconstruction,* 261–71; and Castel, *Presidency of Andrew Johnson,* 90–95.

23. James McPherson, *Ordeal by Fire,* 521–24, 527–28, 538.

24. Johnson suspended Stanton because, under the Tenure of Office Act, he could not remove the controversial secretary of war, without Senate approval. See *Diary of Orville Hickman Browning,* 2:154–56.

25. This summary is largely from Castel, *The Presidency of Andrew Johnson,* 185–86.

26. The Republican senator from Ohio was president pro tempore of the Senate and, in the absence of a sitting vice president, was next in line for the presidency.

For more on Wade, see Hans Trefousse, *Benjamin F. Wade: Radical Republican from Ohio* (New York: Twayne Publishing, 1963), 274–301.

27. Kenneth Stampp, *The Era of Reconstruction: 1865–1877* (New York: Alfred A. Knopf, 1965), 54–55; and Johnson to William W. Peppers, July 17, 1854, in *Papers of Andrew Johnson,* 2:237.

28. See, for instance, "Speech Opposing an Increase in Federal Clerks," January 24, 1848, in *Johnson Papers,* 1:400–3; "Remarks Opposing an Appropriation to Pave Washington Streets," July 17, 1848, in *Johnson Papers,* 441–44; and "Amendment on Funeral Expenses of John Quincy Adams, June 20, 1848, in *Johnson Papers,* 1:440 (quote).

29. "Speech on Homestead Bill," May 20, 1858, in *Papers of Andrew Johnson,* 3:138–39. See also the following passages in the *Papers of Andrew Johnson,* "Speech on Homestead Bill, July 25, 1850, 2:557–72 (both clerk and appendix versions), and "Remarks on the Homestead Bill," January 23, 1851, 2:598–600, 608–10. See also Andrew Johnson to Horace Greeley, December 15, 1861, in *Papers of Andrew Johnson,* 2:631–33.

30. "Speech at Raleigh, Tennessee, July 24, 1857, *Papers of Andrew Johnson,* 2:477; "Speech on Harper's Ferry Incident, December 12, 1859, *Papers of Andrew Johnson,* 318–52 (quote, 335).

31. "Speech at Evans' Crossroads, Greene County," May 26, 1849, in *Papers of Andrew Johnson,* 1:500; Johnson to Sam Milligan, November 23, 1856, in *Papers of Andrew Johnson,* 2:452; and "Speech on Popular Sovereignty and the Right of Instruction," February 23, 1858, 3:43–73 (quote, 56). On Johnson's opposition to the position of the fire eaters, see, for instance, Johnson to George W. Jones, March 13, 1860, in *Papers of Andrew Johnson,* 3:466–68.

32. "Interview with John A. Logan," May 31, 1865, in *Papers of Andrew Johnson,* 8:154; "Interview with Pennsylvania Delegation," May 3, 1865, in *Papers of Andrew Johnson,* 8:21–23 (quote, 21); and "Third Annual Message," December 3, 1867, in *Papers of Andrew Johnson,* 13:282.

33. "Reply to Delegation of Black Ministers," May 11, 1865, in *Papers of Andrew Johnson,* 8:61–63 (quote, 62); John Martin to Johnson, May 28, 1865, in *Papers of Andrew Johnson,* 8:125–26; and "Third Annual Message," December 3, 1867, in *Papers of Andrew Johnson,* 14:286–87 (quote, 287).

34. "Third Annual Message," December 3, 1867, in *Papers of Andrew Johnson,* 14:280–306 (quote, 284); and "Interview with the Cincinnati *Commercial* Correspondent," December 31, 1867, in *Papers of Andrew Johnson,* 14:392–99 (the correspondent was Joseph McCullough).

FURTHER READING

Michael Les Benedict, *The Impeachment and Trial of Andrew Johnson* (New York: W. W. Norton, 1973); Albert Castel, "Andrew Johnson." In Henry F. Graff, ed. *The Presidents in American History* (New York: Charles Scribner's Sons, 1984); idem., *The Presidency of Andrew Johnson* (Lawrence: Regents Press of Kansas, 1979); Eric L. McKitrick, *Andrew Johnson and Reconstruction* (Chicago: University of Chicago Press, 1960); George Fort Milton, *The Age of Hate: Andrew John-*

son and the Radicals (New York: Coward, McCann, 1930); Brooks Simpson, *The Reconstruction Presidents* (Lawrence: University Press of Kansas, 1998); Hans Trefousse, *Andrew Johnson: A Biography* (New York: W.W. Norton & Company, 1989); and idem., *Impeachment of a President: Andrew Johnson, the Blacks, and Reconstruction* (Knoxville: University of Tennessee Press, 1975).

ROBERT E. LEE
(1807–1870)

Duty and Stoicism

LIFE

Robert Edward Lee was born on January 19, 1807, at Stratford Hall in Westmoreland County, Virginia, the fourth child of parents Henry Lee and Ann Hill Carter Lee. Lee's father was the famed "Light-Horse Harry," who had led slashing cavalry raids against the British during the American Revolution. Harry Lee and Ann had five children, and Lee had three children from a former marriage. Robert E. Lee was born into a socially prominent family in Virginia society with an extended kinship network. Unfortunately, a cloud of disgrace hung over the Lee family because of the actions of Lee's father and half-brother. Harry Lee, the dashing cavalry commander of the Revolution, was a spectacularly unsuccessful speculator. He had married Matilda Lee, a second cousin, in 1782; they had three children before her early death in 1790. Lee had squandered much of the property his first wife brought to the marriage, so much so that as Matilda lay dying after the birth of her last child, she altered her will to place her remaining property in a trust beyond her husband's control. Lee went on to court and win Ann Hill Carter, daughter of Charles Carter, a prominent and wealthy figure and the owner of the magnificent Shirley estate. Carter was against the marriage but eventually gave his reluctant consent. After marrying Ann on June 18, 1793, Lee continued his profligate and disastrous speculations until creditors and process servers constantly hounded him. Lee even gave his former commander, George Washington, a bogus note in repayment of a debt.

Lee became governor of Virginia, but the Virginia legislature ousted him in 1794 for leading the state militia to Pennsylvania to suppress the Whiskey Rebellion. He served in Congress, and then soon lost his seat after taking "loans" from the Spanish government. Convinced that the Jeffersonians were to blame for his misfortunes, Lee wrote violent screeds condemning Thomas Jefferson. In 1809, he was imprisoned for debt. After his release, he was savagely beaten in Baltimore while personally defending an antiwar editor from a mob. His health broken, Lee left his wife and children, by then living in Alexandria, Virginia, and sailed to self-imposed exile in the Caribbean. He died en route back to the United States in 1818 and was buried on Cumberland Island off the Georgia coast. In a society that valued personal honor, which was in essence an individual's community standing, Harry Lee's disgrace was complete.

His son Henry, his child by his first wife Matilda, inherited his late mother's Stratford estate in 1808 and his father's poor judgment. Henry married Anne McCarty and subsequently accepted the role of guardian to Anne's younger sister Elizabeth, or Betsy. When their young daughter was killed in a tragic accident, both Anne and Henry chose to cope with their grief in destructive ways. Anne became an opium addict. Henry seduced his ward and sister-in-law Betsy. She was "ruined" in polite society and fled back to her mortified family. They in turn sued Lee for the return of funds Betsy had entrusted to him as her guardian. His father's son, Henry had squandered them. Forced to sell Stratford to pay the debt, "Black Horse Harry," as Henry came to be known, was soon as penniless and disgraced as his father had been.

This grim legacy haunted Robert E. Lee for his adult life. It hung over him like a dark cloud, a constant reminder of what fate had in store should he violate the honor code and the duties and obligations of a gentleman. Fortunately, Lee's mother was a formidable woman. Ann Carter Lee raised five children and got them off to decent beginnings in life with little assistance from her wastrel husband. In 1810, Ann had moved to Alexandria, Virginia, and it was here that Robert grew to young manhood. Ann was able to support the family from a trust fund her father set up on her behalf prior to his death. She was a devout Christian; when her eldest son Carter went off to Harvard, Ann sent him letters adjuring him to pray for faith in Jesus Christ as his sole salvation. She held up George Washington as a moral exemplar and urged her boys to emulate his example of probity and dignity.

Robert appears, in every account, as a good boy. His father abandoned the family when he was six years old. His mother took him in hand, and Lee was educated at Eastern View in Fauquier County, and at the Alexandria Academy. The Alexandria area included many Carter and Lee relatives, and Robert often followed his mother on visits to the homes of extended family members. He was a shy fellow, perhaps uncomfortable with the necessity of repeatedly adjusting to unfamiliar surroundings and people. However, he was not disconsolate, but was happy and cheerful with family and close friends. Lee had to grow up quickly. His mother's health began to falter, perhaps because of progressive tuberculosis. Lee had to take care of her and the household as a young teen, including overseeing the household slaves. With no patrimonial inheritance or guidance, Lee gravitated to a military career. He won an appointment to West Point in 1824 after a personal interview with the stern John C. Calhoun, then secretary of war. Lee entered the academy in June 1825.

With his father's dissolute life as a constant warning of the consequences of bad behavior, and his mother's example of dignity and religious devotion in the face of adversity, Lee compiled an exemplary record as a cadet. He adapted to the harsh discipline and spartan accommodations of the academy. At an age when many young people are inclined to flout rules and rebel against authority, Lee completed his four years without a single demerit. He also demonstrated mathematical ability at what was essentially an engineering school. He was even appointed to be a tutor and acting assistant professor. Lee graduated second in his class in 1829 and was given his brevet second lieutenant commission in the Corps of Engineers. Lee would spend the bulk of his more than thirty-year military career as an engineer.

After graduation, Lee returned home to his ailing mother. As she aged, Ann spent much time at the beautiful Ravensworth estate, owned by William Fitzhugh. She died there of tuberculosis on July 26, 1829. Having lost his mother, Lee was in the process of acquiring a wife. The Lee family had on occasion visited the Arlington estate owned by George Washington Parke Custis, an eccentric grandson of George and Martha Washington. Lee had visited the estate while on furlough in 1827 and had enjoyed the company of Custis's only child, Mary. Now, in the summer of 1829, Lee returned to Mary, and the relationship began to ripen into more than simple friendship. Lee eventually married Mary Parke Custis in Alexandria on June 30, 1831. They had seven children: George Washington (1832), Mary Custis (1835), William Henry Fitzhugh (1837), Anne (1839), Agnes (1841), Robert Edward Jr. (1843), and Mildred (1846).

Marriage united Lee with an illustrious family linked to George Washington. G. W. Parke Custis was Washington's adopted grandson, and he turned his Arlington mansion into a shrine to the general's memory. It was filled with old tents, sabers, clothing, china, and other bits of Washington memorabilia. Lee's mother had held up Washington as a man worth emulating; now Lee was marrying a Washington descendant. He had tied himself to a more illustrious lineage than the darkened shadows of the Lee family. Yet, his choice of wife could not have been more different from him on a personal level. Lee was stoic and frugal, religious but not a church member until his forties, reserved, even shy, but a young man who enjoyed the company of pretty women. He had an immense capacity for self-denial and self-discipline. By contrast, Mary Parke Custis was the spoiled only child of doting parents who lavished attention on her. She tended to self-absorption and self-pity, and she was neither a good housekeeper nor particularly industrious. She had a religious epiphany in 1830, brought on characteristically after she felt guilty for her selfish worrying that the death of an uncle would compel her to wear mourning clothing during the social season. She became aggressively devout and hectored Lee on the necessity of saving his soul. She was inclined to nag and, indeed, rebuked Lee at table for his tardiness to dinner immediately prior to his fatal stroke in 1870. She only reluctantly left Arlington for stints with Lee at his duty stations, fleeing back to the estate as soon as she could. To all intents, it continued to be her home residence throughout her marriage until she was forced to abandon it to Union troops in 1861.

Lee began his professional life with the Corps of Engineers. It is notable that, except for a brief sojourn in command of cavalry in Texas, Lee worked as an engineering officer for his entire military career. He was typically assigned to build or strengthen forts and fortifications. His first assignment was to Cockspur Island at the mouth of the Savannah River, where Lee tried to drain the marshes so a fort could be constructed. He labored at Fort Monroe at Old Point, Virginia (1831–1834); served a stint in Washington, D.C., as a staff officer (1834–1837); then went to St. Louis, Missouri (1837–1840), to improve the navigation of the Mississippi River. That assignment was followed by duty at Fort Hamilton, New York (1840–1846), before the Mexican War intervened. Lee established a reputation for professional competence and reliability. His work on the Mississippi River, where he saved the port of St. Louis from a sandbar, was particularly well done. He chafed on occasion at the dullness of routine garrison duty and the glacial pace of the army's promotions. He contemplated leaving the service, as other engineering officers had done, but remained in uniform. Lee may have been hesitant to leave the army because to do so was to embark on a kind of speculative, get-rich-quick adventure. Changing careers from the staid army to something flashy and profitable, like working for the newfangled railroad, may have struck Lee as precisely the path his ne'er-do-well father would have taken. Lee always avoided his father's disastrous habits.

Service in the Mexican War marked a dramatic departure from Lee's typical routine. His subsequent war record established him as one of the army's best officers, bringing the notice and patronage of its legendary commander-in-chief, Winfield Scott. Lee was first assigned to General John Wool's army, which marched from Texas into Mexico in the fall of 1846. As an engineering officer, Lee was supposed to improve roads and bridge rivers. But there were few maps of the Mexican interior, so Lee and other engineers became scouts, forging ahead of the army to find the best route of march to the day's objective. His duties brought him into regular contact with general officers and, indeed, made him a crucial advisor at command level.

In January 1847, Lee was ordered to join Winfield Scott's staff. Scott was gathering an army to invade the Mexican interior and capture the capital,

Mexico City. Lee landed with Scott's army at Veracruz on March 10, 1847, and helped place artillery that quickly battered the city into submission. Lee then scouted ahead of the army on its march to Mexico City. Finding Mexican forces blocking the national road, Lee found a route for an attack on the Mexican flank and rear. Scott ordered an attack based on Lee's reports, and ordered Lee to guide the American force. The ensuing battle resulted in victory at Cerro Gordo in April 1847, earning Lee brevet promotion to major for his gallantry and efficiency.

After Cerro Gordo, there was a lull in fighting during which Lee prepared accurate maps at Scott's order to be used in the assault on Mexico City. With the road into the capital strongly defended, Scott again employed Lee to find a way around the fortified positions. Lee found favorable paths for attacking forces that led to victories at Contreras and Churubusco. For those exploits, Lee received another brevet promotion to lieutenant colonel. Lee then provided crucial intelligence that helped defeat the Chapultepec fortress and worked to place artillery to force the gates of Mexico City, finally collapsing from exhaustion and a minor wound. Lee was awarded a third brevet promotion to colonel for his last exploit. Throughout the successful campaign, Scott mentioned Lee in dispatches, complimenting him for intelligence, energy, and courage.

Serving with Scott was Lee's professional training in how to manage an army and conduct a campaign. A brilliant officer, Scott maneuvered his outnumbered force around fortifications and obstacles, staying on the offensive to keep the initiative. He lectured his staff officers on strategy and tactics at dinners in his quarters. He recognized Lee's talents and considered him the finest officer in the army. Lee learned those lessons, and he also came to the self-realization that he was a skilled soldier capable of forming quick and accurate judgments of terrain and the employment of troops.

Still, Lee's Mexican tour ended on a sour note as the conquering army's officer corps bickered over credit or blame for the success of the campaign. Lee was forced to testify before Courts of Inquiry called to adjudicate disputes. He had hoped that his exploits would earn him promotion and important duties, but 1848 found him back in the United States assigned to Baltimore and the construction of another fort. Four years later, Lee became superintendent of West Point, an assignment he resisted as not to his taste. In 1855, Lee was appointed second in command of the Second Cavalry, which was stationed in Texas. He remained in command in the field until the secession crisis called him back to Washington in 1861. He took an extended leave in 1857 when his father-in-law died and Lee was obliged to help settle the estate. While on leave in 1859, Lee led the force that crushed John Brown's raid on Harpers Ferry, an event that hardened sectional animosity between North and South.

The breaking point for Virginia came in April 1861. Recalled to Washington, Lee told friends and colleagues that he was a strong supporter of the Union but could never raise his hand against "his country," by which he meant Virginia. Both Winfield Scott and Francis P. Blair Sr. offered Lee command of the Union Army, but he refused. When a Virginia convention voted to adopt a secession resolution, Lee resigned his commission with a heavy heart. As he explained, "With all my devotion to the Union, and the feeling of loyalty and duty of an American citizen, I have not been able to make up my mind to raise my hand against my relatives, my children, my home." He was summoned to Richmond and given command of Virginia's armed forces, at which he remained until those forces were absorbed into the Confederate Army. He became an administrative staff officer to Jefferson Davis, the Confederate president, a role he wished to leave for field duty.[1]

Lee believed the war would be long and bloody, and his candor about his views gave him a gloomy cast that was unpopular in the euphoria of the early days of secession. It was commonly believed that the South would easily and quickly defeat the North and win independence. Victory at Bull Run in July 1861 seemed confirmation of the correctness of those attitudes. Soon after Bull Run, Lee left Richmond for western Virginia. Confederate forces had suffered a series of reverses at the hands of Union forces under George B. McClellan. Jefferson Davis ordered Lee to organize disparate Confederate armies in the region to fight in a coordinated fashion. Lee struggled in the assignment; he lacked clear authority and gave orders more in the nature of suggestions. Characteristically, Lee would not provoke a personal confrontation. When the campaign ended on an inconclusive note, Richmond newspapers criticized Lee for lack of daring. He was "Granny Lee," too much the patrician to stomach the bloody work of killing Yankees. In November 1861, Lee was sent to the Carolina coast to shore up coastal defenses. Again, the nature of the task, building fortifications, obstructing rivers, and consolidating lines of defense that involved abandoning offshore islands with profitable plantations and influential owners, necessarily entailed unpopular decisions. Luckily, Lee had the consistent support of Jefferson Davis, who brought Lee back to Richmond in March 1862.

That spring, George B. McClellan moved the massive Army of the Potomac to the peninsula between the York and the James Rivers just east of Richmond. Confederate forces under command of Lee's West Point classmate, Joseph Johnston, opposed him. In May 1862, Johnston conducted a fighting withdrawal of his forces in the face of McClellan's horde. Just as it appeared that Johnston would be forced into the Richmond fortifications, he launched an attack on May 31, 1862, against two Union corps isolated from the remainder of the federal army by the rain-swollen Chickahominy River. Johnston was wounded in the fighting, and Davis replaced him with Lee, whose moment had arrived.

For the next year, Lee and his Army of Northern Virginia consistently defeated the numerically superior, though lumbering, Union Army of the Potomac. He adopted the tactics he had learned in Mexico from Winfield Scott, aided by able lieutenants like Thomas "Stonewall" Jackson, another West Point graduate and a former professor at the Virginia Military Institute. Like Scott, Lee took the offensive and employed flanking attacks, often dividing his army in the face of the opposing force. His offensive operations were based on aggressive reconnaissance that yielded intelligence, the same scouting missions that he had conducted as a staff officer for Scott. Lee's command style with subordinates was to provide an overall plan and leave the tactical details to them. In doing so, Lee wanted to destroy the Union Army, not simply stop it. He disliked personal confrontations and avoided them; unlike Johnston, who had been secretive about his plans, Lee kept Davis apprised of his intentions, working to build a relationship of trust with the prickly Confederate president.

Immediately after taking over from Johnston, Lee disengaged the Confederate Army while he formulated his plan. Lee decided to strike McClellan on the right flank and rear with two-thirds of his army while the other third held the Union army in place. The campaign, called the Seven Days, began on June 25, 1862, and continued to July 1 with Lee repeatedly attacking the Union force. Unfortunately, the assaults were often poorly coordinated and executed, resulting in higher casualties. Lee had hoped to turn the federals out of their prepared defenses by flanking attacks, but often his forces attacked more directly. Despite the flawed execution, McClellan was unnerved. Instead of interpreting Lee's attacks and high casualties as evidence of the success of his strategy to force the Confederate Army to attack him, McClellan believed they corroborated the inflated estimates of Confederate troop strength he received from his spy chief, Allan Pinkerton. He acted in a purely reactive, defensive manner, switching his base and conducting a fighting retreat.

With McClellan checked at Harrison's Landing, Virginia, Lee faced another federal army moving on him from the North. Under the command of John Pope, the federal Army of Virginia, some 50,000 strong, was made up of troops from the Shenandoah Valley and from the Washington, D.C., garrison. Lee moved his army against Pope in August 1862. Dividing his outnumbered forces in half, Lee sent Jackson and 24,000 men on a wide flanking march to the rear of Pope's army. Jackson marched on August 25, 1862. He was soon destroying railroads and supply depots. Pope tried to crush Jackson; the latter took up a strong defensive position at Sudley Springs. When Pope attacked Jackson, Lee approached with his other corps under James Longstreet and struck Pope's left flank on August 30, 1862. Pope's army broke and fled. The battle of Second Manassas demonstrated Lee at his best, taking great risks and relying on excellent reconnaissance and superior battlefield leadership, to rout a larger foe.

With Pope and McClellan back in the Washington fortifications, Lee strove to retain the initiative. He determined to invade Maryland and moved his army into the state, making Frederick his headquarters. He hoped to again tempt the Union Army into striking at him, complete its destruction, and win Confederate independence. He sent Stonewall Jackson off to capture the small Union garrison at Harpers Ferry. McClellan had the great fortune to intercept a copy of Lee's orders that revealed that the Confederate Army was again divided. The Union commander could have struck quickly and destroyed the Confederate Army in detail. Instead, he waited and allowed Lee to gather his forces and give battle. Lee took position near Sharpsburg on hills near Antietam Creek, and on September 17, 1862, McClellan launched a series of uncoordinated assaults on Lee's line. Lee made tactical command decisions during the fighting, shuttling troops and artillery to weak points in his defensive line. The carnage at Antietam was terrible, the worst in a very bloody war, and the outcome indecisive. When McClellan was inactive on September 18, Lee slipped back across the Potomac River. The Maryland campaign accomplished little and cost the Army of Northern Virginia precious lives it could not afford to lose.

Frustrated at McClellan's failure to trap and destroy Lee's army north of the Potomac River, Abraham Lincoln dismissed him and installed Ambrose Burnside. Known for his decisiveness on the battlefield, Burnside was under no illusions as to the reasons for his abrupt elevation—the president wanted the army to attack. Hoping to steal a march on Lee, whose forces were at Culpeper Court House, Burnside marched east to Fredericksburg, where he waited for pontoon bridges that would enable him to cross the Rappahannock River. The bridges were late in arriving, and the delay permitted Lee to shift his army to the heights south of Fredericksburg. The game was up, but Burnside went forward nonetheless, forcing a bloody river crossing on December 11, 1862. After spending a day gathering his forces, Burnside attacked the heights on December 13. Lee had assisted in locating his more than 300 cannon into effective killing positions. The carnage was simply awful, as wave after wave of regiments with colors streaming brightly in the wind were slaughtered on the gentle slopes of Marye's Heights and Prospect Hill. As Lee watched the magnificent yet bloodcurdling spectacle, he remarked, "It is well that war is so terrible; we should grow too fond of it." Lee had won another smashing victory, but he allowed Burnside to retire across the Rappahannock on the night of December 14.[2]

Lee took the army into winter quarters in 1862–1863. The months of active campaigning, with its bad food and primitive camping, had taken a toll on Lee's health. He fell ill in March 1863 with a bad cold that grew progressively worse until his doctors ordered him to bed in April. He spent two weeks bedridden before emerging pale and weak. Lee biographer

Emory Thomas has argued that Lee's health was permanently harmed by this episode. He began to experience angina and other symptoms of atherosclerosis. Back at his headquarters in mid-April 1863, Lee hoped to again defeat the federal army and thereby aid the Northern peace movement.

Joseph Hooker had replaced the hapless Ambrose Burnside as commander of the Army of the Potomac in the interval. He sent his cavalry charging into the rear of the Army of Northern Virginia on April 29, 1863, beginning a spring campaign. As usual, Lee was outnumbered with an army of 60,000 facing Hooker's 133,000. Hooker sent two corps across the Rappahannock to fix Lee in his fortified positions at Fredericksburg, then marched his army west and crossed with five corps, moving on Chancellorsville to flank Lee. Instead of striking Lee's left and rear, Hooker paused. Leaving 10,000 men at Fredericksburg, Lee moved the rest of his army west to confront Hooker's masses. He employed his battle-tested techniques in the face of seemingly insurmountable odds. With Hooker immobile, aggressive Confederate scouting discovered that Hooker's right was vulnerable. Lee and Stonewall Jackson planned and executed a flanking attack on Hooker's right on May 2, taking the incredible risk of sending 26,000 men while leaving a mere 17,000 to face Hooker. Jackson's slashing flank attack wrecked the Union Eleventh Corps, disrupted the Union advance, and unnerved Hooker. Jackson paid for the success of Confederate arms with his life; he was mistakenly shot by his own troops on May 2. Lee took a portion of his forces and drove the Union host at Fredericksburg back across the river before they could assist Hooker. Dazed after being concussed when shellfire knocked a porch pillar down on his head, Hooker withdrew the army to his starting point on May 6. Victorious again, Lee contemptuously referred to Hooker, whose sobriquet was "Fighting Joe," as "Mr. F. J. Hooker."

After his success at Chancellorsville, Lee was determined to grasp the strategic initiative and invade the North. A march into Pennsylvania would accomplish a number of goals. Lee's army needed supplies, and better to confiscate them from Pennsylvania farmers than depend on depleted Virginia farms. He would be taking the war to the enemy, and thereby frustrating the Army of the Potomac's campaign plans. Lee hoped that an invasion of the North would strengthen the Northern peace movement, which in turn could pressure the Lincoln administration to end the war. Lee believed that time favored the North, and that if the Confederacy was to survive, the war had to be brought to a swift conclusion. With that in mind, Lee hoped, most importantly, to bring on a major battle at a place and time of his choosing. Ideally, Lee wanted to strike the Army of the Potomac on the march; defeat it in detail, that is, attack portions of the enemy's army, and destroy each in turn. Once victorious, he would march his army to Washington, D.C., and dictate terms, as he had with Winfield

Scott at Mexico City. Lee even requested that an envoy travel with the army, empowered to treat for peace with the Lincoln administration.

Lee traveled to Richmond in May and convinced Jefferson Davis and Secretary of War James Seddon of the merit of his plan. In June 1863, three corps of the Army of Northern Virginia moved west into the Shenandoah Valley and then north, employing the Blue Ridge Mountains as a natural screen for its movement. In addition, J.E.B. Stuart's cavalry blocked the mountain passes and kept federal scouting parties at bay. Stuart smarted from a near-defeat at Brandy Station just as the campaign was to begin. Seeking to restore his reputation, Stuart convinced Lee to permit a raid behind the Union Army, another of his fabled encircling rides that made great headlines in Richmond newspapers. Hubris and general contempt for the federal army, which had been repeatedly bested, brought on this decision. It proved a fatal error, as Lee was deprived of effective reconnaissance, essential to his audacious plan for the campaign. He could not strike the enemy at a time and place of his choosing if he had no idea where the enemy was located.

In consequence of Stuart's absence, Lee's infantry acted as cavalry, a role to which they were unsuited. On July 1, 1863, Third Corps commander A. P. Hill sent an entire division to reconnoiter Gettysburg, Pennsylvania, where federal troops had been observed. Hill's force blundered into Union cavalry and elements of the Union First Corps, and a major engagement ensued. Lee had specifically ordered Hill not to bring on a general engagement, but with his blood aroused, Hill disregarded the command. In a hard day of fighting, Hill drove Union forces out of Gettysburg and right into good defensive positions on hills outside of town. Lee ordered Hill to assault and drive out Union forces from the heights, but Hill did not comply.

The action on July 1 left Lee upset and anxious. Because he had given Stuart too much autonomy, he found himself suddenly facing the Union Army. George Meade, who had replaced the failed Hooker, quickly concentrated the Army of the Potomac on the heights near Gettysburg. Anxious to keep the initiative, and excessively confident because of previous victories, Lee decided to attack even though the terrain favored the enemy. He found himself opposed by First Corps commander James Longstreet, who preferred a flanking march that would put the army between Meade and Washington, D.C. Lee insisted on his plan, and two days of bloody fighting followed, culminating in the famous repulse of George Pickett's division on July 3. His losses forced Lee to retreat south.

In the Gettysburg campaign, all of the characteristics of Lee's leadership style that had proven so advantageous in previous battles suddenly became liabilities. He relied on aggressive reconnaissance and good intelligence to form his plans; he deprived himself of both when he released Stuart. He typically gave general orders and allowed his generals to work out the tactical specifics, avoiding personal confrontations. At Gettysburg, Lee's generals made poor decisions, ignored his orders, disputed his plans, and forced him to involve himself at the tactical level. He was an aggressive commander who preferred offensive operations and was prepared to take risks. Lee hazarded too much when he assaulted the heights at Gettysburg.

After Gettysburg, Lee offered his resignation to Jefferson Davis, but the Confederate president would not hear of it. Lee was compelled to send James Longstreet and his corps to the western theater, where Confederate armies had suffered a series of setbacks. In the East, Lee and Meade spent the remainder of the year fencing, maneuvering for advantage, and occasionally skirmishing. The absence of Longstreet's corps hampered Lee's penchant for the offensive. As the winter approached, Meade settled into winter quarters. Lee spent another winter begging Richmond for supplies. His health suffered, as he continued to experience angina. His wife Mary was living in Richmond over his objections; she organized the local women into a knitting circle that produced a flurry of socks and gloves for the army.

In April 1864, Longstreet returned to the Army of Northern Virginia. Soon after, the Army of the Potomac began crossing the Rapidan River. The Union force was under the command of Meade, but traveling with the army was the new general-in-chief of all federal armies, Ulysses S. Grant. The implacable Grant had been a successful commander in the West and had been called to Washington for the supreme command and to deal with the Army of Northern Virginia. A series of bloody battles followed in May and June 1864: the Wilderness, Spotsylvania Court House, and Cold Harbor. After each battle, Grant shifted the army to the east and south in a flanking maneuver, and Lee struggled to catch up and set up a blocking position. Lee tried to retake the initiative with counterattacks, but as time wore on and casualties mounted, he lacked the manpower to maneuver. He relied on entrenchments to offset his numerical inferiority. In June, Grant had managed to move south of Richmond near Petersburg. The two armies spent the summer of 1864 locked in trench warfare, with continual skirmishes. Grant inched south, trying to cut the railroad and roads leading into Richmond.

The winter of 1864–1865 was depressing and frustrating for Lee. His army, scarcely fed by the ineffectual Confederate government, began to melt away. Perhaps, too, the men could sense the inevitability of defeat. Desertion became a terrible problem. Lee was supremely discomfited. Committed to offensive action as the only path to military victory, he faced a trench war of attrition that he could not win. He lacked the troops to break out and maneuver. In April, Grant's flanking operations turned Lee out of his trenches and forced him to retreat. The withdrawal was clumsily managed and a mere prelude to the end.

Lee surrendered his much-reduced Army of Northern Virginia on April 9, 1865, at Appomattox Court House. Ulysses Grant arrived for the surrender meeting in a uniform filthy from the now-victorious pursuit. Lee was clad in a new uniform with an immaculate sword. The choice of attire of the two principals was emblematic of the passing of the plantation aristocracy, finally giving way to the common man Andrew Jackson had ushered into American democracy three decades previous. Grant offered generous terms, allowing Confederates to keep their horses and mules, and Lee accepted.

In his report to Jefferson Davis on the demise of his army, Lee urged that the war end finally and totally, dismissing any thoughts of a guerrilla war. His concluding comments set the tone for Lee's postwar years, the final five years of his life. In his view, the conflict was over. Lee always believed that Southerners had to reunite with their Northern brethren and make the best of a bad situation. Though he believed the cause for which he had fought was just, he urged conciliation of the sections. That was Lee's public face. His private correspondence contains expressions of outrage and anger at Reconstruction policies.

Lee returned to Richmond, to Mary and his family, where in the weeks to come thrill-seekers pestered him whenever he ventured outdoors. He was indicted for treason on June 7, 1865, but nothing came of the indictment, which was eventually dismissed. Grant was adamant that Lee's formal surrender precluded any further action against him, and he so expressed himself in strong terms to President Andrew Johnson. In August 1865, the trustees of Washington College in Lexington, Virginia, elected Lee president of the school. Lee had little desire to teach, but he was anxious to make a living. The college had fallen into disrepair, and enrollment was quite low. The trustees hoped that Lee's luster would draw money and students. Lee succeeded as president of the college. His celebrity brought financial contributions as hoped, and he had the kind of credibility that allowed him to lobby the Virginia legislature for funds. He took steps to modernize the curriculum, and he paved the way for a more progressive educational institution. He took a strong interest in the students, and tried to learn their names and intervene for good when they had trouble. He also worked on a building program, and he was active in the local church. His health was in decline, however, most likely from heart disease. On September 28, 1870, Lee attended a church vestry meeting late on a cold, rainy afternoon. Returning home for dinner, Lee arrived at table, where Mary rebuked him for being late. He was suddenly unable to speak and, sitting heavily down, had clearly suffered a stroke. Physicians were called, but could do little. Lee lingered for nearly two weeks, then passed peacefully away on October 12, 1870.

PRINCIPAL IDEAS

Political Ideas

Lee believed in a social hierarchy, in which those of good breeding and wealth should govern those who had neither. He was suspicious of democracy, of leveling. He considered himself a Whig, and he thought the Mexican War an unjust bullying of a weaker neighboring country. Yet politics scarcely appears in his personal correspondence until the sectional crisis after the 1854 Kansas-Nebraska Act. Lee was an adherent to the honor code, which meant that a gentleman acted in a manner that preserved his personal standing with his community. The personal disasters of Lee's father and half-brother reinforced his desire to maintain his personal honor. He thought slavery was a terrible evil, and he supported colonization for blacks. However, he owned slaves and believed that blacks were fortunate to be in the United States. Slavery, Lee argued, helped prepare blacks for a better life when they were freed at some amorphous future date. He blamed abolitionists for sectional tensions, and the North writ large for abandoning the Constitution. Lee's wife was a strong Confederate partisan. He ultimately chose to serve the Confederacy because it was impossible for him to side against his wife, family, friends, and Virginia, which Lee called his county.

Military Ideas

Robert E. Lee was an exponent of offensive warfare. Like his mentor, Winfield Scott, Lee sought to defeat his numerically superior foe by seizing and keeping the initiative, launching flanking attacks based on aggressive reconnaissance. In Lee's opinion, only the quick defeat of the Union Army would insure ultimate Confederate victory. If the war dragged on for any length of time, Lee believed that the North's overwhelming superiority in population and material wealth would begin to tell. In consequence of those beliefs, Lee's preferred battlefield tactics neatly coincided with his strategic conception.

The central critique of Lee's wartime leadership is that his excessive offensive-mindedness drained the Southern army of manpower it could not replace, thereby insuring defeat. Lee's tactics were Napoleonic in an era when defensive weaponry, such as rifled muskets and cannons wielded by entrenched troops, outmatched offensive tactics, such as massed infantry attacks in tight formations. Had the South remained on the defensive, it could have bled the North, which was obligated to attack, in a war of attrition until the Northern peace movement forced an end to the conflict.

Lee argued that only by taking the strategic initiative could he keep the numerically superior North from defeating his army and capturing Richmond. Had Lee taken a defensive posture, he would have, he argued, been forced back into the Richmond fortifications. Once bottled up, his army would have inevitably succumbed to siege warfare. Indeed, that is precisely what happened in 1864–1865 when Lee's dwindling manpower rendered offensive action impossible. Lee preferred to take the offensive to lure the Army of the Potomac into battle at a time and place of his choosing. He would destroy the Union Army and march on Washington to dictate terms, as he and Winfield Scott had marched on Mexico City in 1847. Lee's tactics probably saved the Confederate government in 1862 and prolonged the war. As George B. McClellan's massive Army of the Potomac approached Richmond from the Peninsula (the area between the York and James rivers), Lee's predecessor as commander, Joseph Johnston, had slowly yielded ground, withdrawing to Richmond where in time he and his army would have been locked into a doomed siege. After Johnston was wounded, Lee took command and launched a series of slashing attacks, the Seven Days battles. Lee's attacks unnerved McClellan and convinced him of the correctness of his wildly inflated estimates of the size of the Confederate forces. Lee's aggression locked his enemy into a defeatist mindset and ended a potent threat to the Confederate nation. The cost in casualties was horrific, but the resulting success gave more time for the Confederacy to survive. As mentioned, Lee believed that the Confederacy had to win the war quickly in order to survive. The speedy destruction of the Northern army he faced would do more than anything to ensure the survival of the Confederate nation.

CONCLUSION

The audacity and offensive-mindedness of Robert E. Lee extended the life of the Confederacy, as time and again he outwitted and defeated opposing Union generals. He conducted himself with courage, stoicism, and dignity, enduring personal and professional frustrations with little complaint. By nature conservative and prudent, Lee sundered his allegiance to the army he had served for decades and allied himself with the secession movement because of state and family ties.

NOTES

1. Emory M. Thomas, *Robert E. Lee* (New York: W. W. Norton, 1995), 188.
2. Thomas, *Robert E. Lee*, 271.

FURTHER READING

Thomas L. Connelly, *The Marble Man: Robert E. Lee and His Image in American Society* (Baton Rouge: Louisiana State University Press, 1977); Douglas Southall Freeman, *R. E. Lee: A Biography*, 4 vols. (New York: Charles Scribner's Sons, 1934–1935); Richard B. McCaslin, *Lee in the Shadow of Washington* (Baton Rouge: Louisiana State University Press, 2001); Paul C. Nagel, *The Lees of Virginia: Seven Generations in an American Family* (New York: Oxford University Press, 1990); and Emory M. Thomas, *Robert E. Lee* (New York: W. W. Norton, 1995).

ABRAHAM LINCOLN
(1809–1865)

The House Divided

LIFE

The log cabin came into vogue in American politics in the presidential election of 1840, when the Whigs capitalized on the log cabin origins of their nominee, William Henry Harrison, to counter Democratic claims of Whig elitism. The log cabin began to symbolize both humble birth and the upward mobility of American society. Daniel Webster, the prestigious Massachusetts senator and perennial Whig presidential hopeful, remarked somewhat painfully that he had not been born in a log cabin, but wished that he had been. A scant twenty years after the election of 1840, the newly formed Republican party nominated its own log cabin candidate when it chose an obscure Illinois lawyer and politician, Abraham Lincoln, to be its second presidential nominee.[1]

Abraham Lincoln was neither proud of his log cabin birth nor particularly forthcoming about the details of his early life. When Chicago journalist John L. Scripps interviewed Lincoln in order to write a campaign biography, Lincoln bluntly asserted, "Why Scripps it is a great piece of folly to attempt to make anything out of my early life. It can all be condensed into a single sentence, and that sentence you will find in Gray's Elegy: 'The short and simple annals of the poor.' That's my life, and that's all you or any one else can make of it." Ashamed of his humble origins, by 1860 Lincoln had reached the pinnacle of success in American political life. He had risen above his obscure frontier origins to achieve the office of the presidency.[2]

Born on February 12, 1809, near Hodgenville, Kentucky, Abraham Lincoln was the son of Thomas and Nancy Hanks Lincoln. Little is known about Nancy Hanks. Illiterate and possibly illegitimate, Abraham Lincoln had cherished but few memories of his natural mother. More is known about Thomas Lincoln. Thomas was the son of Abraham Lincoln, a fairly well-to-do Virginia farmer. Since Thomas was a younger son and, therefore, according to Virginia law, received no inheritance, he eventually left Virginia for Kentucky. Through working odd jobs and carpentry, Thomas acquired a 300-acre farm near Hodgenville known as Sinking Springs. The land was of poor quality, so shortly after Abraham's birth, Thomas moved his family to a smaller but more fertile farm on Knob Creek, near present-day Bardstown, Kentucky. Preceded by a sister, Sarah, who was born in 1807, Lincoln also had a brother, Thomas, born at Knob Creek, who died in infancy.

In 1816, trouble with land titles forced Thomas Lincoln to take a hard look at his Kentucky life. Lacking money for attorney's fees to prove the authenticity of his title to the lands, Thomas instead traveled to southern Indiana and acquired land in Spencer County, near the small town of Gentryville on Pidgeon Creek. Here were Lincoln's clearest memories of his frontier childhood. Tragedy soon struck, however, when the rural community was struck by a bout of brucellosis, or milk sickness, which claimed Lincoln's mother, Nancy Hanks. Undaunted, Thomas Lincoln traveled back to Elizabethtown, Kentucky, where he quickly arranged a marriage with Sarah "Sally" Bush Johnston. Sarah Lincoln had an immediate positive effect on the family. In addition to her three children, Sally also brought furniture and kitchen utensils, forcing Thomas to adopt a touch of domesticity in the crude frontier environment. For young Abraham, the new stepmother was a productive influence, encouraging him to pursue education and providing emotional nurturing that he never got from his father.

Although Lincoln had attended school in Kentucky, the bulk of his "formal" education took place in Spencer County. Lincoln was educated in what was known as a "blab" school, where children recited lessons aloud. While the education was crude and unsophisticated, Lincoln did learn the basics of arithmetic, reading, and writing. Indeed, Lincoln soon voraciously devoured any book he came across, committing large portions of books to memory. By the time he was a young man, Lincoln's quest for intellectual achievement came into conflict with the goals and aspirations of his father.

Lincoln biographers have made much of the alienation between Abraham and Thomas Lincoln. In several respects, they were very much alike. The younger Lincoln excelled at storytelling and amusing friends and neighbors with numerous anecdotes. However, the elder Lincoln rivaled or even surpassed the son in this regard. As the younger Lincoln became a teenager and moved toward adulthood, a substantial rift developed between father and son. Never particularly fond of manual labor, Abraham resented the work he was obliged to perform for Thomas. When the elder Lincoln joined the Pidgeon Creek Primitive Baptist Church, Abraham refused to join. By early adulthood, Lincoln had repudiated entirely the world of his father. As historian Alan Guelzo observes, the elder Lincoln was a traditional Jacksonian subsistence farmer, content to satisfy the basic needs of life, but wanting little else. Abraham, conversely, was striving for goals well beyond the narrow confines of the Pidgeon Creek locale.[3]

In 1830, Thomas Lincoln decided to move west, following some of the Hanks family to Macon County, Illinois, near the present-day Decatur. Undoubtedly, the death of daughter Sarah Lincoln Grigsby in 1828, while giving birth, made the Spencer County community less attractive to the Lincolns. Not yet twenty-one, Abraham was obliged to help the family move as he was still a minor. Upon turning twenty-one, Lincoln left Macon County and his parents' home for good. Along with stepbrother John Johnston, Lincoln worked for Denton Offutt, transporting produce in a flatboat to New Orleans. He eventually settled in New Salem, Illinois, on the Sangamon River. With nearly 100 residents, New Salem was the largest place Abraham Lincoln had lived heretofore.

At New Salem, Lincoln would become one of the village's most popular residents. He earned a living by tending store for Denton Offutt. When Offutt's business failed in the spring of 1832, Lincoln volunteered with the Illinois militia to help quell the uprising of Chief Black Hawk. Elected company captain, Lincoln served three months. During this time, he saw a great deal of marching but no military engagements. After his military term was up, Lincoln ran for the state legislature, polling a majority of votes in the New Salem precinct, but finishing eighth out of thirteen candidates. Trying his hand at business, Lincoln then entered into a partnership with William F. Berry, buying out the general store of J. Rowan and James Herndon. It was an ill-fated venture that ended in bankruptcy and saddled Lincoln with debts for many years into the future.

Fortunately Lincoln had many friends in New Salem. Despite his Whig proclivities in a Democratic town, Lincoln's friends got him elected postmaster of New Salem, a job that did not pay much but gave Lincoln some income while allowing him much leisure time to study and read. When an opportunity to become assistant county surveyor arose, Lincoln jumped at the chance. Reading all of the available literature on the topic, Lincoln became a first-rate surveyor. His travels took him all over the surrounding counties and helped form the basis of political support that he would utilize for years to come. Indeed, by the summer of 1834, Lincoln was ready for another run for the state legislature. As one biographer notes, the need for income was an important motive in Lincoln's decision. This time Lincoln finished second among all candidates with 1,376 votes and took a seat at the state legislature at Vandalia in December 1834. While largely silent during his first legislative session, it was the beginning of a lifelong association in politics that would culminate in the White House in 1860.

The New Salem years were important in the shaping of Abraham Lincoln. Here Lincoln made important decisions about the direction that his life would take, for it was in New Salem that he acquired an interest in the law and began to educate himself in the law by reading Blackstone, Chitty, and Joseph Story's works. It was also in New Salem that Lincoln first experienced love, falling for Anne Rutledge, the daughter of tavern owner R. B. Rutledge. When Anne died in August 1835 of typhoid, Lincoln fell into deep depression, revealing a chronic melancholy that would plague his adult life. Finally, it was in New Salem where Lincoln participated in the epic wrestling match with Jack Armstrong, leader of the Clary Grove Gang, a group of local ruffians whose respect Lincoln won by standing up to their leader. Indeed, Lincoln had fond memories of New Salem. When he decided to locate to Springfield to practice law with Whig Congressman John Todd Stuart, he left behind fond memories and many friends.

Reelected to a second term in 1836, Lincoln was part of the Whig delegation known as the Long Nine (named appropriately for the height of each state legislator). His second term in the state legislature was characterized by two central goals: support of internal improvements and a bill to move the state capital to Springfield. While there was strong bipartisan consensus for internal improvement spending, the bill to move the state capital required much more legislative gamesmanship. Nevertheless, the bill was passed on February 28, 1837. The following April, having passed his bar exam, Lincoln moved from New Salem to the new state capital.

Lincoln arrived in Springfield, then a primitive frontier village of 1,500. Despite its crudeness, it was once again the largest place Lincoln had ever lived. Poor but ambitious, Lincoln was determined to achieve economic, social, and political success in this rising Illinois town. Meeting and eventually rooming with Joshua Speed, Lincoln quickly became associated with a like-minded group of ambitious young men including Speed, Milton Hay, James Conkling, James Matheny, and Simeon Francis. As a younger partner of John Todd Stuart, Lincoln gained a wealth of legal experience. At the same time, because of Stuart's social standing in Springfield, Lincoln found opportunities to climb socially using his partner's considerable connections.

Lincoln continued as a state legislator and lawyer in the late 1830s in Springfield (he was reelected in 1836, 1838, 1840, and 1844). His association with Stuart eventually gained Lincoln entrance to the elite social world of Governor Ninian Edwards and the leading citizens of Springfield. It was in the Edwards's social circle that Lincoln first met Mary Todd. Energetic and educated, Mary Todd attracted a host of potential suitors including Lincoln's future political rival, Stephen A. Douglas. Lincoln, insecure in female company, seemed an unlikely match for the headstrong Mary. Nevertheless, sharing an interest in poetry and Whig politics, the two quickly fell in love and were engaged by the end of 1840. Then, in a fit of anxiety and uncertainty, Lincoln got cold feet. When Mary wrote him a letter at the end of that same year releasing him from the engagement, Lincoln suffered a bout of severe depression in January 1841, a bout so severe that friends worried that he was suicidal. A visit to friend Joshua Speed, recently married and resettled in Kentucky, helped Lincoln realize that the doubt he had experienced was typically human and not a sign that he did not love Mary sufficiently. Through the intervention of mutual friends, the couple was eventually reconciled, engaged again, and finally married on November 4, 1842.[4]

By the early 1840s, Abraham Lincoln was one of Springfield's rising young men. In the 1830s, Illinois was heavily Democratic. Sangamon County was a pocket of Whig supremacy surrounded by numerous Democratic counties. Lincoln quickly emerged as a prominent Whig spokesperson for the Sangamon District, becoming a frequent campaigner for other candidates, including the Whig presidential nominees. After serving four successive terms, Lincoln retired from the state legislature and began to focus on a much more prominent prize: a seat in the U.S. House of Representatives.

In addition to building political support, Lincoln continued polishing his legal skills. His partnership with Stuart was dissolved and, in 1841, he became the junior partner of Stephen Logan. Although Lincoln learned much about the law from the older and more experienced Logan, the two eventually parted when Logan wanted to bring his son into the firm. Having twice been the junior partner, Lincoln was determined to be the senior partner in any new partnership. When he approached William H. Herndon, a younger man who fancied himself something of an intellectual, however, Lincoln had another goal in mind besides the legal partnership. Although from a simple frontier background, Lincoln's marriage to Mary Todd identified him with the aristocratic Edwards faction of the Whig Party. Herndon, on the other hand, was closer to the more egalitarian Whig faction, led by Edward D. Baker. Though different in temperament and interests, Lincoln and Herndon formed a prosperous law firm that lasted until Lincoln's election to the presidency in 1860.

While Lincoln's legal and political prospects continued to brighten, his marriage to Mary Todd experienced uneven progress. Lincoln derived a significant part of his income from traveling the Eighth Judicial Circuit, an arduous biannual task that took him out of Springfield for approximately twenty weeks a year. Not only was Mary alone for long periods of time, but after the Lincoln boys were born (Robert Todd in 1843 and Edward in 1846), she also had the complete task of raising them. When Lincoln was home, he was often aloof and introverted. So, too, Mary's living conditions were a far cry from her aristocratic Kentucky upbringing. First, the Lincolns rented rooms in the Globe Tavern on North Adams and then a small house on S. 4th Street. In 1844, Lincoln's rising income allowed him to spend $1,200 on a home at 8th and Jackson. While the Lincoln marriage was often erratic, the couple seemed to share a genuine affection for each other, and Mary, particularly astute on political matters, was increasingly proud of her husband's political accomplishments.[5]

Lincoln's chance for Congress finally came in 1846. While he had coveted the Seventh Congressional seat since retiring from the state legislature in 1841, the reality was that Lincoln faced several more popular Whig rivals including John J. Harding and Edward D. Baker. In the past, he worked hard for all Whig congressional candidates, campaigning first for Harding in 1843 and then for Baker to replace Harding in 1845. Then, in the next general election, Lincoln used his loyalty to the party to justify his nomination for the seat. In the general election, Lincoln faced evangelist Peter Cartwright as his Democratic opponent. Among Cartwright's repertoire of political tricks was the accusation that Lincoln was a religious skeptic who ridiculed religious belief. Cartwright's charges had little effect on the Seventh District electorate, as Lincoln won easily and left for Washington on October 25, 1847.

Lincoln came to Washington as the only Whig representative from Illinois. A devotee of the Whig economic doctrines of Henry Clay, he was intensely devoted to Clay's American system, which stressed national economic developments through federally sponsored internal improvements, protective tariffs, and a national bank. Appointed to the Committee of Post Office and Roads as well as the Committee of Expenditures for the War Department, Lincoln enjoyed his work in the House immensely. He also enjoyed the company of such diverse congressmen as antislavery zealot Joshua R. Giddings of Ohio and Alexander Stephens of Georgia.

Perhaps Lincoln's most notorious accomplishment during his single term in the House was his criticism of American involvement in the Mexican War. While the war had been raging for nearly seven months by the time Lincoln arrived in Congress, Whig congressmen were already using the war to criticize President James K. Polk and to enhance Whig presidential prospects in 1848. On December 22, 1847, Lincoln introduced his so-called spot resolutions, which castigated Polk for claiming that Mexico had started the war by spilling American blood on American soil. Since the territory lying between the Rio Grande and the Nueces River was claimed by both Mexico and the United States, he challenged the president to show the precise spot on American soil where blood had been shed. The move backfired in Lincoln's home district, and the first-term congressman was on the defensive, forced to justify himself to friend and foe alike. "Allow the President to invade a neighboring nation, whenever *he* shall deem it necessary to repel an invasion," Lincoln lectured William H. Herndon, "and you allow him to do so, *wherever he may choose to say* he deems it necessary for such purpose—and you allow him to make war at pleasure." When Stephen Logan, the 1848 Whig nominee, was soundly thrashed in the fall election, it was likely a repudiation of Lincoln's war position.[6]

Having spent the fall of 1848 campaigning for Whig presidential candidate Zachary Taylor, the latter's victory gave Lincoln hope for a prestigious patronage appointment. While he lost out on an appointment as the commissioner of the General Land Office, Lincoln was offered the governorship of the Oregon Territory, an offer he politely refused. Putting politics out of his mind temporarily, Lincoln resumed his law practice with Herndon. Returning to the old Eighth Circuit, Lincoln increasingly began to take on corporate clients and soon was earning lucrative fees representing the Illinois Central Railroad and other industrial/commercial interests. The extra income allowed Lincoln to fund an elaborate addition and renovation to his home on 8th and Jackson.

The early 1850s were also a time of joy and sadness in the Lincoln household. In late 1849, Lincoln's youngest son, Edward, became sick; he died on February 1, 1850. Just prior to that Thomas Lincoln, now living at a farm at Goosenest Prairie (just south of Charleston, Illinois), died. Abraham, never close to his father, did not attend his funeral. The pain of death, however, was quickly counterbalanced with new family additions. William Wallace "Willie" Lincoln was born in 1851, while Thomas "Tad" Lincoln arrived in 1853.

While Lincoln had unofficially retired from politics after his term in Congress, he continued to follow political events and take an interest in promoting Whig candidates. It was not until 1854, however, that he gave serious consideration about returning to the political area. The cause was, of course, Stephen A. Douglas's Kansas-Nebraska Act, which Lincoln viewed as an opportunity to revive not only his own political fortunes but those of the faltering Whig Party as well. Lincoln did not initially speak publicly on the bill, instead waiting until late in the summer of 1854 to offer public comment—lashing out against the bill at a Scott County Whig convention. In early October 1854, Lincoln tried to arrange a joint appearance with Senator Douglas at the Illinois State Fair; however, the more popular Douglas refused, thus forcing Lincoln to arrange his own reply to Douglas's defense of the Kansas-Nebraska Act. Inclement weather forced Lincoln to make his reply at the Illinois state capital, where, with Douglas in attendance, he denounced the bill in a three-hour speech.

Lincoln, like other Whigs, assumed that the anti-Nebraska fervor would serve ultimately to revitalize the Whig Party. When the shifting fusion of anti-Nebraska elements seemed certain to bring about party realignment without the Whigs, Lincoln hesitated on his political direction. Writing to his friend Joshua F. Speed, Lincoln told him, "I think I am a whig; but others say there are no whigs, and that I am an abolitionist. When I was in Washington," he continued, "I voted for the Wilmot Proviso as good as forty times, and I never heard of any one attempting to unwhig me for that. I now do no more than oppose the *extension* of slavery."[7]

Lincoln also hoped to use the Kansas-Nebraska controversy to launch his own political comeback. In particular, he coveted the U.S. Senate seat that was held by James Shields, a Springfield Democrat who had once challenged Lincoln to a duel over a series of inflammatory newspaper articles penned by Lincoln. Although he had been elected to the state legislature in the fall election, Lincoln refused to accept his seat because it would disqualify him from running for the Senate. While Lincoln appeared to be the strongest candidate, a small group of anti-Nebraska Democrats held the balance of power and they were determined to prevent the election of a Whig. Finally, Lincoln faced reality and threw his support to anti-Nebraska Democrat Lyman Trumbull, who was elected on the tenth ballot. Despite this personal setback, Lincoln's role in the Kansas-Nebraska controversy was the beginning of a political comeback that would ultimately lead to the White House.

By early 1856, having spurned the Know-Nothings and concluded that the Whigs were doomed politically, Abraham Lincoln decided to cast his lot with the newly formed Republican Party. Indeed, Lincoln played a prominent role in a February 1856 meeting of newspaper editors at Decatur that is viewed by many historians as the founding of the Republican Party in Illinois. Later that year, he was elected as a Republican delegate to another convention in Bloomington. In fact, Lincoln delivered the concluding speech (the so-called lost speech) at the convention. At the Republican National Convention, Lincoln received consideration for the vice presidential slot, losing to William Dayton of New Jersey by a vote of 253–110. While not personally fond of presidential nominee John C. Frémont, Lincoln nevertheless wholeheartedly embraced the Republican ticket, delivering over fifty stump speeches for the popular "Pathfinder."

Lincoln kept a low profile in 1857, despite continued violence in Kansas over the slavery issue and the controversial Dred Scott decision. As a private citizen, he had devoted much time to political matters since the Kansas-Nebraska Act and needed to focus on his neglected law practice. Still, Lincoln kept his political antennae poised and was considered the leading Republican candidate to challenge incumbent Senator Stephen A. Douglas for reelection in 1858. Yet, as the senatorial election drew near, Lincoln faced another obstacle. Because of Douglas's role in opposing the Lecompton Constitution, the fraudulent proslavery constitution forced on Kansas residents, a number of prominent eastern politicians urged Illinois Republicans to nominate Douglas as their candidate in defiance of the Buchanan administration. Lincoln was determined to thwart such a strategy and, therefore, emphasized the participation of all Democrats in a gigantic proslavery conspiracy. Kicking off his campaign in Chicago on June 16, 1858, with the famous "House Divided" speech, Lincoln contrasted his opposition to the expansion of slavery to the proslavery policies of all Democrats—Douglas included. In a particularly trenchant description, Lincoln asserted,

> We can not *absolutely* know that all these exact adaptations are the result of preconcert. But when we see a lot of framed timbers, different portions of which we know have been gotten out at different times and places and by different workman—Stephen, Franklin, Roger, and James . . . and where we see these timbers joined together, and see they exactly make the frame of a house or a mill . . . in *such* case, we find it impossible to not *believe* that Stephen and Franklin and Roger and James all understood one another from the beginning, and all worked upon a *common* plan or *draft* drawn up before the first lick was ever struck.[8]

In 1858, Illinois Republicans made Lincoln their senatorial nominee, and all Republican state legislators were expected to cast their vote for Lincoln when the new legislature met at Springfield in January 1859. Stephen Douglas was by far the better-known man in 1858. Already a perennial presidential candidate, Douglas was a powerful and well-known senator with a gigantic reputation. When Lincoln began following Douglas's schedule and making a reply to each one of his stump speeches, the incumbent senator finally agreed to a series of joint debates. The debates were to take place in each congressional district, save the ones in which Lincoln and Douglas had already delivered major speeches (Springfield and Chicago). Accordingly, throughout the late summer and fall of 1858, the two engaged in three-hour oratorical warfare waged in Ottawa, Freeport, Jonesboro, Charleston, Galesburg, Quincy, and Alton. While the modern voter looks at such debates as long, repetitive, and boring, nineteenth-century voters deemed them grand and popular entertainment.

Both Lincoln and Douglas stressed familiar themes during the majority of the debates. The combative Douglas continually accused Lincoln of radicalism on the slavery issue, charging him with inconsistency on racial issues, and what Douglas deemed Republican consolidationism—the need for uniformity of law and custom throughout the nation. According to Douglas, Lincoln trimmed his views on slavery and race to suit the particular audience he was addressing, proclaiming white supremacy in "Egypt" (southern Illinois) but endorsing radical abolitionism in the northern part of the state. Advocating popular sovereignty as a way to allow local communities to determine their own customs and institutions, Douglas lambasted Lincoln and the Republicans for denying local control and demanding uniformity of law and custom.

Lincoln, conversely, accused Douglas of harboring a crude moral indifference to the slavery question. "Every thing that emanates from him [Douglas] or his coadjutors in their course of policy," Lincoln told the audience at Galesburg, "carefully excludes the thought that there is any thing wrong in slavery . . . if you will take the Judge's speeches . . . you will see at once that this is perfectly logical, if you do not admit that slavery is wrong." Lincoln's opposition to slavery was rooted in the equality promised in the Declaration of Independence. While Douglas bluntly stated that the Founding Fathers had included only whites in the document, Lincoln viewed the declaration as a promise to all races and groups, challenging the Democratic senator to prove that Thomas Jefferson had ever said it applied to whites only.[9]

Despite President Buchanan's attempt to defeat Douglas by sponsoring another Democratic senatorial candidate, Sidney Breese (the so-called National Democratic candidate), on Election Day, Douglas and Democrats prevailed and thereby maintained control of the Illinois legislature. In January 1859, the legislature reelected Douglas by a margin of 54–46. Once again, Lincoln had come out on the short end of a highly competitive political campaign. Yet despite defeats in two senatorial campaigns, Lincoln was, according to political rumors, mentioned as a possible favorite son candidate for the presidency. With the Republican convention slated for Chicago in May 1860, Lincoln publicly paid little attempt to such rumors. At the same time, however, he carefully worked behind the scenes to advance his candidacy. In the fall of 1859, he made a series of stump speeches in Ohio to counter Douglas, who was campaigning for Democratic candidates. And in February 1860, Lincoln spoke before a young Republican group at New York City's Cooper Union Hall, a successful speech in which Lincoln criticized Douglas's position on slavery in the federal territories and demonstrated his stature to eastern Republicans.

As Republicans looked forward to May 1860, Lincoln was successful in cultivating a strategy of being everyone's second choice. If no candidate emerged as dominant, he might capture the prize as a compromise candidate. He had several advantages. First, his antislavery sentiments were viewed as genuine by the abolition wing of the Republican Party, but he was not viewed as a radical like William H. Seward or Salmon P. Chase. Second, Lincoln had stayed away from the Know-Nothing phenomenon that would cripple candidates like Missouri's Edward Bates, while his views in favor of protectionism would make him popular in important states like Pennsylvania, in contrast to low-tariff free traders like Chase. Finally, as a relative unknown, Lincoln had few enemies like many of the other major candidates. William H. Seward, for instance, was intensely disliked by the Horace Greeley wing of the New York Republican Party, while Salmon Chase feuded with Ohio's senior Senator Benjamin F. Wade.

When the Republican convention opened up in Chicago at a massive structure known as the Wigwam, Lincoln did not attend as was the custom of the day. Instead he left the management of his campaign to others, most notably David Davis, the rotund Bloomington attorney and judge who Lincoln had gotten to know on the Eighth Circuit. When frontrunner William H. Seward did not capture a majority on the first ballot, he began to falter and Lincoln began to pick up strength on subsequent ballots. Eventually the Illinois Republican passed the New Yorker and then surpassed the 234 votes necessary to nominate. The two-time senatorial loser had won the prize of a lifetime: the Republican presidential nomination.

In 1856, first-time Republican nominee John C. Frémont had lost to James Buchanan by a narrow margin. Nineteenth-century Republican spin doctors speculated that a successful candidate in 1860 would have to carry all the states taken by Frémont, and, in addition, Pennsylvania along with either Illinois or Indiana. Without being on the ballot of any Deep South states, the Republican Party was poised to carry out an impressive electoral coup d'etat in its second presidential run. Helping the Republican cause was the division of the Democrats into Northern and Southern wings, represented by Douglas and John C. Breckinridge respectively. Adding to the confusion was the formation of the Constitutional Union Party, composed of former Whigs devoted to the meaningless formula of maintaining the Constitution and the Union. Led by Tennessean John Bell, this fracturing of the opposition assured Lincoln's victory. Although he obtained a mere 39 percent of the popular vote, Lincoln received 180 electoral votes (all in the North) and thereby became the nation's sixteenth president.[10]

When Lincoln arrived in Washington in February 1861, he inherited a chaotic situation. His predecessor, James Buchanan, had watched as seven states of the Deep South seceded. After considerable debate, the two political parties and regions rejected the Crittenden compromise proposals which had offered compromises on slavery. Just after delivering his inaugural address, the newly installed president received word from Major Robert Anderson, commander of the garrison at Fort Sumter in Charleston, South Carolina, that it could hold out only a few more weeks due to lack of supplies.

To give up Sumter might demoralize the North and fellow Republicans; however, to reinforce the garrison against the wishes of South Carolina and the newly formed Confederate government would alienate the crucial states of the Upper South and inevitably compel them to cast their lot with the seceded states of the Deep South. General-in-Chief Winfield Scott and several cabinet ministers, principally Secretary of State William H. Seward, advised Lincoln to abandon the fort; however, urged by Postmaster General Montgomery Blair and Assistant Secretary of the Navy Gustavus Fox, Lincoln eventually decided to reinforce the garrison. If he succeeded, he could maintain the status quo in the Charleston Harbor and buy more time. If he failed and war resulted, he could at least claim that the South had fired the first shots.

When his attempt to resupply Fort Sumter ended in the bombardment and surrender of the fort to Confederate forces, Lincoln immediately asked state governors for 75,000 three-month volunteers to suppress the rebellion. Shortly thereafter, the states of Arkansas, Virginia, North Carolina, and Tennessee seceded, while the border states of Maryland, Missouri, and Kentucky hovered on the precipice of secession. Lincoln now faced the preeminent crisis in American history woefully ignorant of administrative routine, inexperienced in military affairs, and the head of a youthful, internally divided political party. While he would eventually prove equal to the task before him, in the initial days of the crisis, both friends and critics alike questioned not only his policies but also his ability to deal with the crisis. Indeed, throughout the war, Lincoln was faced with three competing and often overlapping tasks. To successfully prosecute the war, he had to find generals who would carry out a style of warfare suited to take advantage of Northern superiority in men and materials. As head of a nation, not only his political party, he had to maintain unity behind the war effort. To do so, however, Lincoln also had to maintain order within the Republican Party and restrain its more radical element on issues such as emancipation, the recruitment of black soldiers, and the confiscation of enemy property.

Northern expectations for a quick and painless victory over the Confederacy were quickly shattered in the summer of 1861. In the east, federal forces under General Irvin McDowell were routed at Manassas on July 21, 1861. A few weeks later, Union forces suffered a devastating defeat in southwest Missouri at the battle of Wilson's Creek. Shortly after the defeat at Wilson's Creek, Lincoln was forced to confront the volatile slavery issue head on. The Department of the West was commanded by the popular antislavery Republican, John C. Frémont. On August 30, 1861, Frémont issued a controversial proclamation, placing Missouri under martial law and, most disturbing to Lincoln, emancipating the slaves of Confederate slaveholders in Missouri.

Frémont's emancipation proclamation created the first real political crisis between Lincoln and Republicans in Congress. Frémont's proclamation departed from the policy established by the recently passed Crittenden-Johnson resolution, which stated that the purpose of the war was solely to restore the Union. At the same time, Frémont's proclamation also went well beyond a recently passed congressional measure, the First Confiscation Act. Signed into law by Lincoln, the bill authorized the seizure of Confederate slaves that were directly used to fight the rebellion; however, it was not a general proclamation of emancipation. Impatience with Union military efforts, however, caused many Republican congressmen to support Frémont's action as necessary to weaken the South and bring about Union military victory. Because Lincoln steadfastly maintained that the war's purpose was to restore the Union, he believed that Frémont's measure would damage the Union cause in the border states and possibly cause the pivotal state of

Kentucky to desert to the Confederacy. Lincoln lectured his Illinois political ally, Orville Browning, "I was so assured, as to think it probably, that the very arms we had furnished Kentucky would be turned against us. I think to lose Kentucky is nearly the same as to lose the whole game. Kentucky gone, we can not hold Missouri, nor, as I think, Maryland. These all against us, and the job on our hands is too large for us."[11]

When Congress met in December 1861, there was plenty of dissatisfaction with the president. After overruling Frémont's proclamation in September, Lincoln removed the popular general from command in November 1861. In the eastern theater, Lincoln replaced Irvin McDowell with the dashing George B. McClellan, who had made a name for himself in West Virginia. While McClellan was determined to turn the Army of the Potomac into a model of efficiency, critics charged that McClellan intended to drill and organize, but never fight. One sure sign of dissatisfaction with Lincoln was the appointment of a special congressional committee to investigate military affairs: the Joint Committee on the Conduct of the War. Chaired by Ohio Republican Ben Wade, the committee included some of the staunchest antislavery advocates in the Republican Party, including Michigan's Zachariah Chandler and Indiana Republican George W. Julian. Throughout the rest of the war, the committee would attempt to direct and prod the president, introducing an unwanted and unwarranted nuisance to Union military efforts. As 1861 turned into 1862, Lincoln had great hopes for Union military fortunes. Unfortunately for the president, the coming year would be perhaps the most frustrating of all his years as commander-in-chief.[12]

1862 began on a positive note when Union forces under Brigadier General Ulysses S. Grant captured Fort Henry and Fort Donelson on the Tennessee and Cumberland Rivers respectively. The inactivity of the Army of the Potomac, however, continued to annoy the president. Lincoln tried to remedy the situation by issuing General Order #1 on January 27, 1862, which directed the forward movement of all federal forces on Washington's birthday, February 22. Although the order did not prompt McClellan to move, it did force him to reveal his military musings to the president, a strategy that McClellan called the Urbanna plan. Under this scheme, federal forces would be transported via naval transport to Urbanna, Virginia, near the mouth of the Rappahannock River, thus placing Union forces between the Confederate capital at Richmond and its principal army stationed near Manassas Junction. Though skeptical, Lincoln eventually assented to the plan and its eventual change to striking Richmond from the east via the Virginia Peninsula when the Confederate Army prematurely withdrew from Manassas Junction southward to the Rappahannock River.

What began as a promising spring ended up in disappointment. McClellan floundered on the Peninsula, becoming indecisive, passive, and convinced that he was drastically outnumbered. By early July, his army languished at Harrison's Landing, having been driven from the outskirts of Richmond by a more aggressive Confederate army under Robert E. Lee. While military affairs were more positive in the western theater, it was the eastern theater that was the focus of national attention. It was in the context of a gloomy military situation that Lincoln began to think seriously about attacking slavery. Although a number of Republican congressmen, including Charles Sumner, Benjamin F. Wade, and Thaddeus Stevens, had urged such action for quite a long while, Lincoln had hesitated. After all, he had conservative members of his own party, the border states, and members of the Democratic Party to consider—and such a move might not be popular with those constituents.

Although Lincoln had resisted the pressure for an outright decree of emancipation, he had endorsed partial measures such as compensated emancipation in the District of Columbia as well as his own plan of voluntary emancipation for the border states. On July 12, 1862, Lincoln met with representatives of the border states, who promptly rejected his plan for voluntary, gradual, and compensated emancipation. With the war at a seeming standstill and this rejection from the border states fresh in his mind, Lincoln made a dramatic announcement to Cabinet members William H. Seward and Gideon Welles while taking a carriage ride with them that July. He told the two of his decision to issue an Emancipation Proclamation. Then, at a July 22 Cabinet meeting, an Emancipation Proclamation was discussed. While the Cabinet was not in total agreement on the policy, Lincoln finally agreed with Secretary of State Seward, who advised Lincoln to hold the proclamation until after a significant military triumph was achieved; otherwise, according to Seward, the proclamation would look like an act of desperation.[13]

Publicly Lincoln maintained the official position that the war was waged soley for the restoration of the Union. Indeed, the president's most famous statement of this position appeared when he responded to *New York Tribune* editor Horace Greeley's editorial entitled "The Prayer of Twenty Millions." "My paramount object in this struggle *is* to save the Union," the president told Greeley, "and *is not* either to save or to destroy slavery." A demoralizing military defeat suffered by Union forces at the second battle of Manassas in late August made it impractical for Lincoln to issue an Emancipation Proclamation. Lincoln had temporarily transferred the bulk of McClellan's Army of the Potomac to the blustering John Pope, a western general that Lincoln had put in charge of the newly formed Army of Virginia. With demoralized Union soldiers retreating toward the capital, Lincoln turned again to McClellan. The "Young Napoleon" responded to the challenge, reorganizing and bolstering the morale of the army once again. When McClellan's Army of the Potomac checked Lee's invading Army of Northern Virginia at the battle of Antietam in Maryland on September 17, Lincoln decided to strike against slavery, issuing a preliminary

Emancipation Proclamation on September 22, 1862. In effect, Lincoln gave the South ninety days to lay down arms and come back into the Union; otherwise, Southerners would lose their slaves forever.[14]

While most Republicans greeted the proclamation with enthusiasm, Democrats denounced the document with venom. Since early summer, the bipartisanship that had characterized the early days of the war had deteriorated for a variety of reasons. Passionately Negrophobic, many Democratic voters were already skeptical about the most minimal attacks against the peculiar institution. For many Democrats, a full-blown proclamation raised the specter of floods of free black laborers surging into the North, displacing white workers and creating a new society based on miscegenation. When the fall 1862 elections went poorly for Republicans, many experts claimed it was not only the state of the war but also the preliminary emancipation proclamation that eroded Republican electoral strength.[15]

Lincoln's problems with the Democrats were scarcely over with the fall electoral setbacks. Despite poor Republican performance in the elections, the president felt strong enough to replace General Don Carlos Buell in the West and the popular McClellan in the East, both of whom opposed emancipation and were incapable of conducting offensive operations. Lincoln replaced McClellan with Ambrose Burnside, who promptly led the Army of the Potomac into a disastrous defeat at the battle of Fredericksburg on December 13, 1862, plunging Northern morale into the depths of despair. Democrats in Congress were emboldened and talked of forcing the president to back down on his final emancipation decree. Angry radical Republicans believed that conservative members of Lincoln's Cabinet, such as William Seward and Montgomery Blair, were responsible for poor military performance. When a caucus of Republican senators called on Lincoln in an effort to force the president to dismiss Seward, Lincoln told Orville Browning, "They wish to get rid of me, and I am sometimes half disposed to gratify them." He added, "We are now on the brink of destruction. It appears to me that the Almighty is against us, and I can hardly see a ray of hope." In the end, Lincoln was able to prevent congressional Republicans from reorganizing his Cabinet; nevertheless, at the end of 1862, the future looked bleak.[16]

With the coming of a new year, Lincoln did not back down from the final Emancipation Proclamation. In fact, the final version even contained provisions for arming African American soldiers, which provided an important boost to Northern armies in the war's final years. Still, the Northern military situation did not markedly improve, a fact that kept the Northern peace Democrats in high spirits. When Lincoln replaced Ambrose Burnside with Joseph Hooker for commander of the Army of the Potomac, Hooker used tough rhetoric, asserting that it was not a matter of "if" but "when" he would take Richmond. Apprised of Hooker's opinion that perhaps a dictatorship was necessary to win the war, Lincoln remind Hooker that only successful generals could become dictators—he would settle for military victory and risk the dictatorship. Hooker proved unfit for the task and suffered a humiliating defeat at Chancellorsville, Virginia, in early May 1863.

With the defeat at Chancellorsville and the arrest of Clement Vallandigham in the same month, antiwar sentiments soared in the North. In Ohio, the arrest and banishment of Vallandigham enabled the Ohio Democrat to gain the Democratic gubernatorial nomination. Enraged New York Democrats sent Lincoln a public letter protesting the arrest of Vallandigham and the curtailment of civil liberties in general. Lincoln publicly responded to such accusations in the so-called Corning Letter, addressed to the leader of the New York Democrats, Erastus Corning. Justifying his actions on the grounds of wartime necessity, Lincoln scolded New York Democrats for a narrow and legalistic view of constitutional liberties. Referring to Vallandigham, the president asked, "Must I shoot a simple-minded soldier boy who deserts, while I must not touch a hair of the wiley agitator who induces him to desert?" Fortunately for Lincoln, the cause of the peace Democrats who were opposed to the war was severely damaged by Union victories at Gettysburg in Pennsylvania on July 1–3 and Vicksburg in Mississippi on July 4. The latter placed the entire Mississippi River in Union hands. The former stopped Robert E. Lee's bid to win a decisive victory in the North and further fuel antiwar sentiment there. Although Lincoln was not happy that General George Gordon Meade, the Union commander at Gettysburg, seemingly allowed Lee's retreating army a free pass across the Potomac River back into Virginia, the victories were enough to stem the tide of Northern antiwar sentiment. In the fall 1863 elections, popular Democratic candidates, derisively known as "Copperheads," went down to defeat, most prominently in the gubernatorial races in Ohio and Pennsylvania, where Republican candidates decisively routed Democratic nominees Clement Vallandigham and jurist George W. Woodward respectively.[17]

In December 1863, with the war's outcome still uncertain but promising, Lincoln contemplated the postwar Reconstruction of the South, making his first major presentation of the subject when he issued his proclamation of amnesty and Reconstruction. Popularly known as the Ten Percent Plan, Lincoln set down minimal conditions to allow states to resume their position in the Union. Whenever 10 percent of a seceded state's 1860 registered voters swore an oath of loyalty to the Constitution (including an oath to obey all acts of Congress as well as presidential proclamations on slavery), that state could hold elections to elect representatives to Congress and assume its place in the Union. A lenient plan, Lincoln's view was consistent with his constitutional perspective on secession, which held that secession was a legal impossibility and that all seceded states were still in the Union. It was only logical, therefore, that restoration would be a relatively brief, painless, and uncomplicated process.[18]

The debate over Reconstruction would be a major bone of contention between various factions within the Republican Party for the duration of the war. Many anti-Lincoln Republicans supported the candidacy of Secretary of Treasury Salmon Chase for the presidency in early 1864. While the Chase candidacy fizzled and Lincoln was unanimously nominated at the June 1864 Baltimore convention, Reconstruction policy was still a volatile issue. Henry Winter Davis, a virulently anti-Lincoln, anti-Blair Maryland Republican, had maneuvered a Reconstruction bill through the House that was much tougher on the Southern states than the president's plan. Cosponsored by Benjamin F. Wade in the Senate, the measure became known as the Wade-Davis bill. Like Lincoln's plan, this bill maintained that seceded states had never left the Union; however, it specified each state to meet a number of requirements before it could assume its place in the Union. First, it stated that 50 percent of the state's 1860 voting population swear an ironclad oath that they had never willingly aided the Confederacy. Wade-Davis also provides that each state constitutionally prohibit slavery, using the clause of the Constitution (Article 4, Section 4) that requires Congress to provide a republican form of government for each state. Lincoln believed that Congress could not force states to abolish slavery. Employing the little-used device of the pocket veto (allowing a bill to die by ignoring it and allowing the session of Congress to end), Lincoln killed the bill a few days after Congress recessed that July. The aftermath of Lincoln's pocket veto divided the Republican Party and almost cost him a second term.

Angered by Lincoln's action, Henry Winter Davis and Benjamin Wade published a scathing rebuke of Lincoln's pocket veto (known as the Wade-Davis manifesto) that appeared in the *New York Tribune*. Wade and Davis now proposed another Republican convention whose purpose would be to force Lincoln to withdraw in favor of another candidate. With John C. Frémont already posing as a third party candidate and military affairs at a stalemate, the potential nomination of George B. McClellan by the Democrats would seriously jeopardized the president's chances for reelection.

Military matters had started off in 1864 on a positive note. Lincoln finally found the generals he believed had the proper fighting attitude in Ulysses S. Grant and William T. Sherman. Promoted to lieutenant general in March 1864, Grant would coordinate overall military strategy and command the Army of the Potomac, while Sherman would handle Union forces in the West. With Sherman moving toward Atlanta, pressuring the Confederate Army under Joseph Johnston, Grant would move on Lee in Virginia. Unlike previous Northern commanders, there would be no turning back. Unfortunately for Lincoln and the country, Grant's strategy led to a number of bloody battles in the late spring and summer of 1864. In the battles of the Wilderness, Spotsylvania, Cold Harbor, and finally Petersburg, Grant by mid-summer sustained casualties of over 75,000 men. At the same time, in the West, Sherman's forces seemed to accomplish little, failing to capture the important city of Atlanta. Grant's high casualties and Sherman's lack of progress temporarily revived antiwar sentiment. Combining the antiwar feeling with Republican factionalism, Lincoln's reelection seemed unlikely even to Lincoln himself.

Yet events rapidly turned in Lincoln's favor. First, Zachariah Chandler, Michigan's senior Republican senator, helped negotiate a deal to unite Republicans behind Lincoln, orchestrating the withdrawal of Frémont as a candidate in exchange for the removal of the hated Montgomery Blair from the Cabinet. Secondly, the Democrats self-destructed when they met in Chicago in late August. Allowing peace advocates a disproportionate degree of influence, Democrats produced a war candidate, George McClellan, on a platform that branded the war a failure. This contradiction played into Republican hands, particularly after Northerners received a positive piece of military news: the fall of Atlanta to Sherman's army on September 2, 1864. Eventually disaffected Republican radicals, including the likes of Wade, Davis, and Salmon P. Chase, realized that Lincoln was preferable to McClellan and supported the Republican ticket. When the election was over, Lincoln had won a resounding victory, winning by a 55 to 45 percent margin in the popular vote and an even more substantial victory in the Electoral College.

As 1865 dawned and the end of the Confederacy was in sight, Congress constitutionally moved against slavery, passing the Thirteenth Amendment, which constitutionally abolished slavery, much to the satisfaction of the president. On the divisive issue of Reconstruction, however, congressional Republicans and the president remained divided. A compromise Reconstruction bill, designed to mediate the differences between the president's Ten Percent Plan and the Wade-Davis bill, could not be passed. Additionally, Congress refused to recognize Louisiana's Reconstruction government, organized under the Ten Percent Plan of the president. Some of Lincoln's public utterances suggest that he continued to favor a lenient, conciliatory Reconstruction. His masterful second inaugural address suggested conciliation: "With malice toward none; with charity toward all; with firmness in the right, as God gives us to see the right, let us strive on to finish the work we are in; to bind up the nation's wounds; to care for him who shall have borne the battle, and for his widow, and his orphan—to do all which may achieve and cherish a just, and a lasting peace, among ourselves, and with all nations." At the same time, while near the end of his life, Lincoln began to show signs of edging toward the more radical position. A cornerstone of radical Reconstruction was the enfranchisement of adult black males. In his last public utterance, with Senator Charles Sumner at his side, Lincoln defended his plan for Louisiana, but, at the same time, suggested open-mindedness on black suffrage. "It is also unsatisfactory to some," Lincoln told his audience, "that the elective franchise is not given to the colored man. I would myself prefer that it were now conferred on the very intelligent, and on those who serve our cause as soldiers."[19]

How Reconstruction would have been implemented in Lincoln's second term is purely speculative. Just after Lee's surrender to Grant at Appomattox, the president was assassinated. The fanatical, alcoholic, pro-Confederate actor John Wilkes Booth ended Lincoln's life and any plans for Reconstruction on April 15, when he assassinated the sixteenth president as he watched a performance of *Our American Cousin* at Ford's Theater. With Lincoln's death early the next morning, perhaps the best chance for a sensible, conciliatory Reconstruction policy ended.

PRINCIPAL IDEAS

Lincoln, Slavery, and Civil Rights

In popular American history, Abraham Lincoln has gained a reputation as a giant in the antislavery movement—sometimes to the detriment of a number of other important Republican politicians who took bolder stands at much earlier junctures of their political lives and at much greater political risks. In reality, Lincoln's conversion to the antislavery movement was somewhat tardy. While there is no hypocrisy in Lincoln's later statements that he had always opposed slavery, it is also true that slavery was not a major issue for him in his early political career. Although he did vote for the Wilmot Proviso, antislavery sentiments did not become the core of Abraham Lincoln's political beliefs until after the passage of the Kansas-Nebraska Act. By that time, such veteran political abolitionists as Salmon Chase, Thaddeus Stevens, Benjamin F. Wade, Charles Sumner, Joshua Giddings, and Lincoln's Illinois colleague, Owen Lovejoy, were well-established figures in the American antislavery movement. Prior to 1854, one looks in vain for an abundance of antislavery sentiment in Lincoln's correspondence or speeches.[20]

When the Kansas-Nebraska Act placed the slavery question at the top of Lincoln's political agenda, it was embraced primarily from the standpoint of antiextensionism. Borrowing liberally from the arguments of other political abolitionists, Lincoln, in speech and letters, skillfully reconstructed the argument that the Founding Fathers had intended freedom to be national, while slavery was to be a local institution without the sanction of national authority. This was the logic of the Northwest Ordinances, the Missouri Compromise of 1820, and, in Lincoln's opinion, even the recent Compromise of 1850. In Lincoln's rejoinder to Stephen Douglas in the senatorial debate at Quincy, Illinois, he stated the following: "When the fathers of the Government cut off the source slavery by the abolition of the slave-trade, and adopted a system of restricting it from the new Territories where it had not existed, I maintain that they placed it where they understood, and all sensible men understood, it was in the course of ultimate extinction; and when Judge Douglas asks me why it cannot continue as our fathers made it, I ask him why he and his friends could not let it remain as our fathers made it?"[21]

The logic that influenced the Founding Fathers, in Lincoln's view, was based on the Declaration of Independence and the promise of equality contained therein. For Lincoln, this promise implicitly included African Americans. While Douglas denied that the promises of the Declaration of Independence extended beyond white Europeans, Lincoln vehemently protested this assertion:

> I believe the entire records of the world, from the date of the Declaration of Independence up to within three years ago, may be searched in vain for one single affirmation, from one single man, that the Negro was not included in the Declaration of Independence; I think I may defy Judge Douglas to show that he ever said so, that Washington ever said so, that any President ever said so, that any member of Congress ever said so, or that any living man upon the whole earth ever said so.[22]

Although Lincoln stated that his position did not entail social and political equality between the races, he did believe that the Declaration of Independence guaranteed all races the right to life, liberty, and the pursuit of happiness. The question, according to Lincoln, depended on how one viewed the status of African Americans. "If he (a black person) is *not* a man, why in that case, he who *is* a man may, as a matter of self-government, do just as he pleases with him. But if the negro *is* a man, is it not to that extent, a total destruction of self-government, to say that he too shall not govern *himself*? . . . If the negro is a *man,* why then my ancient faith teaches me that 'all men are created equal;' and that there can be no moral right in connection with one man's making a slave of another."[23]

Lincoln, then, had assumed the high moral ground in his discourse on slavery in the 1850s, basing his opposition to the expansion of slavery on the principles contained in the Declaration of Independence. At the same time, however, Lincoln's position, particularly during the debates with Douglas, was riddled with ambiguities. Assuring the South that he intended to do nothing to interfere with slavery in states where it already existed, Lincoln filled his speeches with reference to the ultimate abolition of slavery with the imprecise phrase "course of ultimate extinction." Beyond this vague reference, Lincoln's actual plan for abolishing slavery was heavy on rhetoric but woefully short on details.

While claiming blacks were just as human as whites in several speeches, in practically the same breath, Lincoln went out of his way to disavow any hint of social and political equality between whites and blacks. At Charleston in 1858, Lincoln stated,

> I will say then that I am not, nor ever have been, in favor of bringing about in any way the social and political equality of the white and black races—that I am not nor ever have been in favor of making voters or jurors of Negroes, nor of qualifying them to hold office, nor to intermarry with white people; and I will say in addition to this that there is a physical difference between the white and black races which I believe will forever forbid the two races living together on terms of social and political equality. And inasmuch as they cannot so live, while they do remain together there must be the position of superior and inferior, and I as much as any other man am in favor of having the superior position assigned to the white race. I say upon this occasion that I do not perceive that because the white man is to have the superior position the Negro should be denied every thing. I do not understand that because I do not want a Negro woman for a slave I must necessarily want her for a wife. My understanding is that I can just let her alone.[24]

If blacks were covered under the Declaration of Independence, how could Lincoln so callously deny them the right to vote and to be jurors in almost the same breath? Lincoln's inability to confront head-on the emancipated black in free society left his position riddled with ambiguity and contradiction. Understandably, a logical outcome of his position was to fall back on Henry Clay's position with respect to emancipated blacks: colonization. Physical removal to Africa or Central America would, for Lincoln, solve the question of the status of blacks by removing the source of the problem, the emancipated black. Sticking to this concept at the outset of the war, Lincoln backed one ill-fated and foolhardy scheme to set up a free black colony in Chiriqui, Honduras. Obviously, part of Lincoln's ambivalence on the issue of civil rights for African Americans was his familiarity with the bitter Negrophobia that characterized his home state of Illinois and the entire free North. Undoubtedly aware of the numerous legal inequities that plagued the free black community throughout the North, Lincoln was cautious politically when it came to taking firm positions on black civil rights. As Lincoln told a delegation of free black leaders that visited him in the White House during the war, "Your race is suffering in my judgment, the greatest wrong inflicted on any people. But even when you cease to be slaves, you are yet far removed from being placed on equality with the white race. You are cut off from many of the advantages which the other race enjoy." Although Lincoln claimed to not be annoyed with the presence of blacks in society, he was certainly aware of the predominant Negrophobia that characterized the electorate at large. His uncertainty on how to proceed with the emancipated blacks in Northern society was the result of his awareness of the pervasiveness of racial prejudice.[25]

The outbreak of the Civil War brought new challenges to Lincoln's thinking on the slavery issue. Was the war being waged for the abolition of slavery? Could slavery simply be abolished by executive fiat as a war measure? What was to be done with the slave border states that had remained within the Union? While the radicals within the Republican Party were intent on the abolition of slavery by the fall of 1861, Lincoln's position was characterized by caution, pragmatism, and scrupulous regard for constitutional considerations. By the end of 1862, however, it was clear that Lincoln had clearly identified the cause of the Union with the abolition of slavery. Despite his disagreement with the radicals on such issues as the mechanics of Reconstruction, his commitment to constitutionally codifying abolition in the Thirteenth Amendment was firm and unwavering.

Still, the question of the status of African Americans in a free society was not completely resolved in Lincoln's mind when he was assassinated. While evidence suggests that the sixteenth president had abandoned the notion of colonization as impractical, the level of his commitment to full social and political rights for African Americans remains unclear. On the eve of his assassination, the president appeared to moving toward sponsorship of limited franchise for African Americans. Whether the president would have pursued the course endorsed by such radical Republicans as Thaddeus Stevens or Charles Sumner remains an open question.

Lincoln and Republican Economic Theory

Abraham Lincoln's views on slavery were also based on his vision of economics. In much of his correspondence and major speeches, Lincoln espoused the rhetoric of social mobility that resulted from hard work and enterprise. His economic ideas expressed the free labor ideology so popular with members of the Republican Party in the 1850s. The problem with the slave system, according to Lincoln, was that it started from the assumption that the status of the laborer was fixed forever. "They further assume that whoever is once a *hired* laborer, is fatally fixed in that condition for life," Lincoln told his audience at the Wisconsin State Fair in 1859, "and thence again that his condition is as bad as, or worse than that of a slave. This is the '*mud-sill*' theory."[26]

According to Lincoln, in the dynamic, fluid society of the North, effort and diligence determined the final social-economic status of the worker. As Lincoln stated,

The prudent, penniless beginner in the world, labors for wages awhile, saves a surplus with which to buy tools or land, for himself; then labors on his own account another while, and at length hires another new beginner to help him. This, say its advocates, is *free* labor—the just and generous, and prosperous system, which opens the way for all—gives hope to all, and energy, and progress, and improvement of condition to all. If any continue through life in the condition of the hired laborer, it is not the fault of the system, but because of either a dependent nature which prefers it, or improvidence, folly, or singular misfortune.[27]

Lincoln was enamored with the burgeoning market economy that was advancing across various parts of the United States in the 1850s. As an admirer and proponent of Henry Clay's American system, Lincoln rejected the Jeffersonian agrarian ethic of subsistence farming. This was the world of Thomas Lincoln that Abraham rejected early on in his youth. Instead, Lincoln looked to the larger, broader, national economy that was emerging as the result of legislative policies promoting internal improvements, commerce, and manufacturing. Historian Alan Guelzo points out that Lincoln's perspective was national, not local. He was a man who welcomed the competitive individualism brought about by the market economy.[28]

Indeed, as president, Lincoln presided over some of the most significant economic legislation of the nineteenth century, including the passage of the Pacific Railroad bill in addition to some of the highest protective tariff measures in the nation's history. Ironically, many of the measures brought about during the war did not sustain the type of individualistic, competitive society that Lincoln endorsed in many of his letters and lectures. Instead of a fluid society where hired laborers became the petite capitalists, the very situation that Lincoln applauded and endorsed in his address to the Wisconsin State Fair, a different type of American economy emerged in the late nineteenth century. The emergence of national markets, national transportation systems, and large corporations made wage labor the permanent lot of many American laborers. Regardless of whether one views the emergence of the modern United States as something that primarily benefited ordinary Americans or harmed them, the free labor vision of the Republican Party seemed largely irrelevant in the years following the Civil War. It seems doubtful that Lincoln could have been entirely oblivious to the changes taking place in the American economy that would render it increasingly difficult for wage laborers to enter into the class of business ownership. Nevertheless, Lincoln's written speeches and correspondence are what they are. Despite economic forces at work that were rapidly changing the face of the American economy, Lincoln clung to his simple belief in social mobility and small owners/producers. Perhaps this optimism was a recollection of his own history and his own rise from obscurity to the pinnacle of political leadership.

Lincoln and Military Strategy

The most ironic feature of the Lincoln presidency was that it was characterized by war making. Lincoln had almost no usable military experience. He had spent a few months in the Illinois militia chasing Chief Black Hawk; however, he participated in no engagements of any kind. By his own admission, the biggest enemy he faced in the Illinois woods that summer was mosquitoes.[29]

As commander-in-chief, Lincoln came into the crisis with tremendous advantages over his counterpart, Jefferson Davis. Northern superiority in manpower, material resources, transportation, and weaponry are well known. Even the so-called Southern advantages in military experience have been overstated. The Union had as many competent West Point educated generals as did the South. Northern advantages, however, did not translate into inevitable union victory. The key for Lincoln was bringing Northern advantages to bear against the South in ways that would eventually produce military victory.

Popular opinion and impatient congressmen pressured Lincoln's decision making early on in the conflict. Indeed, without extensive military training, Lincoln, too, fell victim to a number of popular misconceptions about warfare. Perhaps the most prevalent was the failure to appreciate how technological innovations in weaponry had given tactical defense tremendous advantages. While popular attitudes believed that frontal assaults, led by brave men armed with smoothbore muskets and bayonets, would carry the day, new rifled muskets equipped with minieball increased the effective accuracy of infantry weapons from 80 yards to 300 yards. Frontal assaults, even by vastly superior numbers, could be picked apart and broken up by well-entrenched defenders. For this reason, with a couple of notable exceptions, frontal assaults were largely ineffective during the Civil War, accomplishing little else than high rates of casualty.

At the war's beginning, Lincoln allowed impatient congressmen and journalists to rush him into action at the first battle of Manassas, and, through the influence of such amateurish groups such as the Committee on the Conduct of the War, he sometimes maintained and promoted inexperienced and incompetent generals. At various times in the war, Lincoln, too, had unrealistic expectations of his generals and succumbed to the popular notion that one grand victory would destroy the Confederacy. Thus, when Union generals McClellan and Meade failed to follow up on a retreating enemy after the battles of Antietam and Gettysburg, Lincoln was convinced that the opportunity for apocalyptic, war-ending battles had been missed. Lincoln failed to realize early on that one dramatic battle was unlike to win the conflict; rather, it was a war of attrition that had to be waged, where through sustained pressure, the enemy's resources would eventually be worn down, causing the erosion of the will to fight and eventual surrender.

Unlike the public, Lincoln also proved that he was capable of learning a great deal concerning military matters. He began the war as a rank amateur, but by the time Lee surrendered to Grant at Appomattox, Lincoln had become a competent commander-in-chief. The principal component to Lincoln's education as a soldier was his mastery of concentrations in time and space, that is, putting pressure on Confederate forces on many fronts simultaneously so that the enemy could not shift troops to meet individual situations, and thus take advantage of interior lines. Already in early January 1862, Lincoln lectured Major General Don Carlos Buell, using this principle. Lincoln told Buell that the only way Union forces could take advantage of numerical superiority was to threaten Confederate forces "at *different* points, at the *same* time." This was also the intent of General Order #1, which mandated the forward movement of all Union armies on Washington's birthday. When Ulysses Grant came to Washington in March 1864 and proposed a strategy of perpetual engagement to prevent Confederate armies from shifting troops to meet individual hot points, Lincoln was jubilant, telling Grant that those who were not skinning could at least hold a leg.[30]

Similarly, Lincoln's thinking on the method of waging war went through a similar evolution. Early on Lincoln, along with much of Congress, endorsed a policy known as conciliation. This view held that the majority of Southerners did not support secession. If the rights of Southerners with respect to property and slaves were honored, the tide of secession, this view argued, would exhaust itself, and wayward Southerners would come back into the Union. While Republican radicals wanted to pursue more rigorous measures early in the conflict, Lincoln resisted their efforts until he was convinced that the timing for such measures as the Emancipation Proclamation, the arming of black soldiers, and the confiscation of property was appropriate. By the beginning of the 1864 campaigns, Lincoln was comfortable with the type of warfare Grant and Sherman were waging in the South, where critical war-making resources and infrastructure were systematically dismantled by invading Union armies. War was more than armed conflict between professionally led armies. As Lincoln learned, it involved entire societies.

CONCLUSION

Abraham Lincoln has earned the reputation as one of the nation's greatest, if not the greatest, presidents. This reputation is hard to deny, given the fact that Lincoln presided over the most tumultuous event in American history. In assessing the Lincoln presidency, one must also realize that the Lincoln who assumed office in March 1861 was a very different Lincoln from the one who died from Booth's bullet. Lincoln was woefully unprepared for the office of the presidency, particularly during a time of grave national crisis. Through hard work and determination, he mastered the presidency and his office of commander-in-chief. Rising from humble beginnings to the office of the presidency, Abraham Lincoln was the embodiment of the ideology of upward mobility that he fervently endorsed in his political speeches and writing. By successfully guiding the nation through civil war, Lincoln kept alive a society promised in the Declaration of Independence that he so cherished.

NOTES

1. See John William Ward, *Andrew Jackson: Symbol for an Age* (New York: Oxford University Press, 1955), 79–97.

2. Lincoln quote is from David Herbert Donald, *Lincoln* (New York: Simon & Schuster, 1995), 19.

3. See Allen C. Guelzo, "Come-Outers and Community Men: Abraham Lincoln and the Idea of Community in Nineteenth-Century American," *Journal of the Abraham Lincoln Association* 21 (Winter 2000): 1–30. The struggle between subsistence farming and the emerging market economy is expertly conveyed in Charles E. Sellers, *The Market Revolution: Jacksonian America, 1815–1846* (New York: Oxford University Press, 1991).

4. Lincoln's courtship struggles are detailed in Douglas L. Wilson, "Abraham Lincoln and 'That Fatal First of January,'" *Civil War History* 38 (June, 1992): 101–30.

5. On Lincoln's relationship with women, see Frank J. Williams, *Judging Lincoln* (Carbondale: Southern Illinois University Press, 2002), 17–33.

6. Lincoln to William H. Herndon, February 15, 1848, in *The Collected Works of Abraham Lincoln*, edited by Roy P. Basler (New Brunswick, NJ: Rutgers University Press, 1953), 1:451–52 (quote, 451).

7. Lincoln to Joshua F. Speed, August 24, 1855, in *Collected Works of Abraham Lincoln*, 2:320–23 (quote, 322–23). This section was also influenced by Robert W. Johannsen, *Lincoln, the South, and Slavery: The Political Dimension* (Baton Rouge: Louisiana State University Press, 1991).

8. Robert W. Johannsen, ed., *The Lincoln-Douglas Debates of 1858* (New York: Oxford University Press, 1965), 18.

9. Johannsen, *Lincoln-Douglas Debates*, 225.

10. James McPherson. *Ordeal by Fire: The Civil War and Reconstruction* (New York: Alfred A. Knopf, 1982), 121–26.

11. Lincoln to Orville Browning, September 22, 1861, in *Collected Works of Abraham Lincoln*, 4:531–33 (quote, 532).

12. Bruce Tap, *Over Lincoln's Shoulder: The Committee on the Conduct of the War* (Lawrence: University of Kansas Press, 1998).

13. Matthew Pinsker, *Lincoln's Sanctuary: Abraham Lincoln and the Soldier's Home* (New York: Oxford University Press, 2003), 40–43; and *The Diary of Gideon Welles, Secretary of the Navy under Lincoln and Johnson*, edited by Howard K. Beale (New York: W. W. Norton & Company, 1928), 1:70–71.

14. Lincoln to Horace Greeley, August 22, 1862, in *Collected Works of Abraham Lincoln*, 5:388–89 (quote, 388).

15. Bruce Tap, "Race, Rhetoric, and Emancipation: The Election of 1862 in Illinois," *Civil War History* 39 (June 1993): 101–25.

16. *The Diary of Orville Hickman Browning,* edited by Theodore Calvin Pease and James G. Randall (Springfield: Illinois State Historical Library, 1925), 1:600.

17. For the Corning letter see Lincoln to Erastus Corning and Others [June 12, 1863], *Collected Works of Abraham Lincoln,* 6:260–69 (quote, 266). On Lincoln's dissatisfaction with Meade's handling of the army after the battle of Gettysburg, see Frank Williams, *Judging Lincoln,* 80–92; and Bruce Tap, " 'Bad Faith Somewhere': George Gordon Meade and the Committee on the Conduct of the War," *North & South* 2 (August 1999): 74–81.

18. Lincoln's views on reconstruction are discussed in William C. Harris, *With Charity for All: Abraham Lincoln and the Restoration of the Union* (Lexington: University of Kentucky Press, 1997).

19. "Second Inaugural Address," March 5, 1865, in *Collected Works of Abraham Lincoln,* 8:332–33 (quote, 333); and "Last Public Address," April 11, 1865, in *Collected Works of Abraham Lincoln,* 8:399–406 (quote, 403).

20. Douglas L. Wilson, *Honor's Voice: The Transformation of Abraham Lincoln* (New York: Alfred A. Knopf, 1998), 164–66. Robert W. Johannsen offers a critical examination of Lincoln's transformation into an antislavery politician during the 1850s; see Johannsen, *Lincoln, the South, and Slavery.*

21. *Lincoln-Douglas Debates,* 277–78.

22. *Lincoln-Douglas Debates,* 219–20.

23. "The Question of Slavery Extension: Speech on the Kansas-Nebraska Act, 1854," in *The Political Thought of Abraham Lincoln,* edited by Richard N. Current (New York: MacMillan, 1967), 72–73.

24. *Lincoln-Douglas Debates,* 162–63.

25. "Remarks to Committee of Colored Men, 1862," in *Collected Works of Abraham Lincoln,* 5:370–75 (quote, 371–72).

26. "Address at the Wisconsin State Fair, 1859," in *Collected Works of Abraham Lincoln,* 3:471–82 (quote, 478). For the Free Labor Argument, see Eric Foner, *Free Soil, Free Labor, Free Men: The Ideology of the Republican Party before the Civil War* (New York: Oxford University Press, 1970).

27. "Address at the Wisconsin State Fair, 1859," 3:478–79.

28. Allen C. Guelzo, *Abraham Lincoln: Redeemer President* (Grand Rapids, MI: William B. Eerdmans Publishing Company, 1999), 26–63. Also see note 3.

29. This section is draws heavily on Bruce Tap, "Amateurs at War: Abraham Lincoln and the Committee on the Conduct of the War," *Journal of the Abraham Lincoln Association* 23 (Summer 2002): 1–18; and idem., "Inevitability, Masculinity, and the American Military Tradition: The Committee on the Conduct of the War Investigates the American Civil War," *American Nineteen Century History* 5 (Summer 2004): 19–46.

30. Lincoln to Don C. Buell, January 13, 1862, in *Collected Works of Abraham Lincoln,* 5:98–99 (quote, 98).

FURTHER READING

Michael Burlingame, *The Inner World of Abraham Lincoln* (Urbana: University of Illinois Press, 1994); Richard J. Carwardine, *Lincoln* (Harlow, UK: Pearson Education, 2003); Richard N. Current, *The Lincoln Nobody Knows* (New York: Mc-

Graw Books, 1958); David Donald, *Lincoln* (New York: Simon & Schuster, 1995); William E. Gienapp, *Abraham Lincoln and Civil War America* (New York: Oxford University Press, 2002); Allen C. Guelzo, *Abraham Lincoln: Redeemer President* (Grand Rapids, MI: William B. Eerdmans, 1999); Reinhold Luthin, *The Real Abraham Lincoln* (Englewood Cliffs, NJ: Prentice Hall, 1960); Mark E. Neely Jr., *The Last Best Hope on Earth: Abraham Lincoln and the Promise of America* (Cambridge, MA: Harvard University Press, 1993); Stephen B. Oates, *With Malice toward None: The Life of Abraham Lincoln* (New York: Harper & Row, 1977); Philip Shaw Paludan, *The Presidency of Abraham Lincoln* (Lawrence: University Press of Kansas, 1994); Matthew Pinsker, *Lincoln's Sanctuary: Abraham Lincoln and the Soldier's Home* (New York: Oxford University Press, 2003); James Garfield Randall, *Lincoln the President*, 4 vols. (New York: Dodd, Meade & Company, 1945); Benjamin Thomas, *Abraham Lincoln: A Biography* (New York: Alfred A. Knopf, 1952); and Douglas L. Wilson, *Honor's Voice: The Transformation of Abraham Lincoln* (New York: Alfred A. Knopf, 1998).

GEORGE BRINTON McCLELLAN
(1826–1885)

The Young Napoleon

LIFE

George Brinton McClellan was born in Philadelphia on December 3, 1826, the son of Dr. George McClellan and Elizabeth Steinmetz Brinton. The oldest of five children (three sons and two daughters), George Brinton McClellan came from a family with long roots in the Americas. McClellan's great grandfather, Samuel, who lived in Woodstock, Connecticut, was a veteran of the French and Indian Wars. Samuel's grandson, George McClellan Sr., was a graduate of Yale University and also earned a medical degree from the University of Pennsylvania in 1819. By the time George Jr. was born, George Sr. was a well-established ophthalmologist and a member of the city's high society. His marriage to Elizabeth Brinton, the daughter of another prominent family, cemented the McClellan family's elite status in Philadelphia society.

George McClellan Jr. was the beneficiary of a first-rate education, attending infant school at age five, followed by five years at a private school run by Harvard graduate and accomplished scientist Sears Cook Walker. McClellan was then tutored by a private teacher, and then spent the next two years at a prestigious Philadelphia prep school before matriculating to the University of Pennsylvania at the youthful age of thirteen. After graduation, McClellan considered a career in law, but eventually opted for the military. Securing an appointment to West Point, McClellan arrived there as the youngest and smallest of the freshmen class. Youth and size, however, would not thwart his desire for success.

Almost every facet of the West Point regimen appealed to George McClellan. He excelled at academics. "I am head of my class at West Point," he bragged to his brother, "a distinction well worth having—rather different than 'taking first honors' at college." In fact, after his three-year stay at the academy, McClellan would graduate second; only classmate Charles Seaford Stewart would finish ahead of him. Nevertheless, many of his classmates regarded McClellan as the star of the class of 1846.[1]

McClellan was also comfortable with the discipline and Spartan routine of the academy. While not opposed to having fun, as witnessed by his occasional visits to Benny Haven's tavern—a local pub that was off-limits to West Point cadets—McClellan thrived in the environment of the military academy. Although critics of West Point accused the academy of fostering an elitist, pro-Southern point of view, McClellan fit nicely into the social structure of the academy. In particular, he often preferred the company of Southern cadets, getting along particularly well with such Southern classmates as Ambrose Powell Hill and Cadmus Wilcox.

After graduation, McClellan received a coveted appointment in the prestigious Army Corps of Engineers. When the war with Mexico erupted in the spring of 1846, he was appointed second lieutenant in an elite engineering company led by Captain Alexander J. Swift. After training at West Point, McClellan and his company arrived in Brazos de Santiago, Mexico, in September 1846. Eventually, McClellan's company accompanied Winfield Scott's army of invasion, which captured Mexico City the following year. McClellan lived up to his reputation, distinguishing himself in a number of battles, including the battle of Contreras and Churubusco.

The Mexican War was an important event in the professional development of McClellan. For the first time, this professionally educated West Pointer saw volunteer soldiers in action. He was not impressed. "They are useless, useless, useless—expensive, wasteful—good for nothing." Undoubtedly, McClellan's low opinion of volunteer soldiers was a factor in his cautious demeanor during the Civil War. The Mexican War also gave him a strong distaste for civilian control of the military. Indeed, he had a less than favorable view of his commander-in-chief, President James K. Polk. The whole notion of ignorant civilians directing professional soldiers was anathema to the young second lieutenant. This attitude, like his distrust of volunteers, carried over into McClellan's Civil War career, particularly in his reluctance to share his plans with President Abraham Lincoln.[2]

After the war with Mexico ended, McClellan stayed in the army, joining the faculty of West Point, where he taught engineering. His politics at this time were decidedly conservative, which was very much in step with the majority of the U.S. officer corps. He had little sympathy for abolitionists and "higher law" fanatics. Although he endorsed Whig candidate Zachary Taylor for president in 1848, McClellan eventually settled into the Democratic Party and its conservative tenets on race, fiscal matters, and social issues.

After spending a few years with the company of engineers at West Point, McClellan spent a couple of years of active duty in the American West, where he served under his future father-in-law, Randolph Marcy. Stationed

at Fort Smith, Arkansas, McClellan served Marcy as both commissary engineer and quartermaster. He was also commissioned during the 1850s to
perform a survey for Congress for a proposed transcontinental railroad.
One biographer, however, argues that McClellan's excessive caution caused
a lackluster performance in this capacity. For instance, any report of Native American activity in the area would slow the overly cautious McClellan's work. Indeed, McClellan's hesitation as a Civil War general was
foreshadowed in his work as an army surveyor.

In 1855 McClellan received a prestigious assignment abroad: he was appointed to a military commission that observed European military affairs
and, in particular, the performance of European armies in the Crimean War.
His official report, which won critical acclaim, was influential in his own
view of military tactics and strategy during the Civil War. The Crimean
War, particularly the siege of Sevastopol by French and British forces,
demonstrated the awesome power of tactical defense, due primarily to the
advent of rifled weaponry and sophisticated defensive fortifications. More
than anything else, this experience contributed to McClellan's tactical views
as a commander during the Civil War.[3]

In 1857, McClellan left the army to pursue a career in the private sector. Although he had been associated with West Point and the U.S. Army
for almost fifteen years, like many West Point graduates, he viewed the
army as a dead end—its small size meant that promotions were few and
far between. Through a personal friendship with Abram Hewitt, an iron-
master for the Illinois Central Railroad, and Samuel Barlow, an able attorney who was well connected to the Democratic Party, McClellan was
hired as chief engineer for the Illinois Central, a position he held for two
years. During this time, he quarreled bitterly over the financial direction of
the company with the company president, William Osborne. Enlisting the
help of Barlow once again, McClellan secured a position with the Ohio &
Mississippi Railroad. Relocating from Chicago to Cincinnati, McClellan
quickly discovered that a change of scenery did not necessarily provide a
solution to his problems. As he had quarreled with Osborne, McClellan
now found himself embroiled in disputes over financial retrenchment with
the new company president, Joseph Alsop. The outbreak of war in 1861
would provide a new and welcome career alternative.

During the latter half of the 1850s, McClellan engaged in amorous pursuits. In 1854, he was introduced to Ellen Marcy, the daughter of Randolph Marcy, who McClellan had briefly served under at Fort Smith,
Arkansas. He was taken with "Miss Nelly" from the start. His only obstacle was the fact that Miss Nelly had little interest in him—despite the
fact that both her parents very much liked McClellan. Instead, Ellen fell
madly in love with McClellan's West Point classmate and friend, the dashing Ambrose Powell Hill, something that alarmed her parents. After much
parental pressure, however, Ellen eventually broke her engagement with

Hill, and a reinvigorated McClellan renewed his pursuit. This time he was successful. In October 1859, the Marcy family visited McClellan at his Chicago home, when Mrs. Marcy and Ellen accompanied Randolph to his new post in Minneapolis. Traveling with the family on an Illinois Central car to Minneapolis, McClellan proposed to Ellen and this time she accepted. The two were married the following year in the Calvary Protestant Episcopal Church in New York City. The couple would have two children, May, born in 1862, and George Brinton ("Max"), born in 1864.

The central drama in McClellan's life was his participation in the Civil War. A supporter of Stephen A. Douglas in the presidential election of 1860, McClellan shared the viewpoint of Douglas that stressed that the secession crisis and eventual eruption of hostilities were the result of "ultras" in the North and the South. Moreover, like Douglas, McClellan did not hesitate to answer the call to restore the Union. His first command was in Ohio, where he was commissioned by Governor William Dennison as a major general of volunteers and put in charge of all state troops. He was quickly appointed to head up the Department of Ohio and promoted to major general in the regular army. When the State of Virginia seceded from the Union, McClellan was dispatched to West Virginia to rally loyal Unionists and drive out invading Confederates. After achieving a seemingly impressive victory at the battle of Rich Mountain (in fact, William S. Rosecrans was more responsible for Union victory), McClellan was summoned to Washington, where he replaced top commander Irvin McDowell after his defeat at the first battle of Manassas. The choice of McClellan was almost a foregone conclusion, as the dashing general now ranked second only to Winfield Scott in the regular army and had an excellent reputation from his service in the Mexican War.

At age thirty-four, McClellan's rise to top command was remarkable, but the "Young Napoleon," as he was called, seemed confident, almost arrogant, in his ability to get the job done. He threw himself energetically into reorganizing, refitting, and retraining the raw masses of recruits that swarmed the Washington camps. As an organizer and administrator, McClellan's talents were considerable. When impatient Northerners, particularly Republican congressmen, began to demand action, McClellan became defensive and critical. The haughty attitude of the military professional toward civilian leaders crept into his actions as well as his correspondence. Perhaps his most famous snubs were administered to President Abraham Lincoln. His contempt for his commander-in-chief is well documented, and throughout his correspondence, he repeatedly referred to Lincoln in derogatory ways, using such terms as the "original gorilla." On one occasion in the fall of 1861, McClellan went to bed after returning from an engagement, deliberately ignoring Lincoln, Secretary of State Seward, and Presidential Secretary John Hay, who were waiting at McClellan's headquarters to confer with the general.

Had McClellan's private correspondence been destroyed, the historical picture of the general would be much more sympathetic. Unfortunately, his correspondence often revealed a vain, arrogant attitude toward superiors, while also demonstrating a tendency toward self-pity and complaining. "It is perfectly sickening to have to work with such people & to see the fate of the nation in such hands," McClellan wrote his wife, ". . . I know that as a nation we have grievously sinned, but I trust that there is a limit to his [God's] wrath & that ere long we will begin to experience his mercy. But it is terrible to stand by & see the cowardice of the Presdt, the vileness of Seward, & the rascality of Cameron—Welles an old woman—Bates an old fool. The only man of courage & sense in the Cabinet is Blair, & I do not altogether fancy him!"[4]

Early on in his tenure as commander of the Army of the Potomac, McClellan deflected criticism about the inactivity of his army by blaming General-in-Chief Winfield Scott. When Scott retired in early November 1861 and was replaced by McClellan, his critics became impatient at the lack of activity in the Army of the Potomac. Impatient congressmen created the Joint Committee on the Conduct of the War to investigate the military disasters at Bull Run and Ball's Bluff, but it was also clear that they intended to use the committee to prod the cautious McClellan into action. When McClellan became ill with typhoid in late December, President Lincoln tried to prod the army along by holding a conference with a number of McClellan's subordinates. McClellan surprised the president by attending a later conference on military strategy on the evening of January 11, 1862. When asked to outline his plan of operations against the rebel army, McClellan refused, whispering to Quartermaster General Montgomery Meigs that the president would blab his plans to the press. Contributing to McClellan's caution was his belief that his Confederate counterparts vastly outnumbered his army. Aided by the inflated estimates of secret service sleuth Allan Pinkerton, McClellan was convinced that rebel forces under General Joseph Johnston at Manassas numbered 200,000; instead, their actual size was just under 50,000. (McClellan's forces numbered 192,000 at the end of 1861.)[5]

Eventually, public pressure and an intense lobbying campaign by the Committee on the Conduct of the War forced President Lincoln to order the forward movement of all armies on February 22, 1862 (General Order #1). The order forced McClellan to reveal his military plans to the president and stimulated an intense discussion between the general-in-chief and the commander-in-chief. Lincoln believed the Confederates ought to be attacked at Manassas Junction. McClellan, on the other hand, had a radically different scheme. Believing that tactical defense was the best offense, McClellan advocated transporting the Army of the Potomac, via water, to Urbanna, Virginia, a small town located on the south bank of the Rappahannock fifty miles east of the Confederate capital of Richmond. McClellan reasoned that it was a short march from Urbanna to Richmond, and he would gain the rear of the rebel army at Manassas, forcing it to retreat to defend Richmond and also forcing it to attack the Army of the Potomac, thereby giving McClellan the advantage of tactical defense. Lincoln, however, was skeptical of the plan, believing that it might unnecessarily expose Washington, D.C., to capture by rebel forces. To appease the president, in early March, McClellan held a council of war with his twelve top divisional commanders. After they voted to adopt the plan 8–4, Lincoln finally assented to his generals' plans, placing a number of stipulations on McClellan, the most important being that McClellan provide for the safety of the capital before the Army of the Potomac sailed.[6]

Anticipating McClellan's move, however, General Joseph Johnston evacuated the rebel army from Manassas to Fredericksburg, forty miles to the south, thereby invalidating the strategic advantage of the Urbanna plan. Moving his army forward the next day to investigate, McClellan discovered that the "formidable" rebel fortifications were far less strong than supposed. The discovery of painted logs, called "Quaker guns," exposed McClellan to the ridicule of the press and government officials. Attorney General Edward Bates remarked that McClellan "went with a finger in his mouth upon a fool's errand, and that he has won a fool's reward." Undaunted, McClellan revised his Peninsula strategy, proposing to land troops at Fortress Monroe on the James-York Peninsula, then marching eastward to Richmond. At a March 13 council of war, McClellan's principal generals unanimously adopted the plan. On March 17, the Army of the Potomac began moving out on naval transports for Fortress Monroe.[7]

The campaign got off to a rocky start. First, just prior to his departure for the Peninsula, McClellan was relieved from his role as general-in-chief. His authority was now confined to the Army of the Potomac. President Lincoln had good reasons for making the decision, believing that a general in the field would be unable to direct all military operations. Unfortunately, McClellan first learned of the demotion in the newspapers instead of through official channels. More importantly, scarcely had the army left Washington, D.C., when a panicked General James Wadsworth, commander of the capitol's defenses, reported to Secretary of War Edwin Stanton that only 18,000 green troops were left to defend Washington. After an investigation of the Washington defenses, President Lincoln determined that the capitol was in jeopardy and ordered 35,000 troops under General Irvin McDowell withheld from McClellan. The outraged general wrote his wife, "The idea of depriving a General of 35,000 troops when actually under fire!" In actuality, there were 70,000 troops in the vicinity of Washington. McClellan intended these to be used to defend the capitol in case Confederate forces made a mad dash upon the city. His penchant for secrecy and distrust of civilian leadership, however, kept him from fully revealing his arrangements to President Lincoln and Secretary of War

Stanton, thus creating the reasonable suspicion that McClellan had not complied with the president's order.[8]

Deprived of McDowell's forces, McClellan's troops arrived at Fortress Monroe and immediately began siege operations against Confederate forces entrenched at Yorktown. Seriously overestimating the number of rebel troops, McClellan waited for almost one month, finally getting large siege guns in place, whereupon rebel forces simply retreated up the York-James Peninsula. Hampered by wet roads and poor maps, the Army of the Potomac pursued the retreating rebels until it found Johnston's forces around the environs of Richmond.

Believing that he was seriously outmanned, McClellan repeatedly called for the transfer of McDowell's troops, then stationed at Fredericksburg, Virginia. While the administration promised to send the troops via a land route to connect with the Army of the Potomac, a diversionary maneuver in the Shenandoah Valley by the Confederate commander, Thomas "Stonewall" Jackson, succeeded in blocking the transfer of McDowell's troops as Lincoln and the War Department panicked about the safety of the capitol. Meanwhile, McClellan's army was positioned on both sides of the Chickahominy River, with the two corps of Generals Erasmus Keyes and Samuel P. Heintzelman isolated on the south side of the river. Sensing an opportunity, Johnston's Confederate forces attacked on May 31, hoping to cut off and annihilate the isolated federal corps. Confederate bungling and quick thinking by McClellan's subordinates saved the day for Union forces.[9]

The most important consequence of the battle of Fair Oak (or Seven Pines, as it is also called) was the almost complete collapse of McClellan's confidence and an almost obsessive need to blame the administration for his military woes. Instead of using his superior numbers to assault Confederate forces (now commanded by Robert E. Lee), McClellan completely surrendered the initiative to his opponent. In a series of battles, known as the Seven Days, Lee's forces repeatedly attacked the Army of the Potomac in pitched battles that cost Lee thousands of casualties. Although McClellan's troops performed admirably well, their commander had already decided to switch his base of operations and retreat to Harrison's Landing on the James River. Even after a decisive repulse of his enemy at Malvern Hill, McClellan refused to counterattack and instead set up camp and waited for reinforcements. Indeed, throughout the battles of the Seven Days, McClellan constantly complained about the lack of support from the Lincoln administration. In a famous June 28, 1862 telegram to Edwin Stanton, McClellan accused Stanton of not properly supporting the army, stating, "you have done your best to sacrifice this Army." Fortunately for McClellan, an astute telegraph operator at the War Department omitted the offensive passage so that neither Stanton nor Lincoln read McClellan's critical comments.[10]

Lincoln's patience with McClellan was wearing thin. Despite McClellan's constant promise to move on Richmond if reinforced, Lincoln decided to try another tact. After Henry Halleck assumed the position of general-in-chief, he decided to remove the Army of the Potomac from Harrison's Landing and transfer it to the newly formed Army of the Virginia, commanded by the outspoken General John Pope. A bitter critic of Pope, McClellan suspected that Secretary of War Stanton was out to embarrass him. When Lee got wind of the removal of McClellan's army, he acted quickly to send his forces north to attack and defeat Pope before he could be sufficiently reinforced by the Army of the Potomac. In what one historian has called some of the most "disturbing" correspondence in American history, McClellan displayed a petulant, selfish jealousy toward John Pope that seemed unconcerned about the fate of Union forces in Virginia. "I believe I have triumphed!!" he wrote Ellen. "Just received a telegram from Halleck stating that Pope & Burnside are very hard pressed—urging me to push forward reinforcements, & *to come myself as soon as I possibly can!*" When Pope's forces were defeated at the second battle of Manassas, many within the Lincoln administration believed that McClellan's tardiness in forwarding his troops to Pope was not only the cause of defeat but also an intentional act.[11]

Despite McClellan's less than admirable performance in the month of August, as the demoralized remnants of Pope's army began filtering back to Washington, D.C., Lincoln felt he had no choice but to call upon the Young Napoleon to organize the dispirited troops and save the capital. "I have now the entire confidence of the Govt & the love of the army—my enemies are crushed, silent & disarmed—if I defeat the rebels I shall be master of the situation." When Lee's army invaded Maryland after the second battle of Manassas, McClellan received the biggest break of his military career. The discovery of Lee's Special Order #19 gave McClellan the knowledge that Lee had divided his army into five distinct units and gave the exact whereabouts of each section. Characteristically, however, McClellan did not act decisively, waiting a full sixteen hours before pushing his troops through the Maryland Mountain passes. By the time he collided with Lee's force near the small Maryland town of Antietam, McClellan had given the Confederate general time to unite most of his divided force. When Union forces attacked on the morning of September 17, McClellan never committed more than 20,000 federal troops at any one time. While the battle ended as a tactical draw, Lee decided to withdraw his army and retreated across the Potomac. McClellan assumed he had won a great victory.[12]

The Lincoln administration was, nevertheless, pleased with the results at Antietam. In fact, the Union victory allowed the president to issue his preliminary Emancipation Proclamation. Yet, Lincoln had hoped McClellan would follow up Antietam by a vigorous pursuit of Lee and eventual destruction of the rebel army. Once again, however, McClellan's excessive caution set in. After he had heard excuse after excuse as to why the rebel army could not be pursued, a frustrated Lincoln finally visited the Army of the Potomac in early October 1862, hoping to prod the general into action. This having failed, the president patiently waited until after the fall elections and then removed McClellan from command, replacing him with Ambrose Burnside on November 10, 1862. McClellan would never return to command.

The end of McClellan's career as an active Civil War commander signaled the beginning of the 1864 presidential race. Although disingenuously claiming that he had no aspirations for the nation's highest office, McClellan immediately surrounded himself with leading Democrats, including August Belmont, Horatio Seymour, John Van Buren, and Dean Richmond. Splitting time between Orange, New Jersey, and a lavish home in New York City, McClellan was considered the leading Democratic contender for the party's nomination.

While not sympathetic to Vallandigham and the radical peace wing of the party, McClellan did make a number of missteps in 1863–1864, which played into the hands of his Republican political opponents. Perhaps his most controversial action was the publication of a letter in October 1863 endorsing Pennsylvania Democratic gubernatorial candidate George W. Woodward, a controversial Pennsylvania Supreme Court justice who criticized the draft and the war. Then, at the 1864 Democratic Convention at Chicago, McClellan advisors were out-maneuvered by peace Democrats led by Ohio Democrat, Clement Vallandigham. Proponents of peace incorporated a plank into the party platform that bluntly characterized the war against the South as a failure. Additionally, peace advocates were able to get one of their supporters on the ticket as Ohio's George Pendleton was nominated for vice-president. Easily winning the nomination on the first ballot, McClellan was forced to publicly disavow the party's peace plank in a September 8 letter. The platform had stated that an immediate armistice would occur followed by negotiations for eventual reunion. McClellan's letter made clear that restoration of the Union was the only terms under which any negotiations would take place.[13]

The seeming division of the Democratic Party at Chicago gave Republican opponents the opportunity to ridicule the party as having nominated a war candidate on a peace platform. This, along with improvements in military affairs—notably, the fall of Atlanta—gave the election to Lincoln, 55 to 45 percent in the popular vote and a whopping 212–12 margin in the Electoral College. McClellan carried only three states: Delaware, Kentucky, and New Jersey. Despite his previous popularity with enlisted men, McClellan trailed Lincoln miserably in the soldiers' voting, gaining a paltry 22 percent to Lincoln's 78 percent. Sorely disappointed with his defeat, McClellan took his family abroad to Europe in January 1865.

Enormously popular and respected in Europe, McClellan remained overseas for several years. In 1867, he took a position as chief engineer for the Steven's battery, a huge ocean ironclad that had been under construction since 1854. Returning to the United States in 1868, McClellan kept a low profile politically, supporting Democratic nominee Horatio Seymour but hardly playing a role in the campaign. In 1870, McClellan resigned his position with the Steven's battery and accepted the position of chief engineer of the New York City Department of Docks. In 1873, he formed his own firm, George B. McClellan & Co., which specialized in helping European investors protect their investments in American railroad securities.

In 1876, McClellan was an enthusiastic booster of Democratic nominee Samuel Tilden, who had led McClellan forces at the Chicago convention in 1864. He made numerous speeches on Tilden's behalf, in which he argued for the end of Reconstruction in the South. Disappointed with Tilden's defeat, McClellan continued to be involved in New Jersey politics and was the compromise candidate for governor in 1877. Winning the election by 12,700 votes, McClellan's three-year term was characterized by financial frugality—both state debt and taxes were reduced—and minimalist government. When his term expired in 1881, McClellan declined to run for reelection. His last political involvement was campaigning for Grover Cleveland in 1884. Expecting an appointment as secretary of war for his support of the newly elected president, McClellan was disappointed when Cleveland overlooked him at the request of New Jersey Senator John McPherson.

McClellan spent a good deal of time in his post–Civil War career as an author. Beginning with his own report of military operations as commander of the Army of the Potomac, published in February 1864, McClellan produced a steady stream of magazine and journal articles on military affairs. These included pieces in *Scribner's, North American Review,* and *Century Magazine.* His biggest project was undoubtedly his memoirs. Unfortunately, the draft copy—uncompleted—was destroyed when the New York warehouse where his research materials were stored burned to the ground. While McClellan began working on a new version, he was unable to complete it before his death. His literary executor, William Prime, who also put together roughly half of the work from McClellan's letters, reports, and other documents, posthumously published *McClellan's Own Story* in 1887.

In October 1885, McClellan's health declined as he suffered from an attack of angina pectoris. While briefly rallying, his symptoms returned and on October 29, 1885, he passed away in his sleep. News of his death was published in all the major newspapers across the country, and numerous public officials and dignitaries attended his funeral. His funeral service was held at Madison Square Presbyterian Church, where he attended services when in New York City. His wife Ellen would survive him by nearly thirty years, passing away in 1914.

PRINCIPAL IDEAS

Political Ideas

As a mid-nineteenth-century Democrat, McClellan shared the conservative, strict constructionist ideas of his contemporary Democrats. An advocate of limited government, McClellan abhorred what he regarded as the centralizing tendencies of the Lincoln administration during the war. In particular, congressional legislation such as the Second Confiscation Act, which authorized the seizure of property, including slaves, from persons supporting the rebellion, and the Enrollment Act, which provided for a military draft of all adult men from age twenty to forty-five, as well as presidential acts, particularly the Emancipation Proclamation, were seen as unwarranted usurpation of federal power at the expense of the rights of states.

Like Vallandigham and many other Democrats, McClellan endorsed conciliation as the proper approach to waging war. Advocates of conciliation believed that secession was the work of a small group of powerful slaveholders. The majority of Southerners had temporarily been swept up in a wave of emotion that occurred in the aftermath of Lincoln's election. If the war was conducted with strict regard for the constitutional rights and property of Southern civilians, loyalty to the Union would be restored and the war ended. Even as the war progressed and numerous bloody battles transpired, George McClellan persisted in the belief that the conciliatory approach would allow for negotiation and a possible compromise solution. The radical Republican position would alienate Southerners, McClellan reasoned, creating an even bloodier war and preventing an effective Reconstruction from taking place even after military victory was achieved.

On slavery and race, McClellan's position was probably more moderate than many in his party. That he regarded African Americans as intellectually inferior to whites was a theme that permeated his letters and correspondence. From the beginning of the war, he sought to assure Southerners that their slave property was safe from Northern armies. "All your rights will be rigorously respected," McClellan told West Virginia residents. "Notwithstanding all that has been said by the traitors to induce you to believe that our advent among you will be signalized by interference with your slaves, understand one thing clearly—not only will we abstain from all such interference but we will on the contrary with an iron hand, crush any attempt at insurrection on their part." At the same time, however, McClellan was hardly a proslavery fanatic, and he was, prior to the war, a believer in a plan of gradual emancipation. His correspondence is also filled with sympathetic thoughts and sentiments toward African Americans that reveal a noblesse oblige mentality. On one occasion, he wrote Ellen, "When I think of some of the features of slavery I cannot help shuddering. Just think for one moment & try to realize that at the will of some brutal master you & I might be separated for ever!"[14]

The most succinct expression of McClellan's political views, especially as they related to the war, is contained in his famous Harrison's Landing letter. Penned just after the Army of the Potomac had arrived on the James River in early July 1862, the letter was McClellan's attempt to influence the Lincoln administration's direction of the war. It was McClellan's attempt to counter the legislative agenda of radical Republicans in Congress, who were considering a variety of controversial measures aimed at confiscating Confederate property and liberating slaves. After telling the president that the war should be conducted "upon the highest principles know[n] to Christian Civilization," McClellan detailed his objections to the policy of radical Republicans:

> Neither confiscation of property, political executions of persons, territorial organization of states or forcible abolition of slavery should be contemplated for the moment. In prosecuting the War, all private property and unarmed persons should be strictly protected; subject only to the necessities of military operations. All private property taken for military use should be paid for or receipted for; pillage and waste should be treated as high crimes.[15]

Unfortunately for McClellan, his ideas on the conduct of the war had little impact on Lincoln's thinking by July 1862.

Military Ideas

As stated earlier, McClellan had a healthy contempt for civilian leaders of the military, an attitude that surfaced at West Point and during the Mexican War. His contempt for civilian leadership was responsible for a strained relationship with President Lincoln and, particularly, Secretary of War Edwin M. Stanton. The animus toward civilian military control was a common attitude among the nation's West Point educated officer corps. From the founding of the republic, many Americans were skeptical about the need of a professional military education, believing in the superiority of citizen soldiers. Indeed, in the rough-and-ready commonsense world of the mid-nineteenth century, there was generally little recognition of professionalism as such. Instead, as consistent with the fluid free labor beliefs of the Republican Party, many Americans believed that common sense and experience, not a separate military curriculum, were all that were needed to master the art of soldiering.

Skeptical of civilian leadership over military affairs, George McClellan felt compelled to prevent civilian overseers from interfering with his strategic planning. At various points in time, Lincoln and other political leaders knew little of the general's strategic plans. Benjamin F. Wade, chairmen of the powerful Joint Committee on the Conduct of the War, complained, "This nation is making an extraordinary effort. Next March we shall be $600,000,000 in debt for what we have already done [and] everybody knows that our finances are not in a condition to keep this up eternally. All this is hanging on one man who keeps his counsels entirely to himself." Indeed, McClellan's penchant for secrecy fueled the notion among radical Republicans that his loyalty was suspect.[16]

Fundamental to understanding McClellan's conception of military strategy was his experience as an observer during the Crimean War. Here he saw firsthand technological innovations in weaponry that gave a powerful advantage to defensive as opposed to offensive operations. In many respects, the Peninsula campaign was his effort to take advantage of the power of defense. By using a water supply route, the Army of the Potomac would have a more secure supply route than would be provided by a direct land march on Richmond. Additionally, McClellan hoped that quick movement would allow him to position his army in the rear of Confederate forces, while, at the same time, placing the Union Army between Richmond and Confederate forces. This would force the Confederate Army to assume offensive operations, allowing Union forces to take advantage of defensive fortifications as well as the awesome power of rifled musketry.

While McClellan's strategic ideas had merit, his execution suffered from excessive caution and an obsessive fear that he was outnumbered. While a number of military historians admire McClellan's organizational skills and mastery of strategic concepts, few regard him as a competent battlefield tactician. Historian Joseph Glatthaar, for instance, believes that McClellan suffered from a "paranoid personality disorder," which manifested itself in such traits as secrecy, distrust of superiors, and excessive hypersensitivity about criticism. In battle after battle, from the Peninsula campaign through Antietam, McClellan proved to be competent when retreating or conducting defensive operations. His cautiousness prevented him from taking the offensive, and when he did, as in the battle of Antietam, his performance suffered from lack of coordination and a failure to totally utilize the forces at his disposal.[17]

Historian Thomas J. Rowland suggests that McClellan was held to higher standards than other Northern generals such as Grant or Sherman. Not only did he operate in the highly scrutinized eastern theatre, but his relatively brief tenure in command also prevented him from growing and changing his approach to generalship, as was the case with many other Northern military figures. Although it is certainly possible that a McClellan commanding in 1865 might have improved as a general, the way McClellan viewed the war and the way he talked and wrote about the war in his later years suggest that any substantial change would be problematic.[18]

McClellan's Own Story

Although George McClellan wrote a number of articles on military strategy and campaigns, his principal work on military history was his memoirs. As noted earlier, the work had to be reconstructed when fire destroyed early drafts. Instead of making it a memoir of his entire career, McClellan now focused on his Civil War career. Almost by necessity, the foundation of the work was his military report on the operations of the Army of the Potomac that was published in February 1864. McClellan himself completed that portion of the work that dealt with the operations of the Army of the Potomac through May 1862. His literary executor arranged the balance of the material.

Although there are a number of accurate observations about the role McClellan played in reorganizing the Army of the Potomac, weeding out incompetent officers, and making soldiers out of raw recruits, the tone of *McClellan's Own Story* is accusatory and conspiratorial. It hardly stands as a work of impartial history—even when one ignores the normal subjective bias in a personal reminiscence. As usual, McClellan plays the role of the victim. Radicals such as Charles Sumner hated him from the beginning because he did not support immediate abolition, while members of his own party damaged him by holding him up as a political candidate against his will, thereby making the Republicans even more intent on bringing about his failure.

Within this framework, McClellan narrates military operations on the central premise that the Republican Party wanted him to fail, particularly Secretary of War Edwin Stanton, who McClellan took great pains to criticize throughout the work. The administration never adequately supported him with troops. Why? In McClellan's words, it was his devotion to restoring the Union and leaving slavery intact. The Republican Party, according to McClellan, was only interested in abolishing the Union and establishing the ascendancy of their political party. "The real object of the radical leaders," writes McClellan, "was not the restoration of the Union, but the permanent ascendancy of their party, and to this they were ready to sacrifice the Union, if necessary." The subsequent narrative then justifies all of McClellan's failures as the result of insufficient support. While filled with interesting letters and other primary sources, the work's polemical tone lessens its usefulness as an objective work of military history.[19]

CONCLUSION

George McClellan began life with unlimited potential. By the age of thirty-four, he had accomplished a great deal: the star of his class at West Point, a brilliant Mexican War record, a successful railroad executive, and the top Northern general early on in the Civil War. In many respects, perhaps his rise to the top was too quick. So much was expected from McClellan, and so many of the expectations were completely unrealistic. The fact that no commander of the Army of the Potomac lived up to the expectations of the politicians and the public (until Grant, who was not technically its commander) should be taken into account when judging McClellan's military performance. At the time he was appointed, he was as good as, if not better than, any other general put in charge of the nation's most visible army.

The principal reason why McClellan has earned a negative assessment by historians is McClellan himself. His constant complaining, excuse making, shifting the blame on others, and, in spite of much evidence to the contrary, constant crying that he was outnumbered have tended to color historians' interpretation of the Young Napoleon. Despite the negative assessment of his generalship, most agree that McClellan emerged on the national scene at a critical time, supplying a much-needed morale bolster after the devastating defeat at the first battle of Manassas. His skills as an organizer, administrator, and his role in selecting competent officers did much to improve the Army of the Potomac. Despite McClellan's organizational talents, the creator of the fighting machine could not competently use the instrument that he created.

NOTES

1. Quoted from John C. Waugh, *The Class of 1846: From West Point to Appomattox: Stonewall Jackson, George McClellan and Their Brothers* (New York: Ballantine Books, 1994), 36.

2. Quoted from Waugh, *Class of 1846*, 80.

3. Edward Hagerman, "The Professionalization of George B. McClellan and Early Field Command," *Civil War History* 21 (1975): 121.

4. McClellan to Mary Ellen McClellan, October 31, 1861, in *The Civil War Papers of George B. McClellan: Selected Correspondence 1860–1865*, edited by Stephen W. Sears (New York: Da Capo Press, 1989), 113–14. Simon Cameron was Lincoln's first Secretary of War. Gideon Welles was Secretary of the Navy. Edward Bates was Attorney General and Montgomery Blair was Post-master General.

5. Bruce Tap, *Over Lincoln's Shoulder: The Committee on the Conduct of the War* (Lawrence: University Press of Kansas, 1998), 101–15. See also comments in Bruce Tap, "Inevitability, Masculinity, and the American Military Tradition: The Committee on the Conduct of the War Investigates the American Civil War," *American Nineteenth Century History* 5 (Summer 2004): 28–32.

6. On the logic of the Peninsula campaign, see Archer Jones, *Civil War Command and Strategy: The Process of Victory and Defeat* (New York: Free Press,

1992), 60–63. For overall assessments of the Peninsula campaign, see Stephen W. Sears, *To the Gates of Richmond: the Peninsula Campaign* (New York: Ticknor & Fields, 1992).

7. *The Diary of Edwin Bates*, edited by Howard K. Beale (1933; reprint, New York: Da Capo Press, 1971), 240.

8. McClellan to Mary Ellen McClellan, April 6, 1862, *Civil War Papers of George B. McClellan*, 230. On the safety of the Washington, see Thomas J. Rowland, " 'Heaven Save a Country Governed by Such Counsels': The Safety of Washington and the Peninsula Campaign," *Civil War History* 42 (1996): 5–17.

9. A good summary of the Lincoln's decision to detach McDowell is provided in Richard Current, *The Lincoln Nobody Knows* (New York: McGraw-Hill Book Company, 1958), 140–51.

10. McClellan to Stanton, June 28, 1862, *Civil War Papers of George McClellan*, 323.

11. McClellan to Mary Ellen McClellan, August 21, 1862, *Civil War Papers of George B. McClellan*, 397–98. The comment about "disturbing" correspondence is from John J. Hennessy, *Return to Bull Run: The Campaign and Battle of the Second Manassas* (New York: Simon & Schuster, 1993), 242.

12. McClellan to Mary Ellen McClellan, September 7, 1862, in *Civil War Papers of George B. McClellan*, 437–38 (quote, 438).

13. The best analysis of the Democratic Party in the 1864 election is Joel Silbey, *"A Respectable Minority": The Democratic Party during the Civil War Era, 1860–1868* (New York: W. W. Norton & Co., 1977). On the particulars of the Chicago convention, see ch. 5. For McClellan's letter, see McClellan to the Democratic Nomination Committee, September 8, 1864, in *Civil War Papers of George B. McClellan*, 595–97. According to biographer Stephen W. Sears, this is the last of several drafts of McClellan's letter. For an early version, see McClellan to the Democratic Nomination Committee, September 4, 1864, in *Civil War Papers of George B. McClellan*, 590–92.

14. "To the Union Men of Western Virginia," May 26, 1861, and McClellan to Mary Ellen McClellan, November 14, 1861, in *Civil War Papers of George B. McClellan*, 26, 132.

15. McClellan to Abraham Lincoln, July 7, 1862 (Harrison's Landing Letter), in *Civil War Papers of George B. McClellan*, 344–45 (quote, 344). On conciliation, see Mark Grimsley, *The Hard Hand of War: Union Military Policy toward Southern Civilians 1861–1865* (Cambridge, MA: Harvard University Press, 1995), 7–46.

16. Wade quote from Detroit Post and Tribune, *Zachariah Chandler: An Outline Sketch of His Life and Public Service* (Detroit: Post and Tribune Company, 1880), 227. On negative attitudes toward West Point, see Tap, "Inevitability, Masculinity, and the American Military Tradition," 32–38; and Thomas J. Goss, *The War within the Union High Command: Politics and Generalship during the Civil War* (Lawrence: University Press of Kansas, 2003).

17. Joseph T. Glatthaar, *Partners in Command: The Relationships between Leaders in the Civil War* (New York: Free Press, 1994), 237–42.

18. Thomas J. Rowland, "In the Shadows of Grant and Sherman: George B. McClellan Revisited," *Civil War History* 40 (September, 1994): 202–25. See also Joseph L. Harsh, "On the McClellan-Go-Round," *Civil War History* 19 (1973): 117.

19. George B. McClellan, *McClellan's Own Story* (New York: Charles L. Webster and Company, 1887), 149.

FURTHER READING

Warren W. Hassler, *George McClellan: Shield of the Union* (Baton Rouge: Louisiana University Press, 1957); George Brinton McClellan, *McClellan's Own Story* (New York: Charles L. Webster, 1887); William Starr Myers, *General George B. McClellan* (New York: Appleton-Century Co., 1954); Thomas J. Rowland, *George B. McClellan & the Civil War: In the Shadow of Grant & Sherman* (Kent, OH: Kent State University Press, 1998); Stephen W. Sears, *George B. McClellan: The Young Napoleon* (New York: Ticknor and Fields, 1988); Joseph Waugh, *The Class of 1846: From West Point to Appomattox: Stonewall Jackson, George McClellan, and Their Brothers* (New York: Ballantine Books, 1994); and T. Harry Williams, *Lincoln and His Generals* (New York: Alfred A. Knopf, 1952).

WILLIAM H. SEWARD
(1801–1872)

Triumphs and Contradictions

LIFE

William Henry Seward was born in Florida, New York, on May 16, 1801, the son of Samuel S. Seward and Mary Jennings Seward. He had three brothers and a sister as siblings. His father, a man of varied professions including doctor and merchant, also speculated in land and achieved substantial wealth. He was a supporter of Thomas Jefferson and his Jeffersonian-Republican party, an affiliation his son Harry, as young William Henry was called, assumed in his young manhood. It became clear as Henry grew up that he had intellectual gifts, and his father determined that his son should be educated with the goal of becoming a lawyer. Harry attended Union College in Schenectady, where he quickly earned a reputation for frivolity, mischief, and intellectual precocity. In January 1819, he quarreled with his father when the latter refused to honor a tailor's bill and, in a fit of pique, left the college. He settled in Georgia, where he briefly taught school before sober second thoughts and family pleas prompted him to return to New York and college. Harry graduated in July 1820 with honors and gave a public address at graduation ceremonies.

Harry dutifully pursued the study of law in Goshen and New York City with various lawyers, earning his license in 1822. He moved to Auburn, New York, and entered into a partnership with Judge Elijah Miller. Seward never had any affection for his legal career, yet one of the defining characteristics of his professional life was a manic energy for work. So he labored incessantly at his legal tasks, though he had little love for them. Meanwhile, he managed to court and marry his law partner's daughter, Frances Adeline Miller, on October 20, 1824. Judge Miller insisted that the newlyweds live in his home because his own wife had died, and Seward agreed. Frances had a devout Christian faith that her new husband did not share; indeed, the newlyweds soon discovered that they had many differences.

Politics, not the law, was Seward's passion, and he quickly entered the political arena. He abandoned the Jeffersonianism of his youth in 1824 for practical and philosophical reasons. He had come to detest the corruption of Martin Van Buren's Democratic machine in New York, and he admired the soaring nationalism and progressive bent of John Quincy Adams, who advocated internal improvements—public works projects such as canals—and education, enthusiasms that Seward shared. Throughout his career, John Quincy Adams remained Seward's beau ideal as a statesman. (He later visited Boston and had an interview with the great man, but found him disappointingly distant and cold, as did many others.) The county in which he resided, Cayuga, also leaned to Adams, so switching enhanced the prospect for a successful run for office. He joined the National Republican movement, and he was an active supporter of Adams. After the National Republicans and Adams were soundly defeated in 1828, Seward drifted into the Antimasonic Party, a reform-minded third party that formed in western New York in response to the perceived threat of the Masonic society. He attended national and state Antimasonic conventions in 1830, and he met and befriended Thurlow Weed, the skilled political operator whose friendship and support proved an essential ingredient in Seward's future political triumphs. Seward gave financial backing for the establishment of an Albany newspaper, the *Evening Journal*, which Weed edited with the goal of advancing their progressive agenda.

With Weed's help, Seward won his first elective office in 1830, when he was elected to the State Senate. He supported the Antimasonic reform agenda for four years at the state house, backing railroad charters, defending the embattled Bank of the United States, and advocating reform of the penal system and the end of imprisonment for debt. At first somewhat hesitating and unsure of himself, Seward found his voice and also established a reputation for friendliness and conviviality with political foes and friends. As the Antimasonic cause faded in the 1830s, Seward supported the formation of a new political coalition opposed to Andrew Jackson. He embraced the Whig Party as it emerged in New York in 1833–1834, and he became the Whig candidate for governor in 1834 against Democrat William L. Marcy. The Democratic Party in New York easily crushed Seward's gubernatorial ambitions, electing Marcy by more than 10,000 votes.

His wife struggled with her husband and his passion for work and politics. Seward's hyperactive nature kept him perpetually on the move, and he was often away from home. In 1833, he traveled to Europe with his father and wrote seventy pieces describing the trip for publication in Weed's *Evening Journal*. Returning to New York after an absence of five months, Seward went to Albany to get a political briefing from Weed before going on to Auburn and reuniting with his wife and family. Such antics were bound to test the affection of any spouse. Frances did not much care for the enforced socializing that is a necessary part of political life, and when Seward was home, politicians, aspiring politicians, favor seekers, and sycophants invaded her domicile. Her health suffered, perhaps a product of the realization that her husband neglected her and also her detestation of the inconveniences of political life. Nonetheless, the two had five children, and she often read Seward's speeches and offered him political advice and commentary.

After his years in the state legislature, Seward managed a land company in Westfield, New York, engaging in speculative investments tied to property. His financial investment suffered in the ensuing Panic of 1837 and the depression that followed, though his ability to handle the company's affairs earned plaudits. Having saddled himself with debt, Seward continued to pursue political office, giving speeches touting his ideas on the benefits of universal education and aggressive spending on transportation improvements. Weed, ever active, assiduously promoted Seward for the Whig nomination for governor, and he achieved that goal at the state Whig convention at Utica in September 1838. With the depression and general unpopularity of the Van Buren administration as a backdrop, Seward easily bested Democratic incumbent William L. Marcy. The prospect of moving to Albany and entertaining horrified Frances, but Seward was delighted, and he acquired a mansion and spent $5,000 decorating it.

Seward served two terms as New York governor, winning reelection in 1842, and his political cohort Thurlow Weed effectively ruled state government during that period. Weed's influence over patronage and even the choice of speaker in the New York Assembly earned him the sobriquet "The Dictator." As governor, Seward strongly championed a reform agenda very much in keeping with the philosophy of the Whig Party. He advocated spending millions on internal improvements each year, from widening the Erie Canal to chartering railroads, despite the chastening experience of the depression. He supported education reforms, better curriculum, and wider educational opportunities for immigrants, such as state funding for schools that taught in native languages rather than English. He adopted a tolerant attitude toward the immigrants flooding into New York, and he formed a friendship and working relationship with Catholic Archbishop John Hughes. He wanted to expand the money supply by supporting the repeal of legislation that prohibited small bills. He continued to urge penal reform on the state legislature. Seward's support for education and internal improvements, and his friendly disposition toward immigrants, particularly the Irish, amounted to a coherent progressive philosophy for continued improvement of the country and people.

Seward embraced, albeit with a degree of moderation, the reform movements that had sprung up in the 1830s. He took a temperance pledge in 1842 and ceased serving alcohol at his Albany mansion. He thought slavery a genuine evil harmful to the country's progress, but favored gradual, compensated emancipation rather than immediate emancipation as some devout abolitionists advocated. Frances was a firm opponent of slavery, considering it anti-Christian, and brought up her children without racism. Seward refused to surrender three black New York citizens to Virginia authorities who had charged the men with aiding in slave escapes. Seward affirmed that people could not be considered property, so the "crime" of stealing an individual could not be recognized. He also condemned Daniel Webster, then secretary of state, for demanding the return of slave mutineers who had taken over an American vessel, sailed into a British Caribbean port, and been freed by the British government. Such stands endeared Seward to the abolition movement and to the free black population, both in New York and the country at large. Still, Seward's attitude on race mirrored the prevailing racist sentiments of the time; he thought blacks deserved equal treatment under the law but believed them inferior to whites and incapable of assimilating into white society.

Seward also clashed with the Tyler administration. In November 1840, a Canadian, Alexander McLeod, was arrested in New York and indicted for murder as a participant in border violence. British authorities strenuously defended McLeod and urged his release, a stand that Daniel Webster echoed. Seward refused to intervene in the case, though he gave assurances that after a change of venue McLeod was likely to win an acquittal, as he believed that showing McLeod any leniency or favoritism would be politically exploited by jingoistic Democrats and fatal to Whigs. President John Tyler, an erstwhile Whig, broke with his party in 1841 over strongly nationalistic economic legislation and was now trying to cooperate with a suspicious Democratic Party. Seward blamed Henry Clay for Tyler's hostility, as Clay had forced the legislation on the president despite repeated veto threats. The spectacle of a Whig president feuding with a Whig Congress demoralized the party and depressed its turnout in fall elections. The Whigs lost both Houses of the New York legislature in 1841, and Seward decided not to run for a third term.

He spent the next several years after surrendering the governor's office reviving his legal practice in an effort to retire the now massive personal debt he owed (some $200,000, by one estimate). In this Seward was quite successful, as he unloaded real estate and came to debt settlement agreements while pursuing legal work with his usual frenetic pace. He secured work as counsel on patent cases that paid on a continuing basis and proved quite lucrative. He soon had remedied his financial problems and by 1855 could enjoy a measure of security. He kept himself in the public eye whenever possible, for example, representing two black men, Henry Wyatt and William Freeman, who had been charged with murder. Seward's brilliant summation in the Freeman case—he affirmed the humanity of black men— was printed and distributed as a pamphlet. He campaigned for the Whig presidential ticket in 1844, condemning Texas annexation and characterizing the Democratic Party as the slavery party. He was considered a leading Whig progressive with his emphasis on rights for blacks and immigrants, education and penal reform, and advocacy of internal improvements. In 1848, he again campaigned for the Whig ticket, emphasizing his opposition to the extension of slavery, the last troublesome, slavery-related issue.

The Free Soil Party had nominated Martin Van Buren for president in 1848, and the resulting split in the New York Democratic Party led to Whig supremacy in the state legislature. Seward was elected to New York's U.S. Senate seat, over the objections of conservative Whigs who thought him too radical on slavery, on February 6, 1849. Seward's gubernatorial tenure had given him a degree of national exposure, but his two terms in the Senate made him a national figure and contender for the presidency as he participated in the congressional debates and controversies that preceded civil war. In his first weeks as a senator, Seward tried to dispel his radical image by giving temperate speeches and putting on his usual charm offensive. It was inevitable that he would clash with Southern senators bent on asserting the positive attributes of slavery, particularly with tensions rising over legislative efforts to exclude slavery from territory acquired in the Mexican War. He cultivated President Zachary Taylor and soon had influence over New York patronage, much to the frustration of Millard Fillmore and New York's conservative Whigs. Seward also supported Taylor's proposal to immediately admit California and New Mexico, an effort to quickly quell the ongoing controversy over slavery's expansion.

In January 1850, Henry Clay introduced a raft of bills in an effort to find a way out of the impasse. Seward denounced Clay's proposals in a famed Senate speech on March 11, 1850, in which he called compromises "vicious" surrenders of principle and conscience. Slavery, Seward insisted, had to be kept out of the territories, as its expansion would lead to despotism or aristocracy. In a turn of phrase he came to regret, Seward averred that a "higher law than the Constitution" mandated a careful stewardship of the national domain for the benefit of humanity, an obligation that necessarily compelled resistance to the spread of slavery. He was mercilessly attacked in the Senate and in the South for allegedly suggesting that he intended to govern as Almighty God's representative, dismissing the Constitution and the rule of law. Thurlow Weed, too, wrote to condemn the use of the phrase, leading to a serious quarrel between the two political confidants that eventually healed, though not without considerable residual bitterness. Seward thought he had been true to his beliefs and felt vindicated by the popularity of the speech, which was often requested. His radical reputation was firmly fixed in the public consciousness for the foreseeable future.

Taylor's unexpected death in July 1850 was a dramatic setback for Seward and Weed and presaged a damaging split in the New York Whig Party.

Millard Fillmore succeeded to the presidency, and New York's conservative Whigs seized control of federal patronage in the state, turning out Seward loyalists and replacing them with conservatives. Clay's compromise measures passed the Congress in the fall over Seward's objections, though he did support California's admission as a state. With the slave controversy in abeyance and Weed trying to assuage conservatives in New York, Seward focused on issues of traditional interest to him, education and internal improvements. He gave a number of speeches that helped give him the patina of a statesman, welcoming Hungarian patriot Lajos Kossuth, giving eulogies for Henry Clay and Daniel Webster, and supporting the peaceful adjustment of a quarrel with Great Britain over fisheries. He backed Winfield Scott, the Whig nominee for the presidency in 1852, although without much enthusiasm because of Scott's nativism.

Glyndon Van Deusen has argued that after 1852, Seward devoted a considerable and increasing amount of his time to foreign affairs. He favored American expansion and dominance of the western hemisphere, but felt the process would be gradual and inevitable and did not wish to acquire any territory by conquest. He opposed the Gadsden Treaty. He supported a protective tariff and a transcontinental railroad. The slavery controversy proved unavoidable whatever Seward's predilections, as anger erupted in the North over enforcement of the Fugitive Slave Law. Then, in January 1854, Stephen A. Douglas, an Illinois Democratic senator, introduced legislation to organize the Nebraska Territory that included an explicit repeal of the Missouri Compromise of 1820, which prohibited slavery north of the southern boundary of Missouri. Seward was a signatory of an appeal gotten up by Ohio senator Salmon Chase protesting the legislation and condemned it in a Senate speech on February 17, 1854. Seward argued that the Founding Fathers had never wanted slavery to spread, and he worried that a "slaveocracy" was bent on putting slavery in every territory and state in the Union. He issued a public address in June 1854 making the same points, and he urged antislavery activist Theodore Parker to redouble his efforts to educate the public on the dangers of slavery.

The Whig Party had broken up in the wake of the 1852 elections, divided on sectional lines and decimated by defections to nativist and other political movements. Seward lamented the passing of the Whig Party, and he could not abide the nativist manifestation that drew the allegiance of many former Whigs. When a state Republican Party formed at a meeting in Saratoga, New York, in August 1854, he found himself gradually drawn to it, mainly because there was little alternative. The following year, Weed engineered Seward's reelection to the Senate on a tide of anti-Nebraska sentiment. Seward kept a high profile in Congress as an advocate of economic progress and an opponent of slavery's extension. He hoped to win the first Republican presidential nomination in 1856, but much to his consternation, he found himself defeated in a stampede for the political neophyte, renowned explorer John C. Frémont. Seward's longstanding opposition to nativism played a significant role in his being passed over for the nomination, as party leaders felt it was essential to attract nativist support, however distasteful.

Seward continued to play an active role in the national debate from his perch in the Senate. He supported homestead legislation, protective tariffs, a transcontinental railroad, and subsidies for a steamship line. His interest in foreign affairs continued unabated; in an 1855 speech, he called for giving Britain a year's notice to withdraw from South America. Perhaps in recognition of his predilection for foreign affairs, he became a member of the Senate Foreign Relations Committee. As Kansas turned into a battleground between Free Soil and proslavery settlers, Seward staunchly advocated the Free Soil cause, rejecting the compromise English bill and insisting on the immediate acceptance of the Topeka Constitution crafted by Free Soil Kansans. He did all he could to foster the split in the Democratic Party that grew out of disagreement on Kansas policy between Stephen A. Douglas and President James Buchanan. His rhetoric grew progressively harsher as he condemned Southern plantation elites for attempting to control the American government by means fair and foul. On October 25, 1858, Seward spoke in Rochester, New York, and declared an "irrepressible conflict" between slave and free labor, a conflict whose ultimate end would be the establishment of either slavery or free labor across the United States.

This tendency to slip into absolutist rhetoric that painted sectional tensions in stark, even bloody, terms did not help Seward's relentless drive for the presidency. When the Republican National Convention met in Chicago, Illinois, on May 16, 1860, Thurlow Weed had packed the New York delegation with Seward supporters, and he had strong support in the party at large. However, political conventions are anxious to choose a winner, and Seward had, in the opinion of many, strong disadvantages. He had firmly cemented an image of radicalism upon himself with his "higher law" and "irrepressible conflict" speeches, and the worry was that he would repel conservative-minded voters. Seward also had been a strong proponent of a progressive and tolerant policy for immigrants, a record sure to offend nativists. A taint of corruption hung about Weed and had fastened itself upon Seward. The eventual nominee, Abraham Lincoln, by contrast, seemed moderate in comparison on the slavery issue, and further, Lincoln had had the foresight to avoid publicly condemning the nativist movement. Seward was in Auburn during the convention, waiting hopefully for news of his nomination, and received the painful intelligence of Lincoln's victory from a telegram, prompting local citizens to quietly haul off a cannon set up to boom a salute when the glad tidings came of Seward's victory. Seward's loss hurt him deeply, and he lashed out at Horace Greeley, the powerful editor of the *New York Tribune*, for not supporting him. Despite his crushing defeat, Seward gave campaign speeches for the Republican ticket in New England and the Midwest. He met Lincoln in Springfield, Illinois, in October, though it appears that the anger and disappointment had yet to heal, and Seward's typical bonhomie was absent when he met the president-elect.

Seward returned to Washington after the election, in which Lincoln and the Republican Party won the presidency for the first time in the party's brief existence. Many in the South had warned that Lincoln's election would prompt a broad secession movement and the establishment of a Southern nation. The process began within days of Lincoln's election when the South Carolina legislature called a secession convention to meet in December 1860. In the pages of the Albany *Journal*, Weed advocated a constitutional convention to adopt amendments to placate Southern firebrands, such as a stronger Fugitive Slave Law and the resurrection of the old Missouri Compromise line to divide slave and free territory. He had migrated to positions he had once regarded as unthinkable in an effort to head off the drive to secession. Seward had never been inclined to grand compromises on slavery such as Henry Clay had favored. However, he soon found himself drawn to the last-minute legislative flailing to prevent the outbreak of war. Charles Francis Adams Sr. and others urged Seward to take the lead, pleas that must have flattered a man with an ego bruised from a losing bid for the Republican presidential nomination. Further praise of a sort came when Lincoln offered Seward the State Department, a post he accepted on December 28, 1860. For the remaining months until the inauguration, Seward flirted with various compromise proposals, but ultimately, Lincoln refused to countenance any concession on the extension of slavery.

Seward's tenure as secretary of state began inauspiciously. He tried to bully Lincoln, threatening to withdraw from the appointment a few days before the inauguration, a bid to force concessions on the incoming president that would have given de facto control of the new administration to Seward. Lincoln fended him off. In the ensuing controversy over continued federal possession of Fort Sumter in the harbor of Charleston, South Carolina, Seward consistently urged Lincoln to abandon the fort because he considered the hostilities necessary to retain it would prompt border states to side with the Confederacy. He sent Lincoln an insulting memorandum in early April in which he criticized the president for having no domestic or foreign policy. Even weeks after hostilities had begun when Confederate batteries opened on Fort Sumter on April 12, 1861, Seward continued to hope that some negotiated settlement could be arranged or that Southerners would collectively come to their senses and return to discarded loyalties. Glyndon Van Deusen has argued that Seward consistently overestimated the prevalence and strength of Unionist sentiment in the South, though in fairness to Seward the same could be said of Lincoln. Seward also suggested to Lincoln that the United States declare war on Spain and France, using the pretext of foreign machinations in the Caribbean. After Britain granted belligerent rights to the Confederacy, Lincoln had to tone down Seward's bellicose written response. Recognition as a belligerent power, which came with Britain's proclamation of neutrality in May, gave the Confederacy a certain international legitimacy along with the right to purchase arms from neutral nations and employ privateers on the seas. Seward thought war with a foreign power might quickly put an end to secession as the wayward states returned to the Union to defend it. Lincoln wisely dismissed these suggestions, which might have led to foreign intervention on the side of the Confederacy and permanent dismemberment of the United States.

After these initial miscues, Seward settled in at the State Department and conducted American foreign policy through a period of tremendous national danger with what is generally acknowledged to be great skill and success. He faced the problem of keeping Britain and France from intervening in the Civil War, a prospect that ebbed and flowed with the course of the conflict and with various crises. The involvement of European nations on the side of the Confederacy could dramatically shift the tide of war against the Union. On November 8, 1861, the USS *San Jacinto* under command of Captain Charles Wilkes stopped the British mail steamer *Trent* on the way from Havana, Cuba, to St. Thomas. Wilkes's sailors captured two Confederate diplomats on board, James M. Mason and John Slidell, and returned them to the United States as prisoners. The act was immensely popular in the North, starved for a victory and unhappy with Britain, while for their part, the British were incensed and demanded the immediate release of the two men. With public approbation at a fever pitch, releasing the men had to be carefully managed, but Seward and Lincoln accomplished it and thereby avoided a potentially catastrophic clash with the British.

Beyond the *Trent* affair, other irritations with the Great Britain occurred during the war. British merchants shipped goods bound for the Confederacy to Matamoros, Mexico, where they were shipped overland to Texas, skirting the Union blockade. When British ships were seized en route to Mexico with cargo, Seward rebuffed British protests. More problematic was the construction of warships in Britain that were then employed by the Confederacy to prey on Union commerce, the two most infamous examples being the *Florida* and *Alabama*, which shipped out of England over American protests and wreaked great havoc. The British government contended that nothing could be done until definitive proof was presented of the warship's destination; since the fact that the vessels were being built for the Confederacy was concealed, British authorities could not act. Seward vigorously protested this policy of inaction. He threatened to issue letters of marque and reprisal, commissioning privateers, and legislation passed Congress giving the administration the power to act. Since the Confederacy had no merchant fleet, neutral merchant ships, of which the British fleet was quite numerous, would be victimized. Seward's bluster worked. British authorities subsequently prevented the transfer to the Confederacy of the ironclad rams built by the Laird Brothers of Birkenhead. The American government continued to press for damages for the depredations caused by Confederate, British-built raiders, a cause Seward championed but could not resolve during his State Department tenure. Despite the tensions, Seward conducted successful negotiations with Britain during the war, such as the settlement of Canadian claims in Oregon, by a treaty signed in 1863.

France too proved a continuing source of diplomatic trouble. Napoleon III, the French ruler, strove to convince Britain to join France in forcing mediation on the American government, a project that once begun would be likely to result in Confederate independence. The emperor also contemplated outright recognition of the Confederacy. Seward warned of the consequences of intervention, which would place France on the side of a rebellion that celebrated slavery and might involve the French in armed conflict. Napoleon also took advantage of American helplessness to send troops to Mexico and place a ruler on a puppet throne. Seward consistently condemned the incursion in Mexico, but could do nothing until the war had concluded. After the restoration of the Union, Seward's strongly worded protests convinced the French to abandon their Mexican adventurism.

Seward's successes were attributable to his intellectual and personal gifts. A canny lawyer, he was an able writer of diplomatic messages and dispatches. Always a convivial fellow with a pronounced sense of humor, he quickly bonded with Abraham Lincoln, who appreciated Seward's jocularity and deep knowledge of politics. Lincoln leaned on Seward to instruct him in the intricacies of protocol at official receptions and dinners, a service for which the president, a western lawyer with little experience in such matters, was profoundly grateful. It was not unusual for Lincoln to stop at Seward's house in the evening to chuckle over an amusing book. Seward's facile conversation also charmed his diplomatic counterparts, or at least made a good rapport easier to achieve.

Though the public perception of Seward for much of his career had been that he was a radical on slavery, the truth was that he was more moderate on the subject—moderate in the sense that he did not demand immediate emancipation. He also considered blacks inherently inferior to whites. That attitude became apparent during the war, when Seward became the target of radical Republicans for what they perceived as his excessive caution on the slavery issue. Seward favored gradual, compensated emancipation, and though he supported equal treatment under the law for black Americans, he accepted the prevailing racist assumptions of their inferiority. Lincoln too had similar Whiggish, conservative opinions, and congressional radicals feared that Seward reinforced them, knowing that when they lobbied Lincoln to free the slaves, Seward deprecated the prospect. He worried emancipation could provoke dire consequences: dissent and even violent opposition in the racist North, a slave insurrection and race war in the

South, foreign intervention to restore order, and the cotton trade disrupted in the slave revolt. He also fretted that the ensuing social revolution would retard national reconciliation and reconstruction. When draft riots later occurred in New York, with much of the violence directed against blacks, Seward argued that the outbreak was precisely what he had feared. Despite these misgivings, he acquiesced when Lincoln proposed emancipation in July 1862 because he recognized the military value of black manpower. He objected to Lincoln's colonization schemes, as he did not favor so blithely dismissing a source of labor.

Seward also tended to involve himself in matters beyond the limits of his department, offering advice on patronage and military appointments, raising troops when manpower totals fell, and meddling in navy affairs, much to the annoyance of the navy secretary, Gideon Welles. Widespread recognition of his power and influence in the administration made him a convenient scapegoat when the war went poorly, as it often did. Radicals disliked and distrusted him for his tepid support for emancipation, and Salmon Chase, secretary of the treasury, encouraged the belief that the Cabinet was torn by disagreements, much of it attributable to Seward. A crisis occurred in December 1862. That month, Seward published diplomatic correspondence that included a dispatch to Adams in which Seward had suggested that Northern abolitionists and Southern slave owners were colluding to foment a slave revolt. The suggestion of moral equivalency between the two sides left congressional radicals fuming. Then came the debacle at Fredericksburg on December 13, when the Confederate army commanded by Robert E. Lee soundly defeated an attacking Union army under Ambrose Burnside. Five days later, a committee of senators visited the White House and demanded that Lincoln sack Seward, accusing the secretary of insufficient zeal for the war and of malicious influence in the administration. Upon learning of the proceedings, Seward sent in his resignation. Lincoln did not want to part with Seward, and he certainly did not wish Chase and his congressional allies to dictate his Cabinet. He invited the disaffected senators to meet with the Cabinet without Seward, during which Lincoln pressed Chase on Cabinet unity, and Chase was forced to concede that the Cabinet was unified, contradicting what he had privately told the senators. Humiliated, Chase resigned, but Lincoln managed to retain both Chase and Seward, refusing to accept the resignations of the Cabinet's prominent representatives of the Republican Party's radical and conservative factions. Seward had survived, yet the enmity of the radicals remained undimmed.

As the war reached and passed its midpoint in 1863, Seward supported Lincoln's Reconstruction plan, which promised Southern states readmission to the Union after 10 percent of the adult males had taken an oath of allegiance. He supported Lincoln for reelection in 1864, holding in abeyance his own undying ambition for the presidency. Within months of Lincoln's victory in November 1864, Seward participated in fruitless peace talks with three Confederate commissioners held on a vessel anchored near Hampton Roads, Virginia. Lincoln too was present, at the recommendation of Ulysses S. Grant. At the conference, Seward rebuffed suggestions by Alexander H. Stephens, one of the commissioners and the vice president of the Confederacy, that the two warring sections unite to expel the French from Mexico as a prelude to reunification. Little came of the meeting other than that old Whigs like Stephens, Lincoln, and Seward had an opportunity to reminisce. Two months later, Seward was severely injured in a carriage accident, breaking his arm and jaw and dislocating his shoulder. He was recovering from these injuries when, on the night of Lincoln's assassination, Lewis Powell, one of John Wilkes Booth's co-conspirators, forced his way into Seward's bedroom and slashed his face and neck with a knife, causing spectacular but not fatal wounds.

Back at work at the State Department in late May 1865, Seward had a new boss in Andrew Johnson, who assumed the presidency after Lincoln's death. Johnson was a War Democrat of reactionary temperament on race issues. Seward had enjoyed a remarkable degree of camaraderie with Lincoln, and though he became a loyal member of Johnson's administration, he never developed the same degree of intimacy with Johnson as he had once enjoyed with Lincoln. Still, the two men shared a belief that conciliation of Southerners was the best path to national reconciliation. Neither favored an aggressive federal role in protecting and safeguarding the newly freed slaves; black civil rights were a matter for state governments. Johnson's stubbornness in insisting on this policy over the objections of powerful members of the Union political coalition put him on a path to conflict with the national legislature. Seward supported the president philosophically, but he favored negotiation and compromise with Congress rather than confrontation. Johnson ruled his administration and overrode Seward's counsel.

The result was a series of presidential vetoes and overrides and eventually the impeachment and trial of the president. At Johnson's request, Seward had provided draft veto messages preceding Johnson's rejection of the Freedmen's Bureau in February 1866, the Civil Rights Bill in March 1866, and a bill to admit Colorado as a state. Seward denounced the Fourteenth Amendment in Cabinet, though he cooperated with the process of sending it out to the states for ratification. He supported Thurlow Weed's effort to place conservatives in control of the Union Party organization in New York, a gambit that ultimately floundered and left Weed with little influence in the state in which he once had dictatorial control. Seward accompanied the president on his disastrous "Swing round the Circle" speaking tour to the Midwest, an effort to elect congressmen who favored Johnson's permissive Reconstruction scheme. With Seward at his side, the president lashed out at his critics in violent language and generally acted in a manner unbecoming to the office he held. The president's language was so rough at times that both he and Seward were accused of drunkenness. Seward picked up a touch of cholera in Louisville, Kentucky, and had to take to a sickbed in Harrisburg, Pennsylvania, nearly dying. The tour accomplished nothing. The radicals triumphed in fall elections, and in New York took control of the state legislature.

The following year, Seward again supplied Johnson with another draft of a veto message, this time for the Tenure of Office Act. Seward thought the act, which required Senate approval for dismissals of executive branch officials, was unconstitutional, and that the president did have the constitutionally sanctioned power to remove federal officeholders. He also proposed drafts of Johnson's annual messages to Congress, though Johnson invariably threw out Seward's conciliatory words for his own combative language. He tried to remain aloof from the impeachment drama, as he was reluctant to be drawn in as a constant advisor to the president in his trial. Inevitably, though, Seward rallied to the president's side. He organized fundraising to pay for Johnson's legal team, and he lobbied senators on Johnson's behalf. The president's acquittal pleased him, as he worried at the consequences for the future if the effort had succeeded.

Seward had hoped to pursue an aggressive diplomatic agenda in Lincoln's second term, but Lincoln's death and the ensuing controversy and bitterness between the Johnson administration and Congress hampered those plans. The secretary believed that American commerce and trade would spread American-style democracy across the globe, prompting the emergence of new republics. To protect American interests, Seward tried to acquire islands in the Caribbean and Pacific that could be employed as coaling stations for the steam-powered navy. He made a bid to purchase islands in the Dutch West Indies, contemplated naval bases in Santo Domingo and Haiti, and negotiated a reciprocity treaty with Hawaii. His efforts floundered in a Congress alienated from and hostile to the Johnson administration and amid public skepticism of the advisability of colonial pursuits instead of focusing on national recovery from the destructive Civil War. Despite these setbacks, Seward negotiated the purchase of Alaska from Russia and shepherded the agreement through the often recalcitrant Senate. The House later appropriated the necessary funds required for payment.

The regime of Napoleon III had taken advantage of American preoccupation with civil war to intervene in Mexico, placing French troops and a puppet ruler over the country. With the end of the war, Seward ratcheted up American complaints with the French presence in Mexico, culminating in a blunt message to the French government in late 1865 that continued French involvement threatened good relations with the United States. The following year, the French government announced a phased withdrawal of troops from Mexico, which was accomplished by March 1867. Glyndon Van Deusen has argued that Seward handled this crisis so well he managed to accomplish his objective—France out of Mexico—without unduly arousing French public opinion and while maintaining good relations between the two countries. Seward was less successful in pursuing American claims for damages against Great Britain for depredations committed by the British-built Confederate sea raiders *Alabama* and *Florida*. He repeatedly approached the British government to establish negotiations leading to payment of the claims only to be rebuffed. Finally, a convention between the two countries was signed in the waning days of Seward's tenure to adjudicate the dispute. Unfortunately, the Senate refused to approve the agreement, foiling another Seward initiative.

The victory of Ulysses S. Grant in the 1868 presidential election spelled the end of Seward's political career, as his association with Andrew Johnson rendered him anathema to the new administration. Always active and energetic, he dreaded the prospect of retirement and reluctantly surrendered his office in 1869. He traveled in his final years, making a strenuous world tour in 1870–1871, a remarkable feat given the primitive nature of transportation and his own advanced age and declining health. A progressively worsening paralysis hampered Seward and kept him from completing a memoir, though he did manage to publish an account of his world tour, which sold well. He died on October 10, 1872, and was buried in Auburn, New York.

PRINCIPAL IDEAS

In his years as a governor and senator, Seward championed a positive agenda that earned him a reputation as a progressive political figure. He was a consistent supporter of government spending on internal improvements and education, a zeal that reflected his belief in American exceptionalism. When critics charged that state spending on canals and railroads led to onerous debt burdens and higher taxation, Seward responded that the economic growth a better transportation system spurred would refill government coffers and reduce and eliminate any deficits. Americans had unique natural advantages: untouched wealth in land just coming into cultivation, and no predatory aristocracy or court and church elite to siphon off state revenue. With a republic possessed of unlimited resources, both the public and private sector should aggressively spend on transportation improvements with the confidence that the result would be greater economic growth and an improved lifestyle.

Education too was a necessary component of Seward's progressive agenda. He acknowledged that the United States already had a higher per capita literacy rate than many other nations. However, Seward argued that the literacy level of many, if not most, Americans was pretty rude, that is, able to read a newspaper or simple documents and sign a name in frontier scrawl. A healthy and perpetual democracy required a greater degree of sophistication, a broader and deeper learning that embraced a widespread familiarity with works of history, geography, morals, government, and science. Seward noted that many American schoolchildren left school just as the more advanced learning was to begin, a practice he strongly deprecated. A highly educated populace was more likely to spurn the appeal of the demagogue and make elections contests of philosophical discussion and disagreement rather than vicious personality feuds. He also favored education for women, and he supported state subsidies for schools that catered to foreign-born students. Though nativist sentiment was strong throughout his political career, Seward persistently backed religious and ethnic toleration in education and in society at large.

In most other areas of public policy, his position was that of a typical Whig. He supported a protective tariff and the Bank of the United States. He emphasized legislative measures that would improve American trade and commerce throughout the world, such as support for a transcontinental railroad and for a transisthumian canal. Seward believed that the United States had an expansive destiny, though expansion would not come through wars of conquest, which he opposed. Rather, as American trade expanded into previously unreachable world markets, so too would American-style democracy, as other nations adopted the political institutions and democratic values embodied in the United States. As secretary of state, he pursued commercial agreements and naval bases in furtherance of his vision of America's destiny.

Seward's attitude toward slavery and African Americans was both progressive and reactionary, a strange and contradictory mix. He considered slavery a threat to the American republic, a corrupter and an embarrassment to the ideals upon which the nation had been founded. In the 1830s, he thought the Southern defenders of slavery a greater threat to the body politic than the abolitionists, and he opposed the gag rule as a potent source of sectional tensions. Still, he counseled moderation as the best path for the abolitionists. When abolitionists queried him on his attitudes, Seward responded that he did not support black suffrage, but he did support jury trials for fugitive slaves if such trials were constitutional. He favored gradual emancipation. His moderation, even conservatism, on slavery and race issues was always present, though he quickly developed a radical reputation because of what seemed like aggressive public condemnations of slavery.

A series of events and speeches in the 1840s and 1850s cemented Seward's supposed radicalism in the public imagination. As New York governor, he refused to honor an extradition request from Virginia for black citizens accused of assisting in a slave escape. He bluntly argued that freedom was a right, and the State of New York did not recognize the crime of stealing people, or that people could be property. He strongly objected to the concept that one person could own another. Black Americans, he believed, were entitled to equality under the law and should be permitted trial by jury and writs of habeas corpus. As a senator, he opposed the extension of slavery and political compromises that he considered a frivolous abandonment of principles in the face of dubious Southern disunion scares. He was skeptical of the widespread assumption that removing barriers to slavery in the unsettled West was a meaningless concession to Southern sentiment because climate and soil rendered slavery impossible in the region. Seward thought slavery as a system might succeed in the West, and he worried that to permit its expansion would lead to forms of aristocracy and despotism in the new territories. In his famed speech of March 11, 1850, Seward argued that a "higher law than the Constitution" required Americans to be careful stewards of the vast wilderness and unique destiny they had been granted, a gift and a responsibility that necessarily entailed hemming in the corrupting slavery system. Though the phrase "higher law" and other appeals to Providence or God were not uncommon, Seward's use of the phrase in conjunction with restricting slavery sparked widespread outrage and criticism in the South. He opposed Douglas's repeal of the Missouri Compromise as embodied in the Kansas-Nebraska Act and openly worried about the relentless expansionary zeal of the slaveocracy. Seward began to speak of the fundamental incompatibility of free labor and slave labor, an argument that he eventually reduced to the declaration, in Rochester, New York, on October 25, 1858, that an "irrepressible conflict" existed between the two systems, a conflict that would resolve itself into a nation all slave or all free labor.

Yet Seward's radicalism was always tempered by an inherent caution with regard to race. He considered blacks inferior to whites and believed them incapable of assimilating into the broader society. When Lincoln broached the idea of emancipation, Seward's first reaction was to draw back. He worried that emancipation might spark a black-white race war in the South, and worried about the potential for a social revolution that would inhibit the reunion of the warring sections. He also fretted over foreign intervention to restore the cotton trade, brought on after the freed slaves abandoned the cultivation and harvesting of crops. He eventually supported emancipation and even black suffrage, but only grudgingly so, in the case of the former, because he recognized its potency as a war measure. After Andrew Johnson became president following Lincoln's death, Seward viewed black civil rights as a matter for each individual state to determine, and he considered federal intervention on behalf of black citizens deprived of rights in Southern states as unconstitutional and subversive of the nature of the federal union. His attitude was grounded in his belief that only by conciliating Southern white sentiment, which was overwhelmingly racist, could the Union be amicably and permanently restored. He was prepared to sacrifice full civil rights for blacks to propitiate Southern white opinion.

CONCLUSION

William Henry Seward has been characterized as one of the most effective secretaries of state in American history, though many of his initiatives were rejected in Congress. Seward helped prevent foreign intervention on the side of the Confederacy in the Civil War. As a governor and senator, he recognized the dangers that the slave system posed for the American republic, though his views on race reflected the racist attitudes then prevalent. His championship of immigrants and willingness to countenance government assistance to the foreign-born provided a potent counterweight to the poisonous nativist movement. His vision of an expansion of American influence and even empire in the world through the spread of trade and democracy anticipated the emergence of the United States as a world power. Unfortunately, his fears of social revolution brought on by emancipation and his desire to placate Southern racist public opinion to restore the Union led him to back away from continuing federal intervention in support of full black civil rights after the Civil War.

FURTHER READING

Eric Foner, *Free Soil, Free Labor, Free Men: The Ideology of the Republican Party before the Civil War* (New York: Oxford University Press, 1970); William E. Gienapp, *The Origins of the Republican Party, 1852–1856* (New York: Oxford University Press, 1987); Daniel Walker Howe, *The Political Culture of the American Whigs* (Chicago: University of Chicago Press, 1979); William Henry Seward, *The Works of William H. Seward*, edited by George E. Baker, 3 vols. (New York: Redfield, 1853); and Glyndon G. Van Deusen, *William Henry Seward* (New York: Oxford University Press, 1967).

ALEXANDER H. STEPHENS
(1812–1883)

A Diminutive Whig Statesman

LIFE

Alexander Hamilton Stephens was the third child of Andrew B. Stephens and Margaret Grier. Born on February 11, 1812, in Wilkes County, Georgia, near Crawfordsville, Stephens never knew his natural mother, a sickly woman who died within months of his birth. His father remarried the following year to Matilda Lindscy, with whom he had an additional five children. Stephens had little regard for his stepmother and in consequence drew closer to his father, whom he idolized. Andrew Stephens was a stout, pious Georgia farmer who combined the ability to work with his hands with a strong intellect and a love of books. He started teaching at age fourteen and used his earnings to purchase a farm. Stern and demanding, he expected his children to act in a moral and upright fashion.

Alexander, or "Aleck," struggled with the chores that came with farm life. He was incredibly slight and frail, and it was soon clear to him that he must make a living in a manner other than the physical labor farming required. His father had reluctantly opened a school at the urging of neighbors. Stephens attended and purportedly demonstrated a prodigious intellect by reciting passages memorized from the Bible. Biographer Thomas E. Schott has written that the praise Stephens earned for his classroom achievements delighted him. He lived in a society in which a man's honor was a product of his reputation in his community. He determined to pursue personal achievement and recognition in his life.

Stephens's physical appearance was striking. He stood five feet seven inches tall and weighed less than 100 pounds. He was so slight that he was almost ethereal, like a human wisp of smoke. Perched on the skeletal frame was a head with a waxen complexion, prominent ears, and piercing eyes. "A malformed ill-shaped half finished thing," Stephens ruefully called himself. He suffered poor health, from stomach ailments and pneumonia to rheumatoid arthritis, and later in life he took huge self-administered doses of morphine for pain. He also imbibed alcohol in tablespoon draughts for the same reason, a practice that led at least one biographer to conclude that Stephens was an alcoholic. Stephens denied the charge when it was raised against him in the aftermath of the Civil War. In Stephens's telling, a doctor suggested in 1842 that he take a tablespoon of brandy after dinner each day. This Stephens did faithfully and then intermittently over the years. He also confessed to taking a tablespoon after major speeches. "I was never drunk in my life," he affirmed, "and I question if all the spirits I ever drank would amount to three gallons." Poor health that came with age may have prompted Stephens to imbibe more than his earlier habits suggest. Despite his puny, sickly body, Stephens eventually entered the rough world of Southern politics, where campaigns could prompt duels and other physical confrontations.[1]

Andrew Stephens died of pneumonia on May 7, 1826. The death of his beloved father wracked Stephens with grief. Upon hearing the sad news, he purportedly fell to the ground and rolled about in despair, like a man overcome at a camp meeting. The awful event marked the beginning of Stephens's lifelong preoccupation with death. He was given to melancholy and bouts of depression, to which his dwelling on the finality and inevitability of death contributed. As his father had died, so with certainty would he. Awareness of his own mortality oppressed him, though later in life he took comfort in religious faith.

Stephens's stepmother soon followed his father to the grave, and the children dispersed to various maternal and paternal relatives. Stephens and his brother Aaron were taken in by his uncle, Aaron Grier, and his sister Elizabeth, which necessitated a move to Raytown in Warren County. Stephens continued his studies with the kind assistance of local patrons, earning a degree from Franklin College. He became a teacher, but the classroom could not satisfy his soaring ambition. He learned the law and established a successful practice in Crawfordsville, staying in the small town despite offers in larger cities because he wanted to buy back his father's land. His emaciated body notwithstanding, Stephens became a great orator, honing his skills on the country juries that sat in judgment on his cases. His reputation grew, and his practice flourished.

Success in the law, skill as an orator, and ambition led to politics. He ran for state representative in 1836, allied with the State Rights faction that was led by George M. Troup. The Troup faction had objected to Andrew Jackson's muscular handling of South Carolina while quelling the nullification crisis. In the campaign for his first elective office, Stephens had a taste of the centrality of slavery in antebellum Georgia politics. He was accused of abolition sympathies because he had opposed the formation of a local vigilante group to safeguard the mail from abolition literature. Stephens thought such an extralegal group a violation of the rule of law.

He angrily denied any ties to abolitionists and won the election. Stephens biographer Thomas E. Schott has argued that the campaign established what would become a pattern in Stephens's political career. He upheld the rule of law, and he was willing to embrace unpopular positions. He also possessed great self-assurance and felt his conclusions were unassailable.

Stephens served in the Georgia House until 1840, and then was elected to the State Senate in 1842. He supported internal improvements: railroads, roads, and waterways. He opposed Democratic efforts to spur state banks to greater loans in an effort to alleviate the suffering brought on by the economic depression of the Panic of 1837. As a state legislator, Stephens tended the requests and queries of constituents and learned a great deal of parliamentary procedure, but did not introduce much legislation. Though he condemned the Whigs in 1839 as revived Federalists, he and the State Rights faction gradually drifted into alliance with the national Whig Party. In 1840, the Georgia State Rights Party endorsed the Whig presidential candidate, William H. Harrison.

Stephens ran for Congress as a Whig in 1843, campaigning statewide for an at-large seat. He defended measures the Whig Congress had championed against the apostate Whig president, John Tyler: the tariff, distribution, and the national bank. Successful yet again, Stephens endorsed Clay for president the following year. Texas annexation became a crucial issue in Georgia, as Democrats trumpeted annexation as essential to Southern rights in the Union and to the protection of slavery. Though he referred to annexation as a humbug gotten up to divide the Whig Party, Stephens did not resist the pro-Texas tide in his native state. He supported the House resolution of Milton Brown to admit Texas as a state, acknowledging that another slave state would increase Southern political influence in the national government, an important factor in guaranteeing the continuation of the slave-based system. He conceded that slavery was a bad institution, but argued it was necessary to keep a proper relation between the races where they lived together, by which he meant blacks subordinate to whites. Other Georgia Whigs continued to oppose annexation. Stephens's bow to public sentiment on the issue helped him become a leading Whig figure.

As Stephens's law practice flourished, he bought extensive tracts of farm land and purchased slaves to work them. He also enjoyed the service of slaves within his household, who acted as valets and cooks. Stephens has been characterized as a permissive master who did not employ corporal punishment or sell slaves and split up families. He allowed his field hands to supplement their diets by gardening, hunting, and fishing. He often overlooked transgressions slaves committed, gave them passes to leave the farm, and treated them at Christmas. With a mixture of hubris and ignorance, Stephens believed himself a beloved figure to blacks. "I never yet knew one of the coloured race who did not like me," he wrote while imprisoned at Fort Warren after the Civil War. "Toward coloured people I have always felt considerable sympathy and it has never failed to be reciprocated." He even contended that he would not keep a slave against his or her will, a bizarre claim based on the false assumption that slaves in the antebellum South had some kind of choice over their fates. In the early years of his congressional career, Stephens conceded slavery was wrong, but he gradually moved to John C. Calhoun's position that the institution was good. His views were bluntly racist; he could never envision blacks as equals. "Equality does not exist between blacks and whites," he wrote. "The one race is by nature inferior in many respects, physically and mentally, to the other. This should be received as a fixed invincible fact in all dealings with the subject."[2]

Though he had bowed to public sentiment in Georgia on the popular annexation of Texas, Stephens became a committed and vociferous foe of President James K. Polk's expansionist agenda. He opposed legislation giving Great Britain notice of the United States' intention to end joint tenancy of the Oregon Territory. Stephens worried that Polk's bellicose claim of the entire territory for the United States would provoke Britain into war. In the end, Polk negotiated a settlement for less territory. It was the president's war against Mexico that most infuriated Stephens. He believed the Mexican War violated the rule of law, the Constitution, and the fundamental principles of the American Republic. Nevertheless, Stephens voted for supplies for the troops in the field.

In August 1846, David Wilmot, a Pennsylvania congressman, introduced a resolution to prohibit slavery in any territory acquired during the war. Southerners considered the Wilmot Proviso an explicit condemnation of the Southern slave system, an affront to Southern dignity and honor. Much to Stephens's chagrin, the House passed the proviso, but the measure was blocked in the Senate. He subsequently introduced resolutions to prohibit any acquisition of territory from Mexico. His resolutions were defeated, but Stephens earned praise from Whigs across the United States. He maintained that acquiring territory threatened the Union because of the sectional tensioned provoked. He also contended that additional territory was no indemnity for the war's cost, as the expense of constructing forts and the associated troops to staff them and protect settlers would outweigh the value of the new territory. Significantly, in the debate over territory, Stephens argued that the Bible and Christianity sanctioned slavery. He had thus abandoned his earlier acknowledgment of slavery's wrongness and moved toward Calhoun's position. Yet Stephens condemned Calhoun's penchant for oracular pronouncements and controversy and, unlike the South Carolinian, he did not want Congress to legislate on slavery at all. Slavery was, in Stephens's opinion, a state institution upon which Congress had little to say.

The ensuing years of sectional strife pushed Stephens away from his moderation and the Whig Party. He played a minor role in the Young Indian movement of congressional Whigs to draft Zachary Taylor for the Whig presidential nomination in 1848. Stephens opposed popular sovereignty, the gambit of Democratic nominee Lewis Cass, which would allow the citizens of territories to decide on slavery. He considered popular sovereignty an insult to the South, a method to deprive his region of just rights while empowering a local populace that might be of a dubious, in Stephens's opinion, racial mixture. In 1848, Stephens blocked a Senate bill to organize Oregon because it threw the issue of slavery to the Supreme Court. Stephens argued that international law mandated that the existing laws of a captured territory remain in force until superceded by new authority. Mexican law abolished slavery and would therefore remain in force until the organization of an American territorial government. Consequently, Stephens felt the Supreme Court would have no choice but to declare free any territory acquired from Mexico. Stephens suggested extending the Missouri Compromise line as a method for ending the territorial stalemate.

Taylor was elected president in November much to Stephens's delight, as he and other Southern Whigs hoped that the slave-owning president would favor the Southern view on slavery's expansion in the territories. Taylor, though, disappointed Stephens and others by endorsing the quick admission of California and New Mexico as free states. The new president seemed to have allied himself to the Free Soil movement that wished to exclude slavery from the territories. Stephens had hoped to be influential in the new Whig administration, but now found himself and his advice largely ignored. Taylor's apostasy on slavery's extension, as Stephens viewed it, helped propel him out of the Whig Party. When the Thirty-first Congress gathered in Washington, D.C., in December 1849, Stephens and fellow Georgian Robert Toombs introduced resolutions at an organizing Whig caucus calling on Congress not to meddle with slavery in the territories or the District of Columbia. When the resolutions were tabled, Stephens, Toombs, and other Southerners stalked out of the caucus and the Whig Party.

The aftermath of the Mexican War brought continued sectional strife and the breakup of political parties in Georgia. In an attempt to find a solution, the aged Henry Clay introduced resolutions in the Senate on January 29, 1850. Stephens had gone to the Senate chamber to listen to Clay's effort and purportedly sat on the floor at his feet while the Great Compromiser spoke. Stephens backed Clay's compromise, which called for the admission of California, among other elements. Clay's effort foundered in July 1850, but the untimely death of President Taylor that same month removed an important obstacle to compromise. (Calhoun had died in March 1850, removing another obstacle.) The compromise legislation eventually passed under the leadership of younger men such as Illinois senator Stephen A. Douglas. In Georgia, new parties formed, grouped around attitudes toward the compromise. Stephens joined the Constitutional Union Party, the procompromise party made up of former Democrats, such as Howell Cobb, and Whigs, such as Stephens and Robert Toombs. The Southern Rights Party formed to oppose the compromise and looked favorably on secession. The Georgia legislature had mandated a state convention to discuss California's admission to the Union, and Governor George Towns scheduled an election for delegates for November 1850. If the radicals dominated the convention, a secession resolution might result. Stephens, Cobb, and Toombs campaigned for the compromise. In the ensuing election, the Unionist cause triumphed. When the convention met in December, the delegates adopted resolutions giving the compromise a qualified endorsement, resolutions that came to be known as the Georgia Platform.

The Constitutional Union Party dominated Georgia politics for a year, but the presidential election year of 1852 saw a reestablishment of old party ties. Georgia Democrats who had joined the Constitutional Union Party drifted back into allegiance with the national Democratic Party, which had placated them with a platform endorsing the compromise and a presidential candidate, Franklin Pierce, who, though a Northern man, was considered right on Southern principles. Stephens and other Southern Whigs did not feel comfortable with the national Whig Party, which they believed unreliable on Southern issues. Stephens endorsed Daniel Webster for president; he mistrusted the Whig nominee, Winfield Scott, but Webster died shortly before the election. Pierce and the Democratic Party triumphed in Georgia.

For the remainder of his antebellum years in Congress, Stephens became progressively more radical, adopting many of the positions and beliefs of the Southern rights zealots he had once condemned. For example, in 1853, Stephens denounced filibustering and the desire of many in the South to acquire Cuba. Soon enough, Stephens abandoned that position and endorsed Cuba's acquisition and filibustering. He also spoke on slavery and race with greater frequency. In December 1850, he argued that blacks were ordained by nature to be slaves and were better off in the South than free blacks in the North, an argument that Calhoun had also advanced while employing bogus statistical data. He supported the Kansas-Nebraska bill, rejecting the belief, held by many in the North, that the Missouri Compromise, which the bill sundered, was an inviolable compact.

When the Kansas-Nebraska bill was stymied in the House, where opponents promised to kill it by attaching an endless stream of amendments, the required discussion of which would consume the allotted time for debate, Stephens used an obscure parliamentary rule to block the amending process and bring the bill to a successful vote. "I took the reins in my own hand and drove with whip & spur until we got the 'wagon' out of the mire," Stephens boasted. Of course it also helped that President Pierce had made the bill an administration measure, forcing Democrats to choose whether to defy their party leader. Stephens considered the passage of the act the capstone of his congressional career.[3]

Stephens seriously contemplated retirement from politics in 1855. The new Know-Nothing, or American Party, had become a potent force in Georgia politics, much to Stephens's dismay. He disliked the secrecy of the movement and thought opposition to white immigrants wrong-headed. In his opinion, white Catholic immigrants were less a threat to the social order than zealous Protestant abolitionists. He deemed calls to extend the naturalization period a gambit by Northern businessmen to secure a disenfranchised immigrant labor force. Concerned at surrendering the political stage to the new party, in the end Stephens ran for reelection. He triumphed in a bitter campaign, as his Know-Nothing foes criticized the Kansas-Nebraska Act and popular sovereignty for surrendering Southern rights. Returning to Washington for the congressional session, Stephens joined the Democratic Party.

Kansas and sectional strife dominated the final two congressional sessions of Stephens's antebellum career. Southern Know-Nothings and states' rights radicals both demanded Kansas come into the Union as a slave state. Stephens agreed on the goal if not the method for reaching it. He favored popular sovereignty as a way to finesse the issue. In 1856, he sponsored a bill to empower the federal government to conduct a census and register votes in Kansas. Violence in Kansas and in the U.S. Senate marked that year. When Massachusetts senator Charles Sumner was bludgeoned on the floor of the Senate by South Carolina congressman Preston Brooks, Stephens was unconcerned. "I have no objection to the liberty of speech when the liberty of the cudgel is left free to combat it," he wrote. He voted against expelling Brooks from the House of Representatives. Brooks resigned from the House in July 1856, but he was promptly reelected to the seat he had vacated. Stephens always considered dueling a necessary remedy for insults. He challenged Benjamin H. Hill to a duel after the 1856 election for remarks Hill made that Stephens considered offensive. Hill refused to fight, and the two dueled in correspondence that was published in Georgia newspapers.[4]

At the following congressional session, the thirty-fifth, Stephens was the chairman of the House Territories Committee. As such, he championed the tainted Lecompton Constitution for Kansas, which President Buchanan had endorsed and made a party measure. Stephen A. Douglas's strong opposition to Lecompton helped galvanize opposition in the Congress. The Senate accepted Lecompton over Douglas's objections, but the House voted to send it back to Kansas voters. Appointed to the conference committee, Stephens again demonstrated his mastery of the legislative process. He devised a bill that would resubmit the controversial Lecompton Constitution to Kansas voters. If they rejected it, the admission of Kansas would be delayed. He recruited William H. English to propose the bill under his name.

The compromise carried. As with the Kansas-Nebraska Act, Stephens's intervention was crucial to the end of the impasse.

Congressional quarrels and bitter Georgia election campaigns, centered on proving fealty to an increasingly radical definition of Southern rights, exhausted Stephens. He always enjoyed the quiet beauty of the country surrounding Crawfordsville, liking nothing better than a stroll down a red-clay path with his beloved Spanish poodle Rio. Though he had become an influential figure in Washington, Stephens decided to retire from Congress. A speech he delivered at a testimonial dinner on July 2, 1859, demonstrated how the decade of recurring sectional tensions had turned the onetime Whig into a staunch advocate of Southern rights. In his speech, Stephens praised filibustering and thoughtfully looked forward to the acquisition of Cuba and northern Mexico. He warned, however, that acquiring new territory brought the problem of peopling it with settlers and slaves. Stephens suggested that reopening the slave trade might be an efficacious action to ensure labor for the exploitation of the new territory. His comments provoked an uproar in the Northern press, and Stephens claimed he had not suggested what he clearly had. The Alexander Stephens of the 1840s would not have proposed something so inflammatory and so inhuman.

Stephens supported Stephen A. Douglas for president in 1860. He viewed as calamitous the breakup of the Democratic nominating convention in Charleston, South Carolina; a Whig earlier in his career, he feared the anarchy that came with political chaos. He saw little need for additional congressional legislation to protect slavery in the territories, as Jefferson Davis demanded. For Stephens, the Cincinnati platform of 1856, which endorsed popular sovereignty, was adequate to protect Southern rights. He feared and opposed secession. "We have nothing to fear from anything so much as unnecessary changes and revolutions in government," he wrote. Yet after Lincoln's election and the movement for secession in Georgia, Stephens was uncharacteristically passive and even defeatist. While Georgia secessionists delivered fiery speeches, Stephens, perhaps the leading Unionist in the state, did nothing. Elected a delegate to the Georgia secession convention, he delivered a brief uninspired speech for continued union. He voted against secession, but ultimately signed the secession ordinance, supporting his state on its misguided path. He was then named a delegate to the convention charged with creating a Confederate government meeting in Montgomery, Alabama.[5]

In Montgomery, Stephens's parliamentary skills and experience were put to use organizing the Provisional Confederate Congress and government. He served on the Rules Committee and was then named to the committee formed to write the new nation's constitution. His name surfaced as a possible president, but his longstanding unionism, up until Georgia's secession, was too temperate for a movement led by Southern extremists. Instead, Democrat and Southern rights zealot Jefferson Davis was selected. Stephens was chosen as vice president, a sop to an important state, Georgia, and to Southern Unionists and moderates. It was hoped that Stephens's visibility in the national government would graft the support of moderates to the new regime. Davis helped that process along by regularly consulting with Stephens, who became a frequent visitor to the president's office. Stephens biographer Thomas E. Schott has suggested that the similarities in character of the two men made long-term cooperation between them unlikely. Both men tended to view criticism of their actions or decisions as a personal affront while remaining unshakably convinced of the correctness of their own positions. Davis's wife Varina candidly admitted her husband's poor personal skills. The new president did not have the ability to soothe damaged egos or gloss over differences.

After the Confederate government moved from Montgomery to Richmond, Virginia, Stephens had increasingly little contact with Davis. From the summer to fall of 1861, he went from presidential confidant and advisor to nonentity. His isolation wounded his vanity and pride and probably contributed to his eventual break with the administration. There were many causes of the estrangement. Davis lacked the political skills to recognize the value of keeping the vice president pacified with at least courtesy meetings. Beyond the similarities of personality that rendered a clash likely, the two men came from opposite political poles. Stephens had been a Whig, while Davis was a Democrat and Southern rights zealot. The new president was also irritated by a speech Stephens delivered in Savannah, Georgia, in March 1861, during which Stephens had proclaimed that the foundation of the Confederate nation was the recognition of black inferiority and subordination to whites. The so-called Cornerstone Speech undercut Davis's emphasis on states' rights and sovereignty as the ideological bases for the rebellion.

Stephens was elected vice president in November 1861 and sworn in the following February in Richmond. But with few substantive duties, he retreated to Crawfordsville, where he spent much of the war. His isolation contributed to his eventual opposition to the extreme measures Davis felt compelled to take in order to wage war. Stephens believed the Confederacy had been formed to protect and uphold personal liberty. In his view, war measures that sacrificed liberty were subversive of the very core principles of the nation and therefore unwise and intolerable. Accordingly, Stephens opposed conscription, impressment, suspension of the writ of habeas corpus, and martial law. He thought conscription unnecessary, believing in the adequacy of relying on volunteers who could elect their own officers. Impressment was also unwise and unjust. Martial law had no basis in the Constitution or laws, and suspending the writ was unnecessary. The latter threatened liberty for no good purpose or reason. He also considered the cotton embargo poor policy; better for the government to purchase cotton and sell or trade it to foreign countries for war supplies. Stephens believed the war should be financed by taxation, and he deprecated the inflationary policy of simply printing additional notes. Given his attitudes, Stephens was naturally supportive of Georgia's governor, Joseph E. Brown, who resisted the Davis administration's dictates.

Despite his opposition to Davis's policies, Stephens continued to be cordial with the president on the rare occasions when they were together, at least through 1863. In June 1863, Stephens proposed undertaking a personal diplomatic mission to the Lincoln administration. He hoped to restart the practice of exchanging prisoners, with an eye to broadening the discussion to a general settlement of the war. Davis embraced the proposal, though his conception was different than Stephens's. Robert E. Lee's Army of Northern Virginia intended to invade the North that month. Davis envisioned Stephens accompanying the army as a diplomatic envoy, as Nicholas Trist had traveled with Winfield Scott during the Mexican War. With Lee victorious, Stephens would be on site for negotiations to end the war on the basis of Southern independence. Stephens objected to traveling with the army, as he felt it unlikely that he would be welcomed as a diplomat if he arrived with an invading force. He also thought Lee's invasion negated any prospect for successful negotiations. In the end, Stephens spent a few days onboard a packet steamer anchored near Fortress Monroe before the Lincoln administration rebuffed the proposed talks.

In 1864, Stephens openly confronted Davis and his controversial policies. He wrote the president at the beginning of the year, urging him to reconsider conscription, impressment, and suspension of habeas corpus. The president did not act on Stephens's suggestions. Governor Brown had called a special session of the Georgia assembly to protest the Davis administration's policies. Stephens addressed it on March 16, 1864, going over familiar ground on his opposition. His principled stand made him the de facto leader of opponents to an administration of which he was a member. He also condemned Davis for not giving sufficient encouragement to the Northern peace movement.

As the Confederacy's plight worsened, Stephens advocated pursuing negotiations with the Lincoln administration. Davis was reluctant to engage in negotiations unless founded on the premise of Southern independence. Stephens preferred to accept any talks, even if predicated on the South rejoining the Union, as he felt negotiations would inevitably lead to peaceful separation. He had an opportunity to pursue diplomacy for peace at the beginning of 1865, when Lincoln allowed venerable politico Francis P. Blair Sr. to visit Richmond. Blair proposed that talks begin for reunification with the unifying mission of expelling the French from Mexico. Under considerable pressure from domestic foes to consider a negotiated settlement, the beleaguered Confederate president Davis agreed to negotiations while insisting on Southern independence. He summoned Stephens to Richmond and insisted that the vice president act as one of three commissioners charged with the diplomatic mission. Stephens hoped the mission could remain low key, but Davis revealed Stephens' mission to quiet his domestic critics.

The Confederate commissioners passed through the lines and spent a few days at City Point with Union army commander-in-chief Ulysses S. Grant. Stephens was impressed with the stoic general and his modest carriage and obvious sincerity. Though Lincoln was reluctant to meet, a message from Grant persuaded him to make the trip. On February 3, 1865, Lincoln and his secretary of state William H. Seward met with Stephens, John A. Campbell, and Robert M. T. Hunter. Little of moment occurred other than colorful anecdotes, such as Lincoln remarking, on witnessing the diminutive Stephens emerge from layers of winter clothing, that such a small nubbin could come from so large a husk. The president refused to countenance an armistice or joint action against the French. He had little incentive for concessions, with Grant poised to take Richmond and Sherman rampaging across the South. Instead, Lincoln urged Stephens to return to Georgia and convince Governor Brown to take his state out of the Confederacy and back into the Union.

With the talks a failure, there was little for Stephens to do but return to Crawfordsville and await events. After the collapse of the Confederacy in April and the assassination of Lincoln, Stephens and other former Confederate leaders were arrested. Federal troops took Stephens from Crawfordsville to Fort Warren near Boston, Massachusetts. Stephens was imprisoned for nearly five months, from May to October 1865. He was initially closely confined to his cell, allowed out for an hour's walk once each day. He leavened his stark existence by ordering books from the prison library and from the sutler. He also purchased food to supplement his diet, though he often had scant appetite. Confinement itself held little terror for Stephens; separation from his brother Linton, other friends and family, and his beloved Crawfordsville hurt the most.

Released in October 1865, Stephens returned to Crawfordsville. He continued to maintain the beliefs in state sovereignty that he had throughout his career. He could not countenance black equality, and he opposed the Fourteenth and Fifteenth Amendments. He thought it unconstitutional to require Georgia to pass the Reconstruction amendments before being readmitted to the Union. The world may have changed, but Stephens had not, and he saw no reason to alter his convictions. Still, he advocated reconciliation between the two regions, giving a speech to that effect before the Georgia legislature in 1866. Over his objections, Stephens was elected U.S. senator, but Congress refused to accept representatives from the state governments organized by President Andrew Johnson.

In September 1866, Stephens signed a contract with the National Publishing Company of Philadelphia to write an account of the Civil War. He received a healthy $4,000 advance. Stephens produced two volumes, the

first in 1868 and the second in 1870, titled *A Constitutional View of the
Late War between the States*. His first volume sold quite well, but the second did poorly. Stephens had written not an action-packed insider's account of the war, but a dreary legalistic justification for his extreme states'
rights opinions. The book received unflattering reviews, prompting
Stephens to write testy rejoinders. He later published a collection of his an-
swers to the poor reviews.

Stephens continued to be involved in politics until the end of his life. He
deprecated the rise of the Ku Klux Klan in Georgia, but defended men who
may have been Klan members from a murder charge. He purchased an interest in an Atlanta newspaper in 1871 and criticized the so-called New
Democrat movement. He opposed Horace Greeley for president in 1872.
He was returned to the House of Representatives in 1873 to fill a seat made
vacant when Ambrose R. Wright died. Incredibly, Stephens served in the
House for nine additional years. His wizened figure on the House floor was
often remarked upon; like John Quincy Adams, he was considered a relic
from a vanished era. In 1882, Stephens was elected governor of Georgia,
the crowning achievement of his career and a fitting finale given his devotion to Georgia and states' rights. The physically taxing demands of the
gubernatorial post were too much for his elderly constitution. He died a
few months into his term on March 4, 1883.

PRINCIPAL IDEAS

Education and temperament drew Alexander H. Stephens to the conservatism and economic nationalism of the Whig Party early in his political
career. His reading of the classics and history in college filled him with a
healthy concern with the maintenance of the rule of law and order to ensure societal stability; revolution and anarchy were to be avoided, as once
the former had begun it could well lead to the latter and potential bloodshed. Despite his diminutive carriage, Stephens could be quite fiery; he challenged several antagonists to duels and engaged in rather pathetic fisticuffs
with one assailant. His own self-awareness of his passionate nature convinced him of the importance of controlling the emotions, particularly for
a legislator, who had a duty to strive for a patriotic and elevated disinter-
estedness. Like many Whigs, Stephens believed that education could shape
good character and create good citizens who in turn guaranteed civic order.
Stephens's own experience suggested that self-improvement through hard
work and striving to an ambitious goal could succeed in the United States.

He supported the key elements of Whig economic policy, backing internal improvements such as railroads, a tariff that offered incidental protection for industry, distribution of the proceeds of land sales, and a strong
national currency. His Whig attitudes extended to a suspicion of the national executive, from which history suggested threats would emerge to civil

liberties in the form of creeping dictatorship, as had been occurring under the presidency of Andrew Jackson. When James K. Polk led the United States into war with Mexico, Stephens excoriated the president for duplicity, involving the nation in a war of conquest while claiming that Mexico had been the aggressor. He considered the war unconstitutional and that Polk had flagrantly violated his powers, and he worried that the unjust war might imperil the stability of the country by weakening the Constitution and the rule of law.

Increasingly, during the antebellum period of Stephens's political career, Southern politics came to be dominated by slavery, as Democrats and Whigs competed for votes by pledging to uphold the institution and societal order. Stephens had initially thought it impossible to defend slavery as anything other than a necessary evil in a region where black and white populations resided together. In time, he vigorously defended slavery as good for blacks and whites, and as a superior economic system that generated prosperity, going so far as to call for the reopening of the slave trade on the eve of the Civil War. Tough but supposedly kind to blacks, his attitudes were bluntly racist throughout his life.

The secession movement always disturbed Stephens, who worried at the consequences of the revolution. Still, he thought secession a legitimate act, and he acquiesced and went along with his state and region when it occurred, accepting the vice presidency of the new Confederacy. His Whiggish concern with tyrannical executive power asserted itself during the war, and he opposed the policies he viewed as violations of liberty, specifically conscription, confiscation, and the suspension of habeas corpus.

CONCLUSION

Alexander H. Stephens lived the Whig ideal, rising to a successful legal and political career through education and hard work despite daunting physical limitations. Aware that the unique advantages of the American nation and democratic system were essential to his rise, he embraced Whig nationalism. He could not, in the end, resist the demagoguery of Southern extremists who made fealty to the slavery system an obligation for continued political success, and he found himself obliged to carry out the wishes of those he once professed to detest.

NOTES

1. Thomas E. Schott, *Alexander H. Stephens of Georgia: A Biography* (Baton Rouge: Louisiana State University Press, 1988), 20; and Alexander H. Stephens, *Recollections of Alexander H. Stephens*, edited by Myra Lockett Avary (New York: Doubleday, Page & Co., 1910), 178.

2. Stephens, *Recollections*, 181, 207.

3. Schott, *Alexander Stephens*, 173.
4. Schott, *Alexander Stephens*, 205.
5. Schott, *Alexander Stephens*, 299.

FURTHER READING

Henry Cleveland, *Alexander Stephens in Public and Private* (Philadelphia: National Publishing Co., 1866); William J. Cooper Jr., *The South and the Politics of Slavery, 1828–1856* (Baton Rouge: Louisiana State University Press, 1978); Daniel Walker Howe, *The Political Culture of the American Whigs* (Chicago: University of Chicago Press, 1979); Thomas E. Scott, *Alexander H. Stephens of Georgia: A Biography* (Baton Rouge: Louisiana State University Press, 1988); and Alexander H. Stephens, *Recollections of Alexander Stephens*, edited by Myra Lockett Avary (New York: Doubleday, Page & Co., 1910).

THADDEUS STEVENS
(1792–1868)

Radical of Radicals

LIFE

In the small town of Danville, Vermont, Thaddeus Stevens was born on April 4, 1792. He was the second of four sons born to Joshua and Sarah Morrill Stevens. Growing up in the predominately farming community of Danville, Stevens's early life was filled with hardships and challenges. Afflicted with a clubfoot at birth, Stevens was often the object of ridicule during his childhood years. At age twelve, Stevens's father, a shoemaker and surveyor of questionable moral character, abandoned his family, leaving the job of raising the family to Sarah Morrill. While Stevens's mother was an intensely religious woman, adhering strictly to the tenets of orthodox Calvinism, she was never able to place the stamp of orthodoxy on young Thaddeus, who rejected formal Christianity early in life and never converted. Sarah was determined that Thaddeus receive a respectable education, and in this endeavor she was successful. Stevens studied at the Caledonia (Vermont) Grammar Academy before matriculating to Dartmouth University, where he studied Latin, grammar, mathematics, philosophy, and astronomy. After spending his junior year at the University of Vermont in Burlington, Stevens graduated from Dartmouth in 1814.

During his college years, many of Stevens's personal traits were evident. Many biographers point out that Stevens's notorious ambition and desire for self-advancement were evident during his college days. Moreover, Stevens also demonstrated a predisposition for conflict and controversy during these years. It was during his college years that Stevens's well-known scorn for aristocracy and elitism first surfaced, earning him the appropriate title of the "great leveler" at Dartmouth. Perhaps most significant was the development of Stevens's well-known oratorical skills. Dripping with irony and sarcasm, Stevens's public oratory could simultaneously put an audience in stitches while, at the same time, demolishing a debating opponent.

After graduation from Dartmouth, Stevens taught school briefly at Peacham, Vermont. He also spent a brief period of time teaching at Calais, Maine. In early 1815, however, Stevens decided to leave his native New England and moved to York, Pennsylvania (York County), where he had a friend, Samuel Merrill, from college days. While at York, Stevens again taught school but also began the study of law under attorney David Cassat. Because of York County Pennsylvania's long residency requirements for law licenses, Stevens traveled to neighboring Maryland the next year, where he successfully passed his bar examination. Apparently there was no provision in the local laws to prevent Stevens from practicing law in York County after he obtained his law license in Maryland, despite the county's residency requirements. Instead of practicing in York, where there were plenty of attorneys, Stevens chose to open his practice in the small town of Gettysburg, about thirty miles to the southwest.

Stevens's law practice began slowly; however, he created a reputation for himself when he defended accused murder James Hunter, using what amounted to an insanity defense. While losing this case, Stevens gained a reputation as a skilled lawyer. Undoubtedly his wit, sarcasm, and exacting style of debate served Stevens well in the legal profession. In just a few short years, Stevens was the most popular attorney in Gettysburg and Adams County. Success as a lawyer translated into material wealth. A shrewd investor, Stevens quickly invested in a number of other enterprises including real estate and the iron-forging industry. As early as 1826, Stevens, with partner J. D. Paxton, created the Mifflin forge and later Maria Furnace. The success that Stevens experienced in law and business created social and political opportunities, and Stevens would play a prominent role in the affairs of Gettysburg. Already in 1825, Stevens was elected trustee of Gettysburg Academy. Indeed, Stevens showed an early interest in education that continued throughout his political career. Prominence in local affairs eventually helped Stevens to make a successful bid for the Pennsylvania legislature in 1832.

Stevens's rise to prominence was accompanied by notoriety. Assertive and aggressive, Stevens's courtroom demeanor had already created many enemies. When he entered the political arena, his blunt, take-no-prisoners approach continued. Throughout his life, his enemies would seize upon any rumor to smear him. In September 1824, for instance, when a young black woman was found dead in a pond near the Gettysburg Presbyterian Church, Stevens's enemies spread the word that Stevens had impregnated the young woman and then killed her to cover his transgressions. Not only would this story resurface a few years later, prompting Stevens to successfully sue a local newspaper that republished the charges, but when Stevens hired a mulatto housekeeper, Lydia Smith, in 1843, rumors again surfaced regarding Steven's alleged sexual irregularities. While little credible evidence exists to either confirm or refute allegations of an illicit relationship with the housekeeper, such attacks were the logical byproduct of Stevens's aggressive methods.

Although Stevens's political outlook was decidedly Whiggish, he entered politics in the 1830s as an anti-Mason. The mysterious murder of Mason member William Morgan in upstate New York in 1826 fueled the rise of the anti-Masonic movement. Because the Masons were a secret society with elaborate, secretive rituals and exclusive membership, they attracted considerable suspicion. Despite his sympathy for staple Whig economic tenets such as protective tariffs and the National Bank, Stevens quickly became enamored with the anti-Masonic movement. Perhaps Stevens was drawn to the movement because of his hatred for aristocracy and political elitism. Since the Masons excluded cripples from their membership, Stevens undoubtedly harbored a powerful grudge against the movement. A delegate to the anti-Masonic national convention at Philadelphia in 1829, Stevens also invested $800 in the formation of an anti-Masonic newspaper, the *Anti-Masonic Star.*[1]

Stevens continued his political activism into the 1830s and was eventually elected to the Pennsylvania Assembly in 1833 as an anti-Masonic representative. During several terms in the assembly, Stevens became a skilled parliamentarian and debater. He was involved in several important legislative initiatives including the establishment of a system of free public education in Pennsylvania. As a supporter of the Bank of the United States, Stevens was a persistent critic of President Andrew Jackson, who he believed was an unprincipled demagogue. "Expose as you will the evils, the errors, the faults and dangerous usurpations of Andrew Jackson," Stevens told the Pennsylvania Assembly, "and the satraps of power immediately surround them with the glory of the Eight of January [Jackson's victory at the battle of New Orleans]. . . . Heaven grant that that victory may not prove the ruin of our country."[2]

While Stevens also advocated the abolition of capital punishment and antislavery measures, during the 1830s his principal legislative avocation was the pursuit of the Masons. In his second term in the assembly, he introduced a bill prohibiting secret societies and procured an appointment to a special committee that investigated such societies. Stevens then proceeded to conduct highly visible hearings in which prominent Masons were interrogated, although none revealed anything substantial to Stevens's committee. When the furor of anti-Masonry receded in the mid-1830s, Stevens eventually paid a political price for his continued support of the movement and was defeated for reelection to the assembly by William McCurdy in 1836. Reelected again in 1837, Stevens found his influence diminished.

Elected to a final term in 1841, Stevens continued to work for issues important to him, but continued to exert little real influence in an assembly controlled by the Democratic Party.

During the 1840s, Stevens focused on his legal practice. Although he joined the Whig Party and supported Henry Clay for president in 1844, Stevens remained largely politically inactive. Primarily for economic reasons, he left Gettysburg in 1842 for nearby Lancaster. As Lancaster was larger than Gettysburg, a skilled attorney could expect more profitable work. A primary focus of Stevens's legal work during the 1840s was fugitive slave cases, where the Lancaster lawyer tried to prevent the return of fugitive slaves to their Southern owners. While antislavery beliefs became a preeminent concern for Stevens at this time, he resisted the appeal of Free Soil advocates such as Ohio's Salmon P. Chase to join the new antislavery party in 1848. "Freesoilism puzzles us all," he confessed to Illinois Whig associate, Abraham Lincoln. When Stevens decided to reenter the political arena as a candidate for the House of Representatives, he did so as a Conscience Whig, firmly committed to preventing the spread of slavery to western territories of the United States. Defeating his Democratic opponent by a sizeable margin in October 1848, Stevens arrived in Washington in December 1849 determined to take up the antislavery cause in the nation's capital.[3]

Unlike other first-term representatives, Stevens came to Washington, D.C., with the reputation of a rising star. In fact, he was even nominated for speaker of the house in his first term. Just as he rose to prominence as a state legislator, Stevens soon established himself as a powerful debater and used his oratorical skills to denounce the slave system. During debates over the Compromise of 1850, Stevens delivered a major speech on June 10, 1850, in which he denounced slavery. Despite the eventual adoption of the compromise measures, including the new Fugitive Slave Law, Stevens remained a vocal critic of the measure and participated in the legal defense of two Quakers indirectly involved in aiding a fugitive slave who had eluded his Maryland owner. While supporting the nomination of Winfield Scott for president in 1852, Stevens was disillusioned with the Whig political platform since it was based on the Compromise of 1850. He chose not to seek reelection in 1852 and instead retired to his law practice in Lancaster.

Like many antislavery Whigs, Thaddeus Stevens saw opportunity in the events surrounding the Kansas-Nebraska Act of 1854. Ironically, instead of reviving the Whig Party, the bill eventually caused the party to implode, forcing antislavery Whigs like Stevens to cast about for new political homes. Initially, Stevens aligned himself with the nativistic Know-Nothing Party. Despite his aversion to the xenophobic orientation of this party, Stevens was convinced that the Know-Nothings would help crush conservative Whiggery and thus advance the antislavery cause. By 1855, however,

Stevens was actively involved in organizing the Republican Party in Pennsylvania, helping unite various anti-Nebraska factions into a viable political party for the 1856 elections. As a delegate to the Republican national convention in Philadelphia, Stevens was not an enthusiastic backer of presidential nominee John C. Frémont; nevertheless, he contributed time and money to the fall campaign. Much to Stevens's chagrin, the Democratic nominee, James Buchanan, who was also a resident of Lancaster, Pennsylvania, defeated Frémont in the fall election.

Shortly after Buchanan assumed office in March 1857, the Supreme Court handed down the controversial Dred Scott case, a decisive factor in motivating Stevens to seek a seat in the House of Representatives in 1858. In the Dred Scott case, the United States Supreme Court denied African American citizenship and also declared that Congress had no authority to exclude slavery from the territories of the United States. Running a campaign that emphasized the unjustness of the Dred Scott decision, Stevens easily defeated Democratic challenger James Hopkins by over 3,000 votes. Stevens would spend the next ten years in Washington, becoming one of the most revered and reviled congressmen of his day.

As the South edged toward secession in the aftermath of Abraham Lincoln's election in 1860, Stevens became one of the principal Northern fire-eaters in the House, denouncing secession and any compromise with the states that seceded from the Union. As the momentum for secession increased, he became an outspoken and vocal critic of incumbent President and fellow Lancastrian James Buchanan. "I do not care to be present while the process of humiliation is going on," Stevens confessed to fellow legislator Edward McPherson. "Buchanan is a very traitor." In a major speech before the House on January 29, 1861, Stevens ridiculed compromise. "Rather than show repentance for the election of Lincoln, with all its consequences," Stevens declared, "I would see this Government crumble into a thousand atoms." He then added a warning, "Let no slave state flatter itself that it can dissolve the Union now, and then reconstruct it on better terms."[4]

Stevens feared that fellow Republican leaders like William H. Seward and Simon Cameron lacked sufficient backbone to stand firm against the cries for concession and compromise. "Mr. Sewards [sic] course has mortified and discouraged me," he confessed to Salmon Chase, "that coupled with the apostacy of Cameron, who is his echo, seems to indicate that our platform and principles are to be sacrificed to peace." Could Lincoln stand up to the likes of Seward and Cameron? That was what worried the radical Lancastrian. While Stevens, who had lost a potential Cabinet seat to the slippery Cameron, obtained the chair of the powerful House Committee of Ways and Means, he believed that he might have better served the nation from the Cabinet, where he could help shore up the inexperienced and, in his opinion, mediocre Lincoln.[5]

After the firing on Fort Sumter, Stevens was among the most vocal Republicans in urging a vigorous prosecution of the war. As chair of the House Ways and Means Committee, Stevens played an important role in the crucial area of wartime finance. Not only did Stevens spearhead the drive to pass the Morrill tariff (a tariff act passed on March 2, 1861 that established the highest protective tariff in the nation's history heretofore), but he also played an important role in several other critical financial measures including a bill authorizing a $250 million loan, financed by 7 percent, twenty-year bonds. On another important issue, however, Stevens vehemently disagreed with the majority in Congress. Passed after the Union defeat at the first battle of Manassas, the Crittenden-Johnson resolution stated that the war was not waged for the abolition of slavery. When the vote on this measure was taken in the summer of 1861, instead of directly opposing his party, Stevens simply abstained. When it came to the manner of waging war, Thaddeus Stevens was also in advance of most Republicans, urging punishing measures against the South including confiscation of rebel property. "In time of war," Stevens told the House in August 1861, "you have the right to confiscate the property of every rebel." For Stevens, this included rebel slaves, who would be considered emancipated. "God forbid that I should ever agree that they [slaves] should be returned again to their masters."[6]

Throughout the early war years, Stevens maintained an uneasy relationship with the president. Admitting that Lincoln was well intentioned, Stevens also believed that the president lacked the depth of conviction to vigorously prosecute the war. When Lincoln removed antislavery General John C. Frémont from command of the Department of the West in November 1861, Stevens was mortified. Since Stevens advocated immediate action against the peculiar institution, he was disappointed with the president's more cautious and conciliatory measures such as his plan for the border states that endorsed gradual emancipation. As Union war fortunes stagnated in early 1862, Stevens blamed Lincoln. As he told one correspondent, "As to future hopes, they are poor as Lincoln is a nobody."[7]

As the war dragged into its second year, Stevens worried about Lincoln's choices for Cabinet positions as well as the military leadership that the president entrusted with directing the war effort. When Lincoln countermanded the emancipation order issued by General David Hunter in the Department of South Carolina in May 1862, Stevens publicly defended Hunter in the House. Criticizing the administration for leaving important military positions in the hands of proslavery generals, an undoubted reference to Democratic generals such as George B. McClellan, Stevens complained that conservative advisors too easily dominated the president. Believing Lincoln honest, Stevens claimed that the president was "too easy and amiable, and to be misled by the malign influence of Kentucky counselors."[8]

Throughout the war, Stevens was an outspoken and persistent critic of Northern Democratic opponents of the war, popularly known as Copperheads. In campaign speeches and spirited debates in Congress, Stevens aimed his oratorical missiles at men who he believed were blackhearted traitors to the Union and opposed to the ideals of the Founding Fathers. "I would as soon acknowledge fellowship with sooty demons, whose business and delight it is, to torture the damned," Stevens told one Pennsylvania audience. Often Stevens's rhetorical fury was aimed at prominent opposition leaders such as Samuel Cox or Clement L. Vallandigham. Chief among his complaints was Democratic Negrophobia and opposition to emancipation. "These traitor democrats," Stevens told a Lancaster audience, "propose to amend the Constitution so as to prohibit liberty in the South, but will not agree to amend it so as to prohibit slavery in the North, and in the free territories. . . . Have they human souls? I doubt if there can be found in the hottest corner of pandemonium cinder black enough and hard enough to make hearts for such inhuman wretches."[9]

Handily winning reelection in 1862, Stevens made a number of important contributions to the Thirty-eighth Congress, including sponsorship of the Indemnity bill (later passed as the Habeas Corpus Act of 1863) that legalized Lincoln's earlier suspension of the writ of habeas corpus as well as a number of other important wartime measures. Nor was war without personal sacrifice. Stevens's nephew, Alanson, was killed at the battle of Chickamauga in September 1863; however, Stevens also suffered great financial loss when the Army of Northern Virginia invaded Pennsylvania in late June 1863. On June 26, Stevens's Caledonia Iron Works was destroyed by troops commanded by Jubal Early. Stevens remained stoic about the loss (some $75,000), commenting, "We must all expect to suffer by this wicked war. I have not felt a moment's trouble for my share of it." Of more immediate concern to Stevens was the fate of several poor families who suffered as a result of the rebel invasion. "I know not what the poor families will do," he told associate Simon Stevens. "I must provide for their present relief."[10]

Stevens continued to disagree with the president on a number of issues. While the Emancipation Proclamation pleased the Pennsylvania Republican, the important issue of Reconstruction loomed as a major issue between the two. While the president proposed his moderate Ten Percent Plan, Stevens emerged as one of the most radical Republicans in Congress on Reconstruction, believing the seceded states were, de facto, out of the Union. Once the North emerged victorious, the formerly seceded states were conquered provinces, according to Stevens, that could be reconstructed wholly on the terms of the victor. Although Stevens's beliefs were more radical than the Wade-Davis bill, when radical Republicans threatened to bolt from the Republican Party and nominate another candidate,

Stevens demurred, believing only Lincoln could lead the party to electoral victory. While his support for the president was hardly enthusiastic, Stevens was relieved when both he and the president were reelected in the fall.[11]

During the closing months of the war, Stevens was gratified to vote for passage of the Thirteenth Amendment, even if he was skeptical of some of the means used to secure a favorable vote. With Lincoln's assassination shortly after Lee's surrender, Stevens faced a new, more intractable foe in the new president, Andrew Johnson, the former senator and military governor of Tennessee. Unlike other Republicans, Stevens was extremely skeptical of Johnson's nomination as vice president. Johnson quickly proved Stevens's point when he unilaterally declared his Reconstruction policies in his North Carolina proclamation in late May 1865 (see chapter on Johnson, pp. 134–135). Stevens believed that the president had overstepped his authority and intruded upon an area of congressional prerogative. "I see our worthy president fancies himself a sovereign power," Stevens complained to Congressman William D. Kelley. "His North Carolina proclamation sickens me . . . by the time Congress meets all will be passed [*sic*] remedy I fear."[12]

Stevens's relationship with Johnson deteriorated quickly over the next several months. The Pennsylvania Republican's Reconstruction goals included—at minimum—equality before the law, black suffrage, punishment of rebel leaders, and confiscation of rebel lands—the latter to be redistributed to newly emancipated and landless slaves. Despite vindictive rhetoric, Andrew Johnson wanted a quick and easy Reconstruction. While accepting the legitimacy of emancipation and the Thirteenth Amendment, Johnson's vision did not include black suffrage or the confiscation and redistribution of rebel lands; moreover, whereas Stevens saw Reconstruction as exclusively congressional, Johnson wanted a significant role for the executive.

While Johnson was determined to bring about a political realignment of the center, Stevens was determined to advance the interests of African Americans as well as the Republican Party. To accomplish both, it was necessary to disenfranchise rebel whites while enfranchising recently emancipated African Americans. Stevens also sincerely believed that the elective franchise was pivotal in protecting black civil rights. In order to advance Republican Reconstruction goals, Stevens persuaded the House to establish the Joint Committee on Reconstruction. Although radical Republicans did not dominate the committee (moderate Senator William Pitt Fessenden was chair), this committee was a powerful check on presidential power and initiated several pieces of legislation on Reconstruction.

While Stevens's position on Reconstruction was much more radical than public opinion, his cause was aided by two untimely and unwise presidential vetoes as well as an undignified display by Andrew Johnson on February 22, 1866. The Freedmen's Bureau had been established in the last year of the war to help newly emancipated slaves make the transition from slavery to freedom. Viewed as necessary to ensure the transition of African Americans from slavery to freedom, congressional Republicans believed the life of the bureau should be extended and, accordingly passed legislation in February 1866 to accomplish this. Most Republicans regarded the extension of the bureau's life as a necessary measure to help African Americans achieve self-sufficiency. Johnson's unexpected veto of the measure on February 14, 1866, puzzled conservative and moderate Republicans, who now questioned the president's commitment to the most basic rights for former slaves. Johnson's subsequent veto of the Civil Rights Act of 1866 was also unnerving for many in Congress. Reported out of the Senate Judiciary Committee on January 5, 1866, the measure guaranteed basic civil rights to all citizens including African Americans and guaranteed that they would have the benefit and protection of all laws. Specifically, the law was an antidote to the infamous black codes that had emerged in the former states of the Confederacy. Designed to prevent labor shortages in the postwar South, the codes outlawed vagrancy; however, the codes also included many discriminatory provisions that led Northern Republicans to charge that they were a legal form of slavery. Sandwiched between these two unwise vetoes was Johnson's foolish speech on Washington's birthday, 1866, when he publicly denounced Charles Sumner, Wendell Phillips, and Stevens as traitors to the Union. When Congress reworked the Civil Rights Act of 1866 into the Fourteenth Amendment and made ratification of the amendment the price for Southern states to be readmitted to the Union, Johnson advised Southern states to reject ratification.

Stevens was convinced as early as the summer of 1866 that impeachment was the only way to deal with the president. On August 31, 1866, he complained to Ohio Congressman Robert Schenk that Johnson was abusing executive patronage. "I am clearly of the opinion that it is an impeachable offense, having first proved that it is done for the purpose of corrupting the people, and compelling them to renounce their principles." Emerging victorious in the election of 1866, Stevens and his fellow Republicans were even more determined to thwart an errant executive. Stevens would play a significant role in a number of Reconstruction measures designed to limit Johnson's power and control of the Reconstruction process. The Tenure of Office Act, for instance, made it illegal for Johnson to remove Cabinet officers without the advice and consent of the Senate. A series of military Reconstruction acts was passed between 1867 and 1868 that specified the process under which Southern states might come back into the Union. Individual states were abolished and replaced by five military districts, governed by the army officers. States could come back into the Union once the commanding general in a military district presided over a constitutional convention, which would form a new state constitution. While adult black males were allowed to participate in the process, all Southern males who had violated an oath to uphold the Constitution were prohibited from participation. Once the newly convened state convention ratified the Fourteenth Amendment, the state would be accepted into the Union. Johnson's persistent vetoes of all these measures enraged Stevens and made him more fervent in his support for impeachment.[13]

Despite advanced age and failing health, Stevens continued to press for impeachment in the Fortieth Congress. While the House Judiciary Committee had investigated impeachment and eventually drafted articles of impeachment at the end of 1867, most congressmen believed the case was weak, and the articles were overwhelmingly defeated. However, Johnson eventually played into the hands of the radicals when he violated the Tenure of Office Act. Since Secretary of War Edwin Stanton was a bitter opponent of Johnson, the president suspended him from office in August 1867 and replaced him with Acting Secretary of War Ulysses S. Grant. When the Senate, in January 1868, rejected this suspension in accordance with the provisions of the Tenure of Office Act, Grant vacated the office. After Stanton had taken possession of the War Department, Johnson appointed General Lorenzo Thomas as interim secretary of war and the feisty Thomas attempted to remove Stanton from the War Department. The attempt to remove Stanton the second time tipped the balance of power in the House to the advocates of impeachment. A resolution was passed and quickly sent to Stevens's special Committee on Reconstruction. On February 22, the committee reported articles of impeachment to the House, which were then debated on February 24. According to Stevens, Johnson was guilty of violating the Tenure of Office Act, and, as a result, was not performing the duties of his office as outlined in the Constitution. "Who, after all, can say that such a man is fit to occupy the executive chair," Stevens declared to the House, "whose duty it is to inculcate obedience to those very laws, and see that they are faithfully obeyed?" Eventually eleven articles of impeachment were agreed upon that accused the president of a variety of offenses from violating the Tenure of Office Act to giving speeches that intended to discredit and disrespect Congress. When the articles passed the House, Stevens was also chosen as one of the impeachment managers.[14]

Once the impeachment articles were presented to the Senate and the president formally replied to the charges on March 23, 1868, the trial opened on March 30. The president compiled a group of highly skilled lawyers to defend him. House managers, on the other hand, were handicapped by Stevens's health, which limited his ability to participate in the trial and substantially weakened the case for conviction. The principal defense of Johnson's lawyers was that the president had indeed violated the Tenure of Office Act; however, the violation was intended merely to get the case into the courts, where a decision might be reached as to the law's constitutionality. As the trial dragged on, a weak and tired Stevens became convinced that his archenemy would escape conviction. Indeed, Washington was rife with rumors that doubtful senators were being bribed to vote for an acquittal. Stevens was to deliver his major speech at the impeachment trial on April 28. His weakened condition prevented him from completing the speech and Benjamin F. Butler, another House manager, was forced to read large portions of the speech to Senate jurors. In the end, the vote of a single senator, Edmund Ross of Kansas, prevented Johnson's removal, although many historians maintain that several senators were prepared to vote for acquittal if Ross failed to do so. As Stevens emerged from Senate chambers after the vote, he shouted, "The country is going to the devil."[15]

Stevens continued to harbor hopes that the seventeenth president might yet be convicted of impeachment. To that end, he drafted five new articles of impeachment in the summer of 1868; however, his House colleagues could not be induced to once again challenge the president. When Grant was nominated as the Republican presidential nominee in 1868, Stevens supported the general but without a great deal of enthusiasm. After Congress adjourned in the summer of 1868, Stevens was too sick to return to Lancaster. Instead, he was confined to his sick bed in Washington with his housekeeper, Lydia Smith, and his doctor, Noble Young, at his side. Longtime friend and associate Simon Stevens also spent a great deal of time with the ailing Pennsylvania radical. He died at midnight, August 11–12, 1868. As fitting with the principles of his life, Stevens was buried at Schreiner's Cemetery in Washington, D.C., undoubtedly chosen because it did not recognize segregation in its burial practices.

PRINCIPAL IDEAS

Slavery and Race

From his earliest public utterances, Thaddeus Stevens was committed to the abolition of slavery and the equality of all men before the law. Although biographer Hans Trefousse points out a single departure from this principle when Stevens defended the right of a slaveholder for the return of a fugitive slave, the balance of Steven's actions and utterances were antislavery. Stevens's antislavery thought did emphasize the free labor argument that stressed the debilitating effects of slavery on free institutions. Stevens applauded the dynamic character of Northern society and criticized the South for its rigid class distinctions. Even more important in Stevens's thought was the fundamental immorality of slavery and its contradiction to the ideals of republican institutions. While never a religious man, Stevens's denunciation of the peculiar institution was permeated with religiously colored language. "I can never acknowledge the right of slavery," Stevens informed one correspondent. "I will bow down to no Deity however worshipped by professing Christians—however dignified by the name of the Goddess of Liberty, whose footstool is the crushed neck of groaning millions, and who rejoices in the resoundings of the tyrant's lash, and the cries of the tortured victims."[16]

Practically speaking, however, Stevens realized that the Founding Fathers had allowed slavery to exist in the United States. In many respects, Stevens parroted the arguments of political abolitionists such as Salmon Chase and Charles Sumner. Although individual states were entirely free to incorporate slavery into the fabric of their society, the federal government, reasoned Stevens, was not required to protect slavery. Moreover, Congress was also empowered to prohibit the institution in areas where it has exclusive jurisdiction. Following the example of the Northwest Ordinances of 1787, Stevens argued that Congress had the right to prohibit slavery in federal territories as well as abolish the institution in the nation's capital.

Stevens forcefully outlined his positions in the House during the debate over the Compromise of 1850. For Stevens, slavery was purely a local creature, protected by appropriate state and local legislation. It was not entitled to the protection of the federal government; therefore, the proposed Fugitive Slave Act was both unconstitutional and unjust. For Stevens, a slave brought into a free state or free territory was no longer a slave. "By *common law*, if a slave escapes from a slave state into a free state, he is free." While the original Fugitive Slave Act of 1793 was bad enough, Stevens regarded the new law as an abomination because it denied slaves the right to a trial by jury as well as habeas corpus provisions of the law. "What would the advocates of English freedom, at any time, have said to those who would strike down the writ of habeas corpus and the right of trial by jury—those vital principles of the Magna Carta and the bill of Rights?" Stevens asked the House. "They would have driven them as enemies in disguise," was his response.[17]

When the Civil War erupted, Stevens was one of the earliest advocates of emancipation. His reasons were both moral and practical. The abolition of slavery was obviously in accordance with the moral dictates of conscience and was advocated by Stevens on ethical grounds. The South rebelled, argued Stevens, because it rejected the teachings of Jefferson and the Declaration of Independence, asserting instead the doctrine of oligarchy and privilege. "They have rebelled for no redress of grievances," Stevens asserted, "but to establish a slave oligarchy which would repudiate the odious doctrine of the Declaration of Independence, and justify the establishment of an empire admitting the principle of Kings, lords, and slaves." From a practical standpoint, slavery had caused secession and the war; hence, it must be ended in order for the Union to be whole. During the course of the war, Stevens focused on the practical reasons for emancipation. How could the South be conquered, wondered Stevens, if slaves were cultivating lands and assisting the South by growing crops, thereby enabling the Confederacy to mobilize a much higher percentage of military-aged men for combat? As Stevens argued, "They need not and they do not withdraw a single hand from the cultivation of the soil. Their freemen never labor. Every able-bodied white man can be spared for the army." If the North issued an emancipation decree, Stevens believed the South would be destabilized due to the threat of servile insurrections. Concerns for security would depopulate Southern armies and hasten Union victory.[18]

Once emancipation was declared, the Thirteenth Amendment passed, and Union victory complete, Stevens demonstrated that his attitude on race was far in advance of that of his contemporaries. Indeed, from his earliest days as a Pennsylvania legislator, Stevens had endorsed the equality of all men before the law and publicly spoke out against discrimination. At a Pennsylvania Constitutional Convention in Harrisburg in June 1837, a measure to prohibit the immigration of free blacks into the state was discussed. Stevens argued that it was "disgraceful to consider the subject at all." He then stated, "It could reflect no credit on the head or heart of this body, to give any countenance to a proposition so totally at war with the principles of the Declaration of Independence, the Bill of Rights, and the spirit of our free institutions."[19]

A persistent advocate of black suffrage, Stevens was unrelenting in his determination to see the ideals of the Declaration of Independence realized. For Stevens, equality before the law, as embodied in the Fourteenth Amendment, and the guarantee of suffrage, as embodied in the Fifteenth Amendment, were essential to reaching these goals. For Stevens, this was consistent with the ideals of the Founding Fathers. "Rejecting the old doctrine of the hereditary succession and the divine right of kings," Stevens declared in an address to the House in early 1867, "they boldly proclaimed the equality of the human race, and asserted that the right of all government was founded on the consent of the governed." He then succinctly concluded,

> South Carolina has two hundred thousand whites and four hundred thousand men of color. Both are men; both have immortal souls. The two hundred thousand absolutely rule the four hundred thousand. They have no voice in anything connected with the government that rules them. Is this a Government deriving its force from the consent of the governed? Shame upon American statesmen, who in this day of their power hold such a vile doctrine! Do not delay, give us now the Republic of the Declaration of Independence, and let the world behold and admire.[20]

Like many abolitionists, Stevens probably never did free himself from a paternalistic attitude toward African Americans. No doubt he probably shared the views of many contemporaries that blacks were inferior to whites in terms of intelligence and other abilities; nevertheless, his commitment to the notion of equality before the law was significant, as was his insistence that newly emancipated slaves were entitled to the right of self-government as outlined in the Declaration of Independence.

Reconstruction

Thaddeus Stevens held controversial views on Reconstruction during the war and throughout the postwar period until his death in 1868. Despite the radicalism of his positions, Stevens's point of view was logically conceived, clearly outlined, and fervently endorsed. For Stevens, the principle question in Reconstruction was the meaning and significance of secession. What had really occurred when South Carolina left the Union in December 1860? Reconstruction conservatives, like Abraham Lincoln and Andrew Johnson, maintained that the Union was indissolvable; it was, therefore, theoretically impossible for states to leave the Union. Secession was, on this view, a rebellion of individuals who had committed treason against the United States and temporarily controlled the government of a seceded state.

For Stevens the conservative argument was both illogical and unrealistic, prompting him to compare it to the idealistic theories of English philosopher George Berkley, who denied the existence of the material world and postulated that all reality consisted of ideas. Seceded states had, according to Stevens, left the Union and formed an independent government. To deny this fact was, for Stevens, as ludicrous as to deny that the sun rose every morning. "They have a congress in which eleven States are represented; they have at least three hundred thousand soldiers in the field; their pickets are almost in sight of Washington," Stevens reminded the House in May 1864. "They have ships of war on the ocean destroying hundred of our ships, and our Government and the Governments of Europe acknowledge and treat them as privateers, not pirates. From who do privateers get their commissions except from a Power independent *de jure* or *de facto*? There is no reasoning against such impudent denials."[21]

Since Confederate states were literally out of the Union, Stevens asserted that they had lost all rights under the Constitution. Unlike Charles Sumner, who argued that seceded states lapsed into a territorial status, Stevens maintained that the states of the Confederacy were like conquered provinces in a foreign war and could, therefore, be dealt with as the victors saw fit. "The future condition of the conquered power," Stevens asserted, "depends on the will of the conqueror." To the argument that only individuals, not a state, could commit treason and wage war, Stevens replied, "The idea that the States could not and did not make war because the Constitution forbids it, and that this must be treated as a war of individuals, is a very injurious and groundless fallacy." He continued, "Individuals cannot make war. They can commit murder. Communities, societies, States, make war." Stevens reiterated this point in a letter to Ohio

Republican John Hutchins, adding, "The idea that the States were not out of the Union because the Constitution forbids it—that they could not do what they did do, is transparent folly."[22]

Since states were out of the Union and thus, on Stevens's account, conquered provinces, the North controlled completely the circumstances under which such entities might come back into the Union—if indeed the victorious power chose to allow the vanquished states to return into the Union. For Stevens, this fact had a number of important consequences. First, as indicated in the previous section, Stevens believed it was wholly appropriate to require seceded states to grant newly emancipated slaves full legal and political rights as a condition for each state's return into the Union. For Stevens, granting blacks these rights, as eventually embodied in the Fourteenth and Fifteenth Amendments to the Constitution, was not only just but also necessary to eradicate the spirit of rebelliousness from the seceded states. It would also help the Republican Party become the majority party in the South. To those who complained that Stevens required the Southern states to do more on behalf of black rights than many Northern states were willing to do, he would certainly have argued that the Northern states had not committed treason and, therefore, were not subject to the same impositions as the seceded states.

Secondly, Stevens's belief that the Southern states were conquered provinces reinforced his belief that it was legitimate to confiscate the property of former rebels and use the proceeds to defray federal debt as well as secure the economic independence of former African American slaves. Surely, Stevens reasoned, it was only logical that those who had caused the rebellion should assist in the repayment of Northern debt. In accordance with his egalitarian principles, Stevens proposed in September 1865 that the federal government seize the property of all rebels who owned more than $10,000 in property. Part of the proceeds could go to African Americans to assist in the establishment of economic independence. Only by making African Americans productive owners of the land could the South be transformed into a virtuous and upwardly mobile republic, similar to the North. "If the South is ever to be made a safe republic," Stevens maintained, "let her land be cultivated by the toil of owners or the free labor of intelligent citizens."[23]

While Stevens's views on Reconstruction clashed with beliefs held by Democrats and conservative Republicans, he also tangled with fellow radical Republicans. Many radical Republicans endorsed the Wade-Davis Reconstruction bill that was put forth as an alternative to Lincoln's Ten Percent Plan. When the Wade-Davis bill was voted on in the House, Stevens abstained. His abstention was based on two important considerations. First, the final version of the Wade-Davis bill did not contain provisions for black suffrage. This provision had been removed in order to guarantee passage of the bill. Second, while the Wade-Davis bill seemed more in line with Stevens's position on Reconstruction than the president's view, there was one important difference. The Wade-Davis bill maintained, along with the president, that seceded states were still in the Union. They were not, as Stevens maintained, out of the Union and equivalent to conquered provinces.[24]

Impeachment

The impeachment proceedings against Andrew Johnson played a prominent role in the career of Thaddeus Stevens. Among his Republican colleagues, Stevens had few peers when it came to his hatred and scorn for the seventeenth president. Not only was Stevens among the first advocates of impeachment, but even when Johnson was acquitted, the feisty Republican wanted to pursue new articles of impeachment in the summer of 1868. What explains this single-minded devotion to the cause of impeachment? Given the fact that many historians dismiss the impeachment effort against the president as shabbily crafted and with little merit, one is tempted to regard Stevens's tenacity as a sign of personal hatred or a manifestation of his well-known political ambition. As his correspondence reveals, Stevens intensely disliked Andrew Johnson, whom he felt was abusing power and compromising the war goals of the Republican Party; however, an examination of Stevens's principal speeches on the topic reveals a motivation that, while perhaps misconceived, was logical and sincerely believed.

Eleven impeachment articles were drafted against the president that ranged from violating the Tenure of Office Act to making speeches that discredited Congress. Stevens's principal argument for conviction stemmed from his belief in the constitutional separation of powers and how this belief influenced his views on political Reconstruction. According to the Pennsylvania Republican, the Reconstruction of the Southern state governments was exclusively a legislative function. Johnson, however, had consistently meddled with congressional prerogatives. Not only had he issued the North Carolina proclamation, but he had also attempted to circumvent other congressional laws with respect to the South, including the Command of Army Act as well as the Military Reconstruction Acts, which, Stevens argued, Johnson implemented and interpreted according to his own political preferences. "When admonished by express act of Congress, more than once repeated, he disregarded the warning," Stevens declared, "and continued his lawless usurpation."[25]

Stevens's central argument addressed Johnson's violation of the Tenure of Office Act. To the argument put forth by Johnson's lawyers that the law did not apply to Stanton, who had been appointed by Lincoln, Stevens counterattacked, asserting that the law did not apply to individuals but to an office. Johnson was not serving his own presidential term, but Lincoln's; therefore, the law did apply to him. Moreover, inasmuch as the principal function of the executive was to enforce the laws passed by Congress, Johnson was obligated to support the provision. Stevens asserted, "The President is sworn to take care that the laws be faithfully executed. In what part of the Constitution or laws does he find it to be his duty to search out defective laws that stand recorded upon the statutes in order that he may advise their infraction?" To the argument that Johnson had removed Stanton from office merely to test the law's constitutionality, Stevens responded with scorn. "But that which is *voluntarily* done is *willfully* done, according to every honest definition; whatever he may allege was his intentions."[26]

His health failing, Stevens was unable to devote his full strength to the impeachment proceedings. Some biographers claim that a younger, more energetic Stevens might have had greater success in the impeachment undertaking. When it turned out that the vote of a single senator saved the president from conviction, Stevens, and many other radical Republicans, were convinced that bribery and other illicit means were used to bring about acquittal. Historians generally have not supported this contention, arguing instead that Johnson's acquittal was earned largely on the merits of a superior constitutional argument. While many of the seventeenth president's activities were politically unwise and even foolish, he had not exceeded his constitutional authority and clearly had committed no impeachable offense.

CONCLUSION

Who was Thaddeus Stevens? Was he an unprincipled fanatic, driven by an almost insatiable ambition? Or was he an honest, principled advocate of equality and civil rights? Throughout the years, historians have run the gambit in an effort to properly categorize the Pennsylvania Republican. Like many human beings, Stevens defies such simplistic categorization and was probably an uneven mixture of ambition, principle, and pragmatism. Perhaps the most important consideration in evaluating Stevens's role in public affairs was his dogged devotion to the abolition of slavery and the equality of all people before the law. While many contemporaries and subsequent historians have criticized Stevens for his inflexible fanaticism, his advocacy of civil rights and racial justice, despite the unpopularity of these causes in some quarters, sets him apart from the vast majority of nineteenth-century political figures.

NOTES

1. On the anti-Masonic movement, see Hans L. Trefousse, *Thaddeus Stevens: Nineteenth-Century Egalitarian* (Chapel Hill: University of North Carolina Press, 1997), 21–23, 34–35.

2. "Speech on the Wolf and Jackson Administrations," March 3, 1834, in *The Selected Papers of Thaddeus Stevens*, edited by Beverly Wilson Smith and Holly Byers Ochoa (Pittsburgh, PA: University of Pittsburgh Press, 1997), 1:16.

3. Thaddeus Stevens to [Abraham] Lincoln, September 7, 1848, in *Selected Papers*, 1:102–3 (quote, 103).

4. Stevens to Edward McPherson, December 19, 1860, in *Selected Papers*, 1:172; and "State of the Union," January 29, 1861, in *Selected Papers*, 1: 180–97 (quotes, 190, 193).

5. Stevens to [Salmon] P. Chase, February 3, 1861, in *Selected Papers*, 1:200.

6. "Speech on Emancipation and Confiscation," August 2, 1861, in *Selected Papers*, 1:221–25 (quotes, 222, 223–24).

7. Stevens to Joseph Gibbons, April 17, 1862, in *Selected Papers*, 1:293.

8. "Attack on General Hunter," July 5, 1862, in *Selected Papers*, 1:309–17 (quote, 310).

9. "Speech on State Elections," [September 17?, 1863, in Christiana?], in *Selected Papers*, 1:406–9 (quote, 407–8); and "Speech on Conquered Provinces, April 4, 1863, to Union League of Lancaster," in *Selected Papers*, 1:384–96 (quote, 393–94).

10. Stevens to [Simon] Stevens, July 6, 1863, in *Selected Papers*, 1:400.

11. Eric Foner, *Reconstruction: America's Unfinished Revolution, 1865–1877* (New York: Harper, 1988).

12. Stevens to William D. Kelley, May 30, 1865, in *Selected Papers*, 2:6–7 (quote, 6).

13. Stevens to [Robert C.] Schenck, August 31, 1866, in *Selected Papers*, 2:191.

14. "Speech on the Johnson Impeachment," February 24, 1868, in *Selected Papers*, 2:352–59 (quote, 356).

15. Quote from Trefousse, *Thaddeus Stevens*, 234.

16. Stevens to Samuel Webb and Committee, May 4, 1838, in *Selected Papers*, 1:65–66; and Trefousse, *Thaddeus Stevens*, 13–14. See also Stevens's "Speech on Equal Rights at the Pennsylvania Convention," July 8, 1837, in *Selected Papers*, 1:55–59.

17. "The California Question," June 10, 1850, in *Selected Papers*, 1:110–30 (quote, 126–27).

18. "Subduing the Rebellion," January 22, 1862, in *Selected Papers*, 1:241–53 (quotes, 241, 244).

19. "Remarks on Blacks' Emigration to Pennsylvania, June 9, 1837, to the Pennsylvania Constitutional Convention, Harrisburg," in *Selected Papers*, 1:52–53.

20. "Remarks on the Declaration of Independence," January 15, 1867, in *Selected Papers*, 2:241–42.

21. "The Government of the Rebellious States," May 2, 1864, in *Selected Papers*, 1:464–75 (quote, 468–69).

22. "Reconstruction," December 18, 1865, in *Selected Papers*, 2:44–56 (quotes, 45, 46); and Stevens to John Hutchins, August 27, 1865, in *Selected Papers*, 2:11.

23. "Reconstruction" (speech in Lancaster), September 6, 1865, in *Selected Papers*, 2:13–25 (quote, 23).

24. On the Wade-Davis bill, see Herman Belz, "Henry Winter Davis and the Origins of Congressional Reconstruction," *Maryland History* 67 (1972): 129.

25. "Speech on Johnson Impeachment," February 24, 1868, in *Selected Papers*, 352–58 (quote, 357).

26. "Speech at the Impeachment Trial of Andrew Johnson," April 27, 1868, in *Selected Papers*, 2:401–18 (quote, 417, 407).

FURTHER READING

Fawn Brodie, *Thaddeus Stevens: Scourge of the South* (New York: W. W. Norton, 1959); Richard N. Current, *Old Thad Stevens: A Question of Ambition* (Madison: University of Wisconsin Press, 1942); Eric Foner, *Free Soil, Free Labor, and Free Men: The Ideology of the Republican Party before the Civil War* (New York: Oxford University Press, 1970); Ralph Korngold, *Thaddeus Stevens: A Being Darkly Wise and Rudely Great* (New York: Harcourt Brace, 1953); Hans Trefousse, *Thaddeus Stevens: Nineteenth-Century Egalitarian* (Chapel Hill: University of North Carolina Press, 1997); idem., *The Radical Republicans: Lincoln's Vanguard for Racial Justice* (New York: Alfred A. Knopf, 1969); and T. Harry Williams, *Lincoln and the Radicals* (Madison: University of Wisconsin Press, 1941).

HARRIET BEECHER STOWE
(1811–1896)

A Literary Soldier in a Noble Cause

LIFE

Harriet Beecher Stowe was born in Litchfield, Connecticut, on June 14, 1811. Her parents, Lyman Beecher and Roxana Foote Beecher, and the families each had brought to the marriage, shaped and influenced the future best-selling author. Intensely dedicated and energetic to the point of manic behavior, Lyman Beecher was a Congregational minister who saw himself as a vehicle for Christ standing athwart the abhorrent rationalism of the eighteenth century. He stressed the importance of conversion experiences, and he badgered his children to have one. He encouraged them to discuss and debate theological issues, and he wanted each to receive a good education.[1]

Roxana Beecher had been raised by her grandfather, Andrew Ward, a general officer and colleague of George Washington during the Revolution. An Episcopalian, Roxana enjoyed literature, spoke French, and had a bevy of interesting relatives beyond General Ward, including a sea captain, Samuel Foote. Harriet's mother was an intellectually curious person who tried to continue reading and searching for knowledge, but found those activities overwhelmed by the demands of childrearing. The Beecher household in Litchfield was a hive of activity, with a large family, servants, extended kin, and even boarders. Exhausted from the rigors of her life, Roxana contracted tuberculosis and died when Harriet was five.

In the wake of her mother's death, Harriet was taken to stay with her mother's sister and her namesake, Harriet Foote, at Nutplains near Guilford. She spent nearly a year with her Foote kin, surrounded by surrogate mothers such as Aunt Harriet and Grandma Roxana Foote, and she learned to sew and knit. The Foote women at Nutplains still engaged in the home manufacture of clothing and were often at the spinning wheel, exposing

Harriet to a vanishing lifestyle that harkened back to the previous century. Aunt Harriet was a great storyteller, a keeper of family lore, and a woman of pronounced opinions and the courage to state them. Samuel Foote, the mariner, upon returning from his latest voyage, would regale the household with tales of strange lands and peoples. Experience in the world at large had taught the ship's captain tolerance for other religious faiths, and he boldly proclaimed that a Catholic might be quite a fine person rather than a devil. Foote brought the works of Walter Scott into Harriet's life, and she became a great aficionado of the novels.

Harriet returned to Litchfield, and her father remarried, to Harriet Porter, in 1817. He sent his children to Sarah Pierce's school, and Harriet had a fine teacher in John Brace. She had demonstrated a talent for memorization and entered the school four years earlier than typically permitted at age eight. Brace stressed the English classics, which his students discussed, and he also had regular writing assignments. Harriet's skills as a writer were purportedly apparent, though her lack of discipline rendered her record as a student uneven. She transferred to the Hartford Female Seminary, a school run by her elder sister Catharine Beecher, in 1824. Harriet also reported to her father that she had a conversion experience after one of his innumerable sermons, though the experience may have been less a religious epiphany than an attempt to earn his approval and stop his nagging.

Hartford Female Seminary had a marked effect on Harriet. She spent three largely successful years as a student at the school before completing her studies, then returned home and found herself lost in a world dominated by her stepmother and her children by Harriet's father. Harriet felt depressed with little prospects, and Catharine recognized her despondency and summoned her back to Hartford, where she became a teacher and stand-in for Catharine. At the seminary, Harriet learned a vocation—teaching—and developed confidence enough that she was able to successfully engage in public speaking. The instruction system was based on moral suasion, persuading the students by example and exhortation to behave properly. Harriet found it difficult to punish students, but she could give a speech on the necessity of good acts. "I was made for a preacher," Harriet wrote, "indeed I can scarcely keep my letters from turning into sermons." Her teaching spurred her interest in continued study and in improving her own writing, as she copied and tried to imitate Samuel Johnson.[2]

In 1832, Lyman Beecher concluded that the West, filling with immigrants who were unbelievers and Catholics, needed a Congregational minister to protect the growing region from such perils. He accepted the presidency of Lane Seminary in Cincinnati, and the Stowe clan migrated together, including Harriet and Catharine, who gave up her Hartford school. A town burgeoning with commerce that traveled on the rivers on whose banks it was nestled, Cincinnati provided Harriet a rich vista of western life for observation, with steamboats clogging the docks, sweat-streaked laborers toiling over barrels and bales, muddy streets with pigs rooting in foul gutters, and the music of regional dialects providing a din of conversation. She took it all in, becoming particularly absorbed in dialects, which she later successfully translated to the page. Her uncle Samuel, the former ship captain, had retired from ocean voyages and moved to Cincinnati too, where he and his wife purchased a large home that became a place for social gatherings featuring the Beechers and prominent citizens.

While teaching at Catharine's latest school, Harriet continued to show literary promise. She wrote and published a geography book for children that sold reasonably well and gave her a taste of life as a paid author. She participated in the informal venues available to women writers confined to the domestic sphere: letter writing and parlor literature. She wrote detailed descriptions of life in the West with novelistic flair in letters dispatched to the extended Beecher clan that had remained in the East. She also wrote parlor literature, prose and verse created to entertain a gathering in a home's parlor on an evening with reference to events that had occurred common to the participants. Harriet and Catharine also joined a literary club, the Semi-Colon Club, which met weekly for readings of parlor literature, often in Samuel Foote's spacious home. Members of the Semi-Colon Club included up-and-comers Salmon P. Chase, future treasury secretary; Calvin Stowe, a professor at Lane Seminary; and James Hall, editor of the *Western Monthly Magazine.* Harriet's literary efforts before the assembled Cincinnati luminaries evidently succeeded, as Hall soon invited her to contribute to his *Western Literary Magazine.*

Fellow member of the Semi-Colon Club Calvin Stowe lost his wife in 1834 while Harriet was visiting relatives in the East. Devastated at the loss of his young spouse, Stowe took solace at Lyman Beecher's home, where the president had invited him to recover among his sympathetic family. Harriet returned and became a great source of comfort to Calvin. Stowe had survived an impoverished childhood to win the support of ministers in Natick, Massachusetts, who paid for him to attend Bowdoin College. He excelled as a student, earning valedictorian honors for the class of 1824. He continued his studies at Andover Theological Seminary, becoming an expert in languages. He accepted a position at Dartmouth College, where he met his first wife, before moving to Lane Seminary. Stowe was a man so preoccupied with books that he lost his own clothes and could not manage his personal finances. He had a tendency toward pessimism and hypochondria.

Harriet had covered Stowe's sermons on the Bible for a Cincinnati newspaper and so had witnessed an exhibition of his scholarly erudition. For his part, Calvin found Harriet a great diversion after the loss of his first wife, so great that he was soon convinced the two should never part. Harriet married Calvin Stowe on January 6, 1836, in a modest ceremony. The two had differing personalities—he was emotionally volatile while she tended to stoicism—but both shared a fondness for intellectual pursuits. They brought seven children into the world, four of whom preceded them in death. Calvin became a strong advocate of Harriet's literary career. "God has written it in his book, that you must be a literary woman. . . . You must make all your calculations to spend the rest of your days with your pen," he told her. At first, though, Harriet was preoccupied with the cycle of child bearing and childrearing that began in earnest with the birth of twin girls on September 29, 1836. A regular feature of the Stowes' marriage was separations; Calvin would go on a business trip to Europe within months of their marriage, and later Harriet retreated to spas for months of rest and recovery. When Calvin was home, he did help with the children, though he often disappeared into his study for long periods of reflection.[3]

Harriet published five stories and sketches in the *Western Monthly Magazine* in 1833–1834. She published a number of stories in *Godey's Ladies Book* and in the *New York Evangelist*. Her work tended to provide a guide to proper behavior: some articles endorsed temperance and others were Christian homilies, through the vehicle of a story or tale that typically included descriptions of domestic life. She earned money that supplemented the household income at a time when Calvin's salary had been cut by the failing Lane Seminary. In 1842, the publisher Harper Brothers approached Harriet with an offer to publish a collection of her stories, another sign of impending success. Harriet's early literary labor touched on many of the themes she would successfully employ in her masterpiece on slavery, *Uncle Tom's Cabin*. Her collected stories appeared in 1843 as *The Mayflower*.

As a resident of Cincinnati and with a father and husband employed at Lane Seminary, Harriet witnessed the violence and social dislocation that accompanied the inception of the abolition movement. In 1834, students at Lane Seminary held a debate on the efficacy of colonization or immediate abolition as solutions for slavery and voted for the more radical immediate abolition. It became fashionable for students to openly socialize with Cincinnati's free black community. The result was a counterreaction. Members of Lane's board of trustees voted to ban student abolition and colonization organizations, which prompted an exodus of students to Oberlin College. Lyman Beecher had tried to straddle the problem, saying he saw merit in the arguments of both sides, and had been rendered a nullity by his own board. Lane fell into a spiral of declining enrollment that meant Calvin's salary was continually reduced, an inducement to Harriet to continue writing for pay.

The debate at Lane presaged anti-abolition riots in Cincinnati, driven by a hostile and racist population that wrecked the printing offices of James G. Birney's abolition publication, the *Philanthropist*, which he had been distributing in town. Mobs went in search for Birney, intent on lynching him, but he had the good sense to leave town when violence impended. Elijah Lovejoy, an abolitionist editor in Alton, Illinois, tried to resist a similarly bloody-minded mob and was shot and killed on November 7, 1837, a tragedy that Harriet's brother Edward witnessed. In Cincinnati, a vigilance committee had to be formed to put down the roving anti-abolition mob, though city authorities had initially given the mob overt approval. Harriet published a letter in the *Cincinnati Journal* against mob action, employing a pseudonym as was then common among women writers who felt compelled to remain in the shadows of the domestic sphere. In 1841, Cincinnati was rocked by a race riot. "No one can have the system of slavery brought before him without an irrepressible desire to *do* something," she wrote, "and what is there to be done?" Harriet had decided against slavery but had yet to discover a way to express her opinion.[4]

The 1840s were difficult years for Harriet and Calvin. With Lane Seminary failing, Calvin's salary was repeatedly reduced. The couple quarreled over money, of which there was never enough, with Calvin fuming at Harriet's inability to keep track of her expenditures. Harriet underwent a second and more meaningful conversion experience in the wake of the suicide of her brother George and the birth of a daughter. Exhausted from the baby's demands and emotionally disquieted by George's self-inflicted death, Harriet threw herself on Christ's mercy and became a devoted disciple, convinced of the necessity to submit to Christ's will. Challenges to her newfound faith came in waves. She suffered miscarriages and bouts of bad health, and she tended to embrace the quack cures on offer in the antebellum period. One remedy that Harriet found particularly attractive, and that may have actually aided her health, was hydropathy, the water cure, whereby the patient is immersed in water inside and out and when not drinking or being swathed in wet blankets, took exercise and ate sensibly. Always fond of travel and long absences from Calvin and family, Harriet spent much of the winter of 1846–1847 in Brattleboro, Vermont, enduring hydrotherapy at a fashionable spa. She returned, refreshed and restored in health, in the spring of 1847 and gave birth to a son, her sixth child, named Samuel Charles in January 1848. A healthy boy whom Harriet found a delight, he was the first of her children she successfully nursed. Tragedy intervened when Charley contracted cholera from the foul water of Cincinnati, and the child died in the heat of the summer in July 1849. The death of Charley deeply affected Harriet, who seemed stunned at the loss of so beloved a child. She had a postmortem photograph made of the boy, as was then fashionable among the middle class, which had begun to cherish and even idolize children while having to cope with the loss of so many to incurable maladies of the nineteenth century. Harriet gave expression in her fiction to the common and comforting belief that often the most promising children died young because God required their presence in the next world or life, that a better future waited them in death. The experience also gave her insight into the grief slave mothers regularly endured. "It was at *his* dying bed, and at *his* grave that I learnt what a poor slave mother may feel when her child is torn away from her," she wrote. In *Uncle Tom's Cabin*, Harriet would successfully convey the emotional losses of black parents so that white citizens, who may also have lost a child, could empathize with those undergoing the horrors of the slave system.[5]

The Stowes moved to Brunswick, Maine, in 1850 after Calvin accepted a position at Bowdoin College. Traveling to Maine, Harriet stopped in Boston for a visit with her brother Edward, a firm abolitionist, and his wife Isabella. Edward described his frustration and anger at the reinvigorated Fugitive Slave Law that was an element of the raft of legislation passed as the Compromise of 1850. Once she arrived in Brunswick, Harriet received regular letters from Isabella, who informed her of the horrors of the new law's enforcement and resistance to it in Boston. She urged Harriet to write something about it. Ill health and the chaos of a houseful of children had kept Harriet from writing much for a number of years. However, she found the new Maine vista invigorating and began writing her typically novelistic letters to family members, and she read her children Walter Scott's novels in the evening. Suppressed anger at the death of her precious child may also have stimulated Harriet's urge to write. Whatever the motive, she began writing a story about slavery.

Harriet Beecher Stowe's masterpiece resulted: *Uncle Tom's Cabin*, which was initially serialized in the *National Era* from June 5, 1851, to April 1, 1852. It was subsequently published as a book by John P. Jewett, who gave Harriet a flat 10 percent of sales. The book was wildly successful, selling 300,000 copies in the United States and 1.5 million copies in Great Britain within a year of publication. Three months after the book appeared, Harriet had received $10,000 in royalty payments. The novel touched on familiar emotional themes that drew a ready response from the reading public: separation from a beloved child, death of a child, with biblical imagery such as a flight to freedom across a river. She had also given voice to the increasing number of Northern citizens who were uncomfortable with slavery and angered at the enforcement of the Fugitive Slave Law in their states and communities. Seemingly overnight, Harriet went from the semi-impoverished wife of a bookish professor to worldwide fame and wealth, the celebrity author and ideal of the abolition movement.

With the success of her novel, Stowe began to play a modest role in the antislavery movement. Her work appeared in the *New York Independent*, and she published a documentary follow-up to the novel that purported to establish its factual basis, *A Key to Uncle Tom's Cabin*. She publicly urged an end to the constant quarreling among antislavery factions, counseling William Lloyd Garrison, often the cause of much feuding, to stop criticizing Frederick Douglass. She traveled to Britain in 1852 in part to accept a massive antislavery petition gotten up in response to the emotional impact of her novel. She was given $20,000 both to compensate her for the royalties she missed because of the absence of an international copyright law and for her use in the antislavery cause. Harriet seems to have spent most of the money on herself, but she did use a portion to finance a petition drive against the Kansas-Nebraska Act in 1854 that managed to delay though not defeat the legislation. For the most part, her main contribution to the movement was her novel. When civil war ensued in Kansas, Harriet wrote a more militant antislavery novel, *Dred: A Tale of the Dismal Swamp*, which appeared in 1856. In this novel, the Old Testament message of condign punishment and retribution replaced the New Testament message of forgiveness and understanding that had characterized *Uncle Tom's Cabin*. Like many of her fellow citizens, Harriet was turning more radical and less favorable to compromise. *Dred* did not sell as well as her previous novel, but still earned $20,000.

With money came affluence at a level unthinkable to Harriet's imagination before *Uncle Tom's Cabin*, yet she readily accommodated herself to prosperity, spending with an almost reckless abandon. She made three trips to Europe in 1853, 1856, and 1859, staying in fashionable and expensive resorts and shopping with little restraint. Calvin worried that every nickel would evaporate, and Harriet would find herself chained to her desk, forced to write to earn the means to maintain solvency. Out of her first European trip came a book of travel letters, *Sunny Memories of Foreign Lands*, which appeared in 1854. Later, she published another novel, *Agnes of Sorrento*, which was serialized in the *Atlantic Monthly* and reflected Harriet's new audience, those who could afford to travel to Europe. She built a large home in Hartford dubbed Oakholm, which became a kind of money trap, absorbing considerable funds. After an 1867 trip to Florida, Harriet purchased land near Mandarin on the St. John's River and regularly traveled south each winter to escape the cold. Her twin girls, Hatty and Eliza, wore the latest fashions, provided by their mother, and were completely dependent upon her.

Wealth did not shield the Stowes from tragedy. On July 9, 1857, their promising son, Henry Ellis Stowe, drowned while swimming in the Connecticut River with friends from Dartmouth College. The sudden parting caused considerable anguish for Harriet and Calvin because Henry had not had a conversion experience prior to his demise. The following year, Harriet wrote *The Minister's Wooing*, a novel that suggested that traditionally minded clergy and religion offered little comfort to the mothers of dead children, an expression of her anguish at Henry's death while unsaved and the Calvinist religious dogma that suggested his soul was damned. It too appeared in the pages of the *Atlantic Monthly*. Another son, Fred, drifted into chronic alcoholism, and Harriet had to pay for him to dry out at spas. Fred served in the Union Army and was hideously wounded in the ear by shell fragments at Gettysburg. After the war, he resumed drinking, perhaps to deal with the pain of his wound, and disappeared after a trip to San Francisco in 1871.

On one of her trips to Europe, Harriet met and befriended James T. Fields, who was the editor of the *Atlantic Monthly*. Fields held progressive views on women's rights and other issues, and championed Harriet's work in the pages of the magazine. Harriet had played an unheralded role in the establishment of the *Atlantic Monthly* and was a regular contributor. During the Civil War, Harriet called for the immediate emancipation of the slaves, lampooning Abraham Lincoln after Lincoln's famed letter to Horace Greeley in August 1862 in which the president maintained his paramount objective was to save the Union. She visited the White House on December 2, 1862, the meeting at which Lincoln greeted her with a quip about Stowe being the little lady who had caused the great war. Harriet found Lincoln's sense of humor irresistible. A few weeks later, on January 1, 1863, a celebration was held at Boston's Music Hall in honor of the end of slavery. The crowd lustily cheered Harriet and forced her to stand and acknowledge the accolades. Sensing the war weariness of the population, particularly women, Harriet wrote a column for the *Atlantic* called "House and Home," which focused on the home and was intended as a purposeful distraction from the calamities of war. Calvin retired in 1863, leaving Harriet as the sole provider, and her profligacy and family obligations compelled her to continue writing, as Calvin had feared. She published in magazines and produced a series of forgettable novels that did not duplicate the success of her earlier work.

Her literary career went into decline after 1870 for two reasons. First, Harriet published an article in the *Atlantic*, "Lady Byron Vindicated," that offended much of the reading public with a blunt report of Lord Byron's incestuous affair with a half-sister. Stowe had met Lady Byron while in England and pitied the poor woman who refused to publicly condemn her estranged husband for his incestuous infidelities. For a woman, even of Stowe's stature, to write about such matters for public consumption was simply beyond the boundaries of taste for the populace in Victorian America. Her career was irreparably damaged. Second, Stowe biographer Joan Hedrick has argued that the increasing professionalization of the literary world and the elevation of literature from the parlor to the male-dominated club effectively excluded women writers. Literary criticism too became professionalized, and literature was judged as an art form that had to meet certain aesthetic standards. The new critics found Stowe's novels overly sentimental and relegated her to an inferior status while celebrating the work of male contemporaries like Nathaniel Hawthorne. James Fields, who had promoted her work, retired from the *Atlantic* in 1871, robbing her of an influential and well-placed friend.

Her last years were marked by a steady though gentle decline that left her unable to labor at her writing desk. She had earned a fortune and had been unable to keep it. She sold her mansion, Oakholm, in 1870, purchasing a more modest home in Hartford, and the Florida property had to be given up too. Calvin died in 1886. Harriet lived another decade, with substantially weakened mental faculties after 1889, nursed by her twins until she died in 1896.

PRINCIPAL IDEAS

Christianity animated Harriet Beecher Stowe's life. She had two separate conversion experiences, and she was a minister's daughter and wife. Her religious faith propelled her interest in reform and was the wellspring of her sympathy for the poor and the downtrodden. Stowe had a gift for descriptive writing and for dialogue, and she used fictional characters to convey different ideas and opinions that might then be dissected using logic and reason. She also had a New Englander's pride in American democracy and its unique institutions and heritage. When an anti-abolition mob ransacked Cincinnati, Stowe condemned mob violence and reaffirmed the rights of free speech and petition. The Fugitive Slave Law outraged her, in part because she thought it wrong to force Northern citizens to obey a law they considered a violation of the tenets of Christianity. Stowe argued that a higher law, God's law, trumped "this miserable wicked fugitive slave business."[6]

Her fictional treatment of African Americans presented a false picture of black docility that emanated from her experience with black servant women in Cincinnati, who could hardly be expected to exhibit defiance or an independent spirit toward someone whose disapproval could send them to penury and famine. Stowe lacked the perception to recognize the harsh limitations on free expression under which black women labored. Her attitudes were often paternalistic and condescending, and may have been influenced by Alexander Kinmont, who spoke in Cincinnati, advancing an argument, referred to as "romantic racialism," that blacks had heightened sensitivities. "The poor slave on whom the burden of domestic bereavement falls heaviest is precisely the creature of all Gods creatures that feels it deepest," she wrote. At the conclusion of *Uncle Tom's Cabin*, Stowe advocated colonization to Africa for the slaves after freedom, though only after the freed slaves had been educated and Christianized so they did not fail in the new land. Later, in her 1852 essay, "What Is to Be Done With Them?" she abandoned colonization and advocated equal treatment for blacks as full citizens.[7]

During the Civil War, Stowe advocated immediate emancipation and joined her voice to the criticism of President Lincoln for not moving quickly enough to abolish slavery. She famously parodied Lincoln's declaration to Horace Greeley that the restoration of the Union was his paramount objective. What, Stowe asked, would Christ say in Lincoln's place: "My paramount object in this struggle is to set at liberty them that are bruised, and *not* either to save or destroy the Union. What I do in favor of the Union,

I do because it helps to free the oppressed; what I forbear, I forbear because it does not help to free the oppressed. I shall do less for the Union whenever it would hurt the cause of the slave, and more when I believe it would help the cause of the slave." She reconciled with Lincoln in a December 1862 meeting at the White House and later wrote essays on the home in an effort to provide a respite from the awful war news.[8]

Though Stowe became an advocate of women's suffrage and her own life was hardly conventional, she remained a staunch supporter of women's traditional role as keeper of home and family. For Stowe, God had bestowed on women unique gifts to accomplish that role. She rebuffed entreaties from Elizabeth Cady Stanton and Susan B. Anthony to join the masthead of the *Revolution*, a women's rights newspaper. Stowe wrote, "We have heard much lately of the restricted sphere of woman. . . . It may be true that there are many women far too great, too wise, too high, for mere housekeeping. But where is the woman in any way too great or too high, or too wise, to spend herself creating a home?" Yet she was better at describing domestic order and bliss than in carrying it out herself, as she was notoriously single-minded and when engrossed in writing, missed meals and left her home strewn with books, papers, and discarded clothing. Calvin Stowe wrote that he enjoyed his wife's absences because it was the only time when the house was neat and clean and meals were served at predictable intervals.[9]

CONCLUSION

Harriet Beecher Stowe brought home the horrors of slavery to the people of the North, employing familiar themes that enabled whites to empathize with the slaves and to thereby acknowledge the humanity of those who suffered under the slavery system. Stowe's broadside had greater impact because women were popularly regarded as the moral watchdogs of home and community. Though condemned by later critics, her novel *Uncle Tom's Cabin* retains the power to move readers, and it provides a window into a time in American history when men and women fled bondage across icy rivers and through darkened forests and fields.

NOTES

1. This essay is based on the following sources: Joan D. Hedrick, *Harriet Beecher Stowe: A Life* (New York: Oxford University Press, 1994); Joan D. Hedrick, ed., *The Oxford Harriet Beecher Stowe Reader* (New York: Oxford University Press, 1999); Kathryn Kish Sklar, *Catharine Beecher: A Study in American Domesticity* (New York: W. W. Norton, 1976); and Charles Edward Stowe and Lyman Beecher Stowe, *Life of Harriet Beecher Stowe: The Story of Her Life* (Boston: Houghton, Mifflin and Co., 1911).

2. Hedrick, *Harriet Beecher Stowe*, 64.

3. Hedrick, *Harriet Beecher Stowe*, 140.

4. Hedrick, *Harriet Beecher Stowe*, 109.

5. Hedrick, *Harriet Beecher Stowe*, 193.

6. Harriet Beecher Stowe to Catharine Beecher, n.d. [1850 or 1851], in Joan Hedrick, ed., *The Oxford Harriet Beecher Stowe Reader* (New York: Oxford University Press, 1999), 61.

7. Harriet Beecher Stowe to Henry Ward Beecher, February 1, 1851, in Hedrick, *Stowe Reader*, 65.

8. "Will You Take a Pilot?" in Hedrick, *Stowe Reader*, 472.

9. "What Is a Home?" in Hedrick, *Stowe Reader*, 493.

FURTHER READING

Joan D. Hedrick, *Harriet Beecher Stowe: A Life* (New York: Oxford University Press, 1994); idem., ed., *The Oxford Harriet Beecher Stowe Reader* (New York: Oxford University Press, 1999); Leonard L. Richards, *"Gentleman of Property and Standing": Anti-Abolition Mobs in Jacksonian America* (New York: Oxford University Press, 1970); Kathryn Kish Sklar, *Catharine Beecher: A Study in American Domesticity* (New York: W. W. Norton, 1976); and Charles Edward Stowe and Lyman Beecher Stowe, *Life of Harriet Beecher Stowe: The Story of Her Life* (Boston: Houghton, Mifflin and Co., 1911).

CHARLES SUMNER
(1811–1874)

The Struggle for Equality

LIFE

Charles Sumner was born on January 6, 1811, in Boston to parents of Puritan lineage and modest means. The Sumner family was English; the original name was "Summoner," denoting an early family association with the legal profession. Sumner's father, Charles Pinckney Sumner, was the illegitimate son of Major Job Sumner, a revolutionary war veteran, and Esther Holmes. Charles Pinckney Sumner graduated from Harvard in 1796 and established a modest law practice. In 1810, he married Relief Jacob of Hanover, Massachusetts. Charles had a twin sister, Matilda, who died in 1832. Altogether the Sumners raised nine children, five boys and four girls.

Sumner's father was an extremely stern and disciplined man who showed little affection toward his eldest son. As a youth, Charles was awkward and unskilled in sports. His friends referred to him as "Gawky" Sumner. As a result, he turned his attention to scholarship. He began his education in an infant school run by his aunt. At the age of six, he entered his neighborhood public school. He then entered the Boston Latin School in 1821, where he thrived on the study of Latin classical literature and history. When the elder Charles Sumner received an appointment as sheriff of Suffolk County, he could afford to send his son to Harvard, where the younger Sumner matriculated in 1826. As a college student, Sumner continued to excel in subjects such as history and Latin. He was mediocre in mathematics and science. Upon graduation, Sumner decided to pursue the law as his vocation.

Sumner attended Harvard Law School for three years. During this time, he became enamored with the law and grew close to one instructor in particular, Joseph Story, who was also an associate justice of the U.S. Supreme Court. In many respects, Story gave Sumner the advice and attention he might have received from his father. After graduating from law school, Sumner worked for one year for Boston lawyer Benjamin Rand and then became partners with George S. Hillard. Sumner's early cases involved largely petty matters, and he devoted a considerable amount of time to writing, contributing a number of articles to the *American Jurist*.

Although not politically active at this stage in his life, Sumner nevertheless took a keen interest in politics and the issues of the day. Sympathetic toward the Whigs, a number of early Sumner letters deal with his concern that the Whig Party be corrupted by demagoguery and "vulgar" appeals to the common people. Commenting on the Whig "Hard Cider and Log Cabin" campaign of 1840, Sumner wrote, "The vulgar appeal has succeeded beyond expectation." Another issue that preoccupied the young Sumner was slavery. His father had earned somewhat of a reputation as an antislavery advocate when he publicly protected abolitionist William Lloyd Garrison from Boston rioters in an 1837 fracas on Broad Street. "We are becoming abolitionists at the North fast," he wrote his friend Francis Lieber. Undoubtedly politics played a major role in the fellowship of the Five of Clubs, an informal group of friends who met every Saturday for dinner and discussion. In addition to Sumner, the group included poet Henry Wadsworth Longfellow; Sumner's law partner George Hillard; Henry Cleveland, proctor at Harvard University; and Cornelius Felton, a Latin professor at Harvard.[1]

Much to his father's dismay, in December 1837 Sumner decided to go to Europe, spending time in France, England, and Italy. Particularly in England, he was exposed to numerous intellectuals and political figures. In Europe, the naïve and prudish Sumner was shocked by course language and frank talk about sex. Not only did his European experience have a tremendous impact on the young Boston lawyer, but for the rest of his life, Sumner also maintained a voluminous correspondence with Europeans, particularly the English. By the time of the American Civil War, Sumner was one of the best-known Americans in England.

When Sumner returned in March 1840, his European trip conferred instant credibility on him among Boston's wealthy Beacon Hill residents. Doors that were previously closed to an obscure, impoverished lawyer were now open. Adding to Sumner's prestige was a steady flow of English travelers who visited him in Boston, the most popular being writer Charles Dickens, who visited Sumner during his tour of the United States in 1842. Not all was rosy upon Sumner's return from Europe, for in 1839, his father had passed away while he was abroad. Never emotionally close to his father, but always seeking to win his approval, the exact impact of Sumner's loss is hard to calculate.

Sumner returned to his law practice and initially his practice flourished, yet, as was soon evident, while Sumner loved the law as an intellectual enterprise, ordinary cases bored him. Exposed to the theology of Unitarian

Minister William Ellery Channing, Sumner increasingly became less interested in law and more involved in such social reforms as public education, prison reform, the peace movement, and abolitionism. Indeed, in the early 1840s, Sumner's later viewpoint on slavery began to take shape. Already in 1842, he was developing ideas that would become the standard diet of the Free Soil Party, claiming that slavery was purely a local institution and could never be supported or sanctioned by the national government. "Slavery is a local institution, deriving its vitality from local laws," he wrote. "If a slave master voluntarily takes his slave beyond this jurisdiction, as into another state . . . he manumits him."[2]

Direct involvement in politics, nonetheless, did not appeal to Sumner; however, the annexation of Texas in 1845 and the subsequent Mexican War drew the young reformer closer to the political sphere. The Mexican War violated Sumner's peace principles, but he also believed the annexation of Texas and the subsequent war were waged purely in the interest of advancing slavery. Sumner, along with other young Bostonians like Charles Francis Adams, became part of a younger, antislavery, Conscience Whig faction. They opposed the older, more commercially oriented, Cotton Whig faction that included Senator Daniel Webster, businessman Nathan Appleton, and Boston Congressman Robert Winthrop. Indeed, it was the latter with whom Sumner frequently clashed over the issue of slavery in the late 1840s. In a letter to Nathan Appleton, Sumner complained that by supporting the Mexican War, Winthrop had *done the worst act that was every done by a Boston representative.*[3]

As the Conscience Whigs struggled and failed to wrest control of the party from the likes of Webster and Winthrop, Sumner moved toward the third party camp, supporting the formation of an independent party based exclusively on antislavery principles. "I *do* trust that we may yet be able to arrange our lives so that all the friends of *Liberty* may act together," he wrote Salmon P. Chase. "I am tired of the anomalous position which is forced upon dissenting Whigs here in Massachusetts." When the Whig Party nominated Southern slaveholder and Mexican War General Zachary Taylor for president in 1848, Sumner and many other Massachusetts Conscience Whigs decided to leave the party, linking their fate to a fusion of antislavery factions in the Free Soil Party. Sumner not only delivered a speech at the Free Soil convention at Worcester, Massachusetts, but he also stumped the state on behalf of Martin Van Buren, the party's first presidential nominee.[4]

Despite the unpopularity of this decision with many of his friends, Sumner stressed, as he would throughout his political career, the priority of principles over political expediency. "There is a breaking up of parties, & old names will soon become mere toys," Sumner wrote Horace Mann. "Let us stick to our *Principles* & to the *men* who will sustain them." Despite Van Buren's defeat and Taylor's election in 1848, Sumner and other Free

Soilers were encouraged with the party's showing in the elections. In Massachusetts, a rising new Free Soiler, Henry Wilson, worked with Sumner on a new fusion strategy with the Democratic Party. Hoping to hold the balance of power between the Whigs and Democrats, Sumner and Wilson hoped to gain a share of political offices. When the election of 1850 produced no clear majority in the Massachusetts House, Free Soilers and Democrats made a deal. The Democrats would get the office of governor, lieutenant governor, and the House speakership, and a U.S. Senate seat with an abbreviated term. Free Soilers, the junior partner in the coalition, would get to name the president of the state senate, a few members of the governor's council, and a six-year seat in the U.S. Senate. Despite the profession of little desire to enter party politics, Sumner was the leading Free Soil candidate for senator. "When I think of the insignificance of the state offices, & the importance of Senator, to our cause I confess the strength of the temptation," Sumner wrote his friend, Samuel Gridley Howe.[5]

Despite a "deal" between the two parties, Sumner's election was not final until April 24, 1851—after twenty-six ballots in the legislature. A group of Democrats led by Massachusetts political veteran, Caleb Cushing, known as the "indomitables," refused to accept Sumner initially, on the grounds of his antislavery fanaticism. Although he wanted the Senate seat, Sumner refused absolutely to enter into any negotiations with Cushing. A few Whigs eventually switched to Sumner, giving him the election. While Sumner had not negotiated to get the seat, rumors of corruption and dishonesty shrouded the entire agreement between the two parties. On more than one occasion, Sumner would be forced to defend himself against the charge that his election was the result of a corrupt bargain.

Sumner was not impressed with Washington, D.C., which he regarded as culturally inferior to Boston and New York City. Renting a room on New York Avenue between 14th and 15th Streets, he made the daily walk of one mile to the Senate chambers. As part of an isolated minority—only Salmon Chase and John Hale were Free Soil senators—Sumner believed that he was stereotyped as a one-issue senator. As a result, instead of immediately speaking out against slavery, Sumner held his tongue, determined to contribute in other areas and wait for the right moment to speak out on the slavery issue. As a result, some of his supporters became impatient. Henry Wilson warned him, "You must not let the session close without speaking. Should you do so, you would be openly denounced by nine-tenths of our people."[6]

After several attempts to gain the floor, Sumner finally succeed in August 1852, introducing an amendment on an appropriation bill. Sumner's amendment stated that no monies could be used for enforcement of the Fugitive Slave Act. It was a typical Sumner speech: longwinded, erudite, filled with Latin quotations and historical anecdotes, and delivered in a condescending tone for three and a quarter hours. Since he was a poor extemporaneous speaker, Sumner carefully memorized and rehearsed his speech prior to delivery. The thrust of his argument was that the Fugitive Slave Law was unconstitutional. Arguing that slavery was a local matter, protected only by state law, there was absolutely no federal responsibility to enforce it. Indeed, by denying trial by jury to suspected fugitive slaves, the law was unconstitutional, violating the due process provisions of the Fifth Amendment. The speech initiated a spirited debate in the Senate as well as severe criticism of Sumner by a number of senators; however, among Sumner's Massachusetts constituents, the speech generated considerable enthusiasm. "I throw the speech down as a gage," Sumner wrote associate John Bigelow. "I believe it presents the true limits of opposition to Slavery with the Constitution. I challenge an answer. The attempts in the Senate were puerile, & ill-tempered."[7]

Charles Sumner sincerely believed in the Slave Power conspiracy, a widespread belief among many antislavery advocates who believed that wealthy Southern slaveholders controlled the federal government. For Sumner, the passage of the Fugitive Slave Law was evidence of such a conspiracy. As his senatorial career continued, Sumner and his political allies assigned sinister motives to the action of Southern senators and their Northern associates. In Sumner's opinion, the most sinister evidence of a proslavery plot was Stephen Douglas's Kansas-Nebraska bill. Introduced in the Senate in early 1854, the act proposed to repeal the Missouri Compromise of 1820 and allow residents of the Kansas-Nebraska territories to decide the question of slavery on the basis of majority preference—what Douglas called popular sovereignty. Along with Salmon Chase of Ohio, Sumner was instrumental in persuading Douglas to delay the debate on the bill so that popular opinion could be aroused. In order to accomplish the latter, Sumner joined with Chase, Ohio Representative Joshua Giddings, and others to draft the "Appeal of the Independent Democrats," a document that denounced the bill and accused Douglas of sponsoring the measure to advance his chances of securing his party's 1856 presidential nomination.

Sumner believed the strategy would crush Douglas. He told John Jay of New York that "Benton [former senator Thomas Hart Benton of Missouri] says that every Northern who sustains Douglas's bill is irretrievably ruined. As for Douglas, if he does not succeed in his plot, he will be kicked by the South; if he does, his brains will be dashed out at the North." But Sumner underestimated the Little Giant in the following weeks. On January 30, Douglas attacked Sumner, Chase, and the supporters of the Appeal, claiming they had misled him in their request to delay the debate. While Sumner answered Douglas in a February 21 speech, it was Douglas who got the last word in a debate finale on March 3. Denouncing the opponents of his bill as "abolition confederates," Douglas inflicted a spirited attack on Sumner, even calling into question the legitimacy of his election to the Senate in 1851. "I must be permitted to remind him [Sumner] of what he can certainly never forget, that when he arrived here to take his seat for the first time, so firmly were senators impressed with the conviction that he had been elected by dishonorable and corrupt means, there were very few who . . . could deem it consistent with personal honor to hold private intercourse with him."[8]

In the end, Douglas prevailed and the bill was passed in the Senate. The rigor of the debates drained Sumner, who told his Massachusetts political ally, E. L. Pierce, "I have been oppressed by wicked-ness at last consummated in the Senate. Upon Chase and myself the whole brunt of the contest has fallen." When the measure was passed by the House in May and signed by President Pierce, Sumner complained to editor James Freeman Clarke, "Unless the North arises, & without the distinction of party, forgetting the effete differences of Whig & Democrat, takes possession of the National Govt., we shall be degraded to a serfdom worse than that of Russia."[9]

In the days that followed the Kansas-Nebraska controversy, Sumner was uncertain of the political future. As the Whig Party collapsed and numerous anti-Nebraska Democrats left their party, a newly constituted Republican Party formed to rally antislavery advocates. At the same time, however, the powerful force of nativism organized politically in the form of the American (Know-Nothing) Party. Exploiting ethnocultural and anti-Catholic prejudice that had arisen in the 1840s as a result of European immigration, the Know-Nothing Party advocated a host of provisions to discriminate against immigrants, particularly Irish Catholic newcomers. What party would become the legitimate replacement of the Whig Party was uncertain until 1856, when the Republican Party was able to attract the majority of Know-Nothings into its organization. For his part, Sumner privately denounced the Know-Nothings. "I am ignorant enough," he told fellow Massachusetts Senator Julius Rockwell, "but I am not a Know Nothing." Yet, despite his devotion to principle, Sumner said little publicly to denounce the Know-Nothings, realizing their support would be crucial to the infant Republican Party that he eventually gravitated toward as the best way to combat the expansion of slavery.[10]

As Republicans looked forward to their first presidential race, events in Kansas preoccupied Sumner. Convinced that the violence and aggression taking place there were the responsibility of the proslavery settlers backed and encouraged by the Pierce administration, Sumner was particularly angry with the way in which Douglas characterized the Free State settlers in the Senate. "You will read Douglas's elaborate assault on the Em. Aid Co. Allow me to suggest to you to have the company present a memorial to the Senate directly responsive to this assault, point by point, & vindicating its simple rights," he advised author Edward Everett Hale. Sumner than began to prepare his own speech on the subject. As he told Salmon

Chase, "I have the floor for next Monday on Kansas, when I shall make a thorough & complete speech of my life. My soul is wrung by this outrage, & I shall pour it forth. How small was all that our fathers endured with the wrongs of Kansas!"[11]

Gaining the floor on May 19, Sumner did more than simply pour out his soul, using his speech to make some of the most viscious personal attacks known to the Senate—despite the era's reputation for lack of civility. As usual, Sumner had researched and laboriously rehearsed his masterpiece, "The Crime against Kansas." Sumner wanted to demonstrate to all that proslavery forces in the country were determined that Kansas be made a slave state no matter what the cost. He began by pointing out a number of absurdities in the arguments of the proslavery supporters. First, there was the Douglas fiction that the territorial legislature of Kansas was a legitimate body, which ignored the massive frauds that had taken place in the elections for this legislature. Second, there was the "apology imbecile," which was President Pierce's claim to be unable to stop the violence in Kansas. Third was the "apology absurd," which sought to fix the blame for violence entirely on the Free State settlers of Kansas. Finally there was the "apology infamous," which blamed the New England Emigrant Society for the Civil War in Kansas.

Sumner uncritically accepted all the information that he received from his sources in Kansas. Nevertheless, most senators assumed that he would take the position he did, and had he gone no further than that, most senators would not have found anything particularly noteworthy in his speech. What shocked the Senate were the attacks that he made on Senator Andrew Butler of South Carolina, Stephen Douglas, and James Mason of Virginia, the author of the fugitive slave bill. Reading Cervantes' *Don Quixote*, Sumner used the main characters to spice up his attacks. Butler was, therefore, the "Don Quixote" of slavery. "Of course he has chosen a mistress, to whom he has made his vows, and who, though ugly to others, is always lovely to him—though polluted in the sight of the world, is chaste in his sight: I mean the harlot slavery." Sumner labeled Douglas as "the squire of Slavery, its very Sancho Panza, ready to do its humiliating offices." Sumner accused Douglas of "piling one mass of elaborate error upon another mass" in his zest to bring Kansas into the Union as a slave state. Mason, Sumner argued, did not represent the Virginia of Washington or Jefferson, but "that other Virginia from which Washington and Jefferson avert their faces, where human beings are bred as cattle for the shambles."[12]

While Butler was absent and could not respond to Sumner, both Douglas and Mason did reply. It was the exchange with Douglas that has become a classic of senatorial debate, quoted by almost all Sumner and Douglas biographers. Sumner accused Douglas of deliberately trying to injure him in past speeches:

Sumner: I say also to the Senator, and I wish him to bear in mind, that no person with the upright form of a man can be allowed————[hesitation]

Douglas: Say it.

Sumner: I will say it,—no person with the upright form of man can be allowed, without violation of all decency, to switch out from his tongue the perpetual stench of offensive personality. Sir that is not a proper weapon of debate, at least, on this floor. The noisome, squat, and nameless animal to which I now refer is not the proper model for an American Senator. Will the Senator from Illinois take notice?

Douglas: I will,—and therefore will not imitate you, Sir.

Sumner: I did not hear the Senator.

Douglas: I said, if that be the case, I would certainly never imitate you in that capacity,—recognizing the force of the illustration.

Sumner: Mr. President, again the Senator switches his tongue, and again he fills the Senate with its offensive odor. But I drop the Senator.[13]

While some Northern newspapers praised his speech, there were many that believed Sumner had gone too far. Predictably, Southern papers denounced Sumner, with some suggesting that he be caned or beaten. Many of Sumner's congressional friends were worried about his safety. During his speech, they had heard Douglas remark in the back Senate Chamber "that damn fool will get himself killed by some other damn fool." When Henry Wilson and others tried to escort Sumner home, the senator replied, "None of that, Wilson."[14]

One Southerner who was determined to carry through on threats of violence was Preston Brooks. A representative from South Carolina, Brooks was an amiable, polite gentleman who happened to be a cousin of Andrew Butler. He was determined to avenge his kinsman's honor. After failing to intercept Sumner at the Capitol on May 21, Brooks caught up with him the next day in Senate chambers. As Sumner was busy franking copies of his speech, Brooks waited until a few ladies had left the lobby. He then approached Sumner, introduced himself, and proceeded to beat the senator with his gutta-percha cane. Sumner, dazed from the first blow, was unable to get up. His desk was bolted to the floor. To get up, he had to push back on his chair, which was on rollers. In his effort to get up, he finally pulled the desk from the floor, but then collapsed in unconsciousness. While Mississippi Congressman Lawrence Keitt helped Brooks get away, Representatives Edwin B. Morgan and Ambrose Murray came to Sumner's aid, summoned a doctor, and got the senator to his home.

In the South, Brooks was canonized as a saint who had avenged the honor of his region. Democratic papers, too, generally regretted the caning, but a few believed that Sumner had earned his fate by his savage rhetoric. As the Illinois *State Register* argued, "But when such crawling, sneaking reptiles as Sumner assume the shield of non-combatancy in order to establish for themselves the exclusive privilege of violating every rule of decorum know among men . . . there is certainly great allowance to be made for gentlemen who momentarily losing their temper, may mete out well merited but possibly illegal punishment to the offenders." Predictably, Republican papers universally condemned Brooks's action as barbarous. Sumner had now become a martyr for the antislavery cause. The beating, when combined with the raid on Lawrence, Kansas, that occurred a few days later, gave Republicans the twin issues of "Bleeding Sumner" and "Bleeding Kansas" for the 1856 elections.[15]

The initial prognosis for Sumner was positive. In just a few days, he even was well enough to make a statement to the House committee that was charged with investigating the assault. Then he suffered a relapse, with a return of fever, rapid pulse, and severe pains in the back of the head as well as back pains. For more than two years, Sumner could not perform his duties in the Senate. Whenever he returned to cast an important vote and to resume his Senate duties, the same symptoms recurred. He sought a variety of medical opinions, tried a number of treatments, and made numerous trips, including several to Europe, seeking cures for his condition. During this time, he made few public appearances. When he did, he appeared frail and aged. Most likely, Sumner's ailment was some variation of a psychosomatic disorder. If away from the Senate and official duties, he seemed to function normally. However, the moment he returned to the routine of the Senate and the scene of the beating, his old symptoms resurfaced. Apparently, only time would heal the root cause of Sumner's malady.

Sumner finally was able to resume his duties in December 1859. While the Brooks beating was an important factor in securing his second term in the Senate, his long absence caused many Massachusetts Republicans—particularly rivals who coveted his seat in the Senate—to call for his resignation on the grounds that he would never resume his duties. His return was timely for his own political career. Resuming duties was easier said than done, as Sumner found himself particularly uninformed on a number of important issues. It did not take the Massachusetts senator a long time to revive his attacks on the South and slavery. On June 4, he delivered a 35,000-word speech entitled "The Barbarism of Slavery," refuting the argument that slavery was a blessing that benefited the enslaved.

While the nomination of Abraham Lincoln surprised Sumner, who barely knew the Illinois Republican, he accepted it and worked for Republican victory in 1860. After Lincoln's victory and the subsequent secession crisis, Sumner pursued the course of many radical Republicans, working against real compromise and gravely underestimating the threat of secession by Southern states. As a peace advocate, he was half inclined to allow the seceding states to leave in peace. When it came to concessions to entice the seceding states back into the Union, Sumner had definite ideas. There would be none. "I am against any offer now, even of a peppercorn," he wrote Salmon Chase. "Let us know if we have a Govt." Dismissing the

Crittenden proposals as spineless compromises, Sumner also had harsh words for any Republicans who inclined toward concessions. When the shots were fired on Fort Sumter, Sumner ironically remarked to Henry Longfellow, "Alas! That I, loving Peace, vowed to Peace, should be called to take such great responsibility in a direful ghastly civil war!"[16]

During the American Civil War, Sumner played major roles in the debate over emancipation, discussions over the Reconstruction of the Southern states, and, as chair of the Senate Committee on Foreign Relations, foreign affairs—particularly relations with Great Britain. Although a peace advocate prior to the war, Sumner endorsed a vigorous prosecution of the war and was a vocal critic of those generals who did not live up to his expectations. During the war, Sumner was a persistent and pesky critic of Abraham Lincoln's war policies; nevertheless, he slowly developed a good working relationship with the chief executive. While they would quarrel bitterly on particular issues, the two never allowed their differences to cause a permanent rift between them.

From the beginning of the war, Sumner was convinced that the institution of slavery must be destroyed. According to his logic, since slavery was the cause of the war, only by getting at the root could the problem ultimately be resolved. Although he abstained from voting on the Crittenden-Johnson resolution, which stated that the destruction of slavery was not the object of the war, he quickly changed his tone. "People who ask for Peace," he wrote Wendell Phillips, "should be told that peace is impossible while Slavery exists. Abolition is the Condition precedent." Early on, he was extremely disappointed with the Lincoln administration's policy on slavery. One particularly upsetting incident occurred in early September, when the president countermanded John C. Frémont's Emancipation Proclamation for the State of Missouri. Sumner was also an outspoken critic of military leaders who returned fugitive slaves to slaveholders. In December 1861, he vehemently attacked Massachusetts Brigadier General Charles Pomeroy Stone for returning fugitive slaves, drawing the ire of Democrats and Massachusetts conservatives.[17]

As the war dragged into its second year, Sumner had some reasons for optimism. The president had developed a scheme for gradual, compensated emancipation in the loyal border states. While none of these states took up Lincoln's offer, it was proof to the Massachusetts Republican that the president was on the right track. A proclamation of emancipation, however, was not forthcoming. Sumner endorsed the action of the radical Republicans in Congress when they took action into their own hands on slavery, passing the Second Confiscation Act, a law that provided for the liberation of slaves who belonged to rebel masters. Sumner was genuinely satisfied when Lincoln issued the preliminary Emancipation Proclamation immediately following the battle of Antietam. According to Sumner, the reason for the president's caution was poor advice that he received from Secretary of State William H. Seward and his political crony, Thurlow

Weed. These two "set themselves against Emancipation, & they both began with Compromise; & with the idea that by some patch-work this great question could be avoided." Despite the devastating defeat at Fredericksburg in December 1862, the president followed through with the Emancipation Proclamation on January 1, 1863, as he had earlier promised. Sumner was greatly relieved.[18]

Early in the conflict, Sumner looked beyond the war, anticipating eventual Union victory and contemplating the shape of a reconstructed South. Unlike most members of the Democratic Party and conservative members of his own party, Sumner was not completely comfortable with the notion that secession was a constitutional impossibility. Those Southern states that had declared secession were de facto out of the Union. They were waging war against the United States. Already on February 11, 1862, Sumner introduced resolutions into the Senate that argued that the Southern states were legally dead. They now existed as territories, and once the federal government took control of these areas, Congress would control the process of returning them to statehood. Focusing on the clause in the Constitution that guarantees each state a republican form of government, Sumner believed that slavery could be legally abolished as a condition for readmittance into the Union. While his ideas seemed to conflict with Lincoln's view of Reconstruction, when the president made his December 10, 1863, proclamation on Reconstruction, Sumner was initially pleased with Lincoln's plan. As he told Orestes Brownson on December 27, 1863, the president's plan made emancipation the "corner-stone of reconstruction." Additionally, Sumner believed that Lincoln now had all but accepted the idea that seceded states were practically out of the Union.[19]

With his extensive connections in Europe and his chairmanship of the Senate Committee on Foreign Relations, Sumner played an important role in Civil War diplomacy. Sumner distrusted Secretary of State William H. Seward because he disagreed with the conciliatory approach the latter played during the secession crisis and his lack of enthusiasm for emancipation. However, Sumner also felt that the New Yorker's blustering rhetoric toward the European powers was both dangerous and irrational. During the *Trent* crisis in November and December 1861, when American naval commander Charles Wilkes seized Confederate envoys, James Mason and John L. Slidell, from a British mail packet, Sumner knew that the envoys would have to be given up. The United States could not afford a war with Britain while engaged in a civil war at home.

Extremely vexing to Sumner throughout the war was the official attitude of the English government. Led by Lord Palmerston, many English cabinet members made no effort to disguise their pro-Confederate sentiments. As the war continued, Sumner grew increasingly impatient with England, particularly when it was common knowledge that sophisticated naval vessels, called "Rams," were being constructed by English companies. Sumner complained to the duke of Argyll, "If one nation can allow its ports

& dock-yards to become the nurseries of belligerent activity against a friendly power, & all for the sake of Slavery . . . we may as well renounce International Law, & all its gathered justice & wisdom." During the summer of 1863, Sumner stated his case against England in a major speech entitled "Our Foreign Relations," where he argued that both the English and the French did not fully comprehend the moral dimension to the American conflict.[20]

While Sumner was disappointed in the course of both the French and British during the war, he also realized that the North could not afford to wage war against either one of the European powers without jeopardizing the chances of suppressing the rebellion. For this reason, he used his influence to squash all actions that might unnecessarily antagonize both the British and the French. In early January 1863, he successfully blocked an attempt by California Senator James McDougall to introduce a resolution condemning French intervention in Mexico. And when Sumner believed Seward was mishandling relations with the French, he met with French Minister Henri Mercer to smooth over the relationship. When the secretary of state sponsored a bill to authorize privateers with letters of marque, Sumner opposed the bill on the grounds that such a measure would grievously antagonize British commerce and worsen relations between the two countries. Although the measure passed both houses of Congress, Sumner successfully lobbied Lincoln not to act on the measure.

During the course of the American Civil War, Sumner's strong rhetoric against the South and slavery made him many enemies among the Democrats and many conservatives in his own party. In Massachusetts, political opponents waged a campaign against Sumner's reelection on the grounds that he was at odds with the president. Conservative Republicans and Democrats in Massachusetts also tried to form a new political organization to oust Sumner, called the People's Party and led by such Sumner opponents as ex–Massachusetts governors Henry Gardner and John Clifford. Sumner's allies, particular influential antislavery insider Francis W. Bird, moved quickly to squelch opposition in Republican ranks, maneuvering an unprecedented resolution of endorsement of Sumner at the Massachusetts Republican state convention at Worcester on September 9, 1862. When Lincoln issued the preliminary Emancipation Proclamation, the argument that Sumner opposed the president's policies evaporated. When the Republicans swept Massachusetts in the fall election, Sumner's third term in the Senate was guaranteed.

As Sumner's enemies worked against him, so, too, did the opponents of Abraham Lincoln work to prevent a second term for the Illinois Republican. As early as February 1864, opposition to the president organized around Treasury Secretary Salmon P. Chase. Throughout the years, Sumner had developed a close relationship with this antislavery advocate; nevertheless, Sumner stayed clear of all intrigue against the president. When

Lincoln's pocket veto of the Wade-Davis bill temporarily drove radicals such as Wade, Davis, and others to contemplate either supporting the candidacy of John C. Frémont or nominating another candidate altogether, Sumner stayed clear of involvement. He was not happy with Lincoln's pocket veto, but, at the same time, Sumner did not think it was wise to divide the party by organizing against the president. When military victories in the late summer of 1864 gave new hope to the Republicans for Lincoln's reelection, Sumner could confidently report to John Bright, "From the beginning I declined to have any thing to do with *adversary* proceedings, partly on the grounds of my personal relations with the Presdt but more because I was satisfied that it would only endanger the result."[21]

The winter session of Congress 1864–1865 produced much satisfaction for the Massachusetts Republican. The passage of the Thirteenth Amendment, abolishing the institution of slavery, was one such example. Ironically, the most forceful voice of the abolition of slavery in Congress played no role in drafting the amendment. Reconstruction, on the other hand, was an area where little was accomplished. At issue was whether Congress would recognize the legitimacy of the Louisiana state government as organized by the president's Ten Percent Plan and implemented by General Nathaniel P. Banks. In late 1864, a compromise seemed to be in the works. In exchange for recognizing the Banks regime without black suffrage, future Reconstruction governments would have universal male suffrage. When the compromise fell apart, Sumner joined several radical Republicans in an unusual alliance with Democrats who he intensely disliked to filibuster discussion on recognition, eventually forcing the measure to be tabled until the Thirty-ninth Congress. Sumner was determined that Congress would hold the cards in Reconstruction and that equality would be its foundation.

While Lincoln was angered over Sumner's course in the Louisiana debate, he as well as Sumner were determined not to break relations. Sumner continued to accompany Mary Lincoln on social engagements and accompanied her to City Point, Virginia, in early April 1865. The president also had asked Sumner to accompany him to the inaugural ball on March 5, 1865. When Sumner heard the news about Lincoln's assassination, he rushed to the president's side, holding his hand all night and crying by his bedside. Using his personal relations with the chief executive, Sumner had hoped to influence the course of Reconstruction. Now Lincoln was gone and in his place was Vice President Andrew Johnson, of whom Sumner already had an unfavorable opinion.

In actuality, Sumner was not well acquainted with Johnson; however, the vice president's performance at the 1865 inauguration, where he delivered an incoherent speech under the influence of alcohol, left a negative initial impression. After meetings with Johnson on April 15 and 16, Sumner revised his assessment. Expressing to Johnson the need for Reconstruction based on black suffrage, the new president seemed supportive. During the next few weeks, additional interviews with Johnson tended to support Sumner's belief that racial equality was high on the chief executive's agenda. "Our new Presdt. makes a good impression," Sumner told John Bright. "His chief topic thus far has been that treason is a crime; but I am satisfied that he is the sincere friend of the negro, & ready to act for him decisively."[22]

In his biography of Sumner, David Donald suggests that Sumner misread Johnson's silence in their many interviews as agreement. By the end of May, Sumner was unpleasantly surprised when the president released the North Carolina proclamations, an executive plan to reorganize the State of North Carolina. Not only had Johnson asserted executive supremacy in the Reconstruction process, but he also made it clear that black civil rights—including suffrage—formed no part of his plans. Blaming this new course on the influence of Seward and the Blair family, Sumner tried to rally radicals to delay the president's course until Congress met in December 1865. Taking matters into his own hands, Sumner visited Johnson on December 2, 1865, intent on forcing Johnson to break with the Republican Party. In an intense two-and-one-half-hour interview, the two tussled. Arguing that blacks in the South needed protection from ex-rebels and that black civil rights ought to be the cornerstone of Reconstruction, Sumner found the president particularly recalcitrant. Sumner related Johnson's reasoning to one correspondent:

> Presdt Mr. S. Do murders ever occur in Mass?
>
> Mr. S. Unhappily yes, Mr. Presdt—
>
> Presdt—Do people ever knock each other down in Boston—
>
> Mr. S Unhappily yes Mr Presdt, sometimes.
>
> Presdt. Would you consent that Mass. Should be excluded from the Union on this accnt.
>
> Mr. S. No, Mr. Presdt; surely not.—[23]

Sumner's goals for Reconstruction included universal male suffrage, irrespective of color; provision for equality before the law; and the requirement that all white males swear an oath of loyalty to the Union while denouncing secession. Many of Sumner's Republican colleagues were skeptical of his program and were loath to break with the president. For this reason, Sumner was left off the influential Joint Committee on Reconstruction that was created in December 1865 to formulate congressional Reconstruction policy. However, in early 1866 Johnson's ill-timed vetoes of moderate Reconstruction legislation began to sway conservative and moderate Republicans to Sumner's point of view. Sumner stepped up his criticism of Johnson in the Senate during the opening months of 1866. As a result of Southern defiance and Johnson's intractability, Congress passed the Fourteenth Amendment and determined that its ratification would be the terms whereby Southern states would be readmitted to the Union. When Johnson encouraged the states to reject the amendment and used this as a campaign issue in the fall 1866 congressional elections, he was repudiated decisively. More than anything else, Johnson's political miscalculation helped Sumner regain influence in the Senate. When Congress returned to Washington in December 1866, it would pass legislation that, in part, reflected Sumner's radical approach. These included a series of Military Reconstruction Acts as well as the Tenure of Office Act.

Meanwhile, Sumner was not satisfied that Congress could pass laws and override Johnson's veto. He was one of the earliest proponents of impeachment in the Congress, and throughout 1866 and 1867, he attacked the president repeatedly in the Senate. When Johnson was finally impeached by the House in February 1868 and tried in the Senate, Sumner had nothing but scorn for the seven Republican senators who eventually voted not guilty and allowed the president to remain in office. "The story of 'the seven' is sad enough," Sumner wrote to one correspondent. "There is little doubt that at least two were corrupted by money, & I hear it said that evidence also affects a third." Although he lost the fight over impeachment, Sumner could take satisfaction because during the struggle with Johnson, the Republican Party generally had adopted many of his positions on Reconstruction. Instead of a lone voice, Sumner's stature had risen in the party.[24]

Sumner's personal life had heretofore been one of a scholar-bachelor turned political figure. He had never been comfortable with women, although he often pitied his loneliness when he compared himself to many of his married friends. Suddenly, in the spring of 1866, Sumner met and fell in love with Alice Mason Hooper, the daughter of Samuel Hooper, a Massachusetts representative and friend of the senator. Although there was a thirty-year age difference, the two decided to marry and a wedding took place on October 17, 1866. The relationship, however, quickly deteriorated. Sumner had little time for a wife, given his Senate duties and scholarly habits. Alice, however, was an independent woman who would not stand for Sumner's lack of attention. She began to socialize on her own, and soon rumors began circulating regarding her relationship with a young Prussian diplomat. In the summer of 1867, Alice left Sumner, and the two never saw or spoke to each other again. Eventually in 1873, Sumner was granted a divorce on the grounds of abandonment. It was an ill-fated relationship that caused Sumner considerable personal pain and public embarrassment.

The election of a new Republican president in 1868 made Sumner cautiously optimistic. Although not close to President-Elect Grant, Sumner was willing to cooperate with him. In the area of foreign affairs, for instance, Sumner expected to yield great influence with new Secretary of State Hamilton Fish. Not only was Fish relatively inexperienced in foreign affairs, but his friendship with Sumner from their early days of the Senate also promised a long and fruitful relationship for the Republican senator. Moreover, not only was Sumner allowed to name his choice for minister to England, his friend John Lathrop Motley, but he also expected to play a major role in the Alabama claims negotiations between the United States and Great Britain that had arisen over shipping damage to the North as a result of Confederate ships built in English ports.

Increasingly, Sumner found himself in the familiar position of isolation. New Republican senators replaced political veterans, and many of the new senators had little respect for Sumner, who they regarded as pompous, verbose, and a hairbrained intellectual. They ridiculed Sumner's cries for civil rights legislation as unrealistic and absurd. When Sumner found himself at odds with President Grant over a treaty to annex the Dominican Republic, he found that he was taking on the entire Republican Party. Assuming the role of the beleaguered opposition was a familiar position for Sumner, but it also wore on the Massachusetts senator as he entered his early sixties.

Sumner did have his own way on foreign affairs early in the Grant administration. On April 13, 1869, for instance, his speech on the Alabama claims was widely applauded in the United States, and Sumner also played an influential role in preventing the United States from granting belligerent status to Cuban rebels who rebelled against Spain. On an evening in January 1870, President Grant paid an unexpected visit to Sumner's home, where the senator was dining with journalists Ben Perley Poore and John W. Forney. Grant had come to pitch a treaty of annexation for the Dominican Republican, recently negotiated by his close associate Orville Babcock. Although Grant claimed that Sumner had promised to back the treaty, Sumner claimed only to promise an honest and open hearing in the Committee on Foreign Relations.

After he had time to examine the treaty, Sumner privately opposed it. Convinced that the Dominican dictator, Buenaventura Baez, was corrupt and stood to gain financially from the treaty, Sumner also believed that many of Grant's associates stood to reap financial rewards from the annexation. Since the island was in the midst of civil war, Sumner also believed that it was unwise to intervene. The black republic ought to be allowed to solve its own internal affairs, and the treaty with Baez was pumping new life into a dictator on the verge of collapse. While Sumner hoped to allow the treaty to die silently in committee, Grant's support and lobbying effort in the Senate forced him to report the treaty to the entire Senate. Here Sumner had the votes to kill the treaty, which he did, earning the president's wrath and the accusation that Sumner had tricked him.

Sumner's opposition to the president made him persona non grata in the Republican Party. Younger senators such as New York's Roscoe Conkling and political rivals such as Benjamin F. Butler repeatedly attacked him. The president punished Sumner by leaving him out of patronage decisions and removing John Lathrop Motley from his position as minister to England. The crowning punishment was the removal of Sumner as chair of the Committee on Foreign Relations at the beginning of the Forty-second Congress in March 1871. It was the ultimate slap in the face, and while Sumner allies and friends in the press denounced the move as an outrage, the Massachusetts Republican was clearly on the losing end of his quarrel with the president.

Without position or influence in the Senate, Sumner continued to speak out on civil rights and against President Grant. His great hope was that the president would not be renominated for president in 1872. As he told New York Republican and former abolitionist Gerrit Smith, "All who have known him [Grant] best testify to his incapacity." In temperament, Sumner was beginning to move toward the Liberal Republicans. Tired of Reconstruction, corruption in government, and the Grant administration, the Liberals stressed issues such as amnesty for the South and civil service reform. While Sumner was sympathetic to civil service reform, he was skeptical of amnesty for the South. He hoped that it might be tied to a civil rights bill that he introduced in the Senate in May 1872. When the Liberals nominated Horace Greeley for president and began making overtures to the Democratic Party, Sumner grew skeptical because he did not trust the Democrats to safeguard black rights in the South. Yet so intense was his hatred and distrust for Grant that by the summer of 1872, Sumner left the Republican Party and cast his lot with the Liberals. No doubt his eventual support of Greeley was telegraphed in a May 31, 1872, speech entitled "Republicanism vs. Grantism," a bitter, vindictive attack on the president for alleged corruption in his administration. Although he had left the Republican Party, Sumner refused to give up his Senate seat, despite leaving the party, and accept the Liberal Republican nominee for governor of Massachusetts. Physically worn out, the aging senator took no part in the fall campaign. Instead, he went to Europe to rest and recuperate.[25]

Sumner's remaining career in the Senate was marked by less work and frequent absences. Plagued by bladder spasms, seizures, and heart pains, Sumner devoted most of his time to editing his works for publication and his pet civil rights bill. He would not achieve either in his lifetime. On the evening of March 9, 1874, his house servant heard him fall in his room. Confined to his bedroom, he was in a semiconscious condition. He repeatedly reminded visiting friends of the importance of both his edited works and the civil rights bill. In the early afternoon of March 11, Sumner vomited and fell on his bed. While gasping for air, he quickly expired.

PRINCIPAL IDEAS

Views on Party Politics

Like many political figures, Charles Sumner was a professional politician who professed to abhor politicians. While it is easy to dismiss such pretensions as self-interested nonsense, in the case of Sumner, his Senate career along with the many unpopular stands he took during his Senate tenure are evidence of a high degree of earnestness when it came to this issue. "I am indifferent to what is called political success," Sumner wrote his brother George. "I am satisfied, if I can in an effective way bear my testimony to a great truth." As Sumner moved from the Whig Party to the Free Soil Party in 1848, he placed commitment to principle over that of party. He told Horace Mann in 1848, "Let us stick to our *Principles* & to the *men* who will sustain them." A few years later, Sumner complained to Mann, "You must expect the coldness & vituperation of *politicians*. This is the tribe I eschew and detest . . . I think you will yet see them as I do. Their trade compels them to be faithless to principles—provided they are true to their *party* & *themselves*."[26]

While Sumner was not above pulling strings on his own behalf, particularly to secure reelection to the Senate, he was, nevertheless, firmly devoted to principles throughout his career. His change of political parties and his willingness to take on the leaders of his own party attest to this. At the same time, however, devotion to principle had a cost. Sumner's devotion to principle was often combined with an attitude of moral superiority. This smug, self-righteous attitude prevented Sumner from becoming an effective legislator. His career in the Senate was marked by few legislative achievements. Despite his devotion to emancipation and civil rights, he played a significant role in practically no major legislative bills. Two factors were his condescending attitude and the assumption that his principles were right, while those of opponents were wrong.

Views on Slavery

From at least 1836, Charles Sumner expressed a negative opinion on the institution of slavery; however, unlike his more radical contemporaries such as William Lloyd Garrison, Sumner did not view political action as ill advised or pointless. Nor did Sumner regard slavery as sanctioned by the Constitution. As a result, he never took the Garrisonian position that condemned the Constitution because it sanctioned slavery. In an 1845 letter to abolitionist Wendell Phillips, Sumner defended political activity, arguing that voting had the possibility of effecting change.

As mentioned previously, the Mexican War caused Sumner to become more vocal and active in his attacks on slavery. In an 1846 address in Boston, entitled "Slavery and the Mexican War," Sumner denounced the peculiar institution. "Slavery is a wrong which justice and humanity alike condemn," Sumner contended. "The Mexican War is an enormity born of Slavery. . . . Base in object, atrocious in beginning, immoral in all its influences, vainly prodigal of treasure and life; it is a war of infamy, which must blot the page of our history." Moreover, Sumner boldly attacked Whig Congressman Robert C. Winthrop during the course of the speech for his lack of forthright opposition to the peculiar institution.[27]

As Sumner became involved in the Free Soil Party and eventually was elected to the Senate in 1851, his views on slavery matured. His address in the Senate in August 1852 provides an accurate description of his evolution on the topic. Built on the views of Salmon P. Chase and Joshua Giddings, the speech, in many respects, was largely based on previous arguments. Yet delivered with force and energy to a hostile audience, it was an impressive oratorical argument against slavery.

Delivered as an amendment to an appropriations bill to deny funding for the Fugitive Slave Law, Sumner chided the Senate for regarding the Compromise of 1850 as the final solution to the problem of slavery. Then, narrowing in on his main point, Sumner attacked the belief that slavery was a national institution. Basing his argument on the omission of the word *slave* in the Constitution, Sumner argued that this omission was deliberate, motivated by the embarrassment that slavery caused the Founding Fathers and the intention to disassociate the national government from the peculiar institution. "A popular belief at this moment makes slavery a national institution," Sumner told the Senate, "and, of course, renders its support a national duty. The extravagance of this error can hardly be surpassed. An institution which our fathers most carefully omitted to name in the Constitution, which, according to the debates in the Convention, they refused to cover with any 'sanction,' and which, at the original organization of the Government, was merely *sectional*, existing nowhere on the *national* territory, is now, above all other things, blazoned as national."[28]

Taking the view that slavery required positive law to sanction its existence, Sumner maintained that the entire tenor of the Constitution argued against slavery. First, it is nowhere mentioned by name or sanctioned in a positive sense. Second, to the extent that slaves were mentioned, they were called persons. When the Constitution promised that no one would be deprived of life and liberty without due process of law, Africans and other persons of all races, reasoned Sumner, were meant to be included. "The word 'person' in the Constitution embraces every human being within its sphere, whether Caucasian, Indian, or African, from the President to the slave," Sumner noted. Since the Constitution was biased toward freedom and contained no positive affirmations of slavery, Sumner maintained that all legislation that committed the federal government to provide protection for slavery was unconstitutional. "The Constitution contains no power to make a king, or to support kingly rule," Sumner asserted. "With similar reason it may be said, that it contains no power to make a slave or to support a system of slavery . . . but if there be no such power, all national legislation upholding slavery must be unconstitutional and void." Denouncing the Fugitive Slave Laws of 1793 and 1850 as unconstitutional, Sumner had particular venom for the most recent act. "Sir, in the name of the Constitution which it violates; of my country which it dishonors; of humanity which it degrades; of Christianity which it offends, I arraign this enactment, and now hold it up to the judgment of the Senate and the world."[29]

In his early declarations on slavery, Sumner had used moral and constitutional reasons to denounce slavery. In June 1860, he employed a somewhat different approach in his "The Barbarism of Slavery." The constitutional and moral arguments were there, but Sumner also incorporated elements of some of the economic arguments against slavery—what historian Eric Foner has dubbed the "Free Labor" argument. Arguing that slavery was founded on violence, slavery, according to Sumner, gave rise to an inferior, barbaric civilization. "Barbarous in origin, barbarous in law, barbarous in the instruments it employs, barbarous in consequence, barbarous in spirit, barbarous wherever it shows itself, Slavery must breed Barbarians, while it develops everywhere alike in the individual and the society to which he belongs, the essential elements of Barbarism." Sumner went to great lengths to demonstrate the superiority of free institutions and society over those of slavery. Using numerous statistical illustrations, he strove to show the North's superiority in education, manufacturing, literacy, property values, and population—all the effects of abolishing slavery. "At every point is the character of Slavery more and more manifest, rising and dilating into an overshadowing Barbarism, darkening the whole land. Through its influence, population, values of all kinds, manufactures, commerce, railroads, canals, charities, the post-office, professional schools, academies, public schools, newspapers, periodicals, books, authorship, inventions, are all stunted, and, under a Government which profess[es] to be founded on the intelligence of the people, one in five of the native white adults in the region [of] Slavery is officially reported as unable to read and write."[30]

Slavery also had a negative impact on whites, which Sumner equated with the arrogant, lawless attitude of slave masters, including a pronounced propensity to violence and personal confrontation. Not only did slave owners have a disproportionate influence in the national government, but they also used that influence to quell free speech and silence all critics of the peculiar institution. Sumner then justified his charges by citing numerous examples in Congress where Southern slaveholders threatened violence, brandished weapons, or challenged Northern opponents to dueling. "It requires no special significance," Sumner told the Senate, "to estimate the insignificance of an argument that can be supported only by violence." "The sacred animosity of Freedom and Slavery can end only with the triumph of Freedom," Sumner predicted optimistically.[31]

Civil Rights

Many Republican political figures, reformers, and philanthropists believed that once the Thirteenth, Fourteenth, and Fifteenth Amendments to the Constitution were passed, the government's obligation to African Americans was fulfilled. The classic Republican free labor argument maintained that equality before the law was the only condition that government ought to provide its citizens. To take positive action to aid African Americans—

such as free land or special protective legislation—would amount to favoritism. To Sumner, such arguments ignored the fact that slavery had placed African Americans in a disadvantaged position. Accordingly, special provisions were necessary to bring about equality before the law.

Even before the war, Sumner had been an advocate of desegregation in the Boston public school system. During the war, he played an important role in repealing Jim Crow laws in the District of Columbia as well as bringing about provisions for equal pay for black soldiers. During Reconstruction, Sumner was a forceful advocate of black suffrage, arguing that color had nothing to do with citizenship and arguing that Northern states might have voluntarily adopted black suffrage had Republican leaders forcefully endorsed it. "The Opposition could never have triumphed on negro suffrage in any Northern state," Sumner bitterly told Hugh McCulloch, "if the Administration had not pointed the way, & encouraged it. The whole country was ready to accept the principles of the Declaration of Indep."[32]

In a February 5, 1869, speech before the Senate, Sumner provided a blunt statement of the principles that motivated his ideas on race and civil rights. Slavery had been replaced by caste, according to Sumner, a caste that was determined by the color of skin. Whereas the doctrine of state's rights previously shielded slavery, now it protected racial discrimination based on skin color. It was the responsibility of the national government to monitor the actions of states and prevent such specious justification for the deprivation of rights. As Sumner stated,

A Republic is where taxation and representation go hand in hand, where all are equal in rights, and no man is excluded from participation in the government, which is the duty of Congress to maintain. Here is a bountiful source of power that cannot be called into question. In the execution of the guaranty Congress may—nay, must—require that there shall be no Inequality, Caste, or Oligarchy of Skin.[33]

While numerous Republican colleagues retreated from the tenets of radicalism as Reconstruction dragged on into the 1870s, Sumner remained devoted to the cause of human equality. In 1870, he introduced a Civil Rights Act, a sweeping measure that banned discrimination in public accommodations, while providing for equal access to public transportation, education facilities, churches, as well as juries and cemeteries. A pet concern of Sumner, it was on his mind when he lay on his death bed and whispered to friend George Hoar, "You must take care of the civil rights bill . . . don't let it fail." As a tribute to Sumner, the Senate and the House eventually passed it, although the final version was a watered-down version of Sumner's bill. The Civil Rights Act of 1875, however, was quickly eroded and undermined by a number of important Reconstruction U.S. Supreme Court cases.[34]

CONCLUSION

Vain, self-righteous, condescending, and often insensitive to the feelings of others, Charles Sumner was a source of irritation to many of his Senate colleagues. Brazenly putting his principles on the side of right, he irritated and offended his Senate colleagues on numerous occasions. Unwillingly to compromise and often wildly unrealistic, Sumner was an ineffective legislator who, in over twenty years in the Senate, could take credit for few legislative achievements. Nevertheless, Sumner was often a voice of conscience for both his Senate colleagues and the nation at large. Boldly endorsing the antislavery cause in a hostile Senate, Sumner never backed down from positions he believed were right, regardless of personal consequences. His continued advocacy of black civil rights and suffrage during the Reconstruction period provides additional evidence of his devotion to principle. Eventually leaving the party that was so dear to him, Sumner ended his career an outcast. Isolated and without influence in the Senate, he went to his grave convinced of the essential rightness of his positions.

NOTES

1. Charles Sumner to Richard Monckton Milnes, July 31, 1840 in *The Selected Letters of Charles Sumner*, edited by Beverly Wilson Palmer (Boston: Northeastern University Press, 1990), 1:92; and Sumner to Francis Lieber, January 9, 1836, in *Selected Letters*, 1:18.

2. Sumner to Lieber, February 10, 1842, in *Selected Letters*, 1:109–110.

3. Sumner to Nathan Appleton, August 11, 1846, *Selected Letters*, 1:172.

4. Sumner to Salmon P. Chase, February 7, 1848, in *Selected Letters*, 1:206. The story of the Free Soil Party is told in Richard Sewell, *Ballots for Freedom: Antislavery Politics in the United States 1837–1860* (New York: Oxford University Press, 1976).

5. Sumner to Horace Mann, June 21, 1848, in *Selected Letters*, 1:233; and Sumner to Samuel Gridley Howe, August 27, 1850, in *Selected Letters*, 1:311.

6. Henry Wilson quote is from E.L. Pierce, *Memoirs and Letters of Charles Sumner* (Boston: Roberts Brothers, 1893), 3:288.

7. Sumner to John Bigelow, [August 30, 1852], in *Selected Letters*, 1:371.

8. Sumner to John Jay, January 21, 1854, in *Selected Letters*, 1:402; and Congressional *Globe*, Thirty-fourth Congress, First Session, 275–82.

9. Sumner to E. L. Pierce, March 8, 1854, in Pierce, *Memoirs*, 3:361–62; and Sumner to James Freeman Clarke, June 10, 1854, in *Selected Letters*, 1:412.

10. Sumner to Julius Rockwell, November 26, 1854, in *Selected Letters*, 1:423.

11. Sumner to Edward Everett Hale, March 13, 1856, in *Selected Letters*, 1:452; and Sumner to Chase, May 15, 1856, in *Selected Letters*, 456.

12. "The Crime against Kansas," in Charles Sumner, *His Complete Works* (New York: Negro University Press, 1969), 5:143–256 (quotes, 144, 149, 244).

13. "Crime against Kansas," 255–56.

14. Quotes from David Donald, *Charles Sumner and the Coming of the Civil War* (New York: Fawcett Columbine, 1960), 285–86, 289.

15. Illinois *State Register*, May 26, 1856, p. 2, col. 2.

16. Sumner to Chase, January 19, 1861, in *Selected Letters*, 2:44; and Sumner to Henry Wadsworth Longfellow, April 17, 1861, *Selected Letters*, 67.

17. Sumner to Wendell Phillips, August 8, 1861, in *Selected Letters*, 2:75. On Frémont's proclamation, see, for instance, William E. Parrish, *Frank Blair: Lincoln's Conservative* (Columbia: University of Missouri Press, 1997), 121–22.

18. Sumner to John Bright, November 18, 1862, in *Selected Letters*, 2:131.

19. Sumner to Orestes Brownson, December 27, 1863, *Selected Letters*, 2:216.

20. Sumner to the duke of Argyll, May 10, 1863, in *Selected Letters*, 2:170.

21. Sumner to John Bright, September 27, 1864, in *Selected Letters*, 2:252–53.

22. Sumner to Bright, April 24, 1865, in *Selected Letters*, 2:297.

23. Quoted from Sumner to Peleg W. Chandler, January 3, 1865 [1866], in *Selected Letters*, 2:352.

24. Sumner to Edward Atchinson, June 3, 1868, in *Selected Letters*, 2: 430.

25. Sumner to Gerrit Smith, August 20, 1871, in *Selected Letters*, 2:570.

26. Sumner to George Sumner, July 31, 1847, in *Selected Letters*, 1:192; Sumner to Mann, June 21, 1848, in *Selected Letters*, 1: 233; and Sumner to Mann, August 5, 1850, in *Selected Letters*, 307.

27. "Slavery and the Mexican War," in *Complete Works*, 1:333–51 (quote, 335–36).

28. Congressional *Globe*, Thirty-second Congress, First Session, 1102–13 (quote, 1103).

29. Congressional *Globe*, 1106.

30. "The Barbarism of Slavery," in *Complete Works*, 6:127, 159.

31. "The Barbarism of Slavery," in *Complete Works*, 6:210, 236.

32. Sumner to Hugh McCulloch, August 28, 1865, in *Selected Letters*, 2:329.

33. Charles Sumner, "Powers of Congress to Prohibit Inequality, Caste, and Oligarchy of the Skin," in *Complete Works*, 17:34–51 (quote, 43).

34. David Donald, *Charles Sumner & the Rights of Man* (New York: Alfred A. Knopf, 1970), 586.

FURTHER READING

Frederick Blue, *Charles Sumner and the Conscience of the North* (Arlington Heights, IL: Harlan Davidson, 1994); David Donald, *Charles Sumner and the Coming of the Civil War* (New York: Fawcett Columbine, 1960); idem., *Charles Sumner & the Rights of Man* (New York: Alfred A. Knopf, 1970); Archibald H. Grimke, *The Life of Charles Sumner* (New York: Funk & Wagnall Co., 1892); Storey Moorefield, *Charles Sumner* (Boston: Houghton Mifflin Co., 1900); and E. L. Pierce, *Memoirs and Letters of Charles Sumner*, 4 vols. (Boston: Roberts Brothers, 1893).

CLEMENT LAIRD VALLANDIGHAM
(1820–1871)

Leader of a "Respectable Minority"

LIFE

Clement Laird Vallandigham (Va-land-ig-ham) was born on July 29, 1820, at New Lisbon, Ohio. He was the third son of the Reverend Clement Vallandigham and Rebecca Laird Vallandigham. The elder Vallandigham was the descendant of Michael Van Lendegham, who immigrated to Virginia in 1690 from Flanders. A generation later, Michael's son (also named Michael) changed the family name to Vallandigham. This Michael Vallandigham then left Virginia for Western Pennsylvania and more promising farming. Clement Vallandigham Sr. was the second son of Michael's son, George, who was also a Revolutionary War veteran.

The elder Clement Vallandigham attended Jefferson College in Cannonsburg, Pennsylvania, where he was trained for the Presbyterian ministry. In 1807, he married Rebecca Laird, the daughter of a Scots-Irish family. The couple then moved to New Lisbon, Ohio (in Columbiana County), where Clement became pastor of the Presbyterian Church. A strict Calvinist with a strong sense of duty and obligation, Clement Sr. instilled this sense of duty into his offspring—particularly in his third son, Clement Laird.

Named after his mother's Scotch-Irish descendants, Clement Laird Vallandigham was educated in a classical school that his father ran in the Vallandigham home. Although the young Vallandigham enjoyed fishing, hunting, and other boyhood diversions, he was a serious scholar who, according to his brother James, sometimes spent as much as twelve hours a day studying Greek, Latin, and classical literature. His classical studies provided an excellent preparation for college. Like his father, Clement Laird also matriculated to Jefferson College, beginning his education in 1837. After a year of study, the family's financial circumstances forced him to leave college and take a position as school teacher in Snow Hill, Maryland, a position Vallandigham held until 1840, when he resumed his studies at Jefferson College.

Perhaps more than any of his siblings, Clement Laird inherited his father's discipline, moral firmness, and sense of duty. For instance, after his return to college in 1840, Vallandigham was expelled after he quarreled with its president over an issue in constitutional law. A few years later, the president realized the foolishness of the quarrel and invited Vallandigham to receive his diploma by merely making an application for it to the college faculty. The proud Vallandigham refused the offer and never received a college degree.

After leaving Jefferson College, Vallandigham returned to New Lisbon, where he devoted himself to the study of law, reading in the office of his older brother, James. Admitted to the bar in 1842, Clement was an able lawyer, whose love of study and research gave him an edge over many of his fellow attorneys. Vallandigham was also an able orator and seemed aptly suited for a political career. Although his Protestant upbringing and support for causes such as temperance might suggest political principles sympathetic to the Whig Party, Vallandigham entered politics as a fervent Jacksonian Democrat, endorsing strict construction of the Constitution, free trade, and the support of agriculture as opposed to manufacturing and commercial interests. While he did regard slavery as wrong in an abstract moral sense, Vallandigham was a bitter opponent of abolitionism, which he regarded as a revolutionary and dangerous doctrine.

Vallandigham won a seat in the Ohio state legislature in 1845 and was reelected the following year. Eventually, the ambitious Vallandigham sought a more promising environment for his goals and relocated to the larger town of Dayton, Ohio, in early 1847. Perhaps the need to expand professional opportunities increased because of his marriage to Louisa A. McMahon on August 27, 1846. A native of Cumberland, Maryland, Louisa was a devoted wife; however, through the years, frequent illness and bouts of depression caused her husband considerable concern. The couple would have one son, Charles, born in 1854.

The new Dayton resident applied himself principally to his law practice, something that paid handsome financial dividends and allowed the purchase of a substantial home located at 323 1st Street—then a fashionable residential area in Dayton. After moving to Dayton, Vallandigham also bought a financial stake in the Democratic Dayton *Empire* from law partner Thomas J. S. Smith. The decision proved to be a sound financial investment for the young attorney, who was also gaining a favorable reputation for his courtroom victories. Politics, however, was never far from Vallandigham's mind, although the young attorney's initial attempts at public office were largely frustrated in his early years in Dayton. In 1850, he lost an election for judge of the Court of Common Pleas. He then ran unsuccessfully for lieutenant governor and two times for the Third Congressional District seat in the U.S. House of Representatives. In 1852 and 1854, Vallandigham lost to Whig candidate Lewis D. Campbell. When nominated by the local Democratic Party again in 1856, Vallandigham ran an extremely competitive race against Campbell only to be defeated narrowly in the general election. Rumors of voting fraud, however, prompted Vallandigham to challenge the election results in the House of Representatives. After a lengthy investigation, on May 25, 1857, the House Committee of Elections upheld Vallandigham's challenge. Reelected by narrow margins in 1858 and 1860, Vallandigham would make the most of his relatively short congressional career.

In the House, Vallandigham supported Stephen Douglas and popular sovereignty. He followed the Little Giant's leadership during the controversy over Kansas and the Lecompton Constitution. Like Douglas, Vallandigham believed that the slavery controversy was becoming a dangerous abstraction; he condemned Northern and Southern radicals, urging conciliation, common sense, and appeals to the political center. In an August 1858 speech in Detroit, Michigan, Vallandigham told his audience: "Men of the North and West have been taught to hate the men of the South, and Southerners have been taught to hate the men of the North and West. This Northern sectionalism and fanaticism has been approaching nearer and nearer to Mason and Dixon's line, while the Southern fanaticism, starting in the Cotton States, has been creeping northwardly, until the two factions have nearly met. What will be the inevitable result of the conflict that must ensue? They must meet if the floods of fanaticism be not checked."[1]

Despite Vallandigham's appeals for moderation, the success of the avowedly sectional Republican Party unsettled the Dayton Democrat. Increasingly, Vallandigham began to place a disproportionate blame on abolitionists and the Republican Party for the nation's problems as opposed to Southern fire-eaters. When John Brown's ill-advised raid on Harpers Ferry failed, Vallandigham traveled to Harpers Ferry on his way home to Ohio to interview the eccentric abolitionist. Vallandigham's intention was to uncover evidence of organized abolitionists' sponsorship of Brown's raid. The wily Brown, however, would not take the bait and Vallandigham returned emptyhanded, although he earned the abuse of numerous Republican papers that accused him of trying to profit politically from Brown's raid.

Elected by his colleagues as secretary of the Democratic Party, Vallandigham was on hand for the disruption of the party at the April 1860 convention at Charleston. Believing that only a united Democratic Party could avert civil war, Vallandigham nevertheless backed Douglas entirely in his dispute with the Southern wing of the Democratic Party. He campaigned enthusiastically for the Little Giant in Michigan, Ohio, and New York. In his native state, Vallandigham faced a challenge from Republican nominee Samuel Craighead. Undoubtedly the high point of the campaign was a visit to Dayton by the Little Giant on September 23, as Vallandigham shared the platform at the Court House Square with the more popular Illinois senator.

Although Vallandigham was elected to his third term in Congress, the election of Abraham Lincoln made him pessimistic about the country's future. Upon returning to Washington in early December for the opening of the last session of the Thirty-sixth Congress, Vallandigham wrote his wife, "They who some centuries hence shall read the history of these times, will be amazed at the folly and blindness of us who live and act now." As congressional moderates put forth a series of compromise measures to mediate sectional tensions, it became increasingly clear that Republicans and Deep South senators were against any compromise. Vallandigham became convinced, however, that congressional Republicans were the real culprits. "Every day proves still more clearly," he wrote his wife on Christmas Eve, 1860, "that it is the fixed purpose of the Republican party not only to refuse all compromise, but to force a *civil war*."[2]

On the subject of war, the Dayton Democrat had already publicly expressed his opposition to all forms of coercion. In a speech given at the famous Cooper's Institute in New York City, Vallandigham declared, "*I never would as a Representative in the Congress of the United States vote one dollar of money whereby one drop of American blood should be shed in a civil war.*" To his congressional colleagues, he declared on December 22, 1860, "*I am all over and altogether a Union man. I would preserve it in all its integrity and worth. But I repeat that this cannot be done by coercion—by the sword.*"[3]

In early 1861, when it was obvious that the Crittenden compromise proposals as well as the Washington Peace Conference had failed, Vallandigham introduced his own compromise proposals in the form of three amendments to the Constitution. The first, a proposed Thirteenth Amendment, was a variation on John C. Calhoun's notion of a concurrent majorities. It divided the nation into four sections: North, South, West, and Pacific. Each section would have an equal number of electors, and the nation's president and vice president could be elected only if a majority of electors from *each* section agreed. The proposed Fourteenth Amendment would have allowed for secession if all the states in a section agreed on it. Finally, the proposed Fifteenth Amendment guaranteed equal rights to all citizens in federal territories, including slaveholders—thus granting the Deep South the moral equivalent of a federal slave code. Predictably Republicans in Congress did not seriously consider Vallandigham's proposals, which died as Congress adjourned in early March just prior to Lincoln's inauguration.[4]

Vallandigham was skeptical of Lincoln's inaugural address, arguing that he could not determine whether the president was for war or for peace. However, when the firing on Fort Sumter took place on April 12, he resisted the tide of public opinion that supported war and stuck to the position that he had articulated since the fall of 1860. When Lincoln called upon the states for 75,000 men to put down the rebellion, Vallandigham publicly commented, "I will not vote to sustain or ratify—never! Millions for defense; not a dollar or a man for aggressive and offensive civil war." During the meeting of the special session of Congress in July 1861, Vallandigham stood almost alone in his opposition to the war. Denouncing many of President Lincoln's actions during May and June—suspending the writ of habeas corpus and increasing the size of the regular army, for instance—as unconstitutional, Vallandigham introduced a number of resolutions criticizing the president for unconstitutional actions. Both Republicans and Democrats joined to table the resolution. Undaunted, Vallandigham persisted in his criticism of the war. "I am for *peace*, speedy, immediate, honorable PEACE, with all its blessings," he told the House of Representatives.[5]

During the first regular session of the Thirty-seventh Congress, Vallandigham continued his opposition to the war. During the winter of 1861–1862, dissatisfaction with Republican policy toward slavery began to slowly erode Democratic support for the war. Beginning with the repeal of the Crittenden-Johnson resolution in December 1861, Lincoln and the Republican Congress began chipping away at the peculiar institution with such proposals as abolishing slavery in Washington, D.C.; forbidding army officers to return fugitive slaves to masters; and finally the president's own proposal for compensated emancipation in the border states. Sensing an opportunity, in the spring of 1862, Vallandigham organized a group of congressional Democrats that formulated "An Address of the Democratic Members of Congress to the Democracy of the United States." Urging conciliation and compromise toward the South, the document emphasized respect for civil liberties and states' rights, and criticized what were perceived as the revolutionary excesses of the Lincoln administration. While hardly representing the majority of Democrats in Congress, the address was, at least, an indication that Vallandigham was no longer a "voice in the wilderness" with respect to his position on the war.[6]

To his fellow Democrats, Vallandigham's views on the war were often annoying and embarrassing. Subject to a regular stream of abuse and ridicule from Republican newspaper editors, particularly in his native state of Ohio, Vallandigham's every action was watched with a critical eye. On the streets of Dayton, he was subject to occasional insults and abuse. Vallandigham and a group of Dayton Democrats met most nights at the office of the Dayton *Empire*. As a result, Republican leaders and editors began to brand these as meetings of the Knights of the Golden Circle, a much exaggerated secret society whose aim and purpose was to aid the Confederacy. Likewise, when Democrats such as Vallandigham refused to unite with War Democrats and Republican in a Union Party, the Dayton congressman and like-minded Democrats were denounced as unpatriotic. As early as the fall elections of 1861, Republican newspaper editors popularized rumors about Democratic treason and association with the Knights of the Golden Circle.[7]

Vallandigham's Republican colleagues in Congress frequently accused him of disloyalty. Vallandigham did not take such accusations lightly. When radical Republican Senator Benjamin F. Wade denounced Vallandigham as a traitor in a speech in Washington, D.C., the Ohio congressman used the House of Representatives to reply to his Republican antagonist. Gaining the floor on April 24, 1862, Vallandigham read a portion of Wade's speech to the House. He then uttered the following words: "Now, Sir, here in my place in the House, as a Representative I denounce . . . the author of that speech as a liar, a scoundrel, and a coward. His name is BENJAMIN F. WADE." House Republicans objected and eventually tried to censure Vallandigham for his remarks, an attempt that proved unsuccessful.[8]

While Vallandigham and his message were largely ignored early on in the war, by the summer and fall of 1862 his message seemed to resonate throughout the Midwest and other areas of the country that were traditionally Democratic strongholds. His message of peace and compromise was particularly popular because of the abysmal state of the war, particularly the failure of General George McClellan and the Army of the Potomac in the Peninsula campaign in the spring and summer of 1862. But there were other reasons. Undoubtedly Republican policy on slavery did much to alienate Democrats and cause them to question their commitment to the war. In the summer of 1862, Congress passed the Second Confiscation Act, which provided for the freedom of African American slaves seized from owners who were loyal to the Confederacy. After the battle of Antietam, Lincoln would further alienate Democrats when he issued his preliminary Emancipation Proclamation. To Democrats, this bolstered Vallandigham's charge that the war was being waged for the abolition of slavery, not the restoration of the Union.[9]

But emancipation was only one of many issues that revitalized Democratic opposition. For well over a year, prominent and not-so-prominent Democrats had languished in jail for expressing criticism of the war. Lincoln had raised eyebrows in May 1861 when he suspended the writ of habeas corpus for a portion of the country. A general suspension of the writ on September 23, 1862, raised howls of protest. Democrats feared that the Civil War would cause the loss of republican traditions and values. Western sectionalism also helped fuel Democratic dissent. Vallandigham and other peace Democrats believed that the Republicans were using the war to satiate the interests of New England capitalists. These western sectionalists could point to such pieces of Republican legislation as the Morrill tariff, the highest tariff in the history of the Republic. Exacerbating the fears of Democrats was the closing of the Mississippi River, which destroyed antebellum trade relationships with the South and subjected mid-western farmers to higher transportation costs as a result of rising railroad rates. For many midwestern Democrats, it seemed as if the agricultural interests of the West were being deliberately sacrificed as a result of the war.[10]

In the fall elections of 1862, the Democratic Party scored a significant number of gains, capturing more seats in the House of Representatives, the legislatures of Indiana and Illinois, as well as the important governorships of New York and New Jersey. Ironically, Vallandigham, the man who arguably did the most to state the Democratic case, went down to defeat. However, his defeat was the result of the Ohio Republican legislature's gerrymandering of his district. Republicans took Preble County, which was equally divided between Democrats and Republicans, out of Vallandigham's district and replaced it with strongly Republican Warren County. This action doomed the Dayton Democrat in the fall election, as veteran Ohio politician and soldier General Robert Schenck defeated Vallandigham in a close race. Setting aside personal disappointment, Vallandigham was encouraged with the overall results of the fall election, and he returned to Washington determined to state his message of peace and conciliation with new vigor.[11]

During the last session of the Thirty-seventh Congress, Clement Vallandigham was a persistent critic of the Lincoln administration and an advocate of peace and reconciliation. Bolstered by the devastating Union defeat at Fredericksburg in December 1862, Vallandigham introduced six separate resolutions, all detailing the failures of the president's policies. On December 22, Vallandigham introduced a resolution calling for the immediate cessation of hostilities and the beginning of peace talks with a view toward mediating all differences between the regions and eventual reunion. Rejected by Republicans in Congress, Vallandigham began working on a major speech to state his views to the nation.

Vallandigham's speech was delivered before packed galleries on January 14, 1863. The current state of the war, argued Vallandigham, demonstrated the failure of Republican policy. Despite millions of dollars and materials expended as well as thousands of lives sacrificed, this war policy was no closer to reuniting the country than at the outset of the war. The people of his section wanted peace, Vallandigham argued, and if the Republicans persisted in their perverse war policy, the Northwest might strike out on its own. War had failed; it was time for compromise and reunion.[12]

Predictably Vallandigham's speech generated a good deal of attention in the press; however, it had little effect on Lincoln's determination to carry the war through. Closing out his congressional term with critical comments on the conscription bill, Vallandigham returned to Dayton as a private citizen. His return was marked by a Democratic rally, where the former congressman delivered a scathing rebuke of the Lincoln administration. For those Republicans who hoped Vallandigham's defeat would silence him, this was a bad omen. And with the help of Ambrose Burnside, Union commander of the Department of the Ohio, Vallandigham would rise to new heights of popularity in the months ahead.[13]

Concerned that Republican power was a threat to constitutional liberties, Vallandigham spoke frequently in Ohio and other parts of the country. The tone of his speeches became increasingly critical of administration policy on civil rights and free speech. A catalyst for Vallandigham's activities was a series of orders issued by Ambrose Burnside for the Department of Ohio. Most prominent was General Order #38, which threatened to punish and imprison individuals who were in the habit of criticizing the government. "The Administration Abolition party is thoroughly consolidated, and unquestionably it is now contending solely for the *unity and a strong centralized government through war*," Vallandigham remarked to one correspondent, "*and, failing in this, then disunion.*"[14]

When Vallandigham and several other prominent Democrats—including Samuel S. Cox, Daniel W. Voorhees, and George Pendleton—were scheduled to speak at Mount Vernon, Ohio, Burnside had several men stationed in the audience to record the speakers' comments. Vallandigham did not disappoint. In fact, he delivered a two-hour diatribe, ridiculing the military proclamations of both Burnside and Department of Indiana Commander Henry Carrington. To thunderous applause, Vallandigham expressed his determination to spit upon the proclamations of Burnside. He would not recognize General Order #38 or any other such military proclamation under the authority of General Order #1: the Constitution of the United States. "The sooner the people inform the minions of usurped power . . . that they will not submit to such restrictions, the better," Vallandigham told his audience.[15]

Once Burnside's men reported back to the general at his Cincinnati headquarters, the departmental commander was determined to arrest the Dayton Democrat and bring him before a military tribunal on charges of violating General Order #38. On the evening of May 4, a small group of soldiers, under the command of Captain Charles G. Hutton, took a late train into Dayton from Cincinnati. Quickly setting out for Vallandigham's home on 1st Street, the soldiers knocked on the door and awoke the former congressman and his family. When Vallandigham refused to grant the soldiers admission, they forcibly broke down the door. The soldiers pursued a retreating Vallandigham into his home amidst the shrieks of his frightened wife. Hoping to attract attention to his plight, Vallandigham fired a gun out the window. Eventually pinned in an interior room with no escape, he eventually surrendered with the words, "You have now broken open my house and over powered me by superior force, and I am obliged to surrender." Quickly boarding the next train to Cincinnati, the soldiers, Vallandigham in tow, were out of town about thirty minutes after arriving.

Vallandigham was deposited at Kemper barracks while he awaited his trial.[16]

The trial that awaited Vallandigham was little more than a formality, as the military tribunal, headed by Brigadier General Robert Potter, was composed of men who were under Burnside's command. Charged with violating General Order #38, Vallandigham's initial strategy was to refuse to enter a plea on the grounds that a military court was inappropriate for the trial of a civilian. Potter thwarted this strategy by entering a not guilty plea for the defendant. Before the trial began, Vallandigham was granted a brief recess to confer with attorneys George Pugh, George Pendleton, and Alexander Ferguson. The trial took two days, and Vallandigham conducted his own defense. To have allowed his lawyers to be present would have given the proceedings undeserved legitimacy. The prosecution presented two witnesses who were present at the Mount Vernon rally, H. R. Hill and John A. Means. Vallandigham also questioned Samuel Cox. The result was a foregone conclusion. Vallandigham was found guilty and sentenced to confinement for the duration of the war. To protest the illegitimacy of the proceedings, Vallandigham submitted a formal protest denying that he had done anything against the Constitution and questioning the legitimacy of a military trial. In addition, his lawyers also filed a writ of habeas corpus with Judge Leavitt of the U.S. Court, Southern District. Leavitt, however, refused to recognize the writ, probably not wanting to alienate General Burnside.

Watching from Washington, D.C., the Lincoln administration was not entirely pleased with Burnside's actions. In a Cabinet meeting on May 19, the majority of Lincoln's advisors believed that Burnside had erred. While Burnside had determined that Vallandigham's imprisonment would take place at Fort Warren, Boston Harbor, one Cabinet member suggested banishment to the Confederacy. Worried that the outspoken Ohio Democrat would become a lightning rod for dissatisfied Democrats throughout the country, this option appealed to Lincoln. This would have the effect of portraying the dissenter as a supporter of Jefferson Davis and might squelch the rising tide of public sentiment in Vallandigham's favor. So, over General Burnside's protest, Secretary of War Edwin Stanton turned over the prisoner to Army of the Cumberland Commander William Rosecrans, with instructions to put Vallandigham through to Confederate lines near Murfreesboro, Tennessee.

Once Vallandigham was in the custody of Confederate General Braxton Bragg, the Confederate government had a dilemma. What were they to do with such an unusual prisoner? He had not come willingly across lines, nor was he in sympathy with the rebellion. In fact, Vallandigham's position was based on reunion through peace, not recognition of the Confederacy. The premise of the Confederacy was to deny reunion and assert independence as a sine qua non. In consultation with Richmond, Bragg directed to send the prisoner to Lynchburg, Virginia. There the Davis administration directed General Robert Ould, commissioner of prisoner exchanges, to interview the so-called prisoner. After Vallandigham was interviewed, he was allowed to leave the Confederacy via a blockade-runner (from Wilmington, North Carolina), and eventually worked his way to Niagara Falls, Canada, staying at a local hotel, the Clifton House.

The real story, however, was in Ohio. Vallandigham's arrest invigorated the peace faction of the Democratic Party. In early May, from his prison cell in Cincinnati, Vallandigham penned a letter entitled "To the Democracy of Ohio." "I am here in a military bastile," he wrote on May 5, 1863, "for no other offense than my political opinions, and the defence of them and of the rights of the people, and of your constitutional liberties." Later, on May 23, Vallandigham offered the following advice: "I will not doubt that the people of Ohio, cowering not a moment before the threats of arbitrary power, will, in every trial, prove themselves worthy to be called freemen." The fact that General Burnside had put Montgomery County under martial law after angry Vallandigham supporters sacked and vandalized the offices of the Republican *Dayton Journal* gave substance to the prisoner's accusations. With the embarrassing defeat of Union forces at Chancellorsville on May 2–3 and the inactivity of both Rosecrans's and Grant's armies in the West, many Ohio Democrats began to believe that the only real casualties of the war might be their constitutional liberties.[17]

Democratic Party leaders were wary of Vallandigham's rising popularity and wanted to stop his potential gubernatorial nomination at the party's state convention at Columbus in July. In fact, most party leaders wanted to renominate unsuccessful 1862 candidate Hugh C. Jewett, but party leaders were unable to control the delegates at the convention. They unanimously endorsed Vallandigham to oppose Republican nominee John Brough.

From the Clifton House in Niagara, along with his wife, son Charles, and numerous political friends, Vallandigham accepted the nomination in another public letter entitled "To the Democracy of Ohio." Not yet confident that he could return to Ohio to campaign, Vallandigham was content to watch developments from Canada and allow his political allies to campaign for him. Unfortunately for Vallandigham, Union victories at Gettysburg and Vicksburg stemmed the high tide of the antiwar feeling in the North. Vallandigham lost the October election to Brough by 100,000 votes. While he accepted defeat, Vallandigham believed he had won a more important battle. "You were beaten," he told Ohio Democrats, "but a nobler battle for constitutional liberty and free popular government never was fought by any people." The gubernatorial nomination was the high point of Vallandigham's nationwide popularity. While he remained active in politics and influential, the degree of his influence would never again compare with this popularity in the summer of 1863.[18]

Remaining in Canada until the summer of 1864, Vallandigham was the object of much attention at the Clifton House in Niagara, so much so that he eventually moved to Windsor, where he would be near the solidly Democratic stronghold of Detroit, Michigan. Worried federal agents tracked his every move and reported faithfully to General Burnside. In Windsor, Vallandigham was visited by numerous Democratic leaders, including representatives of the newly organized Sons of Liberty. Formed to offset the propaganda of the Republican-sponsored Union leagues, the Sons of Liberty was a secret society, complete with elaborate rituals. Its primary methods were political and aimed at Democratic victory at the ballot box; however, a small group of dissidents including Indiana Democrats Harrison H. Dodd and Lambdin Milligan were convinced that violent methods and even active cooperation with the Confederacy were necessary to defeat the tyranny of the Republican Party. While Vallandigham was skeptical of secret societies and regarded the organization's rituals as unnecessary, even comical, he did agree to serve in the official capacity of "supreme grand commander" for one year. While Republicans made much of this association and played the treason card routinely, in reality Vallandigham's connection with the group was a mere formality. He played little role in the affairs of the organization, and the suggestion that he was a participant in treasonous activities is untrue.

Vallandigham's principal goal for 1864 was to get back into the United States so that he could use his influence in selecting the Democratic nominee to oppose Lincoln's reelection. To accomplish this, Vallandigham finally gathered up enough nerve to return to Ohio. A disguised Vallandigham crossed the border into Detroit and made his way toward Hamilton, Ohio. Vallandigham timed his return to Ohio with a surprise appearance at the Montgomery County Democratic Convention, held at Hamilton, Ohio, where he electrified delegates with an address that featured pointed criticisms of Ambrose Burnside and the Lincoln administration.

For the Democrats, the major event of the summer was the party's convention, which took place in Chicago at the end of August. Overlooked as a delegate-at-large by the Ohio State Convention, Vallandigham was chosen as a delegate by the Third Congressional District. His principal aim was to influence the platform as well as to derail the candidacy of George McClellan. For peace Democrats such as Vallandigham and New York's Fernando Wood, McClellan was a war candidate, committed to restoring the Union through military force, while Vallandigham and many peace Democrats argued for a cessation of hostilities and then peaceable reunion.

At the opening of the convention in Chicago, it was apparent that the divided state of the party might seriously hamper the Democrats. McClel-

lan, the favorite, had no problem securing the nomination; and principal
McClellan backer Samuel S. Cox did secure a pledge from Vallandigham
to support the nominee. As a concession to the peace wing of the party,
Vallandigham was given a seat on the important Committee of Resolutions,
charged with composing the party platform. Most controversial was the
second resolution, authored by Vallandigham and Dr. John McElwee. It declared that the attempt to restore the Union by force had failed and that
an armistice should be declared, a convention of states held, and all outstanding issues between the North and South adjudicated. While controversial, the convention nevertheless adopted the platform. However, when
McClellan repudiated the controversial peace plank in his acceptance letter, Vallandigham's support for the nominee wavered. In the end, however,
Vallandigham reasoned that the "Young Napoleon" was preferable to Lincoln and actively campaigned for the Democratic nominee.[19]

While Democrats had gone into the fall campaign confident that Lincoln
would not be reelected, a number of actions and events quickly tempered
Democratic optimism. The Democrats' own action at the Chicago convention was significant. Republicans ridiculed the party as featuring a war candidate on a peace platform—a strategy that paid dividends. Equally
important were changing military fortunes. During the summer of 1864,
Grant's high casualties in Virginia and the failure of Sherman to deliver a
knockout punch in Georgia contributed to war weariness. By the fall, however, the situation had changed. Sherman had taken Atlanta, David Farragut had taken Mobile Bay, while Grant was increasing his pressure on
Robert E. Lee's Army of Northern Virginia in the trenches near Petersburg,
Virginia. Finally, provisions for the voting of soldiers was guaranteed to
give the Republican ticket a decided advantage. With Lincoln's reelection
in November 1864, Vallandigham's hope of peaceful reunion was crushed,
as was his hope for a return to the republic of antebellum times.

After the war, Vallandigham returned to his law practice. Although he
continued to harbor political ambitions, he was never again elected to public office. While he was a vociferous critic of Lincoln during the war, he
tended to favor the more moderate sixteenth president against the radical
Republicans during the initial phases of the debate over political Reconstruction of the South, and he expressed shock and genuine remorse when
he learned of Lincoln's assassination in April 1865.

The Democratic Party after the war was plagued by charges of disloyalty.
Republican campaign strategy of "waving the bloody shirt" predominated
in many political races irrespective of the positions taken by candidates. Understandably, Vallandigham's positions during the war played a major role
in this Republican strategy and provide an important clue as to why the
Ohio Democrat never again won elective office, despite aspirations to the
Senate seats of both John Sherman and Benjamin F. Wade. Indeed, nothing
better illustrates the controversy surrounding Vallandigham than his sup-

port and participation in the so-called arm-in-arm convention in Philadelphia in the summer of 1866. A movement of Democrats and conservative Republican supporters of Andrew Johnson, the convention was an attempt to create a new political alliance of the center, providing an alternative to the controversial Reconstruction policies of the radical Republicans. Vallandigham was named as a representative of the Third Ohio Congressional District; however, fellow Ohio politicians Hugh Jewett and Lewis D. Campbell worked behind the scenes to have the convention adopt a resolution of censure against the former Ohio congressman. Worried that the association with prominent Copperheads such as Vallandigham would discredit the new political organization, Jewett and Campbell wanted to distance the organization from such individuals as Vallandigham. To save face, Vallandigham, who was ill and suffering from dysentery, decided not to attend the convention in exchange for having the resolution of censure dropped.

To engineer his own political comeback and restore credibility to the Democratic Party, Vallandigham endorsed a new political philosophy called the "New Departure." In essence, Vallandigham was ready to concede the controversial political issues of the Civil War to the Republican Party. There was no sense in debating the issue of emancipation or the passage of the postwar amendments. Instead, the party ought to focus on new issues, such as monetary reform, and pursue them with the same zeal and fire as the old, antebellum Democratic Party.

Vallandigham's attempt at a political comeback was cut short by his untimely death on June 16, 1871. While defending a local rowdy, Thomas McGehan, on murder charges, Vallandigham attempted to show the jury how the murder victim had accidentally shot himself. Somehow the lawyer got his weapons mixed up, and when he pulled the trigger of what he thought was an unloaded gun, the gun fired and Vallandigham exclaimed to the jury, "My God, I've shot myself!" A mere twelve hours later, the controversial Ohio Democrat was dead. Buried in Woodland cemetery in Dayton, Vallandigham's funeral was attended by numerous political luminaries including Samuel Cox, Salmon Chase, George Pugh, and numerous unnamed Ohio Democrats. It was an unexpected ending to an unusual political career.

PRINCIPAL IDEAS

Political Philosophy

Clement Vallandigham began politics as a Jacksonian Democrat and never deviated from that course in his public life. Devoted to states' rights and a strict construction of the Constitution, he was skeptical of unwarranted assumptions of power on the part of the federal government. As a Jacksonian Democrat, he was perpetually critical of government measures to promote industrial and commercial development. In many respects, he had a Jeffersonian devotion to farming and agricultural interests—something that he regarded as more fundamental to the concerns of his constituents. His was a backward-looking, almost nostalgic desire for the country to remain devoted to small agricultural concerns and only marginally concerned with industrial and financial development. Vallandigham called himself a western sectionalist, and he sought to advance the agricultural interests of his constituents as opposed to the manufacturing and commercial interests of the East.

Steeped in the writings of English philosopher Edmund Burke, Vallandigham was a conservative who was devoted to stability, order, and tradition. For this reason, he was a bitter critic and opponent of abolitionism. As early as 1850, Vallandigham publicly announced his opposition to slavery; however, since the Constitution granted Southern states the right to maintain the peculiar institution, abolitionists, maintained Vallandigham, wanted something that was unjust to the South. In 1855, Vallandigham told a Dayton audience, "Patriotism above mock philanthropy; the Constitution before any miscalled higher laws of morals or religion; and the Union of more value than many negroes." To Vallandigham, the abolitionists' appeal to a higher law was unacceptable and potentially destabilizing.[20]

Vallandigham's political opinions were fairly typical of the antebellum Democratic Party; however, the tenacity with which Vallandigham held his principles and his unwillingness to compromise, even when unpopular, certainly made him unique among nineteenth-century American political leaders—Republican or Democrat.

Peace through Compromise and Conciliation

Clement Vallandigham went to his grave believing the course that he had pursued in the Civil War was correct. Since the Lincoln administration chose to pursue war as a means of restoring the Union, Vallandigham could argue that his philosophy of peace and reunion was never seriously pursued. While Republicans argued that they had restored the Union, Vallandigham could point to the bloody consequences of this policy. Ironically, throughout his political career, Vallandigham certainly was no pacifist. He had supported the Mexican War. Why did he pursue a different course with respect to the Civil War? Precisely because it was a civil war, with region pitted against region, state pitted against state, and brother fighting against brother. The Mexican War was between two different peoples and cultures. The Civil War, conversely, was a war between what had been equal states in a political Union. The best approach to end a family quarrel was through reason, reconciliation, and a return to the status quo antebellum.

Probably the best statement of Vallandigham's position on the war is contained in one of his last congressional speeches, delivered to the House of

Representatives on January 14, 1863. Vallandigham placed the blame for the war squarely on the Republican Party. Motivated by fanatical abolitionism, Republicans could not accept the fact that the nation had existed half slave and half free for over three-quarters of a century. Hence, when the secession crisis erupted, Republicans abandoned the policy of conciliation pursued by President Buchanan and deliberately fomented the Civil War. For Vallandigham, there was no "irrepressible conflict" between the North and South, between free and slave labor. "There is not an 'irrepressible conflict' between slave labor and free labor," Vallandigham asserted. "There is no conflict at all. Both exist together in perfect harmony in the South . . . the fundamental idea of the Constitution is the perfect and eternal compatibility of the union of States 'part slave and part free.' "[21]

Not only had the Republican Party inaugurated civil war on behalf of abolition, but the war policy, argued Vallandigham, had also been a miserable failure. With the recent defeat at Fredericksburg in the immediate background, Vallandigham believed that the Confederacy could not be conquered. "Twenty, sixty, ninety, three hundred, six hundred days have passed; a thousand millions have been expended; and three hundred thousand lives lost or bodies mangled," Vallandigham maintained, "and to-day the confederate flag is still near the Potomac and the Ohio, and the confederate government stronger, many times, that at the beginning." For Vallandigham, all hope of military victory over the Confederacy was a dangerous illusion that would simply cost more dollars and lives.[22]

Yet if the Confederacy, as Vallandigham maintained, was perfectly capable of maintaining its independence, what possible inducements might bring about the peaceable reunion that he envisioned? Certainly at the war's beginning, one might argue, the philosophy of conciliation, rigorously pursued, might have prevented the outbreak of hostilities, particularly if reasonable compromise measures could have been negotiated that protected the slavery to the satisfaction of the South; however, once hostilities erupted and war had been waged for almost two years, how did Vallandigham envision peaceable Reconstruction? The Ohio Democrat believed that it was necessary that Northern radical abolitionism be replaced by a more latitudinarian conservatism that was comfortable and tolerant of sectional differences. "The price of the Union," Vallandigham argued, "is the utter suppression of the abolitionism or anti-slavery as a political element, and the complete subordination of the spirit of fanaticism and intermeddling which gave it birth . . . whoever hates negro slavery more than he loves the Union, must demand separation at last."[23]

Even if the North suppressed the spirit of abolitionism, how would a confident and independent Confederacy be induced to reunite with the federal Union? For Vallandigham, the process would be subtle and gradual. From the start, there would have to be a de facto recognition of separation; however, it would not be acknowledged as permanent. "But certainly what I propose is informal, practical recognition. And that is precisely what exists to-day, and has existed, more or less defined, from the first." Vallandigham did hold out the possibility of foreign mediation, perhaps through the agency of the French or English. Most importantly, Vallandigham believed that the cessation of hostility would allow tempers and passions to subside. Eventually trade and travel would transpire between the regions, followed by the resumption of religious and fraternal organizations between the two regions. As long as the doctrine of abolitionism was suppressed, eventually the two would reunite under a common government. "It cost thirty years of desperate and most wicked impatience and industry to destroy or impair the magnificent temple of the Union. Let us be content," Vallandigham told the House, "if, within three years, we shall be able to restore it."[24]

Civil Liberties

Like many Democrats who were nervous about the centralizing tendencies inherent in a civil war, Vallandigham was afraid that overzealous federal officials and military personnel would use the war as a means of restricting and eventually destroying civil liberties. Harkening back to a tradition of Whig opposition to the excesses of the crown in seventeenth-century England, Vallandigham believed it was important to curb executive excesses during the war before they became a precedent for peacetime activities. If a war for the preservation of the Union resulted in the restriction of rights and the erosion of republican values, such a war would have little value for Vallandigham. This point was stressed over and over by him in speeches delivered throughout the East, the Midwest, and the halls of Congress. In his last congressional speech, Vallandigham stated,

> But I have denounced from the beginning the usurpations and the infractions, one and all, of law and Constitution by the President and those under him; their repeated and persistent arbitrary arrests, the suppression of the writ of *habeas corpus,* the violation of freedom of the mails, of the private house, of the press and of speech, and all the other multiplied wrongs and outrages upon public liberty and private right which have made this country one of the worst despotisms on earth for the past twenty months; and I will continue to denounce them to the end.[25]

The actions taken by the Lincoln administration—the suspension of the writ of habeas corpus, the arbitrary arrests of thousands of administration critics who were held without trial, military trials in place of civilian courts, and controversial unconstitutional laws (in Vallandigham's opinion)—these were all abundant proof that constitutional liberties were being sacrificed for the war. They were examples of the federal government wildly expanding its power at the expense of state governments and the rights of ordinary citizens. The result, in Vallandigham's opinion, could only be an arbitrary despotism. "We have a Constitution yet, and laws yet," Vallandigham told the House of Representatives. "To them I appeal. Give us our rights; give us known and fixed laws; give us a judiciary; arrest us only upon due process of law . . . give us free speech and a free press."[26]

Radical Republicans argued that the restoration of the Union took precedent over constitutional fine points, declaring that such a position hampered the execution of the war and would end with the destruction of constitutional government. Vallandigham, conversely, maintained that a war that violated constitutional rights and liberties was not worth fighting. Indeed, in his July 15, 1863, "To the Democracy of Ohio," Vallandigham went to great lengths to demonstrate the absurdity of waging a war to maintain the Constitution while, at the same time, trampling on constitutional rights and liberties. "It is vain to invite the States and the people of the South to return to a Union without a Constitution, and dishonored and polluted by repeated and most aggravated exertions of tyrannic power." What were the reasons, Vallandigham asked, for violations of civil liberties? "Military necessity. But if, indeed, all these be demanded by military necessity, then, believe me, your liberties are gone, and tyranny is perpetual."[27]

CONCLUSION

Clement Vallandigham was perhaps the most colorful Northern political figure during the Civil War. Devoted to principle, confident, even arrogant, he expressed a point of view that is often ignored or even misrepresented today. Although the Ohio Democrat lost his seat in the House of Representatives during the war and lost the 1863 gubernatorial election, his message was perhaps more prominent than the messenger. While Vallandigham's support for slavery and use of Negrophobic rhetoric to gain votes are not acceptable, many of his critical comments regarding violations of civil liberties were legitimate and thought-provoking. They express important political opinions that are still controversial today. To what extent can a democratic government suspend constitutional liberties? At what point does the circumvention of political and constitutional rights to protect the nation violate the very purpose and intent of the nation? Vallandigham's message is one worth considering in any democratic society when issues of national security conflict with basic constitutional liberties.

NOTES

1. Quoted from James L. Vallandigham, *A Life of Clement L. Vallandigham* (Baltimore: Turnbull Brothers, 1872), 140.

2. Vallandigham to wife, December 3, 1860, and December 24, 1860, in Vallandigham, *Life of Clement L. Vallandigham*, 144, 151. See also Vallandigham's speech in the House, "The Great American Revolution of 1861," *Appendix to the Congressional Globe*, Thirty-sixth Congress, Second Session, 235–43.

3. Vallandigham speech in the House, December 22, 1860, quoted in Vallandigham, *Life of Clement L. Vallandigham*, 141–42, 149.

4. On the Washington Peace Conference, see James McPherson, *Ordeal by Fire: The Civil War and Reconstruction* (New York: Alfred A. Knopf, 1982), 138; and Frank L. Klement, *The Copperheads in the Middlewest* (Gloucester, MA: Peter Smith, 1972), 107.

5. Quoted from Vallandigham, *Life of Clement L. Vallandigham*, 162, 166. For Vallandigham's amendments, see Congressional *Globe*, Thirty-sixth Congress, Second Session (appendix), 242–43.

6. On Democratic opposition to the antislavery policies of the Republican Party, see Klement, *Lincoln's Critics: The Copperheads of the North* (Shippensburg, PA: White Mane Books, 1999), 109–17; and V. Jacque Voegeli, "The Northwest and the Race Issue, 1861–1862," *Mississippi Valley Historical Review* 50 (September 1963): 235–51.

7. Frank L. Klement, *Dark Lanterns: Secret Political Societies, Conspiracies, and Treason Trials in the Civil War* (Baton Rouge: Louisiana State University Press, 1984), 7–33. Until the scholarship of Frank Klement, the traditional nationalist view of Democratic dissenters was that they constituted a dangerous and disloyal minority. See the following works: George Fort Milton, *Abraham Lincoln and the Fifth Column* (New York, 1943); Wood Gray, *The Hidden Civil War: The Story of the Copperheads* (New York: Viking Press, 1942); Mayo Fesler, "Secret Political Societies in the North during the Civil War," *Indiana Magazine of History* 14 (1918): 183–286; and Bethania Meradith Smith, "Civil War Subversives," *Journal of the Illinois State Historical Society* 45 (Autumn 1952): 220–40. Recently, however, a few historians have suggested that Klement underestimated the danger represented by secret societies and Democrats intent on violent overthrow of the Lincoln administration. See, for instance, David E. Long, *The Jewel of Liberty: Abraham Lincoln's Re-election and the End of Slavery* (New York: Da Capo Press, 1994); and William A. Tidwell, *April '65: Confederate Covert Action in the American Civil War* (Kent, OH: Kent State University Press, 1995).

8. Vallandigham, *Life of Clement L. Vallandigham*, 192–202 (quote, 193).

9. Klement, *Copperheads in the Middlewest*, 43–52, 113–14; and McPherson, *Ordeal By Fire*, 272–75. On the impact of the preliminary Emancipation Proclamation on specific states, see Bruce Tap, "Race, Rhetoric, and Emancipation: The Election of 1862 in Illinois," *Civil War History* 39 (June 1993): 101–25.

10. Klement, *Lincoln's Critics*, 43–63.

11. Bruce Tap, "The Election of 1862," in *The Encyclopedia of the American Civil War* (Denver: ABC-CLIO, 2000), 2:639–40.

12. The speech was originally named "The Constitution—Peace—Reunion," and

appeared in the appendix of the Congressional *Globe*, Thirty-seventh Congress, Third Session, 53–60. It was subsequently published as a pamphlet. See also Frank L. Klement, *The Limits of Dissent: Clement L. Vallandigham & The Civil War* (New York: Fordham University Press, 1998), 123–31.

13. For Vallandigham's remarks on the conscription bill, see appendix to the Congressional *Globe*, Thirty-seventh Congress, Third Session, 172–77.

14. Vallandigham to Alfred Sanderson, April 24, 1863, in Vallandigham, *Clement L. Vallandigham*, 246.

15. Quoted from Klement, *The Limits of Dissent*, 154.

16. Vallandigham quote from Vallandigham, *Clement L. Vallandigham*, 257.

17. Vallandigham to "the Democracy of Ohio," May 5, 1863, and May 22, 1863, in Vallandigham, *Clement L. Vallandigham*, 260, 297.

18. "To the Democracy of Ohio," July 15, 1863, in Vallandigham, *Clement L. Vallandigham*, 318–21; and "Democrats of Ohio," October 14, 1863, in Vallandigham, *Clement L. Vallandigham*, 334–35 (quote, 334). For an analysis of the Vallandigham's electoral defeat, see Eugene H. Roseboom, "Southern Ohio and the Union 1863," *Mississippi Valley Historical Review* 39 (June 1952): 29–44; and James A. Rawley, *The Politics of the Union: Northern Politics during the Civil War* (Hinsdale, IL: Dryden Press, 1974), 131–34.

19. On the Democratic Party, the Chicago Convention, and the controversy over the platform, see the following: Joel Silbey, *"A Respectable Minority": The Democratic Party in the Civil War Era, 1860–1868* (New York: W. W. Norton, 1977), 115–36; Stephen Sears, *George B. McClellan: The Young Napoleon* (New York: Ticknor & Fields, 1988), 344–86; and Stephen W. Sears, "McClellan the Peace Plank of 1864: A Re-appraisal," *Civil War History* 36 (March 1990): 57–64.

20. Quote from Vallandigham, *Clement L. Vallandigham*, 80.

21. Congressional *Globe*, Thirty-seventh Congress, Third Session (appendix), 54–57 (quote, 57).

22. Congressional *Globe* (appendix), 54–55 (quote, 54).

23. Congressional *Globe* (appendix), 56–59 (quote, 58).

24. Congressional *Globe* (appendix), 59.

25. Congressional *Globe* (appendix), 54. On the Democrats and civil liberties, see the works of Frank L. Klement already cited in this chapter. Also see Jean Baker, *Affairs of Party: The Political Culture of Northern Democrats in the Mid-Nineteenth Century* (Ithaca, NY: Cornell University Press, 1983), 147–60; and Mark E. Neeley Jr., *The Fate of Liberty: Abraham Lincoln and Civil Liberties* (New York: Oxford University Press, 1991).

26. Congressional *Globe*, Thirty-seventh Congress, Third Session (appendix), 177.

27. "To the Democracy of Ohio," July 15, 1863, in Vallandigham, *Clement L. Vallandigham*, 319–20.

FURTHER READING

Joanna D. Cowden, *"Heaven Will Frown on Such a Cause as This": Six Democrats Who Opposed Lincoln's War* (New York: University Press of America, 2001); Charles F. Howlett, "Clement Laird Vallandigham, 1820-1871," in *Encyclopedia of the American Civil War*, edited by David L. and Jeanne T. Heidler (Denver: ABC-CLIO, 2000), 4:2011–13; Edward Chase Kirkland, *The Peacemakers of 1864* (New York: MacMillan Co., 1927); Frank L. Klement, *The Copperheads in the Middlewest* (Gloucester, MA: Peter Smith, 1972); idem., *Dark Lanterns: Secret Political Societies, Conspiracies, and Treason Trials in the Civil War* (Baton Rouge: Louisiana State University Press, 1984); *The Limits of Dissent: Clement L. Vallandigham & The Civil War* (New York: Fordham University Press, 1998); idem., *Lincoln's Critics: The Copperheads of the North* (Shippensburg, PA: White Mane Books, 1999); and James Vallandigham, *A Life of Clement L. Vallandigham* (Baltimore: Turnbull Brothers, 1872).

WILLIAM LOWNDES YANCEY
(1814–1863)

Submission or Secession: A Tragic Career

LIFE

William Lowndes Yancey was born on August 10, 1814, at "the Aviary," the home of his maternal grandfather, William Bird, in Warren County, Georgia. Bird's daughter Caroline had married a South Carolina lawyer, Benjamin Cudworth Yancey, in 1808. Yancey took his bride back to South Carolina, where he was considered a talented young member of the state bar. He ran as a Federalist for Congress in 1812, challenging John C. Calhoun, but was defeated by the rising star of South Carolina politics. The Abbeville District elected Yancey to the state legislature that same year, and he was chosen chairman of the judiciary committee. He lost reelection in 1814 because the Calhoun faction worked hard to defeat him.[1]

The following year Yancey and Caroline moved to Charleston, and he became a law partner of Daniel E. Huger and James L. Petigru. Yancey was elected to the state legislature again in 1816 and served another stint as chairman of the judiciary committee, a testament to his legal reputation. In 1817, a yellow fever epidemic raged, and Yancey packed up his wife and two boys, William Lowndes and younger brother Benjamin, and fled for the upcountry. Unfortunately, Yancey contracted the fever near the Edisto River. He was taken to a friend's plantation and nursed until he died on October 26, 1817.

After the death of her husband, Caroline returned to Georgia to live with her mother. She subsequently took her boys to Mount Zion Academy in Hancock County, Georgia, a Presbyterian School operated by Nathan Sidney Smith Beman. A harsh disciplinarian, Beman was a New England native who had been in Georgia since 1812. An affection blossomed between the widow and the clergyman, and Beman and Caroline married in 1821.

Two years after the marriage, Beman accepted a call to be pastor of the

First Presbyterian Church in Troy, New York. He became an important figure in the religious revivals that swept much of New York, advocating a more lenient doctrine of God's grace for all, not just the elect. Beman conducted emotionally wrenching revivals that featured harsh condemnations of sin and sinners. At the same time, Beman and Yancey's mother began quarreling, and their marriage remained stormy and generally unhappy. Young William Lowndes did not adjust well to his new situation in Troy, where he was surrounded by religious fervor and constant bickering between his mother and stepfather. Beman also employed corporal punishment on both William and Benjamin.

According to family lore, Yancey's mother regaled her young son with tales of his natural father's distinguished, albeit brief, career and tragic end. He also learned about the family forebears who had fought in the American Revolution. Caroline purportedly made William recite from a book of oratorical addresses then commonly employed as training in public speaking. Yancey attended local academies in preparation for Williams College in Massachusetts, which he entered in 1830. He was an average student at Williams, more given to reverie than study. Yancey later credited his skills as a public speaker to his mother and to Edward Dorr Griffin, president of Williams while he was a student.

In 1833, Yancey abruptly left Williams College for reasons that remain unclear. He may have had to leave after committing a breach of discipline. He may also have wanted to escape from a tyrannical stepfather and the discord associated with his mother's unhappy marriage. Significantly, Yancey moved south to Sparta, Georgia, where he studied law with Nathan Sayre. The next year, Yancey moved to Greenville, South Carolina, where he lived on the plantation of his uncle, Robert Cunningham, working as a clerk and bookkeeper. He soon resumed his legal studies under the direction of Benjamin F. Perry.

Life in South Carolina was an invigorating change for a young man who had spent years in a household carried away with stifling religious zeal. Horse racing, dancing, socials, and barbeques featuring attractive young women—Yancey embraced the whirlwind of activities that would have been unthinkable in the Beman home. He abandoned the Presbyterianism his stepfather represented and joined the Episcopal Church. An exciting political controversy also gripped the state, as South Carolinians divided into those who supported nullification and those who opposed it. Yancey's father's colleagues, Petigru and Huger, were Unionists, as was his uncle. He mustered with a Unionist militia unit and took to carrying a pistol, willingly adopting the martial spirit of the state. In 1834, Yancey gave his first public address, a Fourth of July oration in the Abbeville District, in which he linked the heroes of the Revolution to the antinullification cause. He became editor of the Greenville *Mountaineer* in November, writing editorials that touted the virtues of Union and condemned nullification and secession.

Yancey resigned from the newspaper in May 1835 and a few months later, on August 13, 1835, he married Sarah Caroline Earle. His new bride came from wealth and brought thirty-five slaves to the marriage, prompting Yancey to abandon his legal career and take up the life of a gentleman planter. He purchased land near Cahawba, Alabama; transported his slave labor force to the area; and began an effort to make a fortune in cotton. An uncle and aunt, Jesse Beene and Catherine Bird Beene, owned a plantation near Cahawba, and Yancey stayed with them on trips to his property. Beene was a states' rights Democrat, an admirer of Andrew Jackson, and he explained and advocated his strong political beliefs to Yancey.

While in Greenville in September 1838, preparing to move his wife permanently to Alabama, Yancey fought a street brawl with his wife's uncle, Dr. Robinson Earle. The dispute, a fatal encounter for Earle, had its origins in the honor code that Southern gentlemen were expected to abide by and that Yancey had evidently internalized. After Earle called Yancey a liar, a fighting word for Southern gentlemen, Yancey pulled a pistol and the two struggled for control of it. In the ensuing melee, which included knives and an unsheathed sword stick, Yancey shot and stabbed Earle, who later died of his wounds. Convicted of manslaughter, Yancey served three months of a year's sentence in prison until South Carolina governor Patrick Noble pardoned him. He returned to Alabama in January 1839.

His effort to establish himself as a planter in Alabama failed miserably, plagued by his poor business sense, indolence, and bad luck. In the wake of the Panic of 1837, cotton prices plummeted, and a depression afflicted the country. To compound that difficulty, an overseer from a rival plantation purportedly poisoned Yancey's slaves, killing some and sickening others. Unable to harvest his 1839 crop, Yancey was wiped out. He had earlier purchased a newspaper in Cahawba; he sold that paper and purchased the Wetumpka *Argus*, moving to Wetumpka, Alabama. Financial ruin made Yancey less inclined to sympathize with the Whig Party, as he associated it with economic policies and interests, such as the national bank, that were, in his opinion, fatal to his prosperity.

The hated stepfather, Nathan Beman, had also become an abolitionist and forced Yancey's mother to return to the South, effectively ending the marriage. Yancey felt Beman had cheated his mother out of property and money she had brought to the union. To him, Beman's moral abolition crusade masked an abusive husband, and that personal experience inflamed and informed Yancey's reaction to the burgeoning abolition movement. In *Argus* editorials, Yancey urged the North to put down abolitionism lest Southern secession become necessary. By 1840, Yancey had abandoned his earlier Unionism and had transferred his allegiance to the Democratic Party, becoming a strident advocate for Southern rights.

While running the *Argus*, Yancey took up his law books again and began studying for his law license. Admitted to the Alabama bar in November

1841, he started a law practice with Sampson W. Harris at Wetumpka. He subsequently sold the newspaper and devoted himself to the law. Yancey's passionate attachment to the Southern cause and extraordinary ability as a speaker drew him to the political arena. He was a naturally gifted orator in an age when lengthy speeches were much admired as a kind of performance art, though he also had an unfortunate tendency to employ sarcasm and attack political foes in offensive terms. Often, Yancey's harsh terms were delivered in a tone described as soothing or melodious, which did little to soften their power to hurt the unfortunate targets of the abuse. He attended the 1839 state Democratic convention as a delegate. In the ensuing presidential campaign, Yancey delivered speeches touting the virtues of incumbent president Martin Van Buren.

His gifts as a speaker were rewarded with election to the Alabama House in 1841 and then to the Alabama Senate in 1843. In the state legislature, Yancey pursued a number of progressive reforms. He promoted the rights of women to retain ownership of property brought into a marriage. Perhaps as a result of his own experience in prison, Yancey backed a state penitentiary and the abolishment of flogging and branding as punishments for crime. He considered education the best crime prevention and advocated a system of public education. His record was not entirely progressive, however, as Yancey also sought to weaken penalties for dueling and gambling.

When Alabama congressman Dixon Lewis was appointed to the Senate in 1844 to replace Alabama senator William Rufus King, who had been elevated to minister to France, a district convention appointed Yancey to fill Lewis's place. He then defeated Whig Daniel Watrous in August 1844 to win the seat. Serving in the final session of the Twenty-eighth Congress, Yancey avowed the standard principles of a Southern Democrat: a strict construction of the Constitution, economy in federal spending, low tariff, the independent treasury, and Texas annexation. He witnessed the repeal of the gag rule at the beginning of the session, a procedural rule that had prohibited abolition petitions from being read in the House. The vote to repeal broke down on sectional rather than party lines, with Northern Whigs joining Northern Democrats to end the practice, while Southern representatives voted as a bloc to uphold the rule.

In a January 6, 1845, floor speech, Whig representative Thomas L. Clingman of North Carolina condemned Texas annexation, Secretary of State John C. Calhoun, and Democratic fraud in the recent elections. Clingman had been the sole Southern vote for repealing the gag rule the previous month. Scheduled to speak the next day in defense of annexation, Yancey found himself drafted by Southern Democrats to respond to Clingman. He had a personal interview with Calhoun at the latter's request so the secretary could advise him on his reply, which would also be his maiden floor speech. In his remarks, Yancey quickly demonstrated his penchant for giving offense as he harshly denounced Clingman. Employing loaded terms,

Yancey called Clingman a betrayer and traitor to the South, and he unfavorably compared the Whig congressman's character to that of North Carolina's famed patriot, Nathaniel Macon. Adhering to the Southern honor code, Clingman requested an explanation with a disavowal on Yancey's part of any intent to defame him. When Yancey refused to provide it, a challenge from Clingman followed. The two congressmen repaired to Maryland with a retinue of seconds and fought a brief duel, exchanging fruitless pistol shots at ten paces before local police arrived and broke up the exchange. Violence or the threat of violence clung to Yancey throughout his political career.

The duel with Clingman only enhanced Yancey's reputation despite an Alabama statute that prohibited dueling by elected officials; the Alabama legislature obligingly repealed it to exempt Yancey. He was widely acclaimed in Southern newspapers and became a sought-after guest on the Washington, D.C., social circuit. He was reelected and served in the Twenty-ninth Congress, in which he continued to act as a Southern rights zealot. He opposed giving notice to Great Britain, a necessary prelude to substantive negotiations for a final settlement of the joint occupation of Oregon, as required by treaty, an act that angered western and Northern Democrats who felt their support for Texas annexation had earned the backing of Southern Democrats for Oregon. In similar fashion, Yancey refused to modify his opposition to internal improvements legislation beneficial to the West, though western Democrats had voted for lower tariff rates that the South desired. Ralph Draughon has argued that Yancey's constant complaints exacerbated sectional tensions in Congress, setting the stage for greater bitterness when the Wilmot Proviso was introduced.

During his congressional career, Yancey rejoined the Presbyterian Church and experienced a religious awakening of sorts, a not uncommon phenomenon in the 1840s. The revitalized piety and the fame he had won in the Clingman affair encouraged him to see himself as a righteous warrior defending the noble South. He retained his sharp tongue and propensity for giving offense. After Whig congressman Alexander Stephens condemned the Mexican War in a floor speech, Yancey answered him and linked Stephens to abolitionists, a tough charge against a man representing a district in Georgia. Stephens acted, Yancey alleged, "in unison with the contemptible horde of Abolitionists who infest this Hall." Once again, a flurry of correspondence occurred preliminary to a formal duel, but the affair was amicably adjusted.[2]

Yancey resigned his congressional seat in June 1846, explaining in a circular that he needed to earn a better living to support his family. He moved to Montgomery, Alabama, and began a law partnership with John A. Elmore, a man who, like Yancey, came from a distinguished South Carolina family. In his circular, Yancey condemned Northern Democrats for supposedly cheating the South, for not being sufficiently orthodox on taxation and other party-backed legislation. "My observation here convinces me," he wrote, "that in such a party organization the South, which is the only portion of the party sound on these questions, is used merely to *foot the bill* and to aid in securing to the party a power which shall give to our northern brethren the spoils." Yancey had concluded that Northern Democrats cared only for patronage posts and had little concern for issues of principle, such as protecting the Southern slave-based economic system. The Polk administration had reduced tariff rates, engaged in an expensive war that added potential slave territory to the Union, and vetoed popular internal improvement legislation. For Yancey, it was not enough to keep him from condemning the Democratic Party for pro-Northern bias harmful to the South. "Party has no charms for me," he said, "if not based on principle." Intense Southern partisanship had warped his judgment, and his allegiance to the Democratic Party became nominal at best.[3]

Despite his skepticism of political parties, politics continued to interest Yancey, though he also worked hard at developing his law practice. He attended the Alabama State Democratic Convention in February 1848 and cowrote, with John A. Campbell, a series of resolutions protective of Southern rights that was dubbed the Alabama Platform. During an evening session, with the delegates groggy from the day's labor, Yancey delivered a dramatic speech that swept the convention into endorsing the Alabama Platform, an act many Democrats deprecated when its import became clear. The resolutions stated that Congress could not keep slavery out of the territories, but had a duty to protect it. Also, the citizens of a territory could not exclude slavery until the constitutional convention held prior to state admission into the Union. Yancey and Campbell included a resolution requiring the Alabama delegation to the Democratic National Convention to reject any presidential candidate who supported popular sovereignty or the Wilmot Proviso.

The Democratic National Convention met at Baltimore beginning May 22, 1848, and Yancey attended as a delegate-at-large. He wanted the party to adopt the Alabama resolutions as the national platform, thereby committing the Democrats to the federal protection of slavery in the territories. But the national Democratic Party could not be bullied. Lewis Cass, a Michigan Democrat, received the nomination, and he was an advocate of popular sovereignty, or allowing the people of the territories to determine the status of slavery. When the platform committee met, the absolutist edicts of the Alabama Platform were considerably weakened in tone and content. Once it was certain that an unalloyed version of the Alabama Platform would not be adopted, Yancey walked out of the convention. His fellow Alabama delegates, with a single exception, chose to remain and endorse Cass, a decision Yancey denounced in a slashing speech at Charleston, South Carolina. He refused to support the Cass ticket, despite pleas from other Democrats, maintaining a studied neutrality during the presidential campaign.

Yancey strongly backed Calhoun's 1849 call for united Southern action regardless of party in the face of Northern aggression. The Compromise of 1850 enraged Yancey, who considered the omnibus of bills unjust to the South and a victory for abolitionism. "The issue, then, is before us," he intoned. "Congress has boldly tendered it—submission or secession." He helped form Southern Rights Associations in Alabama and played an important role in state Southern rights conventions. In February 1851, Southern rights advocates met in Montgomery, and Yancey wrote a Secession Address that the convention issued. The delegates denounced national political parties as vehicles that duped Southerners into unwarranted concessions. Yancey argued that Alabama had to prepare for secession, which was now inevitable. He and his cohorts considered themselves freedom fighters, like the Hungarian patriot Louis Kossuth, to whom they compared themselves, beset by a despotic North bent on seizing control of the federal government and subverting Southern rights. Unfortunately for Yancey, Alabama Unionists triumphed in the 1851 elections, dealing the secessionists a severe rebuke. Still, though outright secession did not have broad support in Alabama, Yancey confidently predicted that, given time, his fiery rhetoric, and Northern provocations, his views would become mainstream opinion in Alabama.

By 1852, while maintaining he was aloof from party, Yancey had decided that he could better realize his goals with at least a tacit alliance with the Democratic Party. He became the leader of an Alabama Southern rights faction that considered it legitimate to work within political parties. Other Southern rights zealots believed that cooperating with political parties was useless and preferred to agitate outside the political party system. Yancey endorsed Franklin Pierce, the New Hampshire native and Democratic presidential candidate, in 1852. He backed Pierce at the Southern rights state conventions held in Alabama, though unsuccessfully, as the Southern rights men nominated George M. Troup for president and John A. Quitman for vice president. Shortly before the election, Yancey announced he was voting for Troup, but that he would have supported Pierce if the contest was close with Whig candidate Winfield Scott.

The 1854 Kansas-Nebraska Act and the resulting bloody turmoil in Kansas roiled South and North as both regions vied to rush settlers to the newly organized territories. Yancey considered the Missouri Compromise unconstitutional and approved the explicit repudiation of it that was included in the final version of the act. He continued to condemn popular sovereignty. He also acted as treasurer for a fund established to aid Southerners emigrating to Kansas. His reputation in the Democratic Party continued to grow, particularly after he savagely denounced nativism and the

American Party. He worried about the secrecy prized in the nativist move-ment, and he condemned the American Party's vague references in favor of Union without an exact definition of what the term *Union* represented. The nativists simply were not reliable enough on slavery for Yancey and indeed were prepared to leave the question to the judiciary. Yancey also abhorred the idea of political proscription for Catholics, reminding listeners in his speeches that many prominent Catholics had been friendly to the South. His strong criticism of the nativist third party movement further endeared him to the leadership of the Democratic Party, and in September 1855, Yancey explicitly announced his Democratic allegiance.

The party was delighted to have him, and Yancey was named a delegate to the Democratic National Convention that met at Cincinnati, Ohio, in 1856. J. Mills Thornton has argued that Yancey's uncompromising South-ern rights rhetoric, delivered in his inimitable style on countless occasions in the 1850s, attracted young lawyers and other upwardly mobile profes-sionals who saw Yancey as a rising star in politics. He could soon depend upon and influence a reliable voting bloc, and this made him all the more worth cultivating for the Democratic Party. He attracted new members to the party; indeed, the ascendance of James Buchanan, considered reliably pro-Southern, seemed to validate Yancey's decision to work within an ex-isting political party. Staunch Southern rights extremists, fire-eaters previ-ously skeptical of party, worked for Buchanan and rallied to the Democratic banner. After Buchanan's victory, Yancey was spoken of as a possible cab-inet member, but the new president contented himself with appointing Yancey's brother Benjamin to a minor diplomatic post.

The optimism over Buchanan proved short-lived, as disappointment with the inability of the administration to admit Kansas as a slave state led many Southern rights advocates, who had joined the party in 1856 and 1857, to bolt and resume an aloof stance. Yancey had emerged as a power in the Al-abama Democratic Party, but the defection and alienation of Southern rights extremists from the party weakened his position. To recoup, Yancey challenged Benjamin Fitzpatrick for a Senate seat in 1859, accusing Fitz-patrick of insufficient zealotry for Southern rights in Congress. Fitzpatrick was fairly orthodox on Southern rights, so Yancey sought to differentiate the two by suggesting that the federal prohibition against the slave trade was an insult to the South and unconstitutional. He argued that regulation of the slave trade properly belonged to state governments, who could bet-ter decide whether the practice was desirable. The state legislature post-poned the election for senator until 1861, a moral victory for Yancey as his supporters had deadlocked the state legislature, which chose to await the results of the forthcoming presidential election before selecting a senator.

The presidential election of 1860 allowed Yancey to reprise his role of 1848. At the state Democratic convention, in January 1860, he carried the delegates to an endorsement of the Alabama Platform, suitably modified to take into account recent events such as the Dred Scott decision. The central demand was a national platform that committed the Democratic Party to federal protection for slavery in the territories without which the resolutions instructed the Alabama delegation to walk out of the national convention. Yancey could not abide popular sovereignty or its champion and potential Democratic presidential nominee, Stephen A. Douglas. Selected as a delegate to the national convention, Yancey was in Charleston, South Carolina, in April 1860 for the ill-fated meeting. J. Mills Thornton has argued that Yancey did not attend the convention with the fixed intention of breaking up the party. He hoped that united Southern resolve would persuade the delegates to make concessions on Southern rights. Yancey delivered an eloquent and passionate speech in an attempt to browbeat the convention, as he had so successfully done to other gatherings, into accepting Southern demands, but Ohio senator George E. Pugh responded with equal force. When Douglas's delegates insisted on their man and his cardinal principal, popular sovereignty, Yancey led the Alabama delegation out of the convention. Other Southern delegations followed, and the convention broke up. When the Democrats reassembled in Baltimore, Yancey's platform demands were rejected again and his Alabama delegation refused seats. In the end, with the Democratic Party sundered, Yancey supported John C. Breckenridge for president.

Since Alabamians believed abolitionists dominated and controlled the Republican Party, Lincoln's victory in 1860 fulfilled the dire predictions Yancey had been preaching for more than a decade. He participated as a delegate in the Alabama secession convention and helped draw up the ordinance of secession. Yancey turned down a cabinet post in the new Confederate government, but he accepted a diplomatic appointment from the new president, Jefferson Davis, though he knew little of Europe, foreign affairs, or the intricacies of diplomacy. Robert Barnwell Rhett had suggested sending three commissioners to Europe in an effort to secure diplomatic recognition of the new nation. Davis chose Yancey as one of the three. Yancey spent much of 1861 overseas in pursuit of that goal and was singularly unsuccessful. He complained in correspondence that every British citizen had read and internalized Harriet Beecher Stowe's unflattering fictional account of Southern slavery. At the end of a disappointing year, the Alabama legislature elected Yancey to the Confederate Senate, and he returned to assume those duties.

As a Confederate senator, Yancey could not abide the aggressive measures the exigencies of the war compelled the Davis administration to take. He strongly objected to impressment and conscription. Earlier in his career, Yancey had supported egalitarian measures, such as penal reform and property rights for married women. Now, he was the servant of the planter class,

sponsoring legislation that exempted plantation overseers from military service. He thought not enough Alabamians had been elevated to general officer and advocated apportionment of general and staff officer appointments
among the states. He bitterly complained when Davis ignored his choices
for patronage posts in Alabama, and he came to dislike and despise the president, though he thought it unwise to remove him in the midst of an ongoing war. His penchant for cutting sarcasm, violence, and invective
continued when, during a debate on the powers of the Confederate Supreme
Court, he argued and fought with Georgia senator Benjamin Hill on the
floor of the Confederate Senate, with Hill hurling an inkwell at Yancey's
head. In the heat of the Alabama summer of 1863, Yancey contracted an
infection in his urinary tract, and he died in Montgomery on July 27, 1863.

PRINCIPAL IDEAS

Though he began his political life as a Unionist, Yancey became a
staunch Southern rights partisan, an attitude that Ralph B. Draughon and
J. Mills Thornton have argued was a product of his distaste for his New
Englander stepfather, a minister and abolitionist who had treated his
mother poorly. By 1840, Yancey had completed his transition to Southern
rights Democrat. He considered himself a political moralist, a term he defined as someone who sought to make politics a "branch of morals." He
avowed a Benthamite objective as a legislator, "the promotion of the greatest good of the greatest number." With that goal in mind, Yancey backed
certain reform measures in the Alabama legislature, such as penal and education improvements.[4]

His congressional career was marked by an often harsh advocacy of his
Southern rights views. Yancey declared that the attempt to keep slavery out
of the territories and prevent Texas annexation was an effort to surround
the South with free territories and revolutionize Southern government. He
characterized slavery as the "chief source of wealth and power" of the
South and as a constitutionally protected institution. Slavery, he argued,
ought to be embraced by Northern Democrats because it liberated poor
whites from menial labor. Slavery had also been ordained by God himself
as the proper fate for black Americans. Like many Southerners, Yancey
felt the Wilmot Proviso was an insult, a legislative measure that condemned
the Southern way of life and the Southern people. Honor, he felt, compelled
the South to secede from the Union. He believed the Union was a compact
of sovereign states, with the states retaining all rights not explicitly surrendered to the federal government, including the right to withdraw from
the compact. His congressional experience prompted Yancey to modify his
Benthamite objective: "The greatest good of the greatest number, consistent with the inalienable rights of the minority, is now the chief aim of legislation."[5] Like Calhoun, Yancey thought loyalty to the South should

transcend any loyalty to a political party, and indeed, for a time, he held himself largely aloof from the Democratic Party.

Yancey strongly denounced the Compromise of 1850 as inequitable to the South. He favored and advocated immediate secession, framing the choice before Southerners in Manichean terms: submission or secession. He dismissed suggestions of an economic boycott of the North as unmanly: "If you resist at all, resist effectually and manfully, use swords, not pins, cannon and iron balls, not paper pellets." He was a divisive leader of the Southern rights movement in Alabama because of his insistence on ideological purity. Convinced that states should secede whenever they wished without reference to other states, he denounced those who also favored secession but only as a unified bloc of Southern states.

Though his time in Congress led him to conclude that the Democratic Party was a mere vehicle for Northern patronage, he eventually decided that remaining aloof from the party was a mistake. The victory of Alabama Unionists in the 1851 elections convinced Yancey that a tactical retreat was necessary. In 1852, Yancey cooperated with the Alabama Democratic Party and advocated converting the party to a Southern rights course, to turn the party from an instrument for patronage to an instrument for advancing ideology, the ideology of Southern nationalism. He no longer favored immediate secession, but advocated a policy of continued agitation within the Democratic Party for his Southern rights views. By 1860, his work of conversion had enjoyed considerable success in both the Alabama Democratic Party and the state at large.

CONCLUSION

Every account agrees that William Lowndes Yancey possessed great oratorical gifts in an age when good stump speaking was almost a requirement for a political career. Tragically, he chose to employ his considerable talent in defense of the indefensible system of chattel slavery. His biographers have wistfully speculated on the possible impact Yancey might have had if he had followed his stepfather's example and joined the abolition movement. Garrison's eloquent pen might have had an oratorical counterpart. As it was, though, the war Yancey had so confidently predicted and even welcomed laid waste to the region he so loved, though he died before he could witness the doleful final act.

NOTES

1. This essay is based on the following sources: William J. Cooper Jr., *The South and the Politics of Slavery, 1828–1856* (Baton Rouge: Louisiana State University Press, 1978); Ralph B. Draughon Jr., "William Lowndes Yancey: From Unionist to

Secessionist, 1814–1852" (Ph.D. diss., University of North Carolina at Chapel Hill, 1968); John Witherspoon DuBose, *The Life and Times of William Lowndes Yancey* (Birmingham, AL: Roberts and Son, 1892); J. Mills Thornton, *Politics and Power in a Slave Society: Alabama, 1800–1860* (Baton Rouge: Louisiana State University Press, 1978); and Wilfred B. Yearns, *The Confederate Congress* (Athens: University of Georgia Press, 1960).

2. Congressional *Globe*, Twenty-ninth Congress, First Session (appendix), 951.

3. DuBose, *The Life and Times*, 153–54; and Draughon, "William Lowndes Yancey," 156.

4. Draughon, "William Lowndes Yancey," 101.

5. DuBose, *Life and Times*, 301; and Draughon, "William Lowndes Yancey," 168.

FURTHER READING

William J. Cooper Jr., *The South and the Politics of Slavery, 1828–1856* (Baton Rouge: Louisiana State University Press, 1978); William C. Davis, *Rhett: The Turbulent Life and Times of a Fire-Eater* (Columbia: University of South Carolina Press, 2001); Ralph Brown Draughon Jr., "William Lowndes Yancey: From Unionist to Secessionist, 1814–1852" (Ph.D. diss., University of North Carolina at Chapel Hill, 1968); John Witherspoon DuBose, *The Life and Times of William Lowndes Yancey* (Birmingham, AL: Roberts and Son, 1892); J. Mills Thornton, *Politics and Power in a Slave Society: Alabama, 1800–1860* (Baton Rouge: Louisiana State University Press, 1978); Eric Walther, *The Fire-Eaters* (Baton Rouge: Louisiana State University Press, 1992); and Wilfred Buck Yearns, *The Confederate Congress* (Athens: University of Georgia Press, 1960).

APPENDIX: BRIEF BIOGRAPHIES

Adams, Charles Francis (1807–1886). Union Diplomat. The son of John Quincy Adams, Charles Francis Adams spent much time in Europe as his father served both as minister to Russia and England. Trained as a lawyer, Adams gravitated to politics and was involved in the formation of the Free Soil Party in Massachusetts. Elected to Congress in 1858, Adams was subsequently appointed minister to England, where he represented the Union cause during the Civil War. After the war, he continued in this role and played an important part in the negotiations of the *Alabama* claims. After retiring from public life, Adams spent the rest of his career working on his father's papers. *Source*: Duberman, Martin. *Charles Francis Adams, 1807–1886* (1968).

Anderson, Robert (1805–1871). Union General. Born at Louisville, Kentucky, Robert Anderson graduated from West Point in 1825. He served in the Black Hawk, Seminole, and Mexican Wars. As a major in the U.S. Army, he commanded Fort Sumter at the outbreak of the secession crisis and ultimately surrendered the garrison to Southern forces on April 14, 1861. Anderson commanded the Department of Kentucky, but retired from active service in October 1861. He died in Nice, France. *Source*: Swanberg, W. A. *First Blood: The Story of Fort Sumter* (1957).

Anderson, William "Bloody Bill" (1839–1864). Confederate Guerrilla. A native of Kentucky, Bloody Bill Anderson moved with his family to Missouri, and then in 1857 to Council Grove, Kansas. Prior to the war, Anderson became a bandit, affiliating with both antislavery and proslavery bushwhackers. In 1863, Anderson joined the guerrilla band of William Quantrill. In 1864, Anderson formed his own band of guerrillas and terrorized the State of Missouri, climaxing with a raid of Centralia on September 27, 1864. Anderson was killed when ambushed by Union troops at Albany, Missouri, in October 1864. *Source*: Castel, Albert and Goodrich, Thomas. *Bloody Bill Anderson: The Short, Savage Life of a Civil War Guerrilla* (1998).

Andrew, John Albion (1818–1867). Massachusetts Governor. Born in Maine, John Andrew moved to Boston, Massachusetts, where he practiced law. He became involved in the Free Soil Party and then the Republican Party. Elected to five successive terms as governor of Massachusetts, Andrew began his first term in January 1861. An advocate of rights for African Americans, Andrew enthusiastically endorsed the use of African American troops and played an important role in raising the 54th Massachusetts, a prominent black regiment. *Source*: Pearson, Henry Greenleaf. *The Life of John A. Andrew, Governor of Massachusetts, 1861–1865* (1904).

Anthony, Susan Brownell (1820–1906). Advocate of Abolition and Women's Rights. A native of Adams, Massachusetts, Susan B. Anthony migrated to New York in the early 1850s, where she taught school in the town of Center Falls. An enthusiastic proponent of reforms, Anthony became a prominent speaker and advocate of antislavery and women's rights. During the Civil War, Anthony temporarily abandoned the demand for women's rights to focus on the struggle for emancipation. With Elizabeth Cady Stanton, Anthony formed the National Woman's Suffrage Association in 1869. Moving to Rochester, New York, in 1890, Anthony worked for the cause of suffrage until her death in 1906. *Source*: Venet, Wendy Hamand. *Neither Ballots Nor Bullets: Women Abolitionists and the Civil War* (1991).

Atchison, David Rice (1806–1887). United States Senator. Born in Kentucky, David Rice Atchison moved to Liberty, Missouri, to practice law. A member of the Missouri State Legislature in the 1830s, Atchison was appointed senator in 1843 and subsequently served Missouri in the U.S. Senate until 1856. A critic of the Wilmot Proviso, Atchison became identified with the extreme Southern states' rights position of John C. Calhoun and other proslavery Southerners. During the Civil War, Atchison supported the Confederacy and the Missouri rump government of Claiborne Fox Jackson. After the war, Atchison settled in Clinton County, Missouri, where he farmed. *Source*: Parrish, William E. *David Rice Atchison of Missouri, Border Politician* (1961).

Baker, Edward Dickinson (1811–1861). Politician and Union General. Born in England, Edward Baker migrated to the United States in 1815 and eventually settled in Springfield, Illinois, where he practiced law and became involved in Whig politics. He was also a close friend of Abraham

Lincoln. After service in the Mexican War, Baker migrated to California, where he practiced law in San Francisco. To advance his political career, Baker moved to Oregon, where he was elected as the Republican senator to the U.S. Senate. After the Civil War broke out, Baker remained in the Senate but also was appointed colonel of the 71st Pennsylvania. Baker was killed at the battle of Ball's Bluff on October 21, 1861, when his troops were surprised and overwhelmed by Confederate forces. *Source*: Blair, Harry C., and Rebecca Tarshis. *The Life of Colonel Edward D. Baker, Lincoln's Constant Ally, Together with Four of His Great Orations* (1960).

Banks, Nathaniel Prentice (1816–1894). Republican Politician and Union General. Born at Waltham, Massachusetts, Nathaniel Banks worked in the mill in his local town and earned the name "bobbin boy of Massachusetts" for his efforts. Trained as a lawyer, Banks launched his political career in 1849. First, a Free Soil Democrat, Banks eventually joined the Republican Party and was elected governor of Massachusetts in 1857. When the Civil War erupted, Banks was given a military commission. Banks was defeated and befuddled repeatedly by Thomas "Stonewall" Jackson in the Shenandoah Valley Campaign in 1862 and presided over the disastrous Red River Expedition in May 1864. After the war, Banks served several terms as a Republican representative from Massachusetts. He briefly switched to the Democratic Party before returning to the Republicans in 1876. *Source*: Harrington, Fred Harvey. *The Fighting Politician: Major General N. P. Banks* (1948; reprint, 1970).

Barton, Clara (1812–1921). Union Nurse. Clara Barton became known as the "angel of the battlefield" for her philanthropic efforts during the Civil War. Barton was born in Massachusetts and became an educator in the 1830s. During the Civil War, Barton became increasingly interested in relief work, collecting supplies from her native North Oxford, Massachusetts, and distributing them to wounded Union soldiers. She also gained experience in extracting bullets and treating wounds after the battle of Antietam. Barton spent periods of time in the Sea Islands; Port Royal, South Carolina; and Point of Rocks, Virginia. During the war, Barton constantly battled for her status and saw her duties frequently circumscribed because she was a female. After the war, Barton lectured frequently and headed the American Red Cross for twenty-three years. *Source*: Burton, David H. *Clara Barton: In the Service of Humanity* (1995).

Bates, Edward (1793–1869). Attorney General of the United States. Edward Bates was born in Virginia. He served in the War of 1812 and then moved to St. Louis, Missouri, where he practiced law with his elder brother, Frederick. Associated with the Whig Party, Bates was elected to one term in Congress. While frustrated in attempts at election to the U.S. Senate,

Bates was the most prominent Whig in Missouri. A hesitant member of the Republican Party, Bates was nevertheless a leading candidate for the party's nomination in 1860. Appointed as attorney general, Bates was considered too conservative for many Republicans. He resigned from office on November 30, 1864, and returned to Missouri, where he became increasing critical of radical Republicans in his home state. *Source*: Cain, Marvin R. *Lincoln's Attorney General: Edward Bates of Missouri* (1965).

Beauregard, Pierre Gustave Toutant (1818–1893). Confederate General. Pierre Beauregard was born near New Orleans into a powerful Southern family. He enrolled at West Point in 1834 and graduated second in his class four years later. Beauregard served in the Mexican War and, prior to the Civil War, was the superintendent engineer of U.S. Customs installation for the City of New Orleans. He oversaw the surrender of Fort Sumter and played a significant role in the first battle of Bull Run. Transferred to the western theater in early 1862, Beauregard saw his role in Confederate military operations gradually diminished, undoubtedly the result of criticism of his actions after the battle of Shiloh and the lack of confidence on the part of Jefferson Davis. After the war, Beauregard was nominally involved in Democratic politics and also served as president of the Great Northern Railroad Company. *Source*: Williams, T. Harry. *P.G.T. Beauregard: Napoleon in Gray* (1955).

Beecher, Henry Ward (1813–1887). Minister and Social Reformer. Henry Ward Beecher was born into a prominent American family, the son of abolitionist minister Lyman Beecher and the brother of Harriet Beecher Stowe. A graduate of Lane Seminary in Cincinnati, Beecher became one of the most prominent ministers in the nineteenth century, known primarily for his oratorical skills. After ministerial calls in Lawrenceburg and Indianapolis, Indiana, Beecher was called to the prestigious Plymouth Church in Brooklyn, New York. While strongly opposed to the institution of slavery, Beecher did not question prevailing attitudes about black inferiority. In 1872, Beecher was accused of adultery with the wife of New York journalist, Theodore Tilton. Church and civil proceedings exonerated Beecher of the adultery charge. *Source*: Clark, Clifford Jr. *Henry Ward Beecher: Spokesman for Middle-Class America* (1978).

Bell, John (1796–1869). Politician. A native of Mill Creek, Tennessee, John Bell pursued the profession of law. By 1822, he moved his family to Nashville, where he practiced law and pursued a variety of elected offices including election to both the U.S. House of Representatives and Senate. An opponent of Andrew Jackson, Bell became one of Tennessee's most prominent Whigs. In 1860, Bell became the presidential nominee of the short-lived Constitutional Union Party, which hoped to squelch sectional controversy by vague appeals to the Union and the Constitution. Once Tennessee seceded from the Union, Bell accepted the decision, although he played no active role in the war. After the war, Bell devoted his life to private business interests and never returned to public life. *Source*: Parks, Joseph H. *John Bell of Tennessee* (1950).

Benjamin, Judah Philip (1811–1884). United States Senator and Confederate Cabinet Officer. A native of Charleston, South Carolina, Judah P. Benjamin went to Yale University, but did not graduate. He later moved to New Orleans, where he found work as a clerk. Since Benjamin was Jewish, New Orleans was one of the more hospitable cities in the South for the practice of his religious principles. In New Orleans, Benjamin practiced law and soon earned enough money to become a planter. As a member of the upper class, entry into politics was inevitable. Benjamin began as a Louisiana legislator and was eventually elected as a Whig U.S. senator in 1852. After the secession of his state, Benjamin resigned from the Senate and served his friend Jefferson Davis in a variety of offices including attorney general, secretary of war, and secretary of state. After the war, Benjamin fled to England, where he was eventually admitted to the bar. He died in Paris in 1884. *Source*: Evans, Eli. *Judah P. Benjamin: The Jewish Confederate* (1988).

Bennett, James Gordon (1795–1872). Journalist and Publisher. The well-known editor and publisher of the *New York Herald* was born in Scotland and immigrated to the United States in 1819. After working in the publishing industry in a variety of areas, he eventually began the *Herald* in 1835. His style of journalism was both cutting edge and controversial, as Bennett pioneered such techniques as the "anonymous source" and used photography to detail battlefield carnage. Bennett supported primarily Democratic candidates for office, the one exception being Republican John C. Frémont in 1856. In 1867, Bennett retired and turned over the paper to his son. He died of a paralytic stroke on June 1, 1872. *Source*: Fermer, James. *James Gordon Bennett and the* New York Herald: *A Study of Editorial Opinion in the Civil War Era* (1986).

Blair, Francis Preston (1791–1876). Editor and Political Advisor. Francis Preston Blair was a Virginian who grew up in Kentucky. A newspaper editor who supported Andrew Jackson's campaign for president, Blair became editor of the Washington *Globe*, a pro-Jackson paper in the nation's capitol. Blair sold the paper after the election of James K. Polk, but continued to influence politics from his Silver Springs, Maryland, home. Blair and his two sons, Montgomery and Francis Jr. ("Frank"), became members of the

Republican Party in the 1850s. A proponent of a mild Reconstruction, Blair followed his son Frank back into the Democratic Party in 1868. *Source*: Smith, Elbert. *Francis Preston Blair* (1980).

Blair, Francis Preston Jr. (1821–1875). Politician and Union General. Francis Preston Blair Jr. was the son of newspaper editor Francis Preston Blair. Frank Blair studied law at Transylvania University and moved to Missouri, where he joined his brother, Montgomery, in the law office of powerful Missouri senator Thomas Hart Benton. Opposed to the extension of slavery, Frank Blair edged into the Republican Party in the 1850s. Elected to Congress in 1860, Blair was a powerful supporter of the Union in Missouri and served as a brigadier general under Generals Grant and Sherman. Alienated by radical Republican policies, Blair joined the Democratic Party after the war and was the party's 1868 vice presidential nominee. His early death in 1875 was the result of a stroke. *Source*: William Parrish, *Frank Blair: Lincoln's Conservative* (1997).

Blair, Montgomery (1813–1883). Politician and Cabinet Officer. Montgomery Blair was the oldest son of Francis Preston Blair. A graduate of West Point, Blair spent time in the army before choosing the legal profession and practicing law under the direction of Missouri senator Thomas Hart Benton. He joined the Republican Party in the 1850s. The Blair family's support for Abraham Lincoln in 1860 was rewarded by the appointment of Montgomery as postmaster general. A conservative member of the Cabinet, Blair was often at odds with Salmon Chase and other radicals. His 1864 resignation was tendered in an effort to preserve party unity and promote the reelection of Lincoln to a second term. Blair supported Andrew Johnson's policies after the war and returned to the Democratic Party. He remained active in Maryland politics until his 1883 death. *Source*: Monroney, Rita. *Montgomery Blair: Postmaster General* (1963).

Booth, John Wilkes (1838–1865). Actor and Assassin. John Wilkes Booth was the son of popular actor Junius Brutus Booth and the brother of noted actor Edwin Booth. A supporter of the Confederacy, Booth decided on assassination of the president once the Confederacy was doomed. With a group of co-conspirators, he formulated a plan to assassinate Lincoln and leading Cabinet officers. On April 14, 1865, Booth shot the president after gaining access to his box at Ford's Theater. Although he was able to escape and leave Washington, D.C., Booth and co-conspirator David Herold were eventually cornered at a farm near Port Royal, Virginia. Booth was shot during the attempt of federal forces to apprehend him. *Source*: Tidwell, William A., James O. Hall, and David Winfred Gaddy. *Come Retribution: The Confederate Secret Service and the Assassination of Lincoln* (1988).

Botts, John Minor (1802–1869). Virginia Unionist and Political Figure. John Minor Botts was a moderate Democrat who opposed both Southern fire-eaters as well as Northern abolitionists. An opponent of the secession of Virginia, Botts played no role in the government of Virginia after it seceded from the Union. Botts declined an offer to be the Unionist's nominee for the U.S. Senate under the Virginia Unionist government of Frances Pierpont. After the war, Botts became a Republican and participated in party politics until retiring from public life in 1867. *Source*: Lapidus, Robert D. "A Southern Enigma: The Unwavering Unionism of John Minor Botts." M.A. thesis; Ohio University, 1972.

Boyd, Maria Isabella "Belle" (1843–1900). Confederate Spy. Belle Boyd was born in Martinsburg, Virginia. As a resident of the Shenandoah Valley town of Fort Royal, she had ample opportunity to provide useful information to Confederate officers operating in the area. She provided useful information to General Thomas J. "Stonewall" Jackson that benefited his campaign against Union forces in the area in the spring of 1862. Boyd was eventually betrayed and spent about one month in the Old Capitol Prison in the summer of 1862. She was arrested again in 1863, but shortly released. She spent the remainder of the war in England. *Source*: Scarborough, Ruth. *Belle Boyd: Siren of the South* (1983).

Brady, Matthew B. (1823–1896). Journalist and Photographer. Matthew Brady was a native of New York who was initially trained as a portrait painter. He became interested in photography as a result of improvements in the field pioneered principally by Louis J. M. Daguerre. He opened photography studios, first in New York and then in Washington, D.C. When the war erupted, Brady accompanied Union forces in an effort to capture realistic images of the fighting. Many of the actual images that appeared in Union papers were probably the work of Brady's many assistants, since Brady's poor eyesight limited his photographic work. *Source*: Horan, James D. *Matthew Brady: Historian with a Camera* (1955).

Bragg, Braxton (1817–1876). Confederate General. Braxton Bragg was a native of North Carolina and an 1837 graduate of West Point. He served during the Seminole War in Florida and then during the Mexican War. He retired from the U.S. Army in 1856 to pursue farming in Louisiana. Because he had good relations with Confederate President Jefferson Davis, Bragg rose quickly in the ranks of Confederate military leadership. Bragg began his Confederate service commanding the Department of Louisiana, but was eventually appointed commander of the Army of Tennessee, the Confederacy's principal army in the western theater. He presided over the Confederate invasion of Kentucky in the fall of 1862 and commanded the Army of Tennessee in the battles of Perrysville, Murfreesboro, Chickamauga, and Chattanooga. Failure to follow up on a stunning victory at Chickamauga and disputes with subordinates forced Davis to remove Bragg from command. Bragg spent the remainder of the war as a presidential advisor and eventually returned to the Department of North Carolina as a divisional commander. *Source*: McWhiney, Grady C. *Braxton Bragg and Confederate Defeat* (1969).

Breckinridge, John Cabell (1821–1875). United States Senator, Vice President, and Confederate General. Kentuckian John C. Breckinridge was trained as a lawyer and practiced law before the outbreak of the Civil War. A veteran of the Mexican War, the Kentuckian was also drawn to politics. Elected to the Kentucky legislature and then to the U.S. House of Representatives, Breckinridge was elected vice president in 1856. He was subsequently elected U.S. senator after his vice presidential term expired in 1861. In the presidential election of 1860, Breckinridge was the nominee of Southern states' rights Democrats. A proponent of Kentucky neutrality, Breckinridge eventually rallied to the Confederate cause and served in a variety of military assignments. Toward the end of the war, Breckinridge was appointed secretary of war, and in that capacity, he served until the end of the war. After the war, Breckinridge fled to Cuba and then to England. When he returned to the United States in 1869, he resumed the practice of law until he died in 1875. *Source*: Davis, William C. *Breckinridge: Statesman, Soldier, and Symbol* (1974).

Brooks, Preston Smith "Bully" (1819–1857). United States Congressman. Preston Brooks was known as "Bully" Brooks throughout the country because of his highly publicized caning of Senator Charles Sumner. A native of South Carolina, Brooks was elected to the House of Representatives in 1853. Prior to his election, Brooks was a veteran in the war against Mexico. Brooks attacked Charles Sumner because of a controversial speech that Sumner delivered entitled "The Crime against Kansas." The speech savaged Andrew Butler, a relative of Brooks and a senator from South Carolina. Although the House of Representatives failed to expel Brooks, he resigned from the House. He was subsequently reelected to his House seat by approving constituents. He died in 1857 when a cold brought on serious medical problems. *Source*: Nevins, Allan. *Ordeal of the Union: A House Dividing, 1852–1857* (1947).

Brough, John (1811–1865). Governor of Ohio. John Brough was a prominent Ohio Democrat. Prior to the war, Brough was a journalist and held positions in the railroad industry. Once the war broke out, Brough repudiated the positions held by Northern Democrats who sympathized with the South (known as Copperheads). In an effort to discredit Clement Vallandigham, Brough accepted the Unionist's nomination for governor of

Ohio in 1863 and easily defeated Democratic nominee Vallandigham. Shortly after the war ended, in August 1865, Brough died while governor of Ohio. *Source*: Reid, Whitlaw. *Ohio in the War: Her Statesmen, Her Generals and Soldiers* (1868).

Brown, Albert Gallatin (1813–1880). United States and Confederate Politician. Albert Gallatin Brown was born in South Carolina; however, he immigrated to Mississippi, where he was trained as a lawyer. He was elected to the Mississippi State Legislature, the U.S. House of Representatives, and the U.S. Senate. An advocate of federal protection of slavery in federal territories, Brown garnered the reputation of a Southern extremist on the issue of slavery. After secession, Brown briefly served the Confederate armed forces before his election to the Confederate Senate, where he served for the duration of the war. After the war, Brown endorsed a conciliatory approach to Reconstruction and was popularly known as "submissionist." *Source*: Ranck, James B. *Albert Gallatin Brown: Radical Southern Nationalist* (1937).

Brown, Joseph Emerson (1821–1894). Governor of Georgia. Joseph Brown was born in South Carolina; however, he spent most of his childhood in northern Georgia. Like many political leaders, he was trained as a lawyer at Yale Law School and practiced law before entering politics. Brown began as a state legislator, but in 1857 he was elected to the first of four terms as governor of Georgia. During the war, Brown was a states' rights purist who spoke out against many of the policies of Jefferson Davis and the Richmond government. After the war, Brown aligned himself with the Republican Party. In 1880, Brown returned to the Democratic Party and was appointed to fill a vacancy in the U.S. Senate. Brown remained in the Senate until his retirement in 1891. *Source*: Parks, Joseph H. *Joseph E. Brown of Georgia* (1977).

Browning, Orville Hickman (1806–1881). United States Senator and Cabinet Officer. Orville Hickman Browning is probably best known as an Illinois political crony of Abraham Lincoln. Like Lincoln, he was born in Kentucky, trained as a lawyer, and practiced law in his Illinois home at Quincy. Originally a member of the Whig Party, Browning, like Lincoln, eventually joined the Republican Party. During the Civil War, Browning came to Washington, D.C., when he was chosen to replace the deceased Stephen Douglas in the Senate. William A. Richardson defeated him for reelection in 1863. After the war, Browning served Andrew Johnson as secretary of the interior. He was a bitter opponent of radical Reconstruction. When Johnson's term was over, he returned to Illinois and resumed his law practice. *Source*: Baxter, Maurice Glen. *Orville H. Browning: Lincoln's Friend and Critic* (1957).

Brownlow, William Gannaway "Parson" (1805–1877). Clergyman, Editor, and Politician. A native of Virginia, William Brownlow was a Methodist minister before he entered the world of journalism. He eventually landed in Knoxville, where he edited the Knoxville *Whig*. Brownlow hated Democrats and abolitionists. When the war came, Brownlow was a bitter critic of secession and the Confederacy. Consequently, he was imprisoned and expelled from the Confederacy. Returning to east Tennessee in 1864, Brownlow aligned himself with the Republican Party and played a prominent role in Reconstruction politics. He was governor of Tennessee and then chosen as senator. He retired from politics in 1875 and resumed a career in journalism until his death. *Source*: E. Merton Coulter. *William G. Brownlow: Fighting Parson of the Southern Highlands* (1937).

Buell, Don Carlos (1818–1898). Union General. Like many Civil War generals, Don Carlos Buell was a regular army officer when the Civil War began. While he was born in Ohio, the 1841 West Point graduate was raised in Indiana. Buell saw service in the Mexican War and was wounded at the battle of Churubusco. At the war's beginning, Buell was stationed on the west coast. Buell was eventually given command of the Army of Ohio in November 1861. Failing to respond to the political demands of his position, Buell refused to liberate Unionist east Tennessee as Abraham Lincoln and other Republican politicians wanted. In the fall of 1862, he stopped the advance of Confederate forces under Braxton Bragg at Perryville, Kentucky. His failure to attack the retreating Confederate Army prompted President Lincoln to remove him from command on October 8, 1862. Buell would play no additional role in the war. He spent the rest of his life engaged in Kentucky business interests. *Source*: Engle, Stephen D. *Don Carlos Buell: Most Promising of All* (1999).

Burnside, Ambrose Everett (1824–1881). Union General and United States Senator. Ambrose Burnside was born in Indiana and graduated from West Point in 1847. He served in Mexico and on the western frontier before retiring from the military in 1853. He then moved to Rhode Island, where he started a rifle manufacturing business. He returned to the military when the Civil War began. He was appointed brigadier general on August 6, 1861, and saw success early on in the conflict when he led a successful expedition on the North Carolina coast. Twice offered command of the Army of the Potomac, twice he refused. Appointed to command of the Army of the Potomac in November 1862, Burnside suffered a humiliating defeat at Fredericksburg and was removed from command after the disastrous mud march in early January 1863. His attempt to take the offensive was thwarted by two days of heavy rain that turned the roads into mud bogs. He continued to generate controversy when he arrested Clement Vallandigham while commanding the Department of Ohio. In August 1864,

Burnside presided over the controversial and disastrous battle of the Crater, near Petersburg, Virginia. He eventually resigned from the army on April 15, 1865. After the war, Burnside served as both governor and U.S. Senator from Rhode Island. *Source*: Marvel, William. *Burnside* (1991).

Butler, Benjamin Franklin (1818–1893). Attorney, Union General, and Politician. Benjamin F. Butler's career was as varied as it was controversial. Born in New Hampshire, Butler moved to Massachusetts, where he was a prominent attorney and held a variety of state offices. Initially a member of the Democratic Party and a supporter of John C. Breckinridge in 1860, Butler rallied to the Union in 1861 and became one of the most prominent War Democrats. Sensing the political winds, Butler aligned himself with radical Republicans. While his tenure as military commander at New Orleans was successful, Butler's field commands were mixed. After he bungled the attack on Fort Fisher, North Carolina, in late 1864, Grant prevented him from playing a prominent role in the war. After the war, Butler's political career blossomed. He served five terms in the House and played the principal role in the impeachment trial of Andrew Johnson. He served one term as governor of Massachusetts and was the 1884 presidential nominee of the Greenback Party. *Source*: Trefousse, Hans L. *Ben Butler: The South Called Him Beast!* (1957).

Calhoun, John Caldwell (1782–1850). United States Senator, Cabinet Officer, and Political Theorist. One of the most vigorous proponents of states' rights, John C. Calhoun was born near Abbeville, South Carolina. He studied at Yale University and became a lawyer. He was elected to the U.S. House of Representatives in 1811. He served as secretary of war under James Monroe. During the 1820s, Calhoun backed away from the so-called National Republicans and became a vigorous proponent of states' rights and nullification. After serving as vice president under Andrew Jackson and subsequently resigning as a result of the nullification crisis, Calhoun was elected to the U.S. Senate. He resigned in 1843, then served briefly as secretary of state under John Tyler before going back to the Senate in 1845, where he spent the balance of his career until his death in 1850. Calhoun's writings, including the "Exposition and Protest," played a major role in influencing Southern fire-eaters and proponents of secession. *Source*: Wilson, Clyde N. *John C. Calhoun: A Bibliography* (1990).

Cameron, Simon (1799–1889). United States Senator and Cabinet Officer. Simon Cameron was born in Maytown, Pennsylvania. He was trained as a journalist and became interested in Pennsylvania and national politics. At first affiliated with the Democratic Party, Cameron was an ally of James Buchanan. In 1845, Cameron acquired a seat in the U.S. Senate by garnering the support of Whigs, causing Democrats to question his political loyalty. Briefly aligning himself with the American Party in 1855, Cameron finally migrated into the Republican Party in 1856, and in 1857 returned to the U.S. Senate. A candidate for the presidential nomination in 1860, Cameron was eventually appointed secretary of war because of his support of Lincoln's candidacy. Dogged by rumors of financial improprieties and bogged down by the sheer size of mobilizing the North for war, Cameron was forced out of office in early 1862. He served briefly as minister to Russia before returning to his native Pennsylvania, where he continued to play the role of the consummate political insider. In 1867 he reentered the U.S. Senate, where he allied himself with the radical Republicans. He retired from politics in 1877, but continued to remain active in politics and business until his death in 1889. *Source*: Bradley, Ervin Stanley. *Simon Cameron: Lincoln's Secretary of War, A Political Biography* (1966).

Cass, Lewis (1782–1866). United States Senator, Cabinet Officer, and Presidential Candidate. Lewis Cass was Michigan's most dominant political figure prior to the Civil War. Born at Exeter, New Hampshire, Cass saw military service in the War of 1812. He was subsequently appointed governor of Michigan Territory, a post he held for eighteen years. After serving as secretary of war in the Jackson administration, Cass was elected U.S. senator from Michigan. In 1848, Cass became the Democratic presidential nominee, endorsing popular or squatter sovereignty as a way of dealing with the issue of slavery in federal territories. Cass remained in the Senate until 1857, when James Buchanan appointed him secretary of state. He resigned the position in December 1860. During the war, Cass was not politically active as his health slowly deteriorated. *Source*: Klunder, Willard Carl. *Lewis Cass and the Politics of Moderation* (1996).

Chandler, Zachariah (1813–1879). United States Senator and Cabinet Officer. Born at Bedford, New Hampshire, Zachariah Chandler migrated to Michigan, where he became a prominent Detroit businessman. Involved in Whig politics, Chandler was elected mayor of Detroit in 1851. An unsuccessful candidate for governor of Michigan, in 1857, he replaced Lewis Cass in the U.S. Senate. Chandler quickly became a powerful voice against slavery and Southern domination of the Union. During the secession crisis, he was a forceful voice against compromise, and once war erupted, he urged vigorous prosecution. As a member of the Committee on the Conduct of the War, Chandler was in a good position to advance the goals of the Republican Party. After the war, Chandler was an advocate of radical Reconstruction and a determined opponent of Andrew Johnson. Defeated for reelection in 1875, Chandler served briefly as President Grant's secretary of the interior. Reelected to the Senate in 1879, Chandler died unexpectedly in a Chicago hotel. *Source*: George, Sister Mary Karl. *Zachariah Chandler: A Political Biography* (1969).

Chestnut, James, Jr. (1815–1885). Attorney, Politician, and Presidential Advisor. Born to a wealthy plantation family, James Chestnut was educated at Princeton University and, upon returning to his native South Carolina, practiced law in his hometown of Camden. Beginning in 1840, Chestnut served in the South Carolina legislature until his election to the U.S. Senate in 1858. A proponent of secession, Chestnut favored South Carolina's withdrawal from the Union after the election of Abraham Lincoln. After serving in the Confederate Army under Pierre Beauregard, Chestnut was elected to the Confederate Congress. He served as chief of the Department of the Executive Council of South Carolina, but returned to Richmond in the fall of 1862 to serve as a military advisor to President Davis. In April 1864, Chestnut was given an active command, appointed to command the reserves of South Carolina. He performed in this capacity until the end of the war. After the war, James Chestnut practiced law and remained involved in Democratic politics. Chestnut was married to diarist Mary Chestnut. *Source*: Woodward, C. Vann and Elisabeth Muhlenfeld. *The Private Mary Chestnut: The Unpublished Civil War Diaries* (1984).

Chestnut, Mary Boykin (1823–1886). Diarist. Known principally for the diary she kept during the Civil War, Mary Boykin Chestnut was born into a life of privilege, the daughter of a wealthy South Carolina planter. She subsequently married another wealthy planter aristocrat, James Chestnut Jr. Since her husband would occupy a prominent position in the government of the Confederate States of America, Mary Chestnut was in a unique position for an insider's view of the Richmond government. After the war, Chestnut devoted much time to revising her Civil War diary. Bitter about Southern defeat, Chestnut and her husband suffered major financial losses from which they never recovered. *Source*: Woodward, C. Vann and Elisabeth Muhlenfeld. *The Private Mary Chestnut: The Unpublished Civil War Diaries* (1984).

Child, Lydia Maria Francis (1802–1880). Abolitionist, Reformer, and Writer. Lydia Maria Child became an important female abolitionist in the antebellum United States. In 1828, she was married to David L. Child, a prominent Boston attorney. She was already known as a writer, editing a magazine called *Juvenile Miscellany*. In the 1830s she began her involvement in antislavery activities. In 1833, she published *An Appeal in Favor of That Class of Americans Called Africans*. After John Brown's raid on Harpers Ferry, Child created a stir when she asked Virginia governor Henry Wise if she might be allowed to care for the incarcerated abolitionist. Once war broke out, Child was a critic of Lincoln's seemingly cautious policy on slavery; however, as the war dragged on, she changed her mind about the president and supported his reelection in 1864. After the war, Child was much less involved in public affairs. *Source*: Karcher, Carolyn L. *The First*

Woman in the Republic: A Cultural Biography of Lydia Maria Child (1994).

Clay, Cassius Marcellus (1810–1903). Antislavery Advocate, Union General, and Diplomat. Cassius Clay was born on a Kentucky plantation where slavery was practiced. He attended St. Joseph's College and Transylvania University before matriculating to Yale in 1831. Clay then practiced law. He was elected to the Kentucky legislature as a Whig in 1837. His rejection of slavery ended his political career in Kentucky after one term. Clay did not favor the immediate abolition of slavery, but endorsed gradual emancipation. Clay joined the Republican Party in the 1850s. After Lincoln's election, Clay held the position as minister to Russia until 1862. He then secured a major general's commission, but never commanded in the field. He returned to Russia as minister from 1863 to 1869. After the war, Clay eventually migrated into the Democratic Party. Although he lived until 1903, his behavior became increasingly unpredictable. In 1878, he divorced his wife, and at the age of eighty-four he married a teenaged farm hand. *Source*: Richardson, H. Edward. *Cassius Marcellus Clay: Firebrand for Freedom* (1976).

Clay, Henry (1777–1852). United States Congressman, Senator, and Presidential Candidate. Henry Clay never achieved his lifelong ambition of the presidency; nevertheless, the Virginia-born Kentucky resident was the most prominent politician of the first half of the nineteenth century. Trained as a lawyer, Clay was elected to the U.S. Senate in 1806. He was elected to the House in 1811, and quickly became speaker. He was known for the development of a comprehensive economic program known as the American system. Clay was also noted for his work in diffusing sectional tensions as evidenced in the Missouri Crisis of 1820 and the Nullification Crisis of 1832–1833. Clay ran for president in 1824 and 1832. As one of the principal founders of the Whig Party, he captured the nomination one last time in 1844. Clay spent his final years in the Senate, where he tried to moderate the increasingly divisive slavery issue. While he played a role in the Compromise of 1850, he was not the central figure in bringing about this compromise. *Source*: Remini, Robert V. *Henry Clay: Statesman for the Union* (1991).

Cobb, Howell (1815–1868). Congressman and Confederate General. Howell Cobb was born in Jefferson County, Georgia, but grew up in Athens. After graduating from the nearby University of Georgia, Cobb began practicing law in his native town. Elected to the U.S. House of Representatives in 1842, Cobb acquired an excellent reputation as a legislator that led to his election as speaker in 1849. While Cobb briefly left the Democratic Party in the early 1850s and was elected governor as a Unionist in 1851, he returned to the Democratic Party in 1853 as a matter of political expediency. He returned to the House in 1855 and, after the election of James Buchanan, was appointed as secretary of the treasury. Supporting John Breckinridge in 1860, Cobb became a determined supporter of secession. During the war, he served in the Confederate Provisional Congress as well as the military. As a brigadier general, Cobb performed a number of duties including participation in the Peninsula campaign and the Antietam campaign. After the war, Cobb was pardoned by President Johnson and resumed his law practice in Macon, Georgia. *Source*: Montgomery, Horace. *Howell Cobb's Confederate Career* (1959).

Colfax, Schuyler (1823–1885). Congressman and Vice President. Schuyler Colfax was born in New York City. After the death of his father, his mother migrated to Indiana. He became interested in journalism, investing in a South Bend newspaper at the age of twenty-three. A persistent advocate of reform, Colfax was elected to Congress in 1854 as an antislavery Whig, but cast his lot with the Republican Party after the Kansas-Nebraska Act. During the war, Colfax remained in Congress and was elected speaker in 1863. During the Reconstruction period, Colfax favored the impeachment of Andrew Johnson, and, in 1868, was elected vice president of the United States. Implicated in the Credit Mobilier scandal, in which congressmen received preferential treatment in the form of stock and money from the construction company created to build a transcontinental railroad, Colfax was not renominated for the office of vice president in 1872 and retired from public life. Colfax passed the rest of his days as a lecturer. *Source*: Smith, Willard H. *Schuyler Colfax: The Changing Fortunes of a Political Idol* (1952).

Conkling, Roscoe (1829–1888). United States Congressman and Senator. A native of Albany, New York, Roscoe Conkling became a lawyer and established a practice in nearby Utica. Possessing a charismatic personality, Conkling launched a successful political career when he was elected to the House in 1858. In 1867, he entered the U.S. Senate, where he would serve until he resigned from office in 1881. In a career characterized by combative, personal confrontations, Conkling became identified with the Stalwart wing of the Republican Party. Conkling was defeated in an attempt to return to the Senate after he retired in 1881. He spent the rest of his career practicing law. *Source*: Conkling, Alfred A. *The Life and Letters of Roscoe Conkling, Orator, Statesman, Advocate* (1889).

Cox, Samuel Sullivan "Sunset" (1824–1889). United States Congressman. Samuel Cox was a native of Zanesville, Ohio, and was educated at both Ohio University and Brown University. An excellent writer, Cox began a career in journalism, editing the *Ohio Statesman* and gaining the nickname

"Sunset" for his descriptive literary style. Attracted to the Democratic Party, Cox was nominated and elected to Congress in 1856. A moderate, Cox worked for compromise on the slavery issue. During the war, Cox associated with the pro-Southern Copperheads, an association that was undoubtedly exaggerated by Cox's friendship with Clement L. Vallandigham. While defeated for reelection in 1864, Cox was elected again in 1869. He would remain in Congress for almost twenty straight years, until his death in 1889, absent only in 1885–1886 as a result of his appointment as minister to Turkey. *Source*: Lindsey, David. *"Sunset" Cox: Irrepressible Democrat* (1959).

Crittenden, John Jordan (1786–1863). Senator, Congressman, Attorney General of the United States. Kentuckian John J. Crittenden spent over fifty years in public service, starting with his election to the Kentucky House in 1811. After service in the War of 1812, Crittenden was elected to the U.S. Senate in 1817. William Henry Harrison chose Crittenden as attorney general; however, he resigned in 1841 because of frequent disagreements with John Tyler and was returned to the Senate. After serving as attorney general under Millard Fillmore, Crittenden returned to the Senate in 1855. His most famous work was the formulation of the so-called Crittenden compromise measures in December 1860, which proposed a series of compromises on the slavery issue that might diffuse the secession crisis. Crittenden served a single term in the House, 1861–1863, then retired. He died shortly thereafter. *Source*: Kirwan, Albert D. *John J. Crittenden: The Struggle for the Union* (1962).

Dana, Charles Anderson (1819–1897). Journalist and Assistant Secretary of War. Charles Dana was born into a New England family of modest means. An 1839 graduate of Harvard University, Dana was involved with Brook Farm—a utopian community founded by George Ripley—before moving to New York, where he joined the staff of the *New York Tribune*. Dana left the paper in April 1862 after his relationship soured with editor Horace Greeley. Dana then worked for War Secretary Edwin Stanton, performing a variety of tasks until he was appointed assistant secretary of war in early 1864. It was largely through reports filed by Dana that Ulysses Grant acquired a favorable reputation in the Lincoln administration. After the war, Dana reentered the profession of journalism. He became editor of the *New York Sun* until his death in 1897. *Source*: Steele, Janet E. *The Sun Shines for All: Journalism and Ideology in the Life of Charles A. Dana* (1993).

Davis, David (1815–1886). United States Supreme Court Justice. Portly David Davis was born in Cecil County, Maryland. He attended college at Kenyon College in Ohio. After studying law with Henry Lenox in Massachusetts, Davis then studied at Yale University, then called the New Haven Law School. After his graduation, Davis moved to Bloomington, Illinois. He was elected circuit judge of the Illinois Eighth Judicial Circuit. During his fourteen years on the circuit, Davis became friends with fellow Whig attorney Abraham Lincoln. In 1860, Davis played a crucial role in managing efforts to secure Lincoln's nomination as the Republican Party's presidential nominee. Davis was appointed to the U.S. Supreme Court in 1862. He played a role in major court decisions that disagreed with the policies of Lincoln on civil liberties, including the 1866 *Ex Parte Milligan* that determined that civil courts had jurisdiction over military tribunals in areas outside the theater of war. After the war, Davis remained on the court until 1877. He served in the U.S. Senate as a Democrat prior to his death in 1886. *Source*: King, Willard L. *Lincoln's Manager, David Davis* (1960).

Davis, Henry Winter (1817–1865). United States Congressman. A cousin of Lincoln associate David Davis, Henry Winter Davis was born at Annapolis, Maryland. He was educated at Kenyon College and the University of Virginia. A successful trial lawyer, Davis's oratory also made him successful in the Whig Party. After he moved to Baltimore in 1849, Davis became active in Whig politics. After the Whig Party disintegrated, Davis cast his lot with the xenophobic American Party and was elected to the U.S. House of Representatives in 1855, 1857, and 1859 as an American candidate. Davis cooperated with the Republican Party in the secession crisis and during the Civil War. Defeated for election in 1861, Davis was elected in 1863 as a radical Republican. Davis became an opponent of Lincoln's Reconstruction policies. His Wade-Davis bill was the radical alternative to Lincoln's Ten Percent Plan. Denied the nomination for his seat in Congress in 1864, Davis died a year later from pneumonia. *Source*: Henig, Gerald S. *Henry Winter Davis: Antebellum and Civil War Congressman from Maryland* (1973).

Davis, Varina Howell (1826–1906). First Lady of the Confederacy. Varina Howell Davis was seventeen years younger than her famous husband, Jefferson Davis. Born in Mississippi, the daughter of a wealthy slave owner, Varina received a first-rate education from both tutors and attendance at a female academy in Philadelphia. Intelligent and independent, her marriage to Jefferson Davis in 1845 was often trying and turbulent. Varina Davis spent long periods of time at the couple's Davis Bend plantation without her husband. After her husband's election to the Senate and appointment to the War Department, Varina moved to Washington, where she became comfortable with the social life of the nation's capitol. Skeptical of secession, Varina Davis accepted her role as first lady, although she was widely criticized for her supposed less than enthusiastic support for the Confederacy. After the war, Varina Davis was beset by financial hardships, as Jefferson Davis's business ventures were largely unsuccessful. After he died in 1889, Varina published a highly reverential memoir of her husband. She moved to Manhattan, where she wrote occasional articles for newspapers and lived the rest of her life. *Source*: Rowland, Eron. *Varina Howell: The Wife of Jefferson Davis*, 2 vols. (1927).

DeBow, James Dunwoody Brownson (1820–1867). Journalist and Editor. James DeBow was a native of Charleston, South Carolina. His father was a prosperous merchant who died while James was still a young boy. Through hard work, James put himself through the College of Charleston. DeBow studied law after graduation, but was more interested in economics and journalism. After relocating to New Orleans, DeBow launched the *Commercial Review of the South and Southwest,* later called *DeBow's Review*. The journal promoted the economic interests of the South as well as defended the peculiar institution. DeBow was an enthusiastic supporter of secession, and, during the war, aided the Confederate government by functioning as an agent to purchase and sell cotton. After the war, DeBow resumed the publication of his journal in 1866 (he had suspended regular publication in 1862 due to wartime hardships). He died of pleurisy in 1867 while visiting relatives in New Jersey. *Source*: Eric Walther H. *The Fire Eaters* (1992).

Dennison, William (1815–1882). Governor of Ohio and Postmaster General of the United States. Born in Cincinnati, Ohio, William Dennison attended Miami University and then studied law. After establishing a law practice in his native Cincinnati, Dennison became involved in politics. Initially a member of the Whig Party, Dennison, who opposed the expansion of slavery into the federal territories, aligned himself with the Republican Party. He was nominated for governor in 1859 and served a two-year term beginning in 1860. While Dennison was energetic in his preparations to put Ohio on a war footing, his actions alienated some segments of the community. As a result, Dennison gave way to David Tod as the Republican nominee for governor in 1861. In 1864, Dennison was chair of the Republican National Committee and was appointed to the Cabinet post of postmaster general, a position he held through the first year of Andrew Johnson's presidency. After leaving Washington, Dennison devoted his time to business pursuits until his death in 1882. *Source*: Mulligan, Thomas C. "Lest the Rebels Come to Power: The Life of William Dennison." Ph.D. dissertation, Ohio State University, 1994.

Doolittle, James Rood (1815–1897). United States Senator. Born in New York, James Doolittle was a graduate of Geneva College. He was also trained as a lawyer. He moved to Racine, Wisconsin, in 1851. A Free Soil Democrat, Doolittle eventually joined the Republican Party and was elected

Republican senator in 1857. While opposed to the extension of slavery, Doolittle was a conservative whose support for emancipation was linked to the colonization of free African Americans. Eventually, Doolittle's conservatism led him back into the Democratic Party. After leaving the Senate in 1869, Doolittle moved to Chicago and established a law practice. *Source*: Marone, Biagino. "Senator James Rood Doolittle and the Struggle against Radicalism, 1857–1866." Master's thesis, Marquette University, 1955.

Durant, Thomas Jefferson (1817–1882). Louisiana Unionist. A native of Pennsylvania, Thomas Durant moved to New Orleans when he was seventeen years old. While Durant volunteered for service in the Confederate forces in 1861, after the city fell to federal forces in 1862, he made an about turn of face. A close ally of Benjamin Butler, Durant became associated with radical Republicans and became an advocate of racial equality. When Nathaniel Banks replaced Butler in Louisiana, Durant became a hardened opponent of Banks's more cautious plans to reconstruct Louisiana. While appointed attorney general of the reconstructed Louisiana regime, Durant's opposition to Banks eventually prompted his resignation. After the war, Durant moved to New York, practiced law, and argued a number of important cases before the U.S. Supreme Court. *Source*: Tregle, Joseph G., Jr. "Thomas J. Durant, Utopian Socialism, and the Failure of Presidential Reconstruction in Louisiana." *Journal of Southern History* (1979).

Early, Jubal Anderson (1816–1894). Politician and Confederate General. Jubal Early was a native of Virginia. An 1837 graduate of West Point, Early spent time in the army after the war, serving in Florida's second Seminole War. Early retired from the army in 1838, returning to Virginia to pursue the practice of law. He returned to the army in 1846 when the Mexican War began. Resuming his law practice and political activities after the war with Mexico, Early was an opponent of secession; however, once Virginia seceded, he joined Confederate forces. Early rendered steady and brilliant service as a brigadier general (eventually a major general) and divisional commander in the Army of Northern Virginia. Perhaps his most notable accomplishment was his generalship in the summer of 1864, when Early defeated a force in the Shenandoah Valley and threatened the city of Washington, D.C. After the war, Early fled the country, living in Mexico and Canada. He returned to his native Virginia in 1867. He died in Lynchburg, Virginia, in 1894. *Source*: Osborne, Charles C. *Jubal: The Life and Times of General Jubal A. Early* (1992).

Emerson, Ralph Waldo (1803–1882). Writer, Orator, and Philosopher. Ralph Waldo Emerson was a native of Boston, Massachusetts, and a graduate of Harvard University. Although trained in theology, Emerson left the ministerial profession in 1832. He became one of the most popular and influential American thinkers of the day. Credited as one of the founders of transcendentalism, Emerson gained famed for his well-known essays, including "Nature" and "Self-Reliance." Although an early opponent of slavery, Emerson was suspicious of political activism until the passage of the 1850 Fugitive Slave Law. Endorsing the "higher law" position of radical abolitionists, Emerson now began speaking out forcefully against slavery. During the Civil War, Emerson was a powerful voice in support of the Union, viewing the Northern cause as advancing the side of freedom and morality. After the war, Emerson was involved in such organizations as the National Academy of Arts and Literature. *Source*: Allen, Gay Wilson. *Waldo Emerson: A Biography* (1981).

Ericsson, John (1803–1886). Inventor and Naval Architect. Known chiefly as the inventor of the USS *Monitor*, John Ericsson was a native of Sweden. A member of the Swedish Corps of Cadets, Ericsson showed an unusual mechanical aptitude early in life. In 1844, Ericsson came to the United States, largely through the efforts of Robert Field Stockton, a U.S. naval officer. Ericsson designed the USS *Princeton*; however, a fatal accident during the ship's trial tarnished Ericsson's reputation until the Civil War. During the Civil War, the navy commissioned Ericsson to build the *Monitor*, largely to counteract the Confederate ironclad, *Merrimack*. The success of the *Monitor* in neutralizing the *Merrimack* was a personal triumph for Ericsson, who was subsequently commissioned to build four additional classes of ironclads by the Department of the Navy. After the war, Ericsson continued to be involved in the development of new technologies and inventions. *Source*: DeKay, James T. *Monitor: The Story of the Legendary Civil War Ironclad and the Man Whose Invention Changed the Course of History* (1997).

Everett, Edward (1794–1865). Politician, Orator, and Diplomat. One of the foremost orators of his day, Edward Everett had successful careers in several areas. Everett was an ordained minister, a professor at Harvard University, as well as editor of the prestigious *North American Review*. Everett held a variety of political offices including U.S. congressman, governor of Massachusetts, minister to England, U.S. senator, and secretary of state under Millard Fillmore. Everett was also the vice presidential nominee of the Constitutional Union Party. Everett was the featured speaker at the dedication of the Gettysburg National Cemetery. He did not live to see the Union restored, as he passed away on January 15, 1865. *Source*: Frothingham, Paul Revere. *Edward Everett* (1925).

Ewell, Richard Stoddert "Old Bald Head" (1817–1872). Confederate General. Born in Washington, D.C., and reared in Prince William County, Virginia, Richard Ewell entered West Point in 1836. After graduating, Ewell entered a career of service in the regular army, serving in the American West, performing distinguished service in the Mexican War, and returning to service on the frontier after the war. When Virginia seceded from the Union, Ewell tendered his service to the Confederate government. He gained a reputation for effective generalship during the Shenandoah campaign of May 1862 and during the Peninsula campaign, where he served under Robert E. Lee. Wounded at the battle of Groveton, Ewell lost a leg; however, he eventually returned to active duty, replacing Thomas "Stonewall" Jackson as commander of the 2nd corps of the Army of Northern Virginia. Playing a major role at the battle of Gettysburg, some have blamed Confederate fortunes on Ewell's indecisiveness on the first day of battle. Wounded again at the battle of Spotsylvania, Ewell again returned to active command and commanded the defenses of Richmond until the end of the war. *Source*: Pfanz, Donald C. *Richard S. Ewell: A Soldier's Life* (1998).

Ewing, Thomas, Jr. (1829–1896). Union General. Born in Lancaster, Ohio, Thomas Ewing was the son of the politically powerful Thomas Ewing Sr. After graduating from Brown University, Ewing returned to Ohio, where he studied law. He then immigrated to Kansas, where he began a business with brother Hugh and their foster brother, William Tecumseh Sherman. Ewing became a prominent Free State leader in the political struggle in Kansas in the 1850s. When war erupted in 1861, he became a colonel in the 11th Kansas regiment. He was promoted brigadier general for his meritorious service at the battle of Prairie Grove, Arkansas. Placed in command of the district of the border, Ewing had the unenviable task of dealing with Confederate guerrillas. Prompted by Quantrill's raid on Lawrence, Ewing issued the controversial General Order #11, which forced the residents of four Missouri counties to vacate in an effort to deny guerrillas support. After the war, Ewing moved to Washington, D.C., where he practiced law. He later returned to Ohio, where he became involved in Democratic and Greenback Party politics. *Source*: Castel, Albert. *Civil War Kansas: Reaping the Whirlwind* (1997).

Farragut, David Glasgow (1801–1870). Union Naval Officer. The son of George Farragut, David Farragut was born in Tennessee; however, at an early age, David (originally James) was placed under the guardianship of David Porter, a naval officer and father of David Dixon Porter. At the age of twelve, David Farragut became a midshipman in the U.S. Navy, serving on the USS *Essex*. He then served an apprenticeship in the navy in the Mediterranean. Farragut is best known for his Civil War service. He commanded the naval force that captured New Orleans. In addition, he captured a number of other Confederate ports including Galveston, Corpus

Christi, and Sabine Pass. He assisted in military operations against Port Hudson on the Mississippi. Perhaps his most significant naval operation was the taking of the Port of Mobile, a critical Union victory that created momentum for the reelection of Abraham Lincoln. While Farragut commanded the European squadron after the war, his life was cut short by a heart attack in 1870. *Source*: Hearn, Chester G. *David Glasgow Farragut: The Civil War Years* (1997).

Fessenden, William Pitt (1806–1869). United States Senator and Cabinet Officer. William Pitt Fessenden was born in Maine and a graduate of Bowdoin College. Following the example of his father, William became a lawyer in Portland, Maine. Successful at this career, Fessenden became involved in Whig politics. He served in the Maine legislature and the U.S. House of Representatives, and, in 1854, was chosen to represent Maine in the U.S. Senate. While a moderate Republican, Fessenden was one of the most powerful and influential members of the Senate. Fessenden served briefly as secretary of the Treasury after Salmon Chase resigned in 1864. He returned to the Senate and chaired the powerful Joint Committee on Reconstruction. Fessenden became unpopular with fellow Republicans when he voted to acquit Andrew Johnson during the impeachment trial. Unpopular for this decision, Fessenden died before he stood for reelection to the Senate. *Source*: Jellison, Charles A. *Fessenden of Maine: Civil War Senator* (1962).

Floyd, John Buchanan (1806–1863). Governor of Virginia, Cabinet Officer, and Confederate General. John Floyd was born in Montgomery County, Virginia. A graduate of South Carolina College, Floyd practice law, farmed, and eventually became interested in Democratic politics in Virginia. He was elected governor of Virginia in 1848, and, in 1857, became Secretary of War. In the latter position, Floyd's administration was riddled with charges of corruption and nepotism. During the secession crisis, Floyd urged President Buchanan to surrender Fort Sumter. When his native state seceded, Floyd volunteered for Confederate military service. Sent West, Floyd's performance at Fort Donelson in February 1862 was less than admirable. For this, Jefferson Davis eventually removed him from command. After his health deteriorated, Floyd died in 1863. *Source*: Pinnegar, Charles. *Brand of Infamy: A Biography of John Buchanan Floyd* (2002).

Foote, Andrew Hull (1806–1863). Union Navy Admiral. Andrew Foote played a significant role in naval operations in the western theater of the American Civil War. A native of New Haven, Connecticut, Foote joined the U.S. Navy as a midshipman in the early 1820s. He saw duty in the West Indies, off the southwest coast of Africa, and in Asia. Foote was a unique naval officer as a result of his devotion to spreading Christianity as well as the temperance cause. During the Civil War, Foote commanded ironclad vessels on the Mississippi River, participating in such battles as Fort Henry, Fort Donelson, New Madrid, and Island No. 10 on the Mississippi River between Tennessee and Missouri. Wounded in actions against Fort Donelson, Foote eventually took a leave of absence. Just before returning to duty in June 1863, he contracted Bright's disease and died. *Source*: Tucker, Spencer C. *Admiral Andrew H. Foote* (1999).

Forrest, Nathan Bedford (1821–1877). Confederate General. Without the benefit of formal education, Nathaniel Forrest was nevertheless an economic success in antebellum Tennessee. Born in Tennessee, Forrest also lived in northern Mississippi. Prior to the Civil War, Forrest amassed a considerable fortune through slave trading and other business ventures. At the eve of the war, he lived in Memphis. Although lacking military experience and education, he became one of the Confederacy's most competent and daring cavalry commanders. While participating in numerous battles, Forrest's name in history is often linked to the Fort Pillow massacre, which took place on April 12, 1864, just north of Memphis. Fort Pillow was famous because of the slaughter of African-American troops, who fought for the union. After the war, Forrest invested in railroads and dabbled in politics. A determined opponent of African American rights, Forrest became a prominent leader of the Ku Klux Klan. *Source*: Hurst, Jack. *Nathan Bedford Forrest: A Biography* (1993).

Fox, Gustavus Vasa (1821–1883). Assistant Secretary of the Navy and Union Naval Officer. Gustavus Fox left his Saugus, Massachusetts, home at the age of sixteen, when he became a midshipman in the U.S. Navy. After eighteen years of service, he left the navy for a business career. During the secession crisis, Fox was called to Washington to act as an advisor to Winfield Scott. His plan to reprovision Fort Sumter was rejected by President Buchanan. Eventually President Lincoln adopted the plan; however, it failed, in part because key naval vessels were withheld from the expedition. A relative of the powerful Blair family, Fox was eventually appointed assistant secretary of the navy. Throughout the war, Fox was a fervent proponent of ironclad monitors. After leaving the Department of the Navy in 1866, Fox participated in the diplomatic team that worked on the purchase of Alaska. He then returned to the woolens business in Massachusetts. *Source*: Musicant, Ivan. *Divided Waters: The Naval History of the Civil War* (1995).

Frémont, Jessie Benton (1824–1902). Political Activist and Writer. Married to the controversial John C. Frémont, Jessie Benton Frémont came from a politically active family, the daughter of Missouri Senator Thomas Hart Benton. Jessie Benton Frémont was a tireless promoter of her husband's political career, playing an active role in the presidential campaign of 1856.

During the Civil War, Jessie went to Washington to defend her husband's emancipation decree, arguing Frémont's case with President Lincoln. After the war, the Frémonts experienced financial difficulty and Jessie Benton contributed to the family income through publications. After John Frémont's death, she retired to Los Angeles, where she composed her memoirs. *Source*: Herr, Paula. *Jesse Benton Frémont: A Biography* (1987).

Frémont, John Charles "The Pathfinder" (1813–1890). Politician and Union General. The son of a French immigrant, John Frémont was born in Savannah, Georgia, and educated in South Carolina. After briefly teaching mathematics, he joined the army and was assigned to the topological engineers. In 1841, he married Jessie Benton. He gained wide popularity for his explorations in the West in the 1840s and 1850s. He was chosen as the first presidential nominee of the Republican Party in 1856, but lost to Democratic nominee James Buchanan. During the Civil War, he served as commander of the Department of the West and in the Shenandoah Valley. His performance in both commands was lackluster. After resigning in 1862, he played no further role in military affairs. A third party presidential candidate in 1864, Frémont eventually withdrew from the race, aiding to the reelection of Abraham Lincoln. After the war, Frémont struggled financially, investing in risky railroad ventures. He also served as governor of Arizona Territory from 1878 to 1883. *Source*: Nevins, Allan. *Frémont: Pathmarker of the West* (1955).

Gamble, Hamilton Rowan (1798–1864). Jurist and Governor of Missouri. Hamilton Rowan Gamble was born at Winchester, Virginia. Moving to St. Louis, Gamble embarked on a successful career as a lawyer, politician, and jurist. After serving in the Missouri state legislature a single term, Gamble won a seat on the Missouri Supreme Court in 1851. Gamble played a pivotal role in Missouri's March 1861 convention that considered, but did not accept, secession from the Union. After current Governor Claiborne Fox Jackson vacated Jefferson City, another state convention chose Gamble governor of the provisional government of Missouri. Gamble's tenure in office was marked by bitter controversy as the governor fought with Union military commanders such as John Frémont and an increasingly large group of radical Republicans determined to force emancipation on Missouri. Gamble died in office on January 31, 1864. *Source*: Parrish, William E. *Turbulent Partnership: Missouri and the Union, 1861–1865* (1963).

Garfield, James Abram (1831–1881). Congressman, Union General, and President of the United States. Born in the Western Reserve region of Ohio, James Garfield was influenced by his religious upbringing. In 1856 he graduated from Williams College in Massachusetts. After teaching for a few years, he was elected to the Ohio legislature as a Republican representative. During the Civil War, he saw active duty and was eventually commissioned a brigadier general and then a major general. He saw action in the western theater, serving with both the Army of the Ohio and the Cumberland. Elected to Congress in the 1862 fall elections, Garfield resigned from the army in December 1863. After the war, Garfield continued to serve in Congress. He was elected to the presidency in 1880, but had served only four months when he was assasinated by a disappointed patronage seeker. *Source*: Peskin, Allan. *Garfield: A Biography* (1978).

Garrison, William Lloyd (1805–1879). Editor and Abolitionist. Born at Newburyport, Massachusetts, William Lloyd Garrison was one of the most prominent abolitionists in the nineteenth-century United States. At first a journalist, Garrison worked for different newspapers. Attracted to anti-slavery ideas, Garrison established the *Liberator* in 1831, a radical anti-slavery newspaper that demanded the immediate, unconditional abolition of slavery. In 1832, Garrison founded the New England Anti-Slavery Society that eventually merged with other abolition societies to form the American Anti-Slavery Society. A suasionist who spurned political activity, Garrison rejected the Liberty Party and later the Free Soil Party, which tried to use the political system to abolish slavery. While a pacifist, Garrison eventually supported Lincoln, particularly when the war was tied to the emancipation of slaves. During the postwar years, Garrison largely supported the Reconstruction programs of the Republican radicals. *Source*: Stewart, James B. *William Lloyd Garrison and the Challenge of Emancipation* (1992).

Giddings, Joshua Reed (1795–1864). United States Congressman. Born in Pennsylvania, Joshua Giddings eventually settled in the radical Western Reserve area of Ohio. He became a lawyer in 1821 and became active in Whig politics. In 1838, he was elected to the U.S. House, where he became an outspoken critic of slavery. He joined the Free Soil Party in 1848 and then moved into the Republican Party in 1854. During the Civil War, he served as consul general in Montreal, Canada, where he died in 1864. *Source*: Stewart, James B. *Joshua Giddings and the Tactics of Radical Politics* (1970).

Grant, Ulysses S. (1822–1885). Union General and Eighteenth President of the United States. Without the Civil War, Ulysses S. Grant might have remained an obscure figure in American history. An Ohio native and 1843 graduate of West Point, Grant served with competent distinction in the Mexican War. Trouble with drinking, however, forced him out of the army in 1854, and Grant undertook a number of business pursuits with little success. On the eve of the war, Grant was clerking in a harness shop in Galena, Illinois, owned by his father and operated by his younger brothers. Appointed colonel of the 21st Illinois, Grant slowly made his way to the top position of military leadership. Winning victories at Fort Henry and Fort Donelson made Grant a household name in the North. Grant would eventually command the Army of the Tennessee when Henry Halleck was sent east. He orchestrated the brilliant Vicksburg campaign, which culminated in the surrender of the Confederate stronghold on July 4, 1863. After becoming the top commander in the West and presiding over victorious Union forces at the battle of Chattanooga, Grant was appointed lieutenant general and general-in-chief. While orchestrating overall Union strategy for all armies, Grant traveled with the Army of the Potomac and presided over some of the bloodiest battles of the war: the Wilderness, Spotsylvania, Cold Harbor, and Petersburg. When he accepted Lee's surrender at Appomattox Court House on April 9, 1865, Ulysses Grant was the most popular military figure in the country. After the war, Grant continued as general-in-chief. He was inevitably drawn into the field of presidential politics, and elected president in 1868 and again in 1872. Although Grant tried to enforce civil rights legislation and protect the rights of African Americans in the South, his tenure in office was often distracted by numerous scandals that plagued his two terms. He published his memoirs just prior to his 1885 death from cancer. *Source*: Perrot, Geoffrey. *Ulysses S. Grant: Soldier & President* (1997).

Greenhow, Rose O'Neal (1817–1864). Confederate Spy. Hailing from Maryland, Rose Greenhow lived in Washington, D.C., when the Civil War began. An attractive, wealthy widow, she was well connected in Washington's social circles. Known for Southern sympathies, she used her connections to advance the cause of the Confederacy. She provided useful information to General Pierre Beauregard before the first battle of Manassas. Union officials eventually imprisoned Greenhow for her espionage activities in January 1862. Released in June 1862, Greenhow then traveled to England. She died on the way back when her ship, the *Condor*, sank off the coast of North Carolina. *Source*: Fishel, Edwin C. *The Secret War for the Union: The Untold Story of Military Intelligence in the Civil War* (1996).

Grimke, Angelina (1805–1879). Abolitionist and Feminist. The more radical of the antislavery Grimke sisters, Angelina was born in Charleston, South Carolina. Educated at Charleston Seminary, Grimke questioned the morality of slavery at an early age. While in Philadelphia with sister, Sarah, Angelina joined the Philadelphia Female Anti-Slavery Society. Influenced by William Lloyd Garrison, Grimke joined the American Anti-Slavery Society and married abolitionist Theodore Dwight Weld. Grimke wrote two pamphlets to help the cause of slavery and women's rights: *An Appeal to the Christian Women of the South* (1836) and *Appeal to the Women of the*

Nominally Free States (1837). Grimke eventually supported the war when she realized it would lead to emancipation. In 1870, she settled in Hyde Park, Massachusetts. *Source*: Lumpkin, Katharine Du Pre. *The Emancipation of Angelina Grimke* (1974).

Grimke, Sarah Moore (1792–1873). Abolitionist and Feminist. Born in Charleston, South Carolina, Sarah Grimke was Angelina Grimke's older sister. Although born into a wealthy slaveholding family, Grimke opposed slavery and treated African Americans as equals at an early age. Unhappy with the position of women in Southern society, Grimke joined the Quaker church and moved to Philadelphia in 1821. She soon joined her sister in antislavery work for the American Anti-Slavery Society. She helped Angelina and husband Theodore Dwight Weld put together *American Slavery As It Is*, which appeared in 1838. A pacifist, Grimke still supported the Union during the Civil War. She eventually retired with the Welds to Hyde Park, Massachusetts. *Source*: Lerner, Gerda. *The Grimke Sisters from South Carolina: Rebels against Slavery* (1967).

Grow, Galusha Aaron (1822–1907). United States Congressman. Born in Connecticut, Galusha Grow moved to Glenwood, Pennsylvania, at the age of twelve. After graduating from Amherst College, Grow studied law and became active in Democratic politics. Grow was elected to Congress in 1850 as a compromise candidate, replacing law partner David Wilmot, the incumbent congressman. Grow moved into the Republican Party in the mid-1850s. He eventually became speaker in 1861. Defeated for reelection in 1862, he returned to the House in 1893 and served until 1903. *Source*: Ilisevich, Robert D. *Galusha A. Grow: The People's Candidate* (1988).

Halleck, Henry Wager "Old Brains" (1815–1872). Union General. At the beginning of the Civil War, Henry Halleck was one of the foremost authorities on military matters in the United States. Originally from Westernville, New York, Halleck entered West Point in 1837. After graduation, he served in the prestigious Army Corps of Engineers. He also published works on military science, including *Elements of Military Arts & Science* in 1846. During the Mexican War, Halleck served in California. At the beginning of the Civil War, his close association with Winfield Scott resulted in a commission as major general. He succeeded John C. Frémont in the West and quickly demonstrated his knack for administrative order. After several successes in the West, Halleck was appointed general-in-chief and relocated to Washington, D.C. Although largely unsuccessful in this role, Halleck nonetheless played an important role in establishing order in the Union military bureaucracy. After the war, Halleck commanded forces in Richmond, the west coast, and Louisville, Kentucky, where he died in 1872. *Source*: Ambrose, Stephen. *Halleck: Lincoln's Chief of Staff* (1962).

Hamlin, Hannibal "Carthaginian of Maine" (1809–1891). United States Senator and Vice President. A native of Paris Hill, Maine, Hannibal Hamlin was not formally educated; however, he learned to read and studied law with two Portland, Maine, attorneys. In 1835, Hamlin was elected to the Maine legislature. Hamlin acquired a reputation as a brilliant orator. Devoted to the ideology of Andrew Jackson, Hamlin also developed a deep hatred for slavery. An advocate of the Wilmot Proviso, Hamlin was elected to the U.S. Senate in 1848 after serving in the House since 1843. He resigned his seat in 1856, leaving the Democratic Party in the aftermath of the Kansas-Nebraska Act. Joining the Republican Party, Hamlin was quickly elected governor of Maine in 1856, but then resigned to return to the Senate a year later. Nominated and elected vice president in 1860, Hamlin moved closer to the positions of the Republican radicals. Andrew Johnson replaced him on the ticket in 1864. In 1869, he was elected senator from Maine, remaining in the Senate until 1881. After serving one year as minister to Spain, Hamlin retired in 1882. *Source*: Scroggins, Mark. *Hannibal Hamlin: The Life of Lincoln's First Vice President* (1994).

Hammond, James Henry (1807–1864). United States Senator and Governor of South Carolina. Known for coining the phrase *King Cotton*, James Henry Hammond was a South Carolina native. He graduated from South Carolina College in Columbia and taught school before becoming an attorney. An ally of John C. Calhoun, Hammond endorsed the doctrine of nullification. In 1835, Hammond was elected to the House of Representatives. After losing the South Carolina gubernatorial race in 1840, he was elected to the position two years later. In 1857, Hammond was elected to the U.S. Senate. Although a believer in states' rights, Hammond was not enthusiastic about secession from the Union after Lincoln's election in 1860. He was a persistent critic of Confederate President Jefferson Davis for his intrusion into the rights of states. He did not live to experience Confederate defeat, dying on his plantation home in 1864. *Source*: Faust, Drew Gilpin. *James Henry Hammond and the Old South: A Plan for Mastery* (1982).

Hancock, Winfield Scott "Hancock the Superb" (1824–1886). Union General and Democratic Presidential Nominee. Born at Montgomery Square, Pennsylvania, Winfield Scott Hancock graduated from West Point in 1844. He stayed in the U.S. Army, where he saw service in the Mexican War, in Kansas, and when fighting Native American tribes during the third Seminole War. When the Civil War erupted, Hancock traveled back from duty in California where he was last stationed. He was quickly commissioned as a brigadier general. He served with distinction in the majority of battles in the eastern theater, including the Peninsula campaign, Antietam, Fredericksburg, Chancellorsville, Gettysburg, the Wilderness, Spotsylvania,

Cold Harbor, and Petersburg. After the war, Hancock remained active, overseeing the execution of the Lincoln assassination conspirators. In 1880, Hancock was nominated by the Democrats for president, but lost to Republican James Garfield. Hancock remained in the army until his 1886 death. *Source*: Jordan, David M. *Winfield Scott Hancock: A Soldier's Life* (1988).

Harris, Isham Green (1818–1897). Governor of Tennessee. Although born in Tullahoma, Tennessee, Isham Harris moved to Mississippi, where he practiced law and became politically active. In 1847, Harris was elected to the state senate of Mississippi. After serving two terms in the U.S. House of Representatives, Harris moved back to his native Tennessee, starting the practice of law in the larger city of Memphis. Harris succeeded Andrew Johnson as governor in 1857. After the attack on Fort Sumter, Harris was able to steer Tennessee into the Confederacy. During the war, Harris also served as an aide to General Albert Sidney Johnston as well as a number of other generals in the western theater. After the war, Harris fled the country as the Tennessee legislature offered a reward for his capture. Through the efforts of William Brownlow, Harris eventually returned to Memphis in 1876. He was subsequently elected to the U.S. Senate in 1877. He remained in the Senate until his death in 1897. *Source*: Watters, George Wayne. "Isham Green Harris, Civil War Governor and Senator from Tennessee, 1818–1897." Ph.D. dissertation, Florida State University, 1977.

Hawthorne, Nathaniel (1804–1864). American Writer. Writer and novelist Nathaniel Hawthorne had already acquired a reputation as a leading American writer at the time of the Civil War. Known for such novels as *The Scarlet Letter*, *The House of Seven Gables*, and *The Blithedale Romance*, the Salem, Massachusetts, native was also a Democratic partisan and friend of former President Franklin Pierce. Prior to the Civil War, Hawthorne accepted patronage positions from the party including an appointment as an inspector in the Boston Customs House. Hawthorne's chief contribution to the Civil War years was his publication in the *Atlantic Monthly* of an article highly critical of the Union war effort and somewhat sympathetic to the cause of the South. Roundly criticized by Northerners, Hawthorne's health began to deteriorate and he died before the war ended, passing away on May 18, 1864. *Source*: Turner, Arlin. *Nathaniel Hawthorne: A Biography* (1980).

Hay, John Milton (1838–1905). Presidential Secretary, Historian, and Secretary of State. John Hay was born in Indiana, but moved to Warsaw, Illinois, at an early age. He graduated from Brown University in 1858. After graduation, he studied law at his uncle's office in Springfield, Illinois, where he also became acquainted with Abraham Lincoln. Along with journalist

John Nicolay, Hay went to Washington, D.C., where he served as a presidential secretary. With Nicolay, Hay wrote an eight-volume biography of the sixteenth president, published in 1895. Appointed assistant secretary of state under Garfield, Hay was appointed to the top position in the state department by William McKinley in 1897. *Source*: Dennett, Tyler. *John Hay: From Poetry to Politics* (1963).

Hayes, Rutherford Birchard (1822–1893). Union General and Nineteenth President of the United States. Born and raised in Ohio, Rutherford Hayes was trained as a lawyer and was living in Cincinnati when the war began. Although lacking military experience, Hayes would rise to the rank of brigadier general in 1864. He saw action in West Virginia, the Antietam campaign, and the Shenandoah campaign of 1864 under Philip Sheridan. In 1863, Hayes participated in the pursuit and capture of Confederate raider John Hunt Morgan. After the war, Hayes was a radical Republican congressman, governor of Ohio, and finally the nineteenth president of the United States. His election in 1876 is often viewed as the end of Reconstruction in the South. *Source*: Hoogenboom, Ari. *Rutherford B. Hayes: Warrior and President* (1995).

Helper, Hinton Rowan (1829–1909). Antislavery Writer. Born in Rowan County, North Carolina, Hinton Helper was born into a poor farming family. Helper became an indentured servant, but ran away to New York after embezzling money. Although a bitter Negrophobe, Helper blamed the lot of poor whites in the South on slavery. In 1857, he published *The Impending Crisis of the South: How to Meet It*, a book highly critical of slavery. Not only did the book enrage Southerners, but it also made Helper persona non grata in the South. The newly formed Republican Party championed Helper's book. After the Civil War, Helper looked to Andrew Johnson as the type of leader who might transform the South. In his later years, Helper dabbled in real estate, but also continued to write and publish. *Source*: Bailey, Hugh C. *Hinton Rowan Helper: Abolitionist-Racist* (1965).

Hill, Ambrose Powell "Little Powell" (1825–1865). Confederate General. A native of Culpepper County, Virginia, Ambrose Powell Hill was an 1846 graduate of West Point and a veteran of the Mexican War. During the secession crisis, Hill resigned from the U.S. Army to serve the Confederacy. He earned a reputation as a skilled general. Serving in the eastern theater, Hill was initially a brigade commander, but was eventually promoted to major general and a divisional commander in the Army of Northern Virginia. He participated in numerous battles including Williamsburg, the Seven Days, Cedar Mountain, Second Manassas, Antietam, Fredericksburg, and Chancellorsville. After the death of "Stonewall" Jackson, Hill became a corps commander in the Army of Northern Virginia. Illness caused his performance to suffer at Gettysburg, and during the spring campaign of 1864, Hill was frequently absent due to illness. Hill was killed in action near Petersburg, Virginia, on April 2, 1865. *Source*: Robertson, James I., Jr. *A. P. Hill: The Story of a Confederate Warrior* (1987).

Hill, Daniel Harvey (1821–1889). Confederate General. Daniel Harvey Hill was born in South Carolina and graduated from West Point in 1842. He served in the Mexican War. After the war, he taught mathematics at Washington College in Lexington, Virginia, and then at Davidson College in North Carolina. When the Civil War erupted, Hill volunteered for Confederate service and was put in charge of the 1st North Carolina Infantry. Hill was eventually made brigadier and then major general. He served under both Joseph Johnston and Robert E. Lee, and participated in most of the major battles in the eastern theater including the Seven Days, Antietam, and Fredericksburg. He was then promoted to lieutenant general (later revoked) and sent west, where he participated in the battle of Chickamauga. After the war, Hill edited a journal and returned to teaching. *Source*: Bridges, Hal. *Lee's Maverick General: Daniel Harvey Hill* (1961; reprint, 1991).

Holden, William Woods (1818–1892). Journalist and Southern Peace Advocate. William W. Holden was a Raleigh, North Carolina, lawyer and journalist. A member of the Democratic Party, Holden was a vigorous advocate of secession and states' rights in the 1850s. When aspirations for political office were frustrated, Holden became much more conciliatory in his approach toward secession from the Union. After the firing on Fort Sumter, Holden supported the Confederacy; however, he was a persistent critic of the methods of Jefferson Davis, particularly in the columns of his *North Carolina Standard*. By 1863, Holden was calling for peace and sponsoring peace rallies. He ran for governor on a platform endorsing separate peace negotiations for North Carolina with the Union. Incumbent Governor Zebulon Vance overwhelmingly defeated him. After the war, Holden became a Republican and provisional governor. After he was impeached and removed from his position, he returned to private life. *Source*: Harris, William C. *William Woods Holden: Firebrand of North Carolina Politics* (1987).

Hooker, Joseph "Fighting Joe" (1814–1879). Union General. A native of Hadley, Massachusetts, Joseph Hooker graduated from West Point in 1837. After serving in the Mexican War, he resigned from the army in 1853; however, he quickly volunteered for military service once the Civil War began. He was extremely ambitious and looked for opportunities to promote himself. He performed admirably under McClellan during the Peninsula campaign. He participated in the second battle of Manassas and was wounded during the battle of Antietam. After the battle of Fredericksburg, Hooker was promoted to commander of the Army of the Potomac. After suffering defeat at Chancellorsville, Hooker resigned from command just prior to the battle of Gettysburg. Hooker was sent west, where he was a corps commander in the Army of the Cumberland and participated in the battles of Chickamauga, Chattanooga, and the Atlanta campaign. Angered by his treatment by top general in the West, William T. Sherman, Hooker resigned and spent the rest of the war in Chicago, supervising reserves. *Source*: Hebert, Walter H. *Fighting Joe Hooker* (1944).

Houston, Sam (1793–1863). United States Senator and Governor of Texas. Born in Virginia and raised in Tennessee, Sam Houston spent a good deal of his early life living with the Cherokee Indians in eastern Tennessee. He fought under Andrew Jackson in the War of 1812. After practicing law in Tennessee, Houston became involved in politics and was elected to the U.S. House of Representatives in 1823. He worked as an Indian negotiator in Arkansas and Texas. When Texas successfully revolted from Mexico, Houston was elected president. When Texas later joined the United States, Houston became a U.S. senator. In 1859, he was elected governor. An opponent of secession, Houston attempted to keep Texas in the Union and even attempted to establish another Texas Republic. Houston left office in 1861 and died in 1863 before the war concluded. *Source*: Williams, John Hoyt. *Sam Houston: A Biography of the Father of Texas* (1993).

Howe, Julia Ward (1819–1910). Social Reformer. Born into a wealthy New York City family, Julia Ward received a first-rate education from private tutors. She married Boston reformer Samuel Gridley Howe in 1843, and she bore six children. Howe was active as a writer, editing the antislavery periodical *Commonwealth*. She also published literary works including the play *Leonora* (1857) and *A Trip to Cuba* (1860). During the Civil War, she composed the poem "Battle Hymn of the Republic," later set to music. When the war ended, Howe stayed involved in reform movements, particularly the peace movement and women's suffrage. *Source*: Clifford, Deborah Pickman. *Mine Eyes Have Seen the Glory: A Biography of Julia Ward Howe* (1979).

Hunter, David (1802–1886). Union General. A native of the District of Columbia, David Hunter was an 1822 graduate of West Point. After service in both the Mexican War and Kansas Territory, Hunter had an extensive career in the Civil War. Appointed brigadier general and then major general, Hunter commanded in the Department of the West, the Department of Kansas, the Department of the South, and the Department of West Virginia. When Hunter issued a May 7, 1862 emancipation proclamation in the Department of the South, he inspired the radicals; however, Abraham

Lincoln quickly overruled him. After an ignominious defeat in the Shenandoah Valley in June 1864, Hunter would not see field service again. After the war, he took part in the military trial of the Lincoln assassination conspirators. *Source*: Hubell, John T., and James W. Geary, eds. *Biographical Dictionary of the Union: Northern Leaders of the Civil War* (1995).

Jackson, Claiborne Fox (1806–1862). Governor of Missouri. A Kentucky native, Claiborne Jackson moved to Missouri in the 1820s. He was elected to the Missouri House in 1836 and to the Missouri Senate in 1848. In 1860, he was elected to the governorship of Missouri. Although a supporter of Stephen A. Douglas, Jackson favored secession. Alienated by the actions of Nathaniel Lyon and Frank Blair in the spring of 1861, Jackson took measures to move the state into the Confederacy. Jackson was eventually forced to flee Jefferson City to avoid federal forces under Lyon. Jackson spent little time as governor in exile, as he died of pneumonia in December 1862. *Source*: Yearns, Buck, ed. *The Confederate Governors* (1985).

Jackson, Thomas Jonathan "Stonewall" (1824–1863). Confederate General. Thomas Jonathan Jackson was born in Clarksburg, Virginia (now West Virginia). A graduate of the famous West Point class of 1846, Jackson followed his graduation with distinguished service in the Mexican War. After the war, he went on to a teaching career at Virginia Military Institute in Lexington, Virginia. When the South seceded, Jackson quickly answered the call to service and would become one of the South's legendary heroes. Earning the nickname "Stonewall" at the first battle of Manassas, Brigadier General Jackson earned his reputation for genius in his Shenandoah campaign of May 1862. His service under Robert E. Lee in the Peninsula campaign was mediocre; however, he recovered his competency at the second battle of Manassas. For the remainder of his life, Jackson (subsequently appointed major general and lieutenant general) would play a major role in every battle of the Army of Northern Virginia. At the battle of Chancellorsville, Jackson conducted a long flanking maneuver that surprised the 11th corps of the Army of the Potomac. He was subsequently shot by his own men while conducting reconnaissance of federal positions. He died a few days later on May 10, 1863. *Source*: Robertson, James I., Jr. *Stonewall Jackson: The Man, The Soldier, The Legend* (1997).

Johnson, Herschel Vespasian (1812–1880). United States and Confederate Senator. A Georgia native, Herschel Johnson graduated from the University of Georgia and then practiced law in Augusta. He briefly served in the U.S. Senate (1848–1849) before he was elected to consecutive terms as Democratic governor of Georgia (1853–1857). A moderate on the slavery expansion issue, Johnson endorsed the position of Stephen Douglas and was Douglas's running mate in 1860. An opponent of secession, when

Georgia seceded, Johnson felt compelled to follow his state. He served in the Confederate Senate, where he was a sometime critic of the Davis administration. During the Reconstruction era, Johnson sought a conciliatory approach toward the Republican Party. Appointed a circuit court judge in 1873, Johnson died while still in office. *Source*: Flippin, Percy Scott. *Herschel V. Johnson of Georgia: States' Rights Unionist* (1931).

Johnston, Albert Sidney (1803–1862). Confederate General. Albert Sidney Johnston hailed from Washington, Kentucky. An 1826 graduate of West Point Military Academy, Johnston served in the armed forces of the United States and the Republic of Texas against Mexico. After the Mexican War, Johnston left the army briefly but returned in 1855 after his Texas plantation yielded sparse profits. He led U.S. forces to Utah in the so-called Mormon War. When Texas seceded from the Union, Johnston tendered his services to Jefferson Davis. Appointed principal commander of the West, Johnston was killed during the battle of Shiloh. *Source*: Roland, Charles P. *Albert Sidney Johnston: Soldier of Three Republics* (1964).

Johnston, Joseph Eggleston (1807–1891). Confederate General. Born in the vicinity of Farmville, Virginia, Joseph Johnston was the highest-ranking regular army officer to resign his commission and join the Confederacy. An 1840 West Point graduate, Johnston saw action in the Seminole and Mexican Wars. Initially skeptical of secession, Johnston sided with the Confederacy after President Lincoln called for troops to suppress the rebellion. Johnston participated in the first battle of Manassas and was the principal commander of Confederate forces at the beginning of the Peninsula campaign. Injured at the battle of Fair Oaks, Johnston was replaced by Robert E. Lee. After recovering from wounds, Johnston was sent West. He would eventually command the Army of the Tennessee during the Atlanta campaign, but was ultimately removed from command by Jefferson Davis for not conducting a more aggressive campaign. In the spring of 1865, Johnston was moved East and eventually negotiated a surrender with Sherman in April 1865. After the war, Johnston published his memoirs, which were highly critical of Jefferson Davis. *Source*: Symonds, Craig L. *Joseph E. Johnston: A Civil War Biography* (1998).

Julian, George Washington (1817–1899). United States Congressman and Reformer. George Julian was born near Centreville, Indiana. He was trained to be a lawyer in New Boston, Illinois. Eventually he returned to his native town to establish a law practice. At an early age, Julian became interested in reform activities, particularly the antislavery movement. He initially joined the Whig Party, but migrated into the Free Soil Party. He was elected to Congress as a Free Soiler in 1848 and was the party's vice presidential nominee in 1852. He later joined the Republican Party and was elected to Congress, where he served five successive terms. An outspoken opponent of slavery, Julian also served on the Joint Committee on the Conduct of the War. After the war, Julian practiced law in Indianapolis. He eventually migrated into the Democratic Party before his death in 1899. *Source*: Riddleburger, Patrick W. *George Washington Julian, Radical Republican: A Study in Nineteenth-Century Politics and Reform* (1966).

Keitt, Lawrence Massillon (1824–1864). Politician and Confederate Officer. Lawrence Keitt was born in the Orangeburg District of South Carolina. After graduation from South Carolina College, he became an attorney. A devoted advocate of Southern rights, Keitt was interested in politics and was elected to the South Carolina legislature in 1848. He was subsequently elected to the U.S. House of Representatives in 1853. When South Carolina left the Union, Keitt resigned his seat in the House and raised a regiment, the 20th South Carolina. His principal duties pertained to the defense of Charleston Harbor. Late in the war, his unit was called north to assist the depleted Army of Northern Virginia. Keitt was killed at the battle of Cold Harbor. *Source*: Merchant, John Holt. "Lawrence M. Keitt: South Carolina Fire-Eater." Ph.D. dissertation, University of Alabama, 1976.

Lamon, Ward Hill (1819–1893). Attorney and Presidential Advisor. Ward Hill Lamon was born in Virginia, but migrated to Illinois in 1847. After settling in Danville, he read law and became an attorney. He became associated with Abraham Lincoln through their mutual travels on the Eight Illinois Judicial Circuit. Lamon helped Lincoln in his 1858 senatorial and 1860 presidential campaigns. He became marshal of the District of Columbia after Lincoln's election to the presidency. After the war, Lamon published a biography of Lincoln, ghostwritten by Chauncey Black. Lamon eventually relocated to Colorado, where he practiced law. *Source*: Hamand, Lavern. "Ward Hill Lamon: Lincoln's Particular Friend." Ph.D. dissertation, University of Illinois, 1949.

Lane, James Henry (1814–1866). United States Senator and Union General. James Henry Lane was one of the most colorful and controversial politicians of the Civil War era. Born near Lawrenceburg, Indiana, Lane studied and practiced law in Indiana. When the war with Mexico broke out, Lane volunteered for service. He was elected lieutenant governor of Indiana (1849–1853) before moving to the Kansas Territory in 1855. Although initially a Democrat, Lane became heavily involved in the Free State movement in Kansas. A legendary orator, Lane quickly became one of the principals in the Free State movement. When Kansas became a state, Lane was chosen as a U.S. senator in 1861. When the war erupted, Lane became a brigadier general. He operated on the border region of Kansas and Missouri, taking part in jayhawking expeditions. While a radical during the war, after the war Lane sided with Andrew Johnson and opposed civil rights measures for blacks. Suspected of bribery, Lane committed suicide on July 11, 1866. *Source*: Castel, Albert. *Civil War Kansas: Reaping the Whirlwind* (1997).

Letcher, John (1813–1884). Governor of Virginia. A native of Lexington, Virginia, John Letcher attended Washington College. He was active in law, journalism, and the politics of the Democratic Party. He was elected to the U.S. House of Representatives in 1851. In 1858, he was elected governor of Virginia. While a moderate Democrat and an ally of Stephen Douglas, Letcher eventually supported secession after the bombardment of Fort Sumter. Letcher's support for the Davis administration and willingness to subordinate the rights of Virginia to those of the national government made him unpopular in the state. He was defeated for a seat in the Confederate Congress after his term as governor expired. After the war, Letcher returned to Lexington, where he played a prominent role in securing support for Washington College and the Virginia Military Institute. He was elected to one term in the Virginia House of Delegates in 1875. *Source*: Boney, F. N. *John Letcher of Virginia* (1966).

Lincoln, Mary Todd (1818–1882). First Lady. Mary Todd Lincoln was born in Lexington, Kentucky, the daughter of a prominent planter and Whig politician. Well educated, she moved to Springfield in 1839, where she resided with her sister, the wife of Illinois Governor Ninian Edwards. After a rocky romance, she married Abraham Lincoln. She had four children: Robert Todd, Edward, William (Willie), and Thomas (Tad). Only Robert Todd lived to mature adulthood. Politically shrewd, Mary promoted her husband's political career. While first lady, Mary Lincoln carried on a major redecoration of the White House. She was also widely criticized and accused of having Southern sympathies. Having experienced the death of three children and a husband, Mary Lincoln suffered from emotional stress at the end of her life. In 1875, she was committed to a mental institution for a short period of time. She eventually traveled to France to avoid recommitment, where she died in 1882. *Source*: Baker, Jean H. *Mary Todd Lincoln: A Biography* (1987).

Lincoln, Robert Todd (1843–1926). Attorney and Son of Abraham Lincoln. Robert Todd Lincoln was the first son of Abraham and Mary Lincoln. Born in Springfield, he was educated at Harvard University and Harvard Law School. He served briefly on the staff of Ulysses Grant during the Civil War. He became politically involved in the latter half of the nineteenth century, serving as secretary of war for James Garfield and Chester Arthur as well as minister to England under Benjamin Harrison. From 1897 to 1911, he was president of the Pullman Company. Never particularly close to his more famous father, Robert Todd refused to run for office using his father's name for political advantage. *Source*: Goff, John F. *Robert Todd Lincoln: A Man in His Own Right* (1969).

Logan, John Alexander "Black Jack" (1826–1886). United State Congressman, Union General, and Senator. A native of Jackson County in southern Illinois, John A. Logan was educated at Brownsville and then Shiloh Academy in Randolph County. After service in the Mexican War, John studied to become a lawyer. He quickly abandoned law for politics and was subsequently elected to the Illinois Assembly in 1852. In 1858, Logan was sent to the U.S. House of Representatives. During the secession crisis, Logan was initially ambivalent but eventually supported the Union. He volunteered for military service and would blossom into one of the finest political generals in the war. He saw action in the western theater, serving under Grant and Sherman. He was eventually appointed major general in March 1863. Initially a divisional commander in the Army of the Tennessee, he eventually commanded the 15th corps. After the war, Logan joined the Republican Party, winning election to the House in 1866 and to the U.S. Senate in 1871. A founding member of the Grand Army of the Republic, Logan died while holding his Senate seat. *Source*: Cottingham, Carl D., Preston Michael Jones, and Gary Gallagher. *General John A. Logan: His Life and Times* (1989).

Longstreet, James "Old Pete" (1821–1804). Confederate General. Born near Edgefield, South Carolina, James Longstreet became one of the most famous generals of the Confederacy. Graduating from West Point in 1842, Longstreet served with distinction in the Mexican War. At the beginning of the Civil War, Longstreet resigned his commission in the U.S. Army. He initially was commissioned to command Alabama troops as a brigadier general. By the fall of 1861, Longstreet was commissioned as a major general. He saw service in almost all of the principal battles of the eastern theater, including First and Second Manassas, the Peninsula campaign, Antietam, Fredericksburg, Gettysburg, and the Wilderness, where he was wounded and out of command until October 1864. After the war, Longstreet was involved in business, but eventually joined the Republican Party—making him a "scalawag" and subject to public criticism. He served in a number of public offices including minister to Turkey (1880–1881). He died at Gainesville, Georgia, in 1904. *Source*: Wert, Jeffrey D. *General James Longstreet: The Confederacy's Most Controversial Soldier* (1993).

Lovejoy, Owen (1811–1864). Abolitionist and United States Congressman. The brother of martyred antislavery advocate Elijah Lovejoy, Owen Lovejoy was born in Albion, Maine. Although trained as a lawyer, Lovejoy chose to study theology and became a minister. He followed brother Elijah to

Alton, Illinois, where he joined in antislavery activities. After Elijah's murder, Lovejoy completed ministerial studies and became a minister at a Congregational church in Princeton, Illinois. Preaching antislavery from his pulpit, Lovejoy also became involved in Underground Railroad activities. Involved in organizing the Republican Party in Illinois, Lovejoy won a seat to Congress in 1856, where he stayed until his death in 1864. A powerful orator, Lovejoy was one of the most outspoken critics of the institution of slavery. While he lived to see the Emancipation Proclamation, Lovejoy died in 1864, before the passage and ratification of the Thirteenth Amendment. *Source*: Magdol, Edward. *Owen Lovejoy: Abolitionist in Congress* (1967).

Lyon, Nathaniel (1818–1861). Union General. A career soldier, Nathaniel Lyon was born in Connecticut and graduated from West Point in 1841. Prior to the Civil War, he served in Florida, the Mexican War, Kansas, and California. After the Civil War began, he was sent to Missouri. Along with Francis Preston Blair Jr., Lyon moved to thwart the designs of pro-Confederate Governor Claiborne Fox Jackson to take Missouri into the Confederacy. Lyon's seizure of the pro-Confederate militia at Fort Jackson in St. Louis enraged pro-Confederate Missourians. In the summer of 1861, Lyon moved into southwest Missouri in an effort to drive out Confederate forces. Attacking a larger force under Ben McCulloch and Sterling Price at Wilson's Creek, Lyon's forces were eventually routed and Lyon was killed in the battle. *Source*: Price, Richard Scott. *Nathaniel Lyon: Harbinger from Kansas* (1990).

Magoffin, Beriah (1815–1885). Governor of Kentucky. Beriah Magoffin was trained as an attorney. He practiced law in both Kentucky and Mississippi before becoming interested in Kentucky politics. A member of the Democratic Party, Magoffin was an unsuccessful candidate for lieutenant governor of Kentucky in 1855; nonetheless, he became governor of the state in 1859. After the firing on Fort Sumter, Magoffin wanted to organize a convention to secede from the Union; however, a pro-Union Kentucky legislature thwarted his plans. Instead, Magoffin strove to make Kentucky a neutral state, issuing a neutrality proclamation in May 1861. Frustrated with the course of Kentucky during the war, Magoffin resigned his office in August 1862. Toward the end of the war, Magoffin realized that slavery was doomed; consequently, he accepted the Thirteenth Amendment. After the war, he even supported civil rights for newly emancipated slaves. *Source*: Coulter, E. Merton. *The Civil War and Readjustment in Kentucky* (1926).

Mahan, Dennis Hart (1802–1871). West Point Professor and Union Officer. Dennis Hart Mahan was born in New York City, but was raised in Norfolk, Virginia. An 1824 graduate of West Point, he excelled in drawing and mathematics. Although commissioned in the corps of engineers after graduation, Mahan remained at West Point, where he taught mathematics. After an extended tour of Europe, where he studied engineering, Mahan returned to West Point as a professor of engineering. By 1838, Mahan was the dean of West Point and, in 1843, his principal class was Engineering and the Science of War. Mahan was the author of numerous books on military matters, including *An Elementary Treatise on Advanced-Guard, Out-Post, and Detachment Service of Troops* (1847). Influenced by French military theorist Antoine-Henri Jomini, Mahan influenced a generation of American military leaders, including Henry Halleck, George McClellan, and Ulysses Grant. *Source*: Ambrose, Stephen E. *Duty, Honor, and Country: A History of West Point* (1966).

Mason, James Murray (1798–1871). United States Senator and Confederate Diplomat. Born into a wealthy Washington, D.C., family, James Murray Mason was educated at the University of Pennsylvania and the College of William and Mary. He moved to Winchester, Virginia, where he began a law practice. Drawn to politics, he was elected to the Virginia House of Delegates in 1826. By 1837, he returned to his birthplace as a member of the U.S. House of Representatives. In 1847, he was chosen as Virginia's U.S. senator. A staunch advocate of states' rights, slavery, and the Democratic Party, Mason crafted the new Fugitive Slave Act of 1850. He advocated secession and was eventually selected as envoy to England. Briefly incarcerated as a result of the *Trent* affair, Mason spent the rest of the war in England and in France, where he unsuccessfully lobbied for recognition of the Confederacy. After the war ended, Mason stayed on in England before moving to Canada, where he joined his family. Eventually pardoned, Mason returned to his native Virginia, where he died in 1871. *Source*: Young, Robert W. *Senator James Murray Mason: Defender of the Old South* (1998).

McClernand, John Alexander (1812–1900). Politician and Union General. John McClernand was the textbook Civil War political general. A native of Kentucky, McClernand moved to Illinois at a young age. As with many aspiring politicians, McClernand first became an attorney, but in 1836, he was elected as a Democratic member to the state assembly. Eventually elected to the U.S. House of Representatives, he became a close ally of Stephen A. Douglas. He served in the House from 1843 to 1851 and again from 1859 to 1861. Because of his popularity in the West, President Lincoln appointed him brigadier general. He saw action at the battle of Belmont, Fort Henry, Fort Donelson, Shiloh, and Vicksburg. In the fall of 1862, he lobbied Lincoln for an independent command; however, the command eventually became incorporated into Grant's Army of the Tennessee. Because of poor relations with Grant, McClernand was eventually removed from command. After a brief stint under Nathaniel Banks in Louisiana, he became ill and never served again. After the war, McClernand continued in law and politics, eventually becoming a judge. *Source*: Meyers, Christopher C. "John Alexander McClernand and the Politics of Command in Grant's Army of the Tennessee." *Columbiad* (1998).

McCulloch, Ben (1811–1862). Texas Ranger and Confederate General. A native of Tennessee, Ben McCulloch moved to Texas in 1835, where he eventually joined the Texas army led by Sam Houston, a family friend. He served with distinction in the battle of San Jacinto. Shortly after this battle, McCulloch left the army to take up surveying. He also became a Texas Ranger. He served a single term in the Texas legislature. During the Mexican War, he served with distinction under Zachary Taylor. After moving to California in search of gold, McCulloch received an appointment as U.S. marshal for the district of eastern Texas. When Texas seceded from the Union, Jefferson Davis appointed McCulloch brigadier general in May 1861. In charge of Indian Territory and headquartered in Little Rock, Arkansas, McCulloch participated with Sterling Prince at the battle of Wilson's Creek. McCulloch was killed the following spring at the battle of Pea Ridge. *Source*: Cutrer, Thomas W. *Ben McCulloch and the Frontier Military Tradition* (1993).

McDowell, Irvin (1818–1885). Union General. Irvin McDowell was the Union's first principal commander in the eastern theater. Born at Columbus, Ohio, McDowell was an 1838 graduate of West Point. After graduation, he taught at West Point and saw action in the Mexican War. After the war, he served on the staff of General-in-Chief Winfield Scott. Because of his close relationship with Scott and his excellent record, McDowell was appointed commander of the Department of Northeastern Virginia at the war's beginning. Defeat at the first battle of Manassas led to McDowell's demotion. He served as a corps commander under McClellan. McDowell's role in the Union defeat at the second battle of Manassas was the end of his active role in the war. He served on the west coast for the remainder of the war in largely administrative roles. After the war, McDowell served as commander of the Department of the West, the Department of the South, and then the Department of the Pacific. He was appointed major general in 1872. *Source*: Hennessy, John J. *Return to Bull Run: The Campaign and Battle of Second Manassas* (1993).

Meade, George Gordon "Old Snapping Turtle" (1815–1872). Union General. Born in Spain, the son of a wealthy Philadelphia merchant, George Gordon Meade was educated at West Point, graduating in 1835. After seeing action in the Seminole War, Meade left the army briefly to pursue civil engineering. In the early 1840s, he rejoined the army. He saw action in the

Mexican War and was involved in various engineering projects prior to the Civil War. Commissioned as a brigadier general for Pennsylvania volunteers in August 1861, Meade saw extensive action in the eastern theater. Promoted to major general in November 1862, Meade's division played an important role in the battle of Fredericksburg. Just prior to the battle of Gettysburg, Meade was appointed commander of the Army of the Potomac. He bested Lee at Gettysburg, but was criticized for not pursuing Lee rapidly after the battle. Meade remained at the helm of the Army of the Potomac for the remainder of the war. After the war, Meade remained in the army, commanding the Department of the Atlantic as well as the Third Military District. *Source*: Cleaves, Freeman. *Meade of Gettysburg* (1960).

Medill, Joseph (1823–1899). Journalist, Editor, and Publisher. Joseph Medill was Canadian born, but moved to the United States at age nine, settling in Ohio where he became a lawyer. He became involved in journalism early in his career when he bought the *Coshocton Whig* with his brothers. In the mid-1850s, he invested in the *Chicago Tribune*. Acting as managing editor, he eventually acquired a majority interest in 1874 and retained this until his death in 1899. An early supporter of the Republican Party and Abraham Lincoln, Medill transformed the *Tribune* into the major voice of the Republican Party in the Northwest. Mirroring the work of James Gordon Bennett, Medill's paper performed pioneering work in the area of war reporting. After the war and before he took majority interest in the *Tribune*, Medill served a single term as mayor of Chicago. *Source*: Kinsley, Philip. *The Chicago Tribune: Its First Hundred Years* (1943).

Meigs, Montgomery Cunningham (1816–1892). Quartermaster General of the United States Army. Montgomery Meigs was Southern by birth, born at Augusta, Georgia. Educated at West Point, Meigs graduated in 1836, fifth in a class of forty-nine. A regular army careerist, he was appointed to the Army Corps of Engineers and worked on a variety of projects including construction of an aqueduct system for Washington, D.C. After the Civil War began, Meigs was promoted to brigadier general and given the arduous task of quartermaster general. He performed his task with efficiency, organizing the army's supply network in an orderly, systematic manner. After the war, Meigs continued as quartermaster general until retirement in 1882. *Source*: Weigley, Russell F. *Quartermaster General of the Army: A Biography of M. C. Meigs* (1959).

Miles, William Porcher (1822–1899). United States and Confederate Congressman. Charleston, South Carolina, attorney William Porcher Miles was born at Walterboro, South Carolina, and educated at the College of Charleston. After practicing and teaching law for a few years, Miles entered politics, serving as mayor of Charleston and in the U.S. House of Representative from 1857 to 1860. A staunch supporter of Southern rights and secession, Miles resigned from the House after Abraham Lincoln's election. He served as a delegate to South Carolina's secession convention. During the war, he served as an aide to Pierre Beauregard but was also elected as a representative to the Confederate Congress in Richmond. A supporter of Davis, Miles became less sympathetic with Davis as Confederate prospects dimmed. After the war, Miles was president of the University of South Carolina before moving to Louisiana to run the plantation of his wife's family. *Source*: Walthers, Eric. *The Fire Eaters* (1992).

Morgan, John Hunt (1825–1864). Confederate General. John Morgan conducted some of the most dangerous and daring raids during the American Civil War. While born at Huntsville, Alabama, Morgan was reared in Lexington, Kentucky. He joined the army and served in Mexico as a lieutenant in the 1st Kentucky Cavalry. Before the Civil War, Morgan became a prosperous hemp farmer in Kentucky. When Kentucky stayed loyal to the Union, Morgan continued to support the Confederacy. He became one of the most legendary Southern cavalry commanders. His most notorious raid came in July 1863 when, largely for diversionary purposes, Morgan and his 2,400 men went on a 1,100-mile ride through the states of Ohio and Indiana. Eventually captured, Morgan made a successful escape in November 1863. He was killed in 1864 near Greeneville, Tennessee, shortly after a raid against Union-controlled Knoxville, Tennessee. *Source*: Ramage, James. *Rebel Raider: The Life of John Hunt Morgan* (1986).

Morrill, Justin Smith (1810–1898). United States Representative and Senator. Born in Strafford, Vermont, Justin Morrill is often referred to as the "father of the land grant college." Marginally educated, Morrill made a small fortune as a merchant, retired from business in 1848, and began to dabble in politics. He was elected as a Whig representative to Congress in 1854. He would serve for six consecutive terms. His principal accomplishment in Congress was the introduction of the Morrill Land Grant Act, which helped establish land grant universities throughout the country and the Morrill Tariff of 1861. In 1867, the Vermont legislature selected Morrill as a U.S. senator, a position he held until his 1898 death. *Source*: Parker, William B. *The Life and Public Service of Justin Smith Morrill* (1971).

Nicolay, John George (1832–1901). Secretary to President Lincoln and United States Consul. At age five, John Nicolay emigrated from Bavaria, Germany, to Pike County, Illinois. He became involved in the newspaper business, eventually purchasing and running a local paper in Pittsfield, Illinois. He later moved to Springfield, where he became a law clerk. In Springfield, he became acquainted with Abraham Lincoln. He became Lincoln's private secretary after the election of 1860. With John Hay, Nicolay wrote an eight-volume biography of Abraham Lincoln. *Source*: Nicolay, Helen. *Lincoln's Secretary: A Biography of John G. Nicolay* (1948).

Northrop, Lucius Bellinger (1811–1894). Commissary General of the Confederacy. Lucius Northrop was born in Charleston, South Carolina, and in 1831 graduated from West Point. He saw service in the second Seminole War, where he was wounded. Due to injury, Northrop served in the Commissary Department. He also studied and practiced medicine. He followed his state, South Carolina, when it seceded and became commissary general of the Confederacy in June 1861. In this capacity, Northrop struggled with a poor transportation infrastructure, which made it difficult to distribute food to both troops and prisoners of war. Northrop was widely criticized for food shortages by commanders in the field. After the war, he farmed in Virginia until his 1894 death. *Source*: Moore, Jerrold Northrop. *Confederate Commissary General: Lucius Bellinger Northrop and the Subsistence Bureau of the Southern Army* (1996).

Palmer, John McCauley (1817–1900). Politician and Union General. While born in Kentucky, John Palmer moved to Illinois in 1831. He was elected to the Illinois state legislature in 1851. One of the founders of the Republican Party in Illinois, Palmer attended the 1860 national convention in Chicago. When the Civil War began, Palmer volunteered and was appointed brigadier general in December 1861. He eventually became a divisional commander, then a corps commander, in the Army of the Cumberland and participated in important battles such as Stone's River, Chickamauga, Chattanooga, and the Atlanta Campaign. After the war, he reentered the political sphere and was elected governor of Illinois in 1868. In 1872, he cast his lot with the Liberal Republicans. He eventually joined the Democratic Party and was elected to the U.S. Senate in 1891. *Source*: Palmer, George T. *A Conscientious Turncoat: The Story of John M. Palmer* (1941).

Parker, Joel (1816–1888). Governor of New Jersey. Joel Parker was born near Freehold, New Jersey, and educated at the College of New Jersey (now Princeton University). Involved in state Democratic politics, Parker was also a brigadier general in the New Jersey state militia. In the election of 1860, Parker supported Stephen A. Douglas. In the Democratic resurgence in 1862, Parker was elected governor of New Jersey. He supported the war but opposed emancipation and other Republican policies. After his term expired in 1866, Parker practiced law. He was elected governor again in 1871. After a brief tenure as state attorney general, Parker was appointed to the New Jersey Supreme Court in 1880. He died while still a member of the court. *Source*: Gillette, William. *Jersey Blue: Civil War Politics in New Jersey* (1994).

Parker, Theodore (1810–1860). Theologian and Abolitionist. Born in Lexington, Massachusetts, Theodore Parker graduated from Harvard Divinity School in 1836. A brilliant student, he became minister at West Roxbury, Massachusetts. Joining the Unitarian denomination in the 1840s, Parker eventually formed his own church in Boston in 1846. Popular for his sermons, Parker also embraced reform causes, particularly the antislavery movement. He publicly condemned the Fugitive Slave Act and advocated forcible resistance to it. Parker was one of the secret six, a group of individuals that provided financial assistance to John Brown for his raid on Harpers Ferry. When Brown was captured, Parker was abroad in Italy, suffering from tuberculosis. He died in Florence. *Source*: Commager, Henry S. *Theodore Parker: Yankee Crusader* (1936).

Patterson, Robert (1792–1881). Union General. Robert Patterson was the scapegoat for Union defeat at the first battle of Manassas. Born in Ireland, Patterson came to Pennsylvania in 1798. A veteran of the War of 1812, Patterson also served under Winfield Scott in the Mexican War. A prosperous Philadelphia businessman, Patterson was appointed major general of the Pennsylvania volunteers at the beginning of the Civil War. His failure to check the movement of Joseph Johnston at Winchester, Virginia, allowed the latter to reinforce Beauregard at Manassas and contributed to the defeat of Union forces. He was widely ridiculed for this failure. When his ninety-day commission expired, Patterson was not given another field command. He remained active in business until his death in 1881. *Source*: Patterson, Robert. *A Narrative of the Campaign in the Valley of the Shenandoah in 1861* (1865).

Pemberton, John Clifford (1814–1881). Confederate General. John Pemberton was one of the few northern-born Confederates. A Pennsylvania native, Pemberton used a family friendship with Andrew Jackson to secure an appointment to West Point. He served in the second Seminole War as well as the Mexican War. His wife, Martha Thompson, was a Norfolk, Virginia, native, which may explain Pemberton's future loyalty to the Confederacy. When Virginia seceded from the Union, Pemberton was commissioned by the State of Virginia and later became a brigadier general in the Confederate Army. Initially stationed in the East, in October 1862, Pemberton was given command of the District of Mississippi and Eastern Louisiana. He presided over the surrender of Vicksburg on July 4, 1863, a surrender that prompted rumors about Pemberton's loyalty to the Confederacy. After he was paroled, he served with artillery units defending Richmond. After the war, Pemberton farmed in Virginia before moving back to his native Pennsylvania. *Source*: Ballard, Michael B. *Pemberton: A Biography* (1991).

Pendleton, George Hunt (1825–1889). Ohio Congressman and Vice Presidential Candidate. A native of Cincinnati, Ohio, George Pendleton became a prominent antiwar Democrat in the Civil War. Educated at Cincinnati College, Pendleton began a law practice in his native city. Elected to the Ohio state senate in 1853, Pendleton was then elected to the U.S. House of Representatives in 1856. An opponent of the Civil War and the policies of Abraham Lincoln, Pendleton was the vice presidential nominee of the Democratic Party in 1864. Along with George McClellan, Pendleton went down to defeat. After the war, Pendleton favored the issuance of paper currency and endorsed the so-called Ohio Plan, which championed paper currency. In 1878, he was elected to the U.S. Senate. Appointed as minister to Germany in 1885, Pendleton died in Brussels. *Source*: Mach, Thomas S. " 'Gentleman George' Hunt Pendleton: A Study in Political Continuity." Ph.D. dissertation, University of Alabama, 1996.

Phillips, Wendell (1811–1884). Abolitionist and Reformer. Wendell Phillips was a patrician reformer, born into a wealthy Boston family and educated at Harvard University and Harvard Law School. Phillips practiced law for a scant three years, becoming much more attracted to Garrisonian abolitionism. He was a frequent antislavery speaker and activist. Like Garrison, Phillips spurned politics for moral suasion. During the Civil War, Phillips was often critical of Abraham Lincoln for moving to slowly to abolish slavery. After the war, Phillips embraced a variety of reform causes. In 1870 he was an unsuccessful candidate for governor of Massachusetts, running on the Labor Reform and Prohibitionist Party tickets. *Source*: Stewart, James B. *Wendell Phillips: Liberty's Hero* (1986).

Pickens, Francis Wilkinson (1805–1869). Governor of South Carolina. Francis Pickens was the son of South Carolina Governor Andrew Pickens. Francis studied law, but opted to run his family's plantation. He was elected to the U.S. House of Representatives and served from 1834 to 1843. Appointed minister to Russia in 1856, Pickens was then elected governor of South Carolina in 1860. Although he opposed secession, he devoted his time as governor to defense of the state. He presided over the Fort Sumter crisis that eventually ended with the firing on the fort and its surrender on April 12, 1861. When his gubernatorial term was up, Pickens retired to private life and played no active role in the war. *Source*: Edmunds, John B. *Francis W. Pickens and the Politics of Destruction* (1986).

Pickett, George Edward (1825–1875). Confederate General. Best known as the leader of Pickett's Charge on the third day of Gettysburg, George Pickett was born in Henrico County, Virginia. He entered West Point in 1842, and graduated with an undistinguished academic record in 1846. He served in the Mexican War, on the Texas frontier, and then in the Pacific Northwest. After Virginia seceded, Pickett resigned from the U.S. Army and was quickly appointed a brigadier general in the Confederate Army in February 1861. Wounded during the Peninsula campaign, Pickett did not see significant action until the battle of Gettysburg. He led the brilliant but tragically failed assault on the Union center on the third day of the battle. His last battle was the Five Forks, where Confederate forces were routed, partially as a result of Pickett's neglect. After the war, Pickett entered the insurance business. His health slowly declined and he died at age fifty. *Source*: Gordon, Lesley J. *General George E. Pickett in Life and Legend* (1998).

Polk, Leonidas (1806–1864). Bishop and Confederate General. Leonidas Polk was born in Raleigh, North Carolina. He graduated from West Point in 1827. He then began studies at Virginia Theological Seminary. Polk became an Episcopal priest in May 1831. After marriage, Polk moved to Tennessee. He farmed and resumed ministerial duties. A few years later, he relocated to Thibodaux, Louisiana, where he planted and assumed the duties of the priesthood. After Louisiana seceded, Polk returned to the military, commissioned as a major general and then lieutenant general. He commanded Department Number Two in the West and participated in the battle of Belmont, Shiloh, Perrysville, Stone's River, and Chickamauga. After quarreling with his superior, Braxton Bragg, Polk was transferred to command of the Department of Alabama, Mississippi, and East Tennessee. He rejoined the Army of the Tennessee during the Atlanta campaign but was killed by artillery fire on June 14, 1864. *Source*: Parks, Joseph H. *General Leonidas Polk, C. S. A.: The Fighting Bishop* (1962).

Pope, John (1822–1892). Union General. John Pope's rise to fame was meteoric; his descent into obscurity was equally rapid. Born in Kentucky and reared in Illinois, Pope graduated from West Point in 1842. During the Mexican War, he served under Zachary Taylor. When the Civil War erupted, Pope was appointed brigadier general of volunteers. Serving in the West, he gained a reputation for aggressiveness and success. After distinguished service at New Madrid and Island No. 10, Pope came east. He was put in command of the newly formed Army of Virginia. After a humiliating defeat at the second battle of Manassas, he quickly fell from favor. He was sent to the Northwest to fight the Sioux. After the war, he continued in military service fighting Native American tribes in the Southwest, particularly the Apache. Pope died in Sandusky, Ohio. *Source*: Schutz, Wallace J., and Walter N. Trenerry. *Abandoned by Lincoln: A Military Biography of General John Pope* (1990).

Porter, David Dixon (1813–1891). United States Naval Officer. David Dixon Porter was the son of the outspoken Commodore David Porter. He joined the U.S. Navy in 1829 and saw almost continuous service up until the outbreak of the Civil War. During the war, Porter was promoted to commander and participated in the expedition against New Orleans. He also saw action in the Vicksburg and Red River campaigns as well as the expeditions against Fort Fisher. After the war, Porter served as superintendent of the Naval Academy. He was promoted to admiral in 1870. *Source*: West, Richard S., Jr. *The Second Admiral: A Life of David Dixon Porter* (1937).

Porter, Fitz John (1822–1901). Union General. Fitz John Porter was one of the most controversial generals of the Civil War. A native of Portsmouth, New Hampshire, Porter graduated from West Point in 1845. He served in the Mexican War and on the American frontier prior to the outbreak of the Civil War. Porter became a divisional commander and later a corps commander in the Army of the Potomac and part of George B. McClellan's inner circle. He distinguished himself during the Peninsula campaign, particularly at the battle of Seven Pines and Gaines Mill. Promoted to major general on July 4, 1862, Porter was accused of dereliction of duty at the second battle of Manassas. He participated in the battle of Antietam, but was court-martialed and relieved of command in November 1862. He was convicted and cashiered from the army in January 1863. Porter spent the next sixteen years trying to exonerate his name. Finally, in 1879 a review board overturned the court-martial. In 1886, Porter was given a colonel's commission in the U.S. Army. *Source*: Eisenschiml, Otto. *The Celebrated Case of Fitz John Porter: An American Dreyfuss Affair* (1950).

Price, Sterling "Old Pap" (1809–1867). Confederate General. Although born a Virginian, Sterling Price migrated to Missouri in 1831. A brigadier general in the Mexican War, Price was also an experienced politician serving as governor of Missouri, a state legislator, as well as a U.S. representative. When the secession crisis erupted, Price was initially a conditional Unionist; however, the actions of Nathaniel Lyon drove him permanently into the Southern camp. Price became one of the Confederacy's principal commanders in the trans-Mississippi theater. He won decisive victories at Wilson's Creek (August 1861) and Lexington, Missouri (September 1861). Price also participated in the battles of Pea Ridge, Iuka, and Corinth. In August 1864, Price led Confederate forces on a raid into Missouri. Initially successful, Price was eventually forced to retreat into Arkansas and then Texas. After the war, Price fled to Mexico; however, he returned to St. Louis in 1867. *Source*: Castel, Albert. *General Sterling Price and the Civil War in the West* (1968).

Quantrill, William Clark (1837–1865). Confederate Guerrilla. William Clark Quantrill was born in Canal Dover, Ohio. After teaching school for several years, Quantrill relocated to Kansas in 1857. Initially associated with Kansas "Jayhawkers"—armed bands of antislavery raiders who attacked proslavery residents of Kansas—Quantrill eventually switched to the proslavery side in Kansas affairs. During the Civil War, he emerged as the leading guerrilla figure in the Kansas-Missouri border region. His most controversial deed was undoubtedly his August 21, 1863, raid on Lawrence, Kansas. During the spring of 1864, rival George Todd displaced Quantrill as leader of Quantrill's band of guerrillas. Quantrill eventually led a small band of irregulars to Kentucky, where he was wounded and apprehended by federal forces. He died on June 6, 1865. *Source*: Castel, Albert. *William Clarke Quantrill: His Life and Times* (1962; reprint, 1998).

Raymond, Henry Jarvis (1820–1869). Journalist and Politician. Henry Raymond was born in Lima, New York. A graduate of the Genesee Wesleyan Seminary and the University of Vermont, Raymond entered the field of journalism. He gained valuable experience from *New York Tribune* editor Horace Greeley, but arguments with Greeley led to Raymond's departure. Raymond held a number of other journalistic jobs but was also elected to the New York Assembly in 1849 as a Whig. He also served as lieutenant governor of New York from 1854 to 1859. In the 1850s, he founded the *Times,* a Republican paper that attempted to steer a moderate course. In 1864, Raymond was elected to the U.S. House of Representatives. During Reconstruction, Raymond opposed the policies of the radical Republicans. He died unexpectedly in 1869. *Source*: Brown, Francis. *Raymond of the* Times (1970).

Reynolds, John Fulton (1820–1863). Union General. Born at Lancaster, Pennsylvania, John F. Reynolds secured the help of fellow Lancastrian, James Buchanan, to get accepted into West Point. After graduating in 1841, Reynolds served in Florida and in the war against Mexico. When the Civil War began, Reynolds was commandant of cadets at West Point. Reynolds was appointed brigadier general and given a command in the Army of the Potomac. He participated in the Peninsula campaign, but was taken prisoner. After his release, he participated in the second battle of Manassas. After the battle of Chancellorsville, President Lincoln considered Reynolds for top command of the Army of the Potomac. Reynolds's decisive action at Gettysburg forced the battle to take place. He was killed during the first day of fighting. *Source*: Riley, Michael A. *"For God's Sake, Forward": General John F. Reynolds* (1995).

Rhett, Robert Barnwell, Sr. (1800–1876). Journalist and Confederate Congressman. Dubbed the "father of secession," Robert Barnwell Rhett was born in the vicinity of Beaufort, South Carolina. He practiced law and engaged in farming. A disciple of John C. Calhoun, Rhett served in the U.S. House of Representatives from 1837 to 1849. With his son, he owned an interest in the Charleston *Mercury*, which expressed his extreme views on Southern rights and nationalism. He supported secession but was disillusioned with Jefferson Davis, who he thought was too moderate. He held Davis responsible for the defeat of the Confederacy. During the war, Rhett led the opposition to Davis in the Confederate Congress. After the war, Rhett eventually settled in New Orleans. His postwar years were marred by debt and disappointment. *Source*: Heidler, David T. *Pulling the Temple Down: The Fire-eaters and the Destruction of the Union* (1998).

Rosecrans, William Starke "Old Rosy" (1819–1898). Union General. William Rosecrans came from a military family. A native of Delaware County, Ohio, Rosecrans enrolled in West Point and graduated fifth in the class of 1842. He served in the prestigious Army Corps of Engineers until his retirement from the regular army in 1854. During the Civil War, he began service on the staff of George B. McClellan, serving with success in West Virginia. He then served under Henry Halleck in the West, commanding the Army of Mississippi and then replacing Don Carlos Buell as commander of the Army of the Cumberland in late October 1862. While gaining a victory at Murfreesboro, Rosecrans was defeated at Chickamauga in September 1863 and subsequently trapped by rebel forces at Chattanooga. Rosecrans was relieved of command and sent to command the Department of Missouri, where he remained until December 1864. He held no other command during the war. After the war, Rosecrans was appointed minister to Mexico (1868) and served two terms in Congress (1880–1885). *Source*: Lamers, William M. *The Edge of Glory: A Biography of William S. Rosecrans* (1961; reprint, 1999).

Ruffin, Edmund (1794–1865). Secession Advocate and Agriculturalist. Born in Prince George County, Virginia, Edmund Ruffin became a leading advocate of secession. After briefly attending the College of William and Mary and volunteering for military duty in the War of 1812, Ruffin directed the affairs of his family plantation at Coggin's Point. Interested in agricultural experiments, Ruffin published a journal on agricultural affairs entitled *Farmer's Register*. After serving a partial term in the Virginia Senate, Ruffin began to write on political topics. He opposed the federal tariff and argued for the necessity of slavery. An advocate of states' rights, Ruffin believed in the necessity of secession. During the crisis over secession, Ruffin left his native Virginia for the more radical South Carolina. He participated in the bombardment of Fort Sumter. After returning to Virginia, Ruffin became disillusioned with Southern defeat. On June 17, 1865, he took his own life. *Source*: Matthew, W. M. *Edmund Ruffin and the Crisis of Slavery* (1988).

Russell, William Howard "Bull Run Russell" (1820–1907). British Journalist. Born in County Dublin, Ireland, William Howard Russell attended Trinity College, but took a job with the *London Times* before graduating. Russell gained experience as a war correspondent during the Crimean War. When the outbreak of war was expected in the United States, Russell was sent to cover the anticipated conflict. He traveled extensively through the North and South during the spring of 1861. After the first battle of Bull Run, Russell described the Northern retreat in unflattering terms. As a result, he was mercilessly criticized in the American press. In April 1862, he was forbidden to travel with the Army of the Potomac. Russell returned to England, where he continued his career in journalism. *Source*: Russell, William Howard. *My Diary North and South*. Edited by Eugene Berwanger (1988).

Schofield, John McAllister (1831–1906). Union General. Born in Gerry, New York, John Schofield graduated from West Point in 1853. After a few years of active duty, he returned to his alma mater to teach philosophy. When the Civil War began, Schofield served under Nathaniel Lyon in Missouri and was appointed a brigadier general in November 1861. He was eventually named commander of the Department of Missouri. In early 1864, he left Missouri when he was given command of the Army of Ohio. He participated in the Atlanta campaign as well as the battles of Franklin and Nashville. After the war, Schofield served as military commander in Virginia as part of the Military Reconstruction Acts. He served as secretary of war in 1868 and held a number of different command posts, including superintendent of West Point. *Source*: Schofield, John McAllister. *Forty-Six Years in the Army* (1897).

Schurz, Carl (1829–1906). Union General and United States Senator. A native of the German Rhineland, Carl Schurz arrived in the United States in 1852 after the failed revolutions of 1848. Migrating to Wisconsin, Schurz quickly identified with the antislavery movement and sought a political career. Joining the Republican Party, Schurz was a frequent political speaker on behalf of Republican candidates. Schurz played an important role in securing German American votes for Abraham Lincoln in 1860. During the war, Schurz served as minister to Spain, but then was commissioned as a brigadier general and saw service in several battles, including Chancellorsville and Gettysburg. A supporter of radical Reconstruction, Schurz moved to Missouri after the war and was elected to the U.S. Senate in 1869. He went on to serve as secretary of the interior under Rutherford Hayes. Schurz eventually moved into the Democratic Party, supporting Grover Cleveland in three campaigns for the presidency. *Source*: Trefousse, Hans. *Carl Schurz: A Biography* (1982).

Scott, Dred (1795–1858). United States Supreme Court Plaintiff. Born to slave parents in Virginia, little is known about Dred Scott's early life. Eventually Peter Blow, who moved him to St. Louis, purchased Scott. He was later sold to surgeon John Emerson, who as an assistant surgeon in the army took Scott with him on active duty. When Emerson died, Scott tried to buy his and his wife's freedom from Emerson's widow. Failing, he filed suit in the Missouri Circuit Court. After a series of trials and appeals, Scott finally lost his case in 1852 in the Missouri Supreme Court. When Emerson's widow remarried, Scott was placed in the care of John Sanford, an antislavery congressman who would free Scott in 1857. In March 1857, the U.S. Supreme Court denied Scott's right to sue for freedom in the case that bears his name. Just one year later, an emancipated Scott passed away. *Source*: Fehrenbacher, Don E. *The Dred Scott Case: Its Significance for American Law and Politics* (1978).

Scott, Winfield "Old Fuss and Feathers" (1786–1866). General-in-Chief of the United States Army. A native of Virginia, Winfield Scott was the United States' most visible war hero at the outset of the Civil War. Serving in the War of 1812, Scott's most distinguished service came in the Mexican War, when he landed an expeditionary force at Veracruz and then captured Mexico City after skillfully outflanking his Mexican opponents in several battles. At the onset of the Civil War, Scott was old, infirm, and suffering from vertigo. Conflict with George McClellan eventually led to Scott's retirement. He passed away in 1866. *Source*: Johnson, Timothy D. *Winfield Scott: The Quest for Military Glory* (1998).

Seddon, James Alexander (1815–1880). United States Representative and Confederate Secretary of War. James Seddon was born in Fredericksburg, Virginia. Educated at the University of Virginia, he became a lawyer and practiced at Richmond. Twice elected to the U.S. House of Representatives (1844, 1848), Seddon spent the 1850s as a planter. During the secession crisis, Seddon returned to public life. He served as Confederate secretary of war from November 1862 to February 1865. Criticized for his support of Jefferson Davis, Seddon resigned from office. After the war, he lived on his plantation at Sabot Hill, Goochland County, Virginia. *Source*: Stearns, Merton Everett. *The Public Life of James A. Seddon* (1924).

Sedgwick, John "Uncle John" (1813–1864). Union General. Connecticut native John Sedgwick graduated from West Point in 1837 and was assigned to the artillery. After serving in the second Seminole War and the Mexican War, Sedgwick spent the 1850s in the military, serving in the Mormon War as well as in Kansas Territory. During the Civil War, he was commissioned as a brigadier general and served under Samuel P. Heintzleman in the Army of the Potomac. Wounded at Antietam, Sedgwick was eventually promoted to major general and commanded the 6th Corps, Army of the Potomac. He directed Union forces at the second battle of Fredericksburg and led the attack at Salem's Church. Sedgwick was killed at the battle of Spotsylvania on May 9, 1864. *Source*: Winslow, Richard E., III. *General John Sedgwick: The Story of a Union Corps Commander* (1982).

Seymour, Horatio (1810–1886). Governor of New York. Horatio Seymour was born at Pompey Hill, New York. He became a lawyer and acquired an interest in Democratic politics through his connection with William L. Marcy. He was elected to the New York Assembly in 1841 and 1844. During the Civil War, Seymour was elected governor of New York in 1862. Although he criticized the draft and Republican policies on civil liberties, Seymour did not identify with the peace wing of the Democratic Party. After the war, he was the Democratic standard-bearer in 1868, defeated by Republican nominee Ulysses S. Grant. After his defeat, Seymour remained active in state politics until his death in 1886. *Source*: Stewart, Mitchell. *Horatio Seymour of New York* (1938; reprint, 1970).

Seymour, Thomas Hart (1807–1868). Governor of Connecticut. A native of Hartford, Connecticut, Thomas Seymour was educated at a military academy but chose the law as his profession. Seymour was interested in Democratic politics and was elected to the U.S. House of Representatives in 1842. He served in the Mexican War and in 1850 was elected governor of Connecticut. He was subsequently reelected for three successive terms. Seymour served as minister to Russia in 1853–1857. During the election of 1860, Seymour supported John C. Breckinridge. When Southern states seceded, Seymour opposed the use of force to restore the Union. He became a prominent critic of the war and was mentioned as a possible presidential nominee in 1864. In 1863, he ran for governor of Connecticut but was narrowly defeated. After the war, he retired to private life until his death in 1868. *Source*: Cowden, Joanna D. *"Heaven Will Frown on Such a Cause as This": Six Democrats Who Opposed Lincoln's War* (2001).

Shaw, Robert Gould (1837–1863). Union Officer. Born in Boston, Robert Gould Shaw came from an aristocratic Boston family known for its wealth and connections to the antislavery movement. Failing to graduate from Harvard University, Shaw entered the business world and, on the outbreak of Civil War, was working in a New York City firm owned by his uncles. After the war erupted, he joined the 2nd Massachusetts as a second lieutenant. Shaw's most prominent role would come when he was chosen as colonel of the 54th Massachusetts, an African American regiment. Shaw died leading the regiment on an assault of Fort Wagner in Charleston Harbor on July 18, 1863. *Source*: Duncan, Russell, ed. *Blue-Eyed Child of Fortune: The Civil War Letters of Colonel Robert Gould Shaw* (1992).

Sheridan, Philip Henry "Little Phil" (1831–1888). Union General. Although born in Albany, New York, Philip Sheridan was raised in Somerset, Ohio. He graduated from West Point in 1853 with a mediocre record. Sheridan began his Civil War service as a quartermaster in the Department of the West under Henry Halleck. He then received a colonel's commission in the 2nd Michigan Cavalry. Throughout the remainder of the war, Sheridan earned high marks for his service, both as a cavalry and infantry commander. He participated in the battles of Perrysville, Murfreesboro, Chickamauga, and Chattanooga. In 1864, he oversaw cavalry operations in the eastern theater and conducted a devastating campaign in the Shenandoah Valley. After the war, Sheridan was active as a commander under the Military Reconstruction Acts. He also participated in wars against the Native American tribes of the Great Plains. *Source*: Morris, Roy. *The Life and Wars of General Phil Sheridan* (1992).

Sherman, John (1823–1900). United States Congressman and Senator. Like his older brother, William Tecumseh, John Sherman was born in Lancaster. He practiced law with his oldest brother, Charles, in Mansfield, Ohio. Affiliated with the Whig Party, Sherman was elected to the U.S. House of Representatives in 1854 as an anti-Nebraska candidate. He eventually affiliated with the Republican Party and in 1861 was elected as a Republican senator from Ohio. He served several terms in the Senate, interrupted by service as secretary of the treasury under Rutherford B. Hayes. Appointed secretary of state by William McKinley, Sherman resigned in 1898 due to poor health. He died two years later. *Source*: Wheeler, Kenneth W., ed. *For the Union: Ohio Leaders in the Civil War* (1998).

Sherman, William Tecumseh "Cump" (1820–1891). Union General. Born in Lancaster, Ohio, William Sherman was raised by the powerful Ewing family after the death of his father in 1829. An 1840 graduate of West Point, Sherman was in California during the Mexican War and left the army in 1853. He pursued a number of business enterprises that ended in failure. When the war broke out, Sherman was living in Louisiana, where he was the superintendent of a military academy. Sherman commanded a brigade in the Union Army that fought at the first battle of Manassas. While performing well at Manassas, Sherman's subsequent performance in the West was erratic. He eventually took a leave of absence due to mental exhaustion. Associated with the rising general of the West, Ulysses Grant, Sherman's return to active duty was increasingly successful. When Grant was appointed as general-in-chief, Sherman was given the top position in the West. His Atlanta campaign culminated in the fall of Atlanta and led to his famous march to Savannah. At the war's conclusion, Sherman was a bona fide war hero, second only to Grant. After the war, Sherman remained in the army, appointed as commanding general in 1869. He remained a popular figure as well as writer and speaker. *Source*: Marzalek, John. *Sherman: A Soldier's Passion for Order* (1993).

Sigel, Franz (1842–1902). Union General. Franz Sigel was born in the Grand Duchy of Baden (now part of Germany). He originally settled in New York City, where he was involved in a number of different professions including teaching and surveying. When the Civil War began, he volunteered for military service and became a colonel in the 3rd Missouri. Popular among the German American community, Sigel's popularity contributed to the advancement of his military career. He participated in the battles of Wilson's Creek and Pea Ridge, and the battle of New Market in the Shenandoah Valley. While many questioned his military abilities, Sigel's popularity with the German American community accounted for high-profile positions in the military. After the war, Sigel stayed active in New York City politics and business. *Source*: Engle, Stephen D. *Yankee Dutchman: The Life of Franz Sigel* (1999).

Simms, William Gilmore (1806–1870). Southern Writer. A native of Charleston, South Carolina, William Gilmore Simms became a prominent Southern writer. Raised by his maternal grandmother, he married a wealthy plantation heiress, thus allowing him the freedom to write. Among his most prominent works were the novels *Woodcraft* and *Joscelyn; A Tale of the Revolution;* and *The History of South Carolina*. Simms was also politically active, elected to the Carolina legislature in 1844. He supported Southern rights and secession, as evidenced by his correspondence and friendship with Edmund Ruffin, James Hammond, and William Porcher Miles. After the war, Simms wrote for the *Charleston Daily South Carolinian*. He also wrote a number of short stories for magazines. *Source*: Watson, Charles S. *From Nationalism to Secession: The Changing Fiction of William Gilmore Simms* (1993).

Slidell, John (1793–1871). United States Senator and Confederate Diplomat. Although born in the North, John Slidell moved to New Orleans as a young man, where he practiced law. He was eventually elected to the U.S. House of Representative in 1843. During the Mexican War, he was President Polk's special envoy to Mexico. During the 1850s, Slidell, elected to the U.S. Senate in 1853, was increasingly identified with the proslavery wing of the Democratic Party. When the Civil War began, Slidell was tapped as minister to France. After being briefly detained in Boston as a result of the *Trent* affair, Slidell spent the bulk of the war in Paris, where he was unsuccessful in gaining French recognition of the Confederacy. After the war, Slidell remained in Europe as an exile. While in England, he died in 1871. *Source*: Sears, Louis Martin. *John Slidell* (1925).

Smith, Gerrit (1797–1874). United States Congressman, Abolitionist, and Reformer. Born in Utica, New York, into a wealthy family, Gerrit Smith became one of the most prominent antislavery figures of the antebellum period. Inheriting most of his family's land, Smith resided in Peterboro, New York. He became involved in antislavery activities in the 1830s and was involved in the formation of both the Liberty and the Free Soil political parties. Elected to Congress without political affiliation in 1852, Smith was an outspoken critic of the Fugitive Slave Act. Smith was a member of the secret six, a group of antislavery supporters of John Brown's raid on Harpers Ferry. During the war, he eventually joined the Republican Party. While a proponent of black rights, Smith also endorsed a somewhat mild Reconstruction policy toward the South. *Source*: Taylor, Edward Livingston. *Gerrit Smith* (1909).

Stanton, Edwin McMasters (1814–1869). Secretary of War. A native of Steubenville, Ohio, Edwin Stanton was one of the most prominent attorneys in the United States on the eve of the Civil War. Attorney general in the final months of the Buchanan administration, the War Democrat was tapped by Abraham Lincoln to succeed Simon Cameron as secretary of war in January 1862, primarily because of his reputation as a skilled administrator. While always controversial and hot tempered, most agree that Stanton was a skilled organizer whose methods at the War Department played a major role in eventual Union victory. During the Reconstruction period, Stanton became embroiled in controversy with President Andrew Johnson. The latter's attempt to removed Stanton from office ultimately resulted in the impeachment of the seventeenth president. Stanton died in 1869, just after newly elected President Grant had appointed him to the U.S. Supreme Court. *Source*: Thomas, Benjamin P., and Harold M. Hyman. *Stanton: The Life and Times of Lincoln's Secretary of War* (1962).

Stanton, Elizabeth Cady (1815–1902). Reformer and Women's Rights Advocate. A native of Johnstown, New York, Elizabeth Cady Stanton graduated from the Troy Female Seminary in 1832. Initially attracted to the antislavery cause, she married abolitionist Henry Stanton in 1840. Offended at discriminatory treatment by male abolitionists, Stanton became active in the cause of women's rights, playing a major role in the organization of the 1848 convention at Seneca Falls, New York. During the Civil War, Stanton focused more on the emancipation issue than she did on women's rights. She was critical of Lincoln's conservatism and supported the candidacy of John C. Frémont in 1864. After the war, Stanton continued to promote the cause of female rights and belonged to the American Equal Rights Association, the National Woman Suffrage Association, and finally, in 1892, the National American Woman Suffrage Association. *Source*: Griffith, Elisabeth. *In Her Own Right: The Life of Elizabeth Cady Stanton* (1984).

Stone, Charles Pomeroy (1824–1887). Union General. Known primarily for his imprisonment after the battle of Ball's Bluff, Charles Stone was born at Greenfield, Massachusetts. He graduated from West Point in 1845 and saw service in the Mexican War and on the west coast. During the Civil War, he was a divisional commander under George McClellan. When Union forces were defeated at Ball's Bluff, Stone became the scapegoat and was eventually imprisoned for 189 days without being charged. He served briefly for Nathaniel Banks in Louisiana after his release. After the war, Stone traveled to Egypt, where he served as chief of staff for the khedive of Egypt. He later returned to the United States, where he oversaw the construction of the Statue of Liberty's foundation. *Source*: Tap, Bruce. *Over Lincoln's Shoulder: The Committee on the Conduct of the War* (1998).

Surratt, Mary Eugenia (1823–1865). Lincoln Assassination Conspirator. A native of Maryland, Mary Surratt was married to John Surratt, a Maryland planter. While Surratt was initially financially successful, his addiction to liquor quickly erased this success. As a result, Mary eventually moved to Washington, D.C., where she ran a boardinghouse. Through her son, John Jr., Mary was drawn into the plot to assassinate the president. John Wilkes Booth was often at the boardinghouse, and several of the Lincoln conspirators lived there. Mary Surratt was arrested on April 17, 1865. She was tried and eventually convicted on June 28, 1865. On July 7, 1865, despite protestations of innocence, Mary Surratt was hanged. *Source*: Hanchett, William. *The Lincoln Murder Conspiracies* (1983).

Taney, Roger Brooke (1777–1864). Chief Justice of the Supreme Court of the United States. A native of Maryland, Roger Taney was trained as a lawyer. Initially a Federalist, Taney was eventually drawn into the Cabinet of Andrew Jackson, serving first as attorney general and then as secretary of the treasury. In 1836, Jackson appointed Taney as chief justice of the U.S. Supreme Court, a position Taney held until his 1864 death. While on the court for twenty-eight years, Taney is best known for writing the majority opinion in the Dred Scott case, a case that denied that African Americans were citizens and denied the power of Congress to prohibit slavery in the territories of the United States. *Source*: Lewis, Walker. *Without Fear or Favor: A Biography of Chief Justice Roger Brooke Taney* (1965).

Thomas, George Henry "Pap" and "Rock of Chickamauga" (1816–1870). Union General. Although Virginia born, George Thomas remained loyal to the Union. An 1840 graduate of West Point, Thomas saw action in the second Seminole and Mexican Wars. When the Civil War began, he was appointed brigadier general in August, 1861. After seeing some action in the East, he was sent to the western theater. He was appointed major general of volunteers in 1862 (and in the regular army in 1864). He served in different capacities in the armies of Ohio, Cumberland, and Tennessee. He participated in the battles of Perrysburg, Stones River, Chickamauga, Chattanooga, Atlanta, and Nashville. His heroic action at Chickamauga earned the sobriquet "Rock of Chickamauga." When the war concluded, Thomas continued to command in Tennessee, but was eventually transferred to the west coast. He died in 1870. *Source*: Cleaves, Freeman. *The Rock of Chickamauga: The Life of General George H. Thomas* (1948; reprint, 1974).

Thompson, Jacob (1810–1885). United States Congressman and Confederate Officer. A native of North Carolina, Jacob Thompson studied law before relocating to Oxford, Mississippi. In addition to the practice of law, Thompson became politically active and was elected to the U.S. House of Representatives in 1838. In 1856, for loyal service to James Buchanan, Thompson was chosen as secretary of the interior. When the war erupted, Thompson served as an officer in the Confederate armies; however, his most prominent role was his involvement in Confederate espionage and his role in cultivating Northern support for the peace movement. *Source*: Tidwell, William A. *April '65: Confederate Covert Action in the American Civil War* (1995).

Tod, David (1805–1868). Governor of Ohio. Born near Youngstown, Ohio, David Tod was trained as a lawyer and established a practice in nearby Warren. Active in Democratic politics, he was appointed minister to Brazil in 1847 and served until 1857. A supporter of Stephen A. Douglas, Tod was a committed War Democrat at the outset of the Civil War. Temporarily setting aside partisanship, Tod was nominated and elected as Unionist governor of Ohio in 1861. When he left office in 1863, Tod pursued private business interests. He remained interested in politics and joined the Republican Party. *Source*: Abbot, Richard H. *Ohio's War Governors* (1962).

Toombs, Robert Alexander (1810–1885). United States Senator, Confederate Secretary of State, and General. The descendant of wealthy Georgian planters, Robert Toombs had a long career in politics, and was elected to the U.S. House of Representatives in 1844 and the U.S. Senate in 1850. A skilled lawyer and brilliant orator, Toombs was often a voice of compromise prior to the war. Once secession was accomplished, he rallied to the

Southern cause. Although appointed secretary of state, Toombs stayed in the position for only five months. Elected to the Confederate Congress, Toombs held a legislative seat as well as a commission as a brigadier general. His generalship was mediocre and often controversial. A persistent critic of Jefferson Davis, Toombs allied himself with Alexander Stephens and Governor Joe Brown in opposing the Davis administration. After the war, Toombs fled to Europe but returned to Georgia in 1867. He never renounced secession or his course of action during the Civil War. *Source*: Thompson, William Y. *Robert Toombs of Georgia* (1966).

Trumbull, Lyman (1813–1896). United States Senator. A native of Connecticut, Lyman Trumbull moved to Belleville, Illinois, in 1836, where he began a law practice. In 1855, Trumbull was elected to the U.S. Senate as an anti-Nebraska candidate. During the Civil War, Trumbull had a somewhat uneasy relationship with Lincoln, initially pushing the president toward vigorous prosecution of the war. Toward the end of the war and into the Reconstruction period, Trumbull became more moderate. Initially an opponent of Andrew Johnson, Trumbull was one of the seven senators who voted not guilty during the impeachment trial. Alienated by the policies of Grant, Trumbull would eventually leave the Republican Party altogether during Grant's first term. *Source*: Krug, Mark M. *Lyman Trumbull: Conservative Radical* (1965).

Truth, Sojourner (1797–1883). Abolitionist. Originally named Isabella Baumfree, Sojourner Truth was born a slave in New York. Gaining her freedom in 1826, Truth became a persistent and outspoken advocate of abolitionism. After she converted to Christianity, Baumfree adopted the name Sojourner Truth in 1843. She was a frequent speaker on behalf of women's rights and abolitionism. During the war, she was active in the recruitment of African American troops. After the war, she was a powerful advocate of the distribution of western lands to former slaves. She died in Battle Creek, Michigan. *Source*: Painter, Nell Irvin. *Sojourner Truth: A Life, a Symbol* (1996).

Tubman, Harriet (1821–1913). Abolitionist, Nurse, and Union Scout. Born into slavery in Maryland, Harriet Tubman (originally named Araminta Ross) experienced firsthand the brutality of plantation slavery. In 1849, she fled to Philadelphia to escape slavery and immediately began working to bring other slaves to freedom. During the Civil War, Tubman was a fervent advocate of the Union, equating Union victory with the abolition of slavery. She served as a scout for David Hunter in the Department of South Carolina. She also served as a nurse in hospitals for Union soldiers. After the war, she continued her interest in improving the lot of recently emancipated slaves. *Source*: Clinton, Catherine. *Harriet Tubman: The Road to Freedom* (2004).

Van Dorn, Earl (1820–1863). Confederate General. Port Gibson, Mississippi, native Earl Van Dorn graduated from West Point in 1842. He gained experience in the Mexican War and, during the 1850s, fought Native American tribes in the West. He joined Confederate forces shortly after the secession crisis, commissioned as a brigadier general by June 1861 and as a major general in September 1861. Van Dorn's major theater of action was in the trans-Mississippi region. He saw action at Pea Ridge and Corinth. Skilled in cavalry operations, Van Dorn gained praise for his actions against Ulysses S. Grant at Holly Springs, Mississippi, in December 1862. He was killed on May 7, 1863, when the jealous husband of a lover shot and killed him. *Source*: Hartje, Robert G. *Van Dorn: The Life and Times of a Confederate General* (1967; reprint, 1994).

Van Lew, Elizabeth (1818–1900). Southern Unionist. Although a native of Richmond, Virginia, Elizabeth Van Lew was educated in Philadelphia. As a result of her education, she disliked the institution of slavery. Not only did she assist runaway slaves in Virginia, but during the Civil War she also began cooperating with Union army officers, particularly during the 1864–1865 campaign. To cover her espionage activities, Van Lew adopted the demeanor of a person of questionable mental stability. After the war, Van Lew was isolated and poor, ostracized by most Richmond residents. *Source*: Ryan, David D. *A Yankee Spy in Richmond: The Civil War Diary of "Crazy Bet" Van Lew* (1996).

Vance, Zebulon Baird (1830–1894). Governor of North Carolina. Zebulon Vance was born in western North Carolina. His political affiliation was initially Whig, then Know-Nothing, and finally the Constitutional Union Party in 1860. Elected to the U.S. House of Representatives in 1858, Vance was not an ardent secessionist. When North Carolina seceded, Vance finally cast his lot with the Confederacy. Elected governor of North Carolina in 1862, Vance became a determined critic of Jefferson Davis, particularly because the war's burdens fell disproportionately on North Carolina residents. In the 1864 campaign against Democrat William W. Holden, Vance endorsed peace through negotiations. After the war, Vance continued to be active in public affairs, serving both as governor and as U.S. senator. *Source*: Yearns, W. Buck, ed. *The Confederate Governors* (1985).

Wade, Benjamin Franklin "Bluff Ben" (1800–1878). United States Senator. Benjamin Wade was born at Feeding Hill, Massachusetts, but, as a young man, relocated to Jefferson, Ohio. Trained as an attorney, Wade formed a partnership with Joshua R. Giddings. After spending time as a Whig state senator and judge, Wade was elected U.S. senator in 1850. He spoke out forcefully against slavery. During the Civil War, Wade chaired the powerful Joint Committee on the Conduct of the War and cosponsored the Wade-Davis Reconstruction bill. After the war, Wade was one of the principal radical Republicans who disagreed with Andrew Johnson. In 1869, he stepped down from his Senate seat. *Source*: Trefousse, Hans L. *Benjamin F. Wade: Radical Republican from Ohio* (1963).

Washburne, Elihu Benjamin (1816–1887). United States Congressman. A resident of Galena, Illinois, Elihu Washburne migrated from Maine. Beginning in 1852, he served nine successive terms in the U.S. House of Representatives. Originally a Whig, Washburne later joined the Republican Party. During the war, Washburne served on the House Committee on Government Contracts. He was also an advisor and sponsor of Ulysses S. Grant. After the war, Washburne eventually sided with radical Republicans against Andrew Johnson. During Grant's presidency, Washburne served as minister to France, a position he held until 1877. *Source*: Washburne, Mark. *A Biography of Elihu Benjamin Washburne* (2002).

Weed, Thurlow (1797–1882). Political Advisor and Journalist. Thurlow Weed was the consummate nineteenth-century political insider. Born in New York, Weed gravitated toward a career in journalism. As editor of the *Albany Evening Journal*, Weed advanced the Whig economic agenda of commercial development. Through his Whig political involvement, Weed became a close political friend of William H. Seward. After gravitating into the Republican Party in the 1850s, during the Civil War Weed advocated a more cautious and conservative approach to the war than that endorsed by radical Republicans. At time, his support for the reelection of Abraham Lincoln wavered. After the war, Weed stayed actively involved in political issues, dispensing his counsel on political appointments and the issues of the day. *Source*: Van Deusen, Glyndon. *Thurlow Weed: Wizard of the Lobby* (1947).

Weld, Theodore Dwight (1803–1895). Minister and Social Reformer. A Connecticut native, Theodore Dwight Weld moved to New York early in life and was educated at Hamilton College and the Oneida Institute. Influenced by the antislavery sentiments of Charles Grandison Finney, Weld played a role in the establishment of Lane Seminary in Cincinnati, which was dedicated to preparing antislavery clergy. Engaged by the American Anti-Slavery Society, Weld spoke and wrote extensively on abolition. His *American Slavery As It Is* (1839) was an influential polemic against the peculiar institution. Married to female abolitionists Angelina Grimke, Weld eventually grew alienated with the political and public side of abolitionism and retreated from public affairs by the late 1840s. He nevertheless supported the abolition of slavery, and after the Civil War favored the establishment of equal rights for former slaves. *Source*: Abzug, Robert H. *Passionate Liberator: Theodore Dwight Weld and the Dilemma of Reform* (1980).

Whitman, Walt (1819–1892). Poet and Journalist. Walt Whitman is among the United States' most celebrated poets. Born in Huntington, New York, Whitman worked as a journalist prior to the war. His 1855 *Leaves of Grass* is among his best-known works, but received little public acclaim at the time. During the Civil War, Whitman went to Washington, D.C., where he volunteered as a nurse's assistant in Union hospitals. His publication *Drum-Taps* was a collection of forty-three poems inspired by Whitman's experiences in the war. After the war, Whitman continued to write poetry and continued to look toward the Civil War as a central event in the history of the republic. Some of his most popular poems included "The Death of Abraham Lincoln" and "O Captain!" *Source*: Allen, Gay Wilson. *The Solitary Singer: A Critical Biography of Walt Whitman* (1955; reprint, 1985).

Wigfall, Louis Trezevant (1816–1874). United States Senator, Confederate Senator, and General. Louis Wigfall was a native of South Carolina, born in Edgefield. A student of the law, Wigfall practiced law but was also attracted to politics. He moved to Texas in 1848 and in 1859 was chosen as U.S. senator. A determined opponent of the Republican Party, he led the secession movement in Texas after Lincoln's election. He initially served in the Confederate Army as a colonel in the 1st Texas regiment. Elected to the Confederate Senate in 1861, Wigfall resigned his military commission in early 1862. For the balance of the war, Wigfall became a persistent opponent of Jefferson Davis, blaming the Confederate president for Southern military failures. After the war, Wigfall fled to Great Britain before returning to the United States in 1872. *Source*: King, Alvy L. *Louis T. Wigfall, Southern Fire-Eater* (1970).

Wilkes, Charles (1798–1877). Union Naval Officer. Known primarily for his seizure of the British ship *Trent*, Charles Wilkes began life in New York City. He joined the navy in 1818 and gained a reputation in the early 1840s as a result of his role in commanding naval expeditions of exploration and surveying. During the Civil War, he commanded the USS *San Jacinto*. His seizure of the British mail ship *Trent* off the coast of Cuba caused a diplomatic crisis with Great Britain. Although Wilkes was regarded as a national hero, the Lincoln administration was forced to capitulated and return Confederate envoys James Mason and John Slidell, who had been taken from the vessel. Wilkes remained on active command until he was court-martialed in April 1864 as a result of public criticism of Naval Secretary Gideon Welles. He returned to duty for brief periods of time after the war and was eventually promoted to rear admiral (retired) in 1866. *Source*: Anderson, Bern. *By Sea and by River: The Naval History of the Civil War* (1962).

Wilmot, David (1814–1868). United States Congressman and Senator. Pennsylvania native David Wilmot was best known for his antislavery measure, the Wilmot Proviso, introduced into the House in August 1846. The measure helped inflame the slavery controversy in the United States. Initially a Democrat, Wilmot would eventually migrate into the Republican Party after participation in the Free Soil Party. An unsuccessful Republican candidate for governor of Pennsylvania in 1857, Wilmot was elected senator in 1861 to finish the term of Simon Cameron. When his term expired in 1863, Wilmot was appointed by the Lincoln administration to the Court of Claims. Wilmot died in 1868 while a member of the court. *Source*: Going, Charles Buxton. *David Wilmot: Free Soiler* (1924).

Wilson, Henry (1812–1875). United States Senator. Henry Wilson was born to a New Hampshire family named Colbath. Living in Natick, Massachusetts, Wilson practiced his acquired trade, shoe cobbling, and eventually earned enough money to open his own factory. Interested in politics, Wilson was elected to the Massachusetts legislature as a Whig representative. An opponent of slavery, he joined the Free Soil Party and then the Republicans, after briefly flirting with the nativistic Know-Nothing Party. He was elected to the U.S. Senate in 1855 and chaired the Senate Committee on Military Affairs during the Civil War. During the Reconstruction period, Wilson endorsed radical Reconstruction. He was eventually rewarded for his loyalty to his party by receiving his party's vice presidential nomination in 1872. Suffering a stroke in 1875, Wilson died before his term of office in the second Grant administration was over. *Source*: McKay, Ernest A. *Henry Wilson: Practical Radical* (1971).

Wood, Fernando (1812–1881). United States Congressman and Mayor of New York City. Born in Philadelphia, Fernando Wood was raised in New York City. Receiving little education because his family was poor, Wood worked at a variety of laboring jobs. He was interested in politics, however, and joined the Democratic Tammany Society. Appealing to immigrants, Wood was elected to the U.S. House of Representatives in 1840. An unsuccessful candidate for mayor of New York City in 1850, Wood was elected in 1854. During the Civil War, Wood was elected to the House in 1862. He became a prominent Peace Democrat. His peace principles cost him reelection in 1864. After the war, Wood returned to Congress and remained in the House until his death in 1881. *Source*: Mushkat, Jerome. *Fernando Wood: A Political Biography* (1990).

Woodward, George Washington (1809–1875). Judge and Pennsylvania Gubernatorial Candidate. A native of Bethany, Pennsylvania, George Woodward descended from a long line of lawyers. Woodward proved to be a skilled attorney and also became interested in Democratic state politics. By 1841 he was appointed as judge of the Fourth Judicial District Court of Pennsylvania. Increasingly conservative, Woodward supported John C. Breckinridge for president in 1860. During the war, Woodward was a vocal critic of the Lincoln administration. In 1863, he was nominated for governor of Pennsylvania but was defeated by Andrew Curtin. After the war, he served in the U.S. House of Representatives for two terms. He died while abroad in Italy. *Source*: Shankman, Arnold M. *The Pennsylvania Anti-War Movement, 1861–1865* (1980).

Yates, Richard (1815–1873). United States Congressman and Governor of Illinois. Richard Yates moved to Illinois from Kentucky at an early age. After practicing law, he entered politics, serving in the Illinois state legislature as well as two terms in the U.S. House of Representatives. A leading Republican in the State of Illinois, Yates was elected governor in 1860. Despite a strong Democratic opposition during the war, Yates was one of the nation's most prominent Unionist governors. After the war, Yates was elected to the U.S. Senate. In 1873, he passed away as the result of an unexpected heart attack. *Source*: Krenkel, John H. *Richard Yates: Civil War Governor* (1966).

INDEX

About the Authors

DAN MONROE is the author of *The Republican Vision of John Tyler* and *At Home with Illinois Governors: A Social History of the Illinois Executive Mansion*.

BRUCE TAP is an independent historian and the author of *Over Lincoln's Shoulder: The Committee on the Conduct of the War*, which was selected as a Choice Outstanding Academic Book. He has also published in *Civil War History*, *Journal of the Abraham Lincoln Association*, *Illinois Historical Journal*, and *American Nineteenth Century History*.